SLAVERY AND SLAVING IN WORLD HISTORY

Volume II

SLAVERY AND SLAVING IN WORLD HISTORY

A BIBLIOGRAPHY

Volume II, 1992–1996

JOSEPH C. MILLER
EDITOR

M.E. Sharpe
Armonk, New York
London, England

Library of Congress Cataloging-in-Publication Data

Miller, Joseph Calder.
Slavery and slaving in world history : a bibliography / Joseph C. Miller.
p. cm.
Vol. 1 originally published: New York : Kraus International Pub., 1993.
Includes bibliographical references and index.
Contents: v. 1. 1900–1991 — v. 2. 1992–1996.
ISBN 0-7656-0281-4 (set: alk. paper).—ISBN 0-7656-0279-2 (v. 1: alk. paper).
ISBN 0-7656-0280-6 (v. 2: alk. paper)
1. Slavery—Bibliography. I. Title.
Z7164.S6M544 1998
[HT861]
016.3063′62—DC21 97-32908
CIP

Printed in the United States of America

The paper used in this publication meets the minimum requirements of
American National Standard for Information Sciences—
Permanence of Paper for Printed Library Materials,
ANSI Z 39.48-1984.

IBT (c) 10 9 8 7 6 5 4 3 2 1

Contents

* Prepared on the basis of references graciously provided by Dr. Wim Hoogbergen, of the Universiteit Utrecht.

** Prepared on the basis of references graciously provided by Dr. Walter Scheidel, of the Cambridge University.

Introduction to the Second Volume

THIS BIBLIOGRAPHY[1] of course reflects the new emphases in the scholarship on slavery that have developed during the early 1990s. For earlier academic trends, users are referred to previous compilations of the materials[2] and to the introduction to the first volume of this set.

---

[1] Originally, annual installments in *Slavery and Abolition* (London: Frank Cass, vol. 1 = 1980), with retrospective coverage continuing through about 1985.

Starting in 1983, these annual "supplements" drew heavily on the skills of a talented series of collaborators, all graduate students at the University of Virginia:

Larissa V. Brown for "Slavery: Annual Bibliographical Supplement (1983)",, which appeared in *Slavery and Abolition*, 4, 2 (1983), pp. 163-208 (Part I), and 4, 3 (1983), pp. 232-74 (Part II). She also contributed importantly to production of the 1985 consolidation (see note 2).

James V. Skalnik for "Slavery: Annual Bibliographical Supplement (1984)" and "Slavery: Annual Bibliographical Supplement (1985)", *Slavery and Abolition*, 6, 1 (1985), pp. 59-92; and 7, 3 (1986), pp. 315-88.

David F. Appleby for "Slavery: Current Bibliographical Supplement (1986)" and "Slavery: Current Bibliographical Supplement (1987)", in *Slavery and Abolition*, 8, 3 (1987), pp. 353-86; and 9, 2 (1988), pp. 207-45.

Randolph C. Head for "Slavery: Current Bibliographical Supplement (1988)", "Slavery: Annual Bibliographical Supplement (1990)",; and "Slavery: Annual Bibliographical Supplement (1991)", in *Slavery and Abolition*, 10, 2 (1988), pp. 231-71; 13, 3 (1992), pp. 244-315; and 12, 3 (1991), pp. 259-312. And vitally also to the 1993 compilation of all materials accumulated through 1991 (see note 2).

Jena R. Gaines for "Slavery: Annual Bibliographical Supplement (1989)" in *Slavery and Abolition*, 11, 2 (1990), pp. 251-308.

Those who contributed to the yearly updates included in this volume are:

Emlyn Eisenach for "Slavery: Annual Bibliographical Supplement (1992)", in *Slavery and Abolition*, 14, 3 (1993), pp. 264-304 .

Janis M. Gibbs for "Slavery: Annual Bibliographical Supplement (1993)," *Slavery and Abolition*, 15, 3 (1994), pp. 134-97; "Slavery: Annual Bibliographical Supplement (1994)," *Slavery and Abolition*, 16, 3 (1995), pp. 398-460; and "Slavery: Annual Bibliographical Supplement (1995)," *Slavery and Abolition*, 17, 3 (1996), pp. 270-339.

John R. Holloran for "Slavery: Annual Bibliographical Supplement (1996)," *Slavery and Abolition*, 18, 3 (1997), forthcoming.

[2] The first elements of this bibliography -- some 1651 items -- appeared as *Slavery: A Comparative Teaching Bibliography* (Waltham MA: Crossroads Press, 1977). Materials accumulated through 1983 (5177 entries)

The rate of publication of studies sufficiently focused on slavery and the slave trade to meet the standards established for inclusion in this bibliography[3] remained approximately constant between 1991 and 1996, at some 700 to 800 titles each year. The academic emphases within this literature followed general scholarly trends away from the social and quantitative style that had defined the modern study of slavery during the 1960s, with its characteristic focus on social aggregates, and also beyond the marxist extensions of its underlying focus on structures and institutions in much of the scholarship of the 1970s and 1980s. Collectivities and structural abstractions of these sorts were then thought to constitute the only available ways to recover the experiences of the often anonymous victims of slavery, inarticulate in the historical record as individuals.

During the last five years, historians of slavery have increasingly re-invented themselves as historians of the slaves and their varied experiences of enslavement. They have teased the meanings of slavery and freedom to enslaved people from the vast research in previously unused primary sources that had characterized the previous three decades. Novelty has recently come less from discovery of additional evidence than from re-examination of relatively familiar records in search of new insight, as scholarly sensibilities have distinguished the women, children and older people, who in fact made lives of their own under slavery from the stereotypical "young adult males" that the slaveholders idealized as the "prime" slaves they tried to own and exploit, and which earlier views of slavery tended to reproduce.

---

appeared in Joseph C. Miller, *Slavery: A Worldwide Bibliography, 1900-1982* (White Plains NY: Kraus International, 1985). All materials compiled from 1983 through 1991 were corrected and consolidated during 1992, integrated with corrected entries from the 1985 consolidation, and published in 1993 in a new single-volume indexed bibliography (10,344 entries), *Slavery and Slaving in World History: A Bibliography, 1900-1991* (Millwood NY: Kraus International).

[3] Secondary scholarly writings published since 1900 in western European languages on slavery or the slave trade anywhere in the world: monographs, notes and articles in scholarly periodicals, substantial reviews and review essays, conference papers, and chapters in edited volumes and *Festschriften* focused primarily on slavery or slave trading. Scholarly materials in electronic media, as well as some audio and visual, have been mentioned since 1995. Although a few older titles continue to appear, the bibliography for 1992-96 basically covers only current research.

The bibliography takes a single author's intellectual product as the unit defining eligibility for inclusion. Hence, it does not usually include chapters on slavery -- even important ones -- in single-authored books conceived in terms of other subjects, e.g. Spanish administrative practice, the history of sugar, urban or agricultural history, race relations, the Roman family, or abolitionism in British politics. Specialists in every field will therefore notice the absence of recognized contributions to knowledge of slavery that appear in the context of the broader scholarship in their areas. Indeed, the significance of such thinking on slavery may derive precisely from its embeddedness in its full historical context.

It is from such area specialists, and the references they make in the works cited here to such broader, relevant studies, that the full utility of this bibliography ultimately derives. Here the aim is to cover an otherwise boundless literature at a level of introductory comprehensivness, one that gives readers full access to all relevant literature on slavery within a single additional research step.

An asterisk (*) indicates a title for which a reference has been encountered but that has not been verified by direct inspection or by consultation of such standard bibliographical sources as the OCLC on-line catalog. Items with asterisks are offered without assurance of accuracy, or even of existence.

With this growing visibility of the human beings who actually lived behind the "mask of obedience" has come greater attention to family, play, the ambiguities and ambivalences of the human feelings and interactions behind legalities defined by legislators, but always modified in their implementation by magistrates, masters, and the men and women who on whom fell the restraints they aimed to create. Hence, current scholarship extends beyond the burden of living under slavery to consider the implications of living with slavery for the masters, and for bystanders as well. The field in 1996 had become richer in humane sensibility than it was in 1991, realizing more of the potential established by key works pointing in this direction during the 1980s.

This second volume of the bibliography accordingly contains selected references to the considerable number of recent works drawing on literary theory, and often reflecting on the meanings of slavery for all those concerned, as works of literature have represented them. The criterion governing inclusion in the bibliography of such materials -- often very different in style from the behavioralist premises of preceding studies -- has been a distinction that excludes works using representations of slavery to study literary concerns (language, genre, theory) but includes those employing literary techniques to understand human domination and subjugation, often represented in its most extreme forms by slavery. A complementing search for the meanings of slavery has developed through a marked interest in the small corpus of writings by slaves themselves; the results are mostly included in Section II.11, *Biographies and Autobiographies.*

Some indication of the maturation of the field, and of its incorporation in general teaching, may be inferred from the fact that 5.4% of the publications on slavery between 1992 and 1996 represented anthologized reprints of materials published previously as original monographic research.

The distribution of publications across the geographical regions that structure the bibliography has remained roughly constant, with modestly increased concentration in the broad "General and Comparative" and "North America" sections, as indicated in the following table. The higher percentages in these categories derive in part from a considerable number of reprints in them, very likely prompted by the popularity of this level of the field for increasingly inclusive and diverse college and university instruction in the United States.

Regional Distribution of Bibliography Contents

Regional Category		*% 1900-91*	*% 1992-96*
I.	General and Comparative	7.9	9.8
II.	North America	22.0	30.2
III.	Spanish Mainland	3.4	2.7
IV.	Brazil	9.0	6.2
V.	Caribbean	13.5	16.0
VI.	Africa	4.6	5.0
VII.	Muslim	3.3	3.0
VIII.	Ancient	16.2	10.8
IX.	Medieval/Early Modern Europe	3.5	2.4
X.	Other	3.1	3.2
XI.	Slave Trade	13.0	10.8
	Atlantic - General	[9.3	7.5]
	Other, from Africa	[1.2	0.8]
	Africa, effects on, internal	[1.3	1.8]
	Other	[1.1	0.6]

The relative decline in the appearance of new work listed on ancient slavery may reflect several factors. The maturity of ancient history, and particularly Roman law, as fields of historical study covered in Volume I, particularly during the first half of the twentieth century, produced higher percentages in the "Ancient" category for that period than for the remainder of the world, where systematic study of slavery acquired momentum only in the 1950s.[4] The study of slavery in modern times, directly driven by contemporary concerns with race relations and human rights, has thrived, while the classic debates over slavery in the ancient Mediterranean, stimulated by similar concerns in the nineteenth century,[5] have waned with the decline during the 1980s of Cold-War-era debate between marxists and partisans of other visions of ancient economies and societies.

Known weakness of coverage in this volume of the bibliography lies principally in Brazil, where dozens of university departments of history have recently inaugurated newsletters and journals that frequently include studies of slavery based on local archives. It has not yet proved possible to identify all of these, or to locate accessible copies of those identified.

Coverage of similarly difficult-to-locate publications has expanded in this volume for the Dutch Caribbean, owing to the expertise and generosity of Dr. Wim Hoogbergen, who has contributed his knowledge of that field for every year covered in it.

Growing attention to modern conditions of servitude, domination, and violation of human rights as "slavery" -- as well as concern for contemporary forms of exploitation that continue earlier practices of enslavement -- has prompted the addition of a section on "Modern" forms of slavery (Section X.8). Definitions of certain other regional sections have been refined (e.g. "Muslim India" has been subsumed in "Muslim Asia", Section VII.9, with the remaining "India" section, X.4, limited to slavery in the context of other cultures). Precise statements of the criteria defining other categories have been added as footnotes to the headings of the sections concerned.

This volume has utilized electronic databases and other new methods of identifying publications, with the result that some previously unavailable categories of material (e.g., non-U.S. doctoral dissertations, undergraduate theses in the U.S., certain private and ephemeral publications) are listed more fully than has earlier been the case. The bibliography also now extends -- undoubtedly only inconsistently -- into the brave new realm of electronic publication itself: CDs, electronic journals, and specialized websites.[6]

The principal substantive development in understanding slavery during the last five years, beyond individuation and humanization of the slaves, has come in historicizing slavery as a process, through which slaves and masters may be seen to have moved in varying ways, creating and then recreating new cultures of their own, working out tense accommodations among themselves, and jointly setting the terms of cultures of domination and resistance specific to each moment and space, within similarly evolving economies and societies -- more structured and abstracted concepts of time and place.

---

4 It is unlikely that the apparent decrease reflects less complete coverage of this highly specialized field, without recourse to the exhaustive specialist bibliographies available for earlier decades. Dr. Walter Scheidel has contributed the fruits of his own research each year since 1993. If this confidence is ill-founded, the contributions of those able to guide us to the works not listed will be gratefully received.

5 Moses I. Finley, *Ancient Slavery and Modern Ideology* (New York: Viking Press, 1980).

6 E.g., #136, 206, 334, 379, 1496, 1499, 1520, 3475, 3852.

Among "general and comparative" studies, this historical emphasis has lessened the yawning gap between abstract concepts of slavery and other forms of human domination opened by structuralist efforts to define clear theoretical distinctions among them. Current work tends to embed the abstractions within the blur of human lives as experienced and thus to treat "slavery" within a broader category of domination, exploring similarities and differences among the many manifestations of this apparently elemental quality of human social and psychological life in varying personal and historical circumstances. "Serfdom" and "slavery", for example, now come up in the setting of a single conference.[7] The implications of Orlando Patterson's *Freedom* continue to anchor explorations of slavery in the context of historically changing meanings of its opposite.[8] The proceedings of several of the francophone conferences held in 1989 to commemorate the bicentennial of the French Revolution have also extended this sort of contextualization of slavery into the development of modern notions of liberty and human rights.[9]

Maturation of the field, and acceptance of enslavement -- or, at least, human domination, aggression, defiance, and survival -- as basic aspects of human existence, have led increasingly to academically responsible representations of slavery in popular forums. Major publishers have no fewer than three general encyclopedias of *Slavery* in preparation, with publication scheduled as early as 1998.[10] Museum exhibitions on the slave trade in the United Kingdom, Germany, France, and elsewhere have followed on the inclusion of the slave experience in the 1992 commemorations of the Columbian quincentennial, with publication of several -- sometimes lavishly -- illustrated exhibition catalogues.[11] The UNESCO "Slave

---

[7] #52 M[ichael] L. Bush, ed. *Serfdom and Slavery: Studies in Legal Bondage* (London: Longman, 1996).

[8] Orlando Patterson, *Freedom in the Making of Western Culture* (New York: Basic Books, 1991). Recently, for the United States, #463 Paul Finkelman, *Slavery and the Founders: Race and Liberty in the Age of Jefferson* (Armonk NY: M. E. Sharpe, 1996).

[9] E.g., #2230 Catherine Coquery-Vidrovitch, ed., *Esclavage, colonisation, libérations nationales de 1789 à nos jours* (Colloque, 24-26 février 1989, Université Paris VIII à Saint-Dénis) (Paris: Harmattan, 1990); #2250 Marcel Dorigny, ed., *Les abolitions de l'esclavage: de L. F. Sonthonax à V. Schoelcher, 1793, 1794, 1848* (Actes du Colloque International tenu à l'Université de Paris VIII les 3, 4 et 5 février 1994) (Saint-Dénis (France): Presses Universitaires de Vincennes, 1995, and Paris: UNESCO, 1995).

[10] See listings #111, 112, 113. Also see index for other large encyclopedia projects (African-American culture and history, Black women, Latin America, the North American colonies, the Civil War, the Confederacy, American social history) including essays relevant to slavery.

In addition, (#566) Randall M. Miller and John David Smith, comps. *Dictionary of Afro-American Slavery* ("Updated, with a new introduction and bibliography" - Westport CT: Praeger, 1996).

[11] #3692 *"Les Anneaux de la Mémoire": Nantes, Europe, Afrique, Amériques* (Exposition: Nantes, Château des Ducs de Bretagne, 5 déc. 1992 - 4 févr. 1994) (Rochefort: Centre International de la Mer-Corderie Royale, 1992); #157 Hamburgisches Museum für Volkerkunde. *Afrika in Amerika: Hamburgisches Museum für Volkerkunde 1992* (ed. Corinna Raddatz, Hamburg: Das Museum, 1992) (Exhibition catalog. "Ein Lesebuch zum Thema Sklaverei und ihren Folgen"); #3683, Anthony Tibbles, ed. *Transatlantic Slavery: Against Human Dignity* (National Museums & Galleries on Merseyside) (London: HMSO, 1994).

Also see #3677 *A Slave Ship Speaks: The Wreck of the Henrietta Marie* (Key West FL: Mel Fisher Maritime Heritage Society, 1995); #819 Theresa A. Singleton, Review of *Carter's Grove: The Winthrop Rockefeller Archaeology Museum, Wolstenholme Towne, the Slave Quarter, and the Mansion* (long-term exhibition at Colonial Williamsburg), *American Anthropologist*, 95, 2 (1993), pp. 525-28.

The bibliography does not include Barry Unsworth's Booker-prize-winning *Sacred* Hunger (New York: Norton, 1992),a work of historical fiction that has prompted serious discussion among professional historians. It does, however, list (#3503) Tom Feelings' evocative drawings of *The Middle Passage* (New York: Dial Press, 1995).

Route Project", inaugurated with a significant international conference in 1994 at the former slave-embarkation port of Ouidah (Whydah) in Bénin,[12] and its program includes development of Ouidah, Elmina, Gorée Island and other African coastal sites associated with the slave trade for international tourism. The terms on which the experience of enslavement there will be presented are subjects of intense negotiation.[13]

Though the emergence of world history as a focus of theoretical reflection and reconceptualization of the regional histories within it has not yet led directly to global syntheses on slavery *per se*, it has accelerated thinking on the "Atlantic economy",[14] including the colonial commodity exports, plantations, and slaves that produced them from the time of Columbus until well into the nineteenth century. The principal new historical synthesis on the Atlantic world is that of Robin Blackburn.[15]

Renewed interest in African American cultures, much of it stimulated by John Thornton's emphasis on *Africa and Africans in the Making of the Atlantic World*,[16] has generated productive debate on the extent to which slaves in the Americas drew on their backgrounds in Africa to create new lives for themselves, even under the constraints they endured.[17] A number of scholars have adapted the concept of the "African diaspora" to this emphasis on the continuities in cultural creativity among the slaves.[18]

The production of coffee-table representations of the trade has continued in 1997: Rosemarie Robotham, ed., *Spirits of the Passage: The Transatlantic Slave Trade in the Seventeenth Century* (New York: Simon and Schuster Editions, 1997). Text by Madeleine Burnside; foreword by Cornel West.

[12] #3870 La route de l'esclave - Colloque International. "De la traite négrière au defi du développement: réflexion sur les conditions de la paix mondiale" (Ouidah, Bénin - 1-5 September 1994).

[13] #3479 Edward M. Bruner, "Tourism in Ghana: the Representation of Slavery and the Return of the Black Diaspora," *American Anthropologist*, 98, 2 (1996), pp. 290-304.

[14] Evident in several indirect ways, including conferences comparing labor systems on all shores of the Atlantic. E. g. Paul E. Lovejoy and Nicholas Rogers, eds. *Unfree Labour in the Development of the Atlantic World* (London: Frank Cass, 1994) (also as a special issue of *Slavery and Abolition*, 15, 2 [1994]); Michael Twaddle, ed., *The Wages of Slavery: From Chattel Slavery to Wage Labour in Africa, the Caribbean and England* (London: Frank Cass, 1993) (also as special issue, *Slavery and Abolition*, 14, 1 [1993]); in addition to #271 Stephan Palmié, ed., *Slave Cultures and the Cultures of Slavery* (Knoxville: University of Tennessee Press, 1995).

[15] #40 Robin Blackburn, *The Making of New World Slavery: From the Baroque to the Creole* (London, New York: Verso, 1996).

[16] John K. Thornton, *Africa and Africans in the Making of the Atlantic World, 1400-1680* (New York: Cambridge University Press, 1992).

[17] E.g., #171 Wim Hoogbergen, ed., *Born out of Resistance: On Caribbean Cultural Creativity* (Utrecht: ISOR-Press, 1995); Palmié, ed., *Slave Cultures and the Cultures of Slavery.*

[18] #183 Alusine Jalloh and Stephen E. Maizlish, eds., *The African Diaspora* (College Station: Texas A&M University Press, 1996). Also see forthcoming publication of the proceedings of conferences held in connection with "The Development of the African Diaspora: The Slave Trade of the Nigerian Hinterland" (Coordinated by Paul E. Lovejoy and Robin Law in collaboration with the UNESCO "Slave Route Project"); see note 48 and the subject/keyword index for details.

Wide-ranging scholarship in gender and women's history has provided perhaps the second most innovative current in recent scholarship on slavery, extending beyond its earlier beginnings to nearly all regions.[19]

In terms of methodologies, historical archaeology has contribute the greatest quantity of new data on what we know about slaves' lives.[20] Legal history has also been prominently elaborated.[21]

Within the regions, developments in the study of North American slavery have continued to differentiate the formative encounters of English and Africans, and others, in the seventeenth century from the increasingly routinized and conscious, regionally distinct institutions of slavery characteristic of the eighteenth century -- in the Chesapeake, in low-country Carolina and Georgia, in the lower Mississippi Valley -- and each of those in turn from the quasi-industrial plantations of the nineteenth century Cotton Kingdom and the farms of Piedmont Virginia and the Upper South.[22] Accordingly, work on slavery in specific places has extended into colonies, counties, and states not previously explored systematically,

---

[19] See the subject/keyword index. Among the major collections: see (#510) Darlene Clark Hine, "The Making of Black Women in America: an Historical Encyclopedia," in Linda K. Kerber, Alice Kessler-Harris, and Kathryn Kish Sklar, eds., *U.S. History as Women's History: New Feminist Essays* (Chapel Hill: University of North Carolina Press, 1995), pp. 335-47; (#579) Patricia Morton, ed., *Discovering the Women in Slavery: Emancipating Perspectives on the American Past* (Athens: University of Georgia Press, 1996).

#145 David Barry Gaspar and Darlene Clark Hine, eds., *More Than Chattel: Black Women and Slavery in the Americas* (Bloomington: Indiana University Press, 1996); #2506 Verene S. Shepherd, Bridget Brereton, and Barbara Bailey, eds., *Engendering History: Caribbean Women in Historical Perspective* (New York: St. Martin's Press, Kingston: Ian Randle, and London: James Currey, 1995); #2846/2857 "Femme-esclave: modèles d'interprétation anthropologique, économique et juridique" (Groupe International de Recherches sur l'Esclavage Antique [GIREA], Colloque, 1994, Naples).

[20] #314 Theresa A. Singleton and Mark D. Bograd, *The Archaeology of the African Diaspora in the Americas* (N.p.: Society for Historical Archaeology, 1995) (Guides to the Archaeological Literature of the Immigrant Experience in North America, no. 2); Charles E. Orser, ed., *Images of the Recent Past: Readings in Historical Archaeology* (Walnut Creek CA: Alta Mira Press, 1996); and #1789-93 and #1815-18, especially Charles E. Orser, Jr., "Toward a Global Historical Archaeology: An Example from Brazil," *Historical Archaeology*, 28, 1 (1994), pp. 5-22.. See index for primary research.

[21] #467 Paul Finkelman, ed., *Race, Law, and American History 1700-1990: The African-American Experience* (11 vols.) (New York: Garland, 1992); #411 "Bondage, Freedom & the Constitution: The New Slavery Scholarship and Its Impact on Law and Legal Historiography," *Cardozo Law Review*, 17, 6 (1996), special issue; #815 Philip J. Schwarz, *Slave Laws in Virginia* (Athens: University of Georgia Press, 1996).

[22] The only new synthesis -- #539 Peter Kolchin, *American Slavery, 1619-1877* (New York: Hill and Wang, 1993) -- emphasizes historical distinctions of this sort. See also #398 Ira Berlin, "From Creole to African: Atlantic Creoles and the Origins of African-American Society in Mainland North America," *William and Mary Quarterly*, 53, 2 (1996), pp. 251-88.

particularly in New England and the Middle Colonies,[23] Florida,[24] and Louisiana.[25] A noticeable portion of the materials listed for North America are republications or extend work initiated before 1992.[26]

Current interests in slavery in mainland Spanish America have developed most productively in Mexico[27] and Peru,[28] the colonies with the principal concentrations of Africans under Spanish rule. Production in Colombia and Venezuela has languished.

In Brazil, where the New World's first, and long its largest, population of enslaved Africans and their freed descendants lived, commemorations of the centennial of abolition in 1988-89,[29] growing national debate about the nation's contemporary race relations,[30] and growing activism among darker-skinned Brazilians have turned attention there to the tercentennial of the defeat of the maroon colony of Palmares (1694)[31] and have extended the prevailing social-economic style of scholarship into new localities and regions. In the United States slavery in Brazil, revealed in all its horrors during the three preceding decades of research, appears to have lost its fascination as an imagined contrast with North Americans' cruelties toward their own slaves, and little has appeared in English beyond convenient syntheses.[32]

---

[23] E.g., #678 Patience Essah, *A House Divided: Slavery and Emancipation in Delaware, 1638-1865* (Charlottesville: University Press of Virginia, 1996), and #725 William Henry Williams, *Slavery and Freedom in Delaware, 1639-1865* (Wilmington DE: SR Books, 1996).

[24] Section II.7.

[25] Section II.9.

[26] Notably, #479 Robert W. Fogel and Stanley L. Engerman, eds., *Without Consent or Contract: Technical Papers* (2 vols.)

[27] #1603 Luz María Martínez Montiel, coord., *Presencia africana en México* (México: Dirección General de Publicaciones, 1994).

[28] #1648 Peter Blanchard, *Slavery and Abolition in Early Republican Peru* (Wilmington DE.: Scholarly Resources Inc., 1992); #1653 Christine Hünefeldt, *Paying the Price of Freedom: Family and Labor among Lima's Slaves, 1800-1854* (Berkeley and Los Angeles: University of California Press, 1994); #1654 Fernando Romero, *Safari africano y compraventa de esclavos para el Perú* (Lima: Instituto de Estudios Peruanos, Universidad Nacional San Cristóbal de Huamanga, 1994); #1655 Jean-Pierre Tardieu, *L'église et les noirs au Pérou: XVIe et XVIIe siècles* (Saint-Dénis and Paris: Université de la Réunion, Faculté des Lettres et des Sciences Humaines and Harmattan, 1993).

[29] #273 Maria Verônica de Pas, coord., *Anais do Seminário internacional da escravidão* (Seminário Internacional da Escravidão, Universidade Federal do Espírito Santo, Vitória, Espírito Santo, 15-17 de junho de 1988) (Ed. Fundação Ceciliano Abel de Almeida, 1992).

[30] #1671 Luiz Claudio Barcelos, Olivia Maria Gomes da Cunha, and Tereza Christina Nascimento Araújo, *Escravidão e relações raciais no Brasil: cadastro da produção intelectual (1970-1990)* (Rio de Janeiro: Centro de Estudos Afro-Asiáticos, 1991). Also see #309 Ronald Segal, *The Black Diaspora* (New York: Farrar, Straus and Giroux, 1995).

[31] #1742 João José Reis and Flávio dos Santos Gomes, eds., *Liberdade por um fio: história dos quilombos no Brasil* (São Paulo: Companhia das Letras, 1996).

[32] Reissue of Robert Conrad's *Children of God's Fire: A Documentary History of Black Slavery in Brazil* (University Park: Pennsylvania State University Press, 1994) and *The Destruction of Brazilian Slavery, 1850-1888* (2nd ed. Melbourne FL: Krieger, 1993) (#1682-83); #1753 Stuart B. Schwartz, *Slaves, Peasants, and Rebels: Reconsidering Brazilian Slavery* (Urbana: University of Illinois Press, 1992);

Anglophone Caribbean scholars have built actively on the bases laid during the 1970s and 1980s, though without widespread new departures in approach. The bicentennial of the French Revolution turned scholarship on the French islands strongly toward abolition and the revolutionary eras, 1789-1805 and 1848.[33] Scholarship on the Dutch-speaking portions of the area, principally Suriname, showed the greatest increase in activity, advancing from 12.2% of the Caribbean entries through 1991 to 35.2% during the last five years.[34] Equally clear is a new interest in slavery in the Danish Virgin Islands.[35]

For Africa, after two decades of intense exploration of the extent and implications of slavery throughout the continent, beyond the activities of European slave-buyers along the coast, attention to domination has turned toward patriarchy and colonial discourse and other forms of it characteristic of more recent times. As a result, three conference-based collections -- one in German and two in English, one of these on Cameroon and the other on pawnship (a system of temporary dependency closely linked in Africa to slavery) -- account for much of the recent scholarship on the bulk of the continent.[36]

At the Cape of Good Hope, slavery has attracted more continuing attention and interest in the history of forced labor has expanded to much of the rest of in southern Africa, in part as a side effect of intense current debate over the historiography of a country that passed through a profound revision of its national identity between 1992 and 1996; the 75 entries in the bibliography for this five-year period multiplied the rate of scholarly publication in this field tenfold from 1.5 titles per year (before 1992) to 15. Studies of slavery at the Cape have long evolved with scholarship on North American slavery, and the discrimination of regional, local, and temporal variation there now parallels distinctions in South Africa among urban slavery in Cape Town, slavery on the wine and wheat farms of the western Cape, and rural slavery to the north and east.

Elsewhere in Africa, a notable addition to the literature in 1996 was the UNESCO "Slave Route"-linked conference on slavery in Madagascar that produced extensive national commentary on that island's history of forced labor.[37]

Outside of Muslim Africa, scholarship on Islamic slavery showed no more than scattered activity. Revisions and republications of the work of two leading scholars, David Ayalon's well-known studies of Egyptian and other military slaves (*mamluks*) and Ehud Toledano's studies of Ottoman slavery, account

---

[33] In addition to the collections noted in note 10, #2333 Michel L. Martin and Alain Yacou, eds., *Mourir pour les Antilles: indépendance nègre ou esclavage (1802-1804)* (Paris: Editions Caribéennes, 1991)

[34] Some -- though not all -- of the growth in this category of the bibliography is obviously owing to the thorough coverage provided by Wim Hoogbergen.

[35] #2506 Arnold R. Highfield, *Slavery in the Danish West Indies: A Bibliography* (St. Croix: The Virgin Islands Humanities Council, 1994), and other works listed in Section V.6.

[36] #2535 Helmut Bley, Clemens Dillmann, Gesine Krüger, and Hans-Hermann Pogarell, eds., *Sklaverei in Afrika: Afrikanische Gesellschaftsformen im Zusammenhang von europäischer und interner Sklaverei und Sklavenhandel.* (Pfaffenweiler: Centaurus-Verlagsgesellschaft, 1991); #2542 Bongfen Chem-Langhëë, ed., "Slavery and Slave-Dealing in Cameroon in the Nineteenth and Early Twentieth Centuries," *Paideuma* (special issue), 41 (1995); #2549 Toyin Falola and Paul E. Lovejoy, eds., *Pawnship in Africa: Perspectives on Debt Bondage* (Boulder: Westview Press, 1993).

[37] #2688 *Fanandevozana ou esclavage* (Proceedings of Colloque international sur l'esclavage à Madagascar, 24-28 sept. 1996) (Antananarivo: Musée d'Art et d'Archéologie de l'Université d'Antananarivo, coord. Rajaoson François).

for a significant portion of the listings.[38] The somewhat more active scholarship on North Africa included a noticeable emphasis on Christian captives from the sixteenth through the eighteenth centuries. The most striking novelty within the Muslim world was the appearance of a small number of works -- virtually the first -- on central Asia.[39]

Scholarship on slavery in the ancient Mediterranean has drawn significant impetus in recent years from the Groupe International de Recherches sur l'Esclavage Antique (GIREA) based at the *Centre de recherches d'histoire ancienne* at the Université de Besançon. Papers presented at its annual conferences, each intending to define a new emphasis in the study of ancient slavery, account for 53 of the 418 entries. Jacques Annequin and others associated with the group have published annual surveys of current work in the field.[40] Much of the recent work slavery in the ancient Mediterranean reflects relatively specialized research, and little of it appears in English. The only recent synthesis in English is that of Keith Bradley.[41]

Interest in slavery in medieval and Renaissance Europe, on the other hand, has intensified during the last five years, particularly in Spain and its island possessions in the eastern Atlantic.[42] The first systematic work on slavery and other forms of servitude in medieval England appeared also during these years.[43] Virtually no new work turned up on Russia and northern Europe.

In Asia, the conventionally narrow focus in India on labor as "bonded" and on society as constructed out of "castes" widened significantly to admit scholarship conceived in terms of slavery. This new emphasis extended beyond Muslim India (Section VII.9) to include ancient times,[44] Portuguese India, and British East India Company trading in slave labor in the Indian Ocean during more recent centuries.

Studies on slave trading remained heavily concentrated on the Atlantic "middle passage" and on the effects on the African continent itself of the seventeenth-nineteenth-century era of intensified European commerce along its shores.[45] The most noteworthy development during the last five years has been the

---

[38] #2721 David Ayalon, *Islam and the Abode of War: Military Slaves and Islamic Adversaries* (Aldershot: Variorum, 1994); #2763 Ehud R. Toledano, *Slavery & Abolition: Studies in Ottoman Social History* (Seattle: University of Washington Press, forthcoming).

[39] See Section VII.9.

[40] For GIREA, see main listings #2841, 2855, 2858, 2859, 2860.

The annual surveys, published in *Dialogues d'histoire ancienne*, for 1990 and 1992-94 are listed as #2836, 2839, 2840, and 2873, and it is to be hoped that time will bring further such compilations. Also see #2853 for other activities of the Centre.

[41] #3012 *Slavery and Society at Rome* (New York: Cambridge University Press, 1994).

[42] Section IX.4.

[43] #3330 Allen J. Frantzen and Douglas Moffat, eds., *The Work of Work: Servitude, Slavery, and Labor in Medieval England* (Glasgow: Cruithne Press, 1994), and #3338 David Anthony Edgell Pelteret, *Slavery in Early Mediaeval England: From the Reign of Alfred until the Twelfth Century* (Woodbridge, Suffolk, and Rochester NY: Boydell Press, 1995).

[44] See the very useful bibliography by #3372 Jonathan A. Silk, "A Bibliography on Ancient Indian Slavery," *Studien zur Indologie und Iranistik*, 16-17 (1992), pp. 277-85.

[45] For generalizing reviews, mostly of the publications of the late 1980s, see #3481 W[illiam] Gervase Clarence-Smith, "The Dynamics of the African Slave Trade (review essay: Miller, *Way of Death*; Law, *Slave Coast of West Africa*; Thornton, *Africa and Africans in the Making of the Atlantic World*; Savage, ed., *Human Commodity*;

advance toward completion of the "Harvard Database" of quantitative data on Atlantic slaving voyages.[46] Its publication will culminate the three decades of quantitative research inspired by Philip Curtin's *Atlantic Slave Trade A Census*[47] and will provide a fully integrated set of the data generated to support a new generation of quantitative studies of slaving in the Atlantic at previously inaccessible levels of detail, complexity, and comprehensiveness. Initial exploration of this extraordinary compilation of some 25,000 voyages, with data distributed through 170 analytical fields, produced several studies between 1993 and 1996 that extended the conventional style of "volume and direction" to bear on new and current issues.[48] A secondary style of scholarship continued to emphasis the relationship between economic developments in the Atlantic and the growth of European economies.[49]

Innovation in studies of the Atlantic trade took the form of renewed interest in the cultural consequences of the delivery of slaves to the Americas, supported by closer examination of the captives' backgrounds in Africa and their experience of the Middle Passage itself, generally questioning the prevailing assumption that the trade so disoriented its victims, and so dispersed the members of African communities, that slaves seldom drew on shared cultures to adjust to life under slavery.[50]

In terms of new regional emphasis, Brazilian historians have begun to investigate more thoroughly the trade that landed the majority of that nation's population prior to the late nineteenth century.[51] The

---

Solow, ed., *Slavery and the Rise of the Atlantic System*; Inikori and Engerman, eds., *Atlantic Slave Trade*; Manning, *Slavery and African Life*; Wright, *Strategies of Slaves and Women*; and Meillassoux, *Anthropology of Slavery*)," *Africa*, 64, 2 (1994), pp. 275-86, and [listed in volume 1, #5883] Janet J. Ewald, "Slavery in Africa and the Slave Trades from Africa (review essay: Clarence-Smith, ed., *Economics of the Indian Ocean Slave Trade*; Lovejoy, *Transformations in Slavery*; Manning, *Slavery and African Life*; Miers and Roberts, eds., *End of Slavery in Africa*; Miller, *Way of Death*; Roberts, *Warriors, Merchants, and Slaves*; and Sheriff, *Slaves, Spices and Ivory in Zanzibar*)," *American Historical Review*, 97, 2 (1992), pp. 465-85.

46 "The Transatlantic Slave Trade: A Database", under the direction of David Eltis, David Richardson, Stephen D. Behrendt, and Herbert S. Klein, at the W. E. B. Dubois Institute for Afro-American Research, Harvard University. The completed project will be released through Cambridge University Press as a CD in the fall of 1997.

47 Volume 1, #9040.

48 By the directors of the project; see author index for these publications. Also see listings for the original data sets, #3608, 3609, 3610, 3625, 3638, 3639 (and 3648), 3643, 3653, 3654, 3672, 3700, 3711, 3723, 3724, 3771.

49 Beyond that stimulated by the fiftieth anniversary of Eric Williams' classic statement of the case for a close linkage between (#55) "*Capitalism and Slavery* Fifty Years Later: Eric Williams and the Post Colonial Caribbean" (Colloquium, 24-28 September 1996, University of the West Indies, St. Augustine, Trinidad). See #55.

50 See author index for recent publications of John K. Thornton; also the UNESCO "Slave Route"-linked project directed by Paul E. Lovejoy and Robin C. C. Law: #91 "The Development of the African Diaspora: The Slave Trade of the Nigerian Hinterland"; #5 "The African Diaspora and the Nigerian Hinterland: Towards a Research Agenda" (Conference, York University, Toronto, 2-3 February 1996); #328 "Source Material for Studying the Slave Trade and the African Diaspora" (Conference, University of Stirling, Scotland, 13-14 April 1996).

51 Notably #3601 Manolo Garcia Florentino, *Em costas negras: uma história do tráfico Atlântico de escravos entre a África e o Rio de Janeiro (séculos XVIII e XIX)* (Rio de Janeiro: Arquivo Nacional, 1995); #3603 João Luís Ribeiro Fragoso, *Homens de grossa aventura: acumulação e hierarquia na praça mercantil do Rio de Janeiro (1790-1830)* (Rio de Janeiro: Arquivo Nacional, 1992); and #3598 Roquinaldo Amaral Ferreira, "Dos sertões ao Atlântico: tráfico ilegal de escravos e comércio lícito em Angola, 1830-1860" (Dissertação de Mestrado, Universidade Federal do Rio de Janeiro - Instituto de Filosofia e Ciências Sociais, Programa de Pós-Graduação em História Social, n.d. [1996]). For a synthesis with extensive, expensively reproduced illustrations, prepared in connection

noteworthy Danish interest in slavery extended to the supporting slave trade.[52] Interest in the effects of this slaving on Africa has moved productively from the older emphasis on "underdevelopment" relative to Europe to the specific ways in which Africans utilized Atlantic trading, depending on time, region, social position, gender, and other differentiating factors within Africa.[53]

---

with the UNESCO "Slave Route" project, #3613 João Medina and Isabel Castro Henriques, *A rota dos escravos: Angola e a rede do comércio negreiro* (Lisbon: Cegia, 1996).

[52] #3763 George F. Tyson and Arnold R. Highfield, eds., *The Danish West Indian Slave Trade: Virgin Islands Perspectives* (St. Croix VI: Virgin Islands Humanities Council, 1994); #3758 Per O. Hernaes, *Slaves, Danes and the African Coast Society: The Danish Slave Trade from West Africa and Afro-Danish Relations on the Eighteenth-Century Gold Coast* (Trondheim: Department of History - University of Trondheim, 1995).

[53] E.g., the studies in #3853 Robin [C. C.] Law, ed., *From Slave Trade to "Legitimate" Commerce: The Commercial Transition in Nineteenth-Century West Africa* (New York: Cambridge University Press, 1995).

Acknowledgments

Credit for the comprehensiveness of this bibliography rests squarely on the shoulders of the skilled graduate students at the University of Virginia who have collaborated with the principal compiler in preparing the annual bibliographical supplements from which all the entries in this bibliography derive. Emlyn Eisenach worked effectively on the supplement for 1992, and Janis M. Gibbs definitively expanded search methodologies and thoroughness of procedure from 1993 to 1995 -- even beyond the high levels set by her now-numerous predecessors.[54] John R. Holloran creatively maintained those standards for 1996 and will contribute similarly to the 1997 supplement, in preparation as these words are written. They have all claimed well-earned, full professional credit as co-compilers of the annual supplements.

For several of those years, as noted in the introductions to the resulting publications, the Carter G. Woodson Institute for African-American and African Studies at the University of Virginia provided welcome financial support for the project.

The process of detecting and correcting remaining errors, consolidating five separate listings, eliminating duplicated references, and indexing are my responsibility. Although I of course accept blame for the errors and omissions that inevitably still remain (and the previously undetected duplications noted in the indexes), I will do so most gratefully from colleagues who provide the details and additions that will improve future revisions of these materials.

Frank Cass, Ltd., the publishers of *Slavery & Abolition*, in which all of the annual bibliographical supplements appeared, have been consistently and generously gracious in allowing me to compile their contents in occasional comprehensive bibliographies, like this one. They certainly share my own interest in providing the added accuracy and accessibility that integrated, ordered listings offer to students and researchers in the field. I am very grateful for their collaboration.

Members of the professional staff in the Department of History at the University of Virginia -- in particular Lottie McCauley and Kathleen Miller -- have once again numbered the entries and generated the alphabetized list of entries from which the author index has been created.

Charlottesville, Virginia
September 1997

[54] See note 2 for a full listing.

I: General and Comparative

1. Abasiattai, Monday B. "The Search for Independence: New World Blacks in Sierra Leone and Liberia, 1787-1847," *Journal of Black Studies*, 23, 1 (1992), pp. 107-16.

2. Adande, Joseph C. E. "Influence de l'art africain dans l'art américaine" (Unpublished paper, UNESCO conference on "La route de l'esclave", Ouidah, Bénin, 1-5 Sept. 1994).

3. Adler, Joyce Sparer. "*Benito Cereno*: Slavery and Violence in the Americas," in idem, *War in Melville's Imagination* (New York: New York University Press, 1981), pp. 88-110.

Reprinted in Burkholder, ed., *Critical Essays on Herman Melville's "Benito Cereno"*, pp. 76-93.

4. Adoukonou, Barthélemy. "Les religions et les philosophies face à l'esclavage noir" (Unpublished paper, UNESCO conference on "La route de l'esclave", Ouidah, Bénin, 1-5 Sept. 1994).

5. "The African Diaspora and the Nigerian Hinterland: Towards a Research Agenda" (Conference, York University, Toronto, 2-3 February 1996).

For papers see Chambers, Eltis, Hawkins and Morgan, Law, Law and Lovejoy, Lovejoy (2), Philips, Reynolds, Richardson and Behrendt, and Thornton.

6. "Against the Odds: Free Blacks in the Slave Societies of the Americas," special issue of *Slavery and Abolition*, 17, 1 (1996), edited by Jane G. Landers.

For contents see Landers, ed., "Against the Odds".

7. Akkerman, T. "Liberal Feminism and the Language of Slavery: A Legacy of the Colonial Past?" *European Legacy*, 1, 3 (1996), pp. 975-80. (Special Issue: 4th International conference, International Society for the Study of European Ideas: "The European Legacy: Toward New Paradigms" [Graz, Austria, 1994])

8. Allen, Theodore W. *The Invention of the White Race*. New York: Verso, 1993.

9. Almeida, Irène d'. "Toni Morrison et le mythe de l'Africain ailé" (Unpublished paper, UNESCO conference on "La route de l'esclave", Ouidah, Bénin, 1-5 Sept. 1994).

10. Álvarez Alonso, Clara. "Libertad y propiedad: el primer liberalismo y la esclavitud," *Anuario de historia del derecho español*, 65 (1995), pp. 559-83.

11. Annequin, Jacques. "La parole froide de Mérimée sur l'esclavage" (Unpublished paper, Groupe International de Recherches sur l'Esclavage Antique [GIREA]. Colloque [19ème] sur "Captifs et prisonniers de guerre dans leurs rapports avec l'esclavage", 2 - 5 October, 1991, Palma, Mallorca).

12. Aponte-Ramos, Dolores T. "La representación del africano subsahárico en el discurso colonial, 1450-1618" (PhD diss., Northwestern University, 1992).

13. Artis, David Michael. "Princes and Humble Friends: Representations of Africa and Africans in Eighteenth Century British Literature" (PhD diss., Stanford University, 1991).

14. Ashworth, John. "Capitalism, Class and Antislavery."

Reprinted in Bender, *The Antislavery Debate*, pp. 263-89.

15. Ashworth, John. "The Relationship Between Capitalism and Humanitarianism."

Reprinted in Bender, *The Antislavery Debate*, pp. 180-99.

16. Aubrey, Bryan. "Slavery," in Susan Auerbach, ed., *Encyclopedia of Multiculturalism* (New York: Cavendish, 1994), vol. 6, pp. 1533-37.

17. Austen, Ralph. "The Uncomfortable Relationship: African Enslavement in the Common History of Blacks and Jews," *Tikkun*, 9, 2 (1994), pp. 65-68.

18. Azevedo, Célia Maria Marinho de. *Abolitionism in the United States and Brazil: A Comparative Perspective*. New York: Garland, 1995.

19. Azevedo, Célia Maria Marinho de. "Irmão ou inimigo: o escravo no imaginário abolicionista nos Estados Unidos e no Brasil," *Revista USP* (Universidade de São Paulo), 28 (1996), pp. 96-109.

20. Bailey, Ronald. "'Those Valuable People, the Africans': U.S. Slavery, the Slave(ry) Trade, and the Industrial Revolution in Great Britain and the U.S."

(Unpublished paper, Annual Meeting of the African Studies Association, Seattle, 20-23 November 1992).

21. Bassiouni, M. Cherif. "Enslavement as an International Crime," *New York University Journal of International Law and Politics*, 23, 2 (1991), pp. 445-517.

22. Bateman, Rebecca B. "Africans and Indians: A Comparative Study of the Black Carib and Black Seminole".

Reprinted in Davis, ed., *Slavery and Beyond*, pp. 29-54.

23. Bauer, Arnold J. "Christian Servitude: Slave Management in Colonial South America," in Mats Lundahl and Thommy Svensson, eds., *Agrarian Society in History: Essays in Honor of Magnus Mörner* (New York: Routledge, 1990), pp. 89-107.

24. Baum, Joan. *Mind-forg'd Manacles: Slavery and the English Romantic Poets*. Hamden CT: Archon, 1994.

25. Beaubestre, Jean. "Négritude et esclavage," *La généalogie aujourd'hui*, no. 137 (1995), pp. 42-44.

26. Beckles, Hilary McD. "Caribbean and European Anti-Slavery: Finding the Core" (Unpublished paper, Annual Meeting of the African Studies Association, Seattle, 20-23 November 1992).

27. Behanzin, Joseph-Noël. "De quelques survivances de l'Afrique dans la culture populaire profane aux Amériques" (Unpublished paper, UNESCO conference on "La route de l'esclave", Ouidah, Bénin, 1-5 Sept. 1994).

28. Bell, Alison K. "African-American Patterns of Adaptation to Plantation Life in the New World" (Unpublished paper, Annual Meeting of the Society for Historical Archaeology, Kingston, Jamaica, January 1992).

29. Bender, Thomas. *The Anti-Slavery Debate: Capitalism and Abolitionism as a Problem in Historical Interpretation*. Berkeley and Los Angeles: University of California Press, 1992.

For contents see Ashworth (2), Davis (3), and Haskell (2).

30. Benoît, Norbert. "Anciens affranchis africains: inventaire et conclusions" (Unpublished paper, UNESCO conference on "La route de l'esclave", Ouidah, Bénin, 1-5 Sept. 1994).

31. Bénot, Yves. "Chronologie sommaire des abolitions de la traite des Noirs et de l'esclavage," in Dorigny, ed. *Les abolitions de l'esclavage*, pp. 403-07.

32. Berlin, Ira, and Philip D. Morgan. "Labor and the Shaping of Slave Life in the Americas," in Berlin and Morgan, eds., *Cultivation and Culture*, pp. 1-45.

33. Berlin, Ira, and Philip D. Morgan, eds. *Cultivation and Culture: Labor and the Shaping of Slave Life in the Americas*. Charlottesville: University Press of Virginia, 1993.

For contents see Berlin and Morgan, Campbell, Dunn, Gaspar, Geggus, Marshall, McDonald, Miller, Tomich, Trouillot, and Walsh.

34. Best, Felton O'Neal. *Black Resistance Movements in the United States and Africa, 1800-1993: Oppression and Retaliation*. Lewiston: E. Mellen Press, 1995. (African studies, v. 38)

35. Biezunska-Malowist, Iza, and Marian Malowist. "L'esclavage antique et modern: les possibilités de recherches comparées," in Marie-Madeleine Mactoux and Evelyne Geny, eds., *Mélanges Pierre Lévêque: 2, Anthropologie et société* (Paris: Belles Lettres, 1989), pp. 17-31. (Annales littéraires de l'Université de Besançon, 377; Centre de recherches d'histoire ancienne, vol. 82)

36. Billacois, François. "Figures de l'esclave: métaphores de la condition humaine?" in Bresc, ed., *Figures de l'esclave*, pp. 263-69.

37. Binder, Guyora. "On Hegel, On Slavery, But Not on My Head!" *Cardozo Law Review*, 11, 3 (1990), pp. 563-94.

Hegel and Legal Theory: a Response.

38. Binder, Wolfgang, ed. *Slavery in the Americas*. Würzburg: Königshausen & Neumann, 1993.

For contents see Andrews, Binder, Bolner, Bremer, Cooke, Ensslen, Everaert, G. Fabre, M. Fabre, Fleischmann, Hentschke, Heuman, Hoogbergen, König, Kossek, Kremser, Krüger-Kahloula, Kubik, Littlefield, Lüsebrink, Martin, Meindl, Menard and Schwartz, Mintz, Mörner, Ostendorf, Palmié (2), Späth, Speiser, Vauthier, and Wentklaff-Eggebert.

39. Blackburn, Robin. "The Elementary Structures of Enslavement and the Peculiarities of Slave Exploitation" (Unpublished paper, Conference on

"Serfdom and Slavery", University of Manchester, 5-7 Sept. 1994).

40. Blackburn, Robin. *The Making of New World Slavery: From the Baroque to the Modern*. London, New York: Verso, 1996.

41. Blackburn, Robin. "Slave Exploitation and the Elementary Structures of Enslavement," in Bush, ed., *Serfdom and Slavery*, pp. 158-80.

42. Blight, David W. "'Analyze the Sounds': Frederick Douglass's Invitation to Modern Historians of Slavery," in Palmié, ed., *Slave Cultures and the Cultures of Slavery*, pp. 1-11.

43. Bolland, O. Nigel. "Proto-Proletarians? Slave Wages in the Americas - Between Slave Labour and Free Labour," in Turner, ed., *From Chattel Slaves to Wage Slaves*, pp. 123-47.

44. Brackman, Harold. *Farrakhan's Reign of Historical Error: The Truth Behind The Secret Relationship between Blacks and Jews*. New York: Simon Wiesenthal Center, 1992.

45. Bresc, Henri, ed. *Figures de l'esclave au Moyen-Âge et dans le monde moderne* (Actes de la table ronde organisée les 27 et 28 octobre 1992 par le Centre d'Histoire Sociale et Culturelle de l'Occident de l'Université de Paris-X, Nanterre). Paris: L'Harmattan, 1996.

For contents see Balard, Billacois, Bresc, Calvo, Cheikh-Moussa, Fontenay, Larquié, Mauro, Ragib, Stella, Tardieu, Vauchez, and Vincent.

46. Brett, Stephen F. *Slavery and the Catholic Tradition: Rights in the Balance*. New York: Peter Lang, 1994.

47. Brommer, Bea, and Pieter C. Emmer. "Van Spartacus tot Equiano: slavenhandel en slavernij in de westelijke wereld, 1500-1900," in Brommer, ed., *Ik ben eigendom van ...*, pp. 17-29.

48. Bryan, Patrick. (review: Voelz, *Slave and Soldier*), *Journal of Caribbean History*, 28, 2 (1994), pp. 262-66.

49. Burkholder, Robert E., ed. *Critical Essays on Herman Melville's "Benito Cereno"*. New York: G. K. Hall, 1992.

For contents see Adler, Fiedler, Karcher, Sundquist, Swann, and Vanderbilt.

50. Bush, Jonathan A. "Free to Enslave: The Foundations of Colonial American Slave Law," *Yale Journal of Law and the Humanities*, 5, 2 (1993), pp. 417-70.

51. Bush, Michael [L.]. "Introduction (to 'Comparative Studies of Serfdom and Slavery')," in idem, ed., *Serfdom and Slavery*, pp. 1-17.

52. Bush, M[ichael] L., ed. *Serfdom and Slavery: Studies in Legal Bondage*. London: Longman, 1996.

For contents see Blackburn, Bush, Engerman, Kolchin, Morris, Phillips, Rihll, Saller, Temperley, and Turley.

53. Campbell, Mavis C. "Early Resistance to Colonialism: Montague James and the Maroons in Jamaica, Nova Scotia and Sierra Leone," in J. F. Ade Ajayi and J. D. Y. Peel, eds., *People and Empires in African History: Essays in Honor of Michael Crowder* (London: Longman, 1992), pp. 89-105.

54. Cannon, Katie Geneva. "Slave Ideology and Biblical Interpretation," in Randall C. Bailey and Jacquelyn Grant, eds., *The Recovery of Black Presence: An Interdisciplinary Exploration (Essays in honor of Dr. Charles B. Copher)* (Nashville: Abingdon Press, 1995), pp. 119-28.

55. "*Capitalism and Slavery* Fifty Years Later: Eric Williams and the Post Colonial Caribbean" (Colloquium, 24-28 September 1996, University of the West Indies, St. Augustine, Trinidad).

For contents see Darity, Drescher, Inikori, Morgan, Mulvey, O'Shaughnessy, Ryden, and Sundiata.

56. Carew, Jan. "The Undefeated: Joint Struggles of Native Americans and Peoples of the African Diaspora," in Sudarkasa, Nwachuku, Millette, and Thomas, eds., *The African-American Experience*, pp. 53-70.

57. Carretta, Vincent J., ed. *Unchained Voices: An Anthology of Black Authors in the English-speaking World of the Eighteenth Century*. Lexington: University Press of Kentucky, 1996.

58. Carroll, Patrick J. "Recent Literature on Latin American Slavery (review essay: Blanchard, *Slavery and Abolition in Early Republican Peru*; Bush, *Slave Women in Caribbean Society*; Inikori and Engerman, eds., *Atlantic Slave Trade*; Meillassoux,

Antropologia de la esclavitud; Pérez, *Slaves, Sugar, and Colonial Society*; Solow, ed., *Slavery and the Rise of the Atlantic System*; Thornton, *Africa and Africans in the Making of the Atlantic World*)," *Latin American Research Review*, 31, 1 (1996), pp. 135-47.

59. Carter, George E. "A Review of Slavery and Abolition in South Africa and the United States in the Eighteenth Century," *American Studies International*, 29, 2 (1991), pp. 69-76.

60. Carvalho, José Murilo de. "Luso-Brazilian Thought on Slavery and Abolition," *Itinerario*, 17, 1 (1993), pp. 79-91.

61. Cavalieri, Paola, and Peter Singer. "The Great Ape Project - and Beyond," in Paola Cavalieri and Peter Singer, eds., *The Great Ape Project: Equality Behind Humanity* (London: Fourth Estate, 1993), pp. 304-12.

62. Chambers, Douglas B. "Source Material for Studying the Igbo in the Diaspora: Problems and Possibilities" (Unpublished paper presented at conference on "Source Material for Studying the Slave Trade and the African Diaspora", Stirling, Scotland, 13-14 April 1996).

63. Chambers, Jim. *Philosophy, Slavery and Socio-Economic Disorder*. Langley Park: IAAS Publishers, 1993.

64. Clark, Stephen R. L. "Slaves and Citizens," *Philosophy*, 60 (no. 231) (1985), pp. 27-46.

65. Clarke, John Henrik. *Christopher Columbus and the Afrikan Holocaust: Slavery and the Rise of European Capitalism*. Brooklyn: A&B Books Publishers, 1992.

Also Brooklyn NY: A & B Brooks, 1994.

66. Clarke, John Henrik. *Critical Lessons in Slavery and the Slavetrade: Essential Studies and Commentaries on Slavery, in General, and the African Slavetrade, in Particular*. (Newly expanded and rev. 2nd ed.) Richmond: Native Sun Publishers, 1996.

67. Claxton, Joseph E. "Slavery and Race: An Essay on New Ideas and Enduring Shibboleths in the Interpretation of the American Constitutional System," *Mercer Law Review*, 44, 2 (1993), pp. 637-52.

68. Collins, Merle. "'To Be Free is Very Sweet' (review essay: Ferguson, *Subject to Others*, and *The Hart Sisters*)," *Slavery and Abolition*, 15, 3 (1994), pp. 96-103.

69. Conniff, Michael L., and Thomas J. Davis, eds. *Africans in the Americas: A History of the Black Diaspora*. New York: St. Martin's Press, 1994. With Patrick Carroll, David Eltis, Patience Essah, Alfred D. Frederick, Dale T. Graden, Linda M. Heywood, Richard Lobban, Colin A. Palmer, Joseph P. Reidy, John Thornton, Ronald Walters, Ashton Welch, and Winthrop R. Wright.

Includes chapters (individually authored, but not attributed) on "Early African Experiences in the Americas" (in Part I: Africa, Europe, and the Americas), "Africans in the Caribbean," "Africans in Brazil," "Africans in Mainland Spanish America," "Africans in the Thirteen British Colonies" (all in Part II: The Slave Trade and Slavery in the Americas), and "Abolition of the Atlantic Slave Trade," "Emancipation in the Caribbean and Spanish America," "Emancipation in the United States," and "Emancipation in Brazil" (all in Part III: Ending the Slave Trade and Slavery).

70. Cooke, Michael G. "The Metaphor of Slavery in Recent African-American and Caribbean Fiction," in Binder, ed., *Slavery in the Americas*, pp. 581-600.

71. Cosby, Bruce. "Technological Politics and the Political History of African-Americans" (PhD diss., Clark Atlanta University, 1995).

72. Costa e Silva, Alberto da. "Brasil, África y el Atlántico en el siglo XIX," *Amèrica negra*, 9 (1995), pp. 135-56.

73. Crane, Brian. "Colono and Criollo Ware Pottery from Charleston, South Carolina, and San Juan, Puerto Rico, in Comparative Perspective" (Unpublished paper, Annual Meeting of the Society for Historical Archaeology, Kingston, Jamaica, January 1992).

74. Craton, Michael. "Slave Revolts and the End of Slavery".

Reprinted (excerpted from *Out of Slavery*) in Northrup, ed., *The Atlantic Slave Trade*, pp. 203-17.

75. Crosby, Michael H. "Twentieth Century Slavery Prosecutions: The Sharpening Sword," *Criminal Justice Journal*, 8, 1 (1985), pp. 47-88.

76. Curtin, Philip D. "O açucar e a estrutura produtiva da plantação" (Presentation at "Seminário internacional: Escravos com e sem açucar", Madeira, 17-21 June 1996).

77. Dabla, Séwanou Jean-Jacques. "La mémoire des anneaux ou le souvenir de l'esclavage des noirs dans l'enseignement et la litterature en France" (Unpublished paper, UNESCO conference on "La route de l'esclave", Ouidah, Bénin, 1-5 Sept. 1994).

78. Daniels, Christine. "'Without Any Limitation of Time': Debt Servitude in Colonial America," *Labor History*, 36, 2 (1995), pp. 232-50.

79. Darity, William, Jr. "Eric Williams and the Changing Historiography of the First Industrial Revolution" (Unpublished paper, "*Capitalism and Slavery* Fifty Years Later").

80. Darity, William, Jr. "A Model of 'Original Sin': Rise of the West and Lag of the Rest," *American Economic Review*, 82, 2 (1992), pp. 162-67.

81. Davidson, Basil. "Columbus: The Bones and Blood of Racism," *Race & Class*, 33, 3 (1992), pp. 17-25.

82. Davis, Darién J., ed. *Slavery and Beyond: The African Impact on Latin America and the Caribbean*. Wilmington DE: SR Books, 1995.

For contents see Gerhard and Montejo.

83. Davis, David Brion. "The Perils of Doing History by Ahistorical Abstraction: A Reply to Thomas L. Haskell's *AHR Forum* Reply."

Reprinted in Bender, *The Antislavery Debate*, pp. 290-309.

84. Davis, David Brion. Selections from *The Problem of Slavery in the Age of Revolution, 1770-1823*.

Reprinted in Bender, *The Antislavery Debate*, pp. 15-103.

85. Davis, David Brion. "Reflections on Abolitionism and Ideological Hegemony."

Reprinted in Bender, *The Antislavery Debate*, pp. 161-79.

86. Davis, David Brion. "Sugar and Slavery from the Old to the New World".

Reprinted (from *Slavery and Human Progress*) in Northrup, ed., *The Atlantic Slave Trade*, pp. 25-35.

87. De Assis, Sebastian. "Slavery in the Post-Industrial Revolution Era" (PhD diss., California State University - Dominguez Hills, 1996).

88. Delle, James A. "The West Indian Origins of New England Racism" (Unpublished paper, Annual Meeting of the Society for Historical Archaeology, Kingston, Jamaica, January 1992).

89. "Les dépendances serviles: une approche comparative" (Colloque, École des Hautes Études en Sciences Sociales, Paris, 19-22 juin 1996). Orgs. Myriam Cottias, Rebecca Scott, Alessandro Stella, and Bernard Vincent.

For contributions see Annequin, Bazémo, Berlin, Chase, Cottias, Furio, Garlan, Gerbeau, Klein, Kolendo, Kolchin, Lahon, Martin, Mattoso, Mossé, Reis, Saville, J. Scott, R. Scott, Solow, Stella, Tardieu, and Trabelsi.

90. Derry, Linda. "The Problem with 'Plantation Archaeology': A Feminist Perspective" (Unpublished paper, Annual Meeting of the Society for Historical Archaeology, Kingston, Jamaica, January 1992).

91. "The Development of the African Diaspora: The Slave Trade of the Nigerian Hinterland". Coordinated by Paul E. Lovejoy and Robin Law. (In collaboration with the UNESCO "Slave Route Project")

For current projects see "The African Diaspora and the Nigerian Hinterland: Towards a Research Agenda" and "Source Material for Studying the Slave Trade and the African Diaspora".

92. Diagne, Pathé. "Migrations africaines précolombiennes et économie politique de l'esclavage" (Unpublished paper, UNESCO conference on "La route de l'esclave", Ouidah, Bénin, 1-5 Sept. 1994).

93. Dixon, Chris. "An Ambivalent Black Nationalism: Haiti, Africa, and Antebellum African-American Emigrationism," *Australasian Journal of American Studies*, 10, 2 (1991), pp. 10-25.

94. ["Documenting the Black Holocaust"] (1994).

1 videocassette (VHS) (145 min.): licensed off-the-air recording made by Northeastern University Library Media

95. Dorigny, Marcel. "Les abolitions de l'esclavage: 1793-1794-1848" (Unpublished paper, UNESCO conference on "La route de l'esclave", Ouidah, Bénin, 1-5 Sept. 1994).

96. Drescher, Seymour. "*Capitalism and Slavery* after Fifty Years" (Unpublished paper, "*Capitalism and Slavery* Fifty Years Later").

97. Drescher, Seymour. "Esclavage et réflexion morale au sujet de l'esclavage," in Monique Canto-Sperber, ed., *Dictionnaire d'éthique et de philosophie morale* (Paris: Presses Universitaires de France, 1996), pp. 518-24.

98. Duharte, Rafael. "La rebeldía esclava en el Caribe y la América Latina," *Del Caribe*, 6, 15 (1989), pp. 88-96.

99. Edwards, Paul. "Unreconciled Strivings and Ironic Strategies: Three Afro-British Authors of the Georgian Era: Ignatius Sancho, Olaudah Equiano, Robert Wedderburn" (Edinburgh: University of Edinburgh, Centre of African Studies, 1992). (Occasional papers, University of Edinburgh, Centre of African Studies. no. 34)

100. Elbourne, Elizabeth. "Freedom at Issue: Vagrancy Legislation and the Meaning of Freedom in Britain and the Cape Colony, 1799-1842," in Lovejoy and Rogers, eds., *Unfree Labour in the Development of the Atlantic World*, pp. 114-50.

101. Ellis, Richard J. "The Social Construction of Slavery," in Dennis J. Coyle and Richard J. Ellis, eds., *Politics, Policy, and Culture* (Boulder: Westview Press, 1994), pp. 117-35.

102. Eltis, David. "Europeans and the Rise and Fall of African Slavery in the Americas: An Interpretation," *American Historical Review*, 98, 5 (1993), pp. 1399-423.

103. Eltis, David. "Labour and Coercion in the English Atlantic World from the Seventeenth to the Early Twentieth Century," in Twaddle, ed., *The Wages of Slavery*, pp. 207-26.

104. Emert, Phyllis Raybin, ed. *Colonial Triangular Trade: An Economy Based on Human Misery*. Carlisle MA: Discovery Enterprises, 1995.

105. Emmer, Pieter C. "Afrika in Amerika, Nederland en de opkomst en neergang van de slavenhandel en de slavernij in de Nieuwe Wereld, 1500-1900," in J. Lechner and H. Ph. Vogel, eds., *De Nieuwe Wereld en de lage landen: onbekende aspecten van vijfhonderd jaar ontmoetingen tussen Latijns-Amerika en Nederland* (Amsterdam: Meulenhoff, 1992), pp. 47-73.

106. Emmer, Pieter C. "Afrikanischer Sklavenhandel und Sklaverei im Atlantischen Gebiet, 1500-1900," in Raddatz, ed., *Afrika in Amerika*, pp. 63-79.

107. Emmer, Pieter C. "The Constraints of Change in Postemancipation America," in Frank McGlynn and Seymour Drescher, eds., *The Meaning of Freedom: Economics, Politics, and Culture after Slavery* (Pittsburgh: University of Pittsburgh Press, 1992), pp. 23-47. (Pitt Latin American Series)

108. Emmer, Pieter C. "The Dutch and the Making of the Second Atlantic System," in Solow, ed., *Slavery and the Rise of the Atlantic System*, pp. 75-96.

109. Emmer, Pieter C. "European Expansion and Migration: the European Colonial Past and Intercontinental Migration: An Overview," in Pieter C. Emmer and Magnus Mörner, eds., *European Expansion and Migration: Essays on the Intercontinental Migration from Africa, Asia and Europe* (New York: Berg, 1992), pp. 1-12.

110. Emmer, P[ieter] C. "Nederlandse handelaren, kolonisten en planters in de Nieuwe Wereld," in H. W. van den Doel, idem, and [H.] Ph. Vogel, eds., *Nederland en de Nieuwe Wereld* (Utrecht: Spectrum, 1992), pp. 9-80.

111. *Encyclopedia of Slavery*. Seymour Drescher and Stanley L. Engerman, eds. New York: Garland, in preparation.

112. *Encyclopedia of Slavery*. Paul Finkelman and Joseph C. Miller, eds. New York: Simon and Schuster, in preparation.

113. *Encyclopedia of World Slavery*. Jerusalem: Jerusalem Publishing House, in preparation.

114. Engerman, Stanley L. "The Atlantic Economy of the Eighteenth Century: Some Speculations on Economic Development in Britain, America, Africa and Elsewhere," *European Journal of Economic History*, 24, 1 (1995), pp. 145-75.

115. Engerman, Stanley L. "Chicken Little, Anna Karenina, and the Economics of Slavery: Two Reflections on Historical Analysis, with Examples

Drawn Mostly from the Study of Slavery," *Social Science History*, 17, 2 (1993), pp. 161-71.

116. Engerman, Stanley L. "The Economics of Forced Labor," *Itinerario*, 17, 1 (1993), pp. 59-78.

117. Engerman, Stanley L. "Emancipations in Comparative Perspective: A Long and Wide View," in Oostindie, ed., *Fifty Years Later*, pp. 223-43.

118. Engerman, Stanley L. "The Extent of Slavery and Freedom Throughout the Ages, in the World as a Whole and in Major Subareas," in Julian Lincoln Simon, ed., *The State of Humanity* (Oxford: Blackwell, in association with the Cato Institute, 1995), pp. 171-77.

119. Engerman, Stanley L. "Slavery and Emancipation in Comparative Perspective".

Reprinted in Goodheart, Brown, and Rabe, eds., *Slavery in American Society*, pp. 217-34.

120. Engerman, Stanley L. "Slavery, Serfdom and Other Forms of Coerced Labor: Similarities and Differences," in Bush, ed., *Serfdom and Slavery*, pp. 18-41.

121. Ensslen, Klaus. "The Renaissance of the Slave Narrative in Recent Critical and Fictional Discourse," in Binder, ed., *Slavery in the Americas*, pp. 601-26.

122. *Esclavage, colonisation, libérations nationales de 1789 à nos jours* (Colloque organisé les 24, 25 et 26 février 1989 à l'Université Paris VIII). Paris: Harmattan, 1990.

For contents see Bangou, Bonnet, Cauna, Chrysostome, Daget, Duharte Jimenez, Etienne, Halpern, Legra Hernandez, and Vidaud.

123. Faber, Eli. *Slavery and the Jews: A Historical Inquiry*. (New York): Hunter College of the City University of New York, 1995. (Occasional Papers in Jewish History and Thought, no. 2)

124. Farrakhan, Louis. *The Controversy with the Jews: The True History of Slavery in the Americas*. Chicago: Final Call, Inc., 1994.

Sound recording, three cassettes. (Speech delivered at the University of Massachusetts at Amherst, 9 March 1994)

125. Ferguson, Moira. *Subject to Others: British Women Writers and Colonial Slavery, 1670-1834*. New York: Routledge, 1992.

126. Fiedler, Leslie A. "'Benito Cereno' and the Gothic Horror of Slavery," in idem, ed., *Love and Death in the American Novel* (New York: Stein and Day, rev. ed., 1966), pp. 400-01.

Reprinted in Burkholder, ed., *Critical Essays on Herman Melville's "Benito Cereno"*, pp. 48-49.

127. Field, Ron. *African Peoples of the Americas: From Slavery to Civil Rights*. Cambridge: Cambridge University Press, 1995. (Cambridge History Programme. Key stage 3)

128. Finley, Moses I. *Ancient Slavery and Modern Ideology*.

Translated as *Escravidão antiga e ideologia moderna* (Rio de Janeiro: Graal, 1991).

129. Fleischman, Ulrich. "Maroons, Writers, and History," in Binder, ed., *Slavery in the Americas*, pp. 565-79.

130. Fogel, Robert W. "A Comparison between the Value of Slave Capital in the Share of Total British Wealth (c. 1811) and in the Share of Total Southern Wealth (c. 1860)," in Fogel, Galantine, and Manning, eds., *Evidence and Methods* (*Without Consent or Contract*), pp. 397-98.

131. Fogel, Robert W. "A Note on the Effect of Moral Issues on the Debates among Cliometricians," in Fogel, Galantine, and Manning, eds., *Evidence and Methods* (*Without Consent or Contract*), pp. 589-91.

132. Fogel, Robert W. "The Origin and History of Economic Issues in the American Slavery Debate," in Fogel, Galantine, and Manning, eds., *Evidence and Methods* (*Without Consent or Contract*), pp. 154-63.

Condensation of chapter 5 (pp. 170-86), Fogel and Engerman, *Time on the Cross*.

133. Fogel, Robert W. "Risks and Rewards of Planters in the New World," in Fogel, Galantine, and Manning, eds., *Evidence and Methods* (*Without Consent or Contract*), pp. 47-50.

134. Fogel, Robert W. "Slavery in the New World".

Reprinted (from *Without Consent or Contract*) in Goodheart, Brown, and Rabe, eds., *Slavery in American Society*, pp. 21-34.

135. Fredrickson, George M. "The Origins of Racial Slavery in Virginia and South Africa".

Reprinted (from *White Supremacy*) in Goodheart, Brown, and Rabe, eds., *Slavery in American Society*, pp. 197-207.

136. Friedemann, N. de. "Proyecto: puente Africa-América en la Ruta del Esclavo," *Studies in the World History of Slavery Abolition, and Emancipation* (Aug. 1996).

http://h-net.msu.edu/~slavery

137. Friedman, Gerald, Ralph A. Galantine, and Robert W. Fogel. "The Debate over the Economic Viability of Slavery," in Fogel, Galantine, and Manning, eds., *Evidence and Methods* (*Without Consent or Contract*), pp. 199-205.

138. Funari, Pedro Paulo A. "The Archaeology of Palmares and its Contribution to the Understanding of the History of African-American Culture," *Historical Archaeology in Latin America*, 7 (1995), pp. 1-41.

139. Funari, Pedro Paulo A. "A arqueologia e a cultura africana nas Américas," *Estudos ibero-americanos*, 17, 2 (1991), pp. 61-71.

Also in Francisca L. Nogueira de Azevedo and John Manuel Monteiro, eds., *Raízes da América Latina* (São Paulo: Ed. Universidade de São Paulo, Expressão e Cultura, 1996), pp. 535-46.

140. Funari, Pedro Paulo A. "La cultura material y la arqueología en el estudio de la cultura africana en las Américas," *América negra*, 8 (1994), pp. 33-47.

141. Galenson, David W. "The Market Evaluation of Human Capital: The Case of Indentured Servitude," *Journal of Political Economy*, 89, 3 (1981), pp. 446-67.

Reprinted in Fogel and Engerman, eds., *Markets and Production: Technical Papers*, vol. 1 (*Without Consent or Contract*), pp. 14-30.

142. Galenson, David W. "White Servitude and the Growth of Black Slavery in Colonial America".

Excerpted in Fogel and Engerman, eds., *Markets and Production: Technical Papers*, vol. 1 (*Without Consent or Contract*), pp. 5-13.

143. Galloway, J. H. *The Sugar Cane Industry: An Historical Geography from its Origins to 1914*. Cambridge: Cambridge University Press, 1989.

144. Garcia, Jesús. "La contribución musical de África subsahariana al mosaico musical de las Americas y los Caribes" (Unpublished paper, UNESCO conference on "La route de l'esclave", Ouidah, Bénin, 1-5 Sept. 1994).

145. Gaspar, David Barry, and Darlene Clark Hine, eds. *More Than Chattel: Black Women and Slavery in the Americas*. Bloomington: Indiana University Press, 1996. (Blacks in the Diaspora)

For contents see Beckles, Bush, Cody, Gaspar, Geggus, Gould, Karasch, King, Moitt, Naylor-Ojurongbe and Gaspar, Olwell, Robertson, Slenes, Socolow, Steckel, and Stevenson.

146. Gautier, Arlette. "Nouvelles problematiques dans l'histoire de l'esclavage: l'étude des rapports sociaux de sexe," in Pas, coord., *Anais do Seminário internacional da escravidão*, pp. 107-19. (Section: "Mulheres escravas: nouvelles problematiques dans l'histoire de l'esclavage: l'étude des rapports sociaux de sexe")

Translated as "Novas problemáticas na história da escravidão: estudo das relações sociais de sexo (trans. Josina Nunes Drumond)," in Pas, coord., *Anais do Seminário internacional da escravidão*, pp. 123-35.

147. Gemery, Henry A., and Jan S. Hogendorn. "Technological Change, Slavery, and the Slave Trade".

Reprinted in Michael Adas, ed., *Technology and European Overseas Enterprise: Diffusion, Adaption, and Adoption* (Brookfield VT: Variorum, 1996), pp. 157-80.

148. Gerbeau, Hubert, and Éric Saugera, eds. *La dernière traite: fragments d'histoire en hommage à Serge Daget*. Paris: Société Française d'Histoire d'Outre-Mer, 1994.

For contents see Daget, Ekanza, Follez, Gerbeau (2), Kodjo, Quénum, Renault, Saugera (2), Villiers, and Weber.

149. Gilroy, Paul. *The Black Atlantic: Modernity and Double Consciousness*. London: Verso, 1993.

150. Glaberman, Martin. "Slaves and Proletarians: The Debate Continues," *Labour/Le Travail*, 36 (1995), pp. 209-14.

With reply by Noel Ignatiev, pp. 215-16.

151. Glissant, Edouard. "Creolization in the Making of the Americas," in Hyatt and Nettleford, eds., *Race, Discourse, and the Origin of the Americas*, pp. 268-75.

152. Goldin, Claudia. "The Economics of Emancipation".

Reprinted with revisions in Fogel and Engerman, eds., *Conditions of Life and the Transition to Freedom: Technical Papers*, vol. 2 (*Without Consent or Contract*), pp. 614-28.

153. Greenberg, Kenneth S. "The Meaning of Death in Slave Society," *Research in Law, Deviance & Social Control*, 8 (1986), pp. 113-30.

154. Grupo América Negra, Colombia-Venezuela. "Proyecto 'Puente Africa-América' en La Ruta del esclavo," *América negra*, 10 (1996), pp. 211-24.

155. Hall, Catherine. (Review of Temperley, *White Dreams, Black Africa*, and Turley, *Culture of English Antislavery*), *History Workshop*, 35 (1993), pp. 230-37.

156. Hall, Gwendolyn Midlo. *Social Control in Slave Plantation Societies: A Comparison of St. Domingue and Cuba.*

Reprinted, Baton Rouge: Louisiana State University Press, 1996.

157. Hamburgisches Museum für Volkerkunde. *Afrika in Amerika: Hamburgisches Museum für Volkerkunde 1992*. Ed. Corinna Raddatz. Hamburg: Das Museum, 1992. (Exhibition catalog. "Ein Lesebuch zum Thema Sklaverei und ihren Folgen")

158. Hanes, Christopher. "Turnover Cost and the Distribution of Slave Labor in Anglo-America," *Journal of Economic History*, 56, 2 (1996), pp. 307-29.

159. Hansen, João Adolfo. "Malhado ou malhadiço: a escravidão na sátira barroca," *Revista de história* (São Paulo), no. 120 (1989), pp. 163-82.

160. Hardy, Kenneth V. "The Psychological Residuals of Slavery" (Topeka KS: Equal Partners Productions, 1995). (Videocassette)

161. Hare, R. M. "What Is Wrong with Slavery," *Philosophy and Public Affairs*, 8, 2 (1979), pp. 103-21.

162. Harris, Joseph E. "The African Diaspora in the Old and New Worlds," in B. A. Ogot, ed., *General History of Africa, Vol. 5: Africa from the Sixteenth to the Eighteenth Century* (Berkeley/Paris/London: University of California Press/UNESCO/Heinemann, 1992), pp. 113-36.

163. Harris, Joseph E. "The Dynamics of the Global African Diaspora," in Jalloh and Maizlish, eds., *African Diaspora*, pp. 7-21.

164. Harris, Joseph E., ed. *Global Dimensions of the African Diaspora*. 2nd ed. Washington DC: Howard University Press, 1993.

For contents see Bryce-Laport, Harris, Hunwick, Kaké, Levine, Montillus, Palmer, Raboteau, Shyllon, Skidmore, Steady, and Uya.

165. Haskell, Thomas L. "Capitalism and the Origins of the Humanitarian Sensibility (parts 1 and 2)."

Reprinted in Bender, *The Antislavery Debate*, pp. 107-60.

166. Haskell, Thomas L. "Convention and Hegemonic Interest in the Debate over Antislavery: A Reply to Davis and Ashworth."

Reprinted in Bender, *The Antislavery Debate*, pp. 200-59.

167. Hawkins, Sean, and Philip Morgan. "Patterns of Cultural Transmission: Diffusion, Destruction, and Development in the African Diaspora" (Unpublished paper, "The African Diaspora and the Nigerian Hinterland").

168. Heller, Henry. "Bodin on Slavery and Primitive Accumulation," *Sixteenth Century Journal*, 25, 1 (1994), pp. 53-65.

169. Hoering, Uwe, ed. *Zum Beispiel Sklaverei*. Göttingen: Lamur, 1995.

170. Hoffman, Martha K. "Channing on the Place of Material Treatment in the Moral Indictment of Slavery," in Fogel, Galantine, and Manning, eds., *Evidence and Methods* (*Without Consent or Contract*), pp. 591-93.

171. Hoogbergen, Wim, ed. *Born out of Resistance: On Caribbean Cultural Creativity*. Utrecht: ISOR-Press, 1995.

For contents see Bilby, Blanchard, Bush, Duharte Jiménez, de Groot, Heuman, Moitt, Neumayer, and Serrano López.

172. Horowitz, Maryanne Cline. "Introduction: Race, Class, Gender, and Human Unity," in Horowitz, ed., *Race, Class and Gender in Nineteenth-Century Culture*, pp. ix-xix.

173. Horowitz, Maryanne Cline, ed. *Race, Class and Gender in Nineteenth-Century Culture.* Rochester NY: University of Rochester Press, 1991.

For contents see Cline, D'Elia, Horowitz, Vander Zanden, and Wish.

174. Horsley-Meacham, Gloria. "The Monastic Slaver: Images and Meaning in 'Benito Cereno'," *New England Quarterly*, 56, 2 (1983), pp. 261-66.

Reprinted in Burkholder, ed., *Critical Essays on Herman Melville's "Benito Cereno"*, pp. 94-98.

175. Howard University. Black Diaspora Committee. *The African Diaspora: Africans and Their Descendants in the Wider World 1800 to the Present.* Needham Heights MA: Simon & Schuster Custom Publishing, 1996.

Revised edition of *The African Diaspora: Africans and Their Descendants in the Wider World to 1800.*

176. Hunt, Alfred N. *Haiti's Influence on Antebellum America: Slumbering Volcano in the Caribbean.* Baton Rouge: Louisiana State University Press, 1988.

177. Hyatt, Vera Lawrence, and Rex Nettleford, eds. *Race, Discourse, and the Origin of the Americas: A New World View.* Washington: Smithsonian Institution Press, 1995. (Symposium held at the Smithsonian Institution, 1991)

For contents see Glissant, Kelley, Russell-Wood, Thornton, and Van Sertima.

178. Ifill, Max B. *Slavery, Social Death or Communal Victory: A Critical Appraisal of* Slavery and Social Death *by Dr. Orlando Patterson.* Port of Spain, Trinidad: Economics and Business Research, 1996.

179. Inikori, Joseph E. "*Capitalism and Slavery* After Fifty Years" (Unpublished paper, conference on "*Capitalism and Slavery* Fifty Years Later").

180. Inikori, Joseph E. "Slavery and Atlantic Commerce, 1650-1800," *American Economic Review*, 82, 2 (1992), pp. 151-57.

181. Inikori, Joseph E. *Slavery and the Rise of Capitalism.* Mona: Department of History, University of the West Indies, 1993. (Elsa Goveia Memorial Lecture)

182. Irele, Abiola. "Harlem, Haiti and the Negritude Movement" (Unpublished paper, UNESCO conference on "La route de l'esclave", Ouidah, Bénin, 1-5 Sept. 1994).

183. Jalloh, Alusine, and Stephen E. Maizlish, eds. *The African Diaspora.* College Station: Texas A&M University Press, 1996.

For contents see Chambers, Graden, Harris, Inikori, and Palmer.

184. Jamieson, Ross W. "Material Culture and Social Death: African-American Burial Practices," *Historical Archaeology*, 29, 4 (1995), pp. 39-58.

185. Jenkins, Everett. *Pan-African Chronology: A Comprehensive Reference to the Black Quest for Freedom in Africa, the Americas, Europe and Asia, 1400-1865.* Jefferson NC: McFarland & Co., 1996.

186. Jordan, Winthrop D. "The Simultaneous Invention of Slavery and Racism".

Reprinted (excerpted from *White Over Black*) in Northrup, ed., *The Atlantic Slave Trade*, pp. 12-25.

187. Jordan, Winthrop D. "Slavery and the Jews," *Atlantic Monthly*, 276, 3 (Sept. 1995), pp. 109-14.

188. Karcher, Carolyn L. "The Riddle of the Sphinx: Melville's 'Benito Cereno' and the *Amistad* Case," in Burkholder, ed., *Critical Essays on Herman Melville's "Benito Cereno"*, pp. 196-229.

189. Karras, Alan J., and J. R. McNeill, eds. *Atlantic American Societies from Columbus through Abolition 1492-1888.* London: Routledge, 1992.

For contents see Manning, McNeill, Morgan, and Wood.

190. Kelley, David H. "An Essay on Pre-Columbian Contacts Between the Americas and Other Areas, with Special Reference to the Work of Ivan Van Sertima," in Hyatt and Nettleford, eds., *Race, Discourse, and the Origin of the Americas*, pp. 103-22.

191. Ki-zerbo, Joseph. "La route mentale de l'esclave: brèves réflexions à partir de la condition présent des peuples noirs" (Unpublished paper, UNESCO conference on "La route de l'esclave", Ouidah, Bénin, 1-5 Sept. 1994).

192. King, Preston. "On the Meaning and History of Slavery," in Tibbles, ed., *Transatlantic Slavery*, pp. 116-21.

193. *Klein, Herbert S. "The African Slaves," in UNESCO, *History of Latin America* (??), vol. 3, pp. (??).

194. Klein, Martin A. "Coerced Labour and the International Labour Market: Abolition of Slavery in the Colonial Domains of Africa and Asia" (Unpublished paper, conference on "Unfree Labor in the Development of the Atlantic World", 13-14 April 1993, York University, Ontario).

195. Klein, Martin A. "Introduction: Modern European Expansion and Traditional Servitude in Africa and Asia," in idem, ed., *Breaking the Chains*, pp. 1-36.

196. Klein, Martin A. "Slavery, the International Labour Market and the Emancipation of Slaves in the Nineteenth Century," in Lovejoy and Rogers, eds., *Unfree Labour in the Development of the Atlantic World*, pp. 197-221.

197. Klein, Martin A., ed. *Breaking the Chains: Slavery, Bondage, and Emancipation in Modern Africa and Asia*. Madison: University of Wisconsin Press, 1993.

For contents see Clarence-Smith, Feeny, Klein (2), Kumar, Mbodj, Prakash, Reid, and Toledano.

198. Knight, Franklin. "Columbus and Slavery in the New World and Africa" (Unpublished paper, 24th Annual Conference of Caribbean Historians, Nassau, 29 March - 3 April 1992).

199. Kolawole, Mary E. Modupe. "An African View of Transatlantic Slavery and the Role of Oral Testimony in Creating a New Legacy," in Tibbles, ed., *Transatlantic Slavery*, pp. 105-10.

200. Kolchin, Peter. "American Slavery and Russian Serfdom".

Reprinted (from *Unfree Labor*) in Goodheart, Brown, and Rabe, eds., *Slavery in American Society*, pp. 207-16.

201. Kolchin, Peter. "The Comparative Approach to the Study of Slavery: Problems and Prospects" (Presentation at Colloquium on "Les dépendances serviles", Paris 1996).

202. Kolchin, Peter. "Some Controversial Questions Concerning Nineteenth-Century Emancipation from Slavery and Serfdom," in Bush, ed., *Serfdom and Slavery*, pp. 42-67.

203. Kubik, Gerhard. "Transplantation of African Musical Cultures into the New World: Research Topics and Objectives in the Study of African-American Music," in Binder, ed., *Slavery in the Americas*, pp. 421-52.

204. Lamounier, Lucia. "Between Slavery and Free Labour: Early Experiments with Free Labour and Patterns of Slave Emancipation in Brazil and Cuba," in Turner, ed., *From Chattel Slaves to Wage Slaves*, pp. 185-200.

205. Landers, Jane G., ed. "Against the Odds: Free Blacks in the Slave Societies of the Americas," special issue of *Slavery and Abolition*, 17, 1 (1996).

For contents see Garrigus, Hanger, Hoefte, Lachance, Landers, Olwell, and Schafer.

206. Larson, Pier M. HISTORY MUSEUM OF SLAVERY.

http://squash.la.psu.edu/~plarson/smuseum/homepage.html

207. Law, Robin [C. C.], and Paul E. Lovejoy. "Deconstructing the African Diaspora: The Slave Trade of the Nigerian Hinterland" (Unpublished project proposal, "The African Diaspora and the Nigerian Hinterland").

Another version as "The Development of an African Diaspora" (unpublished).

208. LeBlanc, John R. "The Context of Manumission: Imperial Rome and Antebellum Alabama," *Alabama Review*, 46, 4 (1993), pp. 266-87.

209. Lengelle, Maurice. *L'esclavage*. 6e édition. Paris: Presses Universitaires de France, 1992.

210. Leray, Christian. "Chronologie sommaire des abolitions," *Les anneaux de la mémoire* (Exhibition catalogue, Nantes, 1992), pp. 122-23.

211. Lewis, James R. "Images of Captive Rape in the Nineteenth Century," *Journal of American Culture*, 15, 2 (1992), pp. 69-77.

212. Lewis, Rupert. "The Contemporary Significance of the African Diaspora in the

Americas," *Caribbean Quarterly*, 38, 2-3 (1992), pp. 73-80.

213. Lienhard, Martín. "Una tierra sin amos: lectura de los testimonios legales de algunos esclavos fugitivos (Puerto Rico y Brasil, siglo XIX)," *América indígena*, 54, 4 (1994), pp. 209-27.

214. Linde, J. M. van der. *Over Noach met zijn zonen: de Cham-ideologie en de leugens tegen Cham tot vandaag*. Utrecht: Interuniversitair Instituut voor Missiologie en Oecumenica, 1993.

215. Little, Thomas J. "George Liele and the Rise of Independent Black Baptist Churches in the Lower South and Jamaica," *Slavery and Abolition*, 16, 2 (1995), pp. 188-204.

216. Lohse, Wulf. "Afrikanische Sklaverei," in Raddatz, ed., *Afrika in Amerika*, pp. 53-61.

217. Lovejoy, Paul E. "The African Diaspora: Revisionist Interpretations of Ethnicity, Culture and Religion under Slavery" (Unpublished paper, Boston University African Studies Center, Working Papers, 1996).

218. Lovejoy, Paul E. "Biography as Source Material: Towards a Biographical Dictionary of Slavery" (Unpublished paper presented at conference on "Source Material for Studying the Slave Trade and the African Diaspora", Stirling, Scotland, 13-14 April 1996).

219. Lovejoy, Paul E. "The Conditions of Slaves in the Americas" (Unpublished paper, UNESCO conference on "La route de l'esclave", Ouidah, Bénin, 1-5 Sept. 1994).

220. Lovejoy, Paul E., and Nicholas Rogers. "Introduction," in Lovejoy and Rogers, eds., *Unfree Labour in the Development of the Atlantic World*, pp. 1-10.

221. Lovejoy, Paul E., and Nicholas Rogers, eds. *Unfree Labour in the Development of the Atlantic World*. London: Frank Cass, 1994. Also as a special issue of *Slavery and Abolition*, 15, 2 (1994).

For contents see Beckles, Bolland, Elbourne, Falola, Klein, Lovejoy, Lovejoy and Rogers, Naro, and Walvin.

222. Manning, Patrick. "Migrations of Africans to the Americas: The Impact of Africans, Africa, and the New World," *The History Teacher*, 26, 2 (1993), pp. 279-96.

Reprinted in Manning, ed., *Slave Trades, 1500-1800*, pp. 65-82.

223. Manning, Patrick. "Tragedy and Sacrifice in the History of Slavery".

Reprinted (from *Slavery and African Life*) in Karras and McNeill, eds., *Atlantic American Societies*, pp. 40-72.

224. Martin, Peter. *Schwarze Teufel, edle Mohren: Afrikaner in Geschichte und Bewußtsein der Deutschen*. Hamburg: Junius, 1993.

225. Mason, John E. "Notes on Slavery, Emancipation, and the Reconstruction of Racial Identities in South Africa and the United States" (Unpublished paper, Southern Historical Association, New Orleans, 9-12 Nov. 1995).

226. Mason, John E. "Social Death and Resurrection: Conversion, Resistance and the Ambiguities of Islam in Bahia and the Cape" (Unpublished paper presented to Institute for Historical Research, University of the Western Cape, August 1995).

227. McAuley, Christopher Anthony. "The Amerindian and African Foundations of Modern Capitalism: Black Political Economy and the Atlantic World" (PhD diss., University of Michigan, 1995).

228. McDonald, Roderick A. *The Economy and Material Culture of Slaves: Goods and Chattels on the Sugar Plantations of Jamaica and Louisiana*. Baton Rouge: Louisiana State University Press, 1993.

229. McGary, Howard, and Bill E. Lawson. *Between Slavery and Freedom: Philosophy and American Slavery*. Bloomington: Indiana University Press, 1993.

230. McNeill, J. R. "The End of the Old Atlantic World: America, Africa, Europe, 1770-1888," in Karras and McNeill, eds., *Atlantic American Societies*, pp. 245-68.

231. Meltzer, Milton. *Slavery: A World History*. New York: Da Capo Press, 1993.

232. Menard, Russell, and Stuart B. Schwartz. "Why African Slavery? Labor Force Transitions in Brazil, Mexico, and the Carolina Lowcountry," in Binder, ed., *Slavery in the Americas*, pp. 89-114.

233. Merkel, W. G. "From the Haitian Revolution to Slave Trade Abolition: The Hardening of West Indian and Southern Attitudes toward Slavery, 1791-1808" (MLitt, Oxford University, 1995).

234. Meyer, Jean. "Le voyage des plantes tropicales," *Les anneaux de la mémoire* (Exhibition catalogue, Nantes, 1992), pp. 140-42.

235. Midgley, Clare. *Women Against Slavery: The British Campaigns, 1780-1870*. London: Routledge, 1992.

236. Miller, Joseph C. "The Abolition of the Slave Trade and Slavery: Historical Foundations" (Unpublished paper, UNESCO conference on "La route de l'esclave", Ouidah, Bénin, 1-5 Sept. 1994).

237. Miller, Joseph C. *Slavery and Slaving in World History: A Bibliography, 1900-1991*. Millwood NY: Kraus International, 1993.

238. Miller, Joseph C., and Emlyn Eisenach. "Slavery: Annual Bibliographical Supplement (1992)," *Slavery and Abolition*, 14, 3 (1993), pp. 264-308.

239. Miller, Joseph C., and Janis M. Gibbs. "Slavery: Annual Bibliographical Supplement (1993)," *Slavery and Abolition*, 15, 3 (1994), pp. 134-97.

240. Miller, Joseph C., and Janis M. Gibbs. "Annual Bibliographical Supplement (1994)," *Slavery and Abolition*, 16, 2 (1995), pp. 398-460.

241. Miller, Joseph C., and Janis M. Gibbs. "Slavery: Annual Bibliographical Supplement (1995)," *Slavery and Abolition*, 17, 3 (1996), pp. 270-339.

242. Miller, Joseph C., and Randolph C. Head. "Slavery: Annual Bibliographical Supplement (1991)," *Slavery and Abolition*, 13, 3 (1992), pp. 244-315.

243. Minchinton, Walter. "Abolition and Emancipation: Williams, Drescher and the Continuing Debate," in McDonald, ed., *West Indies Accounts*, pp. 253-73.

244. Mintz, Sidney W. "Tasting Food, Tasting Freedom," in Binder, ed., *Slavery in the Americas*, pp. 257-75.

245. Mintz, Sidney [W.], and Richard Price. *An Anthropological Approach to the Afro-American Past*. Philadelphia: Institute for the Study of Human Issues, 1976.

Republished as *The Birth of African-American Culture: An Anthropological Perspective* (Boston: Beacon Press, 1992).

246. Mintz, Sidney W. *Sweetness and Power*.

Translated as *Sucre blanc, misère noire: le goût et le pouvoir*. Paris: Nathan, 1991.

247. Mintz, Steven "Models of Emancipation During the Age of Revolution," *Slavery and Abolition*, 17, 2 (1996), pp. 1-21.

248. Montilius, Guérin. "Survivances religieuses africaines en Amérique" (Unpublished paper, UNESCO conference on "La route de l'esclave", Ouidah, Bénin, 1-5 Sept. 1994).

249. Moogk, Peter N. "Bound Labor: The French Colonies," in *Encyclopedia of the North American Colonies*, vol. 2, pp. 32-35.

250. Morgan, Jennifer Lyle. "Women in Slavery and the Transatlantic Slave Trade," in Tibbles, ed., *Transatlantic Slavery*, pp. 60-69.

251. Morgan, Kenneth. "Atlantic Trade and British Economic Growth in the Eighteenth Century" (Unpublished paper, "*Capitalism and Slavery* Fifty Years Later").

252. Morgan, Philip D. "Bound Labor: The British and Dutch Colonies," in *Encyclopedia of the North American Colonies*, vol. 2, pp. 19-32.

253. Morgan, Philip D. "The Cultural Implications of the Atlantic Slave Trade: African Regional Origins, American Destinations, and New World Developments" (Unpublished paper, 1996).

254. Mörner, Magnus. "African Slavery in Spanish and Portuguese America: Some Remarks on Historiography and the Present State of Research," in Binder, ed., *Slavery in the Americas*, pp. 57-87.

255. Mullin, Michael. *Africa in America: Slave Acculturation and Resistance in the American South* *and the British Caribbean, 1736-1831*. Urbana: University of Illinois Press, 1992.

256. Mulvey, Christopher. "The Eighteenth Century Liverpool Slaver and the Twentieth Century Post Colonial Scholar" (Unpublished paper, "*Capitalism and Slavery* Fifty Years Later").

257. Murray, D. R. "Slavery and the Slave Trade: New Comparative Approaches (review essay, including Blackburn, *Overthrow of Colonial Slavery*, Curtin, *Rise and Fall of the Plantation Complex*, Galloway, *Sugar Cane Industry*, Hunt, *Haiti's Influence on Antebellum America*, Manning, *Slavery and African Life*, Postma, *Dutch in the Atlantic Slave Trade*, Tomich, *Slavery in the Circuit of Sugar*, and Watson, *Slave Law in the Americas)*," *Latin American Research Review*, 28, 1 (1993), pp. 150-61.

258. Naragon, Michael D. "Communities in Motion: Drapetomania, Work and the Development of African-American Slave Cultures," *Slavery and Abolition*, 15, 3 (1994), pp. 63-87.

259. Nash, Gary B. "Slavery, Black Resistance, and the American Revolution (review essay: Frey, *Water from the Rock*)," *Georgia Historical Quarterly*, 77, 1 (1993), pp. 62-69.

260. Naylor-Ojurongbe, Celia E., and David Barry Gaspar. "Selected Bibliography," in Gaspar and Hine, eds., *More than Chattel*, pp. 315-28.

261. Nederveen Pieterse, Jan. *White on Black: Images of Africa and Blacks in Western Popular Culture*. New Haven: Yale University Press, 1992.

262. Nicholson, Bradley J. "Legal Borrowing and the Origins of Slave Law in the British Colonies," *American Journal of Legal History*, 38, 1 (1994), pp. 38-54.

263. Oldfield, John R. *The "Ties of Soft Humanity": Slavery and Race in British Drama, 1760-1800*. San Marino CA: Huntington Library, 1993.

264. Orser, Charles E., Jr. "Archaeological Approaches to New World Plantation Slavery," in Michael B. Schiffer, ed., *Archaeological Method and Theory* (Tucson: University of Arizona Press, 1990), vol. 2, pp. 111-54.

265. Orser, Charles E., Jr. "Beneath the Material Surface of Things: Commodities, Artifacts, and Slave Plantations," *Historical Archaeology*, 26, 3 (1992), pp. 95-104. Special issue: Barbara J. Little and Paul A. Schackel, eds., "Meanings and Uses of Material Culture".

266. Orser, Charles E., Jr. "Bibliography of Slave and Plantation Archaeology (as of December 31, 1991)," *Slavery and Abolition*, 13, 3 (1992), pp. 316-37.

267. O'Shaughnessy, Andrew. "*Capitalism and Slavery*" (Unpublished paper, "*Capitalism and Slavery* Fifty Years Later").

268. Palmer, Colin A. "Rethinking American Slavery," in Jalloh and Maizlish, eds., *African Diaspora*, pp. 73-99.

269. Palmié, Stephan. "Introduction," in idem, ed., *Slave Cultures and the Cultures of Slavery*, pp. i-xlvii.

270. Palmié, Stephan. "A Taste for Human Commodities: Experiencing the Atlantic System," in idem., *Slave Cultures and the Cultures of Slavery*, pp. 40-54.

271. Palmié, Stephan, ed. *Slave Cultures and the Cultures of Slavery*. Knoxville: University of Tennessee Press, 1995.

For contents see Bartle, Besson, Blight, Jones, Lichtenstein, Meier, Mintz, Olwig, Oostindie and van Stipriaan, Palmié (2), Thoden van Velzen, Usner, and Wetering.

272. Panzer, Joel S. *The Popes and Slavery*. New York: Alba House, 1996.

273. Pas, Maria Verônica de, coord. *Anais do Seminário internacional da escravidão* (Seminário Internacional da Escravidão, Universidade Federal do Espírito Santo, Vitória, Espírito Santo, 15-17 de junho de 1988). Ed. Fundação Ceciliano Abel de Almeida, 1992.

For contents see Bittencourt, Coutinho, Demoner, "Escravidão no Brasil colonial," Gautier, Hünefeldt, Inikori, and Maciel.

274. Patterson, Orlando. "Freedom, Slavery, and the Modern Construction of Rights," in Olwen Hufton, ed., *Historical Change and Human Rights* (New York: BasicBooks, 1995), pp. 131-78. (The Oxford Amnesty Lectures, 1994)

275. Patterson, Orlando. "Slavery, Alienation, and the Female Discovery of Personal Freedom," in Arien Mack, ed., *Home: A Place in the World* (New York: New York University Press, 1993), pp. 159-87.

276. Patterson, Orlando. "Slavery and Social Death".

Reprinted (from *Slavery and Social Death*) in Goodheart, Brown, and Rabe, eds., *Slavery in American Society*, pp. 3-12.

277. Peyrière, Marie-Christine. "L'héritage du regard: réflexions sur l'exposition négrière comme lieu de mémoire" (Unpublished paper, UNESCO conference on "La route de l'esclave", Ouidah, Bénin, 1-5 Sept. 1994).

278. Phillips, William D., Jr. "Continuity and Change in Western Slavery: Ancient to Modern Times," in Bush, ed., *Serfdom and Slavery*, pp. 71-88.

279. Phillips, William D., Jr. "Escravatura: uma visão global" (Presentation at "Seminário internacional: Escravos com e sem açucar", Madeira, 17-21 June 1996).

280. Plasa, Carl. "'Silent Revolt': Slavery and the Politics of Metaphor in *Jane Eyre*," in Plasa and Ring, eds., *Discourse of Slavery*, pp. 64-93.

281. Potter, Jason R. "A Multicultural Curriculum for the Study of Comparative Slave Societies" (Honors paper, Education Department, Albion College, 1995). (Undergraduate research papers - Albion College; v. 50, pt. 32, 1994-95)

282. Price, Richard. "Lutas de resistência escrava e as comunidades cimarrons: novas diretrizes na história etnográfica," in Andrade and Fernandes, eds., *Atualidade & abolição*, pp. 187-98.

283. Price, Richard. *Maroon Societies: Rebel Slave Communities in the Americas.*

Reprinted, Baltimore: Johns Hopkins University Press, 1996.

284. Price, Sally, and Richard Price. "Widerstand, Rebellion und Freiheit: Maroon Societies in Amerika und ihre Kunst," in Corinna Raddatz, ed., *Afrika in Amerika* (Hamburg: Hamburgisches Museum für Völkerkunde, 1992), pp. 157-73.

285. Raboteau, Albert J. "African Religions in America: Theoretical Perspectives," in Harris, ed., *Global Dimensions of the African Diaspora* (2nd ed.), pp. 65-79.

286. Raddatz, Corinna, ed. *Afrika in Amerika.* Hamburg: Hamburgisches Museum für Völkerkunde, 1992.

For contents see Dressendörfer, Emmer, Lohse, Price and Price, Raddatz, Stedman, and Steege (2).

287. Rashad, Adib. *Islam, Black Nationalism and Slavery: A Detailed History.* Beltsville MD: Writers' Inc. International, 1995.

288. *"Renouveau missionnaire et question de l'esclavage," special number of *Mémoire spiritaine: histoire, mission, spiritualité*, 2 (1995).

289. Restrepo, Adriana Maya. "Memorias de esclavitud" (Unpublished paper, UNESCO conference on "La route de l'esclave", Ouidah, Bénin, 1-5 Sept. 1994).

290. Richardson, David. "Across the Desert and the Sea: Trans-Saharan and Atlantic Slavery, 1500-1900 (review essay: Parker, ed., *Europe, America, and the Wider World*; Inikori and Engerman, eds., *Atlantic Slave Trade*; Karras and McNeill, eds., *Atlantic American Societies*; and Savage, ed., *Human Commodity*)," *The Historical Journal*, 38, 1 (1995), pp. 195-204.

291. *Richardson, David. "After *Time on the Cross*: Slavery in the Americas," *Economic History Review* (forthcoming).

292. Richardson, David. "The Slave Trade, Sugar, and British Economic Growth, 1748-1776".

Reprinted in Manning, ed., *Slave Trades, 1500-1800*, pp. 303-33.

293. Robertson, Claire. "Africa into the Americas?" in Gaspar and Hine, eds., *More than Chattel*, pp. 3-40.

294. Robinson, Brian T. "Slavery, Freedom, and Coexistence: Thoughts on the Jaffa/Bradford Debate," in Michael W. McConnell, ed., *Collected Seminar Papers* (Chicago: University of Chicago Law School, Conservative Jurisprudence Seminar, 1993), pp. (various).

295. *Royster, Glenn. *The Slave Master's Religion: Breaking the Last Bonds of Slavery.* [Place??]: Kabila Communications, 1993.

296. Russell-Wood, A. J. R. "Before Columbus: Portugal's African Prelude to the Middle Passage and Contribution to Discourse on Race and Slavery," in Hyatt and Nettleford, eds., *Race, Discourse, and the Origin of the Americas*, pp. 134-68.

297. Rust, Marion. "Invisible Woman: Female Slavery in the New World (review essay: Bush, *Slave Women in Caribbean Society*; Fox-Genovese, *Within the Plantation Household*; Morrissey, *Slave Women in the New World*)," *New West Indian Guide*, 66, 3-4 (1992), pp. 83-88.

298. "La Ruta del Esclavo," *América negra*, 8 (1994), pp. 185-86.

299. "'La Ruta del Esclavo' de UNESCO: presentación en Colombia el 27 de julio de 1995," *América negra*, 10 (1996), pp. 199-210.

300. Ryden, David. "Planters, Slaves and Decline" (Unpublished paper, "*Capitalism and Slavery* Fifty Years Later").

301. Sala Molins, Luis. "L'invisibilité de l'esclave dans la philosophie occidentale médiévale et moderne" (Unpublished paper, "Fanandevozana ou esclavage" [Colloque international, 1996]).

302. Salter, John. "Adam Smith on Feudalism, Commerce and Slavery," *History of Political Thought*, 13, 2 (1992), pp. 219-41.

303. Sánches-Albernoz, Nicolás. "Demographic Change in America and Africa Induced by the European Expansion (1500-1800)" (Unpublished paper, Tenth International Economic History Congress, Leuven, August 1990).

304. Saugera, Éric. "Présentation," in Gerbeau and Saugera, eds., *La dernière traite*, pp. 19-22.

305. Schafer, Daniel L. "Shades of Freedom: Anna Kingsley in Senegal, Florida and Haiti," in Landers, ed., "Against the Odds", pp. 130-54.

306. Scheidel, Walter. "Reflections on the Differential Valuation of Slaves in Diocletian's Price Edict and in the United States," *Münstersche Beiträge zur antiken Handelsgeschichte*, 14 (1995), forthcoming.

307. Scott, Julius S. "Defining Self in an Atlantic World: Afro-Americans in the Eighteenth Century" (Unpublished paper, conference "Through a Glass Darkly: Defining Self in Early America", Institute of Early American History & Culture, College of William and Mary, Williamsburg VA, November 1993).

308. Scott, Rebecca J. "The Boundaries of Freedom: Postemancipation Society in Cuba, Louisiana and Brazil," in Beckles, ed., *Inside Slavery*, pp. 96-118.

309. Segal, Ronald. *The Black Diaspora.* New York: Farrar, Straus and Giroux, 1995.

310. *Seminário Internacional da Escravidão.* See Pas, Maria Verônica de, coord.

311. "Seminário internacional: Escravos com e sem açucar" (Centro de Estudos de História do Atlântico, Funchal, Madeira, 17-21 June 1996) Coord. Alberto Vieira.

For presentations see Curtin, Ferlini, Franco Silva, Galloway, Klein, Knight, Lobo Cabrera, Mintz, Phillips, Rodriguez, Schwartz, and Vieira.

312. "Serfdom and Slavery" (Conference organized by Michael Bush, University of Manchester, 5-7 Sept. 1994).

Participants listed include Blackburn, Davies, Engerman, Iversen, Kolchin, Mironov, Phillips, Rihll, and Saller.

313. Shanley, Mary Lyndon. "Marital Slavery and Friendship: John Stuart Mill's *The Subjugation of Women*," in Neera Kapur Badhwar, ed., *Friendship: A Philosophical Reader* (Ithaca: Cornell University Press, 1993), pp. 267-84.

314. Singleton, Theresa A., and Mark D. Bograd. *The Archaeology of the African Diaspora in the Americas.* N.p.: Society for Historical Archaeology, 1995. (Guides to the Archaeological Literature of the Immigrant Experience in North America, no. 2)

315. SLAVERY@UHUPVM1.EDU.

"Slavery" LISTSERVE, moderator Steven Mintz (SMintz@UH.EDU).

316. *Slavery: An Introduction to the African Holocaust.* (Liverpool?): Black History Resource

Working Group in conjunction with the Race Equality Management Team, 1995.

317. *Slavery and Abolition*, 14, 1 (1993). Special issue, ed. Michael Twaddle, *The Wages of Slavery: From Chattel Slavery to Wage Labour in Africa, the Caribbean and England.*

For contents see entry under Twaddle.

318. *Slavery and the Abolition of the Slave Trade.* Wilmington DE: Scholarly Resources, 1995.

Microfilm, 1 roll, from the holdings of the Schomburg Center for Research in Black Culture and the New York Public Library.

319. *Slavery in the Americas and the Triangular Trade.* Chicago: Encyclopaedia Britannica Educational Corporation, 1992. (videocassette, 15 min.)

320. Small, Stephen. "The General Legacy of the Atlantic Slave Trade," in Tibbles, ed., *Transatlantic Slavery*, pp. 122-26.

321. Small, Stephen. "Racial Group Boundaries and Identities: People of 'Mixed Race' in Slavery Across the Americas," *Slavery and Abolition*, 15, 3 (1994), pp. 13-37.

322. Small, Stephen. "Racist Ideologies," in Tibbles, ed., *Transatlantic Slavery*, pp. 111-15.

323. Smith, J. N. Leith. "Ceramic Use-Wear Analysis: An African Case Study with New World Archaeological Implications" (Unpublished paper, Annual Meeting of the Society for Historical Archaeology, Kingston, Jamaica, January 1992).

324. Smith, Stephen A. "Future Freedom and Freedom of Contract," *Modern Law Review*, 59, 2 (1996), pp. 167-87.

325. Smith, Steven B. "Hegel and the Problem of Slavery in Closed Systems and Open Justice: The Legal Sociology of Niklas Luhmann," *Cardozo Law Review*, 13, 5 (1992), pp. 1771-815.

326. Solow, Barbara. "Marx, Slavery, and American Economic Growth" (Presentation at Colloquium on "Les dépendances serviles", Paris 1996).

327. Somé, Roger. "Slavery, Genocide, and (the?) Holocaust" (Unpublished paper [original in French], UNESCO conference on "La route de l'esclave", Ouidah, Bénin, 1-5 Sept. 1994).

328. "Source Material for Studying the Slave Trade and the African Diaspora" (Conference, University of Stirling, Scotland, 13-14 April 1996).

For papers see Chambers, Law, Lovejoy, Manning, Richardson, Sorensen-Gilmour, Soumonni and Codo, and Yarak.

329. Späth, Eberhard. "Defoe and Slavery," in Binder, ed., *Slavery in the Americas*, pp. 453-69.

330. Speer, Laurel. *Slavery*. Tucson AZ (P.O. Box 12220, Tucson 85732-2220): L. Speer, 1992.

331. Spelman, Elizabeth V. "Slavery and Tragedy," in Roger S. Gottlieb, ed., *Radical Philosophy: Tradition, Counter-Tradition, Politics* (Philadelphia: Temple University Press, 1993), pp. 221-44.

332. Stahlmann, Ines. "Qu'on ne me cite pas les exemples des anciennes republiques! Antike Sklaverei und Französische Revolution," *Klio*, 74 (1992), pp. 447-55.

333. Steady, Filomena Chioma. "Women of Africa and the African Diaspora: Linkages and Influences," in Harris, ed., *Global Dimensions of the African Diaspora* (2nd ed.), pp. 167-87.

334. *Studies in the World History of Slavery Abolition, and Emancipation.*

Electronic journal (eds. Patrick Manning and John Saillant): http://h-net.msu.edu/~slavery.

335. Stufflebeem, Barbara J. "A Skeptical Note on Sexual Exploitation, Slavery, and Cliometry," in Fogel, Galantine, and Manning, eds., *Evidence and Methods (Without Consent or Contract)*, pp. 596-99.

336. Sudarkasa, Niara, Levi Akalazu Nwachuku, Robert E. Millette, and Judith A. W. Thomas, eds. *The African-American Experience: A Multi-Disciplinary Approach*. New York: HarperCollins Custom Books, 1994.

For contents see Carew, Hunter, and Nwachuku.

337. Sundiata, Ibrahim. "Abolition, Capitalism and Slaving" (Unpublished paper, "*Capitalism and Slavery* Fifty Years Later").

338. Sundquist, Eric J. "*Benito Cereno* and New World Slavery," in Sacvan Bercovitch, ed., *Reconstructing American History* (Cambridge MA: Harvard University Press, 1986), pp. 93-122.

Reprinted in Burkholder, ed., *Critical Essays on Herman Melville's "Benito Cereno"*, pp. 146-67.

339. Tannenbaum, Frank. *Slave and Citizen.*

Reprinted, with introduction by Franklin Knight, Boston: Beacon Press, 1991.

340. Tardieu, Jean-Pierre. "De l'évolution de l'esclavage aux Amériques espagnoles" (Presentation at Colloquium on "Les dépendances serviles", Paris 1996).

341. Tavares, Pierre Franklin. "La route de l'esclave hegelien: la deroute du maître, ou comment Hegel s'est inspiré des événements de Saint-Domingue" (Unpublished paper, UNESCO conference on "La route de l'esclave", Ouidah, Bénin, 1-5 Sept. 1994).

342. Taylor, Rupert J. *Slavery: Turning Misery into Money.* Waterloo Ont.: R/L Taylor Pub. Consultants, 1996.

343. Temperly, Howard. "The Idea of Progress".

Reprinted (from "The Ideology of Antislavery") in Northrup, ed., *The Atlantic Slave Trade*, pp. 192-202.

344. Temperley, Howard. "New World Slavery, Old World Slavery," in Bush, ed., *Serfdom and Slavery*, pp. 144-57.

345. Thomas, Laurence Mordekhai. *Vessels of Evil: American Slavery and the Holocaust.* Philadelphia: Temple University Press, 1993.

Also as 6 sound cassettes: New York: Jewish Braille Institute of America, 1995.

346. Thompson, Vincent Bakpetu. "Leadership in the African Diaspora in the Americas Prior to 1860," *Journal of Black Studies*, 24, 1 (1993), pp. 42-76.

347. Thornton, John K. "The Coromantees: An African Cultural Group in Colonial America" (Unpublished paper, 1993).

348. Thornton, John K. "Perspectives on African Christianity," in Hyatt and Nettleford, eds., *Race, Discourse, and the Origin of the Americas*, pp. 169-98.

349. Tibbles, Anthony, ed. *Transatlantic Slavery: Against Human Dignity.* London: HMSO, 1994. (National Museums & Galleries on Merseyside)

350. Tiunov, Oleg I. "Pacta sunt servanda: The Principle of Observing International Treaties in the Epoch of the Slave-Owning Society," *Saint Louis University Law Journal*, 38, 4 (1994), pp. 929-45.

351. Tomich, Dale. "Small Islands and Huge Comparisons: Caribbean Plantations, Historical Unevenness, and Capitalist Modernity," *Social Science History*, 18, 3 (1994), pp. 339-58.

352. Trager, Nat. *Empire of Hate: A Refutation of the Nation of Islam's "The Secret Relationship between Blacks and Jews"*. Fort Lauderdale FL: Coral Reef Books, 1995.

353. Tucker, Joan. *Britain and the Black Peoples of the Americas, 1550-1930.* London: JET, 1992.

354. Turley, David. "Slave Emancipations in Modern History," in Bush, ed., *Serfdom and Slavery*, pp. 181-96.

355. Turley, David. "Slavery in the Americas: Resistance, Liberation, Emancipation (review essay)," *Slavery and Abolition*, 14, 2 (1993), pp. 109-16.

356. Turner, Mary, ed. *From Chattel Slaves to Wage Slaves: The Dynamics of Labour Bargaining in the Americas.* Kingston: Ian Randle/ Bloomington: Indiana University Press/London: James Currey, 1995.

For contents see Bolland, Brana-Shute, Johnson, Lamounier, Mullin, Sheridan, Tomich, Turner, Walsh, and Wood.

357. Twaddle, Michael. "Visible and Invisible Hands," in Twaddle, ed., *The Wages of Slavery*, pp. 1-12.

358. Twaddle, Michael, ed. *The Wages of Slavery: From Chattel Slavery to Wage Labour in Africa, the Caribbean and England.* London: Frank Cass, 1993. (Also as special issue, *Slavery and Abolition*, 14, 1 [1993].)

For contents see Carter, Clarence-Smith, Lovejoy, Eltis, Emmer, Hanson, Hu-Dehart, Ross, Shepherd, Sheridan, and Twaddle.

359. Uya, Okon Edet. *African Diaspora and the Black Experience in New World Slavery*. Rev. ed. New Rochelle NY: Third Press Publishers, 1992.

360. Van Sertima, Ivan. "African Presence in Early America," in Hyatt and Nettleford, eds., *Race, Discourse, and the Origin of the Americas*, pp. 66-102.

361. Vine, Steven. "'That Mild Beam': Enlightenment and Enslavement in William Blake's *Vision of the Daughters of Albion*," in Plasa and Ring, eds., *Discourse of Slavery*, pp. 40-63.

362. Voelz, Peter M. *Slave and Soldier: The Military Impact of Blacks in the Colonial Americas*. New York: Garland, 1993.

363. *The Wages of Slavery: From Chattel Slavery to Wage Labour in Africa, the Caribbean and England*. Ed. Michael Twaddle. Special issue, *Slavery and Abolition*, 14, 1 (1993).

For contents see entry under Twaddle.

364. Wahl, Jenny Bourne. "The Bondsman's Burden: An Economic Analysis of the Jurisprudence of Slaves and Common Carriers," *Journal of Economic History*, 53, 3 (1993), pp. 495-526.

365. Walker, Sheila. "The All-Americas/All-African Diaspora" (Unpublished paper, UNESCO conference on "La route de l'esclave", Ouidah, Bénin, 1-5 Sept. 1994).

366. Walvin, James. "Freedom and Slavery and the Shaping of Victorian Britain," in Lovejoy and Rogers, eds., *Unfree Labour in the Development of the Atlantic World*, pp. 246-59.

367. Walvin, James. *Questioning Slavery*. London: Routledge, 1996.

368. Walvin, James. *Slaves and Slavery: The British Colonial Experience*. Manchester/New York: Manchester University Press, 1992.

369. Walvin, James. "Slaves, Free Time and the Question of Leisure," *Slavery and Abolition*, 16, 1 (1995), pp. 1-13.

370. Weber, Jacques. "Après la traite: le coolie trade," *Les anneaux de la mémoire* (Exhibition catalogue, Nantes, 1992), pp. 143-45.

371. Weiler, Ingomar. "'Schenk dem alternden Freiheit, mein Sohn ... ': Die Beendigung des Sklavereiverhältnisses unter komparativem Aspekt," in Herwig Ebner, Horst Haselsteiner, and Ingeborg Wiesflecker-Friedhuber, eds., *Geschichtsforschung in Graz: Festschrift zum 125-Jahr-Jubiläum des Instituts für Geschichte der Karl-Franzens-Universität Graz* (Graz: Institut für Geschichte an der Karl-Franzens-Universität, 1990), pp. 127-35.

372. Williams, Eric. "Capitalism and Abolitionism".

Reprinted (from *Capitalism and Slavery*) in Northrup, ed., *The Atlantic Slave Trade*, pp. 184-92.

373. Williams, Eric. *Capitalism and Slavery*. With new intro. by Colin A. Palmer. Chapel Hill: University of North Carolina Press, 1994.

374. Williams, Eric. "Economics, Not Racism, as the Root of Slavery".

Reprinted (from *Capitalism and Slavery*) in Northrup, ed., *The Atlantic Slave Trade*, pp. 3-12.

375. Williams-Myers, A. J. "Slavery, Rebellion, and Revolution in the Americas: A Historiographical Scenario on the Theses of Genovese and Others," *Journal of Black Studies*, 26, 4 (1996), pp. 381-400.

376. Wilson, Carter A. *Racism: From Slavery to Advanced Capitalism*. Thousand Oaks CA: Sage Publications, 1996.

377. Wolf, Eric R. "Perilous Ideas: Race, Culture, People," *Current Anthropology*, 35, 1 (1994), pp. 1-7.

With comments by Regna Darnell, p. 7-8; Joel S. Kahn, p. 8; William Roseberry, pp. 8-9; and Immanuel Wallerstein, pp. 9-10. Reply by Wolf, pp. 10-11; bibliography, pp. 11-12.

378. Worden, Nigel. "Slavery and its Aftermath in the Cape Colony: A Comparison with Mauritius," *Omaly sy Anio*, 33-36 (1991-92), pp. 429-52.

Also as "Diverging Histories: Slavery and its Aftermath in the Cape Colony and Mauritius," *South African Historical Journal/Suid-Afrikaanse Historiese Joernaal*, 27 (1992), pp. 3-25.

379. Yai, Olabiyi Babalola. "Survivances et dynamisme des cultures africaines dans les Amériques" (Unpublished paper, UNESCO conference on "La route de l'esclave", Ouidah, Bénin, 1-5 Sept. 1994).

Also in *Studies in the World History of Slavery Abolition, and Emancipation* (Aug. 1996) -- http://h-net.msu.edu/~slavery

380. Ziskind, David. *Emancipation Acts: Quintessential Labor Laws*. Los Angeles: Litlaw Foundation, 1993.

381. Zoller, Rüdiger. "Vorwort," in Zoller, ed., *Amerikaner wider Willen*, pp. 7-10.

382. Zoller, Rüdiger, ed. *Amerikaner wider Willen: Beiträge zur Sklaverei in Lateinamerika und ihren Folgen*. Frankfurt am Main: Vervuert, 1994. (Lateinamerika-Studien, Bd. 32)

For contents see Brübach, Chacon, Hentschke, Kellenbenz, Lüsebrink, Maggie, Santos, Santos-Stubbe, Schelsky, Schüler, Shadow and Rodríguez-Shadow, and Stubbe.

II. NORTH AMERICA[1]

[1] Assignment of materials to sub-categories within the North American section of the bibliography generally privileges regional specificity over the background imperial context; thus, Florida, Louisiana, Texas, and Canada contain all works on those regions, whether in their Spanish, French, or English periods. Similarly, Chesapeake includes the nineteenth century as well as colonial-period studies, even though materials on North and South Carolina are divided between the broader regional categories of "Colonial South" and "Antebellum South". The boundary between Chesapeake and the Middle Colonies is the Mason-Dixon line, so that Baltimore and Maryland belong to the former, while Delaware and Pennsylvania are found in the latter. Arkansas and Missouri are assigned to the Upper South.

The General category once included most of the scholarship which treated "slavery" in North America as a relatively undifferentiated entity, but the proliferation of regionally and chronologically specific research in recent years has left this heading as something of a residual. It now includes mostly law (at the Constitutional level, but not regionally specific state law), race and racism, and works that cover more than a single region.

Individual biographies and slave narratives have their own section, but studies drawing on these materials to investigate slavery in a given time or place are assigned to the respective regional sub-section.

Studies phrased in general terms but drawing heavily on slave narratives and other sources from the middle of the nineteenth century are generally placed in the Antebellum South, by default.

1. General and Comparative

383. Accardo, Anna. *Il racconto della schiavitú negli Stati Uniti d'America*. Rome: Bulzoni, 1996.

384. Accomando, Christina. "Representing Truth and Rewriting Womanhood: Constructions of Race and Gender in Discourses of United States Slavery" (PhD diss., University of California, San Diego, 1994).

385. Adeleke, Tunde. "Slavery, Race and Racism: The Peculiarities and Problems of Southern Studies in Nigeria," *American Studies International*, 31, 1 (1993), pp. 17-20.

386. "The African American Experience" (Eugene OR: Distributed by New Dimension Media, 1995).

2 videocassettes; 2 teaching guides. (African American history series: Pt. 1. 1500-1864; Pt. 2. 1864-1994. Executive producer, Steve Raymen; editor, Martin Brown; narrator, Barry Bell).

387. "African-American History: Slavery to Civil Rights" (Fairfield CT: Queue, 1995).

Windows CD-ROM.

388. Allen, William Francis, Charles Pickard Ware, and Lucy McKim Garrison. *Slave Songs of the United States: With a New Introduction by W. K. McNeil*. Baltimore: Clearfield Co., 1992. (Reprint of 1867 ed.)

389. Anastaplo, George. "Slavery and the Constitution: Explorations," *Texas Tech Law Review*, 20, 3 (1989), pp. 677-786.

390. *Andrews, S. C., and A. L. Young. "Plantations on the Periphery of the Old South: Modeling a New Approach," in Faulkner, ed., *Plantations on the Periphery*, pp. (??).

391. *Antebellum America and Slavery*.

See Schomburg Center for Research in Black Culture, *Guide to the Scholarly Resources Microfilm Edition*.

392. Aptheker, Herbert. *American Negro Slave Revolts*. 5th ed. New York: International Publishers, 1993. Foreword by John H. Bracey.

393 Austin, Allan D. "Islamic Identities in Africans in North America in the Days of Slavery (1731-

1865)," *Islam et sociétés au sud du Sahara*, 7 (1993), pp. 205-19.

394. Bailyn, Bernard. "Jefferson and the Ambiguities of Freedom," *Proceedings of the American Philosophical Society*, 137, 4 (1993), pp. 498-515.

395. Barnett, Todd Harold. "The Evolution of 'North' and 'South': The Settlement of Slavery on American's Sectional Border, 1650-1810" (PhD diss., The University of Pennsylvania, 1993).

396. Baum, Rosalie Murphy. "Early American Literature: Reassessing the Black Contribution," in Zimbardo and Montgomery, eds., "African-American Culture in the Eighteenth Century," pp. 533-50.

397. Bell, Derrick. "Learning the Three 'I's' of America's Slave Heritage," *Chicago-Kent Law Review*, 68, 3 (Symposium on the Law of Slavery) (1993), pp. 1037-49.

398. Berlin, Ira. "From Creole to African: Atlantic Creoles and the Origins of African-American Society in Mainland North America," *William and Mary Quarterly*, 53, 2 (1996), pp. 251-88.

Another version as "Les dépendances serviles" (Paris 1996).

399. Berlin, Ira. "The Slave Trade and the Development of Afro-American Society in English Mainland North America, 1619-1775".

Reprinted in *Southern Studies*, n.s. 2, 3-4 (1991), pp. 335-49.

400. Berlin, Ira. "Time, Space, and the Evolution of African-American Society".

Reprinted in Goodheart, Brown, and Rabe, eds., *Slavery in American Society*, pp. 34-69.

401. Berlin, Ira, *et al.*, eds. *Free at Last: A Documentary History of Slavery, Freedom, and the Civil War*. New York: The New Press, 1992.

402. Berry, Mary Frances. "Slavery, the Constitution, and the Founding Fathers: The African American Vision," in John Hope Franklin and Genna Rae McNeil, eds., *African Americans and the Living Constitution* (Washington DC: Smithsonian Institution Press, 1995), pp. 11-20.

403. Berry, Mary Frances, and Claire Conway. "Slavery, the Constitution, and the Founding Fathers," *Update On Law-Related Education*, 12, 3 (Symposium: Afro-Americans and the Evolution of a Living Constitution) (1988), pp. 3(6).

404. Binder, Guyora. "Did the Slaves Author the Thirteenth Amendment? An Essay in Redemptive History," *Yale Journal of Law and the Humanities*, 5, 2 (1993), pp. 471-505.

405. Binder, Guyora. "The Slavery of Emancipation," *Cardozo Law Review*, 17, 6 (1996), pp. 2063-2102.

Comment by Michael Les Benedict, "Comment on Guyora Binder, 'The Slavery of Emancipation'," pp. 2103-12.

Comment by Eric Foner, "Bondage, Freedom & the Constitution," pp. 2113-14.

406. Black, Jane. *Y Blanhigfa Gotwm yn Neheudir America yn y 18fed a'r 19eg ganrif: pecyn adnoddau athrawon a disgyblion*. Aberystwyth: Canolfan Astudiaethau Addysg, 1994. (Uned astudio hanes: Byd gwaith, 21)

407. *Black Women in America: An Historical Encyclopedia*. Darlene Clark Hine, Elsa Barkley Brown, and Rosalyn Terborg-Penn, eds. 2 vols. Brooklyn: Carlson Publishing, 1993.

For contents see Alexander and Gould, Clinton, Jones, Lowance, McKinley, and Stevenson (2).

408. Block, Sharon. "Coerced Sex in British North America, 1700-1820" (PhD diss., Princeton University, 1995).

409. Block, Sharon. "Coercing Sex within the Bonds of Servitude, 1720-1820" (Unpublished paper, American Historical Association, Chicago, 5-8 Jan. 1995).

410. Bolner, James, Dr. "Slavery and the United States Constitution," in Binder, ed., *Slavery in the Americas*, pp. 225-40.

411. "Bondage, Freedom & the Constitution: The New Slavery Scholarship and Its Impact on Law and Legal Historiography," *Cardozo Law Review*, 17, 6 (1996), special issue.

For contents see Akhil Reed Amar, Benedict, Binder, Burt, Finkelman, Fiss, Foner, Higginbotham, Kaczorowski, Kennedy, Levinson, Maltz, Niemann, Oakes, Stampp, VanderVelde, Wang, Wedgwood, Weisberg, and Wiecek.

412. Bowers, Detine Lee. "A Strange Speech of an Estranged People: Theory and Practice of Antebellum African-American Freedom Day Orators" (PhD diss., Purdue University, 1992).

413. Boxill, Bernard R. "Dignity, Slavery and the Thirteenth Amendment," in Michael J. Meyer and William A. Parent, eds., *The Constitution of Rights: Human Dignity and American Values* (Ithaca: Cornell University Press, 1992), pp. 102-17.

414. Brandon, Mark E. "Free in the World: American Slavery and Constitutional Failure" (PhD diss., Princeton University, 1992).

415. Brawley, Lisa C. "Fugitive Nation: Slavery, Travel and Technologies of American Identity, 1830-1860" (PhD diss., University of Chicago, 1995).

416. Bruce, Dickson D., Jr. "National Identity and African-American Colonization, 1773-1817," *The Historian*, 58, 1 (1995), pp. 15-28.

417. Burgess, Norma J., and Hayward Derrick Horton. "African American Women and Work: A Socio-Historical Perspective," *Journal of Family History*, 18, 1 (1993), pp. 53-63.

418. Burnham, Margaret A. "An Impossible Marriage: Slave Law and Family Law," *Law & Inequality: A Journal of Theory and Practice*, 5, 2 (1987), pp. 187-225.

Reprinted in Finkelman, ed., *Race, Law and American History*, vol. 2 (*Race and Law Before Emancipation*), pp. 1-39.

419. Burroughs, Tony. "You Don't Go from the Census to the Slave Schedules in African-American Genealogy". [Indiana]: Repeat Performances, 1994.

Recording of program presented at Great Lakes Conference, "When East Meets West" (Fort Wayne IN, 4-6 Aug. 1994).

420. Bush, Jonathan A. "Free to Enslave: The Foundations of Colonial American Slave Law," *Yale Journal of Law & the Humanities*, 5, 2 (1993), pp. 417-70.

421. Bynum, Victoria E. "Misshapen Identity: Memory, Folklore, and the Legend of Rachel Knight," in Morton, ed., *Discovering the Women in Slavery*, pp. 29-46.

422. Chambers, Douglas B. "Eboe, Kongo, Mandingo: African Ethnic Groups and the Development of Regional Slave Societies in Mainland North America, 1700-1820" (Working paper no. 96-14, International Seminar on the History of the Atlantic World, 1500-1800, Harvard University, September 1996).

423. Claxton, Joseph E. "Slavery and Race: An Essay on New Ideas and Enduring Shibboleths in the Interpretation of the American Constitutional System," *Mercer Law Review*, 44, 2 (1993), pp. 637-52.

424. Clifton, James M. "The Plantation," in *Encyclopedia of American Social History*, vol. 2, pp. 1197-1208.

425. Coombs, Norman. *The Black Experience in America*. N.p.: N. Coombs, Project Gutenberg, 1993. Electronic text based on original publication, New York: Twayne, 1972.

Ftp site MRCNEXT.CsO.UIUC.EDU; log in as "anonymous"; password = your e-mail address; file name: BLEXP10.TXT or BLEXP10.ZIP.

426. Cost, Jennifer Farrell. "Rhetorical, Political, and Religious Subversity in the Narratives of Ex-slaves and Native American Captives" (MA thesis, San Diego State University, 1994).

427. Cottrol, Robert J. "Liberalism and Paternalism: Ideology, Economic Interest and the Business Law of Slavery," *American Journal of Legal History*, 31, 4 (1987), pp. 359-73.

428. D'Souza, Dinesh. "An American Dilemma: Was Slavery a Racist Institution?" in *The End of Racism: Principles for a Multiracial Society* (New York: Free Press, 1995), pp. 67-114.

429. Dain, Bruce Russell. "A Hideous Monster of the Mind: American Race Theory, 1787-1859" (PhD diss., Princeton University, 1996).

430. Davis, David Brion. *The Emancipation Moment*. [Gettysburg PA]: Gettysburg College, 1983. (22nd Annual Robert Fortenbaugh Memorial Lecture)

431. Davis, David Brion. "The Uncertain Antislavery Commitment of Thomas Jefferson".

Reprinted (from *Problem of Slavery in the Age of Revolution*) in Goodheart, Brown, and Rabe, eds., *Slavery in American Society*, pp. 83-95.

432. Davis, Olga Idriss. "It Be's Hard Sometimes: The Rhetorical Invention of Black Female Persona in Pre-Emancipatory Slave Narratives" (PhD diss., The University of Nebraska-Lincoln, 1994).

433. Dent, Jonathon, and David Drew. "Digging for Slaves" (50-min. cassette). Princeton: Films for the Humanities and Social Sciences, 1993. (Originally 1989)

434. Diamond, Raymond T. "No Call to Glory: Thurgood Marshall's Thesis on the Intent of a Pro-Slavery Constitution," *Vanderbilt Law Review*, 42, 1 (1989), 93-131.

See Marshall, "Constitution's Bicentennial".

Reprinted in Finkelman, ed., *Race, Law and American History*, vol. 1 (*African Americans and the Law*), pp. 329-67.

435. Dillard, Philip David. "Arming the Slaves: Transformation of the Public Mind" (MA thesis, University of Georgia, 1994).

436. "Documenting the African American Experience" (New York: Readex, 1995). (Machine-readable data, Documentary Sources Database, Unit I, American Multiculturalism Series).

Mode of access: Internet. Host: www.lib.virginia.edu (University of Virginia Library, Electronic Text Center).

Includes: Antibiastes, "Observations on the slaves and the indented servants, inlisted in the army, and in the navy of the United States" (Early American imprints. 1st series; no. 15239)

Benjamin Banneker, Copy of a letter from Benjamin Banneker to the Secretary of State, with his answer. (Early American imprints. 1st series; no. 24073)

Peter Bestes, Letter: Boston, April 20th, 1773. (Early American Imprints. 1st series; no. 42416)

437. Dovonon, Valentin. "La constitution américaine et l'esclavage" (Unpublished paper, UNESCO conference on "La route de l'esclave", Ouidah, Bénin, 1-5 Sept. 1994).

438. Drobak, John N. "The Courts and Slavery in the United States: Property Rights and Credible Commitment," in William A. Barnett, Melvin J. Hinich, and Norman J. Schofield, eds., *Political Economy: Institutions, Competition, and Representation* (Proceedings of the Seventh International Symposium in Economic Theory and Econometrics) (New York: Cambridge University Press, 1993), pp. 223-45.

439. Dudley, William, ed. *Slavery: Opposing Viewpoints*. San Diego CA: Greenhaven Press, 1992.

440. Durham, Michael S. "The Word is 'Slaves': A Trip into Black History," *American Heritage*, 43, 2 (April 1992), pp. 89-99.

441. Durham, William H., E. Valentine Daniel, and Bambi Schieffelin, eds. "[Reviews of Singleton, *The Archaeology of Slavery in North America*]," in *Annual Review of Anthropology*, 24 (1995), pp. 119-40.

442. Edwards, Ywone, and Maria Franklin. "Archaeology and the Material Culture of Enslaved Africans and African Americans," *Research Review* (Colonial Williamsburg Foundation), 6, 1 (1995-96), pp. 22-24.

443. Eisgruber, Christopher L. "Justice Story, Slavery, and the Natural Law Foundations of American Constitutionalism," *University of Chicago Law Review*, 55, 1 (1988), pp. 273-327.

444. *Encyclopedia of American Social History*. Mary Kupiec Cayton, Elliot J. Gorn, and Peter W. Williams, eds. 3 vols. New York: Charles Scribner's Sons, 1992.

For contents see Clifton, Lowe, Morgan, Oakes, Oestreicher, Salinger, and Wood.

445. *Encyclopedia of the North American Colonies*. Jacob Ernest Cooke, ed. in chief. 3 vols. New York: Charles Scribner's Sons, 1993.

For contents see Brugge, Goodfriend, Hall, McColley, Miller, Moogk, Morgan, and Usner.

446. Engerman, Stanley L. "Concluding Reflections," in Hudson, Jr., ed., *Working Toward Freedom*, pp. 233-41.

447. Erkkila, Betsy. "Phyllis Wheatley and the Black American Revolution," in Frank Shuffelton, ed., *A Mixed Race: Ethnicity in Early America* (New York: Oxford University Press, 1993), pp. 225-40.

448. Fabl, M. Giulia. "The 'Unguarded Expressions of the Feelings of the Negroes': Gender, Slave Resistance, and William Wells Brown's Revisions of *Clotel*," *African American Review*, 27, 4 (1993), pp. 639-54.

449. *Faulkner, C. H., ed. *Plantations on the Periphery: The Archaeology of Small Slave Holding Sites*. Knoxville TN: University of Tennessee Press, 1992.

For contents see Andrews and Young ... .

450. Faust, Drew Gilpin. "Slavery in the American Experience," in Campbell, with Rice, eds., *Before Freedom Came*, pp. 1-19.

451. Fears, Mary L. Jackson. *Slave Ancestral Research: It's Something Else*. Bowie MD, Daytona Beach FL: Heritage Books; Book orders to M. L. J. Fears, 1995.

452. Fede, Andrew. *People Without Rights: An Interpretation of the Fundamentals of the Law of Slavery in the U.S. South*. New York: Garland, 1992.

453. Ferguson, Leland. *Uncommon Ground: Archaeology and Early African America, 1650-1800*. Washington: Smithsonian Institution Press, 1992.

454. Finkelman, Paul. "The Centrality of the Peculiar Institution in American Legal Development," *Chicago-Kent Law Review*, 68, 3 (Symposium on the Law of Slavery) (1993), pp. 1009-33.

455. Finkelman, Paul. "The Crime of Color," *Tulane Law Review*, 67, 6 (1993), pp. 2063-112. (Symposium: Criminal Law, Criminal Justice, and Race)

456. Finkelman, Paul. "Fugitive Slaves, Midwestern Racial Tolerance, and the Value of 'Justice Delayed'," *Iowa Law Review*, 78, 1 (1992), pp. 89-141.

457. Finkelman, Paul. "Jefferson and Slavery: 'Treason Against the Hopes of the World'," in Peter S. Onuf, ed., *Jeffersonian Legacies* (Charlottesville: University Press of Virginia, 1993), pp. 181-221.

458. Finkelman, Paul. "The Kidnapping of John Davis and the Adoption of the Fugitive Slave Law of 1793," *Journal of Southern History*, 56, 3 (1990), pp. 397-422.

Reprinted in Finkelman, ed., *Race, Law and American History*, vol. 2 (*Race and Law Before Emancipation*), pp. 133-58.

459. Finkelman, Paul. "'The Law, and Not Conscience, Constitutes the Rule of Action': The South Bend Fugitive Slave Case and the Value of 'Justice Delayed'," in Donald G. Nieman, ed., *The Constitution, Law, and American Life: Critical Aspects of the Nineteenth-Century Experience* (Athens: University of Georgia Press, 1992), pp. 23-51.

460. Finkelman, Paul. "Legal Ethics and Fugitive Slaves: The Anthony Burns Case, Judge Loring, and Abolitionist Attorneys," *Cardozo Law Review*, 17, 6 (1996), pp. 1793-1858.

Comment by Owen M. Fiss, "Can A Lawyer Ever Do Right?" pp. 1859-63.

Comment by Ruth Wedgwood, "Ethics Under Slavery's Constitution: Edward Loring and William Wetmore Story," pp. 1865-73.

461. Finkelman, Paul. "Slavery and the Constitution," in Jack Salzman, David Lionel Smith, and Cornel West, eds., *Encyclopedia of African-American Culture and History* (New York: Macmillan Library Reference, 1996), vol. 5, pp. 2469-71.

462. Finkelman, Paul. "Slavery and the Constitutional Convention".

Reprinted in Finkelman, ed., *Race, Law and American History*, vol. 1 (*African Americans and the Law*), pp. 30-67.

463. Finkelman, Paul. *Slavery and the Founders: Race and Liberty in the Age of Jefferson*. Armonk NY: M. E. Sharpe, 1996.

464. Finkelman, Paul. "Sorting out Prigg v. Pennsylvania," *Rutgers Law Journal*, 24, 3 (1993), pp. 605-65. (Race Relations and the United States Constitution: From Fugitive Slaves to Affirmative Action)

For responses see Cottrol and Maltz.

465. Finkelman, Paul. "The Stories Justice Joseph Told: Prigg v. Pennsylvania and the Creation of False Facts and a Mythical Past" (Unpublished paper, American Historical Association, San Francisco, 6-9 Jan. 1994).

466. Finkelman, Paul. "Thomas Jefferson and Antislavery: The Myth Goes On," *Virginia Magazine of History and Biography*, 102, 2 (1994), pp. 193-228.

467. Finkelman, Paul, ed. *Race, Law, and American History 1700-1990: The African-American Experience*. New York: Garland, 1992. 11 volumes.

Vol 1. *African-Americans and the Law*. New York: Garland, 1992.

For contents see Diamond, Finkelman, and Marshall.

Vol. 2. *Race and Law Before Emancipation*. New York: Garland, 1992.

For contents see Calligan, Currier, Dykstra, Erickson, Finkelman (2), Fischer, Fishback, Kousser, Kutler, Litwack, Morris, Nash, Rogers, Ruchames (2), Senese, Soifer, and Walker (2).

468. Finkenbine, Roy E. "Blacks, the Fugitive Slave Law, and the Forging of Community Resistance" (Unpublished paper, Annual Meeting of the Southern Historical Association, Atlanta, 1992).

469. Fisch, Audrey A. "'Repetitious Accounts So Piteous and So Harrowing': Ideological Work of American Slave Narratives in England," *Journal of Victorian Culture*, 1, 1 (1996), pp. 16-34.

470. Fisher, David Hackett. "Afro-American Folkways in America" (Unpublished paper, Annual Meeting of the Southern Historical Association, Atlanta, 1992).

471. Fisher, William W., III. "Ideology and Imagery in the Law of Slavery," *Chicago-Kent Law Review*, 68, 3 (Symposium on the Law of Slavery) (1993), pp. 1051-83.

472. Fogel, Robert W. "An Estimate of the Generational Distribution of U.S. Blacks," in Fogel, Galantine, and Manning, eds., *Evidence and Methods* (*Without Consent or Contract*), pp. 62-65.

473. Fogel, Robert W[illiam]. *The Quest for the Moral Problem of Slavery: An Historiographic Odyssey*. [Gettysburg PA]: Gettysburg College, 1994. (33rd Annual Robert Fortenbaugh Memorial Lecture)

474. Fogel, Robert W. "Revised Estimates of the U.S. Slave Trade and of the Native-Born Share of the Black Population," in Fogel, Galantine, and Manning, eds., *Evidence and Methods* (*Without Consent or Contract*), pp. 53-58.

475. Fogel, Robert W., and Stanley L. Engerman. "Philanthropy at Bargain Prices".

Reprinted from *Urban Slavery in the American South*, in Fogel and Engerman, eds., *Conditions of Slave: Life and the Transition to Freedom: Technical Papers*, vol. 2 (*Without Consent or Contract*), pp. 587-605.

476. Fogel, Robert W., and Stanley L. Engerman, eds. *Conditions of Slave Life and the Transition to Freedom: Technical Papers*, vol. 2 (*Without Consent or Contract*).

For contents see Crawford, Fogel and Engerman (2), John, Kahn (2), Klein and Engerman, Kotlikoff and Rupert, Margo and Steckel, Mello, Steckel (3), Trussel and Steckel, and Webb.

477. Fogel, Robert W., and Stanley L. Engerman, eds. *Evidence and Methods* (*Without Consent or Contract*).

For contents see Cardell and Hopkins, Crawford (2), Fogel (16), Fogel and Engerman (2), Friedman (5), Friedman and Galantine, Friedman and Manning (2), Friedman, Galantine and Fogel, Galantine (2), Hoffman (2), Hopkins and Cardell (2), Kotlikoff, Manning (2), Manning and Fogel, Manning and Friedman, Pinera and Kotlikoff, Stufflebeem, and Wilcox (2).

478. Fogel, Robert W., and Stanley L. Engerman, eds. *Markets and Production: Technical Papers*, vol. 1 (*Without Consent or Contract*).

For contents see Fogel and Engerman (2), Galenson (2), Goldin, Kotlikoff, Kotlikoff and Pinera, Margo, Mello, Metzer, Olson (2), and Rosenfield.

479. Fogel, Robert W., and Stanley L. Engerman, eds. *Without Consent or Contract: Technical Papers*. 2 vols.

For contents see listings as *Markets and Production: Technical Papers*, vol. 1 (*Without Consent or Contract*); and *Conditions of Slave Life and the Transition to Freedom: Technical Papers*, vol. 2 (*Without Consent or Contract*). Also see *Evidence and Methods*.

480. Foluke, Gyasi A. *The Real Holocaust: A Wholistic Analysis of the African-American Experience, 1441-1994*. New York: Carlton Press Corp., 1995.

481. Foner, Eric. *Slavery and Freedom in Nineteenth-Century America: An Inaugural Lecture Delivered Before the University of Oxford on 17 May 1994*. Oxford: Clarendon Press, 1994.

482. Forbes, Robert P. "Slavery and the Monrovian State" (Unpublished paper, American Historical Association, Chicago, 5-8 Jan. 1995).

483. Forbes, Robert P[rice]. "Slavery and the Meaning of America, 1819-1837" (PhD diss., Yale University, 1994).

484. Foster, Vonita White. *Slavery in America: A Catalogue of Nineteenth Century Pamphlets in the Library of Virginia Union University on Arguments Pro and Con*. Richmond VA: The Library, 1995. (Library Bibliography Series, Virginia Union University)

485. Frank, Andrew K. "Peculiar Institutions: Cultural Imperatives in the Law of Slavery" (Typescript, Senior honors thesis, Brandeis University, Waltham MA, 1992).

486. Franklin, John Hope. "Race and the Constitution in the Nineteenth Century," in John Hope Franklin and Genna Rae McNeil, eds., *African Americans and the Living Constitution* (Washington DC: Smithsonian Institution Press, 1995), pp. 21-32.

487. Franklin, John Hope. "Slaves Virtually Free in Antebellum North Carolina."

Reprinted in John Hope Franklin, *Race and History: Selected Essays 1938-1988* (Baton Rouge: Louisiana State University Press, 1989), pp. 73-91.

488. Franklin, John Hope, and Alfred A. Moss. *From Slavery to Freedom: A History of African Americans*. 7th ed. New York: Alfred A. Knopf, 1994.

489. Frederick, David C. "John Quincy Adams, Slavery, and the Disappearance of the Right of Petition," *Law and History Review*, 9, 1 (1991), pp. 113-55.

490. Freeman, Lynn Anne McCallum. "Miscegenation and Slavery: A Problem in American Historiography" (PhD diss., Queen's University [Kingston, Ont.], 1991).

491. French, Scot A., and Edward L. Ayers. "The Strange Career of Thomas Jefferson: Race and Slavery in America, 1943-1993," in Peter S. Onuf, ed., *Jeffersonian Legacies* (Charlottesville: University Press of Virginia, 1993), pp. 418-56.

492. Frey, Sylvia R. "Slavery and Anti-Slavery," in *Blackwell Encyclopedia of the American Revolution* (Cambridge MA: Blackwell Reference, 1991), pp. 379-98.

493. Frey, Sylvia R. *Water from the Rock: Black Resistance in a Revolutionary Age*. Princeton: Princeton University Press, 1991.

494. Friedman, Gerald. "Fluctuations in the U.S. Production and Prices of Indigo, Rice, and Tobacco," in Fogel, Galantine, and Manning, eds., *Evidence and Methods* (*Without Consent or Contract*), pp. 190-92.

495. Galantine, Ralph A. "The Slave Labor Force before the American Revolution," in Fogel, Galantine, and Manning, eds., *Evidence and Methods* (*Without Consent or Contract*), pp. 58-61.

496. Galenson, David W. "The Rise and Fall of Indentured Servitude in the Americas".

Reprinted in Whaples and Betts, eds., *Historical Perspectives on the American Economy*, pp. 110-40.

497. Gates, E. Nathaniel. "Bondage, Freedom and the Constitution: The New Slavery Scholarship and Its Impact on Law and Legal Historiography," *Cardozo Law Review*, 17, 6 (1996), pp. 1685-88.

498. Genovese, Eugene D. *The Southern Front: History and Politics in the Cultural War*. Columbia: University of Missouri Press, 1995.

499. George, Christopher T. "Mirage of Freedom: African Americans in the War of 1812," *Maryland Historical Magazine*, 91, 4 (1996), pp. 427-50.

500. Goldin, Claudia D. "An Explanation for the Relative Decline of Urban Slavery".

Reprinted from *Urban Slavery in the American South*, in Fogel and Engerman, eds., *Markets and Production: Technical Papers*, vol. 1 (*Without Consent or Contract*), pp. 95-131.

501. Gomez, Michael A. "Muslims in Early America," *Journal of Southern History*, 60, 4 (1994), pp. 671-710.

502. Goodheart, Lawrence B., Richard D. Brown, and Stephen G. Rabe, eds. *Slavery in American Society*. 3rd ed. Lexington MA: D. C. Heath, 1993. (Problems in American Civilization series)

For contents see Berlin, Davis, Engerman, Faust, Fogel, Foner, Fox-Genovese, Fredrickson, Genovese (2), Gutman, Kiple and King, Kolchin, Kulikoff, Levine, Morgan, Patterson, and Raboteau.

503. Gravely, Will B. "The Rise of African Churches in America (1786-1822): Re-examining the

Contexts," *Journal of Religious Thought*, 41 (1984), pp. 58-73.

Reprinted in Fulop and Raboteau, eds., *African American Religion*, pp. 133-51.

504. Grayson, Sandra M. "African Culture as Tradition: A Reading of 'Tales of the Congaree', Middle Passage', 'Benito Cereno', and 'Black Thunder" (PhD diss., University of California - Riverside, 1994).

505. Gruwell, Leeann R. "Freedom Found: An Examination of Oral Tradition as Resistance" (Honors thesis, Coe College, n.d.).

506. Gutman, Herbert G. "Family Life".

Reprinted (from *Black Family in Slavery and Freedom*) in Goodheart, Brown, and Rabe, eds., *Slavery in American Society*, pp. 161-66.

507. Hamilton, Virginia. *Many Thousand Gone: African Americans from Slavery to Freedom*. New York: Knopf, 1993.

508. Higginbotham, A. Leon. "The Ten Precepts of American Slavery Jurisprudence: Chief Justice Roger Taney's Defense and Justice Thurgood Marshall's Condemnation of the Precept of Black Inferiority," *Cardozo Law Review*, 17, 6 (1996), pp. 1695-1710.

509. Higgs, Robert, and Robert A. Margo. "Black Americans: Income and Standard of Living from the Days of Slavery to the Present," in Julian Lincoln Simon, ed., *The State of Humanity* (Oxford: Blackwell in association with the Cato Institute, 1995), pp. 178-87.

510. Hine, Darlene Clark. "The Making of Black Women in America: an Historical Encyclopedia," in Linda K. Kerber, Alice Kessler-Harris, and Kathryn Kish Sklar, eds., *U.S. History as Women's History: New Feminist Essays* (Chapel Hill: University of North Carolina Press, 1995), pp. 335-47.

511. Hodges, Graham R. "Violence and Religion in the Black American Revolution (review essay: Frey, *Water from the Rock*)," *Reviews in American History*, 20, 2 (1992), pp. 157-62.

512. Hodges, Graham Russell, ed. *The Black Loyalist Directory: African Americans in Exile After the American Revolution*. New York: Garland, 1996.

513. Hoffman, Michael A. *They Were White and They Were Slaves: The Untold History of the Enslavement of Whites in Early America*. 4th ed. Dresden NY: Wiswell Ruffin House, 1992.

514. Hogge, Amy. "Where Else Can We Go But To The Lord: A Study of Slave Conversion Experiences" (BA thesis, James Madison University, 1992).

515. Holloway, Joseph E. "The Origins of African-American Culture," in idem, ed., *Africanisms in American Culture* (Bloomington: Indiana University Press, 1990), pp. 1-18.

516. Holt, Sharon Ann. "Symbol, Memory, and Service: Resistance and Family Formation in Nineteenth-Century African America," in Hudson, Jr., ed., *Working Toward Freedom*, pp. 192-210.

517. Huggins, Nathan Irvin, and Brenda Smith Huggins. *Revelations: American History, American Myths*. New York: Oxford University Press, 1995.

Includes: "The Historical Odyssey of Nathan Irvin Huggins," by Lawrence W. Levine, pp. 3-20; "Harlem on My Mind," pp. 21-28; "Pilgrimage for Black Americans: the Slave Castles of West Africa," pp. 29-35; "Slavery and Its Defense," pp. 232-41.

518. Humphreys, Hugh C. *Agitate! Agitate Agitate!: The Great Fugitive Slave Law Convention and its Rare Daguerreotype*. Oneida NY: Madison County Heritage, 1994.

519. Hunt, Patricia K. "The Struggle to Achieve Individual Expression through Clothing and Adornment: African American Women under and after Slavery," in Morton, ed., *Discovering the Women in Slavery*, pp. 227-40.

520. Hunter, Gary J. "The Political Economy of Slavery in the United States 1607-1865," in Sudarkasa, Nwachuku, Millette, and Thomas, eds., *The African-American Experience*, pp. 42-52.

521. Hutchison, G. Whit. "The Bible and Slavery, A Test of Ethical Method: Biblical Interpretation, Social Ethics, and the Hermeneutics of Race In America, 1830-1861" (PhD diss., Union Theological Seminary, 1996).

522. Ignatiev, Noel. "The Revolution as an African-American Exuberance," in Zimbardo and Montgomery, eds., "African-American Culture in the Eighteenth Century," pp. 605-14.

523. Ingersol, Thomas N. "Clergy, Markets, and Slaves in Colonial North American Atlantic Perspective" (Unpublished paper, American Historical Association, Washington DC, 27-30 Dec. 1992).

524. Johnson, Kirstin Marie. "The Symptoms of Posttraumatic Stress Disorder in the African-American Slave Experience: A Project Based upon an Independent Investigation" (MS thesis, Smith College School for Social Work, 1995).

525. Jones, Danny. "Jefferson and Slavery: The Paradox of the Age of Reason" (Honors essay, Dept. of History, University of North Carolina - Chapel Hill, 1992).

526. Jones, Jacqueline. "Back to the Future with The Bell Curve: Jim Crow, Slavery, and G," in Steve Fraser, ed., *The Bell Curve Wars: Race, Intelligence, and the Future of America* (New York: BasicBooks, 1995), pp. 80-93.

527. Jones, Jacqueline. *Labor of Love, Labor of Sorrow: Black Women, Work, and the Family from Slavery to the Present*. New York: Vintage Books, 1995.

528. Jones, Jacqueline. "Race, Sex, and Self-Evident Truths: The Status of Slave Women during the Era of the American Revolution," in Ronald J. Hoffman and Peter J. Albert, eds., *Women in the Age of the American Revolution* (Charlottesville: University Press of Virginia, 1989), pp. 293-337.

Reprinted in Clinton, ed., *Half Sisters of History*, pp. 18-35.

529. Jordan, Winthrop D. "Enslavement of Negroes in America to 1700".

Reprinted in Stanley N. Katz, John M. Murrin, and Douglas Greenberg, eds., *Colonial America: Essays in Politics and Social Development* (4th ed.) (New York: McGraw-Hill, 1993), pp. 288-329.

530. Joyner, Charles. "'Believer I Know': The Emergence of African-American Christianity," in Paul E. Johnson, ed., *African-American Christianity: Essays in History* (Berkeley: University of California Press, 1994), pp. 18-46.

531. Joyner, Charles. "Digging Common Ground: African American History and Historical Archaeology" (Unpublished paper, Annual Meeting of the Society for Historical Archaeology, Kingston, Jamaica, January 1992).

532. Joyner, Charles. "Texts, Texture, and Context: Toward an Ethnographic History of Slave Resistance," in Salmond and Clayton, eds., *Varieties of Southern History*, pp. 21-40.

533. Kain, John F. "The Cumulative Impacts of Slavery, Jim Crow, and Housing Market Discrimination on Black Welfare" (Cambridge MA: Harvard Institute of Economic Research, Harvard University, 1992).

534. Kaminski, John P., ed. *A Necessary Evil?: Slavery and the Debate over the Constitution*. Madison WI: Madison House, 1995. (Constitutional Heritage Series, vol. 2. Published for the Center for the Study of the American Constitution)

535. Kardatzke, Tim, and April Hayes. "Jewelry Use in an African-American Slave Community" (Unpublished paper, Annual Meeting of the Society for Historical Archaeology, Kingston, Jamaica, January 1992).

536. Kellow, Margaret M. R. "The Divided Mind of Antislavery Feminism: Lydia Maria Child and the Construction of African American Womanhood," in Morton, ed., *Discovering the Women in Slavery*, pp. 107-26.

537. Kemble, Jean. *American Slavery: Pre-1866 Imprints*. (London): Eccles Centre for American Studies, The British Library, 1995.

538. Kluver, Martina. "Die Darstellung der Schwarzen und die Auseinandersetzung mit der Sklaverei in der Kurzprosa amerikanischer Zeitschriften des späten 18. Jahrhunderts" (PhD diss., Universität Tübingen, 1995).

539. Kolchin, Peter. *American Slavery, 1619-1877*. New York: Hill and Wang, 1993.

540. Koonce, Kenneth T., Jr. "On the Threshold of Involuntary Servitude," *Pepperdine Law Review*, 16, 3 (1989), pp. 689-708.

541. Kujoory, Parvin. *Black Slavery in America: An Annotated Mediagraphy*. Lanham MD: Scarecrow Press, 1995.

542. Kukla, Jon. "On the Irrelevance and Relevance of Saints George and Thomas," *Virginia Magazine of History and Biography*, 102, 2 (1994), pp. 261-70.

543. Lacey, Barbara E. "Visual Images of Blacks in Early American Imprints," *William and Mary Quarterly*, 53, 1 (1996), pp. 137-80.

544. Lambert, Frank. "'I Saw the Book Talk': Slave Readings of the First Great Awakening," *Journal of Negro History*, 77, 4 (1992), pp. 185-98.

545. Langum, David J. "The Role of Intellect and Fortuity in Legal Change: An Incident from the Law of Slavery," *American Journal of Legal History*, 28, 1 (1987), pp. 1-16.

546. Lawrence-McIntyre, Charshee Charlotte. *Criminalizing a Race: Free Blacks During Slavery*. Queens: Kayode, 1993.

547. Lecaudey, Hélène. "Behind the Mask: Ex-Slave Women and Interracial Sexual Relations," in Morton, ed., *Discovering the Women in Slavery*, pp. 260-77.

548. Levesque, George A. "Slavery in the Ideology and Politics of the Revolutionary Generation, 1750-1783: An Afro-American Perspective," *Howard Law Journal*, 30, 4 (We the People: A Celebration of the Bicentennial of the United States Constitution) (1987), pp. 1051-65.

549. Levine, Lawrence W. "African Culture and Slavery in the United States," in Harris, ed., *Global Dimensions of the African Diaspora* (2nd ed.), pp. 99-107.

550. Levine, Lawrence W. "Slave Songs and Slave Consciousness: An Exploration in Neglected Sources".

Reprinted from in Fulop and Raboteau, eds., *African American Religion*, pp. 57-87.

551. Levinson, Sanford. "Slavery In the Canon of Constitutional Law," *Chicago-Kent Law Review*, 68, 3 (Symposium on the Law of Slavery) (1993), pp. 1087-111.

552. Lewis, Earl. "'To Turn as on a Pivot': Writing African Americans into a History of Overlapping Diasporas," *American Historical Review*, 100, 3 (1995), pp. 765-87.

553. Littlefield, Daniel C. "From Phillips to Genovese: The Historiography of American Slavery Before *Time on the Cross*," in Binder, ed., *Slavery in the Americas*, pp. 1-23.

554. Litwack, Leon F. "The Federal Government and the Free Negro, 1790-1860," *Journal of Negro History*, 43, 4 (1958), pp. 261-78.

Reprinted in Finkelman, ed., *Race, Law and American History*, vol. 2 (*Race and Law Before Emancipation*), pp. 313-30.

555. Lively, Donald E. *The Constitution and Race*. New York: Praeger, 1992.

556. Lowe, Eugene Y., Jr. "Racial Ideology," in *Encyclopedia of American Social History*, vol. 1, pp. 335-46.

557. Lyerly, Cynthia Lynn. "Religion, Gender, and Identity: Black Methodist Women in a Slave Society, 1770-1810," in Morton, ed., *Discovering the Women in Slavery*, pp. 202-26.

558. Maltz, Earl M. "Slavery, Federalism, and the Structure of the Constitution," *American Journal of Legal History*, 36, 4 (1992), pp. 466-98.

559. Maltz, Earl M. "The Unlikely Hero of *Dred Scott*: Benjamin Robbins Curtis and the Constitutional Law of Slavery," *Cardozo Law Review*, 17, 6 (1996), pp. 1995-2016.

Comment by Kenneth M. Stampp, "The Unlikely Hero of Dred Scott: Benjamin Robbins Curtis and the Constitutional Law of Slavery: Comment," pp. 2017-22.

560. Marienstras, Elise. "Les Lumières et l'esclavage en Amérique du Nord au XVIIIe siècle," in Dorigny, ed. *Les abolitions de l'esclavage*, pp. 111-32.

561. Marshall, Thurgood. "The Constitution's Bicentennial: Commemorating the Wrong Document?" *Vanderbilt Law Review*, 40, 6 (1987), pp. 1337-42.

See also Reynolds and Diamond.

Reprinted in Finkelman, ed., *Race, Law and American History*, vol. 1 (*African Americans and the Law*), pp. 313-18.

562. McColley, Robert. "Slavery: The British Colonies," in *Encyclopedia of the North American Colonies*, vol. 2, pp. 67-87.

563. McGary, Howard. *Between Slavery and Freedom: Philosophy and American Slavery.* Bloomington: Indiana University Press, 1992.

564. Mintz, Steven. "Introduction," in *African American Voices: The Life Cycle of Slavery.* St. James NY: Brandywine Press, 1993.

565. Miller, Randall M. "Slavery," in Jack Salzman, David Lionel Smith, and Cornel West, eds., *Encyclopedia of African-American Culture and History* (New York: Macmillan Library Reference, 1996), vol. 5, pp. 2454-69.

566. Miller, Randall M., and John David Smith. *Dictionary of Afro-American Slavery.*

"Updated, with a new introduction and bibliography" (Westport CT: Praeger, 1996).

567. Miller, William Lee. *Arguing About Slavery: The Great Battle in the United States Congress.* New York: A. A. Knopf, 1996.

568. Mitchell, Theodore Fuller. "John Belton O'Neall, Criminal Law, and Slavery in Antebellum South Carolina" (MA thesis, Clemson University, 1992).

569. Mitchell, Verner D. "To Steal Away Home: Tracing Race, Slavery and Difference in Selected Writings of Thomas Jefferson, David Walker, William Wells Brown, Ralph Waldo Emerson and Pauline Elizabeth Hopkins" (PhD diss., Rutgers, The State University of New Jersey - New Brunswick, 1995).

570. Montgomery, Benilde. "White Captives, African Slaves: A Drama of Abolition," in Zimbardo and Montgomery, eds., "African-American Culture in the Eighteenth Century," pp. 615-30.

571. Moore, Jane. "Sex, Slavery and Rights in Mary Wollstonecraft's *Vindications*," in Plasa and Ring, eds., *Discourse of Slavery*, pp. 18-39.

572. Moore, Jesse T., Jr. "Alex Haley's *Roots*: Ten Years Later," *Western Journal of Black Studies*, 18, 2 (1994), pp. 70-76.

573. Morgan, Edmund S. "Slavery and Freedom: The American Paradox".

Reprinted in Stanley N. Katz, John M. Murrin, and Douglas Greenberg, eds., *Colonial America: Essays in Politics and Social Development* (4th ed.) (New York: McGraw-Hill, 1993), pp. 263-88.

Reprinted in Goodheart, Brown, and Rabe, eds., *Slavery in American Society*, pp. 69-82.

574. Morgan, Michael J. "Rock and Roll Unplugged: African-American Music in Eighteenth-Century America," in Zimbardo and Montgomery, eds., "African-American Culture in the Eighteenth Century," pp. 649-62.

575. Morris, Christopher. "Challenging the Masters: Recent Studies on Slavery and Freedom (review essay: Jones, *Born a Child of Freedom*, Malone, *Sweet Chariot*, Berlin and Morgan, eds., *Cultivation and Culture*, Berlin *et al.*, eds., *Freedom: A Documentary History of Emancipation*, series 1, vol. 3)," *Florida Historical Quarterly*, 73, 2 (1994), pp. 218-24.

576. Morris, Thomas D. "Slaves and the Rules of Evidence in Criminal Trials," *Chicago-Kent Law Review*, 68, 3 (Symposium on the Law of Slavery) (1993), pp. 1209-40.

577. Morris, Thomas D. *Southern Slavery and the Law, 1619-1860.* Chapel Hill: University of North Carolina Press, 1996.

578. Morton, Patricia. "Introduction," to idem, ed., *Discovering the Women in Slavery*, pp. 1-26.

579. Morton, Patricia, ed. *Discovering the Women in Slavery: Emancipating Perspectives on the American Past.* Athens: University of Georgia Press, 1996.

For contents see Bynum, Gould, Hanger, Hunt, Inscoe, Kattner, Kellow, King, Lecaudey, Lyerly, Morton, Powell, Schwartz, Sheinin, and Weiner.

580. Mullins, Paul R. "'Men in Different Attitudes': The Integrity of African-American Resistance" (Unpublished paper, Annual Meeting of the Society for Historical Archaeology, Kingston, Jamaica, January 1992).

581. Nash, A. E. Keir. "In Re Radical Interpretations of American Law: The Relation of Law and History," *Michigan Law Review*, 82, 2 (1983), pp. 274-345.

582. Nieman, Donald G. "From Slaves to Citizens: African-Americans, Rights Consciousness, and

Reconstruction," *Cardozo Law Review*, 17, 6 (1996), pp. 2115-39.

Comment by Robert J. Kaczorowski, "Reflections on 'From Slaves to Citizens'," pp. 2141-47.

Comment by Randall Kennedy, "From Slaves to Citizens: African-Americans, Rights Consciousness, and Reconstruction - Comment," pp. 2149-51.

583. Nieman, Donald G. "The Language of Liberation: African Americans and Equalitarian Constitutionalism, 1830-1950," in idem, ed., *The Constitution, Law, and American Life: Critical Aspects of the Nineteenth-Century Experience* (Athens: University of Georgia Press, 1992), pp. 67-90.

584. Oakes, James. "'The Compromising Expedient': Justifying a Proslavery Constitution," *Cardozo Law Review*, 17, 6 (1996), pp. 2023-56.

Comment by Robert. A. Burt, "Comments on James Oakes, 'The Compromising Expedient'," pp. 2057-61.

585. Oakes, James. "Slavery," in *Encyclopedia of American Social History*, vol. 2, pp. 1407-19.

586. O'Neal, John, Rhonda Fabian, Jerry Baber, Andrew Schlesinger, and Schlesinger Video Productions. "A History of Slavery in America" (Bala Cynwyd PA: Schlessinger Video Productions, 1994). (Video in the series "Black Americans of Achievement. Video Collection II")

587. Painter, Nell Irvin. "Soul Murder and Slavery: Toward a Fully Loaded Cost Accounting," in Linda K. Kerber, Alice Kessler-Harris, and Kathryn Kish Sklar, eds., *U.S. History as Women's History: New Feminist Essays* (Chapel Hill: University of North Carolina Press, 1995), pp. 125-46.

588. Palmié, Stephan. "Slave Culture and the Culture of Slavery in North America: A Few Recent Monographs," in Binder, ed., *Slavery in the Americas*, pp. 25-55.

589. Paludan, Phillip Shaw. "Hercules Unbound: Lincoln, Slavery, and the Intentions of the Framers," in Donald G. Nieman, ed., *The Constitution, Law, and American Life: Critical Aspects of the Nineteenth-Century Experience* (Athens: University of Georgia Press, 1992), pp. 1-22.

590. Parker, Freddie L., ed. *Stealing a Little Freedom: Advertisements for Slave Runaways in North Carolina, 1791-1840*. New York: Garland, 1994.

591. Patten, M. Drake. "The Archaeology of Playtime: Artifacts of African American Games in the Plantation South" (Unpublished paper, Annual Meeting of the Society for Historical Archaeology, Kingston, Jamaica, January 1992).

592. Patton, Venetria Kirsten. "Women in Chains: The Legacy of Slavery in Black Women's Writing" (PhD diss., University of California - Riverside, 1996).

593. Pendleton, Margaret. "Proslavery: A History of the Defense of Slavery in America, 1701-1840," *California Lawyer*, 8, 4 (1988), pp. 28(1).

594. Plasa, Carl, and Betty J. Ring, eds. *The Discourse of Slavery: Aphra Behn to Toni Morrison*. New York: Routledge, 1994. Foreword by Isobel Armstrong.

For contents see Fogarty, Hauss, Moore, Plasa, Ring, Sabiston, and Vine.

595. Potter, Douglas T. "Slave or Abo: Can Chemical Analyses Tell?" (Unpublished paper, Annual Meeting of the Society for Historical Archaeology, Kingston, Jamaica, January 1992).

596. Prude, Jonathan. "To Look upon the 'Lower Sort': Runaway Ads and the Appearance of Unfree Laborers in America, 1750-1800," *Journal of American History*, 78, 1 (1991), pp. 124-59.

597. Przybyszewski, Linda C. A. "Mrs. John Marshall Harlan's Memories: Hierarchies of Gender and Race in the Household and the Polity," *Law and Social Inquiry*, 18, 3 (1993), pp. 453-78.

598. Quarles, Benjamin. *The Negro in the American Revolution*.

Republished, with new introduction by Gary Nash and new Foreword by Thad W. Tate (Chapel Hill: University of North Carolina Press, 1996).

599. Raboteau, Albert J. "African-Americans, Exodus and the American Israel," in Paul E. Johnson, ed., *African-American Christianity: Essays in History* (Berkeley: University of California Press, 1994), pp. 1-17.

600. Rankin-Hill, Lesley. "Uncovering African Americans' Buried Past," *Science Year 1994* (Chicago: World Book, 1993), pp. 117-31.

601. Rath, Richard C. "The Herskovits-Frazier Problem: Conceptual Models and Historical Tests" (Unpublished paper presented at the Annual Meeting of the Southern Historical Association, Atlanta, 1992).

602. Reeves, Matthew B. "A Slave's Viewpoint: Using Ethnography as an Interpretive Tool" (Unpublished paper, Annual Meeting of the Society for Historical Archaeology, Kingston, Jamaica, January 1992).

603. Reynolds, William Bradford. "Another View: Our Magnificent Constitution," *Vanderbilt Law Review*, 40, 6 (1987), 1343-51.

See Marshall, "Constitution's Bicentennial".

Reprinted in Finkelman, ed., *Race, Law and American History*, vol. 1 (*African Americans and the Law*), pp. 319-27.

604. Riga, Peter J. "The American Crisis over Slavery: An Example of the Relationship between Legality and Morality," *American Journal of Jurisprudence*, 26 (1982), pp. 80-111.

605. Ripley, C. Peter, Roy E. Finkenbine, Michael F. Hembree, and Donald Yacovone, eds. *Witness for Freedom: African-American Voices on Race, Slavery, and Emancipation*. Chapel Hill: University of North Carolina Press, 1993.

606. Roberts, Rita. "Patriotism and Political Criticism: The Evolution of Political Consciousness in the Mind of a Black Revolutionary Soldier," in Zimbardo and Montgomery, eds., "African-American Culture in the Eighteenth Century," pp. 569-88.

607. Rothenberg, Winifred B. "Markets without Contracts: The Cliometrics of Slavery (review essay: Fogel, *Without Consent or Contract*, Fogel, Galantine, and Manning, eds., *Without Consent or Contract: Evidence and Methods*, and Fogel and Engerman, *et al.*, *Without Consent or Contract: Technical Papers*)," *Reviews in American History*, 21, 4 (1993), pp. 584-90.

608. Sale, Maggie. "The Slumbering Volcano: Recasting Race, Masculinity, and the Discourse of US American National Identity" (PhD diss., University of California, San Diego, Department of Literature, 1992).

609. Salinger, Sharon V. "Labor: Colonial Times through 1820," in *Encyclopedia of American Social History*, vol. 2, pp. 1433-45.

610. Salmond, John, and Bruce Clayton, eds. *Varieties of Southern History: New Essays on a Region and Its People*. Westport: Greenwood Press, 1996.

For contents see Isaac, Joyner, and White and White.

611. Samford, Patricia. "The Archaeology of African-American Slavery and Material Culture," *William and Mary Quarterly*, 53, 1 (1996), pp. 87-114.

612. Schomburg Center for Research in Black Culture. *Guide to the Scholarly Resources Microfilm Edition*. Wilmington DE: Scholarly Resources, 1995. (Manuscript collections from the Schomburg Center for Research in Black Culture)

(Alternate title: *Antebellum America and Slavery*)

Katz/Prince collection, 1967-1973; Earl Conrad/Harriet Tubman Collection; The Slavery and Abolition Collection.

613. Schwartz, Marie Jenkins. "'At Noon, Oh How I Ran': Breastfeeding and Weaning on Plantation and Farm in Antebellum Virginia and Alabama," in Morton, ed., *Discovering the Women in Slavery*, pp. 241-59.

614. Schwartz, Marie Jenkins. "Born in Bondage: Slave Childhood in the Virginia Piedmont and the Alabama Black Belt 1820 to 1860" (PhD diss., University of Maryland - College Park, 1994).

615. Schwarz, Philip J. "Jefferson and the Wolf: The Sage of Monticello Confronts the Law of Slavery," (Organization of American Historians) *Magazine of History*, 8, 2 (1994), pp. 18-22.

616. Sensbach, Jon F. "Charting a Course in Early African-American History," *William and Mary Quarterly*, 50, 2 (1993), pp. 394-405.

617. Shields, John C. "Phillis Wheatley's Subversive Pastoral," in Zimbardo and Montgomery, eds., "African-American Culture in the Eighteenth Century," pp. 631-48.

618. Shuffleton, Frank. "Circumstantial Accounts, Dangerous Arts: Recognizing African-American Culture in Eighteenth-Century Travelers' Narratives," in Zimbardo and Montgomery, eds., "African-American Culture in the Eighteenth Century," pp. 589-604.

619. Shuffleton, Frank. "Thomas Jefferson: Race, Culture, and the Failure of Anthropological Method," in Frank Shuffelton, ed., *A Mixed Race: Ethnicity in Early America* (New York: Oxford University Press, 1993), pp. 257-77.

620. Singleton, Theresa A. "The Archaeology of Slave Life".

Reprinted in Charles E. Orser, ed., *Images of the Recent Past: Readings in Historical Archaeology* (Walnut Creek CA: Alta Mira Press, 1996), pp. 141-65.

621. Sloat, William A. H. "George Whitefield, African-Americans, and Slavery," *Methodist History*, 33, (1994), pp. 3-13.

622. Smallwood, Stephanie. "After the Atlantic Crossing: The Arrival and Sale of African Migrants in the British Americas, 1672-1693" (Working paper no. 96-13, International Seminar on the History of the Atlantic World, 1500-1800, Harvard University, September 1996).

623. Smedley, Audrey. *Race in North America: Origin and Evolution of a Worldview*. Boulder: Westview, 1993.

624. Smith, John David. "'The World at First Neither Saw nor Understood': Documenting the Emancipation Experience (review essay: Berlin *et al.*, *Freedom: A Documentary History of Emancipation*, series 1, vols. 1-3, series 2)," *North Carolina Historical Review*, 71, 4 (1994), pp. 472-77.

625. Soifer, Aviam. "Status, Contract, and Promises Unkept," *Yale Law Journal*, 96, 8 (1987), pp. 1916-59.

626. Starobin, Robert S., ed. *Blacks in Bondage: Letters of American Slaves*. 2nd ed. New York: M. Wiener, 1994. (Reprint. Originally published: New York: New Viewpoints, 1974. With new foreword)

627. Steckel, Richard. "The Slavery Period and Its Influence on Family Change in the United States," in Elza Berquó and Peter Xenos, eds., *Family Systems and Cultural Change* (Oxford: Clarendon Press, 1992), pp. 144-58.

628. Stepto, Michele. *Our Song, Our Toil: The Story of American Slavery as Told by Slaves*. Brookfield CT: Millbrook Press, 1994.

629. Stevenson, Brenda E. "Abolition Movement," in Hine, Brown, and Terborg-Penn, eds., *Black Women in America*, pp. 3-10.

630. Stevenson, Brenda E. "Slavery," in Hine, Brown, and Terborg-Penn, eds., *Black Women in America*, pp. 1045-70.

631. Streets, David H. *Slave Genealogy: A Research Guide with Case Studies*. Bowie MD: Heritage Books, 1986.

632. Stuckey, Sterling. "Slavery and the Freeing of American History Instruction," *AHA Perspectives*, 33, 4 (1995), pp. 12-15.

633. Tucker, Veta Smith. "Reconstructing Mammy: Fictive Reinterpretations of Mammy's Role in the Slave Community and Image in American Culture" (A.D. [sic], The University of Michigan, 1994).

634. Turkistani, Abdulhafeez Q. "Muslim Slaves and their Narratives: Religious Faith and Cultural Accommodation" (PhD diss., Kent State University, 1995).

635. Tushnet, Mark. "Slave Law and Contract and Hierarchy (review essay: Morris, *Southern Slavery and the Law*)," *Reviews in American History*, 24, 4 (1996), pp. 590-95.

636. Venable, Cornelia Michelle. "'Slave' and 'Woman' in the Pauline Epistles and New Testament Paradigms in the Slave Narratives of African American Women: A Comparative Study" (PhD diss., Temple University, 1995).

637. Vorenberg, Michael. "Final Freedom: the Civil War, the End of Slavery, and the Thirteenth Amendment" (PhD diss., Harvard University, 1995).

638. Wade-Lewis, Margaret. "The Impact of the Turner Herskovits Connection on Anthropology and Linguistics," *Dialectical Anthropology*, 17, 4 (1992), pp. 391-412.

639. Wahl, Jenny B. "American Slavery and the Path of the Law," *Social Science History*, 20, 2 (1996), pp. 281-316.

640. Wahl, Jenny B. "The Jurisprudence of American Slave Sales," *Journal of Economic History*, 56, 1 (1996), pp. 143-69.

641. Walter, Krista Lynn. "Loopholes in History: The Literature of American Slavery as Cultural Critique" (PhD diss., University of California - Irvine, 1991).

642. Wang Xi. "Black Suffrage and the Redefinition of American Freedom, 1860-1870," *Cardozo Law Review*, 17, 6 (1996), pp. 2153-2223.

Comment by Akhil Reed Amar. "The Fifteenth Amendment and 'Political Rights'," pp. 2225-29.

643. Wasser, Hartmut. "'Wir halten den Wolf an den Ohren ...': Thomas Jefferson und das Institut des Sklaverei," *Amerikastudien/American Studies*, 41, 1 (1996), pp. 33-48.

644. Watkins, Mel. *On the Real Side: Laughing, Lying, and Signifying: The Underground Tradition of African-American Humor that Transformed American Culture, from Slavery to Richard Pryor*. New York: Simon & Schuster, 1994.

645. Weisberg, R. "The Hermeneutic of Acceptance and the Discourse of the Grotesque, With a Classroom Exercise on Vichy Law," *Cardozo Law Review*, 17, 6 (1996), pp. 1875-1968.

Comment by Sanford Levinson, "Allocating Honor and Acting Honorably: Some Reflections Provoked by the Cardozo Conference on Slavery," pp. 1969-81.

Comment by Lea VanderVelde, "The Moral Economy of the Purchase of Freedom: Ethical Lessons From the Slave Narratives," pp. 1983-93.

646. Wells, Daniel J. "To Rend the Demon: The Legacy of Slavery, the American People and Historians" (MA thesis, Oakland University, 1996).

647. Whaples, Robert, and Dianne C. Betts, eds. *Historical Perspectives on the American Economy: Selected Readings*. New York: Cambridge University Press, 1995.

For contents see David and Temin, Fogel and Engerman (2), and Galenson.

648. White, Edward L., III. "Another Look at Our Founding Fathers and their Product: A Response to Justice Thurgood Marshall," *Notre Dame Journal of Law, Ethics & Public Policy*, 4, 1 (1989), pp. 73-130.

649. White, Shane. "Digging Up the African-American Past: Historical Archaeology, Photography and Slavery (review essay: Ferguson, *Uncommon Ground*, Frey, *Water from the Rock*, and Campbell Jr., *Before Freedom Came*)," *Australasian Journal of American Studies*, 11, 1 (1992), pp. 37-47.

650. White, Shane, and Graham White. "Reading the Slave Body: Demeanor, Gesture, and African-American Culture," in Salmond and Clayton, eds., *Varieties of Southern History*, pp. 41-61.

651. White, Shane, and Graham White. "Slave Clothing and African-American Culture in the Eighteenth and Nineteenth Centuries," *Past and Present*, no. 148 (1995), pp. 149-86.

652. White, Shane, and Graham White. "Slave Hair and African-American Culture in the Eighteenth and Nineteenth Centuries," *Journal of Southern History*, 61, 1 (1995), pp. 45-76.

653. Whitler, Debra Lynn. "A Quest for Freedom: The Slave Narrative as Romance" (MA thesis, Arizona State University, 1994).

654. Wiecek, William M. "The Origins of the Law of Slavery in British North America," *Cardozo Law Review*, 17, 6 (1996), pp. 1711-92.

655. *Wilkes, Leslie. "The Treatment of Elderly Women in Slavery" (Unpublished paper, 1987).

656. Williams, Armstrong. *Slavery to 1992: A Historical Perspective of Black American Success Through the Free Market System*. Washington DC: The Heritage Foundation, 1992.

657. Williams, Richard E. *Hierarchical Structures and Social Value: The Creation of Black and Irish Identities in the United States*. Cambridge: Cambridge University Press, 1990.

658. Willis, Jay Thomas. "A Theory of the Origins and Dynamics of Heterogeneity Within African American Culture," *Western Journal of Black Studies*, 15, 3 (1991), pp. 178-82.

659. Wilson, Carol. "Freedom at Risk: The Kidnapping of Free Blacks in America, 1780-1865" (PhD diss., West Virginia University, 1991).

660. Wilson, Carol. *Freedom at Risk: The Kidnapping of Free Blacks in America, 1780-1865.* Lexington: University Press of Kentucky, 1994.

661. Wilson, Carol. "'The Thought of Slavery is Death to a Free Man": Abolitionists' Response to the Kidnapping of Free Blacks," *Mid-America: An Historical Review*, 74, 2 (1992), pp. 105-24.

662. Wilson, Joseph T. *The Black Phalanx: African American Soldiers in the War of Independence, the War of 1812, and the Civil War.* New York: Da Capo Press, 1994. (New ed. [original 1890], with foreword by Dydley Raylor Cornish)

663. Windley, Lathan A. A. *Profile of Runaway Slaves in Virginia and South Carolina from 1730 through 1787.* New York: Garland, 1995. (Studies in African American History and Culture)

664. *Wood, Betty C. *Origins of Slavery in the United States.* New York: Hill and Wang, forthcoming. (Critical Issues Series)

665. Wood, Peter H. "Race," in *Encyclopedia of American Social History*, vol. 1, pp. 437-51.

666. Wright, Donald R. *African Americans in the Early Republic, 1789-1831.* Arlington Heights IL: Harlan Davidson, 1993.

667. Young, Jeffrey Robert. "Domesticating Slavery: The Ideological Formation of the Master Class in the Deep South, from Colonization to 1837" (PhD diss., Emory University, 1996).

668. Zanca, Kenneth J. *American Catholics and Slavery, 1789-1866: An Anthology of Primary Documents.* Lanham MD: University Press of America, 1994.

669. Zimbardo, Rose A. "Introduction," in Zimbardo and Montgomery, eds., "African-American Culture in the Eighteenth Century," pp. 527-32.

670. Zimbardo, Rose [A.], and Benilde Montgomery, eds. "African-American Culture in the Eighteenth Century," special issue of *Eighteenth-Century Studies*, 27, 4 (1994).

For contents see Baum, D'Costa, Ignatiev, Montgomery, Morgan, Murphy, Potkay, Roberts, Shields, Shuffleton, and Zimbardo.

2. New England and Middle Colonies

671. Bezis-Selfa, John. "Forging a New Order: Slavery, Free Labor and Sectional Differentiation in the Mid-Atlantic Charcoal Iron Industry, 1715-1840" (PhD diss., University of Pennsylvania, 1995).

672. Breslaw, Elaine G. "The Salem Witch from Barbados: In Search of Tituba's Roots," *Essex Institute Historical Collections*, 128, 4 (1992), pp. 217-38.

673. Breslaw, Elaine G. *Tituba: Reluctant Witch of Salem: Devilish Indians and Puritan Fantasies.* New York: New York University Press, 1996.

674. Calligaro, Lee. "The Negro's Legal Status in Pre-Civil War New Jersey".

Reprinted in Finkelman, ed., *Race, Law and American History*, vol. 2 (*Race and Law Before Emancipation*), pp. 41-54.

675. Chase, Jeanne. "The Bounds of African Life in New York City during the First Half of the Eighteenth Century" (Presentation at Colloquium on "Les dépendances serviles", Paris 1996).

676. Collison, Gary L. "Alexander Burton and Salem's 'Fugitive Slave Riot' of 1851," *Essex Institute Historical Collections*, 128, 1 (1992), pp. 17-26.

677. Ernst, Daniel R. "Legal Positivism, Abolitionist Litigation, and the New Jersey Slave Case of 1845," *Law and History Review*, 4, 2 (1986), pp. 337-65.

678. Essah, Patience. *A House Divided: Slavery and Emancipation in Delaware, 1638-1865.* Charlottesville: University Press of Virginia, 1996.

679. Fabre, Genevieve. "Election Day Celebrations," in Binder, ed., *Slavery in the Americas*, pp. 403-20.

680. Finkelman, Paul. "The Protection of Rights in Seward's New York," *Civil War History*, 34, 3 (1988), pp. 34, 3 (1988), pp. 211-34.

Reprinted in Finkelman, ed., *Race, Law and American History*, vol. 2 (*Race and Law Before Emancipation*), pp. 159-82.

681. Fitts, Robert [K]. "The Archaeology of New England Slavery: Problems and Promises" (Unpublished paper, Annual Meeting of the Society for Historical Archaeology, Kingston, Jamaica, January 1992).

682. Fitts, Robert K. "Inventing New England's Slave Paradise: Master/Slave Relations in Eighteenth-Century Narragansett, Rhode Island" (PhD diss., Brown University, 1995).

683. Fitts, Robert K. "The Landscapes of Northern Bondage," *Historical Archaeology*, 30, 2 (1996), pp. 54-73.

684. Forbes, Ella M. "'But We Have No Country': An Afrocentric Study of the 1851 Christiana Resistance" (PhD diss., Temple University, 1992).

685. Garman, James C. "Viewing the Color Line Through the Material Culture of Death," *Historical Archaeology*, 28, 3 (1994), pp. 74-93.

686. Gilje, Paul A. "Between Slavery and Freedom: New York African Americans in the Early Republic (review essay: White, *Somewhat More Independent*)," *Reviews in American History*, 20, 2 (1992), pp. 163-67.

687. Goodfriend, Joyce D. "Slavery: The Dutch Colonies," in *Encyclopedia of the North American Colonies*, vol. 2, pp. 87-89.

688. Groth, Michael Edward. "Forging Freedom in the Mid-Hudson Valley: The End of Slavery and the Formation of a Free African-American Community in Dutchess County, New York, 1770-1850" (PhD diss., State University of New York at Binghamton, 1994).

689. Handler, Jerome S. "Update #4: New York's African Burial Ground," *African-American Archaeology*, 12 (1994), pp. 1-2.

690. Harrington, Spencer P. M. "Bones and Bureaucrats: New York's Great Cemetery Imbroglio," *Archaeology*, 46, 2 (1993), pp. 28-38.

691. Herring, Paul W. B. "Selected Aspects of the History of the African-American in the Mohawk and Upper Hudson Valley, 1633-1840" (PhD diss., State University of New York - Binghamton, 1992).

692. Hodges, Graham Russell. *Slavery and Freedom in the Rural North: African Americans in Monmouth County, New Jersey, 1665-1865*. Madison WI: Madison House, 1996.

693. Hodges, Graham Russell, and Alan Edward Brown, eds. *"Pretends to be Free": Runaway Slave Advertisements from Colonial and Revolutionary New York and New Jersey*. New York: Garland, 1994.

694. Holden-Smith, Barbara. "Lords of Lash, Loom, and Law: Justice Story, Slavery and Prigg v. Pennsylvania," *Cornell Law Review*, 78, 6 (1993), pp. 1086-151.

695. Hunter, Carol. *To Set the Captives Free: Reverend Jermain Wesley Loguen and the Struggle for Freedom in Central New York, 1835-1872*. New York: Garland, 1993.

696. Kousser, J. Morgan. "'The Supremacy of Equal Rights': The Struggle Against Racial Discrimination in Antebellum Massachusetts and the Foundations of the Fourteenth Amendment," *Northwestern University Law Review*, 82, 4 (1988), pp. 941-1010.

Reprinted in Finkelman, ed., *Race, Law and American History*, vol. 2 (*Race and Law Before Emancipation*), pp. 227-96.

697. Krüger-Kahloula, Angelika. "Homage and Hegemony: African American Grave Inscription and Decoration," in Binder, ed., *Slavery in the Americas*, pp. 317-35.

698. Kutler, Stanley I. "Pennsylvania Courts, the Abolition Act, and Negro Rights, *Pennsylvania History*, 30, 1 (1963), pp. 14-27.

Reprinted in Finkelman, ed., *Race, Law and American History*, vol. 2 (*Race and Law Before Emancipation*), pp. 298-311.

699. Lane, Roger. "An Epic Story, a Nurserytale Moral (review essay: Slaughter, *Bloody Dawn*)," *Reviews in American History*, 20, 2 (1992), pp. 492-500.

700. Lee, Rebekah. "Culture, Community, and Continuity: the Slave Elections of the North, 1750-1865" (AB honors thesis in History and Literature, Harvard University, 1995).

701. Loff, Geary A. "Fugitives from Injustice: The Underground Railroad in Southeastern Pennsylvania,

1780-1860" (MA thesis, East Stroudsburg University, 1992).

702. Mark, Mack E. "New York Burial Ground from the Field to the Laboratory," *African-American Archaeology*, 12 (1994), p. 4.

703. Marshall, Kenneth Edward. "Rebels in Their Midst: A Theoretical Exploration of Gender, Geography and Consciousness as Related to the Resistance and Survival of Female Slaves in New Jersey" (MA thesis, Michigan State University, 1995).

704. McDermott, William P. "Slaves and Slaveowners in Dutchess County," *Afro-Americans in New York Life and History*, 19, 1 (1995), pp. 17-41.

705. McMillan, Timothy J. "Black Magic: Witchcraft, Race and Resistance in Colonial New England," *Journal of Black Studies*, 25, 1 (1994), pp. 99-117.

706. Mead, Jeffrey B. *Chains Unbound: Slave Emancipations in the Town of Greenwich, Connecticut*. Baltimore: Gateway Press, 1995.

707. Melish, Joanne Pope. "Disowning Slavery: Gradual Emancipation and the Cultural Construction of 'Race' in New England, 1780-1860" (PhD dissertation, Brown University, 1996).

708. Mitros, David, comp. and ed. *Slave Records of Morris County, New Jersey: 1756-1841*. Morristown NJ: Morris County Heritage Commission, 1991.

709. Morgan, Gwenda. "Emancipation Studies: The Demise of Slavery in Pennsylvania and New York (review essay: Nash and Soderlund, *Freedom by Degrees*, and White, *Somewhat More Independent*)," *Slavery and Abolition*, 13, 3 (1992), pp. 207-12.

710. Moss, Richard S. *Slavery on Long Island: A Study in Local Institutional and Early Communal Life, 1609-1827*. New York: Garland, 1993.

711. Mulvihill, William. "Slavery on Long Island: An Overview," *Long Island Forum*, 58 (Winter 1995), pp. 13-18.

712. Renaud, Christopher. "Surviving Slavery and Freedom: African-Americans in New York City and Kings County during the Transformation from a Commercial to an Industrial Society" (MA thesis, City College of New York, 1994).

713. Ruchames, Louis. "Jim Crow Railroads in Massachusetts," *American Quarterly*, 8, 1 (1956), pp. 61-75.

Reprinted in Finkelman, ed., *Race, Law and American History*, vol. 2 (*Race and Law Before Emancipation*), pp. 433-47.

'714. Ruchames, Louis. "Race, Marriage, and Abolition in Massachusetts," *Journal of Negro History*, 40, 3 (1955), pp. 250-73.

Reprinted in Finkelman, ed., *Race, Law and American History*, vol. 2 (*Race and Law Before Emancipation*), pp. 448-71.

715. Sernett, Milton. "On Freedom's Threshold: The African American Presence in Central New York, 1760-1940," *Afro-Americans in New York Life and History*, 19, 1 (1995), pp. 43-91.

716. Sheinin, David. "Prudence Crandall, *Amistad*, and Other Episodes in the Dismissal of Connecticut Slave Women from American History," in Morton, ed., *Discovering the Women in Slavery*, pp. 129-52.

717. Shirk, Willis L., Jr. "Testing the Limits of Tolerance: Blacks and the Social Order in Columbia, Pennsylvania, 1800-1851," *Pennsylvania History*, 60, 1 (1993), pp. 35-50.

718. Slaughter, Thomas P. *Bloody Dawn: The Christiana Riot and Racial Violence in the Antebellum North*. New York: Oxford University Press, 1991.

719. "Slavery's Buried Past" (Chicago IL: WTTW, Kurtis Productions Ltd., 1996).

1 videocassette (ca. 60 min.).

720. Soifer, Aviam. "Status, Contract, and Promises Unkept".

Reprinted in Finkelman, ed., *Race, Law and American History*, vol. 2 (*Race and Law Before Emancipation*), pp. 486-529.

721. Swan, Robert J. "John Teasman: African-American Educator and the Emergence of Community in Early Black New York City, 1787-1815," *Journal of the Early Republic*, 12, 3 (1992), pp. 331-56.

722. "Unearthing the Slave Trade" (Discover Communications, 1994). Produced by Tom Naughton and Nicolas Valcour.

723. White, Shane. "'It Was a Proud Day': African Americans, Festivals, and Parades in the North, 1741-1834," *Journal of American History*, 81, 1 (1994), pp. 13-50.

724. White, Shane. "Slavery in New York State in the Early Republic," *Australasian Journal of American Studies*, 14, 2 (1995), pp. 1-29.

725. Williams, William Henry. *Slavery and Freedom in Delaware, 1639-1865*. Wilmington DE: SR Books, 1996.

726. Wilson, Sherrill D. *New York City's Black Slaveowners: A Social and Material Culture History*. New York: Garland, 1994.

727. Wolff, Cynthia Griffin. "Passing Beyond the Middle Passage: Henry 'Box' Brown's Translations of Slavery," *Massachusetts Review*, 37, 1 (1996), pp. 23-44.

3. Chesapeake

728. Allen, Ray Hoyt. "An Historiographical Survey: Thomas Jefferson and Sally Hemings" (MA thesis, California State University, Fresno, 1994).

729. Atkins, Stephen Charles. "An Archaeological Perspective on the African-American Slave Diet at Mount Vernon's House for Families" (MA thesis, The College of William and Mary, 1994).

730. Bardon, John Randolph. "'Flushed with Notions of Freedom': The Growth and Emancipation of a Virginia Slave Community, 1732-1812" (PhD diss., Duke University, 1993).

731. Barnett, Todd H. "Tobacco Planters, Tenants, and Slaves: A Portrait of Montgomery County in 1783," *Maryland Historical Magazine*, 89, 3 (1994), pp. 184-203.

732. Bear, James A., Jr., ed. *Jefferson at Monticello: Memoires of a Monticello Slave and the Private Life of Thomas Jefferson*.

Reprinted Charlottesville: University Press of Virginia, 1996.

733. Berlin, Ira. "Slavery and Freedom in the Chesapeake During the Age of George Washington" (Unpublished paper, conference on "Slavery in the Age of Washington", Mount Vernon VA, 3-4 Nov. 1994).

734. Boulton, Alexander Ormond. "The Architecture of Slavery: Art, Language, and Society in Early Virginia" (PhD diss., College of William and Mary, 1991).

735. *Callcott, Margaret Law. "Inventory of a Maryland Slave Cabin," *Riversdale Letter*, 12, 1 (1995), pp. 2-4.

736. Carr, Lois G., and Lorena S. Walsh. "The Planter's Wife: The Experience of White Women in Seventeenth-Century Maryland".

Reprinted in Stanley N. Katz, John M. Murrin, and Douglas Greenberg, eds., *Colonial America: Essays in Politics and Social Development* (4th ed.) (New York: McGraw-Hill, 1993), pp. 66-95.

737. Chambers, Douglas B. "'He Gwine Sing He Country': Africans, Afro-Virginians, and the Development of Slave Culture in Virginia, 1690-1810" (PhD diss., University of Virginia, 1996).

738. Chambers, Douglas B. "'He is an African But Speaks Plain': Historical Creolization in Eighteenth-Century Virginia," in Jalloh and Maizlish, eds., *African Diaspora*, pp. 100-33.

739. Clayton, Ralph. *Slavery, Slaveholding, and the Free Black Population of Antebellum Baltimore*. Bowie MD: Heritage Books, 1993.

740. Cole, Stephanie. "Changes for Mrs. Thornton's Arthur: Patterns of Domestic Service in Washington, DC, 1800-1835," *Social Science History*, 15, 3 (1992), pp. 367-79.

741. Cornelison, Alice. "History of Blacks in Howard County, Maryland," *Journal of the Afro-American Historical and Genealogical Society*, 10, 2-3 (1989), pp. 117-19.

742. Corrigan, Mary Beth. "'It's a Family Affair': Buying Freedom in the District of Columbia, 1850-1860," in Hudson, Jr., ed., *Working Toward Freedom*, pp. 163-91.

743. Corrigan, Mary Elizabeth. "A Social Union of Heart and Effort: The African-American in the

District of Columbia on the Eve of Emancipation" (PhD diss., University of Maryland - College Park, 1996).

744. Covington, J. Foy. "The Peculiar Leaf and the Peculiar Institution: A History of Tobacco and Slavery in the Virginia District" (MA thesis, Auburn University, 1992).

745. Daniels, Christine. "Gresham's Laws: Labor Management on an Early-Eighteenth-Century Chesapeake Plantation," *Journal of Southern History*, 62, 2 (1996), pp. 205-38.

746. Deal, J. Douglas. *Race and Class in Colonial Virginia: Indians, Englishmen, and Africans on the Eastern Shore During the Seventeenth Century*. New York: Garland, 1993.

747. Deans, Daniel B. "The Free Black in Seventeenth-Century Virginia" (MA thesis, University of Florida, 1992).

748. Deines, Ann. "The Slave Population in 1810 Alexandria, Virginia: A Preservation Plan for Historic Resources" (MA thesis, George Washington University, 1994).

749. Dermody, Larry D. "Fire and Ice: James Madison Ironworks (1762 to 1801)" (Unpublished paper, Annual Meeting of the Society for Historical Archaeology, Kingston, Jamaica, January 1992).

750. Dew, Charles B. *Bond of Iron: Master and Slave at Buffalo Forge*. New York: W. W. Norton, 1995.

751. Dew, Charles [B.] "Lives of the Slaves: The Ironworkers of Buffalo Forge" (Unpublished paper, American Historical Association, San Francisco, 6-9 Jan. 1994).

752. Dew, Charles B. *The Master and the Slaves: William Weaver and the Iron Works of Buffalo Forge*. New York: Norton, 1994.

753. Egerton, Douglas R. "'Fly Across the River': The Easter Slave Conspiracy of 1802," *North Carolina Historical Review*, 68, 2 (1991), pp. 87-110. With rejoinder to Parramore, pp. 122-24.

754. Egerton, Douglas R. *Gabriel's Rebellion: The Virginia Slave Conspiracies of 1800 and 1802*. Chapel Hill: University of North Carolina Press, 1993.

755. Fabricant, Daniel S. "Thomas R. Gray and William Styron: Finally, A Critical Look at the 1831 Confessions of Nat Turner," *American Journal of Legal History*, 37, 3 (1993), pp. 332-61.

756. French, Scot A. "Plotting 'Nat Turner's Rebellion': A Slave Girl's Testimony in Social Memory, 1831-Present" (Unpublished paper, Southern Historical Association, Louisville KY, 9-12 Nov. 1994).

757. Galke, Laura J. "You are Where you Live: Status Differences Between Field and Village Slaves in Piedmont Virginia" (Unpublished paper, Annual Meeting of the Society for Historical Archaeology, Kingston, Jamaica, January 1992).

758. Gavins, Raymond. "Shared Spaces, Separate Lives (review: Valentine Museum [Richmond] exhibit)," *Journal of American History*, 83 (1996), pp. 143-48.

759. Gawalt, Gerard W. "James Monroe, Presidential Planter," *Virginia Magazine of History and Biography*, 101, 2 (1993), pp. 251-72.

760. Gordon-Reed, Annette. *Thomas Jefferson and Sally Hemmings: An American Controversy*. Charlottesville: University Press of Virginia, 1996.

761. Greenberg, Kenneth S. *The Confessions of Nat Turner, and Related Documents*. New York: St. Martin's Press (Bedford Books), 1996.

762. Grubb, Farley, and Tony Stitt. "The Liverpool Emigrant Servant Trade and the Transition to Slave Labor in the Chesapeake, 1697-1707: Market Adjustments to War," *Explorations in Economic History*, 31, 3 (1994), pp. 376-405.

763. Gruber, Anna. "The Archaeology of Mr. Jefferson's Slaves" (MA thesis, University of Delaware, 1990).

764. Gudmestad, Robert Harold. "The Richmond Slave Market, 1840-1860" (MA thesis, University of Richmond, 1993).

765. Hatfield, April Lee. "The Atlantic World and the Development of Slavery in Seventeenth-Century Virginia" (MA thesis, University of Oregon, 1992).

766. Hernigle, Jacqueline L. "You are What You Eat: The Slaves of Portici Plantation" (Unpublished paper, Annual Meeting of the Society for Historical Archaeology, Kingston, Jamaica, January 1992).

767. Higginbotham, A. Leon, Jr., and Anne F. Jacobs. "The 'Law Only as an Enemy': The Legitimization of Racial Powerlessness Through Colonial and Antebellum Criminal Laws of Virginia," *North Carolina Law Review*, 70, 4 (1992), pp. 969-1070.

768. Higginbotham, A. Leon, Jr., and F. Michael Higginbotham. "'Yearning to breathe free': Legal Barriers Against and Options in Favor of Liberty in Antebellum Virginia," *New York University Law Review*, 68, 6 (1993), pp. 1213-71.

769. Hodges, Graham Russel. "Gabriel's Republican Rebellion (review essay: Egerton, *Gabriel's Rebellion*)," *Reviews in American History*, 22, 3 (1994), pp. 428-32.

770. Hunt, Thomas C. "Sectionalism, Slavery, and Schooling in Antebellum Virginia," *West Virginia History*, 46 (1985-86), pp. 125-36.

771. Hurry, Silas D., and Henry M. Miller. "The Varieties and Origins of Chesapeake Red Clay Tobacco Pipes: A Perspective from the Potomac Shore" (Unpublished paper, Annual Meeting of the Society for Historical Archaeology, Kingston, Jamaica, January 1992).

772. Isaac, Rhys. "Imagination and Material Culture: The Enlightenment on a Mid-18th-Century Virginia Plantation," in Anne Elizabeth Yentsch and Mary C. Beaudry, eds., *The Art and Mystery of Historical Archaeology: Essays in Honor of James Deetz* (Boca Raton: CRC Press, 1992), pp. 401-23.

773. Isaac, Rhys. "Kommunikation und Kontrolle: Machtbeziehungen und Metaphern des Autorität auf Colonel Landon Carters Plantage in Virginia, 1752-1778," in Alf Lüdtke, ed., *Herrschaft als soziale Praxis* (Göttingen: Vandenhoeck & Ruprecht, 1991), pp. 362-99.

774. Isaac, Rhys. "Stories of Enslavement: A Person-Centered Ethnography from an Eighteenth-Century Virginia Plantation," in Salmond and Clayton, eds., *Varieties of Southern History*, pp. 3-19.

775. Jordan, Ervin L. [Jr.] *Black Confederates and Afro-Yankees in Civil War Virginia*. Charlottesville: University Press of Virginia, 1995. (A Nation Divided: New Studies in Civil War History)

776. Katz, Ellen D. "African-American Freedom in Antebellum Cumberland County, Virginia," *Chicago-Kent Law Review*, 70, 3 (1995), pp. 927-91. (Symposium on the Law of Freedom, Part 2)

777. Katz, Sarah. "Rumors of Rebellion: Fear of a Slave Uprising in Post-Nat Turner Baltimore," *Maryland Historical Magazine*, 89, 3 (1994), pp. 328-33.

778. Kelso, William M. "Landscape History by Historical Archaeology: Testimony of Thomas Jefferson's Gardens, Grounds, and Slave House at Monticello and Poplar Forest" (Unpublished paper, Annual Meeting of the Society for Historical Archaeology, Kingston, Jamaica, January 1992).

779. Khalifah, H. Khalif, ed. *The Campaign of Nat Turner: The Complete Text of the Confessions of the Leader of the Most Successful Slave Revolt in United States History*. Newport News VA: U.B. and U.S. Communications Systems, 1993.

780. Kimball, Gregg D. "'The South as It Was': Social Order, Slavery, and Illustrators in Virginia, 1830-1877," in Judy L. Larson, with Cynthia Payne, eds., *Graphic Arts and the South: Proceedings of the 1990 North American Print Conference* (Fayetteville: University of Arkansas Press, 1993), pp. 129-57.

781. Klein, Mary O. "'We Shall be Accountable to God': Some Inquiries into the Position of Blacks in Somerset Parish, Maryland, 1692-1865," *Maryland Historical Magazine*, 87, 4 (1992), pp. 399-406.

782. Kulikoff, Allan. "The Life Cycle of Slaves".

Reprinted (from *Tobacco and Slaves*) in Goodheart, Brown, and Rabe, eds., *Slavery in American Society*, pp. 153-60.

783. Kulikoff, Allan. "The Origins of Afro-American Society in Tidewater Maryland and Virginia, 1700 to 1790".

Reprinted in Stanley N. Katz, John M. Murrin, and Douglas Greenberg, eds., *Colonial America: Essays in Politics and Social Development* (4th ed.) (New York: McGraw-Hill, 1993), pp. 452-85.

784. Latimer, Francis B. *Instruments of Freedom: Deeds and Wills of Emancipation, Northampton County, Virginia, 1782-1864*. Bowie MD: Heritage Books, 1993.

785. Ley, Jennifer Page. "The Slave's Story: Interpreting Nineteenth-Century Slave History at Shirley Plantation" (PhD diss., The University of Delaware, 1995).

786. Lichtenstein, Alex. "Coercion Had Its Limits (review essay: Dew, *Bond of Iron*)," *Reviews in American History*, 23, 1 (1995), pp. 20-25.

787. McElvey, Kay Najiyyah. "Early Black Dorchester, 1776-1870: A History of the Struggle of African-Americans in Dorchester County, Maryland, To Be Free to Make Their Own Choices" (PhD diss., University of Maryland, 1991).

788. McKee, Larry. "The Ideals and Realities Behind the Design and Use of 19th Century Virginia Slave Cabins," in Anne Elizabeth Yentsch and Mary C. Beaudry, eds., *The Art and Mystery of Historical Archaeology: Essays in Honor of James Deetz* (Boca Raton: CRC Press, 1992), pp. 195-213.

789. Medford, Edna [Greene]. "Beyond Mount Vernon: Exploring the History of George Washington's Former Slaves and Their Descendants" (Unpublished paper, conference on "Slavery in the Age of Washington", Mount Vernon VA, 3-4 Nov. 1994).

790. Medford, Edna Greene. "'I Was Always a Union Man': The Dilemma of Free Blacks in Confederate Virginia," *Slavery and Abolition*, 15, 3 (1994), pp. 1-16.

791. Menard, Russell R. "From Servant to Freeholder: Status Mobility and Property Accumulation in Seventeenth-Century Maryland".

> Reprinted in Stanley N. Katz, John M. Murrin, and Douglas Greenberg, eds., *Colonial America: Essays in Politics and Social Development* (4th ed.) (New York: McGraw-Hill, 1993), pp. 41-66.

792. Michel, Gregg L. "From Slavery to Freedom: Hickory Hill, 1850-80," in Edward L. Ayers and John C. Willis, eds., *The Edge of the South: Life in Nineteenth-Century Virginia* (Charlottesville: University Press of Virginia, 1991), pp. 109-33.

793. Miles, Mary Jo. "Slave Life at Shadwell, 1741-1799" (MA thesis, Oakland University, 1992).

794. Morgan, Edmund. "The Labor Problem at Jamestown".

> Reprinted in Karras and McNeill, eds., *Atlantic American Societies*, pp. 73-95.

795. Morgan, Lynda J. *Emancipation in Virginia's Tobacco Belt, 1850-1870*. Athens: University of Georgia Press, 1992.

796. Morgan, Philip. "Slave Flight: Mount Vernon, Virginia and the Wider Atlantic World" (Unpublished paper, conference on "Slavery in the Age of Washington", Mount Vernon VA, 3-4 Nov. 1994).

797. Mouer, L. Daniel. "Chesapeake Creole: A Critical Approach to Colonial Folk Culture" (Unpublished paper, Annual Meeting of the Society for Historical Archaeology, Kingston, Jamaica, January 1992).

798. Neville, Barry, and Edward Jones. "Slavery in Worcester County, Maryland, 1688-1766," *Maryland Historical Magazine*, 89, 3 (1994), pp. 319-27.

799. Newby, Cassandra Lynn. "'The World Was All Before Them': A Study of the Black Community in Norfolk, Virginia, 1861-1864" (PhD diss., College of William and Mary, 1992).

800. Papenfuse, Eric Robert. "From Recompense to Revolution: *Mahoney v Ashton* and the Transfiguration of Maryland Culture, 1791-1802," *Slavery and Abolition*, 15, 3 (1994), pp. 38-62.

801. Parramore, Thomas C. "Aborted Takeoff: A Critique of 'Fly Across the River'," *North Carolina Historical Review*, 68, 2 (1991), pp. 111-21.

802. Pearce, Laurie E. "The Cowrie Shell in Virginia: A Critical Evaluation of Potential Archaeological Significance" (MA thesis, College of William and Mary, 1992).

803. Phillips, Christopher [William]. "'Negroes and Other Slaves': The African-American Community of Baltimore, 1790-1860" (PhD diss., University of Georgia, 1992).

804. Phillips, Christopher. "The Roots of Quasi-Freedom: Manumission and Term Slavery in Early

National Baltimore," *Southern Studies*, 4, 1 (1993), pp. 39-66.

805. Pogue, Dennis J. "The Archaeology of Plantation Life: Another Perspective on George Washington's Mount Vernon," *Virginia Cavalcade*, 41 (1991), pp. 74-83.

806. Pogue, Dennis [J]. "Slave Lifeways at Mount Vernon: An Archaeological Perspective" (Unpublished paper, conference on "Slavery in the Age of Washington", Mount Vernon VA, 3-4 Nov. 1994).

807. Richardson, Julia H. "Restoration of the Plains Plantation Family and Slave Cemeteries," *Chronicles of St. Mary's*, 40, 2 (1992), pp. 129-33.

808. Ryder, Robin. "The Social Context of Post-Colonial 'Colono-Ware' in Virginia" (Unpublished paper, Annual Meeting of the Society for Historical Archaeology, Kingston, Jamaica, January 1992).

809. Sanford, Douglas Walker. "The Archaeology of Plantation Slavery at Thomas Jefferson's Monticello: Context and Process in an American Slave Society" (PhD diss., University of Virginia, 1995).

810. *Saxton, Martha. "Black Women's Moral Values in the Eighteenth Century Tidewater" (Unpublished paper, Berkshire Conference on Women's History, New Brunswick NJ, 1990).

811. Schechter, Patricia A. "Free and Slave Labor in the Old South: The Tredegar Ironworkers' Strike of 1847," *Labor History*, 35, 2 (1994), pp. 165-86.

812. Schnittman, Suzanne. "The Dismal Swamp Slaves: Marronage, Slave-hiring, and the Making of a Black Working Class" (Unpublished paper, American Historical Association, San Francisco, 6-9 Jan. 1994).

813. Schwarz, Philip J. "The Developing Law of Slavery in Virginia" (Unpublished paper, conference on "Slavery in the Age of Washington", Mount Vernon VA, 3-4 Nov. 1994).

814. Schwarz, Philip J. "Escape from Slavery: The Newby Family of Virginia and Ohio" (Unpublished paper, American Historical Association, Washington DC, 27-30 Dec. 1992).

815. Schwarz, Philip J. *Slave Laws in Virginia*. Athens: University of Georgia Press, 1996.

816. Short, Wallace Verando. "Benevolent Apartheid: The Decline of Slavery in the District of Columbia, 1800-1850" (MA thesis, University of Virginia, 1995).

817. Sidbury, James. "Gabriel's World: Race Relations in Richmond, Virginia, 1750-1810" (PhD diss., Johns Hopkins University, 1991).

818. Simmons, J. Susanne. "They Too Were Here: African-Americans in Augusta County and Staunton, Virginia" (MA thesis, James Madison University, 1994).

819. Singleton, Theresa A. Review of *Carter's Grove: The Winthrop Rockefeller Archaeology Museum, Wolstenholme Towne, the Slave Quarter, and the Mansion* (long-term exhibition at Colonial Williamsburg), *American Anthropologist*, 95, 2 (1993), pp. 525-28.

820. "Slavery in the Age of Washington" (Conference, Mount Vernon VA, 3-4 November 1994).

Participants: Ira Berlin, Christy Coleman, Rex Ellis, Eric Gable, James Horton, Edna Medford, Philip Morgan, Dennis Pogue, Philip J. Schwarz, Mary Thompson, Dorothy Twohig, and Lorena Walsh.

821. Sorrells, Nancy Lynn Taylor. "'I Mourn in Bitterness over the State of Things': Francis McFarland's Community at War, 1860-1866" (MA thesis, James Madison University, 1995).

822. Spangler, Jewel L. "Presbyterians, Baptists, and the Making of a Slave Society in Virginia, 1740-1820" (PhD diss., University of California - San Diego, 1996).

823. Stanton, Lucia C. "Slavery at Monticello".

Republished as *Slavery at Monticello* ([Charlottesville Va.]: Thomas Jefferson Memorial Foundation, 1996).

824. Stanton, Lucia C. "'Those Who Labor for My Happiness': Thomas Jefferson and His Slaves," in Peter S. Onuf, ed., *Jeffersonian Legacies* (Charlottesville: University Press of Virginia, 1993), pp. 147-80.

825. Stevenson, Brenda E. "Black Family Structure in Colonial and Antebellum Virginia: Amending the Revisionist Perspective," in M. Belinda Tucker and Claudia Mitchell-Kernan, eds., *The Decline in*

Marriage Among African-Americans: Causes, Consequences, and Policy Implications (New York: Russell Sage Foundation, 1995), pp. 27-56.

826. Stevenson, Brenda E. "Distress and Discord in Virginia Slave Families, 1830-1860," in Carol Bleser, ed., *In Joy and in Sorrow: Women, Family, and Marriage in the Victorian South, 1830-1900* (New York: Oxford University Press, 1991), pp. 103-24.

827. Stevenson, Brenda E. "Gender Convention, Ideals, and Identity among Antebellum Virginia Slave Women," in Gaspar and Hine, eds., *More than Chattel*, pp. 169-90.

828. Stevenson, Brenda E. *Life in Black and White: Family and Community in the Slave South*. New York: Oxford University Press, 1996.

829. Strutt, Michael A. "Changes of Space in Time: Interpreting the Role of Slavery and Space Use at Thomas Jefferson's Poplar Forest" (Unpublished paper, Annual Meeting of the Society for Historical Archaeology, Kingston, Jamaica, January 1992).

830. Sydnor, Charles W., Martin Doblmeier, and Timothy A. Finkbinder. "Thomas Jefferson, A View from the Mountain" (Richmond VA: Central and Northern Virginia Public Television, 1995).

1 videocassette (114 min.)

Pt. 1. "A view from the mountain"; Pt. 2. "Slave Revolt; the Jefferson P; the Sally Hemings Scandal".

831. Takagi, Midori. "Slavery in Richmond, Virginia, 1782-1865" (PhD diss., Columbia University, 1994).

832. Thompson, Mary. "'They Appear to Live Comfortable Together': The Private Lives of the Mount Vernon Slaves" (Unpublished paper, conference on "Slavery in the Age of Washington", Mount Vernon VA, 3-4 Nov. 1994).

833. Tomlins, Christopher L. "In Nat Turner's Shadow: Reflections on the Norfolk Dry Dock Affair of 1830-1831," *Labor History*, 33, 4 (1992), pp. 494-518.

834. Towers, Frank. "Serena Johnson and Slave Domestic Servants in Antebellum Baltimore," *Maryland Historical Magazine*, 89, 3 (1994), pp. 334-37.

835. Tragle, Henry Irving. *Nat Turner's Slave Revolt - 1831*. Amawalk NY: Golden Owl Publishing Co., 1995.

836. Trotti, Michael. "Freedmen and Enslaved Soil: A Case Study of Manumission, Migration, and Land," *Virginia Magazine of History and Biography*, 104, 4 (1996), pp. 455-80.

837. Turtle, Gordon Bruce. "Slave Manumission in Virginia, 1782-1806: The Jeffersonian Dilemma in the Age of Liberty" (PhD diss., University of Alberta, 1991).

838. Twohig, Dorothy. "This Species of Property: Washington and Public Policy on Slavery" (Unpublished paper, conference on "Slavery in the Age of Washington", Mount Vernon VA, 3-4 Nov. 1994).

839. Vaughan, Alden T. *Roots of American Racism: Essays on the Colonial Experience*. New York: Oxford University Press, 1995.

Includes "Slaveholders' 'Hellish Principles': A Seventeenth-Century Critique"; "Blacks in Virginia: Evidence from the First Decade"; "The Origins Debate: Slavery and Racism in Seventeenth-Century Virginia".

840. "[A Forum]: The Virginia-North Carolina Slave Conspiracy of 1802," *North Carolina Historical Review*, 68, 2 (1991).

For contents see Edgerton and Parramore.

841. Vlach, John Michael. "Afro-American Domestic Artifacts in Eighteenth-Century Virginia," in M. G. Quimby and Scott T. Swank, eds., *Perspectives on American Folk Art* (New York: Norton, 1980), pp. 177-217.

Reprinted in idem, *By the Work of Their Hands: Studies in Afro-American Folklife* (Charlottesville: University Press of Virginia. 1991), pp. 53-71.

842. Vlach, John Michael. "Afro-American Housing in Virginia's Landscape of Slavery," in idem, *By the Work of Their Hands: Studies in Afro-American Folklife* (Charlottesville: University Press of Virginia. 1991), pp. 215-29.

843. Wallenstein, Peter. "Flawed Keepers of the Flame: The Interpreters of George Mason," *Virginia Magazine of History and Biography*, 102, 2 (1994), pp. 229-60.

844. Walsh, Lorena S. "'A Place in Time' Regained: A Fuller History of Colonial Chesapeake Slavery through Group Biography," in Hudson, Jr., ed., *Working Toward Freedom*, pp. 1-32.

845. Walsh, Lorena S. "Slave Life, Slave Society, and Tobacco Production in the Tidewater Chesapeake, 1620-1820," in Berlin and Morgan, eds., *Cultivation and Culture*, pp. 170-99.

846. Walsh, Lorena S. "Slavery and Architecture at Mount Vernon" (Unpublished paper, conference on "Slavery in the Age of Washington", Mount Vernon VA, 3-4 Nov. 1994).

847. Walsh, Lorena S. "Work and Resistance in the New Republic: The Case of the Chesapeake 1770-1820," in Turner, ed., *From Chattel Slaves to Wage Slaves*, pp. 97-122.

848. Weis, Tracey M. "Negotiating Freedom: Domestic Service and the Landscape of Labor and Household Relations in Richmond, Virginia, 1850-1880" (PhD diss., Rutgers, The State University of New Jersey - New Brunswick, 1994).

849. White, Esther C. "'To Indulge Themselves in all the Luxuries as Well as Necessaries of Life': Comparison of Slave Quarter and Kitchen Midden Assemblages from George Washington's Mount Vernon" (Unpublished paper, Annual Meeting of the Society for Historical Archaeology, Kingston, Jamaica, January 1992).

850. Whitman, Stephen. "Diverse Good Causes: Manumission and the Transformation of Urban Slavery," *Social Science History*, 19, 3 (1995), pp. 333-70.

851. Whitman, T[orrey] Stephen. "Industrial Slavery at the Margin: The Maryland Chemical Works," *Journal of Southern History*, 59, 1 (1993), pp. 31-62.

852. Whitman, T[orrey] Stephen. "Slavery, Manumission, and Free Black Workers in Early National Baltimore" (PhD diss., Johns Hopkins University, 1993).

853. Whitman, T[orrey] Stephen. "Slavery Reconfigured: Manumission and Self-Purchase in the Crafts and Industry in Baltimore" (Unpublished paper, American Historical Association, San Francisco, 6-9 Jan. 1994).

854. Whitman, T[orrey] Stephen. "Transformations in Slavery: The Role of Manumission in Early National Maryland" (Unpublished paper, Southern Historical Association, Louisville KY, 9-12 Nov. 1994).

855. Whitworth, William Maphis, Jr. "Cumberland County, Virginia, in the Late Antebellum Period, 1840-1860" (MA thesis, University of Richmond, 1992).

856. Willis, Anne R. "The Masters' Mercy: Slave Prosecutions and Punishments in York County, Virginia 1700 to 1780" (MA thesis, College of William and Mary, 1995).

857. Willis, John C. "From the Dictates of Pride to the Paths of Righteousness: Slave Honor and Christianity in Antebellum Virginia," in Edward L. Ayers and John C. Willis, eds., *The Edge of the South: Life in Nineteenth-Century Virginia* (Charlottesville: University Press of Virginia, 1991), pp. 37-55.

858. Windham, Joseph E. "Bondage, Bias and the Bench: An Historical Analysis of Maryland Court of Appeals Cases Involving Blacks, 1830-1860" (PhD diss., Howard University, 1990).

859. Yentsch, Anne Elizabeth. *A Chesapeake Family and their Slaves: A Study in Historical Archaeology*. New York: Cambridge University Press, 1994.

860. Yentsch, Anne. "A Note on a 19th Century Description of Below-Ground 'Storage Cellars' Among the Ibo," *African American Archaeology*, 4 (1991), p. 3-4.

See also Douglas Sanford, "A Response to Anne Yentsch's Research Note," *African American Archaeology*, 5 (1991), p. 4-5, and Dan Mouer, "'Root Cellars' Revisited," *African American Archaeology*, 5 (1991), p. 5-6.

Also Douglas B. Chambers, "Afro-Virginian Root Cellars and African Roots?" *African American Archaeology*, 6 (1992), p. 7-10.

4. Colonial South

861. Anzilotti, Cara. "'In the Affairs of the World': Women and Plantation Ownership in the Eighteenth Century South Carolina Lowcountry" (PhD diss., University of California - Santa Barbara, 1994).

862. Baine, Rodney M. "Indian Slaves in Colonial Georgia," *Georgia Historical Quarterly*, 79, 2 (1995), pp. 418-24.

863. Bellamy, Donnie D. "The Legal Status of Black Georgians during the Colonial and Revolutionary Eras," *Journal of Negro History*, 74, 1-4 (1989), pp. 1-10.

864. Carney, Judith A. "From Hands to Tutors: African Expertise in the South Carolina Rice Economy," *Agricultural History*, 67, 3 (1993), pp. 1-30.

865. Carney, Judith [A]. "Landscapes of Technology Transfer: Rice Cultivation and African Continuities," *Technology and Culture*, 37, 1 (1996), pp. 5-35.

866. Chaplin, Joyce E. *An Anxious Pursuit: Agricultural Innovation and Modernity in the Lower South, 1730-1815*. Chapel Hill: University of North Carolina Press, 1993.

867. Chaplin, Joyce E. "Tidal Rice Cultivation and the Problem of Slavery in South Carolina and Georgia, 1760-1815," *William and Mary Quarterly*, 49, 1 (1992), pp. 29-61.

868. Feight, Andrew Lee. "Edmund Botsford and Richard Furman: Slavery in the South Carolina Low Country, 1766-1825" *Furman Humanities Review*, 6 (1993), pp. 1-29.

869. Ferguson, Leland G. *Uncommon Ground: Archaeology and Early African America, 1650-1800*. Washington: Smithsonian Institution Press, 1992.

870. Gardner, Jeffrey W. "Chinese Porceline and Colonoware: Evidence of Colonial Planter-Slave Interaction from a South Carolina Low Country Plantation" (Unpublished paper, Annual Meeting of the Society for Historical Archaeology, Kingston, Jamaica, January 1992).

871. Greene, Jack P. "Colonial South Carolina and the Caribbean Connection".

Reprinted in Stanley N. Katz, John M. Murrin, and Douglas Greenberg, eds., *Colonial America: Essays in Politics and Social Development* (4th ed.) (New York: McGraw-Hill, 1993), pp. 179-98.

872. Hawley, Thomas Earl, Jr. "The Slave Tradition of Singing Among the Gullah of Johns Island, South Carolina" (PhD diss., University of Maryland - Baltimore County, 1993).

873. Jackson, Harvey H., III. "Behind the Lines: Savannah During the War of Jenkins' Ear," *Georgia Historical Quarterly*, 78, 3 (1994), pp. 471-92.

874. Jenkins, Robert L. "Africans in Colonial and Territorial Mississippi," in Barbara Carpenter, ed., *Ethnic Heritage in Mississippi* (Jackson: University Press of Mississippi, for the Mississippi Humanities Council, 1992), pp. 126-54.

875. Kay, Marvin L. Michael, and Lorin Lee Cary. *An African Diaspora: Slavery in North Carolina, 1748-1775*. Chapel Hill: University of North Carolina Press, 1995.

876. Little, Thomas J. "The South Carolina Slave Laws Reconsidered, 1670-1700," *South Carolina Historical Magazine*, 94, 2 (1993), pp. 86-101.

877. Littlefield, Daniel C. "'Abundance of Negroes of that Nation': The Significance of African Ethnicity in Colonial South Carolina," in David R. Chesnutt and Clyde N. Wilson, eds., *The Meaning of South Carolina History: Essays in Honor of George C. Rogers, Jr.* (Columbia: University of South Carolina Press, 1991), pp. 19-38.

878. Littlefield, Daniel C. *Rice and the Making of South Carolina: An Introductory Essay*. Columbia: South Carolina Department of Archives and History, Public Programs Division, 1995.

879. Menard, Russell R. "Slave Demography in the Lowcountry, 1670-1740: From Frontier Society to Plantation Regime," *South Carolina Historical Magazine*, 96, 4 (1995), pp. 280-303.

880. Morgan, Philip D. "Work and Culture: The Task System and the World of Lowcountry Blacks, 1700 to 1880".

Reprinted in Stanley N. Katz, John M. Murrin, and Douglas Greenberg, eds., *Colonial America: Essays in Politics and Social Development* (4th ed.) (New York: McGraw-Hill, 1993), pp. 486-523.

881. Olwell, Robert. "Becoming Free: Manumission and the Genesis of a Free Black Community in South Carolina, 1740-90," in Landers, ed., "Against the Odds", pp. 1-19.

882. Olwell, Robert. "'Loose, Idle and Disorderly': Slave Women in the Eighteenth-Century Charleston Marketplace," in Gaspar and Hine, eds., *More than Chattel*, pp. 97-110.

883. Olwell, Robert. "'A Reckoning of Accounts': Patriarchy, Market Relations, and Control on Henry Laurens's Lowcountry Plantations, 1762-1785," in Hudson, Jr., ed., *Working Toward Freedom*, pp. 33-52.

884. Pearson, Edward A. "'A Countryside Full of Flames': A Reconsideration of the Stono Rebellion and Slave Rebelliousness in the Early Eighteenth-Century South Carolina Low Country," *Slavery and Abolition*, 17, 2 (1996), pp. 22-50.

885. Pearson, Edward A[nthony]. "From Stono to Vesey: Slavery, Resistance, and Ideology in South Carolina, 1739-1822" (PhD diss., University of Wisconsin - Madison, 1992).

886. Pollitzer, William S. "The Relationship of the Gullah-Speaking People of Coastal South Carolina and Georgia to Their African Ancestors," *Historical Methods: A Journal of Quantitative and Interdisciplinary History*, 26, 2 (1993), pp. 53-67.

887. Simpson, Tiwanna Michelle. "The Development of African Slavery in Eighteenth Century Georgia" (MA thesis, Ohio State University, 1996).

888. Wood, Betty C. "'Never on Sunday?': Slavery and the Sabbath in Lowcountry Georgia 1750-1830," in Turner, ed., *From Chattel Slaves to Wage Slaves*, pp. 79-96.

889. Wood, Peter. "Slave Resistance in Colonial South Carolina".

> **Reprinted (from *Black Majority*) in Karras and McNeill, eds., *Atlantic American Societies*, pp. 144-73.**

5. Ante-Bellum South

890. Abrahams, Roger D. *Singing the Master: The Emergence of African American Culture in the Plantation South*. New York: Pantheon, 1992.

891. Adams, Natalie P. "Struggle in the Quarters: The Design, Construction, and Use of Slave Housing in the South Carolina Low Country" (Unpublished paper, Annual Meeting of the Society for Historical Archaeology, Kingston, Jamaica, January 1992).

892. Adams, Russell L. "Surviving Slavery Intact: The Role of Leisure in Antebellum Black America" (Unpublished paper, American Historical Association, Chicago, 5-8 Jan. 1995).

893. Affleck, Rick. "Settlement Pattern Change at Middleburg Plantation, Berkeley County, South Carolina" (Unpublished paper, Annual Meeting of the Society for Historical Archaeology, Kingston, Jamaica, January 1992).

894. Alexander, Adele Logan. *Ambiguous Lives: Free Women of Color in Rural Georgia, 1789-1879*. Fayetteville: University of Arkansas Press, 1991.

895. Alexander, Adele Logan, and Virginia Gould. "Free Black Women in the Antebellum South," in Hine, Brown, and Terborg-Penn, eds., *Black Women in America*, pp. 456-62.

896. Allen, William F., Charles P. Ware, and Lucy M. Garrison, eds. *Slave Songs of the United States*. NewYork: Dover Publications. 1995.

897. Ammons, Elizabeth, ed. (Harriet Beecher Stowe) *Uncle Tom's Cabin: Authoritative Text, Backgrounds and Contexts, Criticism*. New York: Norton, 1994.

898. Annequin, Jacques. "Des hommes libres dans une société esclavagiste (review essay: Cordillot, *Des hommes libres dans une société esclavagiste*)," *Dialogues d'histoire ancienne*, 17, 1 (1991), pp. 466-70.

899. Anz-Meador, Diana. "Locating Sub-surface Foundations Using Ground Penetrating Radar" (Unpublished paper, Annual Meeting of the Society for Historical Archaeology, Kingston, Jamaica, January 1992).

900. Ashworth, John. *Slavery, Capitalism, and Politics in the Antebellum Republic: Volume 1 - Commerce and Compromise, 1820-1850*. New York: Cambridge University Press, 1995.

901. Atkins, Leah Rawls. "High Cotton: The Antebellum Alabama Plantation Mistress and the Cotton Culture," in Whitten, ed., "Eli Whitney's Cotton Gin," pp. 92-104.

902. Bailey, Ben E. "Music in Slave Era Mississippi," *Journal of Mississippi History*, 54, 1 (1992), pp. 29-58.

903. Bailey, Ronald. "The Other Side of Slavery: Black Labor, Cotton, and the Textile Industrialization of Great Britain and the United States," in Whitten, ed., "Eli Whitney's Cotton Gin," pp. 35-50.

904. Bakker, Jan. "Caroline Gilman and the Issue of Slavery in the Rose Magazines, 1832-1839".

Reprinted in *Southern Studies*, n.s. 2, 3-4 (1991), pp. 203-29.

905. Bardaglio, Peter W. "Rape and the Law in the Old South: 'Calculated to Excite Indignation in Every Heart'," *Journal of Southern History*, 60, 4 (1994), pp. 749-72.

906. Barksdale, Richard K. "History, Slavery, and Thematic Irony in *Huckleberry Finn*," in James D. Leonard, Thomas T. Tenney, and Thadious M. Davis, eds., *Satire or Evasion? Black Perspectives on Huckleberry Finn* (Durham: Duke University Press, 1992), pp. 49-61.

907. Bates, Beverly B. "Slavery Decisions of Judge William H. Crawford," *Georgia Journal of Southern Legal History*, 1, 2 (1991), pp. 461-78.

908. Baumgarten, Linda. "Plains, Plaid and Cotton: Woolens for Slave Clothing," *Ars Textrina*, 15 (1991), pp. 203-21.

909. Beoko-Betts, Josephine A. "'She Make Funny Flat Cake She Call Saraka': Gullah Women and Food Practices under Slavery," in Hudson, Jr., ed., *Working Toward Freedom*, pp. 211-31.

910. Berlin, Ira, Barbara J. Fields, Steven F. Miller, Joseph P. Reidy, and Leslie S. Rowland. *Slaves No More: Three Essays on Emancipation and the Civil War*. Cambridge: Cambridge University Press, 1993.

911. Berwanger, Eugene H. "The Case of Stirrup and Edwards, 1861-1870: The Kidnapping and Georgia Enslavement of West Indian Blacks," *Georgia Historical Quarterly*, 76, 1 (1992), pp. 1-18.

912. Berwanger, Eugene H., ed. *The Civil War Era: Historical Viewpoints*. Fort Worth: Harcourt Brace College Publishers, 1994.

For contents see Foner, Oates, and Sellers.

913. Beverly, John M. "Culture and Social Change: The Values and Behaviors of African-American People in the South Carolina Low-Country and Georgia Coastal Region in the Antebellum and Postbellum Periods" (PhD diss., University of California - Berkeley, 1991).

914. "Beyond Brer Tales and Other Stories: New(anced) Approaches to Slave Minds and Slave Studies" (panel, Southern Historical Association, Louisville KY, 9-12 Nov. 1994).

Mechel Sobel, chair; comments by Charles W. Joyner. For papers see Byrd and Smith.

915. Binder, Guyora. "Did the Slaves Author the Thirteenth Amendment? An Essay in Redemptive History," *Yale Journal of Law & the Humanities*, 5, 2 (1993), pp. 471-505.

916. Bland, Sterling Lecater, Jr. "Speaking for Themselves: The Antebellum Slave Narrative and its Traditions (African-Americans)" (PhD diss. New York University, 1996).

917. Blatt, Jacqueline. "When the Children Cried: Memories of Family Life During Slavery" (Senior honors thesis, Brandeis University, 1995).

918. Bleser, Carol [K]. *Secret and Sacred: The Diaries of James Henry Hammond, a Southern Slaveholder*. New York: Oxford University Press, 1988.

919. Bleser, Carol K. "Southern Planter Wives and Slavery," in David R. Chesnutt and Clyde N. Wilson, eds., *The Meaning of South Carolina History: Essays in Honor of George C. Rogers, Jr.* (Columbia: University of South Carolina Press, 1991), pp. 104-20.

920. Brasfield, Curtis. "'To My Daughter and the Heirs of Her Body': Slave Passages as Illustrated by the Latham-Smithwick Family," *National Genealogical Society Quarterly*, 81, 4 (1993), pp. 270-82.

921. Brown, David. "Slavery and the Market Revolution: The South's Place in Jacksonian Historiography," *Southern Studies*, 4, 2 (1993), pp. 189-207.

922. Buckmaster, Henrietta. *Let My People Go: The Story of the Underground Railroad and the Growth* *of the Abolition Movement*. Columbia: University of South Carolina Press, in cooperation with the Institute for Southern Studies and the South Caroliniana Society of the University of South Carolina, 1992.

923. Burnham, Philip. "Selling Poor Steven: The Struggles and Torments of a Forgotten Class in Antebellum America: Black Slaveowners," *American Heritage*, 44, 2 (1993), pp. 90-97.

924. Burton, Orville Vernon. "Society," in *Encyclopedia of the Confederacy*, vol. 4, pp. 1483-93.

925. Burton, Orville Vernon, and Patricia Dora Bonnin. "Cotton," in *Encyclopedia of the Confederacy*, vol. 1, pp. 416-20.

926. Burton, Orville Vernon, and Henry Kamerling. "Tobacco," in *Encyclopedia of the Confederacy*, vol. 4, pp. 1597-99.

927. Byrd, Alexander X. "Gifts to Do Unnatural Things: Africa and Africans in the Oral Tradition and Personal Remembrances of Former Slaves" (Unpublished paper, Southern Historical Association, Louisville KY, 9-12 Nov. 1994).

928. Byrne, William A. "Slave Crime in Savannah, Georgia," *Journal of Negro History*, 79, 4 (1994), pp. 352-62.

929. Campbell, Jr., Edward D. C., with Kym S. Rice, eds. *Before Freedom Came: African-American Life in the Antebellum South*. Charlottesville: Museum of the Confederacy, Richmond, and University Press of Virginia, 1991.

For contents see Faust, Goldfield, Joyner, Singleton, Vlach, and White.

930. Campbell, John. "'A Kind of Freeman'? Slaves' Market Related Activities in the South Carolina Up Country, 1800-1860," in Berlin and Morgan, eds., *Cultivation and Culture*, pp. 243-74.

931. Campbell, John. "'My Constant Companion': Slaves and their Dogs in the Antebellum South," in Hudson, Jr., ed., *Working Toward Freedom*, pp. 53-76.

932. Cardell, N. Scott, and Mark M. Hopkins. "The Effect of Milk Intolerance on the Consumption of Milk by Slaves in 1860," in Fogel, Galantine, and Manning, eds., *Evidence and Methods (Without Consent or Contract)*, pp. 306-10.

933. Castronovo, Russ. *Fathering the Nation: American Genealogies of Slavery and Freedom*. Berkeley: University of California Press, 1995.

934. Cecelski, David S. "The Shores of Freedom: The Maritime Underground Railroad in North Carolina, 1800-1861," *North Carolina Historical Review*, 71, 2 (1994), pp. 174-206.

935. Chapoton, Beth Lynne. "Biracial Female Relationships: A Key to Understanding Historical and Contemporary Fictional Women's Slave Narratives" (MA thesis, University of North Carolina - Chapel Hill, 1992).

936. Chesebrough, David B. *Clergy Dissent in the Old South, 1830-1865*. Carbondale IL: Southern Illinois University Press, 1996.

937. Clark, Elizabeth B. "Matrimonial Bonds: Slavery and Divorce in Nineteenth-Century America," *Law and History Review*, 8, 1 (1990), pp. 25-54.

938. Clarke, Elizabeth D. "Go Down Moses: James Island African Americans, 1830-1876" (MA thesis, University of Charleston and The Citadel, 1995).

939. Clinton, Catherine. "Mammy," in Hine, Brown, and Terborg-Penn, eds., *Black Women in America*, pp. 744-47.

940. Clinton, Catherine. "Plantation," in *Encyclopedia of the Confederacy*, vol. 3, pp. 1214-18.

941. Clinton, Catherine. "Plantation Mistress," in *Encyclopedia of the Confederacy*, vol. 3, pp. 1218-19.

942. Clinton, Catherine. "'Southern Dishonor': Flesh, Blood, Race, and Bondage," in Carol Bleser, ed., *In Joy and in Sorrow: Women, Family, and Marriage in the Victorian South, 1830-1900* (New York: Oxford University Press, 1991), pp. 52-68.

943. Clinton, Catherine. *Tara Revisited: Women, War, and the Plantation Legend*. New York: Abbeville Press, 1995.

944. Clinton, Catherine, ed. *Half Sisters of History: Southern Women and the American Past.* Durham NC: Duke University Press, 1994.

For contents see Jones, Painter, and White.

945. Close, Stacey Kevin. "Elderly Slaves of the Plantation South: Somewhere between Heaven and Earth" (PhD diss. Ohio State University, 1992).

946. Coclanis, Peter. "Slavery, African-American Agency, and the World We Have Lost (review essay: Wood, *Women's Work, Men's Work*)," *Georgia Historical Quarterly*, 79, 4 (1995), pp. 873-84.

947. Cody, Cheryll Ann. "Cycles of Work and Childbearing: Seasonality in Women's Lives on Low Country Plantations," in Gaspar and Hine, eds., *More than Chattel*, pp. 61-78.

948. Cody, Cheryll Ann. "Sale and Separation: Four Crises for Enslaved Women on the Ball Plantations, 1764-1854," in Hudson, Jr., ed., *Working Toward Freedom*, pp. 119-42.

949. Cole, Stephanie. "Servants and Slaves: Domestic Service in the Border Cities, 1800-1850" (PhD diss., University of Florida, 1994).

950. Connor, Kimberly Rae. "To Disembark: The Slave Narrative Tradition," *African American Review*, 30, 1 (1996), pp. 35-57.

951. Conway, Claire, and John Hope Franklin. "Race and the Constitution in the Nineteenth Century," *Update On Law-Related Education*, 12, 3 (Symposium: Afro-Americans and the Evolution of a Living Constitution) (1988), pp. 8(6).

952. Cottrol, Robert J. "Commentary: Perspectives on Fugitive Slaves from Legal and Social History (response to articles by Finkelman and Horton)," *Rutgers Law Journal*, 24, 3 (1993), 695-98. (Race Relations and the United States Constitution: From Fugitive Slaves to Affirmative Action)

953. Covey, Herbert C., and Paul T. Lockman, Jr. "Narrative References to Older African Americans Living under Slavery," *Social Science Journal*, 33, 1 (1996), pp. 23-37.

954. Crawford, Stephen C. "A Note on the Relationship between Plantation Size and Diet Adequacy," in Fogel, Galantine, and Manning, eds., *Evidence and Methods* (*Without Consent or Contract*), pp. 304-06.

955. Crawford, Stephen C. "Problems in the Quantitative Analysis of the Data Contained in WPA and Fisk University Narratives of Ex-Slaves," in Fogel, Galantine, and Manning, eds., *Evidence and Methods* (*Without Consent or Contract*), pp. 331-71.

956. Crawford, Stephen C. "Punishments and Rewards," in Fogel and Engerman, eds., *Conditions of Life and the Transition to Freedom: Technical Papers*, vol. 2 (*Without Consent or Contract*), pp. 536-50.

957. Crawford, Stephen [C]. "The Slave Family: A View from the Slave Narratives," in Claudia Goldin and Hugh Rockoff, eds., *Strategic Factors in Nineteenth Century American Economic History* (Chicago: University of Chicago Press, 1993), pp. 331-50.

958. Crofts, Daniel W. "From Slavery to Sharecropping (review essay, including: Saville, *Work of Reconstruction*)," *Reviews in American History*, 23, 2 (1995), pp. 456-63.

959. Crow, Jeffrey J., Paul D. Escott, and Flora J. Hatley. *A History of African Americans in North Carolina.* Raleigh: North Carolina Division of Archives and History, 1992.

960. Crowther, Edward R. "Mississippi Baptists, Slavery, and Secession, 1806-1861," *Journal of Mississippi History*, 56, 2 (1994), pp. 129-48.

961. Cumberland, Sharon. "The Two-Ply Yarn: Slave Narratives and Slave Owner Narratives in the Antebellum South" (PhD diss., City University of New York, 1994).

962. Currier, James T. "From Slavery to Freedom in Mississippi's Legal System," *Journal of Negro History*, 65, 2 (1980), pp. 112-25.

Reprinted in Finkelman, ed., *Race, Law and American History*, vol. 2 (*Race and Law Before Emancipation*), pp. 56-69.

963. Curtis, Michael Kent. "The 1859 Crisis over Hinton Helper's Book, *The Impending Crisis*: Free Speech, Slavery, and Some Light on the Meaning of the First Section of the Fourteenth Amendment," *Chicago-Kent Law Review*, 68, 3 (Symposium on the Law of Slavery) (1993), pp. 1113-77.

964. D'Elia, Donald J. "Dr. Benjamin Rush and the Negro," in Horowitz, ed., *Race, Class and Gender in Nineteenth-Century Culture*, pp. 67-76.

965. Daniels, David Douglas, III. "The Cultural Renewal of Slave Religion: Charles Price Jones and the Emergence of the Holiness Movement in Mississippi" (PhD diss., Union Theological Seminary, 1992).

966. "Database of African-American Poetry, 1760-1900" (Alexandria VA: Chadwyck-Healy, 1995). (Machine-readable data)

Bell, James Madison. "The Poetry of James Madison Bell" (Taken from "A poem", delivered August 1st, 1862 by J. Madison Bell, at the grand festival to commemorate the emancipation of the slaves in the District of Columbia, and the emancipation of the slaves in the British West Indian Isles [San Francisco: B. F. Sterett, 1862] and *The Poetical Works of James Madison Bell* [Lansing MI: Press of Wynkoop, Hallenbeck, Crawford, c1901])

Fortune, Michael. "New Year's Anthem as Sung in the African Episcopal Church of St. Thomas, Jan. 1, 1808"

Horton, George Moses. "The Poetry of George Moses Horton" (*Taken from Poems by a slave*, 2nd ed. [Philadelphia: s.n., 1837] and *The poetical works of George M. Horton, the colored bard of North-Carolina: to which is prefixed The life of the author / written by himself* [Hillsborough [NC]: D. Heartt, 1845] and *Naked genius by George Moses Horton, the colored bard of North Carolina, author of "The Black poet"* ..., revised and compiled by Will H. S. Banks, Capt. 9th Mich. Cav. [Raleigh: Wm. B. Smith & Co., Southern Field and Fireside Book Publishing House, 1865]).

Prince, Lucy Terry. "Bars fight" (Taken from "Slavery in Old Deerfield," by George Sheldon [*New England Magazine*, 8 (March 1893): pp. 49-60]).

Rogers, Elymas Payson. "The poems of Elymas Payson Rogers" (Taken from *A poem on the fugitive slave law* [Newark: A. Stephen Holbrook, Printer, 1855] and *The repeal of the Missouri Compromise considered* [Newark: A. Stephen Holbrook, Printer, 1856]).

Sidney, Robert Y. "Anthems, Composed by R. Y. Sidney, for the National Jubilee of the Abolition of the Slave Trade, January 1st, 1809"

Simpson, Joshua McCarter. *The poetry of Joshua McCarter Simpson*. (Taken from *The emancipation car: being an original composition of anti-slavery ballads, composed exclusively for the underground railroad* [Zanesville, Ohio: Printed by Sullivan & Brown, 1874]).

Watkins, James Robert. "The Poetry of James Robert Watkins" (Taken from *Poems, original & selected by James Watkins, a fugitive slave* [Manchester: A. Heywood, Printer, 1859?])

Whitman, Albery Allson. *The poetry of Albery Alison Whitman*.

967. David, Paul A., and Peter Temin. "Slavery: The Progressive Institution".

Reprinted in Whaples and Betts, eds., *Historical Perspectives on the American Economy*, pp. 177-225.

968. Davis, Jack E. "Changing Places: Slave Movement in the South," *The Historian*, 55, 4 (1993), pp. 657-76.

969. Davis, Olga Idriss. "It Be's Hard Sometimes: The Rhetorical Invention of Black Female Persona in Pre-emancipatory Slave Narratives" (PhD diss., University of Nebraska at Lincoln, 1994).

970. Dew, Charles B., editorial advisor. *Slavery in Ante-Bellum Southern Industries*. Bethesda MD: University Publications of America, 1995.

(Microform reels: Black studies research resources) (Pt. 1. Mining and smelting industries, 26 reels)

971. Dillard, Philip David. "Arming the Slaves: Transformation of the Public Mind" (MS thesis, University of Georgia, 1994).

972. Dormon, James H., ed. *Creoles of Color of the Gulf South*. Knoxville: University of Tennessee Press, 1996.

For contents see Brasseaux, Gould, Hanger, and Schweninger.

973. Durand, Sally Graham. "The Dress of the Ante-Bellum Field Slave in Louisiana and Mississippi from 1830 to 1860" (MA thesis, Louisiana State University, 1977).

974. Durrill, Wayne K. "Routine of Seasons: Labour Regimes and Social Ritual in an Antebellum Plantation Community," *Slavery and Abolition*, 16, 2 (1995), pp. 161-87.

975. Durrill, Wayne K. "Slavery, Kinship, and Dominance: The Black Community at Somerset Place Plantation [N.C.], 1786-1860," *Slavery and Abolition*, 13, 2 (1992), pp. 1-19.

976. Dusinberre, William. *Them Dark Days: Slavery in the American Rice Swamps*. New York: Oxford University Press, 1995.

977. Edwards, Laura F. "'The Marriage Covenant is the Foundation of All our Rights': The Politics of

Slave Marriages in North Carolina after Emancipation," *Law and History Review*, 14, 1 (1996), pp. 81-124.

978. Egerton, Douglas R. "Markets Without a Market Revolution: Southern Planters and Capitalism," *Journal of the Early Republic*, 16, 2 (1996), pp. 111-36.

979. *Encyclopedia of the Confederacy*. Richard N. Currant, ed. 4 vols. New York: Simon & Schuster, 1993.

For contents see Burton, Burton and Bonnin, Burton and Kamerling, Clinton (2), Engs (3), McKenzie, Miller, Reidy, Roark, Scarborough, Sitterson, Tadman, and Toppin.

980. Engs, Robert Francis. "Antebellum Slavery," in *Encyclopedia of the Confederacy*, vol. 4, pp. 1434-41.

981. Engs, Robert Francis. "Slave Life," in *Encyclopedia of the Confederacy*, vol. 4, pp. 1448-51.

982. Engs, Robert Francis. "Slavery during the Civil War," in *Encyclopedia of the Confederacy*, vol. 4, pp. 1441-48.

983. Fabre, Michel. "Contrabands All: Neither Slaves nor Freemen," in Binder, ed., *Slavery in the Americas*, pp. 241-56.

984. Faust, Drew Gilpin. "Slave Management".

Reprinted (from *James Henry Hammond and the Old South*) in Goodheart, Brown, and Rabe, eds., *Slavery in American Society*, pp. 237-47.

985. Faust, Drew Gilpin. *Southern Stories: Slaveholders in Peace and War*. Columbia: University of Missouri Press, 1992.

986. Faust, Drew Gilpin. "'Trying to Do a Man's Business': Slavery, Violence and Gender in the American Civil War," *Gender and History*, 4, 2 (1992), pp. 197-214.

987. Fede, Andrew. "The American Law of Slavery 1810-1860: Considerations of Humanity and Interest (review essay: Tushnet, *American Law of Slavery*)," *Law and History Review*, 2, 2 (1984), pp. 301-20.

988. Fede, Andrew. "Legitimized Violent Slave Abuse in the American South, 1861-1865: A Case Study of Law and Social Change in Six Southern States," *American Journal of Legal History*, 29, 2 (1985), pp. 93-150.

989. Ferguson, Rebecca Anne. "The Mulatta Text and the Muted Voice in *Louisa Picquet, the Octoroon*: Revising the Genre of the Slave Narrative" (PhD diss., Marquette University, 1995).

990. Field-Hendrey, Elizabeth B. *Were Free Southern Farmers 'Driven to Indolence' by Slavery?: A Stochastic Production Frontier Approach*. Cambridge MA: National Bureau of Economic Research, 1996.

991. Fleischner, Jennifer. *Mastering Slavery: Memory, Family, and Identity in Women's Slave Narratives*. New York: New York University Press, 1996.

992. "Flight to Freedom: The Underground Railroad" (Princeton: Films for the Humanities & Sciences, 1995).

Producers/directors, John Overlan, Ann Spurling; editor, Michael Conolly; music, Kevin Huber. Advisers: Larry Tise (Franklin Foundation), Charles Joyner (Coastal Carolina U.), Larry Gara (Historian), Horace Clarence Boyer (U. of Massachusetts, Amherst), Alvin Parris (Minister), Charles Blockson (Temple U.), Paul Cyr (Historian), Robert Gullo (Librarian), Robert Hayden (Historian).

993. Fogel, Robert W[illiam]. "American Slavery: A Flexible, Highly Developed Form of Capitalism."

Reprinted (from *Without Consent or Contract*) in Harris, ed., *Society and Culture in the Slave South*, pp. 77-99.

994. Fogel, Robert W. "The Body Mass Index of Adult Male Slaves in the U.S. c. 1863 and Its Bearing on Mortality Rates," in Fogel, Galantine, and Manning, eds., *Evidence and Methods* (*Without Consent or Contract*), pp. 311-18.

995. Fogel, Robert W. "The Distribution of U.S. Slaves by Size of Slaveholding in 1850 and 1860," in Fogel, Galantine, and Manning, eds., *Evidence and Methods* (*Without Consent or Contract*), pp. 387-93.

996. Fogel, Robert W. "Estimating the Undercount of Births and Deaths Below Age Three," in Fogel, Galantine, and Manning, eds., *Evidence and Methods* (*Without Consent or Contract*), pp. 286-91.

997. Fogel, Robert W. "The Life Expectation of U.S. Slaves c. 1830," in Fogel, Galantine, and

Manning, eds., *Evidence and Methods* (*Without Consent or Contract*), pp. 285-86.

998. Fogel, Robert W. "A Method of Estimating the Income Distribution of Slaves c. 1860 from the Available Patchy Evidence," in Fogel, Galantine, and Manning, eds., *Evidence and Methods* (*Without Consent or Contract*), pp. 371-79.

999. Fogel, Robert W. "Moral Aspects of the Debate over the 'Extra Income' of Slaves," in Fogel, Galantine, and Manning, eds., *Evidence and Methods* (*Without Consent or Contract*), pp. 593-96.

1000. Fogel, Robert W. "Was the Overwork of Pregnant Slaves Profit Maximizing?," in Fogel, Galantine, and Manning, eds., *Evidence and Methods* (*Without Consent or Contract*), pp. 321-25.

1001. Fogel, Robert W., and Stanley L. Engerman. "The Anatomy of Exploitation".

Reprinted from *Time on the* Cross in Whaples and Betts, eds., *Historical Perspectives on the American Economy*, pp. 141-76.

1002. Fogel, Robert W., and Stanley L. Engerman. "Explaining the Relative Efficiency of Slave Agriculture in the Antebellum South".

Reprinted in Fogel and Engerman, eds., *Markets and Production: Technical Papers*, vol. 1 (*Without Consent or Contract*), pp. 241-65.

Reprinted in Whaples and Betts, eds., *Historical Perspectives on the American Economy*, pp. 226-56.

1003. Fogel, Robert W., and Stanley L. Engerman. "Explaining the Relative Efficiency of Slave Agriculture in the Antebellum South: Reply".

Reprinted with additions in Fogel and Engerman, eds., *Markets and Production: Technical Papers*, vol. 1 (*Without Consent or Contract*), pp. 266-303.

1004. Fogel, Robert W., and Stanley L. Engerman. "The Slave Breeding Thesis," in Fogel and Engerman, eds., *Conditions of Life and the Transition to Freedom: Technical Papers*, vol. 2 (*Without Consent or Contract*), pp. 455-72.

1005. Fogel, Robert W., and Stanley L. Engerman. "The Slave Diet on Large Plantations in 1860," in Fogel, Galantine, and Manning, eds., *Evidence and Methods* (*Without Consent or Contract*), pp. 291-304.

1006. Foner, Eric. "From Slavery to Citizenship: Blacks and the Right to Vote," in Donald Wayne Rogers and Christine Brendel Scriabine, eds., *Voting and the Spirit of American Democracy: Essays on the History of Voting and Voting Rights in America* (Urbana: University of Illinois Press, 1992), pp. 55-65.

1007. Foner, Eric. "Slavery and the Civil War".

Reprinted (from *Politics and Ideology in the Age of the Civil War*) in Goodheart, Brown, and Rabe, eds., *Slavery in American Society*, pp. 259-76.

1008. Foner, Eric. "Slavery and the Republican Ideology".

Reprinted from "Free Soil, Free Labor, Free Men", in Berwanger, ed., *The Civil War Era*, pp. 52-56.

1009. Ford, Lacy K., Jr. "The Conservative Mind of the Old South (review essay: including Genovese, *Slaveholders' Dilemma*)," *Reviews in American History*, 21, 4 (1993), pp. 591-99.

1010. Foreman, P. Gabrielle. "'This Promiscuous Housekeeping': Death, Transgression, and Homoeroticism in *Uncle Tom's Cabin*," *Representations*, no. 43 (1993), pp. 51-72.

1011. Foster, Frances S. *Witnessing Slavery: The Development of Ante-Bellum Slave Narratives*. 2nd ed., rev. Madison: University of Wisconsin Press, 1994. (Reprint, with new introduction, additional material, and supplemental bibliography.)

1012. Fountain, Daniel L. "Historians and Historical Archaeology: Slave Sites," *Journal of Interdisciplinary History*, 26, 1 (1995), pp. 67-77.

1013. Fox-Genovese, Elizabeth. "Contested Meanings: Women and the Problem of Freedom in the Mid-Nineteenth-Century United States," in Olwen Hufton, ed., *Historical Change and Human Rights* (New York: BasicBooks, 1995), pp. 179-215. (The Oxford Amnesty Lectures, 1994).

1014. Fox-Genovese, Elizabeth. "Slave Women".

Reprinted (from *Within the Plantation Household*) in Goodheart, Brown, and Rabe, eds., *Slavery in American Society*, pp. 166-93.

1015. Fox-Genovese, Elizabeth. *To Be Worthy of God's Favor: Southern Women's Defense and Critique of Slavery*. [Gettysburg PA]: Gettysburg

College, 1993. (32nd Annual Robert Fortenbaugh Memorial Lecture)

1016. Fox-Genovese, Elizabeth. "Within the Plantation Household: Women in a Paternalist System."

Reprinted (from *Within the Plantation Household*) in Harris, ed., *Society and Culture in the Slave South*, pp. 48-73.

1017. Fox-Genovese, Elizabeth, and Eugene Genovese. "The Fruits of Merchant Capital: The Slave South as a Paternalist Society".

Reprinted in Harris, ed., *Society and Culture in the Slave South*, pp. 13-47.

1018. Franklin, John Hope. "Slavery and the Martial South."

Reprinted in John Hope Franklin, *Race and History: Selected Essays 1938-1988* (Baton Rouge: Louisiana State University Press, 1989), pp. 92-103.

1019. Freehling, William W. *Slavery, The Civil War, and the Reintegration of American History*. New York: Oxford University Press, 1994.

1020. Frey, Sylvia R. "Shaking the Dry Bones: The Dialectic of Conversion," in Ownby, ed., *Black and White: Cultural Interaction in the Antebellum South*, pp. 23-44.

With commentary by Robert L. Hall, pp. 44-54.

1021. Friedman, Gerald. "The Rise of the New South and the Geographic Regions of Cotton, Rice, and Sugar," in Fogel, Galantine, and Manning, eds., *Evidence and Methods* (*Without Consent or Contract*), pp. 192-94.

1022. Friedman, Gerald. "Sources of Data on Slave Occupations: Their Uses and Limitations," in Fogel, Galantine, and Manning, eds., *Evidence and Methods* (*Without Consent or Contract*), pp. 69-77.

1023. Friedman, Gerald, and Richard L. Manning. "The Rent and Hire of Slaves," in Fogel, Galantine, and Manning, eds., *Evidence and Methods* (*Without Consent or Contract*), pp. 77-78.

1024. Friedman, Gerald, and Richard L. Manning. "Slaves and Free Blacks in Urban Crafts, Rural Crafts, and Managerial Occupations," in Fogel, Galantine, and Manning, eds., *Evidence and Methods* (*Without Consent or Contract*), pp. 78-84.

1025. Friedman, Gerald, Richard L. Manning, and Robert W. Fogel. "Labor Force Participation and Life Cycles in Slave Occupations," in Fogel, Galantine, and Manning, eds., *Evidence and Methods* (*Without Consent or Contract*), pp. 140-50.

1026. Fry, Gladys-Marie. "Harriet Powers: Portrait of a Black Quilter," *SAGE: A Scholarly Journal on Black Women*, 4, 1 (1988), pp. 11-15.

1027. Fry, Gladys-Marie. *Night Riders in Black Folk History*. Knoxville: University of Tennessee Press, 1975.

1028. Fry, Gladys-Marie. "Slave Storytelling Session," in Mildred Bain and Erwin Lewis, eds., *From Freedom to Freedom: African Roots in American Soil* (Milwaukee: Purnell Reference Books, 1977), pp. 245-47.

1029. Fry, Gladys-Marie. *Stitched from the Soul: Slave Quilting in the Ante-Bellum South*. New York: E. P. Dutton, 1990.

1030. Garino, Carla Vittoria. "Motherhood, Domestic Models, and Slavery" (BA honors thesis, Butler University, 1995).

1031. Genovese, Eugene D. "Black Plantation Preachers in the Slave South".

Reprinted in *Southern Studies*, n.s. 2, 3-4 (1991), pp. 203-29.

1032. Genovese, Eugene D. "On Paternalism".

Reprinted (from *Roll, Jordan, Roll*) in Goodheart, Brown, and Rabe, eds., *Slavery in American Society*, pp. 13-17.

1033. Genovese, Eugene D. "'Our Family, White and Black': Family and Household in the Southern Slaveholders' World View," in Carol Bleser, ed., *In Joy and in Sorrow: Women, Family, and Marriage in the Victorian South, 1830-1900* (New York: Oxford University Press, 1991), pp. 69-87.

1034. Genovese, Eugene D. "Slave Revolts".

Reprinted (from *Roll, Jordan, Roll*) in Goodheart, Brown, and Rabe, eds., *Slavery in American Society*, pp. 247-58.

1035. Genovese, Eugene D. *The Slaveholders' Dilemma: Freedom and Progress in Southern Conservative Thought, 1820-1860*. Columbia: University of South Carolina Press, 1992.

1036. Genovese, Eugene D. *"Slavery Ordained of God": The Southern Slaveholder's View of Biblical History and Modern Politics.* [Gettysburg PA]: Gettysburg College, 1985. (24th Annual Robert Fortenbaugh Memorial Lecture)

1037. Genovese, Eugene D. "South Carolina's Contribution to the Doctrine of Slavery in the Abstract," in David R. Chesnutt and Clyde N. Wilson, eds., *The Meaning of South Carolina History: Essays in Honor of George C. Rogers, Jr.* (Columbia: University of South Carolina Press, 1991), pp. 146-60.

1038. Genovese, Eugene D., and Elizabeth Fox-Genovese. "The Fruits of Merchant Capital: The Slave South as a Paternalist Society."

> Reprinted (from *Fruits of Merchant Capital*) in Harris, ed., *Society and Culture in the Slave South*, pp. 13-47.

1039. George, Carol V. R. "Widening the Circle: The Black Church and the Abolitionist Crusade, 1830-1860," in Lewis Perry and Michael Fellman, eds., *Antislavery Reconsidered: New Perspectives on the Abolitionists* (Baton Rouge: Louisiana State University Press, 1979), pp. 75-95.

> Reprinted in Fulop and Raboteau, eds., *African American Religion*, pp. 153-73.

1040. Getman, Karen A. "Sexual Control in the Slaveholding South: The Implementation and Maintenance of a Racial Caste System," *Harvard Women's Law Journal*, 7, 1 (1984), pp. 115-52.

1041. Gibson, Carol J. "The Children Shall Lead: A Study of Slave Children in the Antebellum South" (MA thesis, Ohio State University, 1994).

1042. Gill, Christopher J. "A Year of Residence in the Household of a South Carolina Planter: Teacher, Daughters, Mistress, and Slaves," *South Carolina Historical Magazine*, 97, 4 (1996), pp. 293-309.

1043. Gleason, Johanna. "The Underground Railroad" (MA thesis, California State University, San Bernardino, 1993).

1044. Glymph, Thavolia. "The Second Middle Passage: The Transition from Slavery to Freedom at Davis Bend, Mississippi" (PhD diss., Purdue University, 1994).

1045. Goatley, David Emmanuel. *Were You There?: Godforsakenness in Slave Religion.* Maryknoll NY: Orbis Books, 1996. (Bishop Henry McNeal Turner/Sojourner Truth series, v. 11)

1046. Goldfield, David R. "Black Slaves in the Plantation South," in Campbell, with Rice, eds., *Before Freedom Came*, pp. 123-54.

1047. Gore, Karenna Aitcheson. "Uses of the Past in the New Deal: the WPA Slave Narratives of Mississippi" (BA honors thesis in History and Literature, Harvard University, 1995).

1048. Gould, Virginia Meacham. "The Free Creoles of Color of the Antebellum Gulf Ports of Mobile and Pensacola: A Struggle for the Middle Ground," in Dormon, ed. *Creoles of Color of the Gulf South*, pp. 28-50.

1049. Greenberg, Bradley Craig. "Jimmying the Lock of Domesticity: Women and Slavery in Stowe's *Uncle Tom's Cabin*, Douglass's *Narrative*, and Mary Chesnut's *Journals*" (MA thesis, Kansas State University, 1995).

1050. Greenberg, Kenneth S. *Honor and Slavery: Lies, Duels, Noses, Masks, Dressing as a Woman, Gifts, Strangers, Humanitarianism, Death, Slave Rebellions, the Proslavery Argument, Baseball, Hunting, and Gambling in the Old South.* Princeton: Princeton University Press, 1996.

1051. Griebel, Helen Bradley. "New Raiments of Self: African American Clothing in the Antebellum South" (PhD diss., University of Pennsylvania, 1994).

1052. Griffin, Farah Jasmine. "Textual Healing: Claiming Black Women's Bodies, the Erotic and Resistance in Contemporary Novels of Slavery," *Callaloo*, 19, 2 (1996), pp. 519-36.

1053. Grindle, David J. "Manumission: The Weak Link in Georgia's Law of Slavery," *Mercer Law Review*, 41, 2 (1990), pp. 701-22.

1054. Gross, Ariela J. "Enslaved Women's Character on Trial in the Deep South, 1800-1861" (Unpublished paper, American Historical Association, Chicago, 5-8 Jan. 1995).

1055. Gross, Ariela J. "Pandora's Box: Slave Character on Trial in the Antebellum South," *Yale*

Journal of Law and the Humanities, 7, 2 (1995), pp. 267-316.

1056. Gross, Ariela J[ulie]. "Pandora's Box: Slavery, Character, and Southern Culture in the Courtroom, 1800-1860" (PhD diss., Stanford University, 1996).

1057. Hadden, Sally Elizabeth. "Law Enforcement in a New Nation: Slave Patrols and Public Authority in the Old South, 1700-1865" (PhD diss., Harvard University, 1993).

1058. Hadden, Sally [Elizabeth]. "Remembering and Forgetting Slave Patrols: Former Slaves and Slave Owners Construct their Shared Past" (Unpublished paper, Southern Historical Association, Louisville KY, 9-12 Nov. 1994).

1059. Hahn, Steven. "African-American Life in the Nineteenth-Century South: A Review Essay (including Schweninger, *Black Property Owners*)," *Arkansas Historical Quarterly*, 50, 4 (1991), pp. 352-73.

1060. Hansen, Ellen. *The Underground Railroad: Life on the Road to Freedom*. Lowell MA: Discovery Enterprises, 1993.

1061. Harbeson, Kristen Lynne. *The Other Middle Passage: Resistance, Runaways, and the Underground Railroad*. Amherst MA: [n.p.], 1996.

1062. Harding, Vincent. "Religion and Resistance among Antebellum Slaves, 1800-1860".

Reprinted in Fulop and Raboteau, eds., *African American Religion*, pp. 107-30.

1063. Hardy, James D., Jr., and Robert B. Robinson. "A Peculiarity of the Peculiar Institution: An Alabama Case," *Alabama Review*, 45, 1 (1992), pp. 18-25.

1064. Harrington, J. Drew. "'*Res*' or '*persona*': Roman Civil Law's Influence on Southern Slave Law," *Labeo: rassegna di diritto romano*, 40, 2 (1994), pp. 236-45.

1065. Harris, J. William. "Introduction," in Harris, ed., *Society and Culture in the Slave South*, pp. 1-9.

1066. Harris, J. William, ed. *Society and Culture in the Slave South*. New York: Routledge, 1992.

For contents see Cashin, Fogel, Fox-Genovese, Genovese and Fox-Genovese, Harris, Jones, Stuckey, White, and Wyatt-Brown.

1067. Harrold, Stanley. "John Brown's Forerunners: Slave Rescue Attempts and the Abolitionists, 1841-1851," *Radical History Review*, 55 (1993), pp. 89-110.

1068. Harrold, Stanley [C., Jr.] "Romanticizing the Slave Revolt: Abolitionist Portrayals of Madison, Washington and the *Creole* Mutiny" (Unpublished paper, Southern Historical Association, Louisville KY, 9-12 Nov. 1994).

1069. Harvey, Marcus Gow. "Antebellum Southerners, Miscegenation, and Attitudes Towards Blacks: The Complexities of Race and Racism in a Slave Society" (MA thesis, Queen's University at Kingston [Canada], 1994).

1070. Hauptman, William. "Denmark Vesey's Rebellion" (Miami: WPBT, 1995). (1 Videocassette).

Executive producer, Shep Morgan, producer, Yanna Kroyt Brandt, director, Stan Lathan.

1071. Hawkes, Alta Marcellus. "Food, Clothing, and Shelter of the American Slave" (PhD diss., Southern Methodist University, 1936).

1072. Hawley, Thomas Earl, Jr. "The Slave Tradition of Singing Among the Gullah of Johns Island, South Carolina" (PhD diss., University of Maryland - Baltimore County, 1993).

1073. Hazzard-Gordon, Katrina. "Dancing under the Lash: Sociocultural Disruption, Continuity, and Synthesis," in Kariamu Welsh Asante, ed., *African Dance* (Trenton NJ: Africa World Press, 1996), pp. 99-130.

1074. Herda, D. J. *The Dred Scott Case: Slavery and Citizenship*. Hillside NJ: Enslow Publishers, 1994.

1075. Hess, Karen. *The Carolina Rice Kitchen: The African Connection*. Columbia: University of South Carolina Press, 1992.

1076. Heyward, Duncan Clinch. *Seed from Madagascar*. New introduction by Peter A. Coclanis. Columbia: University of South Carolina Press, 1993.

1077. Hinks, Peter P. "'There Is a Great Work for You to Do': The Evangelical Strategy of David

Walker's *Appeal* and His Early Years in the Carolina Low Country," in Randall M. Miller and John R. McKivigan, eds., *The Moment of Decision: Biographical Essays on American Character and Regional Identity* (Westport CT: Greenwood Press, 1994), pp. 99-114.

1078. Hinks, Peter P[ringle]. "'We Must and Shall Be Free': David Walker, Evangelicalism, and the Problem of Antebellum Black Resistance" (PhD diss., Yale University, 1993).

1079. Hodes, Martha. "The Toleration of Sex Between White Women and Black Men in the Antebellum South" (Unpublished paper, American Historical Association, San Francisco, 6-9 Jan. 1994).

1080. Hoffman, Martha K. "Thoughts on the Treatment of Moral Issues in *Time on the Cross*," in Fogel, Galantine, and Manning, eds., *Evidence and Methods (Without Consent or Contract)*, pp. 599-603.

1081. Hopkins, Mark M., and N. Scott Cardell. "A Correction to the Computation in *Time on the Cross* of the Value of Freedom at Low-Income Levels," in Fogel, Galantine, and Manning, eds., *Evidence and Methods (Without Consent or Contract)*, pp. 379-83.

1082. Hopkins, Mark M., and N. Scott Cardell. "The Relation between the Cost of Calories for Suckling Babies and for Nursing Mothers," in Fogel, Galantine, and Manning, eds., *Evidence and Methods (Without Consent or Contract)*, pp. 310-11.

1083. Horton, James Oliver. "Links to Bondage: Northern Free Blacks and the Underground Railroad," *Rutgers Law Journal*, 24, 3 (1993), pp. 667-90. (Race Relations and the United States Constitution: From Fugitive Slaves to Affirmative Action)

For responses see Cottrol and Maltz.

1084. Horton, James Oliver, and Lois E. Horton. "A Federal Assault: African Americans and the Impact of the Fugitive Slave Law of 1850," *Chicago-Kent Law Review*, 68, 3 (Symposium on the Law of Slavery) (1993), pp. 1179-97.

1085. Howell, Donna Wyant, ed. *I Was a Slave: True Life Stories Told by Former American Slaves in the 1930s*. Washington DC: American Legacy Books, 1995.

1086. Howlett, Scott [Walcott]. "'My Child, Him is Mine': Plantation Slave Children in the Old South" (PhD diss., University of California - Irvine, 1993).

1087. Howlett, Scott. "'My Child, Him is Mine': Slave Children in the Old South" (Unpublished paper, Annual Meeting of the Southern Historical Association, Atlanta, 1992).

1088. Hudson, Larry E., Jr. "'All That Cash': Work and Status in the Slave Quarters," in Hudson, Jr., ed., *Working Toward Freedom*, pp. 77-94.

1089. Hudson, Larry E. [Jr.] "'Thwarted Ambition': South Carolina Slaves Working Towards Freedom" (Unpublished paper, Annual Meeting of the Southern Historical Association, Atlanta, 1992).

1090. Hudson, Larry E., Jr., ed. *Working Toward Freedom: Slave Society and the Domestic Economy in the American South*. Rochester NY: University of Rochester Press, 1994.

For contents see Beoku-Betts, Brown, Campbell, Cody, Corrigan, Engerman, Holt, Hudson Jr., King, Olwell, and Walsh.

1091. Hull, Mark H. "Concerning the Emancipation of the Slaves: A Proposal by Major-General Patrick Cleburne, CSA," *Journal of Mississippi History*, 58, 4 (1996), pp. 377-99.

1092. Hunt, Judith Lee. "The Circle Large and Small: Kinship, Slavery, and the Middleton Plantocracy, a Lowcountry Example" (MA thesis, University of Charleston, 1995).

1093. Hunt, Patricia K. "Fabric Production in the 19th Century African American Slave Community," *Ars Textrina*, 15 (1991), pp. 83-92.

1094. Hunt, Patricia K. "Textile Fragments Recovered from a Slave Cemetery in South Carolina," *Ars Textrina*, 22 (1994), pp. 87-105.

1095. Hunt, Robert. "A Domesticated Slavery: Political Economy in Caroline Hentz's Fiction," *Southern Quarterly*, 34, 4 (1996), pp. 25-35.

1096. [Hurmence, Belinda.] *We Lived in a Little Cabin in the Yard*. Winston-Salem NC: J. F. Blair, 1994.

1097. Huston, Julia Price. "Power Play: Gender, Power, and Economic Control in the Plantation South

1830-1870" (Honors paper, Mount Holyoke College, Department of History, 1995).

1098. Inscoe, John C. "Generation and Gender as Reflected in Carolina Slave Naming Practices: A Challenge to the Gutman Thesis," *South Carolina Historical Magazine*, 94, 4 (1993), pp. 252-63.

1099. James, Anne G. "'You Your Best Thing': African-American Women Writers and the Depiction of Slavery" (BA thesis, Linfield College, 1995).

1100. John, Beverly M. "Culture and Social Change: The Values and Behaviors of African-American People in the South Carolina Lowcountry and Georgia Coastal Region in the Antebellum and Postbellum Periods" (PhD diss., University of California - Berkeley, 1991).

1101. Johnson, Whittington B. "Free African-American Women in Savannah, 1800-1860: Affluence and Autonomy Amid Adversity," *Georgia Historical Quarterly*, 76, 2 (1992), pp. 260-83.

1102. Jones, Jacqueline. "Federal Writers Project Slave Narratives," in Hine, Brown, and Terborg-Penn, eds., *Black Women in America*, pp. 416-18.

1103. Jones, Norrece T., Jr. "The Black Family as a Mechanism of Planter Control."

Reprinted (from *Born a Child of Freedom, Yet a Slave*) in Harris, ed., *Society and Culture in the Slave South*, pp. 162-87.

1104. Jordan, Ervin L., Jr. "Sleeping with the Enemy: Sex, Black Women, and the Civil War," *Western Journal of Black Studies*, 18, 2 (1994), pp. 55-63.

1105. Jordan, Winthrop D. *Tumult and Silence at Second Creek: An Inquiry into a Civil War Slave Conspiracy*. Baton Rouge: Louisiana State University Press, 1993.

1106. Joseph, J. W[alter, III]. "Liberty: An Archaeological Examination of Social Identity within the Plantation Culture of the Lowcountry of Georgia" (PhD diss., University of Pennsylvania, 1993).

1107. Joseph, J. W. "Pattern and Process in the Plantation Archaeology of the Lowcountry of Georgia and South Carolina," *Historical Archaeology*, 23, 1 (1989), pp. 55-68.

1108. Joseph, J. W. "White Columns and Black Hands: Class and Classification in the Plantation Ideology of the Georgia and South Carolina Lowcountry," *Historical Archaeology*, 27, 3 (1993), pp. 57-73.

1109. Joyner, Charles. "A Single Southern Culture: Cultural Interaction in the Old South," in Ownby, ed., *Black and White: Cultural Interaction in the Antebellum South*, pp. 3-22.

1110. Joyner, Charles. "The World of the Plantation Slaves," in Campbell, with Rice, eds., *Before Freedom Came*, pp. 51-100.

1111. Judy, Ronald A. T. *(Dis)forming the American Canon: African-Arabic Slave Narratives and the Vernacular*. Minneapolis: University of Minnesota Press, 1993.

1112. Kahn, Charles. "An Agency Approach to Slave Punishments and Awards," in Fogel and Engerman, eds., *Conditions of Life and the Transition to Freedom: Technical Papers*, vol. 2 (*Without Consent or Contract*), pp. 551-65.

1113. Kahn, Charles. "A Linear-Programming Solution to the Slave Diet," in Fogel and Engerman, eds., *Conditions of Life and the Transition to Freedom: Technical Papers*, vol. 2 (*Without Consent or Contract*), pp. 522-35.

1114. Karcher, Carolyn L. "Rape, Murder, and Revenge in 'Slavery's Pleasant Homes': Lydia Maria Child's Antislavery Fiction and the Limits of Genre," in Shirley Samuels, ed., *The Culture of Sentiment: Race, Gender, and Sentimentality in Nineteenth-Century America* (New York: Oxford University Press, 1992), pp. 58-72.

1115. Kattner, Lauren Ann. "The Diversity of Old South White Women: The Peculiar Worlds of German American Women," in Morton, ed., *Discovering the Women in Slavery*, pp. 299-311.

1116. Katz, William L., ed. *Flight from the Devil: Six Slave Narratives*. Trenton NJ: Africa World Press, 1994.

1117. Kauffman, Susan. "Whispers from the Shadows: Telling the African-American Story at Selected Historic Sites in North Carolina" (MA thesis, University of North Carolina - Charlotte, 1994).

1118. Kellam, John Harris. "The Evolution of Slave Law in North Carolina: Supreme Court Decisions, 1800-1860" (MA thesis, Wake Forest University, 1992).

1119. Kennedy, Vasantha Lynn. "Images and Actualities: Sexual Stereotypes and Miscegenation in the Antebellum South" (MA thesis, Queen's University at Kingston [Canada], 1994).

1120. Kilbride, Daniel. "Slavery and Utilitarianism: Thomas Cooper and the Mind of the Old South," *Journal of Southern History*, 59, 3 (1993), pp. 469-86.

1121. King, Wilma. "'Rais Your Children Up Rite': Parental Guidance and Child Rearing Practices among Slaves in the Nineteenth-Century South," in Hudson, Jr., ed., *Working Toward Freedom*, pp. 143-62.

1122. King, Wilma. *Stolen Childhood: Slave Youth in Nineteenth-Century America*. Bloomington: Indiana University Press, 1995.

1123. King, Wilma. "'Suffer with Them Till Death': Slave Women and their Children in Nineteenth-Century America," in Gaspar and Hine, eds., *More than Chattel*, pp. 147-68.

1124. King, Wilma. "When Day is Done: Play and Leisure Activities of Slave Children and Youth in Nineteenth-Century America" (Unpublished paper, Annual Meeting of the Southern Historical Association, Atlanta, 1992).

1125. King-Teetor, Cynthia Ann. "'Until the Breakin Time Comes': a Study of Alabama Slave Children, 1830-1865" (MA thesis, Auburn University, 1996).

1126. Kiple, Kenneth F., and Virginia H. King. "Nutrition and Nutriments".

Reprinted (from *Another Dimension to the Black Diaspora*) in Goodheart, Brown, and Rabe, eds., *Slavery in American Society*, pp. 134-49.

1127. Koger, Larry. *Black Slaveowners: Free Black Slave Masters in South Carolina, 1790-1860*. Columbia: University of South Carolina Press, 1995.

1128. Kolchin, Peter. "More *Time on the Cross*? An Evaluation of Robert William Fogel's *Without Consent or Contract*," *Journal of Southern History*, 58, 3 (1992), pp. 491-502.

1129. Komlos, John, and Bjorn Alecke. "The Economics of Antebellum Slave Heights Reconsidered," *Journal of Interdisciplinary History*, 26, 3 (1996), pp. 437-57.

1130. Kotlikoff, Laurence J. "A Production Function Framework for Questioning the Existence of Slave Breeding," in Fogel, Galantine, and Manning, eds., *Evidence and Methods* (*Without Consent or Contract*), pp. 326-27.

1131. Kyger, Helen Brennan. "'Better mind how you talk': Comparative Analysis of Slave Testimonies" (MA thesis, Vanderbilt University, 1995).

1132. Lane, Robert. "Dark Deeds Seen Through a Dark Glass: The Historian as Detective (review essay: Jordan, *Tumult and Silence at Second Creek*)," *Reviews in American History*, 22, 1 (1994), pp. 67-72.

1133. Leaming, Hugo P. *Hidden Americans: Maroons of Virginia and the Carolinas*. New York: Garland Publishing, 1995.

1134. Lenz, Peter A. *Voices for Freedom: Documentary Words of African (& Anglo) American Protest, Struggle, Resistance and Liberation: and Against Slavery and Prejudice Before the Civil War as Seen in Black Accounts, Narratives, Black Newspapers, Pamphlets, Letters and Anglo and Garrisonian Words and Press in 2 Volumes*. Norway ME: Dawnfire Publishing Collective, 1996.

1135. Levine, Lawrence. "Slave Spirituals".

Reprinted (from *Black Culture and Black Consciousness*) in Goodheart, Brown, and Rabe, eds., *Slavery in American Society*, pp. 99-115.

1136. Lichtenstein, Alex. "George Rawick's *From Sundown to Sunup* and the Dialectic of Marxian Slave Studies," *Reviews in American History*, 24, 4 (1996), pp. 712-25.

1137. Lichtenstein, Alex. "Theft, Moral Economy, and the Transition from Slavery to Freedom in the American South," in Palmié, ed., *Slave Cultures and the Cultures of Slavery*, pp. 176-86.

1138. Liqwen, Yang. "John Brown's Role in the History of the Emancipation Movement of Black

Americans," *Southern Studies*, 3, 2 (1992), pp. 135-42.

1139. Lowance, Mason. "Slave Narratives," in Hine, Brown, and Terborg-Penn, eds., *Black Women in America*, pp. 1043-45.

1140. Malone, Bill C. "Blacks and Whites and the Music of the Old South," in Ownby, ed., *Black and White: Cultural Interaction in the Antebellum South*, pp. 149-70.

With commentary by Leslie Howard Owens, pp. 170-89.

1141. Maltz, Earl M. "Commentary (Fugitive Slaves and Underground Railroad - response to articles by Finkelman and Horton)," *Rutgers Law Journal*, 24, 3 (1993), pp. 691-93. (Race Relations and the United States Constitution: From Fugitive Slaves to Affirmative Action)

1142. Manning, Richard L. "The Gang System and the Structure of Slave Employment," in Fogel, Galantine, and Manning, eds., *Evidence and Methods* (*Without Consent or Contract*), pp. 109-19.

1143. Manning, Richard L., and Gerald Friedman. "Occupational Determination in Slave Societies," in Fogel, Galantine, and Manning, eds., *Evidence and Methods* (*Without Consent or Contract*), pp. 119-40.

1144. Margo, Robert A. "Civilian Occupations of Ex-Slaves in the Union Army," in Fogel and Engerman, eds., *Markets and Production: Technical Papers*, vol. 1 (*Without Consent or Contract*), pp. 170-85.

1145. Margo, Robert A., and Richard H. Steckel. "The Nutrition and Health of Slaves and Antebellum Southern Whites," in Fogel and Engerman, eds., *Conditions of Life and the Transition to Freedom: Technical Papers*, vol. 2 (*Without Consent or Contract*), pp. 508-21.

1146. Marietta, Jack. "Egoism and Altruism in Quaker Abolition," *Quaker History*, 82, 1 (1993), pp. 1-22.

See also response by Soderlund.

1147. Martin, B. G. "Sapelo Island's Arabic Document: The 'Bilali Diary' in Context," *Georgia Historical Quarterly*, 78, 3 (1994), pp. 589-601.

1148. Massey, Karen G. "Ritual Improvisation: A Challenge to Christian Education from the Nineteenth Century African-American Slave Community" (EdD, Southern Baptist Theological Seminary, 1991).

1149. McDaniel, Antonio, and Carlos Grushka. "Did Africans Live Longer in the Antebellum United States? The Sensitivity of Mortality Estimates of Enslaved Africans," *Historical Methods*, 28, 2 (1995), pp. 97-105.

1150. McDonnell, Lawrence T. "Work, Culture, and Society in the Slave South, 1790-1861," in Ownby, ed., *Black and White: Cultural Interaction in the Antebellum South*, pp. 125-47.

1151. McGee, Val L. "Escape from Slavery: The Milly Walker Trials," *Alabama Review*, 49, 4 (1996), pp. 243-52.

1152. McKenzie, Robert H. "African American Forgeworkers," in *Encyclopedia of the Confederacy*, vol. 1, pp. 3-4.

1153. McKinley, Catherine. "Infanticide and Slave Women," in Hine, Brown, and Terborg-Penn, eds., *Black Women in America*, pp. 607-09.

1154. McKinney, Don Sidney. "Getting Along in Antebellum Georgian Slavery: Dimensions of the Moral Life Heard in the Voices of the Slaves Themselves" (PhD diss., Vanderbilt University, 1992).

1155. McKivigan, John R. "'His Truth Goes Marching On': The Story of John Brown's Followers after the Harpers Ferry Raid" (Unpublished paper, Southern Historical Association, Louisville KY, 9-12 Nov. 1994).

1156. McKivigan, John R., ed. *The Roving Editor: Or, Talks with Slaves in the Southern States, by James Redpath*. University Park: Penn State Press, 1996.

1157. McMichael, Philip. "Slavery in the Regime of Wage Labor: Beyond Paternalism in the US Cotton Culture," *Social Concept*, 6, 1 (1991), pp. 10-28.

1158. McNair, Glenn Maurice. "The Trials of Slaves in Baldwin County, Georgia, 1812-1838" (MA thesis, Georgia College - Milledgeville, 1996).

1159. Metzer, Jacob. "Rational Management, Modern Business Practices, and Economies of Scale in Antebellum Southern Plantations".

Revised in Fogel and Engerman, eds., *Markets and Production: Technical Papers*, vol. 1 (*Without Consent or Contract*), pp. 191-215.

1160. Meyers, Arthur S. "'Come! Let us Fly to Freedom's Sky': The Response of Irish Immigrants in the South to Slavery During the Antebellum Period," *Journal of Southwest Georgia History*, 7 (1989-92), pp. 20-39.

1161. Michie, James L. *Richmond Hill Plantation, 1810-1868: The Discovery of Antebellum Life on a Waccamaw Rice Plantation*. Spartanburg: The Reprint Company, 1990.

1162. Miller, Edward A. *Gullah Statesman: Robert Smalls from Slavery to Congress, 1839-1915*. Columbia: University of South Carolina Press, 1995.

1163. Miller, Randall M. "Slave Drivers," in *Encyclopedia of the Confederacy*, vol. 4, pp. 1433-34.

1164. Miller, Steven F. "Plantation Labor Organization and Slave Life on the Cotton Frontier: The Alabama-Mississippi Black Belt, 1815-1840," in Berlin and Morgan, eds., *Cultivation and Culture*, pp. 155-69.

1165. Mills, Lane, ed. *Neither More nor Less than Men: Slavery in Georgia: A Documentary History*. Savannah: Beehive Press, 1993.

1166. Mitchell, Angelyn. "Signifyin(g) Women: Visions and Revisions of Slavery in Octavia Butler's *Kindred*, Sherley Anne Williams's *Dessa Rose*, and Toni Morrison's *Beloved*" (PhD diss., Howard University, 1992).

1167. Morgan, Winifred. "Gender-Related Difference in the Slave Narratives of Harriet Jacobs and Frederick Douglass," *American Studies*, 35, 2 (1994), pp. 73-94.

1168. Morris, Thomas D. "'Villeinage ... As it Existed in England, Reflects but Little Light on our Subject': The Problem of the 'Sources' of Southern Slave Law," *American Journal of Legal History*, 32, 2 (1988), pp. 95-137.

1169. Mullen, Harryette. "Runaway Tongue: Resistant Orality in *Uncle Tom's Cabin*, *Our Nig*, *Incidents in the Life of a Slave Girl*, and *Beloved*," in Shirley Samuels, ed., *The Culture of Sentiment: Race, Gender, and Sentimentality in Nineteenth-Century America* (New York: Oxford University Press, 1992), pp. 244-64.

1170. Nardinelli, Clark. "Fogel's Farewell to Slavery: A Review Essay (of *Without Consent or Contract*, [1] *Rise and Fall of American Slavery*, [2] Fogel and Engerman, eds., *Technical Papers* [2 vols.], and [3] Fogel, Galantine, and Manning, *Evidence and Methods*)," *Historical Methods: A Journal of Quantitative and Interdisciplinary History*, 27, 3 (1994), pp. 133-39.

1171. Nash, A. E. Keir. "A More Equitable Past? Southern Supreme Courts and the Protection of the Antebellum Negro".

Reprinted in Finkelman, ed., *Race, Law and American History*, vol. 2 (*Race and Law Before Emancipation*), pp. 375-420.

1172. Neal, Diane, and Thomas W. Kremm. "'The King of Revolution is the Bayonet': General Thomas C. Hindman's Proposal to Arm the Slaves," *Journal of Confederate History*, 7 (1991), pp. 81-96.

1173. Oates, Stephen B. "Death Warrant for Slavery"

Reprinted from *Abraham Lincoln: The Man Behind the Myths*, in Berwanger, ed., *The Civil War Era*, pp. 91-96.

1174. O'Brien, Michael. "Conservative Thought in the Old South: A Review Article (on Genovese, *Slaveholders' Dilemma*)," *Comparative Studies in Society and History*, 34, 3 (1992), pp. 566-76.

1175. Oestreicher, Richard. "Labor: The Jacksonian Era through Reconstruction," in *Encyclopedia of American Social History*, vol. 2, pp. 1447-58.

1176. Olliff, Martin T. "Life and Work in a Progressive Cotton Community: Prattville, Alabama, 1846-1860," in Whitten, ed., "Eli Whitney's Cotton Gin," pp. 51-61.

1177. Olson, John F. "Clock Time versus Real Time: A Comparison of the Lengths of the Northern and Southern Agricultural Work Years," in Fogel and Engerman, eds., *Markets and Production: Technical Papers*, vol. 1 (*Without Consent or Contract*), pp. 216-40.

1178. Olson, John F. "The Occupational Structure of Southern Plantations during the Late Antebellum Era," in Fogel and Engerman, eds., *Markets and Production: Technical Papers*, vol. 1 (*Without Consent or Contract*), pp. 137-69.

1179. Orser, Charles E., Jr. "The Archaeology of African-American Slave Religion in the Antebellum South," *Cambridge Archaeological Journal*, 4, 1 (1994), pp. 33-45.

1180. Orser, Charles E., Jr., and Annette M. Nekola. "Plantation Settlement from Slavery to Tenancy: An Example from a Piedmont Plantation in South Carolina".

Reprinted in Charles E. Orser, ed., *Images of the Recent Past: Readings in Historical Archaeology* (Walnut Creek CA: Alta Mira Press, 1996), pp. 392-415.

1181. Outland, Robert B. III. "Slavery, Work, and the Geography of the North Carolina Naval Stores Industry, 1835-1860," *Journal of Southern History*, 62, 1 (1996), pp. 27-56.

1182. Ownby, Ted, ed. *Black and White: Cultural Interaction in the Antebellum South*. Jackson: University Press of Mississippi, 1993.

For contents see Frey, Joyner, Malone, McDonnell, Sobel, and Vlach.

1183. Painter, Nell Irvin. "Of *Lily*, Linda Brent, and Freud: A Non-Exceptionalist Approach to Race, Class, and Gender in the Slave South," *Georgia Historical Quarterly*, 76, 2 (1992), pp. 241-59.

Reprinted in Clinton, ed., *Half Sisters of History*, pp. 93-109.

Another version as "Three Southern Women and Freud: A Non-exceptionalist Approach to Race, Class, and Gender in the Slave South," in Ann-Louise Shapiro, ed., *Feminists Revision History* (New Brunswick NJ: Rutgers University Press, 1994), pp. 195-216.

1184. Parent, Anthony S., Jr., and Susan Brown Wallace. "Childhood and Sexual Identity under Slavery," *Journal of the History of Sexuality*, 3, 3 (1992-93), pp. 363-401.

1185. Parker, Freddie L. *Running for Freedom: Slave Runaways in North Carolina, 1775 to 1840*. New York: Garland, 1993.

1186. Parker, William N. "The Slave Plantation in American Agriculture".

Reprinted in idem, *Europe, America, and the Wider World: Essays on the Economic History of Western Capitalism* – Vol. 2: *America and the Wider World* (New York: Cambridge University Press, 1991), pp. 33-40.

1187. Parker, William N. "Slavery and Economic Development: An Hypothesis and Some Evidence".

Reprinted as "Slavery and Southern Economic Development ... ," in idem, *Europe, America, and the Wider World: Essays on the Economic History of Western Capitalism* – Vol. 2: *America and the Wider World* (New York: Cambridge University Press, 1991), pp. 41-50.

1188. Patton, Phil. "Mammy: Her Life and Times," *American Heritage*, 44, 5 (Sept. 1993), pp. 78-87.

1189. Paulson, Timothy J. *Days of Sorrow, Years of Glory, 1831-1850: From the Nat Turner Revolt to the Fugitive Slave Law*. New York: Chelsea House, 1994.

1190. Pease, Jane H., and William H. Pease. "Law, Slavery, and Petigru: A Study in Paradox," in Randall M. Miller and John R. McKivigan, eds., *The Moment of Decision: Biographical Essays on American Character and Regional Identity* (Westport CT: Greenwood Press, 1994), pp. 36-64.

1191. Pecori, Jeanne Marie. "Rape as a Form of Social Control in the Antebellum South" (BA thesis, James Madison University, 1995).

1192. Perman, Michael. "A Faustfest (review essay: Faust, *Southern Stories*)," *Reviews in American History*, 22, 1 (1994), pp. 62-66.

1193. Pinera, Sebastian, and Laurence J. Kotlikoff. "The Exploitation-Expropriation Debate," in Fogel, Galantine, and Manning, eds., *Evidence and Methods* (*Without Consent or Contract*), pp. 383-87.

1194. Powers, Bernard E. *Black Charlestonians: A Social History, 1882-1885*. Fayetteville: University of Arkansas Press, 1994.

1195. Quist, John W. "Slaveholding Operatives of the Benevolent Empire: Bible, Tract, and Sunday School Societies in Antebellum Tuscaloosa County, Alabama," *Journal of Southern History*, 62, 3 (1996), pp. 481-526.

1196. Raboteau, Albert J. "The Black Experience in American Evangelicalism: The Meaning of Slavery," in Fulop and Raboteau, eds., *African American Religion*, pp. 89-106.

1197. Raboteau, Albert J. "Conjure".

Reprinted (from *Slave Religion*) in Goodheart, Brown, and Rabe, eds., *Slavery in American Society*, pp. 123-34.

1198. Radano, Ronald. "Denoting Difference: the Writing of the Slave Spirituals," *Critical Inquiry*, 22, 3 (1996), pp. 506-44.

1199. Rahe, Lee Wayne. "Residential Furnishings of Deceased Greene County, Alabama Slave Owners, 1845-1860" (PhD diss., University of Tennessee, 1992).

1200. Ramey, Susan E. "Salvation Black or White: Presbyterian Rationale and Protestant Support for the Religious Instruction of Slaves in South Carolina" (MA thesis, University of Nevada, Las Vegas, 1994).

1201. Reid, Richard. "Raising the African Brigade: Early Black Recruitment in Civil War North Carolina," *North Carolina Historical Review*, 70, 3 (1993), pp. 266-301.

1202. Reidy, Joseph P. "Calliope and Clio: The Style and Substance of Recent Historical Writing on the South," *Southern Review*, 32, 2 (1996), pp. 373-89.

1203. Reidy, Joseph P. *From Slavery to Agrarian Capitalism in the Cotton Plantation South: Central Georgia, 1800-1880*. Chapel Hill: University of North Carolina Press, 1992.

1204. Reidy, Joseph P. "Labor: An Overview," in *Encyclopedia of the Confederacy*, vol. 2, pp. 899-902.

1205. Reidy, Joseph P. "Obligation and Right: Patterns of Labor, Subsistence, and Exchange in the Cotton Belt of Georgia, 1790-1860," in Berlin and Morgan, eds., *Cultivation and Culture*, pp. 138-54.

1206. "Remembering Slavery: The Public Testimony and Private Worlds of Sojourner Truth and Nat Turner" (panel, Southern Historical Association, Louisville KY, 9-12 Nov. 1994).

Panel chair, Waldo E. Martin, Jr.; panelists Nell Irvin Painter and Scot A. French; comments by Alan Trachtenberg and Waldo E. Martin, Jr.

1207. Roark, James L. "Hidden Lives: Georgia's Free Women of Color (review essay: Alexander, *Free Women of Color in Rural Georgia*)," *Georgia Historical Quarterly*, 76, 2 (1992), pp. 410-19.

1208. Roark, James L. "Planters," in *Encyclopedia of the Confederacy*, vol. 3, pp. 1219-21.

1209. Rogers, W. McDowell. "Free Negro Legislation in Georgia Before 1865," *Georgia Historical Quarterly*, 16, 1 (1932), pp. 27-37.

Reprinted in Finkelman, ed., *Race, Law and American History*, vol. 2 (*Race and Law Before Emancipation*), pp. 421-31.

1210. Roper, Louis H. "The Unraveling of an Anglo-American Utopia in South Carolina," *Historian*, 58, 2 (1996), pp. 277-88.

1211. Russell, Thomas D[avid]. "Sale Day in Antebellum South Carolina: Slavery, Law, Economy and Court-Supervised Sales" (PhD diss., Stanford University, 1993).

1212. Russell, Thomas D. "South Carolina's Largest Slave Auctioneering Firm," *Chicago-Kent Law Review*, 68, 3 (Symposium on the Law of Slavery) (1993), pp. 1241-82.

1213. Russo, Paul A. "Antebellum Plantation Labor Experience and the Postbellum Economic Viability of African-American Communities: An Archaeological Model" (MA thesis, Wake Forest University, 1991).

1214. Sabiston, Elizabeth Jean. "Anglo-American Connections: Elizabeth Gaskell, Harriet Beecher Stowe and the 'Irony of Slavery'," in Plasa and Ring, eds., *Discourse of Slavery*, pp. 94-117.

1215. Samuels, Shirley. "The Identity of Slavery," in idem, ed., *The Culture of Sentiment: Race, Gender, and Sentimentality in Nineteenth-Century America* (New York: Oxford University Press, 1992), pp. 157-71.

1216. Saraceni, Jessica E. "Secret Religion of Slaves," *Archaeology*, 49, 6 (1996), p. 21.

1217. Saville, Julie. "Grassroots Reconstruction: Agricultural Labour and Collective Action in South Carolina, 1860-1868," *Slavery and Abolition*, 12, 3 (1991), pp. 173-82.

1218. Saville, Julie. "The Political Lives of Ex-Slave Plantation Workers in the Era of the American Civil War and Reconstruction" (Presentation at Colloquium on "Les dépendances serviles", Paris 1996).

1219. Saville, Julie. *The Work of Reconstruction: From Slave to Wage Laborer in South Carolina, 1860-1870.* Cambridge: Cambridge University Press, 1994.

1220. Scarborough, William K. "Overseers," in *Encyclopedia of the Confederacy*, vol. 3, pp. 1174-75.

1221. Schiller, Reuel E. "Conflicting Obligations: Slave Law and the Late Antebellum North Carolina Supreme Court," *Virginia Law Review*, 78, 5 (1992), pp. 1207-51.

1222. Schipper, Martin W., and Kenneth M. Stampp. *A Guide to the Microfilm Edition of Records of Antebellum Southern Plantations from the Revolution to the Civil War: Series L, Selections from the Earl Gregg Swem Library, the College of William and Mary.* Bethesda: University Publications of America, 1994.

Pt. 1. Carter papers, 1667-1862 -- Pt. 2. Jerdone family papers, 1736-1918 -- Pt. 3. Skipwith family papers, 1760-1877 -- Pt. 4. Austin-Twyman papers, 1765-1865 and Charles Brown papers, 1792-1888.

1223. Schwalm, Leslie Ann. "The Meaning of Freedom: African-American Women and Their Transition from Slavery to Freedom in Lowcountry South Carolina" (PhD diss., University of Wisconsin - Madison, 1991).

1224. Schwartz, Marie Jenkins. "'Me an' My Mammy's Gonna Pick a Bale of Cotton': Slave Child Labor in the Alabama Black Belt" (Unpublished paper, Annual Meeting of the Southern Historical Association, Atlanta, 1992).

1225. Schweninger, Loren. *Black Property Owners in the South, 1790-1915.* Champaign-Urbana: University of Illinois Press, 1990.

1226. Schweninger, Loren. "Slave Independence and Enterprise in South Carolina, 1780-1865," *South Carolina Historical Magazine*, 93, 2 (1992), pp. 101-25.

1227. Schweninger, Loren. "Socioeconomic Dynamics among the Gulf Creole Populations: The Antebellum and Civil War Years," in Dormon, ed. *Creoles of Color of the Gulf South*, pp. 51-66.

1228. Scott, Carole E. "Why the Cotton Textile Industry Did Not Develop in the South Sooner," in Whitten, ed., "Eli Whitney's Cotton Gin," pp. 105-21.

1229. Scott, Jennifer L. "Households of Their Own: The Interior Lives of Slave Families" (History honors thesis, St. Lawrence University, 1995).

1230. Sellers, Charles Grier, Jr. "The Travail of Slavery"

Reprinted from *The Southerner as American*, in Berwanger, ed., *The Civil War Era*, pp. 9-19.

1231. Sellers, James B. *Slavery in Alabama.*

New ed., with introduction by Harriet E. Amos Doss. University AL: University of Alabama Press, 1994. (Library of Alabama Classics)

1232. Senese, Donald J. "The Free Negro and the South Carolina Courts, 1790-1860," *South Carolina Historical Magazine*, 68, 3 (1967), p. 140-53.

Reprinted in Finkelman, ed., *Race, Law and American History*, vol. 2 (*Race and Law Before Emancipation*), pp. 472-85.

1233. Sensbach, Jon F. "Culture and Conflict in the Early Black Church: A Moravian Mission Congregation in Antebellum North Carolina," *North Carolina Historical Review*, 71, 4 (1994), pp. 401-29.

1234. Sensbach, Jon F[redericksen]. "A Separate Canaan: The Making of an Afro-Moravian World in North Carolina, 1763-1856" (PhD diss., Duke University, 1991).

1235. Sharpe, Ann. "The History and Legacy of Mississippi Plantation Labor," in Robert C. Kent, Sara Markham, David R. Roediger, and Herbert Shapiro, eds., *Culture, Gender, Race, and U.S. Labor History* (Westport CT: Greenwood Press, 1993), pp. 105-19.

1236. Shaw, Stephanie J. "Mothering under Slavery in the Antebellum South," in Evelyn Nakano Glenn, Grace Chang, and Linda Rennie Forcey, eds., *Mothering: Ideology, Experience, and Agency* (New York: Routledge, 1994), pp. 237-58.

1237. Sheriff, G. Anne. *1850 Federal Slave Census of Pickens District, South Carolina: Eastern Division (Present-Day Pickens County)*. Self-published, 1991.

1238. Sheriff, G. Anne. *1860 Federal Slave Census of Pickens District, South Carolina: 5th Regiment (Present-Day Pickens County)*. Self-published, 1989.

1239. Shlomowitz, Ralph. "The Genesis of Free Labour in the American Civil War (review essay: Berlin *et al.*, *Freedom: A Documentary History*)," *Slavery and Abolition*, 13, 3 (1992), pp. 213-18.

1240. Silverman, Jason H. "Ashley Wilkes Revisited: The Immigrant as Slaveowner in the Old South," *Journal of Confederate History*, 7, 1 (1991), pp. 123-35.

1241. Simms, L. Moody, Jr. "*Gone with the Wind*: The View from China," *Southern Studies*, 23, 1 (1984), pp. 5-19.

Reprinted in *Southern Studies*, n.s. 2, 3-4 (1991), pp. 351-67.

1242. Singleton, Theresa A. "The Archaeology of Slave Life," in Campbell, with Rice, eds., *Before Freedom Came*, pp. 155-75.

1243. Singleton, Theresa A. "Using Written Records in the Archaeological Study of Slavery: An Example from the Butler Island Plantation," in Barbara J. Little, *Text-Aided Archaeology* (Boca Raton FL: CRC Press, 1992), pp. 55-66.

1244. Sinha, Manisha. "The Counter-Revolution of Slavery: Class, Politics and Ideology in Antebellum South Carolina" (PhD diss., Columbia University, 1994).

1245. Sitterson, J. Carlyle. "Sugar," in *Encyclopedia of the Confederacy*, vol. 4, pp. 1559-60.

1246. *Slavery in Ante-Bellum Southern Industries*. (Charles B. Dew, editorial advisor) Bethesda MD: University Publications of America, 1995.

(Microform reels: Black studies research resources) (Pt. 1. Mining and smelting industries, 26 reels)

1247. Smiddy, Linda O. "Judicial Nullification of State Statutes Restricting the Emancipation of Slaves: A Southern Court's Call for Reform," *South Carolina Law Review*, 42, 3 (1991), pp. 589-655.

1248. Smith, Dale Edwyna. "The Slaves of Liberty: Freedom in Amite County, Mississippi, 1820-1868" (PhD diss., Harvard University, 1993).

1249. Smith, John David, ed. *Anti-Abolition Tracts and Anti-Black Stereotypes: General Statements of "the Negro Problem"*. New York: Garland, 1993.

1250. Smith, John David, ed. *The Benefits of Slavery: The New Proslavery Argument*. New York: Garland, 1993.

1251. Smith, John David, ed. *The Biblical and "Scientific" Defense of Slavery: Religion and "the Negro Problem"*. New York: Garland, 1993.

1252. Smith, Mark M. "'My Father was a Timekeeper ... My Mother Kept a Clock'" (Unpublished paper, Southern Historical Association, Louisville KY, 9-12 Nov. 1994).

1253. Smith, Mark M. "Time, Slavery and Plantation Capitalism in the Ante-Bellum American South," *Past and Present*, no. 150 (1996), pp. 142-68.

1254. Smith, R. Drew. "Slavery, Secession, and Southern Protestant Shifts on the Authority of the State," *Journal of Church and State*, 36, 2 (1994), pp. 261-76.

1255. Sobel, Mechal. "Whatever You Do, Treat People Right: Personal Ethics in a Slave Society," in Ownby, ed., *Black and White: Cultural Interaction in the Antebellum South*, pp. 55-82.

With commentary by Elliott J. Gorn, pp. 82-88.

1256. Soderlund, Jean R. "On Quakers and Slavery," *Quaker History*, 82, 1 (1993), pp. 23-27.

Response to Marietta.

1257. Soltow, James H. "Cotton as Religion, Politics, Law, Economics, and Art," in Whitten, ed., "Eli Whitney's Cotton Gin," pp. 6-19.

1258. Spindel, Donna J. "Assessing Memory: Twentieth-Century Slave Narratives Reconsidered," *Journal of Interdisciplinary History*, 27, 2 (1996), pp. 247-61.

1259. Stampp, Kenneth M. *The Peculiar Institution: Slavery in the Ante-Bellum South. Collector's edition*. Norwalk CT: Easton Press, 1995 (c1984).

1260. Stampp, Kenneth M[ilton], and Martin Paul Schipper, eds. *A Guide to the Microfilm Edition of Records of Antebellum Plantations from the Revolution through the Civil War: Series M, Selections from the Virginia Historical Society.* Bethesda MD: University Publications of America, 1995.

Pt. 1. Tayloe family – Pt. 2. Northern Neck of Virginia and Maryland – Pt. 3. Other Tidewater Virginia.

1261. Steckel, Richard H. "Children and Choice: A Comparative Analysis of Slave and White Fertility in the Antebellum South," in Fogel and Engerman, eds., *Conditions of Life and the Transition to Freedom: Technical Papers*, vol. 2 (*Without Consent or Contract*), pp. 369-92.

1262. Steckel, Richard H. "Slave Mortality: Analysis of Evidence from Plantation Records".

Reprinted with revisions and additions in Fogel and Engerman, eds., *Conditions of Life and the Transition to Freedom: Technical Papers*, vol. 2 (*Without Consent or Contract*), pp. 393-412.

1263. Steckel, Richard [H]. "The Slavery Period and its Influence on Family Change in the United States," in Elza Berquó and Peter Xenos, eds., *Family Systems and Cultural Change* (Oxford: Clarendon Press, 1992), pp. 144-58.

1264. Steckel, Richard H. "Women, Work, and Health under Plantation Slavery in the United States," in Gaspar and Hine, eds., *More than Chattel*, pp. 43-60.

1265. Steckel, Richard H. "Work, Disease, and Diet in the Health and Mortality of American Slaves," in Fogel and Engerman, eds., *Conditions of Life and the Transition to Freedom: Technical Papers*, vol. 2 (*Without Consent or Contract*), pp. 489-507.

1266. Stowe, Harriet Beecher. *Uncle Tom's Cabin, or, Life Among the Lowly.* Champaign IL: Project Gutenberg, 1995.

Machine readable data. Available from Project Gutenberg (ftp uiarchive.cso.uiuc.edu); login as "anonymous"; password is [e-mail address]. Directory: /pub/etext/gutenberg/etext95. File names: utomc10.txt or utomc10.zip.

1267. Stuckey, Sterling. *Going Through the Storm: The Influence of African American Art in History.* New York: Oxford University Press, 1994.

Reprints "Through the Prism of Folklore: The Black Ethos in Slavery," "Remembering Denmark Vesey," and "The Skies of Consciousness: African Dance at Pinkster in New York, 1750-1840".

1268. Stuckey, Sterling. "Slavery and the Circle of Culture."

Reprinted (from *Slave Culture*) in Harris, ed., *Society and Culture in the Slave South*, pp. 100-27.

1269. Tandberg, Gerilyn G. "Field Hand Clothing in Louisiana and Mississippi During the Ante-Bellum Period," *Dress*, 5 (1980), pp. 89-104.

1270. Tandberg, Gerilyn G., and Sally Graham Durand. "Dress-Up Clothes for Field Slaves of Ante-Bellum Louisiana and Mississippi," *Costume*, 15 (1981), pp. 40-48.

1271. Tenzer, Lawrence Raymond. *The Forgotten Cause of the Civil War: a New Look at the Slavery Issue.* Manahawkin NJ: Scholars' Pub. House, 1996.

1272. Thurber, Cheryl. "The Development of the Mammy Image and Mythology," in Virginia Bernhard, Betty Brandon, Elizabeth Fox-Genovese, and Theda Perdue, eds., *Southern Women: History and Identities* (Columbia: University of Missouri Press, 1992), pp. 87-108.

1273. Toppin, Edgar A. "African Americans in the Confederacy," in *Encyclopedia of the Confederacy*, pp. 4-9.

1274. Trussel, James, and Richard H. Steckel. "The Age of Slaves at Menarche and Their First Birth".

Revised in Fogel and Engerman, eds., *Conditions of Life and the Transition to Freedom: Technical Papers*, vol. 2 (*Without Consent or Contract*), pp. 435-54.

1275. Tushnet, Mark V. "A Comment on the Critical Method in Legal History," *Cardozo Law Review*, 6, 4 (1985), pp. 997-1011.

Counterresponse to Alan Watson's critical review of *American Law of Slavery.*

1276. *The Underground Railroad: Resources and Sites to Visit.* Wilberforce OH: National Afro-American Museum and Cultural Center, 1995.

1277. Uzzell, Odell. "Free Negro/Slave Marriages and Family Life in Ante-Bellum North Carolina," *Western Journal of Black Studies*, 18, 2 (1994), pp. 64-69.

1278. Vallas, S. "Slavery and Ideologies of Womanhood in Antebellum America," *European Legacy*, 1, 3 (1996), pp. 1010-16. (Special Issue: 4th International conference, International Society for the Study of European Ideas: "The European Legacy: Toward New Paradigms" [Graz, Austria, 1994])

1279. Vander Zanden, James W. "The Ideology of White Supremacy," in Horowitz, ed., *Race, Class and Gender in Nineteenth-Century Culture*, pp. 90-107.

1280. Vauthier, Simone. "When the Dummy Speaks: The Example of William Alexander Caruthers," in Binder, ed., *Slavery in the Americas*, pp. 503-22.

1281. Vernon, Amelia Wallace. *African Americans at Mars Bluff, South Carolina*. Baton Rouge: Louisiana State University Press, 1993.

1282. Vlach, John Michael. *Back of the Big House: The Architecture of Plantation Slavery*. Chapel Hill: University of North Carolina Press, 1993.

1283. Vlach, John Michael. "Not Mansions ... But Good Enough: Slave Quarters as Bi-Cultural Expression," in Ownby, ed., *Black and White: Cultural Interaction in the Antebellum South*, pp. 89-114.

With commentary by Brenda L. Stevenson, pp. 115-23.

1284. Vlach, John Michael. "Plantation Landscapes of the Antebellum South," in Campbell, with Rice, eds., *Before Freedom Came*, pp. 21-49.

1285. Vlach, John Michael. "'Snug Li'l House with Flue and Oven': Nineteenth-Century Reforms in Plantation Slave Housing," in Elizabeth Collins Cromley and Carter L. Hudgins, eds., *Gender, Class, and Shelter* (Knoxville: University of Tennessee Press, 1995), pp. 118-29. (Perspectives in Vernacular Architecture, 5)

1286. Waldrep, Christopher. "Substituting Law for the Lash: Emancipation and Legal Formalism in a Mississippi County Court," *Journal of American History*, 82, 4 (1996), pp. 1425-51.

1287. Walker, Gary C. *Slavery and the Coming War*. Roanoke VA: A & W Enterprise, 1996.

1288. Walter, Krista L. "Loopholes in History: The Literature of American Slavery as Cultural Critique" (PhD diss., University of California - Irvine, 1991).

1289. Washington, Margaret [Creel]. "Community Regulation and Cultural Specialization in Gullah Folk Religion," in Paul E. Johnson, ed., *African-American Christianity: Essays in History* (Berkeley: University of California Press, 1994), pp. 47-79.

1290. Watson, Alan. "The American Law of Slavery, 1810-1860 (review essay: Tushnet, *American Law of Slavery*)," *Yale Law Journal*, 91, 5 (1982), pp. 1034-47.

1291. Watson, Alan. (Correspondence, Tushnet, *American Law of Slavery*), *Cardozo Law Review*, 7, 2 (1986), pp. 641-44.

1292. Watson, Harry L. "Slavery and Development in a Dual Economy: The South and the Market Revolution," in Melvyn Stokes and Stephen Conway, eds., *The Market Revolution in America: Social, Political, and Religious Expressions, 1800-1880* (Charlottesville: University Press of Virginia, 1996), pp. 43-73.

1293. Weaver, John B. "The Agony of Defeat: Calvin H. Wiley and the Proslavery Argument," in Randall M. Miller and John R. McKivigan, eds., *The Moment of Decision: Biographical Essays on American Character and Regional Identity* (Westport CT: Greenwood Press, 1994), pp. 55-73.

1294. Weiner, Marli F. "Mistresses, Morality, and the Dilemmas of Slaveholding: The Ideology and Behavior of Elite Antebellum Women," in Morton, ed., *Discovering the Women in Slavery*, pp. 278-98.

1295. White, Dana F. "Two Perspectives on the Cotton Kingdom: 'Yeoman' and 'Porte Crayon'," in Judy L. Larson, with Cynthia Payne, eds., *Graphic Arts and the South: Proceedings of the 1990 North American Print Conference* (Fayetteville: University of Arkansas Press, 1993), pp. 101-27.

1296. White, Deborah Gray. "Female Slaves: Sex Roles and Status in the Antebellum Plantation South."

Reprinted in Harris, ed., *Society and Culture in the Slave South*, pp. 225-43; also in Clinton, ed., *Half Sisters of History*, pp. 56-75.

1297. White, Deborah Gray. "Female Slaves in the Plantation South," in Campbell, with Rice, eds., *Before Freedom Came*, pp. 101-22.

1298. White, Graham. "Inventing the Past? The Remarkable Story of an African King in Charleston," *Australian Journal of American Studies*, 12, 4 (1993), pp. 1-14.

1299. Whitten, David O., ed. "Eli Whitney's Cotton Gin, 1793-1933: A Symposium," special issue of *Agricultural History*, 68, 2 (1994).

For contents see Atkins, Bailey, Goldfarb, Olliff, Scott, and Soltow.

1300. Whitney, Lisa. "In the Shadow of Uncle Tom's Cabin: Stowe's Vision of Slavery from the Great Dismal Swamp," *New England Historical Quarterly*, 66, 4 (1993), pp. 552-69.

1301. Wiethoff, William E. *A Peculiar Humanism: The Judicial Advocacy of Slavery in High Courts of the Old South, 1820-1850*. Athens: University of Georgia Press, 1996. (Studies in the Legal History of the South)

1302. Wilcox, Nathaniel T. "The Overseer Problem: A New Data Set and Method," in Fogel, Galantine, and Manning, eds., *Evidence and Methods (Without Consent or Contract)*, pp. 84-109.

1303. Wilentz, Sean. "Slavery, Antislavery, and Jacksonian Democracy," in Melvyn Stokes and Stephen Conway, eds., *The Market Revolution in America: Social, Political, and Religious Expressions, 1800-1880* (Charlottesville: University Press of Virginia, 1996), pp. 202-23.

1304. Wilkins, J. Steven. *Southern Slavery, As it Was*. Moscow ID: Canon Press, 1996.

1305. Willis, William S. "Divide and Rule: Red, White, and Black in the Southeast," *Journal of Negro History*, 48, 3 (1963), pp. 157-76.

1306. Willis-Dorsey, Adrienne Courtney. "Authorial Intention and the Slave Narrative" (MA thesis, University of Maryland at College Park, 1994).

1307. Wilson, Carol. "A Monster in Human Shape: The Black Kidnapper in Antebellum America" (Unpublished paper, American Historical Association, San Francisco, 6-9 Jan. 1994).

1308. Wilson, Carol. "'The Thought of Slavery is Death to a Free Man': Abolitionists' Response to the Kidnapping of Free Blacks," *Mid-America*, 74, 2 (1992), pp. 105-24.

1309. Winter, Kari J. *Subjects of Slavery, Agents of Change: Women and Power in Gothic Novels and Slave Narratives, 1790-1865*. Athens: University of Georgia Press, 1992.

1310. Winter Wertheim, Frederick. "Slavery and the Fellow Servant Rule: An Antebellum Dilemma," *New York University Law Review*, 61, 6 (1986), pp. 1112-48.

1311. Wish, Harvey. "Aristotle, Plato and the Mason-Dixon Line," in Horowitz, ed., *Race, Class and Gender in Nineteenth-Century Culture*, pp. 77-89.

1312. Wood, Betty C. "White Women, Black Slaves and the Law in Early National Georgia: The Sunbury Petition of 1791," *Historical Journal*, 35, 3 (1992), pp. 611-22.

1313. Wood, Betty C. *Women's Work, Men's Work: The Informal Slave Economies of Lowcountry Georgia*. Athens: University of Georgia Press, 1995.

1314. Wright, Gavin. "What was Slavery?" *Social Concept*, 6, 1 (1991), pp. 29-51.

1315. Wright, Richard. "Ambivalent Bastions of Slavery: The Peculiar Institution on College Campuses in Antebellum Georgia," *Georgia Historical Quarterly*, 79, 3 (1996), pp. 467-85.

1316. Wyatt-Brown, Bertram. "The Mask of Obedience: Male Slave Psychology in the Old South".

Reprinted (from *Southern Honor*) in Harris, ed., *Society and Culture in the Slave South*, pp. 128-61.

1317. Yeates, Marian. "Domesticating Slavery: Patterns of Cultural Rationalization in the Antebellum South, 1820-1860" (PhD diss., Indiana University, 1996).

1318. Yee, Shirley J. *Black Women Abolitionists: A Study in Activism, 1828-1860*. Knoxville: University of Tennessee Press, 1992.

1319. Young, Jeffrey R. "Ideology and Death on a Savannah River Rice Plantation, 1833-1867: Paternalism amidst 'a Good Supply of Disease and Pain'," *Journal of Southern History*, 59, 4 (1993), pp. 673-706.

1320. Young, Mary. *"All My Trials, Lord": Selections from Women's Slave Narratives*. New York: F. Watts, 1995. (The African-American Experience)

1321. Young, Mary, and Gerald Horne, eds. *Testaments of Courage: Selections from Men's Slave Narratives*. New York: Franklin Watts, 1995.

> Includes Louis Asa-Asa, 1831; Moses Roper, 1837; Lewis Williamson, 1841; Frederick Douglass, 1845; William Wells Brown, 1847; Henry Bibb, 1849; Henry Box Brown, 1851; Josiah Henson, 1851; James Smith, 1852; "A short and true story of a fugitive," 1855; Solomon Northrup, 1853; William and Ellen Craft, 1860; Rev. Noah Davis, 1859; Nat Love, 1907; the oral accounts of ex-slaves, 1938.

1322. Ziev, Kimberly Anne. "'Chained Witnesses': The Response of Southern Plantation Women to Emancipation" (AB Honors thesis, Harvard University, 1993).

6. Ante-Bellum Upper South

1323. Andrews, Susan C., and Amy L. Young. "Plantations on the Periphery: Modeling a New Approach for the Upland South" (Unpublished paper, Annual Meeting of the Society for Historical Archaeology, Kingston, Jamaica, January 1992).

1324. Arroyo, Elizabeth Fortson. "Poor Whites, Slaves, and Free Blacks in Tennessee, 1796-1861," *Tennessee Historical Quarterly*, 55, 1 (1996), pp. 56-65.

1325. Baker, Steve. "Free Blacks in Antebellum Madison County," *Tennessee Historical Quarterly*, 52, 1 (1993), pp. 56-63.

1326. Barnett, Todd Harold. "The Evolution of 'North' and 'South': Settlement and Slavery on America's Sectional Border, 1650-1810" (PhD diss., University of Pennsylvania, 1993).

1327. Betterley, Richard D. "St. John's Episcopal Churchyard: Material Culture and Antebellum Class Distinction," *Tennessee Historical Quarterly*, 53, 2 (1994), pp. 88-99.

1328. Breitburg, Emanuel, and Larry McKee. "Exploring Dietary Diversity Within Archaeological Communities: Some Tennessee Examples" (Unpublished paper, Annual Meeting of the Society for Historical Archaeology, Kingston, Jamaica, January 1992).

1329. Burckin, Alexander I. "A 'Spirit of Perseverance': Free African-Americans in Late Antebellum Louisville," *Filson Club History Quarterly*, 70, 1 (1996), pp. 61-81.

1330. Cole, Stephanie. "Domesticity and the Decline of Slavery: Household Economy in the Urban Upper South, 1800-1850" (Unpublished paper, Annual Meeting of the Southern Historical Association, Atlanta, 1992).

1331. Corre, Jacob I. "Thinking Property at Memphis: An Application of Watson," *Chicago-Kent Law Review*, 68, 3 (Symposium on the Law of Slavery) (1993), pp. 1373-87.

> Response to articles by Alan Watson in this issue, pp. 1343 and 1355-71.

1332. Deblack, Thomas Alfred. "A Garden in the Wilderness: The Johnsons and the Making of Lakeport Plantation, 1831-1876" (PhD diss., University of Arkansas, 1995).

1333. Eslinger, Ellen. "The Shape of Slavery on the Kentucky Frontier, 1775-1800," *Register of the Kentucky Historical Society*, 92, 1 (1994), pp. 1-23.

1334. Finley, Randy. *From Slavery to Uncertain Freedom: The Freedmen's Bureau in Arkansas, 1865-1869*. Fayetteville: University of Arkansas Press, 1996.

1335. Higgins, Billy D. "The Origins and Fate of the Marion County Free Black Community," *Arkansas Historical Quarterly*, 54, 4 (1995), pp. 427-43.

1336. Hoebing, Phil. "'Fr. Gus': The Slave Priest from Ralls County, Missouri," *Missouri Folklore Society Journal*, 15-16 (1993-94), pp. 51-62.

1337. Hurt, R. Douglas. *Agriculture and Slavery in Missouri's Little Dixie*. Columbia: University of Missouri Press, 1992.

1338. Hurt, R. Douglas. "Planters and Slavery in Little Dixie," *Missouri Historical Review*, 88, 4 (1994), pp. 397-415.

1339. Inscoe, John C. "The Civil War's Empowerment of an Appalachian Woman: The 1864 Slave Purchases of Mary Bell," in Morton, ed., *Discovering the Women in Slavery*, pp. 61-81.

1340. Inscoe, John C. "Mountain Masters as Confederate Opportunists: The Profitability of Slavery in Western North Carolina, 1861-65," *Slavery and Abolition*, 16, 1 (1995), pp. 85-100.

1341. Johnson, Celeste Stanton. "Searching for the Roots, Grafting the Branches: The Saulsbury Family of Kentucky, a Black History of Roots Lost in Slavery" (MA thesis, California State University, 1992).

1342. Lovell, Linda Jeanne. "African-American Narratives from Arkansas: A Study from the 1936-1938 Federal Writers' Project 'A Folk History of Slavery in the United States'" (PhD diss., University of Arkansas, 1991).

1343. Lucas, Marion B. *A History of Blacks in Kentucky: Volume 1, From Slavery to Segregation, 1760-1891*. Frankfort: Kentucky Historical Society, 1992.

1344. Lucas, Marion B. "Kentucky Blacks: The Transition from Slavery to Freedom," *Register of the Kentucky Historical Society*, 91, 3 (1993), pp. 403-19.

1345. Lucas, Marion B. "Slave Nonimportation Law," in John E. Kleber, ed., *The Kentucky Encyclopedia* (Lexington: University Press of Kentucky, 1992), pp. 826-27.

1346. McKelway, Henry St. Clair. "Slaves and Masters in the Upland South: Investigations at the Mabry Site" (PhD diss., University of Tennessee, 1994).

1347. Medford, Edna Greene. "Unfree Labor in an Antebellum Mixed Farming Community," *Slavery and Abolition*, 14, 2 (1993), pp. 35-47.

1348. Moneyhon, Carl H. "From Slave to Free Labor: The Federal Plantation Experiment in Arkansas," *Arkansas Historical Quarterly*, 53, 2 (1994), pp. 137-60.

1349. *Moore, George Ellis. "Slavery as a Factor in the Formation of West Virginia" (MA thesis, West Virginia University, 1947).

1350. Murphy, James B. "Slaveholding in Appalachia: A Challenge to the Egalitarian Tradition," *Southern Studies*, 3, 1 (1992), pp. 17-33.

1351. Patrick, Jeff L. "Nothing but Slaves: The Second Kentucky Volunteer Infantry and the Spanish-American War," *Register of the Kentucky Historical Society*, 89, 3 (1991), pp. 287-99.

1352. Roberts, Ida M. Corley. *Rising Above It All: A Tribute to the Rowan Slaves of Federal Hill*. Edited by William Strode. Louisville: Harmony House Publishers, 1994.

1353. Rollins, Richard. "Servants and Soldiers: Tennessee's Black Southerners in Gray," *Journal of Confederate History*, 11 (1994), pp. 75-93.

1354. Shearer, Gary W., ed. *The Civil War and Slavery in Missouri: A Bibliographic Guide to Secondary Sources and Selected Primary Sources*. Angwin CA: n.p., 1995.

1355. Tallant, Harold D., Jr. "Slavery," in John E. Kleber, ed., *The Kentucky Encyclopedia* (Lexington: University Press of Kentucky, 1992), pp. 827-29.

1356. Thomas, Brian William. "Community Among Enslaved African Americans on the Hermitage Plantation, 1820-1850" (PhD diss., State University of New York at Binghamton, 1995).

1357. Walker, Juliet E. [K.] "The Legal Status of Free Blacks in Early Kentucky, 1792-1825" *Filson Club History Quarterly*, 57, 4 (1983), pp. 382-95.

Reprinted in Finkelman, ed., *Race, Law and American History*, vol. 2 (*Race and Law Before Emancipation*), pp. 530-43.

1358. Young, Amy Lambeck. "Risk and Material Conditions of African-American Slaves at Locust Grove: An Archaeological Perspective" (PhD diss., University of Tennessee, 1995).

7. Louisiana

1359. Baade, Hans W. "The Bifurcated Romanist Tradition of Slavery in Louisiana," *Tulane Law Review*, 70, 5 (1996), pp. 1481-99.

1360. Bankole, Katherine Olukemi. "An Afrocentric Analysis of Enslavement and Medicine in the

Southeastern Parishes of Antebellum Louisiana" (PhD diss., Temple University, 1996).

1361. Brasseaux, Carl A. "Creoles of Color in Louisiana's Bayou Country, 1766-1877," in Dormon, ed. *Creoles of Color of the Gulf South*, pp. 67-86.

1362. Brasseaux, Carl A., and Glenn R. Conrad, eds. *The Road to Louisiana: The Saint-Domingue Refugees 1792-1809*. Lafayette LA: Center for Louisiana Studies, University of Southwestern Louisiana, 1992.

For contents see Debien, Debien and Le Gardeur, Fiehrer, and Lachance.

1363. Butler, Rita Babin. *Ascension Parish, Louisiana, 1850 Census, Annotated, and Slave Schedule*. Gonzales [LA?]: R. B. Butler, 1992.

1364. Caron, Peter. "African Ethnicity and Its Implications for the Study of Colonial Louisiana" (Unpublished paper, Louisiana Historical Association, annual meeting, 1995).

1365. Debien, Gabriel, and René de Gardeur. "The Saint-Domingue Refugees in Louisiana, 1792-1804 (trans. David Cheramie)," in Brasseaux and Conrad, eds., *Road to Louisiana*, pp. 113-243.

1366. Din, Gilbert C. "Carondelet, the Cabildo, and Slaves: Louisiana in 1795," *Louisiana History*, 37, 1 (1996), pp. 5-28.

1367. Ellison, Mary. "African-American Music and Muskets in Civil War New Orleans," *Louisiana History*, 35, 3 (1994), pp. 285-319.

1368. Enger, Allen C. "Valid but Not Enforceable: Decrees Issued by the Supreme Court of Louisiana Involving Contracts for Slaves" (MA thesis, University of New Orleans, 1996).

1369. Fiehrer, Thomas. "From La Tortue to La Louisiane: An Unfathomed Legacy," in Brasseaux and Conrad, eds., *Road to Louisiana*, pp. 1-30.

1370. Fischer, Roger A. "Racial Segregation in Ante Bellum New Orleans," *American Historical Review*, 74, 3 (1969), pp. 926-37.

Reprinted in Finkelman, ed., *Race, Law and American History*, vol. 2 (*Race and Law Before Emancipation*), pp. 184-95.

1371. Fourtner, Tyge W. "French Slavery in the Mississippi Valley" (MA thesis, Southern Illinois University at Carbondale, 1996).

1372. Gould, [L.] Virginia Meacham. "'If I Can't Have My Rights, I Can Have My Pleasures, and if They Won't Give Me Wages, I Can Take Them': Gender and Slave Labor in Antebellum New Orleans," in Morton, ed., *Discovering the Women in Slavery*, pp. 179-201.

1373. Gould, [Lois] Virginia Meacham. "In Full Enjoyment of their Liberty: The Free Women of Color of the Gulf Ports of New Orleans, Mobile, and Pensacola, 1769-1860" (PhD diss., Emory University, 1991).

1374. Gould, L. Virginia [Meacham]. "Urban Slavery - Urban Freedom: The Manumission of Jacqueline Lemelle," in Gaspar and Hine, eds., *More than Chattel*, pp. 298-314.

1375. Hall, Gwendolyn Midlo. "The Formation of Afro-Creole Culture," in Arnold R. Hirsch and Joseph Logsdon, eds., *Creole New Orleans: Race and Americanization* (Baton Rouge: Louisiana State University Press, 1992), pp. 58-87.

1376. Hanger, Kimberly S. "Conflicting Loyalties: The French Revolution and Free People of Color in Spanish New Orleans," *Louisiana History*, 34, 1 (1993), pp. 5-34.

1377. Hanger, Kimberly S. "'The Fortunes of Women in America': Spanish New Orleans's Free Women of African Descent and Their Relations with Slave Women," in Morton, ed., *Discovering the Women in Slavery*, pp. 153-78.

1378. Hanger, Kimberly S. "Origins of New Orleans's Free Creoles of Color," in Dormon, ed. *Creoles of Color of the Gulf South*, pp. 1-27.

1379. Hanger, Kimberly S. "Patronage, Property and Persistence: The Emergence of a Free Black Elite in Spanish New Orleans," in Landers, ed., "Against the Odds", pp. 44-64.

1380. Hanger, Kimberly S. "Personas de varias clases y colores: Free People of Color in Spanish New Orleans, 1769-1803" (PhD diss., University of Florida, 1991).

1381. Head, Wanda Volentine. *Bienville Parish, Louisiana 1850 Census with Mortality Schedule and Slave Holders*. Shreveport LA: J & W Enterprises, 1994.

1382. Hirsch, Arnold R., and Joseph Logsdon. "Introduction [to section on Franco-Africans and African-Americans]," in Hirsch and Logsdon, eds., *Creole New Orleans: Race and Americanization* (Baton Rouge: Louisiana State University Press, 1992), pp. 189-200.

1383. Ingersoll, Thomas N. "Slave Codes and Judicial Practice in New Orleans, 1718-1807," *Law and History Review*, 13, 1 (1995), pp. 63-110.

1384. Ingersoll, Thomas N. "The Slave Trade and Ethnic Diversity of Louisiana's Slave Community," *Louisiana History*, 37, 2 (1996), pp. 133-61.

1385. Johnson, Walter. "Masters and Slaves in the Market: Slavery and the New Orleans Trade, 1804-1864" (Unpublished paper, American Historical Association, Chicago, 5-8 Jan. 1995).

1386. Kerr, Derek N. *Petty Felony, Slave Defiance, and Frontier Villainy: Crime and Criminal Justice in Spanish Louisiana, 1770-1803*. New York: Garland, 1993.

1387. Kilbourne, Richard H. *Debt, Investment, Slaves: Credit Relations in East Feliciana Parish, Louisiana, 1825-1885*. Foreword by Gavin Wright. University AL: University of Alabama Press, 1995.

1388. King, Wilma. "The Mistress and Her Maids: White and Black Women in a Louisiana Household, 1858-1868," in Morton, ed., *Discovering the Women in Slavery*, pp. 82-106.

1389. Kotlikoff, Laurence J. "Quantitative Description of the New Orleans Slave Market, 1804 to 1862," in Fogel and Engerman, eds., *Markets and Production: Technical Papers*, vol. 1 (*Without Consent or Contract*), pp. 31-53.

With material from "The Structure of Slave Prices in New Orleans".

1390. Kotlikoff, Laurence J., and Anton J. Rupert. "The Manumission of Slaves in New Orleans, 1827-1846".

Reprinted in Fogel and Engerman, eds., *Conditions of Life and the Transition to Freedom: Technical Papers*, vol. 2 (*Without Consent or Contract*), pp. 606-13.

1391. Lachance, Paul. "The 1809 Immigration of Saint-Domingue Refugees to New Orleans: Reception, Integration, and Impact," in Brasseaux and Conrad, eds., *Road to Louisiana*, pp. 245-84.

1392. Lachance, Paul. "The Limits of Privilege: Where Free Persons of Colour Stood in the Hierarchy of Wealth in Antebellum New Orleans," in Landers, ed., "Against the Odds", pp. 65-84.

1393. Logsdon, Joseph, and Caryn Cossé Bell. "The Americanization of Black New Orleans, 1850-1900," in Arnold R. Hirsch and Joseph Logsdon, eds., *Creole New Orleans: Race and Americanization* (Baton Rouge: Louisiana State University Press, 1992), pp. 201-61.

1394. Malone, Ann Patton. *Sweet Chariot: Slave Family and Household Structure in Nineteenth-Century Louisiana*. Chapel Hill: University of North Carolina Press, 1992.

1395. Mancall, Peter C. "The Moral Economy of the Eighteenth-Century Backcountry (review essay: Usner, *Indians, Settlers, and Slaves*)," *Reviews in American History*, 20, 2 (1992), pp. 453-58.

1396. McDonald, Roderick A. "Independent Economic Production by Slaves on Antebellum Louisiana Sugar Plantations," in Berlin and Morgan, eds., *Cultivation and Culture*, pp. 273-99.

1397. Morazan, Ronald. "Carondelet and the Slave Ordinance of 1795" (Unpublished paper, Louisiana Historical Association, annual meeting, 1995).

1398. Ostendorf, Berndt. "Urban Creole Slavery and its Cultural Legacy: The Case of New Orleans," in Binder, ed., *Slavery in the Americas*, pp. 389-401.

1399. Rodriguez, Junius P. "Always 'En garde': The Effects of Slave Insurrection upon the Louisiana Mentality, 1811-1815," *Louisiana History*, 33, 4 (1992), pp. 399-416.

1400. Rodriguez, Junius P[eter, Jr]."Ripe for Revolt: Louisiana and the Tradition of Slave Insurrection, 1803-1865" (PhD diss., Auburn University, 1992).

1401. Schafer, Judith K[elleher]. "'Details are of a Most Revolting Character': Cruelty to Slaves as Seen in Appeals to the Supreme Court of Louisiana,"

Chicago-Kent Law Review, 68, 3 (Symposium on the Law of Slavery) (1993), pp. 1283-311.

1402. Schafer, Judith Kelleher. "'Guaranteed Against the Vices and Maladies Proscribed by Law': Consumer Protection, the Law of Slave Sales, and the Supreme Court in Antebellum Louisiana," *American Journal of Legal History*, 31, 4 (1987), pp. 306-21.

1403. Schafer, Judith K[elleher]. "Sexual Cruelty to Slaves: The Unreported Case of Humphreys v. Utz (Louisiana)," *Chicago-Kent Law Review*, 68, 3 (Symposium on the Law of Slavery) (1993), pp. 1313-40.

1404. Schafer, Judith Kelleher. *Slavery, the Civil Law, and the Supreme Court of Louisiana*. Baton Rouge: Louisiana State University Press, 1994.

1405. Thompson, Thomas Marshall. "National Newspaper and Legislative Reactions to Louisiana's Deslondes Slave Revolt of 1811," *Louisiana History*, 33, 1 (1992), pp. 5-29.

1406. Thrasher, Albert. *On to New Orleans! Louisiana's Heroic 1811 Slave Revolt.* 2nd ed. New Orleans: Cypress Press, 1996.

1407. Usner, Daniel H., Jr. "'A Death Preferable to Slavery': French-Natchez Relations in Colonial Louisiana" (Unpublished paper, American Historical Association, Washington DC, 27-30 Dec. 1992).

1408. Usner, Daniel H., Jr. "Slavery: The French Colonies," in *Encyclopedia of the North American Colonies*, vol. 2, pp. 89-91.

1409. Whitten, David O. *Andrew Durnford: A Black Sugar Planter in the Antebellum South*. New Brunswick: Rutgers University Press, 1995.

1410. Wiethoff, William E. "The Logic and Rhetoric of Slavery in Early Louisiana Civil Law Reports," *The Legal Studies Forum*, 12, 4 (1988), pp. 441-57.

1411. Wilkie, Laurie A. "'Never Leave Me Alone': An Archaeological Study of African American ethnicity, Race Relations and Community at Oakley Plantation" (PhD diss., University of California - Los Angeles, 1994).

8. Texas[2]

1412. Allison, Randal Scott. "A Dialogue Betweeen Material Remains, Historical Documents, and Oral History: Allen Farm and Rogers Plantation, a Case Study" (PhD diss., Texas A&M University, 1996).

1413. Beeth, Howard, and Cary D. Wintz. "Slavery and Freedom: Blacks in Nineteenth-Century Houston: Introduction," in idem, eds., Black Dixie: Afro-Texan History and Culture in Houston (College Station: Texas A&M Press, 1992), pp. 13-31.

1414. Braswell, Henry. "Laney's Freedom Paper (1845 Suit by Texas Slave for her Freedom)," *Texas Bar Journal*, 5, 4 (no. 11) (1991), pp. 1197(1).

1415. Brown, Kenneth L. "Material Culture and Community Structure: The Slave and Tenant Community at Levi Jordan's Plantation, 1848-1892," in Hudson, Jr., ed., *Working Toward Freedom*, pp. 95-118.

1416. Brown, Kenneth L. "An Overview of History and Archaeology at the Levi Jordan Plantation, Brazoria County, Texas" (Unpublished paper, Annual Meeting of the Society for Historical Archaeology, Kingston, Jamaica, January 1992).

1417. Brown, Kenneth L., and Doreen C. Cooper. "Structural Continuity in an African-American Slave and Tenant Community," *Historical Archaeology*, 24, 4 (1990), pp. 7-19.

1418. Cheatham, Belzora. *Slaves and Slave Owners of Bowie County, Texas, in 1850: 1850 Bowie County Slave Census with Information from the 1850 Free Census*. [Chicago]: B. Cheatham, 1996.

1419. Dismukes, Diane. "Protein in the Slave/Tenant Farmer Diet" (Unpublished paper, Annual Meeting of the Society for Historical Archaeology, Kingston, Jamaica, January 1992).

1420. Haygood, Tamara Miner. "Use and Distribution of Slave Labor in Harris County, Texas, 1836-60," in Howard Beeth and Cary D. Wintz, eds., *Black Dixie: Afro-Texan History and Culture in Houston* (College Station: Texas A&M Press, 1992), pp. 32-53.

[2] Republic, and under United States jurisdiction; for Spanish and Mexican eras, see Mexico (Section III.2).

1421. Jacobson, Andrew T. "Fugitive Slaves in Texas, 1836-1865" (MA thesis, University of Texas - Austin, 1991).

1422. Krawczynski, Keith. "The Agricultural Labor of Black Texans as Slaves and as Freedmen" (MA thesis, Baylor University, 1989).

1423. Kuffner, Cornelia. "Texas-Germans' Attitudes Toward Slavery: Biedermeier Sentiments and Class-Consciousness in Austin, Colorado and Fayette Counties" (MA thesis, University of Houston, 1994).

1424. Marten, James. "'What is to Become of the Negro?': White Reaction to Emancipation in Texas," *Mid-America: An Historical Review*, 73, 2 (1991), pp. 115-33.

1425. Miller, Laura C. "Status and Ceramics: An Archaeological Study of the Slave and Tenant Quarters of the Levi Jordan Plantation in Brazoria County, Texas" (BS honors thesis, Anthropology, University of Houston, 1994).

1426. Parrish, Thomas Michael. "'This Species of Slave Labor': The Convict Lease System in Texas, 1871-1914" (MA thesis, Baylor University, 1976).

1427. Prather, Patricia Smith, and Jane Clements Monday. *From Slave to Statesman: The Legacy of Joshua Houston, Servant to Sam Houston*. Denton TX: University of North Texas Press, 1995.

1428. Prince, Robert. *A History of Dallas: From a Different Perspective*. Austin: Nortex Press, 1993.

1429. Reynolds, Donald R. "Reluctant Martyr: Anthony Bewley and the Texas Slave Insurrection Panic of 1860," *Southwestern Historical Quarterly*, 96, 3 (1993), pp. 345-61.

1430. *Rozek, Barbara. "Galveston Slavery," *Houston Review*, 15, 2 (1993), pp. 67-101.

1431. Smith, Letha B. Griffin. *Blood's Thicker than Prejudice: A Story of Slavery in Texas*. Winnsboro TX: BAC Publications, 1996.

1432. Telbord, Margaret Joan Agnew. "Slave Resistance in Texas" (MA thesis, Southern Methodist University, 1975).

1433. Temple, David P. "Transacting on the Half Shell: The Testing of African Models of Exchange at the Levi Jordan Plantation" (Unpublished paper, Annual Meeting of the Society for Historical Archaeology, Kingston, Jamaica, January 1992).

1434. Vlach, John Michael. "Black Craft Traditions in Texas: An Interpretation of Nineteenth-Century Skills," in idem, *By the Work of Their Hands: Studies in Afro-American Folklife* (Charlottesville: University Press of Virginia. 1991), pp. 73-104.

1435. Winegarten, Ruthe. *Black Texas Women: A Sourcebook: Documents, Biographies, Time Line*. Austin: University of Texas Press, 1996.

9. Florida

1436. Baptist, Edward E. "The Migration of Planters to Antebellum Florida: Kinship and Power," *Journal of Southern History*, 62, 1 (1996), pp. 527-54.

1437. Brown, Canter Jr. "Race Relations in Territorial Florida," *Florida Historical Quarterly*, 73, 3 (1995), pp. 287-307.

1438. *Cantrell, Brent. "First Generation Africans in South Florida" (research in progress).

1439. Colburn, David R. "Introduction," to Colburn and Landers, eds., *African-American Heritage of Florida*, pp. 1-16.

1440. Colburn, David R., and Jane L. Landers, eds. *The African-American Heritage of Florida*. Gainesville: University Press of Florida, 1995.

For contents see Colburn, Hall, Klos, Landers, Rivers, and Schafer (2).

1441. Hall, Robert L. "African Religious Retentions in Florida," in Colburn and Landers, eds., *African-American Heritage of Florida*, pp. 42-70.

1442. Klos, George. "Blacks and the Seminole Removal Debate," in Colburn and Landers, eds., *African-American Heritage of Florida*, pp. 128-56.

1443. Landers, Jane. "Africans in the Land of Ayllón: The Exploration and Settlement of the Southeast," in Jeannine Cook, ed., *Columbus and the Land of Ayllón: The Exploration and Settlement of the Southeast* (Darien GA: Lower Altamaha Historical Society, 1992), pp. 105-23.

1444. Landers, Jane [G]. "Acquisition and Loss on a Spanish Frontier: The Free Black Homesteaders of Florida, 1784-1821," in Landers, ed., "Against the Odds", pp. 85-101.

1445. *Landers, Jane. "Free and Slave" (research in progress).

1446. Landers, Jane. "Gracia Real de Santa Teresa de Mose: A Free Black Town in Spanish Colonial Florida," *American Historical Review*, 95, 1 (1990), pp. 9-30.

1447. Landers, Jane [G]. "Slave Resistance on the Southeastern Frontier: Fugitives, Maroons, and Bandetti in the Age of Revolutions," *El Escribano*, 32 (1995), pp. 12-24.

1448. Landers, Jane. "Spanish Sanctuary: Fugitives in Florida, 1687-1790," *Florida Historical Quarterly*, 62 (1984), pp. 296-313.

1449. Landers, Jane [L]. "Traditions of African American Freedom and Community in Spanish Colonial Florida," in Colburn and Landers, eds., *African-American Heritage of Florida*, pp. 17-41.

1450. *Landers, Jane, and David R. Colburn. "Race and Society in Florida: The African American Heritage from 1565 to the Present" (research in progress).

1451. *Landers, Jane, and Susan Parker. "Florida's Colonial Plantations" (research in progress).

1452. Mulroy, Kevin. "Ethnogenesis and Ethnohistory of the Seminole Maroons," *Journal of World History*, 4, 2 (1993), pp. 287-305.

1453. Mulroy, Kevin. *Freedom on the Border: The Seminole Maroons in Florida, the Indian Territory, Coahuila, and Texas*. Lubbock: Texas Tech University Press, 1993.

1454. Ogunleye, Tolagbe. "The Self-Emancipated Africans of Florida: Pan-African Nationalists in the 'New World'," *Journal of Black Studies*, 27, 1 (1996), pp. 24-38.

1455. Reitz, Elizabeth J. "Zooarchaeological Analysis of a Free African Community: Gracia Real de Santa Teresa de Mose," *Historical Archaeology*, 28, 1 (1994), pp. 23-40.

1456. Riordan, Patrick. "Finding Freedom in Florida: Native People, African Americans, and Colonists, 1670-1816," *Florida Historical Quarterly*, 75, 1 (1996), pp. 24-43.

1457. *Riordan, Patrick. "'Seminole Genesis' Europeans, Africans, and Native Peoples in the Lower South" (research in progress).

1458. *Rivers, Larry E. "The Peculiar Institution in Jackson County, Florida, 1824-1865" (research in progress).

1459. *Rivers, Larry E. "The Role of Female Slaves on the Antebellum Florida Plantation" (research in progress).

1460. *Rivers, Larry E. "The Role of the Florida Overseer, 1821-1865" (research in progress).

1461. *Rivers, Larry E. "A Statistical View of Florida Overseers and Drivers in Florida, 1821-1865" (research in progress).

1462. *Rivers, Larry E. "A Statistical View of Land and Slaveownership in Florida, 1821-1865" (research in progress).

1463. Rivers, Larry E. "A Troublesome Property: Master-Slave Relations in Florida, 1821-1865," in Colburn and Landers, eds., *African-American Heritage of Florida*, pp. 104-27.

1464. Schafer, Daniel L. *Anna Kingsley*. St. Augustine FL: St. Augustine Historical Society, 1994.

1465. Schafer, Daniel L. "'A Class of People Neither Freemen nor Slaves': From Spanish to American Race Relations in Florida, 1821-1861," *Journal of Social History*, 26, 3 (1993), pp. 587-609.

1466. Schafer, Daniel L. "Freedom was as Close as the River: African Americans and the Civil War in Northeast Florida," in Colburn and Landers, eds., *African-American Heritage of Florida*, pp. 157-84.

1467. Schafer, Daniel L. "'Yellow Silk Ferret Tied Round their Wrists': African Americans in British East Florida, 1763-1784," in Colburn and Landers, eds., *African-American Heritage of Florida*, pp. 71-103.

1468. TePaske, John J. "The Fugitive Slave: Intercolonial Rivalry and Spanish Slave Policy," in

Samuel Proctor, ed., *Eighteenth-Century Florida and its Borderlands* (Gainesville: University of Florida Press, 1975), pp. 1-12.

10. Other

1469. Baker, T. Lindsay, and Julie Philips Baker, eds. *The WPA Oklahoma Slave Narratives*. Norman: University of Oklahoma Press, 1996.

1470. Dykstra, Robert R. "White Men, Black Laws: Territorial Iowans and Civil Rights, 1838-1843," *Annals of Iowa*, 46, 6 (1982), pp. 403-40.

Reprinted in Finkelman, ed., *Race, Law and American History*, vol. 2 (*Race and Law Before Emancipation*), pp. 71-108.

1471. Erickson, Leonard. "Politics and Repeal of Ohio's Black Laws, 1837-1849," *Ohio History*, 82, 3-4 (1973), pp. 154-75.

Reprinted in Finkelman, ed., *Race, Law and American History*, vol. 2 (*Race and Law Before Emancipation*), pp. 110-31.

1472. Fishback, Mason McCloud. "Illinois Legislation on Slavery and Free Negroes, 1818-1865," *Transactions of the Illinois State Historical Society*, 9 (1904), pp. 414-32.

Reprinted in Finkelman, ed., *Race, Law and American History*, vol. 2 (*Race and Law Before Emancipation*), pp. 196-214.

1473. Fruehling, Byron D., and Robert H. Smith. "Subterranean Hideaways of the Underground Railroad in Ohio: An Architectural, Archaeological and Historical Critique of Local Traditions," *Ohio History*, 102, 2 (1993), pp. 98-117.

1474. Hardaway, Roger D. "The African American Frontier: Blacks in the Rocky Mountain West, 1535-1912" (PhD diss., University of North Dakota, 1994).

1475. Hudson, Lynn M. "A New Look, or 'I'm Not Mammy to Everybody in California': Mary Ellen Pleasant, a Black Entrepreneur," *Journal of the West*, 32, 3 (1993), pp. 35-40.

1476. McQuilkin, Carol Ann. "Journey of Faith: Mid-Nineteenth Century Migration of Mississippi Mormons and Slaves" (MA thesis, California State University, Fullerton, 1995).

1477. Middleton, Stephen. *The Black Laws in the Old Northwest: A Documentary History*. Westport CT: Greenwood Press, 1993. Foreword by Linda McMurry.

1478. Middleton, Stephen. "The Fugitive Slave Crisis in Cincinnati, 1850-1860: Resitance, Enforcement, and Black Refugees," *Journal of Negro History*, 72, 1-2 (1987), pp. 20-32.

1479. Mintz, John J., and Jerry Hilliard. "The Social and Political Implications of Slavery in the Ozark Pioneer Period" (Unpublished paper, Annual Meeting of the Society for Historical Archaeology, Kingston, Jamaica, January 1992).

1480. Pirtle, Carol. "*Andrew Borders* v. *William Hayes*: Indentured Servitude and the Underground Railroad in Illinois," *Illinois Historical Journal*, 89, 3 (1996), pp. 147-60.

1481. Robbins, Coy D. *Indiana Negro Registers, 1852-1865*. Bowie MD: Heritage Books, 1994.

1482. Rose, Morgan. "Path-Dependence in Emerging Institutional Structures: A Study of Slavery in Frontier Missouri" (MA thesis, University of Missouri - Columbia, 1996).

1483. Schmook, Rebecca. *Gallatin County, Illinois Slave Register, 1815-1839*. Harrisburg IL: R. Schmook, Rocky's Advanced Printing, 1994.

1484. SenGupta, Gunja. *For God and Mammon: Evangelicals and Entrepreneurs, Masters and Slaves in Territorial Kansas, 1854-1860*. Athens: University of Georgia Press, 1996.

1485. Steiner, Mark E., ed. "Abolitionists and Escaped Slaves in Jacksonville: Samuel Willard's 'My First Adventure with a Fugitive Slave: The Story of it and How it Failed'," *Illinois Historical Journal*, 89, 4 (1996), pp. 213-32.

1486. Thornbrough, Emma Lou. *The Negro in Indiana before 1900*. Bloomington: Indiana University Press, 1993. (reprint of 1957 edition, Indianapolis: Historical Press)

1487. Walker, Juliet E. "Legal Processes and Judicial Challenges: Black Land Ownership in Western Illinois," *Western Illinois Regional Studies*, 6, 2 (1983), pp. 23-48.

Reprinted in Finkelman, ed., *Race, Law and American History*, vol. 2 (*Race and Law Before Emancipation*), pp. 545-70.

11. Biographies and Autobiographies

1488. Adams, Virginia M., ed. *On the Altar of Freedom: A Black Soldier's* [Henry Gooding] *Civil War Letters from the Front*. Amherst: University of Massachusetts Press, 1991.

1489. Allison, Robert J., ed. *The Interesting Narrative of the Life of Olaudah Equiano, Written by Himself*. New York: St. Martin's Press, 1995.

1490. Anderson, Robert. *From Slavery to Affluence: Memoirs of Robert Anderson, Ex-Slave*. Steamboat Springs CO: [printed by Northwest Graphics], 1992.

1491. Andrews, William L. "The Changing Rhetoric of the Nineteenth-Century Slave Narrative of the United States," in Binder, ed., *Slavery in the Americas*, pp. 471-86.

1492. Andrews, William L., ed. *Up from Slavery [Booker T. Washington]: An Authoritative Text, Contexts, and Composition History, Criticism*. (2nd ed.) New York: Norton, 1995.

1493. Barker, Anthony J. "Frederick Douglass and Black Abolitionism," *Slavery and Abolition*, 14, 2 (1993), pp. 117-27.

1494. Blight, David W., ed. *Narrative of the Life of Frederick Douglass, An American Slave, Written by Himself*. Boston: St. Martin's Press, 1993.

1495. Boney, F. N[ash], Richard L. Hume, and Rafia Zafar, eds. *"God Made Man, Man Made the Slave": The Autobiography of George Teamoh*. Macon, Ga.: Mercer University Press, 1990.

1496. Brown, William Wells. "Narrative of William W. Brown, an American Slave" (Chapel Hill, NC: Academic Affairs Library, University of North Carolina at Chapel Hill, 1996).

Internet World Wide Web. URL: http://sunsite.unc.edu/docsouth/brown/brown.sgml

1497. Brown, William Wells. *The Travels of William Wells Brown: Including Narrative of William Wells Brown, A Fugitive Slave, and the American Fugitive in Europe: Sketches of Places and People Abroad*. Ed. Paul Jefferson. Edinburgh: Edinburgh University Press, 1991.

1498. Burnham, Michelle. "Loopholes of Resistance: Harriet Jacobs's Slave Narrative and the Critique of Agency in Foucault," *Arizona Quarterly*, 49, 2 (1993), pp. 53-73.

1499. Burton, Annie L. "Memories of Childhood's Slavery Days" (Chapel Hill, NC: Academic Affairs Library, University of North Carolina at Chapel Hill, 1996).

Internet World Wide Web. URL: http://sunsite.unc.edu/docsouth/burton/burton.sgml

1500. Byrne, William A. "The Hiring of Woodson, Slave Carpenter of Savannah," *Georgia Historical Quarterly*, 77, 2 (1993), pp. 245-63.

1501. Carretta, Vincent, ed. *Olaudah Equiano: The Interesting Narrative and Other Writings*. New York: Penguin Books, 1995.

1502. Coleman, Willie E., Jr. "A Study of African American Slave Narratives as a Source for a Contemporary, Constructive Black Theology" (PhD diss., Graduate Theological Union, 1993).

1503. Conteh-Morgan, John. "African Literature in the Age of Slavery: The Case of Olaudah Equiano" (Unpublished paper, UNESCO conference on "La route de l'esclave", Ouidah, Bénin, 1-5 Sept. 1994).

1504. Costanzo, Angelo, ed. *The Legacy of Frederick Douglass*. Shippensburg PA: Shippensburg University, 1995. (*Proteus, A Journal of Ideas*, 12, 1).

1505. Davis, David Brion. "Celia, A Slave (review essay: McLaurin, *Celia: A Slave*)," *New York Review of Books*, 39 (30 Jan. 1992), pp. 6-9.

1506. "Frederick Douglass, an American Life" (Hollywood CA: Distributed by Mike Craven Productions, 1996).

1 videocassette (31 min.)

1507. Douglass, Frederick. *Frederick Douglass, In His Own Words*. (Milton Meltzer, ed.) San Diego: Harcourt Brace, 1995.

1508. Douglass, Frederick. *Life and Times of Frederick Douglass*. New York: Gramercy Books, distributed by Outlet Book Co., 1993.

1509. [Douglass, Frederick]. *Life and Times of Frederick Douglass*. Foreword by John G. Hunt. New York: Random House, 1993.

1510. Douglass, Frederick. "Narrative of the Life of Frederick Douglass, an American Slave" (n.p.: Penguin Audio Books, 1995).

(2 sound cassettes, abridged)

1511. Douglass, Frederick. "Narrative of the Life of Frederick Douglass, an American Slave" ([Paramus N. J.]: Globe Fearon, 1995).

(2 sound cassettes: Pacemaker Classics on Tape)

For book, see Hill, ed., *Narrative of the Life of Frederick Douglass.*

1512. Douglass, Frederick. "Narrative of the Life of Frederick Douglass, an American Slave," in *CD Sourcebook of American History* (Provo UT: Compact University, 1995).

(1 compact disk)

1513. Foster, Frances Smith. "Autobiography after Emancipation: The Example of Elizabeth Keckley," in James Robert Payne, ed., *Multicultural Autobiography: American Lives* (Knoxville: University of Tennessee Press, 1992), pp. 32-63.

1514. Gordon, Grant. *From Slavery to Freedom: The Life of David George, Pioneer Black Baptist Minister*. Hantsport NS: Published by Lancelot Press for Acadia Divinity College and the Baptist Historical Committee of the United Baptist Convention of the Atlantic Provinces, 1992.

1515. Green, James. "The Publishing History of Olaudah Equiano's *Interesting Narrative*," *Slavery and Abolition*, 16, 2 (1995), pp. 362-75.

1516. Half Slave, Half Free [Solomon Northup]. SVS/Triumph Home Video, 1992. (Videocassette release of the television program, c. 1984, 118 min.).

1517. Hill, Prescott, ed. *Narrative of the Life of Frederick Douglass, an American Slave*. Paramus NJ: Globe Fearon, 1995.

For companion sound cassettes, see Douglass, "Narrative of the Life".

1518. Jackson, John Andrew. "The Experience of a Slave in South Carolina" (Chapel Hill NC: Academic Affairs Library, University of North Carolina at Chapel Hill, 1996).

*Internet World Wide Web. URL: http://sunsite.unc.edu/docsouth/jackson/jackson.html

1519. Johnson, Isaac. *Slavery Days in Old Kentucky*. By a former slave, edited by Cornell Reinhart. Canton NY: Friends of the Owen D. Young Library, Saint Lawrence University, 1994.

1520. Knott, Robanna Sumrell. "Harriet Jacobs: The Edenton Biography" (PhD diss., University of North Carolina at Chapel Hill, 1994).

1521. Lampe, Gregory Paul. "Frederick Douglass: Freedom's Voice, 1818-1845" (PhD diss., The University of Wisconsin-Madison, 1995).

1521. Leslie, Kent Anderson. "Amanda America Dickson: An Elite Mulatto Lady in Nineteenth-Century Georgia," in Virginia Bernhard, Betty Brandon, Elizabeth Fox-Genovese, and Theda Perdue, eds., *Southern Women: History and Identities* (Columbia: University of Missouri Press, 1992), pp. 87-108.

1522. Lewis, Earl. "The Social Geography of the Multipositional Self: McFeeley's Frederick Douglass," *Reviews in American History*, 20, 2 (1992), pp. 48-54.

1523. Libby, Jean, ed. *From Slavery to Salvation: The Autobiography of Rev. Thomas W. Henry of the A.M.E. Church*. Oxford: University Press of Mississippi, 1994.

1524. Mabee, Carleton. *Sojourner Truth: Slave, Prophet, Legend*. New York: New York University Press, 1995.

1525. McFeeley, William S. *Frederick Douglass*. New York: Norton, 1991.

1526. McLaurin, Melton A. "Divided We Stand: Echoes of the Racial Struggle in Antebellum America (review essay: Adams, ed., *On the Altar of Freedom*, and Drago, ed., *"Broke by the War"*)," *Reviews in American History*, 20, 2 (1992), pp. 501-04.

1527. Metzcher-Smith, Marilyn K. "The Ties that Bind: Harriet Jacobs's Portrayal of her Grandmother in Jacobs's '*Incidents in the Life of a Slave Girl*

Written by Herself" (MA thesis, Florida Atlantic University, 1995).

1528. Miller, Douglas T. *Frederick Douglass and the Fight for Freedom*. New York: Facts on File, 1993.

1529. Miller, Edward A., Jr. *Gullah Statesman: Robert Smalls from Slavery to Congress, 1839-1915*. Columbia: South Carolina University Press, 1994.

1530. Murphy, Geraldine. "Olaudah Equiano, Accidental Tourist," in Zimbardo and Montgomery, eds., "African-American Culture in the Eighteenth Century," pp. 551-68.

1531. O'Brien, William Patrick. "Hiram Young: Pioneering Black Wagonmaker for the Santa Fe Trade," *Gateway Heritage*, 14, 1 (1993), pp. 56-67.

1532. Painter, Nell Irvin. "Representing Truth: Sojourner Truth's Knowing and Becoming Known," *Journal of American History*, 81, 2 (1994), pp. 461-92.

1533. Parker, John P. *His Promised Land: the Autobiography of John P. Parker, Former Slave and Conductor on the Underground Railroad*. (Stuart Sprague, ed.) New York: Norton, 1996.

1534. Pickard, Kate E. R. *The Kidnapped and the Ransomed: The Narrative of Peter and Vina Still after Forty Years of Slavery*. Lincoln: University of Nebraska Press, 1995.

1535. Potkay, Adam. "Olaudah Equiano and the Art of Spiritual Autobiography," in Zimbardo and Montgomery, eds., "African-American Culture in the Eighteenth Century," pp. 677-92.

1536. Powell, Carolyn J. "In Remembrance of Mira: Reflections on the Death of a Slave Woman," in Morton, ed., *Discovering the Women in Slavery*, pp. 47-60.

1537. Ring, Betty J. "'Painting by Numbers': Figuring Frederick Douglass," in Plasa and Ring, eds., *Discourse of Slavery*, pp. 118-43.

1538. Saunders, Robert S. "John Archibald Campbell: A Biography" (PhD diss., Auburn University, 1994).

1539. Scott, Lesley Thompson. "The Role of the Engaging Narrator in Four Nineteenth-Century American Slave Narratives" (PhD diss., The University of Tulsa, 1995).

1540. Stowe, Harriet Beecher. "Sojourner Truth, the Libyan Sibyl" (Charlottesville, Va.: University of Virginia Library, 1994).

Machine-readable data prepared for the University of Virginia Library Electronic Text Center. Transcribed from: *The Atlantic Monthly: A Magazine of Literature, Art, and Politics*, 11, 66 (April 1863), pp. 473-481 (Boston: Ticknor and Fields, 1863).

1541. Thompson, Robert F., III. "The Strange Case of Paul D. Peacher, Twentieth-Century Slaveholder," *Arkansas Historical Quarterly*, 52, 4 (1993), pp. 426-51.

1542. Trendler, Gerald J. "A Bakhtinian Critical Analysis of Frederick Douglass's Narrative of The Life of Frederick Douglass: an American Slave, Written by Himself" (MA thesis, West Chester University, Pennsylvania, 1994).

1543. Tucker, Phillip Thomas. "John Horse: Forgotten African-American Leader of the Second Seminole War," *Journal of Negro History*, 77, 2 (1992), pp. 74-83.

1544. Voss, Frederick. *Majestic in His Wrath: A Pictorial Life of Frederick Douglass*. Washington DC: Smithsonian Institution Press for the National Portrait Gallery and the National Park Service, 1995.

1545. Washington, Booker T. "Up from Slavery" (Ashland OR: Blackstone Audio Books, 1995).

5 sound cassettes

1546. Zafar, Rafia, and Deborah Garfield, eds. *Harriet Jacobs and Incidents in the Life of a Slave Girl: New Critical Essays*. Cambridge: Cambridge University Press, 1996. (Cambridge Studies in American Literature and Culture)

12. Canada

1547. Anderson, Karen. *Chain Her by One Foot: The Subjugation of Native Women in Seventeenth-Century New France.* New York: Routledge, 1993.

1548. Bell, D. G. "Slavery and the Judges of Loyalist New Brunswick," *University of New Brunswick Law Journal*, 31 (1982), pp. 9-42.

1549. Brode, Patrick. "In the Matter of John Anderson: Canadian Courts and the Fugitive Slave," *Law Society Gazette*, 14, 1 (1980), pp. 92-97.

1550. Cahill, Barry. "Habeas Corpus and Slavery in Nova Scotia: R. v. Hecht ex parte Rachel, 1798," *University of New Brunswick Law Journal*, 44 (Annual 1995), pp. 179-209.

1551. Cahill, Barry. "Slavery and the Judges of Loyalist Nova Scotia," *University of New Brunswick Law Journal*, 43 (1994), pp. 73-135.

1552. Collison, Gary. "'Loyal and Dutiful Subjects of Her Gracious Majesty, Queen Victoria': Fugitive Slaves in Montreal, 1850-1866," *Québec Studies*, 19 (1994-95), pp. 59-70.

1553. Donovan, Kenneth. "Nominal List of Slaves and Their Owners in Ile Royale, 1713-1760," *Nova Scotia Historical Review*, 16, 1 (1996), pp. 151-62.MacDonald, Cheryl. "Mary Ann Shadd in Canada: Last Stop on the Underground Railroad, " *The Beaver*, 70, 1 (1990), pp. 32-38.

1554. Meindl, Dieter. "Canada and American Slavery: The Case of T. C. Haliburton," in Binder, ed., *Slavery in the Americas*, pp. 523-38.

1555. Stouffer, Allen P. *The Light of Nature and the Law of God: Antislavery in Ontario, 1833-1877.* Montreal: McGill-Queen's University Press, 1992.

1556. Trudel, Marcel. *Dictionnaire des esclaves et de leur propriétaires au Canada français.* Ville LaSalle, Québec: Éditions Hurtubise, 1990.

III. SPANISH MAINLAND[3]

1. General and Comparative

1557. "Africans in Spanish American Colonial Society (bibliographical essay)," in Leslie Bethell, ed., *Cambridge History of Latin America* (Cambridge: Cambridge University Press, 1984), vol. 2, pp. 848-53.

1558. Aguirre Beltrán, Gonzalo. *El negro esclavo en Nueva España: la formación colonial, la medicina popular y otros ensayos.* México: Fondo de Cultura Económica, 1994.

1559. Aponte-Ramos, Dolores T. "The Representation of Sub-Saharan Africans in Colonial Discourse, 1450-1618" (PhD diss., Northwestern University, 1992).

1560. Diaz, Rafael Antonio. "Historiografia de la esclavitud negra en América Latina: Temas y problemas generales," *América negra*, 8 (1994), pp. 11-32.

1561. Dressendörfer, Peter. "Mit Schwarzen im Himmel des 'Reinblütigen'? Sklaven und Kirche im spanischen Kolonialamerika," in Raddatz, ed., *Afrika in Amerika*, pp. 90-101.

1562. Eugenio, María Ángeles. "Encadenados a los 'topos': ordenamiento sobre esclavitud indígena," *Ibero-Amerikanisches Archiv*, 20, 3-4 (1994), pp. 247-78.

1563. Helminen, Juha Pekka. "Las Casas, los judíos, los moros y los negros," *Cuadernos hispanoamericanos*, no. 512 (1993), pp. 23-28.

1564. Kazadi wa Mukuna. "Resilience and Transformation in Varieties of African Musical Elements in Latin America" (Unpublished paper, UNESCO conference on "La route de l'esclave", Ouidah, Bénin, 1-5 Sept. 1994).

[3] The dominant organizing principle in sections of the bibliography on tropical America is the colonial power behind the masters: hence, works on Spanish enslavement of Native Americans occur in the same regional sub-sections as enslavement of Africans. See below Section X.6 for Amerindian mastery of slaves.

1565. König, Hans-Joachim. "The Código Negrero of 1789, its Background and its Reverberations," in Binder, ed., *Slavery in the Americas*, pp. 141-50.

1566. Mallo, Silvia C. "La libertad en el discurso del Estado, de amos y esclavos 1780-1830," *Revista de historia de America*, no. 112 (1991), pp. 121-46.

1567. Montiel, Edgar. "Los negros en el mundo andino," *Cuadernos americanos VI*, 6 (nueva época) (1992), pp. 70-85.

1568. Newland, Carlos, and María Jesús San Segundo. "Human Capital and Other Determinants of the Price Life Cycle of a Slave: Peru and La Plata in the Eighteenth Century," *Journal of Economic History*, 56, 3 (1996), pp. 694-701.

1569. Nippel, Wilfried. "Aristoteles und die Indios: 'Gerechter Krieg' und 'Sklaven von Natur' in der spanischen Diskussion des 16. Jahrhunderts," in Christof Dipper and Martin Vogt, eds., *Entdeckungen und frühe Kolonisation* (Darmstadt: Technische Hochschule, 1993), pp. 69-90.

1570. Palmer, Colin [A.] "From Africa to the Americas: Ethnicity in the Early Black Communities of the Americas," *Journal of World History*, 6, 2 (1995), pp. 223-36.

1571. Palmer, Colin A. "Slavery: Spanish America," in *Encyclopedia of Latin American History* (Barbara Tenenbaum, ed.) (New York: Charles Scribner's Sons, 1995), pp. 131-34.

1572. Paquette, Robert L. "Slave Revolts: Spanish America," in *Encyclopedia of Latin American History* (Barbara Tenenbaum, ed.) (New York: Charles Scribner's Sons, 1995), pp. 120-22.

1573. Pérez Fernandez, Isacio. *Fray Bartolome de las Casas, O.P.: de defensor de los indios a defensor de los negros*. Salamanca: Editorial San Esteban, 1995. (Monumenta historica iberoamericana de la Orden de Predicadores, v. 8)

1574. Sala-Molins, Louis. *L'Afrique aux Amériques: le Code Noir espagnol*. Paris: Presses Universitaires de France, 1992.

1575. Scott, Rebecca J. "Slavery: Abolition," in *Encyclopedia of Latin American History* (Barbara Tenenbaum, ed.) (New York: Charles Scribner's Sons, 1995), pp. 135-38.

1576. Yeager, Timothy J. "*Encomienda* or Slavery? The Spanish Crown's Choice of Labor Organization in Sixteenth-Century Spanish America," *Journal of Economic History*, 55, 4 (1995), pp. 842-59.

1577. Yeager, Timothy J. "An Explanation for the Interregional Pattern of Encomiendas and Indian Slavery in Spanish America, 1518 to 1550" (Unpublished paper, 1994).

1578. Zavala, Silvio. "Esclavitud y libertad en la Neuva España," *Estudios de historia social y económica de América* (Universidad de Alcalá, Alcalá de Henares), 6 (1993), pp. 9-10.

2. Mexico

1579. Aguirre Beltrán, Gonzalo. "Etiología de la esclavitud," *México agrario*, 6, 3 (1944), pp. 181-210.

1580. Aguirre Beltrán, Gonzalo. "La esclavitud en los obrajes novoespañoles," in Susana Glantz, ed., *La Heterodoxia recuperada (en torno a Ángel Palerm)* (México: Fondo de Cultura Económica, 1987), pp. 249-59.

1581. Bennett, Herman Lee. "Lovers, Family and Friends: The Formation of Afro-Mexico, 1580-1810" (PhD diss., Duke University, 1993).

1582. Brugge, David M. "Slavery: The Spanish Borderlands," in *Encyclopedia of the North American Colonies*, vol. 2, pp. 91-101.

1583. Calvo, Thomas. "Entre les exigences de l'économie et celles de la démographie: les esclaves de Don Francisco Rodríguez Ponce (Nouvelle-Galice, 1655)," in Alain Bréton, Jean-Pierre Berthe, and Sylvie Lecoin, eds., *Vingt études sur le Mexique et le Guatemala, réunies à la mémoire de Nicole Percheron* (Toulouse: Presses Universitaires du Mirail [avec le concours du Centre d'Études Mexicaines et Centraméricaines], 1991), pp. 243-52.

1584. Calvo, Thomas. "Les esclavages au Mexique: études de cas (XVIe et XVIIe siècles)," in Bresc, ed., *Figures de l'esclave*, pp. 215-45.

1585. Carroll, Patrick J. "Los mexicanos negros, e mestizaje y los fundamentos olvidados de la 'Raza Cósmica': una perspectiva regional," *Historia mexicana*, 44, 3 (1995), pp. 403-38.

1586. Castañón González, Guadalupe. "Asimilación e integración de los africanos en la Nueva España durante los siglos XVI y XVII" (Thesis, Maestría en historia, UNAM, México, 1990).

1587. Chávez Carbajal, María Guadalupe. "La gran negritud en Michoacán, época colonial," in Montiel, coord., *Presencia africana en México*, pp. 79-131.

1588. Chávez Carbajal, María Guadalupe. *Propietarios y esclavos negros en Valladolid de Michoacán, 1600-1650*. Morelia: Universidad Michoacana de San Nicolas de Hidalgo, Instituto de Investigaciones Historicas, 1994.

1589. Cortés Jácome, María Elena. "Los ardides de los amos: la manipulación y la interferencia en la vida conyugal de sus esclavos: siglos XVI-XVII," in *Del dicho al hecho: Transgresiones y pautas culturales en la Nueva España* (México: Instituto Nacional de Antropologia y Historia, Seminario de Historia de la Mentalidades, 1989), pp. 43-57.

1590. Cortés Jácome, María Elena. "El matrimonio y la familia negra en las legislaciones civil y eclesiástica coloniales: siglos XVI-XIX," in *El placer de pecar y el afán de normar* (México: INAH [Instituto Nacional de Antropología y Historia]/Joaquín Mortiz, 1988), pp. 217-48. (Seminario de Historia de las Mentalidades y Religión en México Colonial

1591. Cortés Jácome, María Elena. "Negros amancebados con indias, siglo XVI," in *Familia y sexualidad en Nueva España* (México: SEP/Fondo de Cultura Económica, 1982), pp. 285-93.

1592. García Rodriguez, Gloria. *La esclavitud desde la esclavitud: la visión de los siervos*. [México]: Centro de Investigación Cientifica "Ing. Jorge L. Tamayo", A.C., 1996.

1593. Gerhard, Peter. "A Black Conquistador in Mexico," in Davis, ed., *Slavery and Beyond*, pp. 1-10.

1594. Gomez Danés, Pedro. "Los negros en el Nuevo Reyno de León, siglos XVII y XVIII," in Montiel, coord., *Presencia africana en México*, pp. 199-258.

1595. Guevara Sanginés, María. "Participatión de los africanos en el desarrollo del Guanajuato colonial," in Montiel, coord., *Presencia africana en México*, pp. 133-98.

1596. Hall, Thomas D. "Bound Labor: The Spanish Borderlands," in *Encyclopedia of the North American Colonies*, vol. 2, pp. 35-44.

1597. Herrera Casasús, Ma. Luisa. "Raices africanas en la población de Tamaulipas," in Montiel, coord., *Presencia africana en México*, pp. 463-523.

1598. Hill, Richard. *Black Corps d'Elite: An African Slave Battalion of the Second Empire in Mexico, 1863-1867*. East Lansing: Michigan State University Press, 1993.

1599. Hoyo, Eugenio del. *Esclavitud y encomiendas de indios en el Nuevo Reino de León, siglos XVI y XVII*. Monterrey: Archivo General del Estado de Nuevo León, 1985.

1600. *Lara Tenorio, Blanca. *La esclavitud en Puebla y Tepeaca (1545-1630)*. México: INAH, Centro Regional de Puebla-Tlaxcala, 1976. (Cuadernos de los Centros, 130)

1601. Lavrin, Asunción. "Perfil histórico de la población negra, esclava y libre, en Guadalajara, 1635-1699," *Boletín del Archivo Histórico de Jalisco*, 6, 1 (1982), pp. 2-7.

1602. Lewis, Laura A. "Colonialism and Its Contradictions: Indians, Blacks and Social Power in Sixteenth and Seventeenth Century Mexico," *Journal of Historical Sociology*, 9, 4 (1996), pp. 410-41.

1603. Montiel, Luz María Martínez, coord. *Presencia africana en México*. México: Dirección General de Publicaciones, 1994.

For contents see Chávez Carbajal, Gomez Danés, Guevara Sanginés, Herrera Casasús, Paredes Martínez and Lara Tenorio, Redondo, Reyes G., and Torres.

1604. Moscoso, Francisco. "Encomendero y esclavista: Francisco Manuel de Lando," *Anuario de estudios americanos*, 49 (1992), pp. 119-42.

1605. *Naveda Chávez-Hita, Adriana. *Esclavos negros en las haciendas azucareras de Córdoba, Veracruz, 1690-1830.* Xalapá: Centro de Investigaciones Históricas, Universidad Veracruzana, 1987.

1606. Nelson, William Javier. "Africans in Mexico: The Colonial Period," *Southeastern Latin Americanist*, 39, 2 (1995), pp. 35-44.

1607. Ortiz Fernández, Fernando. *Los negros esclavos.* Havana: Editorial Ciencias Sociales, 1975.

1608. Palmer, Colin. "Afro-Mexican Culture and Consciousness During the Sixteenth and Seventeenth Centuries," in Harris, ed., *Global Dimensions of the African Diaspora* (2nd ed.), pp. 125-35.

1609. Paredes Martínez, Carlos, and Blanca Lara Tenorio. "La población negra en los valles centrales de Puebla: origenes y desarrollo hasta 1681," in Montiel, coord., *Presencia africana en México*, pp. 19-77.

1610. Powelson, Michael. "Slavery in Colonial Chiapas" (Unpublished paper, Southern Historical Association, Louisville KY, 9-12 Nov. 1994).

1611. Redondo, Brígido. "Negritud en Campeche: de la Conquista a nuestros dias," in Montiel, coord., *Presencia africana en México*, pp. 337-421.

1612. *Reyes García, Cayetano. "Los negros en la sociedad indígena de Cholula" (Unpublished paper, Tercer Congreso Nacional de ALADAA, Puebla 1987).

1613. Reyes García, Juan Carlos. "Negros y afromestizos en Colima, siglos XVI-XIX," in Montiel, coord., *Presencia africana en México*, pp. 259-335.

1614. Serrano López, Lilia. "Veracruz y el Caribe, siglo XVII," in Hoogbergen, ed., *Born out of Resistance*, pp. 98-103.

1615. Soriano Hernández, Silvia. "Aportes sobre el mestizaje de esclavos africanos en Chiapas colonial," *Cuadernos americanos*, nueva época, año VIII, 1 (no. 43) (1994), pp. 80-93.

1616. Torres, Juan Andrade. "Historia de la población negra en Tabasco," in Montiel, coord., *Presencia africana en México*, pp. 423-62.

1617. Valdés, Carlos Manuel, and Ildefonso Dávila. *Esclavos negros en Saltillo: siglos XVII a XIX.* Saltillo: Ayuntamiento de Saltillo/UCA, 1989.

1618. *Winfield C., Fernando. "La vida de los cimarrones en Veracruz," in *Nuestra Palabra* (supplement to *El Nacional*), 2, 11 (29 Nov. 1991), pp. (??).

3. Central America

1619. Bolland, O. Nigel. "Colonization and Slavery in Central America," in Lovejoy and Rogers, eds., *Unfree Labour in the Development of the Atlantic World*, pp. 11-25.

1620. Bryce-Laporte, Roy Simon, with Trevor Purcell. "A Lesser-Known Chapter of the African Diaspora: West Indians in Costa Rica, Central America," in Harris, ed., *Global Dimensions of the African Diaspora* (2nd ed.), pp. 137-57.

1621. Newson, Linda A. "Variaciones regionales en el impacto del dominio colonial español en las poblaciones indígenas de Honduras y Nicaragua," *Mesoamérica*, 13 (no. 24) (1992), pp. 297-312.

1622. Palomo de Lewin, A. C. Beatriz. "Esclavos negros en Guatemala (1723-1773)" (Licenciatura en Historia, Universidad del Valle de Guatemala, Facultad de Sciencias Sociales, 1992).

1623. Potthast-Jutkeit, Barbara. "Indians, Blacks and Zambos on the Mosquito Coast: 17th and 18th Century," *América negra*, 6 (1993), pp. 53-68.

4. New Granada and Gran Colombia

1624. Colmenares, Germán. "El tránsito a sociedades campesinas de dos sociedades esclavistas en la Nueva Granada, Cartagena-Popayán 1750-1850," in *[Primer] Congreso internacional de historia economica y social de la cuenca del Caribe 1763-1898* (Centro de Estudios Avanzados de Puerto Rico y el Caribe, San Juan de Puerto Rico, 1992), pp. 77-104.

5. Colombia

1625. Arrazola, Roberto. "El precioso fruto de la paz en los palenques de la Sierra de Maria, Cartagena: la real cédula de Agosto 23 de 1691," *América negra*, 2 (1991), pp. 247-54.

1626. Friedemann, Nina S. de. "Cabildos negros: refugios de Africanía en Colombia," *Montalbán*, 20 (1988), pp. 121-32.

1627. Hansen, Caroline Anne. "Conquest and Colonization in the Colombian Choco, 1510-1740" (PhD thesis, University of Warwick, 1991).

1628. Maya Restrepo, Adriana. "Las brujas de Zaragoza: resistencia y cimarronaje en las minas de Antioquia, Colombia 1619-1622," *América negra*, 4 (1992), pp. 85-100.

1629. Navarette, Maria Cristina. "Cotidianidad y cultura material de los negros de Cartagena en el XVII," *América negra*, 7 (1993-94), pp. 65-82.

1630. Navarrete, Maria Cristina. *Historia social del negro en la colonia: Cartagena, siglo XVII*. Santiago de Cali [Colombia]: Universidad del Valle, 1995.

1631. Romero, Mario Diego. "Sociedades negras: esclavos y libres en la costa Pacífica de Colombia," *América negra*, 2 (1991), pp. 137-56.

1632. Rueda Mendez, David. *Esclavitud y sociedad en la provincia de Tunja, siglo XVIII*. Tunja, Boyaca, Colombia: Editorial de la Universidad Pedagogica y Tecnologica de Colombia, 1995.

1633. Zuluaga R., Francisco U. "Cuadrillas mineras y familias de esclavos, en Nóvita (Chocó, Colombia), siglo XVIII," *América negra*, 10 (1996), pp. 51-84.

6. Venezuela

1634. Belrose, Maurice. *Africa en el corazón de Venezuela*. Maracaibo: Universidad del Zulia, 1988.

1635. Gil Rivas, Pedro A. *La insurrección de los negros de la sierra coriana, 10 de mayo de 1795: notas para la discusión*. Caracas: Dirección de Cultura, Universidad Central de Venezuela, 1996. (Colección Letras de Venezuela ; Serie Ensayo 127)

1636. "1788: causa criminal contra Joaquín de Rivera, esclavo por la muerte que ejecutó en su ama Luiza de Córdoba," *América negra*, 1 (1991), pp. 11-32.

1637. Noel, Jesse. "History and Slavery in Venezuelan Narrative," in Claudette Williams, ed., *History and Time in Caribbean Literature: Proceedings of the XI Conference on Spanish Caribbean Literature, April, 1988* (Kingston, Jamaica: Institute of Caribbean Studies, University of the West Indies, Mona, 1992), pp. 76-80.

1638. Ortega, Miguel Angel. *La esclavitud en el contexto agropecuario colonial: siglo XVIII*. [Caracas, Venezuela]: Editorial APICUM, 1992.

1639. Ramos Guedez, José Marcial. *Bibliografía y hemerografía sobre la insurrección de Jose Leonardo Chirino en la serranía de Coro, 1795-1995*. Caracas: EBUCV, 1996.

1640. Ramos Guedez, José Marcial. "L'insurrection nègre de Coro en 1795 au Venezuela," in Michel L. Martin and Alain Yacou, eds., *De la révolution française aux révolutions créoles et nègres* (Paris: Editions Caribéennes, 1989), pp. 53-60.

1641. Rojas, Reinaldo. "Rebeliones de esclavos negros en Venezuela antes y después de 1789," *Estudios de historia social y económica de América* (Universidad de Alcalá, Alcalá de Henares), 10 (1993), pp. 151-64.

1642. Tronconis de Veracoechea, Ermilia. "Aspecto de la esclavitud negra en Venezuela y el Caribe (1750-1854)," in *[Primer] Congreso internacional de historia economica y social de la cuenca del Caribe 1763-1898* (Centro de Estudios Avanzados de Puerto Rico y el Caribe, San Juan de Puerto Rico, 1992), pp. 41-60.

7. Ecuador

1643. Jurado Noboa, Fernando. *Esclavitud en la costa pacífica*. Quito: Abya-Yala, 1990.

1644. Speiser, Sabine. "Sklaverei in Ekuador: eine Geschichte hinterlässt ihre Spuren," in Binder, ed., *Slavery in the Americas*, pp. 365-88.

8. Peru

1645. Aguirre, Carlos. "Agentes de su propia emancipación: manumisión de esclavos en Lima, Perú 1821-1854," *América negra*, 2 (1991), pp. 101-38.

1646. Aguirre, Carlos. *Agentes de su propria libertad: los esclavos de Lima y la desintegración de la esclavitud, 1821-1854.* Lima: Pontificia Universidad Catolica del Perú, Fondo Editorial, 1993.

1647. Blanchard, Peter. "Slave Resistance in a 'Humane' Slavery System: The Case of Early Republican Peru," in Hoogbergen, ed., *Born out of Resistance*, pp. 86-97.

1648. Blanchard, Peter. *Slavery and Abolition in Early Republican Peru.* Wilmington DE: Scholarly Resources Inc., 1992.

1649. Bühnen, Stephan. "Ethnic Origins of Peruvian Slaves (1584-1650): Figures for Upper Guinea," *Paideuma*, 39 (1993), pp. 57-110.

1650. Chong Lam, Alberto E. "On Human Capital and Development" (PhD diss., Cornell University, 1993).

1651. Hunefeldt, Christine. *Las manuelos, vida cotidiana de una familia negra en la Lima del S. XIX: una reflexión historica sobre la esclavitud urbana.* Lima: Instituto de Estudios Peruanos, 1992.

1652. Hünefeldt, Christine. "Mujeres: entre esclavitud, emociones y libertad: Lima, 1800-1854," in Pas, coord., *Anais do Seminário internacional da escravidão*, pp. 137-69.

1653. Hünefeldt, Christine. *Paying the Price of Freedom: Family and Labor among Lima's Slaves, 1800-1854.* Berkeley and Los Angeles: University of California Press, 1994.

1654. Romero, Fernando. *Safari africano y compraventa de esclavos para el Perú.* Lima: Instituto de Estudios Peruanos, Universidad Nacional San Cristóbal de Huamanga, 1994.

1655. Tardieu, Jean-Pierre. *L'église et les noirs au Pérou: XVIe et XVIIe siècles.* Saint-Dénis and Paris: Université de la Réunion, Faculté des Lettres et des Sciences Humaines and Harmattan, 1993.

9. Bolivia

1656. Soux, Maria Luisa. "Esclavos, peones y mingas: apuntes sobre la fuerza de trabajo en las haciendas yungueñas a principios de la República," *História y cultura*, 21-22 (1992), pp. 51-59.

1657. *Vásquez-Machicado, José. "El alzamiento de esclavos en Santa Cruz en agosto de 1809," in *Obras completas de Humberto Vásquez-Machicado* (La Paz: Editorial Don Bosco, 1988), vol. 7, pp. 615-20.

10. Chile

1658. Powelson, Michael William. "Slave, Forced and Free Labor in Colonial Chiapa" (PhD diss., Columbia University, 1995).

11. Argentina

1659. Johnson, Lyman L. "The Competition of Slave and Free Labor in Artisanal Production: Buenos Aires, 1770-1815," *International Review of Social History*, 40, 3 (1995), pp. 409-24.

1660. Osun Doyo, Ile Ase. "El negro en la historia y la cultura argentinas," *América negra*, 1 (1991), pp. 161-64.

1661. Pistone, J. Catalina. *La esclavatura negra en Santa Fe.* [Argentina]: Junta Provincial de Estudios Historicos de Santa Fe, 1996.

1662. Yanzi Ferreira, Marcela Aspell de. "La regulación jurídica da las formas del trabajo forzado (segunda parte)," *Investigaciones y ensayos*, no. 41 (1991), pp. 349-94.

12. Uruguay

13. Paraguay

IV. Brazil

1. General and Comparative

1663. Aguiar, Petrônio José de. "O valor histórico dos testemunhos e inventários," *História UFRN* (Departamento de História, Universidade Federal do Rio Grande do Norte), 2, 2 ([1988]), pp. 82-87.

1664. Alencastro, Luiz Felipe de. "The Apprenticeship of Colonization".

Reprinted in Manning, ed., *Slave Trades, 1500-1800*, pp. 83-108.

1665. Alinder, Jasmine Amy. "Picturing Themselves: An Interdisciplinary Examination of Nineteenth-Century Photographs of Brazilian Slaves" (MA thesis, University of New Mexico, 1994).

1666. Andrade, Manuel Correia de, and Eliane Moury Fernandes, eds. *Atualidade & abolição*. Pernambuco: Editora Massangana, 1991. (Ciclo de conferências, comemorativo ao Centenário da Abolição da Escravatura Negra, CEHIBRA, Fundação Joaquim Nabuco, agosto de 1987 a fevereiro de 1988)

For contents see Barbosa, Cerqueira, Chacon, Figueiredo, Freitas, Graham, Hoffnagel, Lindoso, Melo, Monteiro, Moura, Price, and Tomich.

1667. Anjos, João Alfredo dos. "Koster e a escravidão negra na América," *Clio: revista de pesquisa histórica*, 15 (1994), pp. 99-112.

1668. *Arrais, Nely F., and Ana P. G. Ribeiro. "Relatório de pesquisa sobre doenças de escravos" (Niterói: Departamento de História, Universidade Federal Fluminense, 1990). (Unpublished relatório, Centro Nacional de Pesquisas)

1669. Arruda, José Jobson. "Os escravos angolanos no Brasil (sécs. XV-XVIII)," in Medina and Castro Henriques, eds., *A rota dos escravos*, pp. 229-38.

1670. Barbosa, Franciso de Assis. "O movimento abolicionista no Brasil," in Andrade and Fernandes, eds., *Atualidade & abolição*, pp. 11-22.

1671. Barcelos, Luiz Claudio, Olivia Maria Gomes da Cunha, and Tereza Christina Nascimento Araújo. *Escravidão e relações raciais no Brasil: cadastro da produção intelectual (1970-1990)*. Rio de Janeiro: Centro de Estudos Afro-Asiáticos, 1991.

1672. Baronov, David Mayer. "The Process of Working-Class Formation: The Abolition of Slavery in 19th-Century Brazil in World-Historical Perspective" (PhD diss., State University of New York at Binghamton, 1995).

1673. Bittencourt, Gabriel. "Processo da emancipação da escravidão no Brasil: uma visão histórico-econômica," in Pas, coord., *Anais do Seminário internacional da escravidão*, pp. 45-58.

1674. "'Boletim das acquisições mais importantes feitas pela Biblioteca Nacional', relativas à extinção da escravidão (em 1888)," *Anais da Biblioteca Nacional*, 108 (1988), pp. 217-41.

1675. Bulcão, Ana Lucia, and Luiz Sergio Dias, eds. *Escravidão urbana*. Rio de Janeiro: Secretaria Municipal de Cultura, Turismo e Esportes, Departamento Geral de Documentação e Informação Cultural, Arquivo Geral da Cidade do Rio de Janeiro, 1992. (Coleção Memória Urbana, 3; Série Estudos e Ensaios, 1)

1676. Carvalho, José Vidigal. "Os conjurados de 1789 e a escravidão," *Revista de história* (São Paulo), no. 119 (1985-88), pp. 91-99.

1677. Cerqueira, José Luciano. "O negro e a abolição," in Andrade and Fernandes, eds., *Atualidade & abolição*, pp. 23-39.

1678. Chacon, Vamireh. "Franz Boas: eine deutsche Quelle des Antirassismus Gilberto Freyres," in Zoller, ed., *Amerikaner wider Willen*, pp. 261-68.

1679. Chacon, Vamireh. "Ideologia e abolição," in Andrade and Fernandes, eds., *Atualidade & abolição*, pp. 41-59.

1680. Chalhoub, Sidney. "Negócios da escravidão: os negros e as transações de compra e venda," *Revista do CEAA* (Centro de Estudos Afro-Asiáticos), 16 (1989), pp. 118-28.

1681. "Colonial Brazil: Plantations and Peripheries (bibliographical essay)," in Leslie Bethell, ed., *Cambridge History of Latin America* (Cambridge: Cambridge University Press, 1984), vol. 2, pp. 856-64.

1682. Conrad, Robert Edgar. *Children of God's Fire: A Documentary History of Black Slavery in Brazil.*

University Park: Pennsylvania State University Press, 1994. (Re-publication)

1683. Conrad, Robert Edgar. *The Destruction of Brazilian Slavery, 1850-1888.* 2nd ed. Melbourne FL: Krieger, 1993.

1684. Conrad, Robert [Edgar]. (review: Eisenberg, *Homens esquecidos*, and Gorender, *Escravidão reabilitada*), *LPH: Revista de história* (Departamento de História, Universidade Federal de Ouro Preto), 3, 1 (1992), pp. 313-16.

1685. Costa, Iraci del Nero da. *Arraia-miuda: um estudo sobre os não-proprietários de escravos no Brasil.* São Paulo: MSGP, 1992.

1686. Coutinho, José Maria. "O darwinismo social e o negro brasileiro," in Pas, coord., *Anais do Seminário internacional da escravidão*, pp. 77-95.

1687. "Documentação: textos e estampas relativos à escravidão e à situação do negro no Brasil," *Anais da Biblioteca Nacional*, 108 (1988), pp. 7-46.

1688. Drescher, Seymour. "Brazilian Abolition in Comparative Perspective".

Translated as "A abolição brasileira em perspectiva comparativa," *História Social* (Revista da Pós-Graduação em História, IFCH-Unicamp [Campinas]), 2 (1995), pp. 115-64.

1689. "Escravidão no Brasil colonial [mesa redonda, resumo]," in Pas, coord., *Anais do Seminário internacional da escravidão*, pp. 99-100.

1690. Faria, Sheila Siqueira de Castro. "Família escrava e legitimidade: estratégias de preservação da autonomia," *Estudos afro-asiáticos*, 23 (1992), pp. 113-32.

1691. Figueiredo, Ariosvaldo. "A resistencia do negro à escravidão," in Andrade and Fernandes, eds., *Atualidade & abolição*, pp. 115-20.

1692. Freitas, Décio. "A liberdade do Índio e a escravidão do negro," in Andrade and Fernandes, eds., *Atualidade & abolição*, pp. 61-66.

1693. Freitas Filho, Almir Pitta. "Tecnologia e escravidão no Brasil: aspectos da modernização agrícola nas exposições nacionais da segunda metade do século XIX (1861-1881)," *Revista brasileira de história*, 11 (no. 22) (1991), pp. 71-92.

1694. Funari, Pedro Paulo Abreu. "O estudo arqueológico de Palmares e a sociedade brasileira" (Unpublished paper, March 1995).

1695. Gadelha, Regina Maria d'Aquino Fonseca. "A lei de terras (1850) e a abolição da escravidão: capitalismo e força de trabalho no Brasil do século XIX," *Revista de história* (São Paulo), no. 120 (1989), pp. 153-62.

1696. Gonçalves, Maria Filgueiras, trans., and Ana Lúcia Louzada Werneck, intro. "[Encontrando quilombos]," *Anais da Biblioteca Nacional*, 108 (1988), pp. 47-113.

1697. Gorender, Jacob. "A escravidão reabilitada," *LPH: Revista de história* (Departamento de História, Universidade Federal de Ouro Preto), 3, 1 (1992), pp. 245-66.

1698. Graham, Richard. "Introduction," to Graham, ed., *Brazil and the World System*, pp. 1-9.

1699. Graham, Richard, ed. *Brazil and the World System.* Austin: University of Texas Press, 1991.

With chapters by Fernando A. Novais, John R. Hall, Luís Carlos Soares.

1700. Graham, Sandra Lauderdale. "A abolição na cidade: armas-secas, contaminação e controle," in Andrade and Fernandes, eds., *Atualidade & abolição*, pp. 75-89.

1701. Hall, John R. "The Patrimonial Dynamic in Colonial Brazil," in Graham, ed., *Brazil and the World System*, pp. 57-88.

1702. Hentschke, Jens. "Plantation Slavery in Brazil and the Discussion about Modes of Production: Some Critical Comments," in Binder, ed., *Slavery in the Americas*, pp. 115-30.

1703. Hentschke, Jens. "Sklavenfrage und Staatsfrage im Brasilien des 19. Jahrhunderts," in Zoller, ed., *Amerikaner wider Willen*, pp. 231-60.

1704. Hofbauer, Andreas. *Afro-Brasilien - vom "Quilombo" zum "Quilombismo": vom Kampf gegen die Sklaverei zur Suche nach einer neuen Kulturellen Identität.* Frankfurt: Verlag für Interkulturelle Kommunikation, 1989.

1705. Kabengele Munanga. "Origem e histórico do quilombo na África," *Revista USP* (Universidade de São Paulo), 28 (1996), pp. 56-63.

1706. Kabengele Munanga. "La présence africaine au Brésil" (Unpublished paper, UNESCO conference on "La route de l'esclave", Ouidah, Bénin, 1-5 Sept. 1994).

1707. Karasch, Mary C. "Slavery: Brazil," in *Encyclopedia of Latin American History* (Barbara Tenenbaum, ed.) (New York: Charles Scribner's Sons, 1995), pp. 129-31.

1708. Knox, Miridan Britto. "A vida escrava: liberdades consentidas," *Clio: revista de pesquisa histórica*, 15 (1994), pp. 153-61.

1709. Kraay, Hendrik. "'The Shelter of the Uniform': The Brazilian Army and Runaway Slaves, 1800-1888," *Journal of Social History*, 29, 3 (1996), pp. 637-57.

1710. Krueger, Robert. "Milhões de vozes, umas páginas preciosas: as narrativas dos escravos brasileiros," in Roger Zapata, ed., *Imágenes de la resistencia indígena y esclava* (Lima: Editorial Wari, 1990), pp. 181-232.

1711. Lara, Silvia Hunold. "L'esclavage africaine et le travailleur esclave au Brésil," *Dialogues d'histoire ancienne*, 19, 1 (1993), pp. 205-30. (Translated by José António Dabdab Trabulsi)

1712. Lara, Silvia H[unold]. "Escravidão no Brasil: um balanço historiográfico," *LPH: Revista de história* (Departamento de História, Universidade Federal de Ouro Preto), 3, 1 (1992), pp. 215-44.

1713. Lara, Silvia Hunold, apres. e trans. [Manoel Ribeiro Rocha] *Etíope resgatado, empenhado, sustentado, corrigido, instruído e libertado.* Campinas: IFCH - UNICAMP, 1991. (Cadernos do Instituto de Filosofia e Ciências Humanas, no. 21)

1714. Libby, Douglas H. "Demografia e escravidão," *LPH: Revista de história* (Departamento de História, Universidade Federal de Ouro Preto), 3, 1 (1992), pp. 267-94.

1715. Longo, Angelo. *O abolicionismo como ideologia de transição, 1878/1888.* Niterói: Editora Cromos, Clube de Literatura, 1993.

1716. Machado, Maria Helena Pereira Toledo. *O plano e o pánico: os movimentos sociais na decada da abolição.* Rio de Janeiro and São Paulo, Editora UFRJ; EDUSP, 1994.

1717. Machado, Maria Helena Pereira Toledo. "A revolta de escravos como estratégia de libertação: Brasil nas vésperas da abolição," *Revista internacional de estudos africanos*, 16-17 (1992-94), pp. 31-48.

1718. Maciel, Cleber. "388 anos de escravidão, 293 anos da morte de Zumbi, 100 anos de Lei Áurea, 488 anos de intolerância," in Pas, coord., *Anais do Seminário internacional da escravidão*, pp. 101-04.

1719. Maestri Filho, Mário. *A servidão negra.*

Translated as *L'esclavage au Brésil*, with foreword by Jacob Gorender. Paris: Karthala, 1991.

1720. Maggie, Yvonne. "Die Illusion des Konkreten: zum System rassischer Klassifikation in Brasilien," in Zoller, ed., *Amerikaner wider Willen*, pp. 289-319.

1721. Marson, Isabel Andrade. "O 'cidadão criminoso': o engendramento da igualdade entre homens livres e escravos no Brasil durante o segundo reinado," *Estudos áfro-asiáticos*, 16 (1989), pp. 141-56.

1722. Mauro, Frédéric. "Esclaves brésiliens des XVIe et XVIIe siècles," in Bresc, ed., *Figures de l'esclave*, pp. 203-14.

1723. Melo, João Wilson Mendes. "Cruz e Souza: o branco e o negro," *História UFRN* (Departamento de História, Universidade Federal do Rio Grande do Norte), 2, 2 ([1988]), pp. 41-44.

1724. Monteiro, John M. "Indian Slavery and Forced Labor," in *Encyclopedia of Latin American History* (Barbara Tenenbaum, ed.) (New York: Charles Scribner's Sons, 1995), pp. 134-35.

1725. Monteiro, Marília Pessoa. "Ser mulher no Brasil: um patriarcalismo renitente (ser mulher, negra e escrava: tríplice discriminação)," in Andrade and Fernandes, eds., *Atualidade & abolição*, pp. 67-74.

1726. Moreira, José Aparecido Gomes. "Escravidão e evangelização indígena no século XVI: o pensamento de Dom Vasco de Quiroga," *REB/51 (Revista esclesiástica brasileira)*, no. 203 (1991), pp. 531-51.

Issue title: "Missionários X escravidão na América latina".

1727. Mota, Márcia Maria Menendes. "Os 'sem terra' e os minifundistas em face à crise do trabalho escravo (1850-1880)," in Jaime da Silva, Patrícia Birman, and Regina Wanderley, orgs., *Cativeiro e liberdade (Seminário do Instituto de Filosofia e Ciências Humanas da Universidade do Estado do Rio de Janeiro)* (Rio de Janeiro: UERJ, 1989), pp. 107-18.

1728. Mott, Luiz [R. B]. "As alternativas eróticas dos africanos e seus descendentes no Brasil," *LPH: Revista de história* (Departamento de História, Universidade Federal de Ouro Preto), 3, 1 (1992), pp. 176-214.

1729. Mott, Luiz. "Santo Antônio, o divino capitão-do-mato," in Reis and Gomes, eds., *Liberdade por um fio*, pp. 110-38.

1730. Mott, Maria Lucia Barros. "Ser mãe: a escrava em face do aborto e do infanticídio," *Revista de história* (São Paulo), no. 120 (1989), pp. 85-96.

1731. *Motta, José Flávio. "Família escrava: uma incursão pela historiografia" (São Paulo, unpublished, n.d.).

1732. Moura, Clóvis. "Os quilombos e sua significação histórica e social (a insurgência escrava no contexto do escravismo tardio)," in Andrade and Fernandes, eds., *Atualidade & abolição*, pp. 91-114.

1733. Naro, Nancy Priscilla [Smith]. "Revision and Persistence: Recent Historiography on the Transition from Slave to Free Labour in Rural Brazil," *Slavery and Abolition*, 13, 2 (1992), pp. 68-85.

1734. Naro, Nancy Priscilla. "The Transition from Slavery to Migrant Labour in Rural Brazil," in Lovejoy and Rogers, eds., *Unfree Labour in the Development of the Atlantic World*, pp. 183-96.

1735. Neves, Erivaldo Fagundes. "Escravismo e policultura," *Clio: revista de pesquisa histórica*, 15 (1994), pp. 73-98.

1736. Neves, Maria de Fatima Rodrigues das. *Documentos sobre a escravidão no Brasil*. São Paulo: Editora Contexto, 1995.

1737. Novais, Fernando A. "Brazil in the Old Colonial System," in Graham, ed., *Brazil and the World System*, pp. 11-55.

1738. Patrocínio, José do. *Campanha abolicionista: coletânea de artigos*. Rio de Janeiro: Fundação Biblioteca Nacional, 1996.

1739. Reis, João José. "Slave Resistance in Brazil" (Presentation at Colloquium on "Les dépendances serviles", Paris 1996).

1740. Reis, João José. "Slave Revolts: Brazil," in *Encyclopedia of Latin American History* (Barbara Tenenbaum, ed.) (New York: Charles Scribner's Sons, 1995), pp. 119-20.

1741. Reis, João José, and Flávio dos Santos Gomes. "Introdução: uma história da liberdade," in Reis and Gomes, eds., *Liberdade por um fio*, pp. 9-25.

1742. Reis, João José, and Flávio dos Santos Gomes, eds. *Liberdade por um fio: história dos quilombos no Brasil*. São Paulo: Companhia das Letras, 1996.

For contents see Assunção, Carvalho, Funari, Funes, Gomes, Guimarães, Karasch, Lara, Maestri, Mott, Price, Ramos, Reis (2), Reis and Gomes, Schwartz, Souza, Vainfas, and Volpato.

1743. Rocha, António Penalves. "A escravidão na economia política," *Revista de história* (São Paulo), no. 120 (1989), pp. 97-108.

1744. Rodrigues, Jaime. "Índios e africanos: do 'pouco ou nenhum fruto' do trabalho à criação de 'uma classe trabalhadora'," *História Social* (Revista da Pós-Graduação em História, IFCH-Unicamp [Campinas]), 2 (1995), pp. 9-24.

1745. Rodrigues, Jaime. "Liberdade, humanidade e propriedade: os escravos e a assembléia constituinte de 1823," *Revista do Instituto de Estudos Brasileiros*, no. 39 (1995), pp. 159-67.

1746. Russell-Wood, A. J. R. "Technology and Society: The Impact of Gold Mining on the Institution of Slavery in Portuguese America".

Reprinted in Michael Adas, ed., *Technology and European Overseas Enterprise: Diffusion, Adaption, and Adoption* (Brookfield VT: Variorum, 1996), pp. 181-206.

1747. Samara, Eny de Mesquita. "A família negra no Brasil," *Revista de história* (São Paulo), no. 120 (1989), pp. 27-44.

1748. Santos, Ana Maria Barros dos. "Quilombos: Sklavenaufstände im Brasilien des 17. Jahrhunderts," in Zoller, ed., *Amerikaner wider Willen*, pp. 161-73.

1749. Santos-Stubbe, Chirly dos. "Formen der weiblichen afrikanischen Sklaverei in Brasilien," in Zoller, ed., *Amerikaner wider Willen*, pp. 175-202.

1750. Schelskly, Detlev. "Die 'questão racial' in Brasilien: einige Anmerkungen," in Zoller, ed., *Amerikaner wider Willen*, pp. 269-87.

1751. Schulz, John. *The Financial Crisis of Abolition*. São Paulo: Instituto Fernand Braudel de Economia Mundial, 1993.

1752. Schwarcz, Lilia Maria, and Letícia Vidar de Sousa Reis, orgs. *Negras imagens*. São Paulo: Editora da Universidade de São Paulo, 1996.

For contents see ... Funari.

1753. Schwartz, Stuart B. *Slaves, Peasants, and Rebels: Reconsidering Brazilian Slavery*. Urbana: University of Illinois Press, 1992.

Includes revised and expanded versions of "Recent Trends in the Study of Slavery in Brazil"; "Resistance and Accommodation in Eighteenth-Century Brazil"; "Mocambos, quilombos e Palmares" (translated); and "Cleansing Original Sin" (with Stephen Gudeman).

1754. Schwartz, Stuart B. "Somebodies and Nobodies in the Body Politic: Mentalities and Social Structures in Colonial Brazil (review essay: *inter alia*, Fragoso, *Homens de grossa aventura*; Fragoso and Florentino, *O arcaismo como projeto*; Mott, *Rosa Egipcíaca*; Costa, *Arraia-miuda*)," *Latin American Research Review*, 31, 1 (1996), pp. 113-34.

1755. Silva, Eduardo da. *Prince of the People: The Life and Times of a Brazilian Free Man of Colour*. London: Verso, 1993.

1756. Skidmore, Thomas E. "Race and Class in Brazil: Historical Perspectives," in Harris, ed., *Global Dimensions of the African Diaspora* (2nd ed.), pp. 189-203.

1757. Slenes, Robert W. "Black Homes, White Homilies: Perceptions of the Slave Family and of Slave Women in Nineteenth-Century Brazil," in Gaspar and Hine, eds., *More than Chattel*, pp. 126-46.

1758. Smutko, Pe. Frei Gregório, OFMCap. "A luta dos Capuchinhos contra a escravidão dos negros durante os séculos XVII e XVIII," *REB/51 (Revista eclesiástica brasileira)*, no. 203 (1991), pp. 531-51. Issue title: "Missionários X escravidão na América latina".

1759. Soares, Luís Carlos. "From Slavery to Dependence: A Historiographical Perspective," in Graham, ed., *Brazil and the World System*, pp. 89-108.

1760. Soares, Luís Carlos. "Historiografia da escravidão: novos rumos (as cidades escravistas brasileiras: algumas reflexões prévias para os estudos de escravidão urbana)," *LPH: Revista de história* (Departamento de História, Universidade Federal de Ouro Preto), 3, 1 (1992), pp. 161-75.

1761. Sousa, Jorge Prata de. *Escravidão ou morte: os escravos brasileiros na Guerra do Paraguai*. Rio de Janeiro: Mauad/ADESA, 1996.

1762. Souza, Itamar de. "A Igreja e a escravidão no Brasil," *História UFRN* (Departamento de História, Universidade Federal do Rio Grande do Norte), 2, 2 ([1988]), pp. 11-22.

1763. Stubbe, Hannes. "Über die Kindheit der afrobrasilianischen Sklaven," in Zoller, ed., *Amerikaner wider Willen*, pp. 203-30.

1764. [Suess, Paulo, ed.] *Etíope resgatado, empenhado, sustentado, corrigido, instruído e libertado: discurso teológico-jurídico sobre a libertação dos escravos no Brasil de 1758*, by Manoel Ribeiro Rocha. Petrópolis: Vozes, 1992. With introduction and bibliography.

1765. Telles, Norma. "Rebeldes, escritoras e abolicionistas," *Revista de história* (São Paulo), no. 120 (1989), pp. 73-84.

1766. Toral, André Amaral de. "A participação dos negros escravos na guerra do Paraguai," *Estudos avançados*, 9 (no. 24) (1995), pp. 287-96.

1767. Worden, Nigel. "Brazilian Slavery: A Survey from the Cape of Recent Literature in English," *Social Dynamics*, 17, 2 (1991), pp. 76-102.

1768. Zoller, Rüdiger, ed. *Amerikaner wider Willen: Beiträge zur Sklaverei in Lateinamerika und ihren Folgen*.

For main entry and contents, see "General and Comparative" section.

2. Northern

1769. Acevedo, Rosa. *Negros do Trombetas: guardiães de matas e rios*. [Belém, Brazil]: Editora Universitária UFPA, 1993.

1770. Araujo, Mundinha. *A invasão do quilombo Limoeiro, 1878*. São Luis: Estado do Maranhão, Secretaria de Estado da Cultura, Arquivo Público do Estado do Maranhão, 1992.

1771. Assunção, Matthias Röhrig. *Pflanzer, Sklaven und Kleinbauern in der brasilianischen Provinz Maranhão 1800-1850*. Frankfurt-am-Main: Vervuert, 1993.

1772. Assunção, Matthias Röhrig. "Quilombos maranhenses," in Reis and Gomes, eds., *Liberdade por um fio*, pp. 433-66.

1773. Funes, Eurípedes A. "'Nasci nas matas, nunca tive senhor': história e memória dos mocambos do baixo Amazonas" (Tese de doutorado, Universidade de São Paulo, 1995).

1774. Funes, Eurípedes A. "'Nasci nas matas, nunca tive senhor': história e memória dos mocambos do baixo Amazonas," in Reis and Gomes, eds., *Liberdade por um fio*, pp. 467-97.

1775. Galvão, Cláudio Augusto Pinto. "Segundo Wanderley, o poeta Norte-Rio-Grandense dos escravos," *História UFRN* (Departamento de História, Universidade Federal do Rio Grande do Norte), 2, 2 ([1988]), pp. 73-81.

1776. Knox, Miridan Britto. *Escravos do sertão: demografia, trabalho e relações sociais - Piauí, 1826-1888*. Paiuí: Fundação Cultural Monsinhos Chaves, 1995.

1777. Maranhão, Arquivo Público do Estado. *A invasão do quilombo Limoeira 1878*. São Luís: Secretaria de Estado da Cultura, 1992.

1778. Mattos, Maria Regina M. Furtado. "Os trabalhadores do sertão do Seridó (RN) na Segunda Metade do Século XIX," *História UFRN* (Departamento de História, Universidade Federal do Rio Grande do Norte), 2, 2 ([1988]), pp. 61-72.

1779. Medeiros, Tarcísio. "O negro escravo: da etnia à abolição e os remanescentes de sua aculturação no Rio Grande do Norte," *História UFRN* (Departamento de História, Universidade Federal do Rio Grande do Norte), 2, 2 ([1988]), pp. 45-60.

1780. Ribeiro, Jalila Ayoub Jorge. *A desagregação do sistema escravista no Maranhão*. São Luis: SIOGE, 1990.

3. Northeast

1781. Abdul-Aleem, Zaid. "African Muslim Survival and Adaptation in Salvador, Brazil: *Os Males* after the Revolt of 1835" (MA thesis, Duke University, 1996).

1782. *Allen, Scott. "Africanisms, Mosaics, and Creativity: The Historical Archaeology of Palmares" (MA thesis, Brown University, 1995).

1783. Barickman, B. J. "'A Bit of Land, Which They Call Roça': Slave Provision Grounds in the Bahian Recôncavo, 1780-1860," *Hispanic American Historical Review*, 74, 4 (1994), pp. 649-87.

1784. Carvalho, Marcus Joaquim M. de. "O quilombo de Malunguinho, o rei das matas de Pernambuco," in Reis and Gomes, eds., *Liberdade por um fio*, pp. 407-32.

1785. Costa, Dora Isabel Paiva da. "Demografia e economia numa região distante dos centros dinâmicos: uma contribuição ao debate sobre a escravidão em unidades exportadoras e não-exportadoras," *Estudos económicos*, 26, 1 (1996), pp. 111-36.

1786. Demoner, Sonia Maria. "A libertação do ventre e o fundo de emancipação no Espírito Santo," in Pas, coord., *Anais do Seminário internacional da escravidão*, pp. 61-74.

1787. Fagan, Brian. "Brazil's Little Angola," *Archaeology*, 46, 4 (July/Aug. 1993), pp. 14-19.

1788. Freitas, Décio. *A revolução dos Malês: insurreições escravas*. Porto Alegre: Editora Movimento, 1985. (2ª ed., revised [*Insurreições escravas*.])

1789. Funari, Pedro Paulo [de] A[breu]. "A arqueologia de Palmares: sua contribuição para o conhecimento da História da cultura afro-americana," in Reis and Gomes, eds., *Liberdade por um fio*, pp. 26-51.

1790. Funari, Pedro Paulo A[breu]. "A cultura material de Palmares: o estudo das relações sociais de um quilombo pela arqueologia," *Idéias* (FDE-SP), 27 (1995), pp. 37-42.

1791. Funari, Pedro Paulo. "Maroon, Race and Gender: Palmares Material Culture and the Social Relations in a Runaway Settlement" (Unpublished paper, World Archaeological Congress, New Delhi, 3 Dec. 1994).

1792. Funari, Pedro Paulo [de] A[breu]. "Novas perspectivas abertas pela arqueologia na Serra da Barriga," in Schwarz and Reis, orgs., *Negras imagens*, pp. 139-51ff.

1793. Funari, Pedro Paulo A[breu]. "A 'República de Palmares' e a arqueologia da Serra da Barriga," *Revista USP* (Universidade de São Paulo), 28 (1995-96), pp. 6-13.

1794. Gomes, Flávio dos Santos. "Um recôncavo, dois sertões e vários mocambos: quilombos na Capitania da Bahia (1575-1808)," *História Social* (Revista da Pós-Graduação em História, IFCH-Unicamp [Campinas]), 2 (1995), pp. 25-54.

1795. Goody, Jack. "Writing, Religion and Revolt in Bahia," *Visible Language*, 20, 3 (1986), pp. 318-43.

1796. *Graden, Dale T. "Candomblé Viewed as Subversion of the Slave Order and Abolitionist Expression in Bahia, Brazil, 1850-1888" (Unpublished paper, annual meeting of the Latin American Studies Association, Washington DC, 1995).

1797. Graden, Dale T[hurston]. "From Slavery to Freedom in Bahia, Brazil, 1791-1900" (PhD diss. University of Connecticut, 1991).

1798. Graden, Dale T. "'This City Has Too Many Slaves Joined Together': The Abolitionist Crisis in Salvador, Bahia, Brazil, 1848-1856," in Jalloh and Maizlish, eds., *African Diaspora*, pp. 143-52.

1799. Graden, Dale T. "Voices from Under: The End of Slavery in Bahia, Brazil," *Review of Latin American Studies*, 3, 2 (1990), pp. 145-69.

Translated as. "La voz de los de abajo: la abolición de la esclavitud africana en Bahía, Brasil," in Roger Zapata, ed., *Imágenes de la resistencia indígena y esclava* (Lima: Editorial Wari, 1990), pp. 159-80.

1800. Hoffnagel, Marc Jay. "O partido liberal de Pernambuco e a questão abolicionista, 1880-88," in Andrade and Fernandes, eds., *Atualidade & abolição*, pp. 139-51.

1801. Kanten, Frank van. "A república dos Palmares," *Oso (Tijdschrift voor Surinaamse Taalkunde, Letterkunde, Cultuur en Geschiedenis)*, 11, 2 (1992), pp. 157-73.

1802. Knox, Miridan Britto. "Vaqueiros e rendeiras: os escravos do sertão," in Sociedade brasileira de pesquisa histórica (SBPH), *Anais da IX reunião anual da SBPH* (São Paulo, 1990), pp. 241-53.

1803. Kraay, Hendrik. "'As Terrifying as Unexpected': The Bahian Sabinada, 1837-1838," *Hispanic American Historical Review*, 72, 4 (1992), pp. 501-27.

1804. *Ladeira, Cadu, and Marcelo Affini. "Palmares: cem anos de sonho," *Super-Interessante* (Sept. 1993), p. 38-43.

1805. Lara, Silvia Hunold. "Do singular ao plural: Palmares, capitães-do-mato e o governo dos escravos," in Reis and Gomes, eds., *Liberdade por um fio*, pp. 81-109.

1806. *Lima, Sélia Jesús de. "Lucas Evangelista: o Lucas da Feira: estudo sobre a rebeldia escrava em Feira de Santana, 1807-1849" (Tese de mestrado, Universidade Federal da Bahia, 1990).

1807. Lindoso, Dirceu. "Negros papa-méis e negros escravos na guerra dos Cabanos," in Andrade and Fernandes, eds., *Atualidade & abolição*, pp. 121-38.

1808. Lovejoy, Paul E. "Background to Rebellion: The Origins of Muslim Slaves in Bahia," in Lovejoy and Rogers, eds., *Unfree Labour in the Development of the Atlantic World*, pp. 151-82.

1809. Melo, José Octávio de. "Racismo e miscigenação na sociologia da Paraíba no início do século," in Andrade and Fernandes, eds., *Atualidade & abolição*, pp. 153-65.

1810. Nishida, Mieko. "Family and Kinship in Urban Slavery: Salvador, Brazil, 1808-1880" (Unpublished papar, 47th International Congress of Americanists, New Orleans, Louisiana, 8-11 July 1991).

1811. Nishida, Mieko. "Gender, Ethnicity, and Kinship in the Urban African Diaspora: Salvador, Brazil, 1808-1880" (PhD diss., Johns Hopkins University, 1991).

1812. Nishida, Mieko. "Manumissions and Ethnicity in Urban Slavery: Salvador, Brazil, 1808-1880," *Hispanic American Historical Review*, 73, 3 (1993), pp. 361-91.

1813. Oliveira, Maria Inês Côrtes de. *O liberto: o seu mundo e os outros: Salvador, 1790/1890*. São Paulo: Corrúpio, 1988.

1814. Oliveira, Maria Inês Côrtes de. "Retrouver une identité: jeux sociaux des Africains de Bahia (vers 1750 - vers 1890)" (Thèse de doctorat, Université de Paris Sorbonne, Paris IV, 1992).

1815. Orser, Charles E., Jr. *In Search of Zumbi: Preliminary Archaeological Research at the Serra da Barriga, State of Alagoas, Brazil*. Normal IL.: Midwestern Archaeological Research Center, Illinois State University, 1992.

1816. Orser, Charles E., Jr. *In Search of Zumbi, the 1993 Season*. Normal IL: Illinois State University, 1993.

1817. Orser, Charles E., Jr. "Toward a Global Historical Archaeology: An Example from Brazil," *Historical Archaeology*, 28, 1 (1994), pp. 5-22.

1818. Orser, Charles E., Jr., and Pedro Paulo A. Funari. "Pesquisa archaeológica inicial em Palmares," *Estudos ibero-americanos*, 18, 2 (1992), pp. 53-69.

1819. Palacios, Guillermo. "Peasantry and Slavery in Brazil: A Contribution to the History of the Free Poor Planters from the Captaincy General of Pernambuco, 1700-1817" (PhD diss., Princeton University, 1993).

1820. Petrauskas, Maria Evilnardes Dantas. "Os escravos de ganho e de aluguel no mercado de Salvador," *História UFRN* (Departamento de História, Universidade Federal do Rio Grande do Norte), 2, 2 ([1988]), pp. 23-29.

1821. Poole, Dillard Marvin. "The Struggle for Self-Affirmation and Self-Determination: Africans and People of African Descent in Salvador da Bahia, 1800-1850" (PhD diss., Indiana University, 1992).

1822. Price, Richard. "Palmares como poderia ter sido," in Reis and Gomes, eds., *Liberdade por um fio*, pp. 52-59.

1823. Quiring-Zoche, Rosemarie. "Glaubenskampf oder Machtkampf? Der Aufstand der Mali von Bahia nach einer islamischen Quelle," *Sudanic Africa: A Journal of Historical Sources*, 6 (1995), pp. 115-24.

1824. Reis, João José. "Différences et résistances: les noirs à Bahia sous l'esclavage," *Cahiers d'études africaines*, 32, 1 (no. 125) (1992), pp. 15-34.

1825. Reis, João José. "Escravos e coiteiros no quilombo do Oitizeiro: Bahia, 1806," in Reis and Gomes, eds., *Liberdade por um fio*, pp. 332-72.

1826. Reis, João José. "A greve negra de 1857 na Bahia," *Revista da Universidade de São Paulo*, 18 (1993), pp. 7-29.

1827. Reis, João José. "[Anexo]: O mapa do Buraco do Tatu," in Reis and Gomes, eds., *Liberdade por um fio*, pp. 501-05.

1828. Reis, João José. "Recôncavo rebelde: revoltas escravas nos engenhos baianos," *Afro-Ásia*, no. 15 (1992), pp. 100-26.

1829. Reis, João José. *Slave Rebellion in Brazil: The Muslim Uprising of 1835 in Bahia*. Rev. and expanded ed. Baltimore: Johns Hopkins University Press, 1993.

Trans. (by Arthur Brakel) of *Rebelião escrava no Brasil*.

1830. Schwartz, Stuart B. "Cantos e quilombos numa conspiração de escravos haussás: Bahia, 1814," in Reis and Gomes, eds., *Liberdade por um fio*, pp. 373-406.

1831. Schwartz, Stuart B. "Slave in the Cane: Slavery in the Sugar Economy of Northeastern Brazil" (Presentation at "Seminário internacional: Escravos com e sem açucar", Madeira, 17-21 June 1996).

1832. Shepherd, Verene. (review of Reis, *Slave Rebellion in Brazil*), *Social and Economic Studies*, 43, 1 (1994), pp. 239-44.

1833. Soares, Cecília Moreira. "Resistência negra e religião: a repressão ao candomblé de Paramerim, 1853," *Estudos afro-asiáticos*, 23 (1992), pp. 133-42.

1834. Vainfas, Ronaldo. "Deus contra Palmares: representações senhoriais e idéias jesuíticas," in Reis and Gomes, eds., *Liberdade por um fio*, pp. 60-80.

4. Center-South

1835. Abrahão, Fernando António. *As ações de liberdade de escravos no Tribunal de Campinas*. Campinas: UNICAMP, Centro de Memória, 1992.

1836. Algranti, Leila Mezan. "Os registros da polícia e seu aproveitamento para a história do Rio de Janeiro: escravos e libertos," *Revista de história* (São Paulo), no. 119 (1985-88), pp. 115-25.

1837. Andrade, Rômulo. "Escravidão e cafeicultura em Minas Gerais: o caso da Zona da Mata," *Revista brasileira de história*, 11 (no. 22) (1991), pp. 93-131.

1838. Barros, Edval de S. "Escravidão, tráfico atlântico e preços de cativos: o caso da província do Rio de Janeiro, 1790-1830" (Niterói: Departamento de História, Universidade Federal Fluminense, 1987). (Unpublished relatório, Centro Nacional de Pesquisas)

1839. Bergad, Laird W. "After the Mining Boom: Demographic and Economic Aspects of Slavery in Mariana, Minas Gerais, 1750-1808," *Latin American Research Review*, 31, 1 (1996), pp. 67-97.

1840. Bergad, Laird W. "Demographic Change in a Post-Export Boom Society: The Population of Minas Gerais, Brazil, 1776-1821," *Journal of Social History*, 29, 4 (1996) pp. 895-932.

1841. Bonnet, Márcia C. Leão. "Produção artística e trabalho escravo no Rio de Janeiro da primeira metade do século XIX: um estudo de caso," *Estudos afro-asiáticos*, 27 (1995), pp. 167-85.

1842. Botelho, Tarcísio Rodrigues. "Demografia da escravidão norte-mineira no século XIX," *LPH: Revista de história* (Departamento de História, Universidade Federal de Ouro Preto), 2, 1 (1991), pp. 103-11. (VII Encontro regional de história da ANPUH-MG, "Crise das Ideologias", Mariana, 24-28 Sept. 1990)

1843. Chalhoub, Sidney. "The Politics of Disease Control: Yellow Fever and Race in Nineteenth Century Rio de Janeiro," *Journal of Latin American Studies*, 25, 3 (1993), pp. 441-63.

1844. Cunha, Waldir da. "A Fazenda de Gericinó e o Visconde de Santo Amaro," *Anais da Biblioteca Nacional*, 108 (1988), pp. 115-27.

1845. Ferlini, Vera. "Escravos e açucar no Brasil: as capitanias do sul" (Presentation at "Seminário internacional: Escravos com e sem açucar", Madeira, 17-21 June 1996).

1846. Fragoso, João Luís Ribeiro, and Manolo Garcia Florentino. "Marcelino, filho de Inocência Crioula, neto de Joana Cabinda: um estudo sobre famílias escravas em Paraíba do Sul (1835-1872)," *Estudos económicos*, 17, 2 (1987), pp. 151-73.

1847. Godoy, Marcelo Magalães. "Reconstituindo o movimento no tempo de uma estrutura da posse de escravos (Bonfim, 1832-1839)," *LPH: Revista de história* (Departamento de História, Universidade Federal de Ouro Preto), 3, 1 (1992), pp. 67-79.

1848. Góes, José Roberto. *O cativeiro imperfeito: um estudo sobre a escravidão no Rio de Janeiro da primeira metade do século XIX*. Vitória: Governo do Estado do Espírito Santo, Secretaria de Estado da Justiça e da Cidadania, Secretaria de Estado da Educação, 1993.

1849. Gomes, Flávio dos Santos. "O 'campo negro' de Iguaçu: escravos, mocambos no Rio de Janeiro (1812-1883)," *Estudos afro-asiáticos*, 25 (1993), pp. 43-72.

1850. Gomes, Flávio dos Santos. *Histórias de quilombolas: mocambos e comunidades de senzalas no Rio de Janeiro, século XIX*. Rio de Janeiro: Arquivo Nacional, 1995.

1851. Gomes, Flávio dos Santos. "Quilombos do Rio de Janeiro no século XIX," in Reis and Gomes, eds., *Liberdade por um fio*, pp. 263-90.

1852. Gomes, Flávio dos Santos. "Seguindo o mapa das Minas: plantas e quilombos mineiros setecentistas," *Estudos afro-asiáticos*, 29 (1996), pp. 113-42.

1853. Grinberg, Keila. *Liberata: a lei da ambiguidade: as ações de liberdade da Corte de Apelação do Rio de Janeiro no século XIX*. Rio de Janeiro: Relume Dumará, 1994.

1854. Grossi, Yonne de Souza. "Constança do Serro Frio: escravos libertos nas Minas Gerais do século XIX," *LPH: Revista de história* (Departamento de História, Universidade Federal de Ouro Preto), 2, 1 (1991), pp. 118-28. (VII Encontro regional de história da ANPUH-MG, "Crise das Ideologias", Mariana, 24-28 Sept. 1990)

1855. Guimarães, Carlos Magno. "Mineração, quilombos e Palmares: Minas Gerais do século XVIII," in Reis and Gomes, eds., *Liberdade por um fio*, pp. 139-63.

1856. Higgins, Kathleen. "Prospects of the Young in Sabará, Minas Gerais: Enslaved Children in Brazil's Colonial Mining Region, 1710-1809" (Unpublished paper, American Historical Association, Chicago, 5-8 Jan. 1995).

1857. Holloway, Thomas H. "O 'saudável terror': repressão policial aos capoeiras e resistência dos escravos no Rio de Janeiro no século XIX," *Estudos afro-asiáticos*, 16 (1989), pp. 129-40.

1858. Klein, Herbert S., and Clotilde Andrade Paiva. "Escravos e livres nas Minas Gerais do século XIX: Campanha em 1831," *Estudos econômicos*, 22, 1 (1992), pp. 129-51.

Translated as "Slave and Free in Nineteenth-Century Minas Gerais: Campanha in 1831," *Slavery and Abolition*, 15, 1 (1994), pp. 1-21.

1859. Johnson, Elizabeth Alice. "Slavery and the Benedictine Order in Late Colonial São Paulo" (MA thesis, University of Texas at Austin, 1996).

1860. Klein, Herbert S. "Freedmen in a Slave Economy: Minas Gerais in 1831," *Journal of Social History*, 29, 4 (1996) pp. 933-62.

1861. *Lima, Carlos Alberto Medeiros. "Trabalho, negócios e escravidão: artífices na cidade do Rio de Janeiro, c. 1790-c. 1808" (Diss. mestrado, Universidade Federal do Rio de Janeiro, Departamento de História, 1993).

1862. Luna, Francisco Vidal, and Herbert S. Klein. "Slaves and Masters in Early Nineteenth-Century Brazil: São Paulo," *Journal of Interdisciplinary History*, 21, 4 (1991), pp. 549-73.

1863. Machado, Humberto Fernandes. *Escravos, senhores & café: a crise da cafeicultura escravista do Vale do Paraíba Fluminense 1860-1888*. Niterói: Clube de Literatura Cromos, 1993.

1864. Machado, Humberto Fernandes. "Violência e resistência na cafeicultura escravista do Rio de Janeiro," *Revista do Rio de Janeiro*, 1, 1 (1993), pp. 24-34.

1865. Machado, Maria Helena Pereira Toledo. "Vivendo na mais perfeita desordem: os libertos e o modo de vida camponês na província de São Paulo do século XIX," *Estudos afro-asiáticos*, 25 (1993), pp. 25-42.

1866. McCann, Bryan Daniel. "Slavery Negotiated: Tension on the Middle Ground, the Paraiba Valley, Brazil, 1835-1889" (MA thesis, University of New Mexico, 1994).

1867. Mello, Pedro C[arvalho] de. "Expectation of Abolition and Sanguinity of Coffee Planters in Brazil, 1871-1881," in Fogel and Engerman, eds., *Markets and Production: Technical Papers*, vol. 1 (*Without Consent or Contract*), pp. 629-46.

1868. Mello, Pedro C[arvalho] de. "Rates of Return on Slave Capital in Brazilian Coffee Plantations, 1871-1881," in Fogel and Engerman, eds., *Markets and Production: Technical Papers*, vol. 1 (*Without Consent or Contract*), pp. 63-79.

1869. Monteiro, John M. "Alforrias, litígios e a desagregação da escravidão indígena em São Paulo," *Revista de história* (São Paulo), no. 120 (1989), pp. 45-58.

1870. Monteiro, John M. "From Indian to Slave: Forced Native Labour and Colonial Society in São Paulo during the Seventeenth Century".

Reprinted in Manning, ed., *Slave Trades, 1500-1800*, pp. 109-32.

1871. Monteiro, John Manuel. *Negros da terra: índios e bandeirantes nas origens de São Paulo*. [São Paulo]: Companhia das Letras, 1994.

1872. Mott, Luiz. *Rosa Egipcíaca: uma santa africana no Brasil*. Rio de Janeiro: Editora Bertrand Brasil, 1993.

1873. Motta, José Flávio. "O advento da cafeicultura e a estrutura da posse de escravos (Bananal, 1801-1829)," *Estudos econômicos*, 21, 3 (1991), pp. 409-34.

1874. Naro, Nancy Priscilla B. "A transição da mão-de-obra escrava para a livre: historiografia recente e comparação de dois casos ilustrativos: Rio Bonito e Vassouras (1870-1890)," *Estudos afro-asiáticos*, 22 (1992), pp. 33-46.

1875. Nazzari, Muriel. "Transition Toward Slavery: Changing Legal Practice Regarding Indians in Seventeenth-Century São Paulo," *The Americas*, 49, 2 (1992), pp. 131-55.

1876. Oliam, José. *O negro na economia mineira*. N.p.: n.p., 1993.

1877. Paiva, Eduardo França. "Coartações e alforrias nas Minas Gerais do século XVIII: as possibilidades de libertação escrava no principal centro colonial," *Revista de História* (FFLCH-Universidade de São Paulo), 2 (no. 133) (1995), pp. 49-57.

1878. Paiva, Eduardo França. *Escravos e libertos nas Minas Gerais do século XVIII: estratégias de resistência através dos testamentos*. São Paulo: ANNABLUME, 1995.

1879. Pinto, Bartolomeu Homem d'El Rei. "Livro de batismo dos pretos pertencentes à paróquia de Irajá," *Anais da Biblioteca Nacional*, 108 (1988), pp. 129-73.

1880. Piratininga Júnior, Luiz Gonzaga. *Dietário dos escravos de São Bento: originários de São Caetano e São Bernardo*. São Paulo/São Caetano do Sul, 1991.

1881. Ramos, Donald. "O quilombo e o sistema escravista em Minas Gerais do século XVIII," in Reis and Gomes, eds., *Liberdade por um fio*, pp. 164-92.

1882. Reis, Liana Maria. "Escravos e abolicionismo na imprensa mineira (1850/1888)," *LPH: Revista de história* (Departamento de História, Universidade Federal de Ouro Preto), 2, 1 (1991), pp. 222-29. (VII Encontro regional de história da ANPUH-MG, "Crise das Ideologias", Mariana, 24-28 Sept. 1990)

1883. Reis, Liana Maria. "Fuga de escravos e formação de mercado de trabalho livre na província mineira (1850/1888)," *Revista brasileira de estudos políticos*, 73 (1991), pp. 203-17.

1884. *Rios, Ana M. L. "Famílias e transição (famílias negras em Paraíba do Sul, 1872-1920)" (Diss. mestrado, Universidade Federal Fluminense, Departamento de História, 1990).

1885. Santos, Ana Maria dos, and Sónia Regina de Mendonça. "Representações sobre o trabalho livre na crise do escravismo fluminense (1870/1903)," *Revista brasileira de história*, 6, 11 (1985-86), pp. 85-98. (Número especial: Déa Ribeiro Fenelon, ed., "Sociedade e trabalho na história")

1886. *Silva, Lúcia Helena Oliveira. "As estratégias de sedução: mulheres escravas apre(e)ndendo a liberdade (1850-1888)" (Diss. mestrado, Pontifícia Universidade Católica de Campinas, 1993).

1887. Silva, Maximiano de Carvalho e. "Partilha de escravos [Pouso Alegre, Minas Gerais, 1878]," *Anais da Biblioteca Nacional*, 108 (1988), pp. 199-215.

1888. *Simonato, Andréa J., *et al.* "Preços de escravos: a lógica demográfica da empresa escravista" (unpublished, Universidade Federal do Rio de Janeiro, Departamento de História, 1990).

1889. *Slenes, Robert. "Central-African Water Spirits in Rio de Janeiro: Slave Identity and Rebellion in Early Nineteenth-Century Brazil" (Unpublished manuscript, UNICAMP, 1995).

1890. Souza, Laura de Mello e. "Violência e práticas culturais no cotidiano de uma expedição contra quilombolas: Minas Gerais, 1769," in Reis and Gomes, eds., *Liberdade por um fio*, pp. 193-212.

1891. Venâncio, Renato Pinto. "A riqueza do senhor: crianças escravas em Minas Gerais do século XIX," *Estudos afro-asiáticos*, 21 (1991), pp. 97-108.

1892. Vogel, Arno, Marco Antonio da Silva Mello, and José Flávio Pessoa de Barros. *A galinha-d'Angola: iniciação e identidade na cultura afro-brasileira*. Rio de Janeiro: Flacso, 1993.

1893. Wissenbach, Maria Cristina Cortez. "Arranjos de sobrevivência escrava na cidade de São Paulo do século XIX," *Revista de história* (São Paulo), no. 119 (1985-88), pp. 101-13.

1894. Wissenbach, Maria Cristina Cortez. (Review essay: Karasch, *Slave Life in Rio de Janeiro*), *Revista de história* (São Paulo), no. 120 (1989), pp. 163-82.

5. South

1895. Maestri, Mário. "Pampa negro: quilombos no Rio Grande do Sul," in Reis and Gomes, eds., *Liberdade por um fio*, pp. 291-331.

1896. Moreira, Paulo Roberto Staudt. *Faces da liberdade, máscaras do cativeiro: experiências de liberdade e escravidão, percebidas através das cartas de alforria: Porto Alegre, 1858-1888*. Porto Alegre: EDIPUCRS, 1996.

1897. Weimar, Gunter. *Trabalho escravo no Rio Grande do Sul*. Porto Alegre: Universidade Federal do Rio Grande do Sul, 1991.

6. West

1898. Corrêa, Lucia Salsa, and Maria do Carmo Brazil Gomes da Silva. "Escravos: conflito e violência em Corumbá (Slavers [sic]: Conflicts and Violence in Corumbá)," *História* (São Paulo), 10 (1991), pp. 141-50.

1899. Karasch, Mary C. "Os quilombos do ouro na capitania de Goiás," in Reis and Gomes, eds., *Liberdade por um fio*, pp. 240-62.

1900. Karasch, Mary C. "Slave Women on the Brazilian Frontier in the Nineteenth Century," in Gaspar and Hine, eds., *More than Chattel*, pp. 79-96.

1901. Salles, Gilka V. F. de. *Economia e escravidão na Capitania de Goiás*. Goiâna: CEGRAF/EFG, 1992. (Coleção Documentos Goianos, 24)

1902. Volpato, Luiza Rios Ricci. *Cativos do sertão: vida cotidiana e escravidão em Cuiabá em 1850-1888*. São Paulo: Marco Zero, and [Cuiabá], Universidade Federal de Mato Grosso, 1993.

1903. Volpato, Luiza Rios Ricci. "Quilombos em Mato Grosso: resistência negra em área de fronteira," in Reis and Gomes, eds., *Liberdade por um fio*, pp. 213-39.

V. CARIBBEAN

1. General and Comparative

1904. Barrow, Christine. *Family in the Caribbean: Themes and Perspectives*. Kingston [Jamaica]: Oxford/I. Randle/ J. Currey, 1996.

1905. Beckles, Hilary McD. *Black Masculinity in Caribbean Slavery*. St. Michael, Barbados: Women and Development Unit, 1996.

1906. Beckles, Hilary McD. "Caribbean Anti-Slavery: The Self-Liberation Etho- of Enslaved Blacks."

Reprinted in Beckles and Shepherd, eds., *Caribbean Slave Society and Economy*, pp. 363-72.

1907. Beckles, Hilary McD. "Kalinago (Carib) Resistance to European Colonisation of the Caribbean," *Caribbean Quarterly*, 38, 2-3 (1992), pp. 1-14.

1908. *Beckles, Hilary McD. "The Leisure Culture of Slaves in the Caribbean" (Conference of Caribbean Historians, San Germán, Puerto Rico, 1994).

1909. Beckles, Hilary McD. "Resistance to Slavery and Colonization by Amerindians in the Lesser Antilles During the 17th Century" (Unpublished paper, 24th Annual Conference of Caribbean Historians, Nassau, 29 March - 3 April 1992).

1910. Beckles, Hilary McD. "Sex and Gender in the Historiography of Caribbean Slavery," in Shepherd, Brereton, and Bailey, eds., *Engendering History*, pp. 125-40.

1911. Beckles, Hilary McD. "Signposts and Insights," in Beckles, ed., *Inside Slavery*, pp. 1-11.

1912. Beckles, Hilary McD. "An Unnatural and Dangerous Independence: The Haitian Revolution and the Political Sociology of Caribbean Slavery," *Journal of Caribbean History*, 25, 1-2 (1991), pp. 160-76.

1913. Beckles, Hilary McD. "White Women and Slavery in the Caribbean," *History Workshop*, 36 (1993), pp. 66-82.

1914. Beckles, Hilary McD., ed. *Inside Slavery: Process and Legacy in the Caribbean Experience.* [Mona, Kingston, Jamaica]: Canoe Press, University of the West Indies, 1996.

For contents see Beckles, Brereton, Craton, Hall, Higman, Scott, and Sheridan. [The Elsa Gouveia Memorial Lectures, 1985-91]

1915. Beckles, Hilary McD., and Verene Shepherd, eds. *Caribbean Slave Society and Economy: A Student Reader.* London: James Currey, 1991.

For contents see Beckles, Carrington, Craton (2), Drescher, Geggus, Goveia, Hall (4), Higman (2), James, Kiple and Kiple, Knight, Lamur (2), Midas, Mintz and Hall, Morrissey, Scarano, Schuler (2), Scott, Shepherd, Sheridan, Sio, Tomich, and Williams.

1916. Beet, Chris de. "Een staat in een staat: een vergelijking tussen de Surinaamse en Jamaicaanse Marrons," *Oso (Tijdschrift voor Surinaamse Taalkunde, Letterkunde, Cultuur en Geschiedenis)*, 11, 2 (1992), pp. 186-93.

1917. Benjamin, Ann. "Some Reflections on Hilary Beckles' Article: 'Caribbean Anti-Slavery: The Self-Liberation Ethos of Enslaved Blacks'," *Journal of CaribbeanHistory*, 26, 1 (1992), pp. 97-108.

Also see Sio.

1918. Berkland, Ellen P., and Mary C. Baudry. "'A Kind of Freedom on His Little Plantation': Documentary Archaeology of Afro-Caribbean Slave Households" (Unpublished paper, Annual Meeting of the Society for Historical Archaeology, Kingston, Jamaica, January 1992).

1919. Bilby, Kenneth. "Oral Traditions in Two Maroon Societies: The Windward Maroons of Jamaica and the Aluku Maroons of French Guiana and Suriname," in Hoogbergen, ed., *Born out of Resistance*, pp. 169-80.

1920. Blackett, Harcourt. *Survivors of the Middle Passage: Affirmation and Change.* Barbados: Caribbean/African American Dialogue and the Caribbean Conference of Churches, 1993.

1921. Bolland, O. Nigel. "Current Caribbean Research Five Centuries After Columbus (review essay, including: Beckles, *A History of Barbados*, Campbell, *Maroons of Jamaica*, Hoogbergen, *Boni Maroon Wars in Suriname*, Price, *Alabi's World*, Bergad, *Cuban Rural Society in the Nineteenth Century*, among others)," *Latin American Research Review*, 29, 3 (1994), pp. 202-19.

1922. Brereton, Bridget. "Searching for the Invisible Woman (review essay: Beckles, *Natural Rebels*, Bush, *Slave Women in Caribbean Society*, and Morrissey, *Slave Women in the New World*)," *Slavery and Abolition*, 13, 2 (1992), pp. 86-96.

1923. Butel, Paul, and Bernard Lavalle, eds. *Commerce et plantation dans la Caraïbe: XVIIIe et XIXe siècles (Actes du Colloque de Bordeaux, 15-16 mars 1991).* Bordeaux: Maison des Pays Ibériques, 1991. (Centre d'Histoire des Espaces Atlantiques)

For contents see Cauna, Daget, Saugera, Tornero Tinajero, Vergé-Franceschi, and Yacou.

1924. [Primer] Congreso International de Historica Economica y Social de la Cuenca del Caribe 1763-1898 (Centro de Estudios Avanzados de Puerto Rico y el Caribe, San Juan de Puerto Rico, 1992).

For contents see Colmenares, Pérez Vega, Tronconis de Veracoechea, and Vila Vilar.

1925. Craton, Michael. "The Transition from Slavery to Free Wage Labour in the Caribbean, 1790-1890: A Survey with Particular Reference to Recent Scholarship," *Slavery and Abolition*, 13, 2 (1992), pp. 37-67.

Translated as "A transição da escravidão para o trabalho livre no Caribe (1780-1890): um estudo com particular referência à recente produção acadêmica," *Estudos afro-asiáticos*, 22 (1992), pp. 5-32.

1926. Cummins, Alissandra. "Caribbean Slave Society," in Tibbles, ed., *Transatlantic Slavery*, pp. 51-59.

1927. Dénis-Lara, Oruno. "La période révolutionnaire aux Caraïbes 1760-1830: mécanismes endogènes et conflits," in Dorothy Carrington, *et al.*, eds., *Le bicentenaire et ces îles que l'on dit françaises* (Séminaire, Université Paris VIII Jussieu, 21-22 janvier 1989) (Bastia: Scritti, 1989), pp. 31-56.

1928. Entiope, Gabriel. *Nègres, danse et resistance: la Caraïbe du XVIIe au XIXe siècle.* Paris: L'Harmattan, 1996.

1929. Goveia, Elsa V. "The West Indian Slave Laws of the Eighteenth Century."

Reprinted in Beckles and Shepherd, eds., *Caribbean Slave Society and Economy*, pp. 346-62.

1930. Hall, Douglas G. "People in Slavery," in Beckles, ed., *Inside Slavery*, pp. 13-30.

1931. Higman, Barry W. "Ecological Determinism in Caribbean History," in Beckles, ed., *Inside Slavery*, pp. 51-77.

1932. *Higman, Barry W., and Stanley L. Engerman. "The Demographic Structure of Caribbean Slave Societies in the Eighteenth and Nineteenth Centuries," in Franklin W. Knight, ed., *UNESCO General History of the Caribbean*, vol. 3 (forthcoming).

1933. Hodges, Graham. "Reconstructing Black Women's History in the Caribbean (review essay: Beckles, *Natural Rebels*; Bush, *Slave Women in Caribbean Society*; Morrissey, *Slave Women in the New World*)," *Journal of American Ethnic History*, 12, 1 (1992), pp. 101-07.

1934. Johnson, Joyce. "'A Voyage at Anchor': Among the Sang-Mélées in the West Indies," *Slavery and Abolition*, 16, 2 (1995), pp. 226-42.

1935. Kiple, Kenneth F., and Virginia H. Kiple. "Deficiency Diseases in the Caribbean."

Reprinted in Beckles and Shepherd, eds., *Caribbean Slave Society and Economy*, pp. 173-82.

1936. Klein, Herbert S. "Antilhas em geral" (Presentation at "Seminário internacional: Escravos com e sem açucar", Madeira, 17-21 June 1996).

1937. Laviña, Javier. "Tambores y cimarrones en el Caribe," *América negra*, 9 (1995), pp. 95-106.

1938. Leroux, Yannick. "The Archaeology of Slavery" (Unpublished paper, 24th Annual Conference of Caribbean Historians, Nassau, 29 March - 3 April 1992).

1939. Martinez-Vergne, Teresita. "Theoretical Perspectives on the Study of Women in the Caribbean During and After Slavery" (Unpublished paper, 24th Annual Conference of Caribbean Historians, Nassau, 29 March - 3 April 1992).

1940. Mintz, Sidney W. "Slave Life on Caribbean Sugar Plantations: Some Unanswered Questions," in Palmié, ed., *Slave Cultures and the Cultures of Slavery*, pp. 12-22.

1941. Moitt, Bernard. "Gender and Slavery: Women and the Plantation Experience in the Caribbean Before 1848," in Hoogbergen, ed., *Born out of Resistance*, pp. 110-25.

1942. Moreau, Jean-Pierre. "Les Caraïbes insulaires et la mer aux XVIe et XVIIe siècles d'après les sources ethnohistoriques," *Journal de la Société des Americanistes*, 77 (1991), pp. 63-75.

1943. Moreno Fraginals, Manuel. "Agricultural Backwardness - Industrial Production: Experiences of Sugar Production in the Caribbean," in Mats Lundahl and Thommy Svensson, eds., *Agrarian Society in History: Essays in Honor of Magnus Mörner* (New York: Routledge, 1990), pp. 125-39.

1944. Mörner, Magnus. "Patterns of Social Stratification in the 18th and 19th Century Caribbean: Some Comparative Clarifications," *Plantation Society in the Americas*, 3, 2 (1993), pp. 1-30.

1945. Morrissey, Marietta. "Gender Relations in Caribbean Slavery" (Unpublished paper, Annual Meeting of the Society for Historical Archaeology, Kingston, Jamaica, January 1992).

1946. Morrissey, Marietta. "Women's Work, Family Formation, and Reproduction Among Caribbean Slaves."

Reprinted in Beckles and Shepherd, eds., *Caribbean Slave Society and Economy*, pp. 274-86.

1947. Munford, Clarence J., and Michael Zeuske. "Black Slavery, Class Struggle, Fear and Revolution in St. Domingue and Cuba, 1785-1795," *Journal of Negro History*, 73, 1-4 (1988), pp. 12-32.

1948. Olivierre, Muriel Mary. "Abekoi: Things will be Made Clear: Socio-Historical Origins of a Caribbean Nation" (PhD diss., Union Institute, 1993).

1949. Olwig, Karen Fog. "Between Tradition and Modernity: National Development in the Caribbean," *Social Analysis: Journal of Cultural and Social Practice*, 33 (1993), pp. 89-104.

1950. Oostindie, Gert [J]. "'Cimarrón': een Spaans-Caraïbisch contrast met Suriname," *Oso (Tijdschrift voor Surinaamse Taalkunde, Letterkunde, Cultuur en Geschiedenis)*, 11, 2 (1992), pp. 194-208.

1951. Ortiz Aguill, J. J. "Culture History and the Elites Within Non-Dominant Groups: Some Observations from Caribbeanist Archaeology" (Unpublished paper, Annual Meeting of the Society for Historical Archaeology, Kingston, Jamaica, January 1992).

1952. Paquette, Robert L., and Stanley L. Engerman, eds. *The Lesser Antilles in the Age of European Expansion*. Gainesville: University Press of Florida, 1996.

For contents see Drescher, Eltis, Emmer, Gaspar, Geggus, Pérotin-Dumon, and O'Shaughnessy.

1953. *Portrait of the Caribbean*. New York: Ambrose Video Pub., 1992. (videocassette, ca. 45 min.)

1954. Pulsipher, Lydia Mihelic. "They Have Saturdays and Sundays to Feed Themselves: Slave Gardens in the Caribbean," *Expedition*, 32, 2 (1990), pp. 24-33.

1955. Shahabuddeen, J. "Slavery and Historiographical Rectification," *West Indian Law Journal* (October, 1985), pp. 29-42.

1956. Shepherd, Verene S., Bridget Brereton, and Barbara Bailey, eds. *Engendering History: Caribbean Women in Historical Perspective*. New York: St. Martin's Press, Kingston: Ian Randle, and London: James Currey, 1995.

For contents see Beckles, Castañeda, Matos-Rodríguez, and Moitt.

1957. Sio, Arnold. "Another Commentary [on Beckles, 'Caribbean Anti-Slavery']," *Journal of Caribbean History*, 26, 1 (1992), pp. 1-36.

Also see Benjamin.

1958. Sio, Arnold. "Marginality and Free Coloured Identity in Caribbean Slavery Society."

Reprinted in Beckles and Shepherd, eds., *Caribbean Slave Society and Economy*, pp. 150-59.

1959. Smorkaloff, Pamela Maria, ed. *If I Could Write This in Fire: An Anthology of Literature from the Caribbean*. New York: New Press, 1994.

Includes James Carnegie, "The Plantation and Maroon Society: Wages Paid"; Esteban Montejo, ed. Miguel Barnet, "The Autobiography of a Runaway Slave"; Rural peasantry: Simone Schwarz-Bart, "Between Two Worlds"; Theoretical Essays: "Identity, Historiography, and the Caribbean Voice," from C. L. R. James, *The Black Jacobins*.

1960. Stinchcomb, Arthur L. "Liberté et oppression des esclaves aux Caraïbes au XVIIIe siècle," *Revue française de science politique*, 44, 5 (1994), pp. 779-810.

1961. Stinchcombe, Arthur L. *Sugar Island Slavery in the Age of Enlightenment: The Political Economy of the Caribbean World*. Princeton: Princeton University Press, 1995.

1962. Stolcke, Verena. "The Slavery Period and Its Influence on Household Structure and the Family in Jamaica, Cuba, and Brazil," in Elza Berquó and Peter Xenos, eds., *Family Systems and Cultural Change* (Oxford: Clarendon Press, 1992), pp. 125-43.

1963. Tardieu, Jean-Pierre. "Quelques visions utopiques de l'esclavage des Noirs aux Indes occidentales (XVIe et XVIIe siècles)," in Bresc, ed., *Figures de l'esclave*, pp. 247-61.

1964. Trouillot, Michel-Rolph. "Coffee Planters and Coffee Slaves in the Antilles: The Impact of a Secondary Crop," in Berlin and Morgan, eds., *Cultivation and Culture*, pp. 124-37.

1965. Turner, Mary. "Introduction," to idem, ed., *From Chattel Slaves to Wage Slaves*, pp. 1-30.

1966. Vergé-Franceschi. "Fortune et plantations des administrateurs coloniaux aux îles d'Amérique aux XVIIe et XVIIIe siècles," in Butel, ed., *Commerce et plantation dans la Caraïbe*, pp. 115-42.

1967. Yacou, Alain. "Essor et déclin du système esclavagiste des habitations sucrières à Cuba et en Guadeloupe," in Butel, ed., *Commerce et plantation dans la Caraïbe*, pp. 191-213.

2. English[4]

1968. Afroz, Sultana. "The Unsung Slaves: Islam in Plantation Jamaica - The African Connection," *Journal of the Institute of Muslim Minority Affairs* (London), 15, 1-2 (1994), pp. 157-70.

Also as "The Unsung Slaves: Islam in the Plantation Society," *Caribbean Quarterly*, 41, 3-4 (1995), pp. 30-44.

---

[4] Including the "ceded" or "neutral" islands: Dominica, St. Vincent, St. Lucia, Antigua, Tobago.

1969. Agorsah, E. Kofi. "The Archaeology of African Maroons in Jamaica" (Unpublished paper, Annual Meeting of the Society for Historical Archaeology, Kingston, Jamaica, January 1992).

1970. Armstrong, Douglas V., and Kenneth Kelly. "Spatial Transformations in African Jamaican Housing at Seville Plantation" (Unpublished paper, Annual Meeting of the Society for Historical Archaeology, Kingston, Jamaica, January 1992).

1971. Banton, Mandy. "The Transition to 'Free' Labour: Regulation and the Role of the Colonial Office in Legislative Development" (Unpublished paper, conference on "Unfree Labor in the Development of the Atlantic World", 13-14 April 1993, York University, Ontario).

1972. Beckles, Hilary McD. "Black Female Slaves and White Households in Barbados," in Gaspar and Hine, eds., *More than Chattel*, pp. 111-25.

1973. Beckles, Hilary McD. "The Colours of Property: Brown, White and Black Chattels and their Responses on the Caribbean Frontier," in Lovejoy and Rogers, eds., *Unfree Labour in the Development of the Atlantic World*, pp. 36-51.

1974. Beckles, Hilary [McD]. "The Concept of 'White Slavery' in the English Caribbean during the Early Seventeenth Century," in John Brewer and Susan Staves, eds., *Early Modern Conceptions of Property* (London: Routledge, 1995), pp. 572-84.

1975. Beckles, Hilary McD. "English Parliamentary Debate on 'White Slavery' in Barbados, 1659," *Journal of the Barbados Museum and Historical Society*, 36, 4 (1982), pp. 344-52.

1976. Beckles, Hilary McD. "Land Distribution and Class Formation in Barbados 1630-1700: The Rise of a Wage Proletariat," *Journal of the Barbados Museum and Historical Society*, 36, 2 (1980), pp. 136-43.

1977. Beckles, Hilary McD. "Property Rights in Pleasure: The Marketing of Slave Women's Sexuality in the West Indies," in McDonald, ed., *West Indies Accounts*, pp. 169-87.

1978. Beckles, Hilary McD. "Sugar and White Servitude: An Analysis of Indentured Labour during the Sugar Revolution of Barbados 1643-1655," *Journal of the Barbados Museum and Historical Society*, 35, 3 (1981), pp. 236-46.

1979. Berleant-Schiller, Riva. "The White Minority and the Emancipation Process in Montserrat, 1811-32," *New West Indian Guide/Nieuwe West-Indische Gids*, 70 (3-4) (1996), pp. 255-82.

1980. Bernhard, Virginia. "Bids for Freedom: Slave Resistance and Rebellion Plots in Bermuda, 1656-1761," *Slavery and Abolition*, 17, 3 (1996), pp. 185-208.

1981. Besson, Jean. "The Creolization of African-American Slave Kinship in Jamaican Free Village and Maroon Communities," in Palmié, ed., *Slave Cultures and the Cultures of Slavery*, pp. 187-209.

1982. Bratton, John. "Yabba Ware and the African Presence at Port Royal" (Unpublished paper, Annual Meeting of the Society for Historical Archaeology, Kingston, Jamaica, January 1992).

1983. Brereton, Bridget. "A Social History of Emancipation Day in the British Caribbean: The First Fifty Years," in Beckles, ed., *Inside Slavery*, pp. 78-95.

1984. Burnard, Trevor. "A Failed Settler Society: Marriage and Demographic Failure in Early Jamaica," *Journal of Social History*, 28, 1 (1994), pp. 63-82.

1985. Bush[-Slimani], Barbara. "Hard Labour: Women, Childbirth and Resistance in British Caribbean Slave Societies," *History Workshop*, 36 (1993), pp. 83-99.

Also in Gaspar and Hine, eds., *More than Chattel*, pp. 193-217.

1986. Bush, Barbara. "Slave Women in the British Caribbean 1650-1834: A Perspective on Identity, Culture and Resistance," in Hoogbergen, ed., *Born out of Resistance*, pp. 126-36.

1987. Bush, Barbara. "Survival and Resistance: Slave Women and Coercive Labour Regimes in the British Caribbean, 1750 to 1838".

Reprinted in Manning, ed., *Slave Trades, 1500-1800*, pp. 291-302.

1988. Butler, Kathleen Mary. *The Economics of Emancipation: Jamaica and Barbados, 1823-1843.*

Chapel Hill: University of North Carolina Press, 1995.

1989. Butler, Lindley S. "Barbadians on the Cape Fear: A West Indian Frontier Plantation" (Unpublished paper, Annual Meeting of the Society for Historical Archaeology, Kingston, Jamaica, January 1992).

1990. Campbell, Carl C. *Cedulants and Capitulants: The Politics of the Coloured Opposition in the Slave Society of Trinidad, 1783-1838*. Trinidad WI: Paria Pub. Co., 1992.

1991. Carrington, Selwyn. "The American Revolution: British Policy and the West Indian Economy 1775-1807" (Unpublished paper, 24th Annual Conference of Caribbean Historians, Nassau, 29 March - 3 April 1992).

1992. Carrington, Selwyn. "The State of the Debate on the Role of Capitalism in the Ending of the Slave System."

Reprinted in Beckles and Shepherd, eds., *Caribbean Slave Society and Economy*, pp. 435-45.

1993. Cash, Philip, Shirley Gordon, and Gail Saunders. *Sources of Bahamian History*. London: Macmillan Caribbean, 1991.

Includes section on "The African Connection": A. Slaves and Free Blacks before 1807; B. Slaves, Apprentices, Free Blacks 1807-38.

1994. Cheek, Charles D. "Setting an English Table: Black Carib Archaeology on the Caribbean Coast of Honduras" (Unpublished paper, Annual Meeting of the Society for Historical Archaeology, Kingston, Jamaica, January 1992).

1995. Costa, Emilia Viotti da. *Crowns of Glory, Tears of Blood: The Demerara Slave Rebellion of 1823*. New York: Oxford University Press, 1994.

1996. Craton, Michael. "The Ambivalencies of Independency: The Transition out of Slavery in the Bahamas, c. 1800-1850," in McDonald, ed., *West Indies Accounts*, pp. 274-96.

1997. Craton, Michael. "Changing Patterns of Slave Families in the British West Indies."

Reprinted in Beckles and Shepherd, eds., *Caribbean Slave Society and Economy*, pp. 228-49.

1998. Craton, Michael. "Death, Disease and Medicine on the Jamaican Slave Plantations: The Example of Worthy Park, 1676-1838."

Reprinted in Beckles and Shepherd, eds., *Caribbean Slave Society and Economy*, pp. 183-96.

1999. Craton, Michael. "Decoding Pitchy-Patchy: The Roots, Branches and Essence of Junkanoo," *Slavery and Abolition*, 16, 1 (1995), pp. 14-44.

2000. Craton, Michael. "Property and Propriety: Land Tenure and Slave Property in the Creation of a British West Indian Plantocracy, 1612-1740," in John Brewer and Susan Staves, eds., *Early Modern Conceptions of Property* (London: Routledge, 1995), pp. 497-529.

2001. Craton, Michael. "A Recipe for the Perfect Calalu: Island and Regional Identity in the British West Indies," in Beckles, ed., *Inside Slavery*, pp. 119-40.

2002. Craton, Michael J. "Reshuffling the Pack: The Transition from Slavery to Other Forms of Labor in the British Caribbean, ca., 1790-1800," *New West Indian Guide/Nieuwe West-Indische Gids*, 68, 1-2 (1994), pp. 23-75.

Translated as "Reembaralhando as cartas: a transição da escravidão para outras formas de trabalho no Caribe britânico," *Estudos afro-asiáticos*, 28 (1995), pp. 31-83.

2003. Craton, Michael, and [D.] Gail Saunders. *Islanders in the Stream: A History of the Bahamian People*. Athens: University of Georgia Press, 1992.

2004. Dawes, Kwame S. N. "An Act of 'Unruly' Savagery: Re-Writing Black Rebellion in the Language of the Colonizer: H. G. deLisser's *The White Witch of Rosehall*," *Caribbean Quarterly*, 40, 1 (1994), pp. 1-12.

2005. D'Costa, Jean. "Oral Literature, Formal Literature: The Formation of Genre in Eighteenth-Century Jamaica," in Zimbardo and Montgomery, eds., "African-American Culture in the Eighteenth Century," pp. 663-76.

2006. De Verteuil, Anthony. *Seven Slaves and Slavery: Trinidad, 1777-1838*. [Port of Spain, Trinidad and Tobago?]: Scrip-J Printers, 1992.

2007. Delle, James Andrew. "An Archaeology of Crisis: The Manipulation of Social Spaces in the Blue Mountain Coffee Plantation Complex of Jamaica,

1790-1865" (PhD diss., University of Massachusetts at Amherst, 1996).

2008. Drescher, Seymour. "The Decline Thesis of British Slavery since *Econocide*."

Reprinted in Beckles and Shepherd, eds., *Caribbean Slave Society and Economy*, pp. 136-49.

2009. Dunn, Richard S. *Moravian Missionaries at Work in a Jamaican Slave Community, 1754-1835*. Minneapolis: The Associates of the James Ford Bell Library, University of Minnesota, 1994. (James Ford Bell lectures, no. 32)

2010. Dunn, Richard S. "The Story of Two Jamaican Slaves: Sarah Affir and Robert McAlpine of Mesopotamia Estate," in McDonald, ed., *West Indies Accounts*, pp. 188-210.

2011. Dunn, Richard S. "Sugar Production and Slave Women in Jamaica," in Berlin and Morgan, eds., *Cultivation and Culture*, pp. 49-72.

2012. Eltis, David. "The Total Product of Barbados, 1664-1701," *Journal of Economic History*, 55, 2 (1995), pp. 321-38.

2013. Engerman, Stanley S. "The Land and Labour Problem at the Time of the Legal Emancipation of the British West Indian Slaves," in McDonald, ed., *West Indies Accounts*, pp. 297-318.

2014. Eubanks, Thomas Hales. "Sugar, Slavery and Emancipation: The Industrial Archaeology of the West Indian Island of Tobago" (PhD diss., University of Florida, 1992).

2015. Fergus, Claudius K. "British Imperial Trusteeship: The Dynamics of Reconstruction of British West Indian Society, with Special Reference to Trinidad, 1783-1838" (PhD diss., University of the West Indies, Saint Augustine, Trinidad and Tobago, 1996).

2016. Ferguson, Moira, ed. *The History of Mary Prince, a West Indian Slave, Related by Herself.* Preface by Ziggi Alexander. Ann Arbor: University of Michigan Press, 1993.

2017. Finamore, Daniel [R]. "English Mariners and African Slaves: Frontier Settlement in the Bay of Honduras" (Unpublished paper, Annual Meeting of the Society for Historical Archaeology, Kingston, Jamaica, January 1992).

2018. Finamore, Daniel R. "Sailors and Slaves on the Wood-Cutting Frontier: Archaeology of the British Bay Settlement, Belize" (PhD diss., Boston University, 1994).

2019. Fleischman, Mark L. "Human Skeletal Material from Seville Settlement, Jamaica" (Unpublished paper, Annual Meeting of the Society for Historical Archaeology, Kingston, Jamaica, January 1992).

2020. Fogel, Robert W. "The Profitability of Sugar Production under Apprenticeship," in Fogel, Galantine, and Manning, eds., *Evidence and Methods* (*Without Consent or Contract*), pp. 166-68.

2021. Friedman, Gerald. "The 'Decline' Theory of West Indian Emancipation," in Fogel, Galantine, and Manning, eds., *Evidence and Methods* (*Without Consent or Contract*), pp. 163-64.

2022. Friedman, Gerald. "The Profitability of West Indian Properties," in Fogel, Galantine, and Manning, eds., *Evidence and Methods* (*Without Consent or Contract*), pp. 165-66.

2023. Galantine, Ralph A. "Some Economic Aspects of the British Slavery Debate," in Fogel, Galantine, and Manning, eds., *Evidence and Methods* (*Without Consent or Contract*), p. 153.

2024. Gaspar, David Barry. "Ameliorating Slavery: The Leeward Islands Slave Act of 1798," in Engerman and Paquette, eds., *The Lesser Antilles in the Age of European Expansion*, pp. 241-58.

2025. Gaspar, David Barry. "From 'the Sense of their Slavery': Slave Women and Resistance in Antigua, 1632-1763," in Gaspar and Hine, eds., *More than Chattel*, pp. 218-38.

2026. Gaspar, David Barry. "Sugar Cultivation and Slave Life in Antigua before 1800," in Berlin and Morgan, eds., *Cultivation and Culture*, pp. 101-23.

2027. Gaspar, David Barry. "Working the System: Antigua Slaves and their Struggle to Live," *Slavery and Abolition*, 13, 3 (1992), pp. 131-55.

2028. Gerace, Kathy, and Timothy King. "Plantation Archaeology on San Salvador Island, Bahamas: The Preliminary Investigation of the Fortune Hill Slave Quarters" (Unpublished paper, Annual Meeting of the Society for Historical Archaeology, Kingston, Jamaica, January 1992).

2029. Gordon, Shirley C. *God Almighty Make me Free: Christianity in Preemancipation Jamaica.* Bloomington: Indiana University Press, 1996.

2030. Gray, Dorrick. "Locally Made Pipes from Port Royal" (Unpublished paper, Annual Meeting of the Society for Historical Archaeology, Kingston, Jamaica, January 1992).

2031. Hall, Catherine. "White Visions, Black Lives: the Free Villages of Jamaica," *History Workshop*, 36 (1993), pp. 100-32.

2032. Handler, Jerome S. "Amerindians and their Contributions to Barbadian Life in the Seventeenth Century," *Journal of the Barbados Museum and Historical Society*, 35, 3 (1977), pp. 189-210.

2033. Handler, Jerome S. "Determining African Birth from Skeletal Remains: A Note on Tooth Mutilation," *Historical Archaeology*, 28, 3 (1994), pp. 113-19.

2034. Handler, Jerome S. "A Prone Burial from a Plantation Slave Cemetery in Barbados, West Indies: Possible Evidence for an African-type Witch or Other Negatively Viewed Person," *Historical Archaeology*, 30, 3 (1996), pp. 76-86.

Summarized as "An African-Type Burial, Newton Plantation, Barbados," *African-American Archaeology*, 15, 1 (1995), pp. 5-6.

2035. Handler, Jerome S. "Slave Medicine and Obeah in Barbados" (Unpublished paper, 1996).

2036. Handler, Jerome S., and JoAnn Jacoby. "Slave Medicine and Plant Use in Barbados," *Journal of the Barbados Museum and Historical Society*, 41 (1993), pp. 74-98.

2037. Handler, Jerome S., and JoAnn Jacoby. "Slave Names and Naming in Barbados, 1650-1830," *William and Mary Quarterly*, 53, 4 (1996), pp. 685-728.

2038. Handler, Jerome S., with Michael D. Conner and Keith P. Jacobi. *Searching for a Plantation Slave Cemetery in Barbados, West Indies: A Bioarcheological and Ethnohistorical Investigation.* Carbondale IL: Center for Archaeological Investigations, Southern Illinois University, 1989.

2039. Hart, Richard. "L'esclavage et les racines du racisme britannique," in Dorigny, ed., *Les abolitions de l'esclavage*, pp. 321-27.

2040. Heidtke, Kenan. "Hand-Modeled Red Clay Pipes from Port Royal, Jamaica: Their Markings and Possible Origins" (Unpublished paper, Annual Meeting of the Society for Historical Archaeology, Kingston, Jamaica, January 1992).

2041. Heuman, Gad. "From Slave Rebellion to Morant Bay: The Tradition of Protest in Jamaica," in Binder, ed., *Slavery in the Americas*, pp. 151-64.

2042. Heuman, Gad. "A Tale of Two Jamaican Rebellions," in Hoogbergen, ed., *Born out of Resistance*, pp. 104-09.

2043. Higman, Barry W. "The Demography of Slavery in Jamaica, 1817-1834," in W. K. Marshall, ed. *Third Annual Conference of Caribbean Historians, Guyana* (Mona: Department of History, University of the West Indies, 1971), pp. 32-40.

2044. Higman, Barry W. "Economic and Social Development of the British West Indies, from Settlement to ca. 1850," in Stanley L. Engerman and Robert E. Gallman, eds., *Cambridge Economic History of the United States* (New York: Cambridge University Press, 1996), vol. 1, pp. 297-336.

2045. Higman, Barry W. "Growth in Afro-Caribbean Slave Populations," *American Journal of Physical Anthropology*, 50, 3 (1979), pp. 373-86.

2046. Higman, Barry W. "Household Structure and Fertility on Jamaican Slave Plantations: A Nineteenth-Century Example."

Reprinted in Beckles and Shepherd, eds., *Caribbean Slave Society and Economy*, pp. 250-73.

2047. Higman, Barry W. "The Internal Economy of Jamaican Pens, 1760-1890," *Social and Economic Studies*, 38, 1 (1989), pp. 61-86.

2048. Higman, Barry W. "Patterns of Exchange within a Plantation Economy: Jamaica at the Time of Emancipation," in McDonald, ed., *West Indies Accounts*, pp. 211-31.

2049. Higman, Barry W. *Slave Population and Economy in Jamaica, 1807-1834.* Kingston: The Press, University of the West Indies, 1995.

2050. Higman, Barry W. *Slave Population of the British Caribbean, 1807-1834.*

Republished, with a new introduction (Kingston, Jamaica: The Press, University of the West Indies, 1996).

2051. Higman, Barry W. "The Slave Populations of the British Caribbean: Some Nineteenth-Century Variations".

Reprinted in Beckles and Shepherd, eds., *Caribbean Slave Society and Economy*, pp. 221-27.

2052. Higman, Barry W. "Slavery Remembered".

Reprinted in *Jamaican Historical Society Bulletin*, 7, 16 (1980), pp. 216-22, and 8, 1 (1981), pp. 2-9.

2053. Higman, Barry W. "Urban Slavery in the British Caribbean," in Elizabeth M. Thomas-Hope, ed., *Perspectives on Caribbean Regional Identity* (Liverpool: Centre for Latin-American Studies, University of Liverpool, 1984), pp. 39-56. (Monograph series, no. 11)

2054. Jabour, Anya. "Slave Health and Health Care in the British Caribbean: Profits, Racism, and the Failure of Amelioration in Trinidad and British Guiana, 1824-1834," *Journal of Caribbean History*, 28, 1 (1994), pp. 1-26.

2055. Jacobi, Keith, Della Collins Cook, Robert S. Corruccini, and Jerome S. Handler. "Congenital Syphilis in the Past: Slaves at Newton Plantation, Barbados, West Indies," *American Journal of Physical Anthropology*, 89, 2 (1992), pp. 145-58.

2056. John, A. Meredith. "Logistic Models of Slave Child Mortality in Trinidad," in Fogel and Engerman, eds., *Conditions of Life and the Transition to Freedom: Technical Papers*, vol. 2 (*Without Consent or Contract*), pp. 413-34.

2057. Johnson, Howard. *The Bahamas from Slavery to Servitude, 1783-1933*. Gainesville FL: University Press of Florida, 1996.

2058. Johnson, Howard. *The Bahamas in Slavery and Freedom*. Kingston: Ian Randle Publishers, 1991.

2059. Johnson, Howard. "The Self-Hire System in the Bahamas During Slavery" (Unpublished paper, Annual Meeting of the Canadian Association of African Studies/Association Canadienne des Études Africaines, Toronto, May 1991).

2060. Johnson, Howard. "Slave Life and Leisure in Nassau, Bahamas, 1783-1838," *Slavery and Abolition*, 16, 1 (1995), pp. 45-64.

2061. Johnson, Howard [D]. "A Slow and Extended Abolition: The Case of the Bahamas 1800-38," in Turner, ed., *From Chattel Slaves to Wage Slaves*, pp. 165-81.

2062. King, Linda M. Y. "Women in the British West Indies: Resisting Slave Amelioration Policies" (MA thesis, Morgan State University, 1994).

2063. Klaus, Sylvia. "Schwarzer Widerstand in Dominica gegen das Gesellschaftssystem der Plantagensklaverei mit besonderer Berücksichtigung der Maroon-Gesellschaften von 1763 bis 1815" (DPhil diss., Universität Wien, 1991).

2064. Kossek, Brigitte. "Racist and Patriarchal Aspects of Plantation Slavery in Greneda: 'White Ladies', 'Black Women Slaves', and 'Rebels'," in Binder, ed., *Slavery in the Americas*, pp. 277-303.

2065. Kowalski, Amy B. "Social Hierarchy and the Slave-Master Relationship on Thomas Thistlewood's Jamaican Provisioning Estate: Implications for the Archaeology of Jamaican Slave Life in the Late Eighteenth Century" (Unpublished paper, Annual Meeting of the Society for Historical Archaeology, Kingston, Jamaica, January 1992).

2066. Krise, Thomas Warren. "Representations of the British West Indies from the Restoration to the American Revolution: Prolegomena to the Field and a Critical Anthology of Early Jamaica" (PhD diss., University of Chicago, 1995).

2067. Lazarus-Black, Mindie. "John Grant's Jamaica: Notes Towards a Reassessment of Courts in the Slave Era," *Journal of Caribbean History*, 27, 2 (1993), pp. 144-59.

2068. Lewis, Andrew. "'An Incendiary Press': British West Indian Newspapers during the Struggle for Abolition," *Slavery and Abolition*, 16, 2 (1995), pp. 346-61.

2069. Luster, Robert E. *The Amelioration of the Slaves in the British Empire, 1790-1833*. New York: Peter Lang Publishing, 1994. (American University Studies. Series IX, History, vol. 134)

2070. Marshall, Woodville K. "Provision Ground and Plantation Labor in Four Windward Islands: Competition for Resources During Slavery," in Berlin and Morgan, eds., *Cultivation and Culture*, pp. 203-20.

2071. Martin, Jean-Pierre. "Samuel Sewall, Witch-hunter and Abolitionist," in Binder, ed., *Slavery in the Americas*, pp. 197-204.

2072. McDaniel, Lorna. "The Philips: A 'Free Mulatto' Family of Grenada," *Journal of Caribbean History*, 24, 2 (1990), pp. 178-94.

2073. McDonald, Roderick A. "Urban Crime and Social Control in St. Vincent during the Apprenticeship," in idem, ed., *West Indies Accounts*, pp. 319-42.

2074. McDonald, Roderick A., ed. *West Indies Accounts: Essays on the History of the British Caribbean and the Atlantic Economy*. Mona: The Press, University of the West Indies, 1996.

For contents see Beckles, Carrington, Craton, Dunn, Engerman, Higman, McDonald, Minchinton, Turner, and Zahedieh.

2075. Mintz, Sidney W., and Douglas Hall. "The Origins of the Jamaican Internal Marketing System."

Reprinted in Beckles and Shepherd, eds., *Caribbean Slave Society and Economy*, pp. 319-34.

2076. Morrin, Douglas S. "The Bitterest Enemy: Planter Struggles over Amelioration in Jamaica, 1823-31" (Honors paper, Duke University, 1996).

2077. Mullin, Michael. "Slave Economic Strategies: Food, Markets and Property," in Turner, ed., *From Chattel Slaves to Wage Slaves*, pp. 68-78.

2078. O'Jon, Eirene. *Slave Society in Early Nineteenth Century Berbice*. Turkeyen, Guyana: History Society, University of Guyana, 1992.

2079. O'Shaughnessy, Andrew. "Redcoats and Slaves in the British Caribbean," in Engerman and Paquette, eds., *The Lesser Antilles in the Age of European Expansion*, pp. 105-27.

2080. Paton, Diana. "Decency, Dependence and the Lash: Gender and the British Debate over Slave Emancipation, 1830-34," *Slavery and Abolition*, 17, 3 (1996), pp. 163-84.

2081. Peterson, James B., David R. Watters, and Desmond V. Nicholson. "'Afro-Caribbean' Ceramics from Antigua and Montserrat: An Investigation of Ethnicity in the Northern Lesser Antilles" (Unpublished paper, Annual Meeting of the Society for Historical Archaeology, Kingston, Jamaica, January 1992).

2082. Phillips, A. "The Origins and Extension of Slave Laws in Barbados, 1636-1700" (Unpublished paper, American Society for Legal History, Washington DC, 1994).

2083. Quintanilla, Mark S. "Late Seventeenth-Century Indentured Servants in Barbados," *Journal of Caribbean History*, 27, 2 (1993), pp. 14-28.

2084. Schuler, Monica. "Akan Slave Rebellions in the British Caribbean."

Reprinted in Beckles and Shepherd, eds., *Caribbean Slave Society and Economy*, pp. 373-86.

2085. Schuler, Monica. "Myalism and the African Religious Tradition in Jamaica."

Reprinted in Beckles and Shepherd, eds., *Caribbean Slave Society and Economy*, pp. 295-303.

2086. Shelton, Robert S. "A Modified Crime: The Apprenticeship System in St. Kitts," *Slavery and Abolition*, 16, 2 (1995), pp. 331-45.

2087. Shepherd, Verene A. "Alternative Husbandry: Slaves and Free Labourers on Livestock Farms in Jamaica in the Eighteenth and Nineteenth Centuries," in Twaddle, ed., *The Wages of Slavery*, pp. 40-66.

2088. Sheridan, Richard B. "The Condition of the Slaves in the Settlement and Economic Development of the British Windward Islands, 1763-1775," *Journal of Caribbean History*, 24, 2 (1990), pp. 121-45.

2089. Sheridan, Richard B. "From Chattel to Wage Slavery in Jamaica, 1740-1860," in Twaddle, ed., *The Wages of Slavery*, pp. 13-40.

2090. Sheridan, Richard B. "Mortality and the Medical Treatment of Slaves in the British West Indies."

Reprinted in Beckles and Shepherd, eds., *Caribbean Slave Society and Economy*, pp. 197-208.

2091. Sheridan, Richard B. "Strategies of Slave Subsistence: The Jamaican Case Reconsidered," in Turner, ed., *From Chattel Slaves to Wage Slaves*, pp. 48-67.

2092. Sheridan, Richard B. *Sugar and Slavery: An Economic History of the British West Indies 1623-1775*. 2nd ed., with foreword by Hilary McD. Beckles. Kingston: Canoe Press, 1995.

2093. Sheridan, Richard B. "Why the Condition of the Slaves was 'Less Intolerable in Barbadoes than in the Other Sugar Colonies'," in Beckles, ed., *Inside Slavery*, pp. 31-50.

2094. Sio, Arnold A. "The Free Coloured of Barbados and Jamaica: A Comparison," *Journal of the Barbados Museum and Historical Society*, 35, 2 (1976), pp. 87-100.

2095. Smith, Kevin D. "A Fragmented Freedom: The Historiography of Emancipation and its Aftermath in the British West Indies," *Slavery and Abolition*, 16, 1 (1995), pp. 101-30.

2096. Southerland, Joseph C., and James A. Delle. "Alternatives to Sugar: The Development of Cattle Pens and Coffee Plantations in Jamaica" (Unpublished paper, Annual Meeting of the Society for Historical Archaeology, Kingston, Jamaica, January 1992).

2097. Steel, M. J. "A Philosophy of Fear: The World View of the Jamaican Plantocracy in a Comparative Perspective," *Journal of Caribbean History*, 27, 1 (1993), pp. 1-20.

2098. Trouillot, Michel-Rolph. "Beyond and Below the Merivale Paradigm: Dominica's First 100 Days of Freedom," in Engerman and Paquette, eds., *The Lesser Antilles in the Age of European Expansion*, pp. 302-21.

2099. Turner, Grace. "An Archaeological Record of Plantation Life in the Bahamas," in *Amerindians, Africans, Americans: Three Papers in Caribbean History* (Mona: Department of History, University of the West Indies, 1993), pp. 107-25. (Presented at the 24th annual conference of the Association of Caribbean Historians, Nassau, The Bahamas).

Also in French: "Vestiges archéologiques du temps des plantations aux Bahamas," pp. 85-105.

2100. Turner, Mary [A]. "Chattel Slaves into Wage Slaves: A Jamaican Case Study," in idem, ed., *From Chattel Slaves to Wage Slaves*, pp. 33-47.

2101. Turner, Mary A. "Planter Profits and Slave Rewards: Amelioration Reconsidered," in McDonald, ed., *West Indies Accounts*, pp. 232-52.

2102. *Turner, Mary A. "Slave Workers into Contract Workers: Investigating the Legal Dimension" (Unpublished paper, International Conference on Master & Servant in History, York University [Toronto], 11-13 April 1996).

2103. Walvin, James. "L'abolition anglaise de l'esclavage des Noirs, 1787-1838," in Dorigny, ed. *Les abolitions de l'esclavage*, pp. 103-10.

2104. Walvin, James. *Slaves and Slavery: The British Colonial Experience*.

Republished as *Black Ivory: A History of British Slavery* (Washington: Howard University Press, 1992).

2105. Watters, David R. "Mortuary Patterns at the Harney Site Slave Cemetery, Montserrat, in Caribbean Perspective," *Historical Archaeology*, 28, 3 (1994), pp. 56-73.

2106. Webb, Steven B. "Saints or Cynics: A Statistical Analysis of Parliament's Decision for Emancipation in 1833," in Fogel and Engerman, eds., *Conditions of Life and the Transition to Freedom: Technical Papers*, vol. 2 (*Without Consent or Contract*), pp. 571-86.

2107. Wedderburn, Robert. *The Horrors of Slavery and Other Writings*. Ed. Iain McCalmon. Edinburgh: Edinburgh University Press, 1991.

2108. Welch, Pedro. "The Urban Context of the Slave Plantation System: Bridgetown, Barbados, 1680-1834" (PhD diss., University of the West Indies - Cave Hill, 1995).

2109. Wilcox, Nathaniel T. "British Sugar Demand, West Indian Production, and the 'Decline' Theory of West Indian Emancipation, 1790 to 1850," in Fogel, Galantine, and Manning, eds., *Evidence and Methods* (*Without Consent or Contract*), pp. 168-90.

2110. Williams, Eric. "Capitalism and Slavery," in Beckles and Shepherd, eds., *Caribbean Slave Society and Economy*, pp. 120-29.

Reprinted from *From Columbus to Castro: The History of the Caribbean, 1492-1969* (London: Andre Deutsch, 1970), pp. 136-55.

2111. Zips, Werner. *Schwarze Rebellen: Afrikanisch-karibischer Freiheitskampf in Jamaica.* Vienna: Promedia, 1993.

3. Spanish[5]

2112. Arrom, José Juan. "Cimarrón: apuntes sobre sus primeras documentaciones y su probable origen," in Arrom and García Arévalo, *Cimarrón*, pp. 13-30.

2113. Arrom, José Juan, and Manuel A. García Arévalo. *Cimarrón*. Santo Domingo: Fundación García-Arevalo, 1986.

2114. Ayorinde, Christine. "Santeria: The Yoruba Religion in Revolutionary Cuba" (Unpublished paper presented at conference on "Source Material for Studying the Slave Trade and the African Diaspora", Stirling, Scotland, 13-14 April 1996).

2115. Benítez Rojo, Antonio. "De la plantación a la plantación," *Cuadernos hispanoamericanos*, nos. 451-52 (1988), pp. 217-39.

2116. Bergad, Laird W., F^{e} I. García, and María del Carmen Barcia. *The Cuban Slave Market, 1790-1880.* Cambridge: Cambridge University Press, 1995. (Cambridge Latin American Series, 79)

2117. Bremer, Thomas. "The Slave Who Wrote Poetry: Comments on the Literary Works and the Autobiography of Juan Francisco Manzano," in Binder, ed., *Slavery in the Americas*, pp. 487-501.

2118. Casanovas Codina, Joan. "Labor and Colonialism in Cuba in the Second Half of the Nineteenth Century" (PhD diss., State University of New York at Stony Brook, 1994).

2119. Casanovas [Codina], Joan. "Slavery, the Labour Movement and Spanish Colonialism in Cuba, 1850-1890," *International Review of Social History*, 40, 3 (1995), pp. 367-82.

2120. Cassá, Roberto, and Genaro Rodíguez Morel. "Consideraciones alternativas acerca de las rebeliones de esclavos en Santo Domingo," *Anuario de estudios americanos*, 50, 1 (1993), pp. 101-31.

2121. Castañeda, Digna. "The Female Slave in Cuba during the First Half of the Nineteenth Century," in Shepherd, Brereton, and Bailey, eds., *Engendering History*, pp. 141-54.

2122. Debien, Gabriel. "The Saint-Domingue Refugees in Cuba, 1793-1815 (trans. David Cheramie)," in Brasseaux and Conrad, eds., *Road to Louisiana*, pp. 31-112.

2123. Deive, Carlos Esteban. *La Espanola y la esclavitud del indio.* Santo Domingo: Fundación Garcia Arevalo, 1995. (Serie documental Fundación Garcia Arevalo, vol. 3).

2124. Del Valle, Rafael. "Historias en blanco y negro: la novela, el cuento y el discurso politico antiesclavistas en Cuba (1819-1886)" (PhD diss., University of Southern California, 1994).

2125. Diaz, Maria Elena. "Constituting Identity: Sociocultural Changes in a Black Colonial Village (El Cobre, Cuba, 1670-1800)" (PhD diss., University of Texas - Austin, 1992).

2126. Dorsey, Joseph C. "Women Without History: Slavery and the International Politics of *Partus Sequitur Ventrem* in the Spanish Caribbean," *Journal of Caribbean History*, 28, 2 (1994), pp. 165-207.

2127. Duharte Jiménez, Rafaël. "L'influence de la Révolution française dans la région orientale de Cuba (1789-1896)," in Coquery-Vidrovitch, ed., *Esclavage, colonisation, libérations nationales de 1789 à nos jours*, pp. 297-307.

2128. Duharte Jiménez, Rafael. *Rebeldía esclava en el Caribe.* Xalapá, Ver.: Comisión Estatal Conmemorativa del V Centenario del Encuentro de Dos Mundos, Gobierno del Estado de Veracruz, 1992.

2129. *Duharte Jiménez, Rafael. "La rebeldia esclava en la sociedad cubana del siglo XIX," in Hoogbergen, ed., *Born out of Resistance*, pp. 104-09.

2130. Fernandez Mendez, Eugenio. *Las encomiendas y esclavitud de los indios de Puerto Rico, 1508-1550.* 6. ed. rev. San Juan, Puerto Rico: Ediciones "El Cemi", 1995.

---

[5] Hispaniola, Cuba, Santo Domingo, Puerto Rico, but not Caribbean regions of mainland Spanish America (Florida, Mexico, Central America).

2131. Figueroa, Luis Antonio. "Facing Freedom: The Transition from Slavery to Free Labor in Guayama, Puerto Rico, 1860-1898" (PhD diss., University of Wisconsin - Madison, 1991).

2132. Fuente García, Alejandro de la. "Introducción al estudio de la trata en Cuba: siglos XVI y XVII," *Santiago* (Cuba), 61 (1986), pp. 155-208.

2133. Fuente García, Alejandro de la. "El mercado esclavista habanero, 1580-1699," *Revista de Índias*, 50 (no. 50) (1990), pp. 371-95.

2134. García Arévalo, Manuel A. "El maniel de José Leta: evidencias arqueológicas de un posible asentamiento cimarrón en la región sudoriental de la isla de Santo Domingo," in Arrom and García Arévalo, *Cimarrón*, pp. 33-55.

2135. Geggus, David P. "Typologizing Slave Revolts: Two Rebellions in the Spanish Caribbean in the mid-1790s" (Unpublished paper presented to American Studies Association Conference, New Orleans, November 1990).

2136. Gil-Blanco, Emiliano. "La politique espagnole en matière d'abolition de l'esclavage au XIXe siècle," in Dorigny, ed. *Les abolitions de l'esclavage*, pp. 329-33.

2137. Goguet, Jean Christian. "Christophe Colomb, le sucre et l'esclavage," *Revue de la Société haïtienne d'histoire et de géographie*, 48, 1 (67e année) (no. 173) (1992), pp. 57-60.

2138. Hu-Dehart, Evelyn. "Chinese Coolie Labour in Cuba in the Nineteenth Century: Free Labour or Neo-Slavery," in Twaddle, ed., *The Wages of Slavery*, pp. 67-86.

2139. Knight, Franklin. "Sugar Slavery and the Transformation of Cuban Society and Economy, 1786-1886" (Presentation at "Seminário internacional: Escravos com e sem açucar", Madeira, 17-21 June 1996).

2140. Knight, Franklin. "The Transformation of Cuban Agriculture, 1763-1838," in Beckles and Shepherd, eds., *Caribbean Slave Society and Economy*, pp. 69-79.

Reprinted from *Slave Society in Cuba*, pp. 3-24.

2141. Labrador-Rodriguez, Sonia Noemi. "Estrategias discursivas en la narrativa antiesclavista cubana" (PhD diss., State University of New York - Stony Brook, 1993).

2142. Landers, Jane. "Cimarrones and Vecinos: African Communities in the Spanish Caribbean" (Unpublished paper, Annual Meeting of the Society for Historical Archaeology, Kingston, Jamaica, January 1992).

2143. Laviña, Javier. "Iglesia y esclavitud en Cuba," *América negra*, 1 (1991), pp. 11-32.

2144. Legra Hernandez, William, and José Cernicharo Gonzalez. "Influence de la Révolution française sur le régime esclavagiste à Cuba," in Coquery-Vidrovitch, ed., *Esclavage, colonisation, libérations nationales de 1789 à nos jours*, pp. 308-12.

2145. Lopez, Humberto J. "The Antislavery Novel: Black Presence and Identity in Cuban Colonial Literature" (PhD diss., Florida State University, 1995).

2146. Manzano, Juan Francisco. *The Autobiography of a Slave (Autobiografía de un esclavo)*. Bilingual ed. Detroit: Wayne State University Press, 1996. Trans. Evelyn Picón Garfield. Introduction and modernized Spanish version by Ivan A. Schulman. (Latin American literature and culture series)

2147. Martínez-Fernández, Luis. "The Havana Anglo-Spanish Mixed Commission for the Suppression of the Slave Trade and Cuba's *Emancipados*," *Slavery and Abolition*, 16, 2 (1995), pp. 205-25.

2148. Martínez-Fernandez, Luis. "The Sweet and the Bitter: Cuban and Puerto Rican Responses to the Mid-Nineteenth-Century Sugar Challenge," *New West Indian Guide/Nieuwe West-Indische Gids*, 67, 1-2 (1993), pp. 47-67.

2149. Matos-Rodríguez, Felix V. "Street Vendors, Pedlars, Shop-Owners and Domestics: Some Aspects of Women's Economic Roles in Nineteenth-Century San Juan, Puerto Rico, 1820-1870," in Shepherd, Brereton, and Bailey, eds., *Engendering History*, pp. 176-93.

2150. Montejo, Estéban. *The Autobiography of a Runaway Slave*. London: Macmillan Caribbean, 1993.

2151. Montejo, Estéban. "A Cuban Slave's Testimony," in Davis, ed., *Slavery and Beyond*, pp. 11-28.

From Barnet, ed., *Autobiography of a Runaway Slave*, pp. 15-44.

2152. Moscoso, Francisco. "Formas de resistencia de los esclavos en Puerto Rico, siglos XVI-XVIII," *América negra*, 10 (1996), pp. 31-50.

2153. Murray, David. "Capitalism and Slavery in Cuba," *Slavery and Abolition*, 17, 3 (1996), pp. 223-37.

2154. Negrón-Portillo, Mariano. *La esclavitud urbana en San Juan de Puerto Rico: estudio del Registro de Esclavos de 1872*. Rio Piedras PR: Ediciones Huracán: Centro de Investigaciones Sociales, Universidad de Puerto Rico, 1992.

2155. Negrón-Portillo, Mariano. "Esclavitud urbana en San Juan de Puerto Rico: estudio del Registro de Esclavos de 1872: primera parte" (MA thesis, Universidad de Puerto Rico, 1995).

Translated as "Urban Slavery in San Juan, Puerto Rico: Study of the Registro de Esclavos de 1872: Part One".

2156. Neumayer, Helga. "Eighteenth-Century Maroons of Spanish Santo Domingo and Their Contemporary Traces," in Hoogbergen, ed., *Born out of Resistance*, pp. 137-41.

2157. Nippel, Wilfried. "Aristoteles und die Indios: 'Gerechter Krieg' und 'Sklaven von Natur' in der spanischen Diskussion des 16. Jahrhunderts," in Christof Dipper and Martin Vogt, eds., *Entdeckungen und frühe Kolonisation* (Darmstadt: Technische Hochschule, 1993), pp. 69-90.

2158. Ordoñez Mercado, Maria E. "La manumisión de esclavos en la pila bautismal en San Juan de Puerto Rico: 1800-1869" (MA thesis, Universidad de Puerto Rico, Recinto de Rio Piedras, Programa Graduade de Historia, 1994).

2159. Palmié, Stephan. "Ethnogenetic Processes and Cultural Transfer in Afro-American Slave Populations," in Binder, ed., *Slavery in the Americas*, pp. 337-63.

2160. Paquette, Robert L., and Joseph C. Dorsey. "The Escoto Papers and Cuban Slave Resistance," *Slavery and Abolition*, 15, 3 (1994), pp. 89-95.

2161. Pérez, Louis A., Jr. *Slaves, Sugar, and Colonial Society: Travel Accounts of Cuba*. Wilmington DE: Scholarly Resources, 1992.

2162. Philip, Jacqueline. *L'esclavage à Cuba au XIXe siècle d'apres les documents de l'Archivo Historico Nacional de Madrid*. Paris: Editions l'Harmattan, 1995. (Publications de l'Équipe de recherche de l'Université de Paris VIII: Histoire des Antilles hispaniques, 14)

2163. Porro Gutiérrez, Jesús Maria. "Inquietudes en la parte española de la isla, sobre la sublevación de los esclavos en Saint-Domingue," *Estudios de historia social y económica de América*, 10 (1993), pp. 165-79.

2164. "Protocolo para el derecho territorial de Palenque de San Basilio," *América negra*, 1 (1991), pp. 201-08.

2165. Robert, Karen. "Slavery and Freedom in the Ten Years' War, Cuba 1868-1878," *Slavery and Abolition*, 13, 3 (1992), pp. 181-200.

2166. Rodríguez Morel, Genero. "El sistema de plantación azucarera en Puerto Rico en el siglo XVI" (Presentation at "Seminário internacional: Escravos com e sem açucar", Madeira, 17-21 June 1996).

2167. Rodríguez Morel, Genaro. "Esclavitud y vida rural en las plantaciones azucareras de Santo Domingo," *Anuario de estudios americanos*, 49 (1992), pp. 89-117.

2168. Scarano, Francisco. "The Origins of Plantation Growth in Puerto Rico," in Beckles and Shepherd, eds., *Caribbean Slave Society and Economy*, pp. 56-68.

Reprinted from *Sugar and Slavery in Puerto Rico*, pp. 16-34.

2169. Scarano, Francisco A. *Sugar and Slavery in Puerto Rico*.

Translated by Mercedes Solis as *Haciendas y barracones: azucar y esclavitud en Ponce, Puerto Rico, 1800-1850* (Rio Piedras PR: Ediciones Huracan, 1993).

2170. Schmidt-Nowara, Christopher Ebert. "The Problem of Slavery in the Age of Capital: Abolitionism, Liberalism and Counter-Hegemony in Spain, Cuba and Puerto Rico, 1833-1886" (PhD diss., University of Michigan, 1995).

2171. Scott, Rebecca J. "Esclavage, salariat et colonat dans les plantations de sucre cubaines, 1870-1917" (Presentation at Colloquium on "Les dépendances serviles", Paris 1996).

2172. Scott, Rebecca J. "Explaining Abolition: Contradiction, Adaptation, and Challenge in Cuban Slave Society, 1860-86."

Reprinted in Beckles and Shepherd, eds., *Caribbean Slave Society and Economy*, pp. 454-71.

2173. *Siempre trabajando: Latinos and Labor*. New York: Deep Dish TV, 1992 (60 min.). (Spanish with English subtitles. Includes "La Historia de todos nosotros = The History of Us" [35 min.])

2174. Smith, E. Valerie. "Early Afro-American Presence on the Island of Hispaniola: A Case Study of the 'Immigrants' of Samanà," *Journal of Negro History*, 72, 1-2 (1987), pp. 33-41.

2175. Stark, David M. "Discovering the Invisible Puerto Rican Slave Family: Demographic Evidence from the Eighteenth Century," *Journal of Family History*, 21, 4 (1996), pp. 395-418.

2176. Tornero Tinajero, Pablo. *Crecimiento economico y transformaciones sociales: esclavos, hacendados y comerciantes en la Cuba colonial (1760-1840)*. Madrid: Ministerio de Trabajo y Seguridad Social, 1996.

2177. Tornero Tinajero, Pablo. "Producción y costes en los ingenios de Cuba: notas para una investigación," in Butel, ed., *Commerce et plantation dans la Caraïbe*, pp. 215-32.

2178. Tovar Pinzón, Hermes. *De una chispa se forma una hoguera: esclavitud, insubordinación y liberación*. Tunja, Boyaca: Posgrado del Magister en Historia, Vice-Rectoria de Investigaciones Cientificas y Extensión Universitaria, Universidad Pedagogica y Tecnologica de Colombia, 1992.

2179. Venegas, Carlos. "La Habana y su región: un proyecto de organización espacial de la plantación esclavista," *Revista de Indias*, 56 (no. 207) (1996), pp. 333-66.

2180. Villaverde, Maria. "Comparación entre el Yoruba tradicional de Nigeria y el Yoruba que se habla en Cuba" (Unpublished paper, UNESCO conference on "La route de l'esclave", Ouidah, Bénin, 1-5 Sept. 1994).

2181. Wentklaff-Eggebert, Harald. "Miguel Barnet's 'novela-testimonio' *Biografla de un cimarrón*: Life Story of a Runaway Slave, Ethnological Study, or Manipulation of Public Opinion?" in Binder, ed., *Slavery in the Americas*, pp. 627-45.

2182. Whitney, Robert. "The Political Economy of Abolition: The Hispano-Cuban Elite and Cuban Slavery, 1868-1873," *Slavery and Abolition*, 13, 2 (1992), pp. 20-36.

2183. Williams, Lorna V. *The Representation of Slavery in Cuban Fiction*. Columbia: University of Missouri Press, 1994.

2184. Yacou, Alain. "La insurgencia negra en la isla de Cuba en la primera mitad del siglo XIX," *Revista de indias*, 53 (no. 197) (1993), pp. 23-51.

4. French

2185. Abénon, Lucien-René. "Port-la-liberté, an III: approche démographique des nouveaux citoyens," in Dorigny, ed. *Les abolitions de l'esclavage*, pp. 241-52.

2186. Abénon, Lucien[-René]. "Toussaint Louverture et ses biographes," in Martin and Yacou, eds., *Mourir pour les Antilles*, pp. 39-44.

2187. *Abénon, Lucien-René. "Travail et liberté en Guadeloupe de 1794 à 1802," in *La période révolutionnaire aux Antilles - Guyane*, pp. 75-85.

2188. *Adélaïde-Merlande, Jacques. "Autour de la proclamation de Sonthonax, août 1793," in *La période révolutionnaire aux Antilles - Guyane*, pp. 65-73.

2189. *Adélaïde-Merlande, Jacques. "Expansion et subversion révolutionnaire aux Antilles, 1794-1799," in *La période révolutionnaire aux Antilles - Guyane*, pp. 88-101.

2190. Adélaïde-Merlande, Jacques. "Lendemains de Baimbridge et Matouba: 'coureurs de bois et brigands'," in Martin and Yacou, eds., *Mourir pour les Antilles*, pp. 203-10.

2191. Amin, Samir. "Autour de l'abolition de l'esclavage par la Première République," in Dorigny, ed. *Les abolitions de l'esclavage*, pp. 397-402.

2192. Arzalier, Francis. "Les mutations de l'idéologie coloniale en France avant 1848: de l'esclavagisme à l'abolitionnisme," in Dorigny, ed. *Les abolitions de l'esclavage*, pp. 299-308.

2193. Bangou, Henri. "Révolution et esclavage dans les colonies françaises des Antilles," in Coquery-Vidrovitch, ed., *Esclavage, colonisation, libérations nationales de 1789 à nos jours*, pp. 152-59.

2194. Barcellini, Serge. "Deux mémoires dans le temps présent: Sonthonax, Schœlcher," in Dorigny, ed. *Les abolitions de l'esclavage*, pp. 383-95.

2195. Barthélemy, Gérard. "Les 'Africains' ou le rôle des bossales dans les luttes de l'Indépendance d'Haïti," *Revue de la Société Haïtienne d'Histoire et de Géographie*, 51 (71ème année) (no. 186) (1995), pp. 19-37.

2196. Bebel-Gisler, Dany. "Le passé inachevé de l'esclavage: l'héritage culturel africain dans le réel, l'inconscient et l'imaginaire social guadeloupéen" (Unpublished paper, UNESCO conference on "La route de l'esclave", Ouidah, Bénin, 1-5 Sept. 1994).

2197. Begot, Danielle. "À l'origine de imaginaire de violence à Saint-Domingue: insurrection servile et iconographie," in Martin and Yacou, eds., *Mourir pour les Antilles*, pp. 95-133.

2198. Bénot, Yves. "La chaîne des insurrections d'esclaves dans les Caraïbes de 1789 à 1791," in Dorigny, ed. *Les abolitions de l'esclavage*, pp. 179-86.

2199. Bénot, Yves. "Comment la Convention a voté l'abolition de l'esclavage (résumé)," in Coquery-Vidrovitch, ed., *Esclavage, colonisation, libérations nationales de 1789 à nos jours*, pp. 133-35.

2200. Bénot, Yves. *La demence coloniale sous Napoleon: essai.* Paris: Editions La Découverte, 1992.

2201. Bénot, Yves. "Les droits de l'Homme et les Noirs: le rapport de Saint-Just sur les colonies," in *Grands figures de la Révolution française en Picardie* (Colloque, Blérancourt Aisne, 17 - 18 juin 1989) (Chauny: B. Vinto, 1990), pp. 73-84.

2202. Benzaken, Jean-Charles. "Saint-Domingue de la colonie française à la indépendance haïtienne: approche d'iconographie numismatique," in Dorigny, ed. *Les abolitions de l'esclavage*, pp. 253-62.

2203. Blackburn, Robin. "Anti-Slavery and the French Revolution," *History Today*, 41 (Nov. 1991), pp. 19-25.

2204. Blavier, Yves. "Un manuscrit anti-esclavagiste de Fournier l'Américain," *Annales historiques de la Révolution française*, 2 (no. 288) (1992), pp. 257-58.

2205. Bléchet, Miguel. "La correspondance de Sonthonax, commissaire délégué par le Directoire à Saint-Domingue, adressée à Toussaint-Louverture," in Toumson (with Porset), eds., *La période révolutionnaire aux Antilles*, pp. 75-89.

2206. Bontems, Claude. "La Révolution française, les droits de l'homme et l'esclavage," in Francis Hamon and Jacques Lelièvre, eds., *L'héritage politique de la Révolution française* (Lille: Presses Universitaires de Lille, Centre Culturel International de Cerisy, 1993), pp. 237-51.

2207. Brahimi, Denise. "Assimilation ou lutte des races: le Toussaint Louverture de Lamartine," in Toumson (with Porset), eds., *La période révolutionnaire aux Antilles*, pp. 91-100.

2208. Breteau, Jean. "Victor Schœlcher: Paris 1804 - Houilles 1893," *Les anneaux de la mémoire* (Exhibition catalogue, Nantes, 1992), p. 120.

2209. Butel, Paul. "L'investissement immobilier des blancs et des gens de couleur dans les villes de Saint-Domingue à la veille de la Révolution: l'exemple du Cap Française et Port-au-Prince," in Toumson (with Porset), eds., *La période révolutionnaire aux Antilles*, pp. 101-14.

2210. Cabanis, André, and Michel L. Martin. "L'indépendance de Haïti devant l'opinion publique française," in Martin and Yacou, eds., *Mourir pour les Antilles*, pp. 221-37.

2211. Cabanis, André [G.], and Michel L. Martin. "La question économique dans le discours révolutionnaire sur l'abolition de l'esclavage, 1791-1794," in Michel L. Martin and Alain Yacou, eds., *De la révolution française aux révolutions créoles et nègres* (Paris: Editions Caribéennes, 1989), pp. 69-80.

2212. Cabral, Vasco. "Révolution française, esclavage et colonisation," in Coquery-Vidrovitch, ed., *Esclavage, colonisation, libérations nationales de 1789 à nos jours*, pp. 291-96.

2213. Camprasse, Philippe. "L'affranchissement d'esclaves dans les colonies françaises d'Amérique," in *Généalogie et histoire de la Caraïbe*, 39 (1992), pp. 592-94.

2214. Castera, Emmanuel. "1791-1991: Bicentenaire du soulèvement général des esclaves de Saint-Domingue," *Revue de la Société haïtienne d'histoire et de géographie*, 48 (no. 172) (1992), pp. 8-14.

2215. Cauna, Jacques [de] "Les comptes de la sucrerie Fleuriau: analyse de la rentabilité d'une plantation de Saint-Domingue au XVIIIe siècle," in Butel, ed., *Commerce et plantation dans la Caraïbe*, pp. 143-67.

2216. Cauna [de Ladévie], Jacques. "Les derniers français de Saint-Domingue: aperçus sur une débâcle sanglante," in Martin and Yacou, eds., *Mourir pour les Antilles*, pp. 163-80.

2217. Cauna, Jacques de. "Formes de résistance à l'esclavage," *Les anneaux de la mémoire* (Exhibition catalogue, Nantes, 1992), pp. 78-79.

2218. Cauna, Jacques de. "Françoise Dominique Toussaint-Louverture (1743-1803)," *Les anneaux de la mémoire* (Exhibition catalogue, Nantes, 1992), p. 118.

2219. Cauna, Jacques [de]. "L'odysée d'un esclave musulman: du Sénégal à Versailles en passant par Tobago," *Revue de la Société haïtienne d'histoire et de géographie*, 46 (66e année, no. 165) (1990), pp. 59-63.

2220. Cauna[-Ladevie], Jacques de. "A Plantation on the Eve of the Haitian Revolution: La Sucrerie Clérisse," *Plantation Society in the Americas*, 3, 2 (1993), pp. 31-49.

2221. Cauna, Jacques [de]. "La Révolution à Saint-Domingue: des luttes blanches à l'insurrection noire (1789-1791)," in Coquery-Vidrovitch, ed., *Esclavage, colonisation, libérations nationales de 1789 à nos jours*, pp. 160-68.

2222. Cauna, Jacques [de]. "The Singularity of the Saint-Domingue Revolution: *Marronage*, Voodoo, and the Color Question," *Plantation Society in the Americas*, 3, 3 (1996), pp. 321-45.

2223. Cauna, Jacques de. "La vie et l'activité d'une plantation aux Antilles au XVIIIe siècle: l'exemple de la sucrerie Fleuriau de Bellevue à Saint-Domingue," *Les anneaux de la mémoire* (Exhibition catalogue, Nantes, 1992), pp. 72-75.

2224. Champion, Jean-Marcel. "30 Floréal: le rétablissement de l'esclavage par Bonaparte," in Dorigny, ed. *Les abolitions de l'esclavage*, pp. 265-71.

2225. Chatillon, Marcel. *Images de la Révolution aux Antilles: catalogue de l'exposition organisée dans le cadre de la commémoration du bicentenaire de la Revolution*. Basse-Terre: Société d'Histoire de Guadeloupe, 1989.

2226. Christian, Francis. "Le travail des esclaves: Haïti au XVIIIe siècle," *La généalogie aujourd'hui*, no. 137 (1995), pp. 13-16.

2227. Chrysostome, Pierre. "L'esprit colonial, un siècle avant la conférence de Berlin: plantations et esclaves d'après quelques instructions de colons (1690-1788)," in Coquery-Vidrovitch, ed., *Esclavage, colonisation, libérations nationales de 1789 à nos jours*, pp. 17-26.

2228. Coeta, René-Claude. *Sinnamary: 1624-1848 : une cité et des hommes*. Paris: Harmattan, 1992.

2229. Cohen, Claudine. "Taxonomie et ségrégation sociale: l'anthropologie de Moreau de Saint-Méry," in Toumson (with Porset), eds., *La période révolutionnaire aux Antilles*, pp. 137-42.

2230. Coquery-Vidrovitch, Catherine, ed. *Esclavage, colonisation, libérations nationales de 1789 à nos jours* (Colloque, 24-26 février 1989, Université Paris VIII à Saint-Dénis). Paris: Harmattan, 1990.

For contents see Bénot, Bangou, Bonnet, Cabral, Cauna, Chrysostome, Cour Grandmaison, Crebouw, Daget, Dorigny, Duharte Jimenez, Elisabeth, Etienne, Fizaine, Halpern, Jurt, Legra Hernandez and Cernicharo Gonzalez, Lesage, Mac-Kit, Plumelle Uribe and Michelot, Remandet, Vermée, and Vidaud.

2231. Corzani, Jack. "De l'aliénation révolutionnaire: Toussaint Louverture et *la Marseillaise* (à propos de l'*Adieu à la Marseillaise* de J. Brierre)," in Martin and Yacou, eds., *Mourir pour les Antilles*, pp. 45-56.

2232. Corzani, Jack. "L'image de l'homme de couleur avant 1848 (Maynard de Queilhe et Levilloux)," in Toumson (with Porset), eds., *La période révolutionnaire aux Antilles*, pp. 181-99.

2233. Cottias, Myriam. "Les règles de la citoyenneté dans les Antilles françaises après l'Émancipation générale" (Presentation at Colloquium on "Les dépendances serviles", Paris 1996).

2234. Cour Grandmaison, Olivier le. "Les Amis des Noirs face à l'esclavage," in *Actes des 115e et 116e Congrès Nationaux des Sociétés Savantes* (Avignon, 1990, and Chambéry, 1991) (Paris: Editions du Comité des Travaux Historiques et Scientifiques, Ministère de l'Éducation Nationale et de la Culture, 1992), vol. 2 ("Histoire politique pendant la Révolution française"), pp. 39-47.

2235. Cour Grandmaison, Olivier le. "Le discours esclavagiste pendant la Révolution," in Coquery-Vidrovitch, ed., *Esclavage, colonisation, libérations nationales de 1789 à nos jours*, pp. 124-32.

2236. Couve de Murville, Maurice N. L. *Slave from Haiti, A Saint for New York?: The Life of Pierre Toussaint*. London: CTS Publications, 1995.

2237. Crebouw, Yvonne. "Les débats sur les droits politiques des hommes de couleur et des Noirs libres devant les assemblées révolutionaires (juin 1789 - Pluviôse An II)," in Coquery-Vidrovitch, ed., *Esclavage, colonisation, libérations nationales de 1789 à nos jours*, pp. 79-87.

2238. Daget, Serge. "Main-d'oeuvre et avatars du peuplement en Guyane française, 1817-1863," *Revue française d'histoire d'outre-mer*, 79, 2 (n° 297) (1992), pp. 449-74.

2239. Dahomay, Jacky. "L'esclavage et le droit: les légitimations d'une insurrection," in Dorigny, ed. *Les abolitions de l'esclavage*, pp. 33-47.

2240. Debbasch, Yvan. "Sous le fouet du commandeur? Note sur l'encadrement des ateliers serviles aux Antilles Françaises (XVIIe - XVIIIe siècles)," in *Convergences: Études offertes à Marcel David* (Quimper: Calligrammes, 1991), pp. 93-106.

2241. Delépine, Édouard. "À propos du 22 mai 1848: contre le 'néo-révisionnisme tropical'," in Dorigny, ed. *Les abolitions de l'esclavage*, pp. 355-58.

2242. Démier, Francis. "Esclavage, économie coloniale et choix de développement français durant la première industrialisation (1802-1840)," in Dorigny, ed. *Les abolitions de l'esclavage*, pp. 273-83.

2243. Desmangles, L. G. *The Faces of the Gods: Voudou and Roman Catholicism in Haiti*. Chapel Hill: University of North Carolina Press, 1992.

2244. Dessalles, Pierre. *Sugar and Slavery, Family and Race: The Letters and Diary of Pierre Dessalles, Planter in Martinique, 1808-1856*. (Elborg Forster and Robert Forster, eds.) Baltimore: Johns Hopkins University Press, 1996. (Johns Hopkins Studies in Atlantic History and Culture)

French title: *Vie d'un colon à la Martinique au xixème siècle.*

2245. Devaux, Olivier. "Une 'bande nègres' devant la Cour d'Assises de Bordeaux en décembre 1815: criminels ou victimes," in Martin and Yacou, eds., *Mourir pour les Antilles*, pp. 211-18.

2246. Dorigny, Marcel. "Les abolitions de l'esclavage (1793-1794-1848): une célébration nécessaire," in Dorigny, ed. *Les abolitions de l'esclavage*, pp. 7-17.

2247. Dorigny, Marcel. "Mirabeau et la Société des Amis des Noirs: quelles voies pour l'abolition de l'esclavage," in Dorigny, ed. *Les abolitions de l'esclavage*, pp. 153-64.

2248. Dorigny, Marcel. "La Société des Amis des Noirs: les Girondins et la question coloniale," in Coquery-Vidrovitch, ed., *Esclavage, colonisation, libérations nationales de 1789 à nos jours*, pp. 69-78.

2249. Dorigny, Marcel. "La Société des Amis des Noirs et les projets de colonisation en Afrique," *Annales historiques de la Révolution française*, 3-4 (nos. 293-94) (1993), pp. 421-29.

2250. Dorigny, Marcel, ed. *Les abolitions de l'esclavage: de L. F. Sonthonax à V. Schoelcher, 1793, 1794, 1848* (Actes du Colloque International tenu à l'Université de Paris VIII les 3, 4 et 5 février

1994). Saint-Dénis (France): Presses Universitaires de Vincennes, 1995, and Paris: UNESCO, 1995.

For contents see Abénon, Amin, Arzalier, Barcellini, Bart, Bénot (2), Benzaken, Champion, Dahomay, Delépine, Démier, Dorigny (2), Ehrard, Élisabeth, Ève, Fotê, Gainot, Gauthier, Gengembre, Gil-Blanco, Gueye, Halpern, Hart, Hurbon, Lara and Fischer-Blanchet, Lara and Schmidt, Largueche, Marienstras, Mesnard, Tarrade, Schmidt, Steiner, Vigier, Walvin, and Wanquet.

2251. Ehrard, Jean. "L'encyclopédie et l'esclavage colonial," in Toumson (with Porset), eds., *La période révolutionnaire aux Antilles*, pp. 229-40.

2252. Ehrard, Jean. "L'esclavage devant la conscience morale des Lumières françaises: indifférence, gêne ou révolte?" in Dorigny, ed. *Les abolitions de l'esclavage*, pp. 143-52.

2253. Elisabeth, Léo. "L'impact de la Révolution française dans les îles françaises du vent (1789-1794)," in Coquery-Vidrovitch, ed., *Esclavage, colonisation, libérations nationales de 1789 à nos jours*, pp. 144-51.

2254. Elisabeth, Léo. "La question de couleur dans la pensée pré-révolutionnaire," in Toumson (with Porset), eds., *La période révolutionnaire aux Antilles*, pp. 241-57.

2255. Élisabeth, Léo. "Résistances des esclaves au XVIIe et XVIIIe siècles dans les colonies françaises d'Amérique, principalement aux îles du Vent," in Dorigny, ed. *Les abolitions de l'esclavage*, pp. 77-86.

2256. Etienne, Eddy. "Bois Caïman et la génèse d'une nation," *Revue de la Société haïtienne d'histoire et de géographie*, 47 (no. 171) (1991), pp. 13-26.

2257. Ève, Prosper. "Les formes de résistance à Bourbon de 1750 à 1789," in Dorigny, ed. *Les abolitions de l'esclavage*, pp. 49-71.

2258. Fallope, Josette. *Esclaves et citoyens: les noirs à la Guadeloupe au XIXe siècle dans les processus de résistance et d'integration: 1802-1910*. Basse-Terre: Société d'Histoire de la Guadeloupe, 1992.

2259. Favre, Marcel. "Le début de la révolte de Saint Domingue dans la Plaine du Cap, vécu par Louis de Calbiac," *Généalogie et histoire de la Caraïbe*, n° 48 (1993), pp. 774-85.

2260. Faye, Jean-Pierre. "L'an II, l'esclavage, l'Europe," *Annales historiques de la Révolution française*, n° 300 (1995), pp. 137-40.

2261. Fick, Carolyn [E]. "The Haitian Revolution in an Atlantic Context," in James Pritchard, ed., *Proceedings of the Nineteenth Meeting of the French Colonial Historical Society* (Providence RI, May 1993) (Cleveland: FCHS, 1994), pp. 128-40.

2262. Fick, Carolyn E. "The Saint Domingue Slave Insurrection of 1791: A Socio-political and Cultural Analysis," *Journal of Caribbean History*, 25, 1-2 (1991), pp. 1-40.

2263. *Fleury, Marie. "Impact de la traite des esclaves sur la phytogéographie: exemple chez les Aluku (Boni) de Guyane française: phytogéographie tropicale: réalités et perspectives," *Journal d'agriculture traditionelle et de botanique appliquée*, 36, 1 (1994), pp. 113-34.

2264. Forster, Robert. "The French Revolution, People of Color, and Slavery," in Joseph Klaits and Michael H. Haltzel, eds., *The Global Ramifications of the French Revolution* (Washington, D.C.: Woodrow Wilson Center Press; Cambridge: Cambridge University Press, 1994), pp. 89-104.

2265. Foubert, Bernard. "Les habitations Laborde à Saint-Domingue dans la second moitié du XVIIIe siècle," *Revue de la Société haïtienne d'histoire et de géographie*, 48 (no. 174) (1992), pp. 3-13.

2266. Foubert, Bernard. "Les habitations Laborde à Saint-Domingue dans la second moitié du XVIIIe siècle: Contribution à l'histoire d'Haïti (plaine des Caves)" (Thèse, Université de Lille III, 1990) (Atelier National de Reproduction des thèses)

2267. Gainot, Bernard. "La constitutionnalisation de la liberté générale sous le Directoire (1795-1800)," in Dorigny, ed. *Les abolitions de l'esclavage*, pp. 213-29.

2268. Galliard, Gust-Klara. "Toussaint Louverture: ou le déstin d'un ancien esclave devenu gouverneur de Saint-Domingue, symbole de l'émancipation des noirs," *Revue de la Société haïtienne d'histoire et de géographie*, 46 (no. 168) (1990), pp. 43-50.

2269. Garrigus, John. "Blue and Brown: Contraband Indigo and the Rise of a Free Colored Planter Class in

French Saint-Domingue," *The Americas*, 50, 2 (1993), pp. 233-63.

2270. Garrigus, John D. "Colour, Class, and Identity on the Eve of the Haitian Revolution: Saint-Domingue's Free Coloured Elite as *colons américains*," in Landers, ed., "Against the Odds", pp. 20-43.

2271. Gauthier, Arlette. "Le rôle des femmes dans l'abolition de l'esclavage," in Marie-France Brive, ed., *Les femmes et la Révolution française: 2 - l'individuel et le social, apparitions et représentations* (Actes du Colloque international, 12 - 14 avril 1989, Université de Toulouse-Le Mirail) (Toulouse: Presses Universitaires du Mirail, 1990), pp. 153-58.

2272. Gauthier, Florence. "Le rôle de la députation de Saint-Domingue dans l'abolition de l'esclavage," in Dorigny, ed., *Les abolitions de l'esclavage*, pp. 199-211.

2273. Gauthier, Florence. "Y a-t-il une politique des colonies en l'an II?" *Annales historiques de la Révolution française*, n° 300 (1995), pp. 223-31.

2274. Geggus, David P. "British Intervention in the Saint Domingue Revolution," *Caribbean Societies Seminar Papers* (London: Institute of Commonwealth Studies, 1985), vol. 2, pp. 78-85.

2275. Geggus, David P. "The Colonies/Les colonies," in Jean-Paul Bertaud, Georges Miraval, and David P. Geggus, eds., *The French Revolution Research Collection: War and the Colonies* (Witney: Micrographix, 1992), pp. 8-23, 32-50, 87-91.

2276. Geggus, David P. "La cérémonie du Bois-Caiman," *Chemins critiques* (Port-au-Prince), 2 (1992), pp. 59-78.

Translated as "The Bois Caiman Ceremony," *Journal of Caribbean History*, 25, 1-2 (1991), pp. 41-57.

2277. Geggus, David P. "The Effects of the American Revolution on France and its Empire," in *Blackwell Encyclopedia of the American Revolution* (Cambridge MA: Blackwell Reference, 1991), pp. 518-27.

2278. Geggus, David P. "The French Revolution, Racial Equality and Slavery" (Unpublished paper presented to International Congress on the French Revolution, Washington, D.C., 1989).

2279. Geggus, David P. "The Haitian Revolution."

Reprinted in Beckles and Shepherd, eds., *Caribbean Slave Society and Economy*, pp. 402-18.

2280. *Geggus, David P. "The Haitian Revolution," in M. Moreno Fraginals and K. Laurence, eds., *UNESCO General History of the Caribbean*, vol. 2 (forthcoming).

2281. Geggus, David P. "The Haitian Revolution: New Approaches," in James Pritchard, ed., *Proceedings of the Nineteenth Meeting of the French Colonial Historical Society* (Providence RI, May 1993) (Cleveland: FCHS, 1994), pp. 141-55.

With commentary by Robert Forster, pp. 156-59, and Carolyn E. Fick, pp. 160-63.

2282. Geggus, David P. "The Haitian Revolution and Resistance to Slavery in the Americas" (Unpublished paper presented to Society for Caribbean Studies, 15th Annual Conference, High Leigh [UK], July 1991).

2283. Geggus, David P. "Haitian Voodoo in the Eighteenth Century: Language, Culture, Resistance," *Jahrbuch für Geschichte von Staat, Wirtschaft und Gesellschaft Lateinamerikas*, 28 (1992), pp. 21-51.

2284. Geggus, David P. "Jamaica and the Saint Domingue Revolution, 1791-1799" (Unpublished paper presented to 17th Conference of Association of Caribbean Historians, Havana, April 1985).

2285. Geggus, David P. "Marronage, Voodoo, and the Saint Domingue Slave Revolt," in Patricia Galloway and Philip Boucher, eds., *Proceedings of the 15th Meeting of the French Colonial Historical Society* (Martinique, 14-20 May 1989) (Lanham MD: University Press of America, 1992), pp. 22-35.

2286. Geggus, David P. "Slave and Free Colored Women in Saint Domingue," in Gaspar and Hine, eds., *More than Chattel*, pp. 259-78.

2287. Geggus, David P. "The Slaves and Free Coloreds of Martinique during the Age of the French and Haitian Revolutions: Three Moments of Resistance," in Engerman and Paquette, eds., *The Lesser Antilles in the Age of European Expansion*, pp. 280-301.

Translated as "Esclaves et gens de couleur libres de la Martinique pendant l'époque révolutionnaire et napoléonienne: trois moments de résistance," *Revue historique*, 120 année, t. 295, 1 (no. 597) (1996), pp. 105-32.

2288. *Geggus, David P. "Le soulèvement de 1791 et ses liens avec le marronage et le vaudou," *Actes du Colloque sur La Révolution française: filiations et ruptures* (Port au Prince, forthcoming).

2289. Geggus, David P. "Sugar and Coffee Cultivation in Saint Domingue and the Shaping of the Slave Labor Force," in Berlin and Morgan, eds., *Cultivation and Culture*, pp. 73-98 (notes 318-24).

2290. Gengembre, Gérard. "De Bug-Jargal à Toussaint Louverture: le romantisme et l'esclave révolté," in Dorigny, ed. *Les abolitions de l'esclavage*, pp. 309-16.

2291. Gueye, M'baye. "Des affranchissements définitifs à l'émancipation de 1848," in Dorigny, ed. *Les abolitions de l'esclavage*, pp. 359-70.

2292. Gusdorf, G. "Considérations intempestives sur l'esclavage," in Toumson (with Porset), eds., *La période révolutionnaire aux Antilles*, pp. 259-304.

2293. Gusdorf, Simone. "Une approche de Machado de Assis: l'écrivain et l'esclavage," in Toumson (with Porset), eds., *La période révolutionnaire aux Antilles*, pp. 305-22.

2294. Hall, Gwendolyn Midlo. "Saint Domingue," in Beckles and Shepherd, eds., *Caribbean Slave Society and Economy*, pp. 160-71.

Reprinted from Cohen and Green, eds., *Neither Slave nor Free*, pp. 172-92.

2295. Halpern, Jean-Claude. "L'esclavage sur la scène révolutionnaire," *Annales historiques de la Révolution française*, 3-4 (nos. 293-94) (1993), pp. 409-20.

2296. Halpern, Jean-Claude. "L'esclavage vu par l'opinion publique: la question coloniale et le colportage de l'information (1775-1815)," *Annales historiques de la Révolution française*, 2 (no. 288) (1992), pp. 193-200.

2297. Halpern, Jean-Claude. "Les fêtes révolutionnaires et l'abolition de l'esclavage en l'an II," in Dorigny, ed. *Les abolitions de l'esclavage*, pp. 187-98.

2298. Halpern, Jean-Claude. "Sans culottes et ci-devant esclaves," in Coquery-Vidrovitch, ed., *Esclavage, colonisation, libérations nationales de 1789 à nos jours*, pp. 136-43.

2299. Hart, David M. "Class, Slavery and the Industrialist Theory of History in French Liberal Thought, 1814-34: The Contribution of Charles Comte and Charles Dunoyer" (PhD diss., University of Cambridge, 1994).

2300. Hazaël-Massieux, Guy. "À propos des sources de l'argumentaire négrophile après la révolution haïtienne," in Toumson (with Porset), eds., *La période révolutionnaire aux Antilles*, pp. 323-41.

2301. Heilbron, Waldo. "Marronage in Haïti: sociaal-politieke en sociaal-demografische aspecten," *Oso (Tijdschrift voor Surinaamse Taalkunde, Letterkunde, Cultuur en Geschiedenis)*, 11, 2 (1992), pp. 174-85.

2302. Hesse, Philippe-Jean. "Le Code Noir," *Les anneaux de la mémoire* (Exhibition catalogue, Nantes, 1992), p. 80.

2303. Hesse, Philippe-Jean. "Grands principes et petits intérêts: l'esclavage d'une abolition à l'autre," in Jean Imbert, and Gérard Chianéa, eds., *Les droits de l'Homme et la conquête des libertés* (Actes du Colloque de Grenoble-Vizille 1986) (Grenoble: Presses Universitaires de Grenoble, 1988), pp. 264-81.

2304. Howson, Jean. "African-West Indian Pottery from Montserrat: Questions of Style and Context" (Unpublished paper, Annual Meeting of the Society for Historical Archaeology, Kingston, Jamaica, January 1992).

2305. Hurbon, Laënne. "Église et esclavage au XVIIIe siècle à Saint-Domingue," in Dorigny, ed. *Les abolitions de l'esclavage*, pp. 87-100.

2306. Jamard, Jean-Luc. "Consomption d'esclaves et production de 'races': l'expérience caraïbéenne," *L'Homme* (Paris), 32 (nos. 122-24) (1992), pp. 209-34.

2307. James, C. L. R. "French Capitalism and Caribbean Slavery," in Beckles and Shepherd, eds., *Caribbean Slave Society and Economy*, pp. 130-35.

Reprinted from *Black Jacobins*, pp. 47-61.

2308. Jennings, Lawrence C. "French Anti-Slavery under the Restoration: the Société de la Morale Chrétienne," *Revue française d'histoire d'outre-mer*, 81, 3 (no. 304) (1994), pp. 321-31.

2309. Jennings, Lawrence C. "Slavery and the Venality of the July Monarchy Press," *French Historical Studies*, 17, 4 (1992), pp. 957-78.

2310. Jeune, Simon. "L'année littéraire 1835 et les problèmes de l'esclavage," in Toumson (with Porset), eds., *La période révolutionnaire aux Antilles*, pp. 355-69.

2311. Jurt, Joseph. "Les écrivains et le débat sur l'esclavage et la colonisation dans la France prérévolutionnaire: de Prévost à Condorcet," in Coquery-Vidrovitch, ed., *Esclavage, colonisation, libérations nationales de 1789 à nos jours*, pp. 43-50.

2312. Jurt, Joseph. "L. S. Mercier et le problème de l'esclavage et des colonies".

Republished in Toumson (with Porset), eds., *La période révolutionnaire aux Antilles*, pp. 371-84.

2313. Kadish, Doris Y., and Françoise Massardier-Kenney, eds. *Translating Slavery: Gender and Race in French Women's Writing, 1783-1823.* Kent OH: Kent State University Press, 1994.

2314. Lacroix, Général Pamphile de. *La révolution de Haiti.* (Ed. Pierre Pluchon) Paris: Karthala, 1995.

2315. Laplaine, Jean, and Daniel Maragnès. "Les Jacobins noirs et Toussaint Louverture," in Toumson (with Porset), eds., *La période révolutionnaire aux Antilles*, pp. 393-404.

2316. Lara, Oruno D., and Iñez Fischer-Blanchet. "Abolition ou destruction du système esclavagiste?" in Dorigny, ed. *Les abolitions de l'esclavage*, pp. 335-43.

2317. Lara, Oruno D., and Nelly Schmidt. "Préambule (to '1848: la suppression de l'esclavage')," in Dorigny, ed. *Les abolitions de l'esclavage*, pp. 319-20.

2318. Laurent-Ropa, Dénis. *Haiti: une colonie française, 1625-1802.* Paris: l'Harmattan, 1993.

2319. Lavoie, Yolande, Francine-M. Mayer, and Carolyn E. Fick. "A Particular Study of Slavery in the Caribbean Island of Saint Barthelemy: 1648-1846," *Caribbean Studies/Estudios del Caribe/Études des Caraïbes*, 28, 2 (1995), pp. 369-403.

2320. Lebrun, François. "Les esclaves noirs de la Révolution," *L'Histoire*, n° 175 (1994), p. 1825.

2321. Léotine, Marie-Hélène. *La révolution anti-esclavagiste de mai 1848 en Martinique.* Fort-de-France: Apal Production, 1991.

2322. Leray, Christian. "Faire du sucre," *Les anneaux de la mémoire* (Exhibition catalogue, Nantes, 1992), pp. 76-77.

2323. Liborel-Pochot, Hugues. "L'imaginaire de l'esclave (esquisses des fondements d'une pensée antillaise)" (Unpublished paper, UNESCO conference on "La route de l'esclave", Ouidah, Bénin, 1-5 Sept. 1994).

2324. Lirius-Galap, Julie. "Diasporas, sociétés pluriculturelles dans la région caraïbe et solidarité entre les peuples" (Unpublished paper, UNESCO conference on "La route de l'esclave", Ouidah, Bénin, 1-5 Sept. 1994).

2325. Loncke, Jocelyne. "Les métamorphoses de l'image du noir dans le roman Bug-Jargal," in Toumson (with Porset), eds., *La période révolutionnaire aux Antilles*, pp. 437-51.

2326. López Segrera, Francisco. "Esclavage et société dans les Caraïbes (1900-1930)" (Unpublished paper, UNESCO conference on "La route de l'esclave", Ouidah, Bénin, 1-5 Sept. 1994).

2327. Lüsebrink, Hans-Jürgen. "Les chaînes de l'esclave: perceptions et formes de conceptualisation de l'esclavage des noirs, des Lumières à la Révolution Française," in Binder, ed., *Slavery in the Americas*, pp. 205-23.

2328. Lüsebrink, Hans-Jürgen. "Grégoire et la 'littérature des nègres': trajectoires d'une perception culturelle d'Haïti et de la Révolution Haïtienne," in Toumson (with Porset), eds., *La période révolutionnaire aux Antilles*, pp. 75-89.

2329. Lüsebrink, Hans-Jurgen. "Von der Geschichte zur Fiktion: die Haitianische Revolution als gesamtamerikanisches Ereignis," in Zoller, ed., *Amerikaner wider Willen*, pp. 145-60.

2330. Mac-Kit, Samuel. "La Révolution de 1789 et le problème des Noirs (en annexe, le Code Noir)," in Coquery-Vidrovitch, ed., *Esclavage, colonisation, libérations nationales de 1789 à nos jours*, pp. 97-111.

2331. Manigat, Sabine. "Qu'est-ce que la liberté générale en 1793?" *Annales historiques de la Révolution française*, 3-4 (nos. 293-94) (1993), pp. 363-72.

2332. Martin, Jean-Clément. "L'abolition de l'esclavage en question pendant la Révolution," *Les anneaux de la mémoire* (Exhibition catalogue, Nantes, 1992), pp. 114-15.

2333. Martin, Michel L., and Alain Yacou, eds. *Mourir pour les Antilles: indépendance nègre ou esclavage (1802-1804)*. Paris: Editions Caribéennes, 1991.

For contents see Abenon, Adélaïde-Merlande, Begot, Cabanis and Martin, Cauna de Ladévie, Corzani, and Devaux.

2334. Mayer, Francine M., and Carolyn E. Fick. "Before and After Emancipation: Slaves and Free Coloreds of Saint-Barthélemy (French West Indies) in the 19th Century," *Scandinavian Journal of History*, 18, 4 (1993), pp. 251-73.

2335. Meeks, Brian. "James, the Dialectic and the Revolutionary Conjuncture," *Social and Economic Studies*, 43, 3 (1994), pp. 75-103.

2336. Mesnard, Éric. "Le mouvements de résistance dans les colonies françaises: l'affaire Bissette (1823-1827)," in Dorigny, ed. *Les abolitions de l'esclavage*, pp. 293-97.

2337. Midas, André. "Victor Schoelcher and Emancipation in the French West Indies (trans. Mrs. V. O. Aicalá)," in Beckles and Shepherd, eds., *Caribbean Slave Society and Economy*, pp. 446-53.

2338. *Middelanis, C. Hermann, ed. *Schwarze Freiheit im Dialog: Saint Domingue 1791 - Haiti 1991*. Bielefeld: Hans Kock, 1991.

2339. Moitt, Bernard. "In Search of a Guilty Verdict: Slave Women Against Masters in French Caribbean Courts During Slavery" (Unpublished paper, Annual Meeting of the Canadian Association of African Studies/Association Canadienne des Études Africaines, Toronto, May 1991).

2340. Moitt, Bernard. "Slave Resistance in Guadeloupe and Martinique, 1791-1848," *Journal of Caribbean History*, 25, 1-2 (1991), pp. 136-59.

2341. Moitt, Bernard. "Slave Women and Resistance in the French Caribbean," in Gaspar and Hine, eds., *More than Chattel*, pp. 239-58.

2342. Moitt, Bernard. "Women, Work and Resistance in the French Caribbean during Slavery, 1700-1848," in Shepherd, Brereton, and Bailey, eds., *Engendering History*, pp. 155-75.

2343. Montillus, Guerin C. "Guinea versus Kongo Lands: Aspects of the Collective Memory in Haiti," in Harris, ed., *Global Dimensions of the African Diaspora* (2nd ed.), pp. 159-65.

2344. Munford, Clarence J. *The Black Ordeal of Slavery and Slave Trading in the French West Indies, 1625-1715*. Lewiston/Queenston/Lampeter: Edward Mellon Press, 1991.

Vol. 1 - Slave Trading in Africa
Vol. 2 - The Middle Passage and the Plantation Economy
Vol. 3 - Culture, Terror, and Resistance

2345. Nault, François, and Francine M. Mayer. "L'abolition de l'esclavage à Saint-Barthélemy vue à travers l'étude de quatre listes nominatives de sa population rurale de 1840 à 1854," *Revue française d'histoire d'outre-mer*, 79, 3 (no. 296) (1992), pp. 305-40.

2346. Ott, Thomas O. *The Haitian Revolution, 1789-1794*. Knoxville: University of Tennessee Press, 1973.

2347. Pérotin-Dumon, Anne. "The Emergence of Politics Among Free Coloureds and Slaves in Revolutionary Guadeloupe," *Journal of Caribbean History*, 25, 1-2 (1991), pp. 100-35.

2348. Pérotin-Dumon, Anne. "Free Coloreds and Slaves in Revolutionary Guadeloupe: Politics and Political Consciousness," in Engerman and Paquette, eds., *The Lesser Antilles in the Age of European Expansion*, pp. 259-79.

2349. Plumelle Uribe, Rosa Amélia, and Jacques Michelot. "Le débat autour de l'esclavage et de son abolition dans les conflits internes à la Révolution," in Coquery-Vidrovitch, ed., *Esclavage, colonisation,* *libérations nationales de 1789 à nos jours*, pp. 112-23.

2350. Quenum, Abbé Alphonse C. "Les Chrétiens et la traite négrière atlantique," *Les anneaux de la mémoire* (Exhibition catalogue, Nantes, 1992), pp. 116-17.

2351. Remandet, Frédérique. "*Les esclaves* d'Edgar Quinet: Spartacus et la Révolution de 1848," in Coquery-Vidrovitch, ed., *Esclavage, colonisation, libérations nationales de 1789 à nos jours*, pp. 223-30.

2352. Rénard, Didier. "Vivre blanchement: les hommes de couleur libres et la Révolution française," in Michel Vovelle, Jean Imbert, and Gérard Chianéa, eds., *Les droits de l'Homme et la conquête des libertés* (Actes du Colloque de Grenoble-Vizille 1986) (Grenoble: Presses Universitaires de Grenoble, 1988), pp. 257-63.

2353. Renard, Rosamunde. "Labour Relations in Martinique and Guadeloupe, 1848-1870," *Journal of Caribbean History*, 26, 1 (1992), pp. 37-61.

2354. Ros, Martin. *Night of Fire: The Black Napoleon and the Battle for Haiti*. New York: Sarpedon, 1994.

2355. Roumeguère-Eberhardt, Jacqueline. "La persistance chez les esclaves des identités claniques au môyen des cultes vodun et orisha" (Unpublished paper, UNESCO conference on "La route de l'esclave", Ouidah, Bénin, 1-5 Sept. 1994).

2356. Sala-Molins, Louis. "Le Code Noir" (Unpublished paper, UNESCO conference on "La route de l'esclave", Ouidah, Bénin, 1-5 Sept. 1994).

2357. Sala-Molins, Louis. *Les misères des Lumières: sous la raison, l'outrage ...* . Paris: Laffont, 1992.

2358. Saugera, Éric. "Henri-Baptiste Grégoire (1770-1831): l'ami des hommes de toutes les couleurs," *Les anneaux de la mémoire* (Exhibition catalogue, Nantes, 1992), p. 119.

2359. Saugera, Éric. "L'introduction des noirs aux Antilles et en Guyane françaises au début du XIXe siècle," in Butel, ed., *Commerce et plantation dans la Caraïbe*, pp. 99-113.

2360. Schmidt, Nelly. "L'élaboration des décrets de 1848: application immédiate et conséquences à long terme," in Dorigny, ed. *Les abolitions de l'esclavage*, pp. 334-53.

2361. Schmidt, Nelly. *Victor Schoelcher et l'abolition de l'esclavage*. [Paris]: Fayard, 1994.

2362. Schüller, Karin. "Sklavenaufstand - Revolution - Unabhängigkeit: Haite, der erste unabhängige Staat Lateinamerikas," in Zoller, ed., *Amerikaner wider Willen*, pp. 125-43.

2363. Smalls, James. "Esclave, nègre, noir: The Representation of Blacks in Late 18th and 19th-Century French Art" (PhD diss., University of California - Los Angeles, 1991).

2364. Socolow, Susan M. "Economic Roles of the Free Women of Color of Cap Français," in Gaspar and Hine, eds., *More than Chattel*, pp. 279-97.

2365. Souza-Ayari, Rachida de. "L'histoire d'Abomey: des signes et des mots," *Les anneaux de la mémoire* (Exhibition catalogue, Nantes, 1992), pp. 130-33.

2366. Steiner, Philippe. "L'esclavage chez les économistes français (1750-1803)," in Dorigny, ed. *Les abolitions de l'esclavage*, pp. 165-75.

2367. Tarrade, Jean. "L'esclavage est-il réformable? Les projets des administrateurs coloniaux à la fin de l'Ancien Régime," in Dorigny, ed. *Les abolitions de l'esclavage*, pp. 133-41.

2368. Thésée, Françoise. "La révolte des esclaves du Carbet à la Martinique (octobre-novembre 1822)," *Revue française d'histoire d'outre-mer*, 80, 4 (no. 301) (1993), pp. 551-84.

2369. Thornton, John K. "African Soldiers in the Haitian Revolution," *Journal of Caribbean History*, 25, 1-2 (1991), pp. 58-80.

2370. Thornton, John K. "'I am the Subject of the King of Congo': African Political Ideology and the Haitian Revolution," *Journal of World History*, 4, 2 (1993), pp. 181-214.

2371. Tomich, Dale. "The Other Face of Slave Labor: Provision Grounds and Internal Marketing in

Martinique," in Beckles and Shepherd, eds., *Caribbean Slave Society and Economy*, pp. 304-18.

Reprinted from *Slavery in the Circuit of Sugar*, pp. 259-80.

Translated as "A outra face da escravidão: campos de produção de bens de subsistencia na Martinica," in Andrade and Fernandes, eds., *Atualidade & abolição*, pp. 167-85.

2372. Tomich, Dale. "*Une petite Guinée*: Provision Ground and Plantation in Martinique, 1830-1848," in Berlin and Morgan, eds., *Cultivation and Culture*, pp. 221-42.

2373. Tomich, Dale. "Visions of Liberty: Martinique in 1848," in James Pritchard, ed., *Proceedings of the Nineteenth Meeting of the French Colonial Historical Society* (Providence RI, May 1993) (Cleveland: FCHS, 1994), pp. 164-72.

2374. Toumson, Roger, with the collaboration of Charles Porset, ed(s). *La période révolutionnaire aux Antilles: images et résonnances* (Colloque international pluridisciplinaire, 26 - 30 novembre 1986, Fort-de-France/Pointe-à-Pitre). Martinique: Groupe de Recherche et d'Étude des Littératures et Civilisations de la Caraïbe et des Amériques Noires, Faculté des Lettres et de Sciences Humaines, Université des Antilles et de la Guyanne, 1987. (Mise en page électronique Graphicom)

For contents see Bléchet, Brahimi, Butel, Chauleau, Cohen, Corzani, Ehrard, Elisabeth, G. Gusdorf, S. Gusdorf, Hazaël-Massieux, Jeune, Jurt, Laplaine and Maragnès, Loncke, Lüsebrink, Rupp-Eisenreich, and Thésée.

2375. Trouillot, Michel-Rolph. "From Planters' Journals to Academia: The Haitian Revolution as Unthinkable History," *Journal of Caribbean History*, 25, 1-2 (1991), pp. 81-99.

2376. Vermée, Guy. "Avancées et limites des discours antiesclavagistes et anticolonialistes des philosophes des Lumières," in Coquery-Vidrovitch, ed., *Esclavage, colonisation, libérations nationales de 1789 à nos jours*, pp. 35-42.

2377. Vidaud, Pierre. "Le Révolution française et l'abolition de l'esclavage et de la traite," in Coquery-Vidrovitch, ed., *Esclavage, colonisation, libérations nationales de 1789 à nos jours*, pp. 88-96.

2378. Vigier, Philippe. "La recomposition du mouvement abolitionniste français sous la monarchie de Juillet," in Dorigny, ed. *Les abolitions de l'esclavage*, pp. 285-91.

2379. Villiers, Patrick. "Flibustiers, négriers, planteurs et engagés dans les Antilles françaises des années 1640 aux années 1680," *Les Normandes et les Amériques: Cahiers havrais de recherche historique*, numéro special (1993), pp. 89-101.

2380. Wimpffen, A. D. de. *Haiti au XVIIIe siècle: richesse et esclavage dans une colonie française*. (Ed. Pierre Pluchon) Paris: Karthala, 1993.

2381. Zorn, Jean-François. "Le combat antiesclavagiste chrétien au XIXe siècle," *Bulletin historique et littéraire de la Société de l'Histoire du Protestantisme Française*, 139, [4] (1993), pp. 635-52.

5. Dutch

2382. Allen, Rose Mary. "Katholicisme en volkscultuur: een dialectische relatie: een aanzet tot de studie van het 'beschavingswerk' van de Curaçaose rooms-katholieke kerk in de periode 1824-1915," in H. B. Boudewijnse, H. Middelbrink, and C. van de Woestijne, eds., *Kerkwandel en lekenhandel: de rooms-katholieke kerk op Curaçao* (Amsterdam: Het Spinhuis, 1992), pp. 15-30.

2383. "De Andere Marrons," special issue of *Oso (Tijdschrift voor Surinaamse Taalkunde, Letterkunde, Cultuur en Geschiedenis)*, 11, 2 (1992).

For contents see Beet, Groot, Heilbron, Hoogbergen, Kanten, Oostindie, and Stipriaan.

2384. Arends, Jacques. "Alabi's taal: over taal en taalgebruuik in 'Alabi's World'," *Oso (Tijdschrift voor Surinaamse Taalkunde, Letterkunde, Cultuur en Geschiedenis)*, 12, 1 (1993), pp. 110-12.

2385. Baesjou, René. "De juffrouw Elisabeth op de kust van Guinea ten tijde van de vierde Engelse oorlog," in Brommer, ed., *Ik ben eigendom van ...* , pp. 49-61.

2386. Bakker, Eveline, Leo Dalhuisen, Maurits Hassankhan, and Frans Steegh. *Geschiedenis van Suriname: van Stam tot Staat*. Zutphen: Walburg Pers, 1993.

Chapters on "De slaven", "De marrons", and "De Creolen".

2387. Barata, Mário. "Um diário de viagem ao Suriname em 1798," in Lima, ed., *Mutirão para o Suriname*, pp. 25-40.

2388. Barka, Norman F. "A Cultural Resource Survey of Saint Maarten" (Unpublished paper, Annual Meeting of the Society for Historical Archaeology, Kingston, Jamaica, January 1992).

2389. Beeldsnijder, Rudie Otto. *'Om werk van jullie te hebben': plantageslaven in Suriname, 1730-1750.* Utrecht: Universiteit Utrecht, 1994. (Bronnen voor de Studie van Afro-Surinaamse Samenlevingen, deel 16)

2390. Beeldsnijder, Ruud. "Een weinig bekende brief over de heelmeester, lukuman en slavenjager Quassie," *Oso (Tijdschrift voor Surinaamse Taalkunde, Letterkunde, Cultuur en Geschiedenis)*, 12, 1 (1993), pp. 82-86.

2391. Beet, Chris de, ed. *Skrekiboekoe = Boek der verschrikkingen: visioenen en historische overleveringen van Johannes King.* Utrecht: Universiteit van Utrecht, Vakgroep Culturele Antropologie, 1995. (Bronnen voor de studie van Afro-Suriname, BSA; 17).

2392. Behn, Aphra. *Oroonoko: an Authoritative Text, Historical Backgrounds, Criticism.* New York: W. W. Norton, 1996.

2393. Bilby, Kenneth M. "The Emergence of an Ethnic Enclave: the Aluku," *SWI Forum voor kunst, cultuur en wetenschap*, 8, 2 (1991), pp. 48-55.

2394. Blakely, Allison. *Blacks in the Dutch World: The Evolution of Racial Imagery in a Modern Society.* Bloomington: Indiana University Press, 1993.

2395. Böhm, Günter. *Los sefardíes en los dominios holandeses de América del Sur y del Caribe, 1630-1750.* Frankfurt am Main: Vervuert Verlag, 1992. (Bibliotheca Ibero-Americana).

2396. Boogaart, Ernst van den, *et al. La expansión holandesa en el Atlántico, 1580-1800.* Madrid: MAPFRE, 1992. (Collección Mar y América).

2397. Boomgaard, Peter. "The Tropical Rain Forests of Suriname: Exploitation and Management 1600-1975," *New West Indian Guide/Nieuwe West-Indische Gids*, 66, 3-4 (1992), pp. 207-35.

2398. Bosz, A. J. A. Quintos. "O desenvolvimento do estatuto legal dos escravos de plantações na história do Suriname," in Lima, ed., *Mutirão para o Suriname*, pp. 161-73.

2399. Bosz, A. J. A. Quintos. "O sistema da grande fazenda agrícola (plantation) no Suriname," in Lima, ed., *Mutirão para o Suriname*, pp. 149-54.

2400. Brana-Shute, Rosemary. "Negotiating Freedom in Urban Suriname, 1760-1830," in Turner, ed., *From Chattel Slaves to Wage Slaves*, pp. 148-64.

2401. Brommer, Bea. "Juffrouw Elisabeth: naar de kust van Guinea: het uitreden van de juffrouw Elisabeth in 1780," in Brommer, ed., *Ik ben eigendom van ...*, pp. 33-49.

2402. Brommer, Bea, ed. *Ik ben eigendom van ... : slavenhandel en plantageleven.* Wijk en Aalburg: Pictures Publishers, 1993.

For contents see Baesjou, Brommer, Brommer and Emmer, Oostindie, Stipriaan, and Voort.

2403. Brown, Enid. *Suriname and the Netherlands Antilles: An Annotated English-Language Bibliography.* Metuchen NJ: Scarecrow Press, 1992.

2404. Capitein, Jacobus Elisa Joannes. *The Agony of Asar: A Doctoral Thesis of an African Slave in the Twilight of Holland's Golden Age.* (Robert Carl-Heinz Shell, ed.) Princeton: Markus Wiener, 1996.

Originally presented as the author's thesis (doctoral), Leyden University, 1742 "Dissertation politico-theologica de servitute liberati Christiani non contraria".

2405. Devonish, Hubert. "A Total Analysis of Some Afro-European Creole Languages," in *Talking in Tones: A Study of Tone in Afro-European Creole Languages* (London: Karia Press, Caribbean Academic Publications, 1989), pp. 24-71.

2406. Drescher, Seymour. "Epilogue: Reflections," in Oostindie, ed., *Fifty Years Later*, pp. 243-62.

2407. Drescher, Seymour. "The Long Goodby: Dutch Capitalism and Anti-slavery in Comparative Perspective," in Oostindie, ed., *Fifty Years Later*, pp. 25-66.

2408. Emmer, Pieter C. "Between Slavery and Freedom: The Period of Apprenticeship in Suriname

(Dutch Guiana), 1863-1873," *Slavery and Abolition*, 14, 1 (1993), pp. 87-113.

2409. Emmer, Pieter C. "De grote terleurstelling: het Caribische gebied, Suriname en de prijs van de vrijheid," in Gobardhan-Rambocus, Hassankhan, and Egger, eds., *De erfenis van de slavernij*, pp. 93-113.

2410. Emmer, Pieter C. "The Ideology of Free Labor and Dutch Colonial Policy, 1830-1870," in Oostindie, ed., *Fifty Years Later*, pp. 207-22.

2411. Fogarty, Anne. "Looks that Kill: Violence and Representation in Aphra Behn's *Oroonoko*," in Plasa and Ring, eds., *Discourse of Slavery*, pp. 1-17.

2412. Gobardhan-Rambocus, Lila. "Het Sranan: ontwikkeling en emancipatie," in Gobardhan-Rambocus, Hassankhan, and Egger, eds., *De erfenis van de slavernij*, pp. 147-71.

2413. Gobardhan-Rambocus, Lila, Maurits S. Hassankhan, and Jerry L Egger, eds. *De erfenis van de slavernij*. Paramaribo: Anton de Kom Universiteit, 1995.

For contents see Emmer, Gobardhan-Rambocus, Hassankhan, Hoogbergen, Lamur, and Stipriaan.

2414. Goslinga, Cornelis Christiaan. *Sjons en slaven: verhalen uit de Antilliaanse slaventijd*. Leiden: Primavera Pers, 1992.

2415. Groot, Silvia W. de. "Charting the Suriname Maroons, 1730-1734," in Hoogbergen, ed., *Born out of Resistance*, pp. 142-56.

2416. Groot, Silvia W. de. "Inleiding (to *De andere marrons*)," *Oso (Tijdschrift voor Surinaamse Taalkunde, Letterkunde, Cultuur en Geschiedenis)*, 11, 2 (1992), pp. 118-21.

2417. Haafner, Jacob. "De neger slaven en de vrije negers, in Suriname, en de Deensche slaven," in J. A. de Moor and P. G. E. I. J. van der Velde, bezorgd en van inl. voorzien, *Verhandeling over het nut der zendelingen en zendelings-genootschappen* (Hilversum: Verloren, 1993), pp. 48-67.

2418. Hassankhan, Maurits S. "Immigratie van contractarbeiders voor en na de afschaffing van de slavernij: voorwaarde tot en gevolg van de emancipatie," in Gobardhan-Rambocus, Hassankhan, and Egger, eds., *De erfenis van de slavernij*, pp. 56-70.

2419. *Haviser, J., and C. De Corse. "African-Caribbean Interaction: A Research Plan for Curaçao Creole Culture," in E. N. Ayubi and J. B. Haviser, eds., *Proceedings of the 13th International Congress for Caribbean Archaeology* (Curaçao: Archaeological Institute of the Netherlands Antilles, 1991), part. 1, pp. 326-37. (Reports, no. 9)

2420. Haviser, Jay B. "Preliminary Investigations at Zuurzak, a 17th Century Dutch Slave Camp on Curaçao" (Unpublished paper, Annual Meeting of the Society for Historical Archaeology, Kingston, Jamaica, January 1992).

2421. Heijer, Henk den. *De geschiedenis van de WIC*. Zutphen: Walburg Pers, 1994.

2422. Heilbron, Waldo. *Colonial Transformations and the Decomposition of Dutch Plantation Slavery in Surinam*. Amsterdam: University of Amsterdam, AWIC, ASC, 1992. Also London: Goldsmiths' College, University of London, 1993.

2423. Heilbron, Waldo. "Nieuwe en oude slavernijstudies: een kritiek op Oostindie," *SWI Forum*, 8, 2 (1991), pp. 56-64.

2424. Heyde, H. *1492-1992: 500 jaar ontdekking van Amerika: een schets over Surinaamse indianen uit het verleden*. [Paramaribo]: [n.p.], 1992.

2425. Hoefte, Roosemarijn. "Free Blacks and Coloureds in Plantation Suriname: The Struggle to Rise," in Landers, ed., "Against the Odds", pp. 102-29.

2426. Hoogbergen, Wim. *"De bosnegers zijn gekomen!": slavernij en rebellie in Suriname*. Amsterdam: Prometheus, 1992.

2427. Hoogbergen, Wim. "De geschiedenis van de Kwinti," *SWI Forum voor kunst, cultuur en wetenschap*, 10, 1 (1993), pp. 49-82.

2428. Hoogbergen, Wim. "Marronage and Slave Rebellions in Suriname," in Binder, ed., *Slavery in the Americas*, pp. 165-95.

2429. Hoogbergen, Wim. "Origins of the Suriname Kwinti Maroons," *New West Indian Guide/Nieuwe West-Indische Gids*, 66, 1-2 (1992), pp. 27-59.

2430. Hoogbergen, Wim. "De slavernij herinnerd," in Gobardhan-Rambocus, Hassankhan, and Egger, eds., *De erfenis van de slavernij*, pp. 71-92.

2431. Hoogbergen, Wim. "De verdwenen Marrons van Krabbeholle," *Oso (Tijdschrift voor Surinaamse Taalkunde, Letterkunde, Cultuur en Geschiedenis)*, 12, 1 (1993), pp. 6-27.

2432. Hoogbergen, Wim. "Vredesverdragen met Marrons," *Oso (Tijdschrift voor Surinaamse Taalkunde, Letterkunde, Cultuur en Geschiedenis)*, 11, 2 (1992), pp. 141-55.

2433. Horlings, Edwin. "An Economic Explanation of the Late Abolition of Slavery in Suriname," in Oostindie, ed., *Fifty Years Later*, pp. 105-17.

2434. Hove, Okke ten. "Surinaamse slavernij: de gescheiden verkoop van moeder en kind(eren)," *Oso (Tijdschrift voor Surinaamse Taalkunde, Letterkunde, Cultuur en Geschiedenis)*, 15, 1 (1996), pp. 41-57.

2435. Janssen, René, Okke ten Hove (bew. door), and Wim Hoogbergen (medew. van). *Historisch-geografisch woordenboek van Suriname* [naar A. J. van der Aa, 1839-1851]. Utrecht: Instituut voor Culturele Antropologie, 1993). (Bronnen voor de studie van Afro-Surinaamse samenlevingen, deel 14)

2436. Klinkers, Ellen. "The Archives of the Moravian Church in Herrnhut, Germany," *Itinerario*, 17, 1 (1993), pp. 99-100.

2437. Klinkers, Ellen. "De zending onder de plantegeslaven in Coronie," *Oso (Tijdschrift voor Surinaamse Taalkunde, Letterkunde, Cultuur en Geschiedenis)*, 12, 1 (1993), pp. 110-12.

2438. Klooster, Wim. "Subordinate but Proud: Curaçao's Free Blacks and Mulattoes in the Eighteenth Century," *New West Indian Guide/Nieuwe West-Indische Gids*, 68, 3-4 (1994), pp. 283-300.

2439. Klooster, Wim, and Gert Oostindie. "El Caribe holandés en la época de la esclavitud," *Historiografía y bibliografía americanistas*, 51 (1994) pp. 233-59.

2440. Koefoed, Geert, and Jacqueline Tarenskeen. "De opbouw van de Sranan woordenschat," *OSO (Tijdschrift voor Surinaamse Taalkunde, Letterkunde, Cultuur en Geschiedenis)*, 11, 1 (1992), pp. 67-82.

2441. Kpobi, David N. A. *Mission in Chains: The Life, Theology and Ministry of the Ex-Slave Jacobus E. J. Capitein (1717-1747), with a Translation of His Major Publications*. Zoetermeer: Uitgeverij Boekencentrum, 1993.

2442. Kuitenbrouwer, Maarten. "The Dutch Case of Antislavery: Late Abolitions and Elitist Abolitionism," in Oostindie, ed., *Fifty Years Later*, pp. 67-88.

2443. Lamur, Humphrey E. "Demographic Performance of Two Slave Populations of the Dutch Speaking Caribbean."

Reprinted in Beckles and Shepherd, eds., *Caribbean Slave Society and Economy*, pp. 209-20.

2444. Lamur, Humphrey [E]. "Drie eeuwen demografische geschiedenis van de slavenbevolking en Creoolse nazaten," in Gobardhan-Rambocus, Hassankhan, and Egger, eds., *De erfenis van de slavernij*, pp. 15-28.

2445. Lamur, Humphrey E. "The Slave Family in Colonial 19th-Century Suriname," *Journal of Black Studies*, 23, 3 (1993), pp. 371-81.

Translated as "A família escrava no Suriname colonial do século XIX," *Estudos afro-asiáticos*, 29 (1996), pp. 103-12.

2446. Lamur, Humphrey E. "Slave Religion on the Vossenburg Plantation (Suriname) and Missionaries' Reaction."

Reprinted in Beckles and Shepherd, eds., *Caribbean Slave Society and Economy*, pp. 287-94.

2447. Lehmann, Manfred R. "Surinam's 'Jodensavanne' and Several of its Religious Leaders," in Jozeph Michman, ed., *Dutch Jewish History: Proceedings of the Fifth Symposium on the History of the Jews in the Netherlands* (25-28 Nov. 1991) (Van Gorcum [etc.]: The Institute for Research on Dutch Jewry, Hebrew University of Jerusalem, 1993), vol. 3, pp. 239-48.

2448. Lenders, Maria. "Strijders voor het lam: Hernhutter-zendelingen in Suriname," *Savante*, 3, 9 (1994), pp. 6-9.

2449. Lima, Nestor dos Santos. "Stedman: um clássico sobre o Suriname," in idem, ed., *Mutirão para o Suriname*, pp. 141-48.

2450. Lima, Nestor dos Santos, ed. *Mutirão para o Suriname: 1976-1982 Paramaribo*. Brasília: [n.p.], 1991.

For contents see Barata, Bosz (2), and Lima.

2451. Linde, Jan M. van der. "Cham in de tijd van de ontdekkingsreizen, westerse zending/missie en kolonialisme (ca. 1500-1800)," in *Over Noach met zijn zonen: de Cham-ideologie en de leugens tegen Cham tot vandaag* (Utrecht: Interuniversitair Instituut voor Missiologie en Oecumenica, 1993), vol. 1, pp. 77-90. (IIMO research publication, 33)

2452. Linde, Jan M. van der. "Cham in de negentiende eeuw en eerste helft van de twintigste eeuw in Afrika, Latijns-Amerika en het Caribische gebied (ca. 1800-1960)," in *Over Noach met zijn zonen: de Cham-ideologie en de leugens tegen Cham tot vandaag* (Utrecht: Interuniversitair Instituut voor Missiologie en Oecumenica, 1993),vol. 1, pp. 119-36. (IIMO research publication; 33)

2453. MacLeod, Cynthia. *Elisabeth Samson: een vrije, zwarte vrouw in het achttiende-eeuwse Suriname*. Utrecht: Vakgroep Culturele Antropologie, Universiteit van Utrecht, 1993. (Bronnen voor de studie van Afro-Suriname, 15).

2454. McGowan, Winston F. *The French Revolutionary Period in Demerara-Essequibo, 1793-1802*. Turkeyen, Guyana: History Society, University of Guyana, 1993. (History Gazette, no. 55)

2455. Oostindie, Gert. "The Economics of Surinam Slavery," *Economic and Social History in the Netherlands*, 5 (1993), pp. 1-24.

2456. Oostindie, Gert. "The Enlightenment, Christianity and the Suriname Slave," *Journal of Caribbean History*, 6, 2 (1992), pp. 147-70.

2457. Oostindie, Gert. "Introduction," in Oostindie, ed., *Fifty Years Later*, pp. 1-24.

2458. Oostindie, Gert. *Roosenburg en Mon Bijou: twee surinamse plantages, 1720-1870*. Dordrecht, and Providence RI: Foris Publications, 1989.

2459. Oostindie, Gert. "Same Old Song? Perspectives on Slavery and Slaves in Suriname and Curaçao," in idem, ed., *Fifty Years Later*, pp. 143-78.

2460. Oostindie, Gert [J.] "Slaaf van de bronnen: de reconstructie van het onherroepelijk verlorene," *Oso (Tijdschrift voor Surinaamse Taalkunde, Letterkunde, Cultuur en Geschiedenis)*, 7, 2 (1988), pp. 135-46.

2461. Oostindie, Gert. "Slavenleven," in Brommer, ed., *Ik ben eigendom van ...* , pp. 95-113.

2462. Oostindie, Gert. "Slavernijstudies en de kleren van de keizer," *SWI Forum voor kunst, cultuur en wetenschap*, 8, 2 (1991), pp. 65-73.

2463. Oostindie, Gert. "Voltaire, Stedman and Suriname Slavery," *Slavery and Abolition*, 14, 2 (1993), pp. 1-34.

2464. Oostindie, Gert. "Zoete dromen, bittere ironie: Nederland in 'Latijns'-Amerika," in J. Lechner and H. Ph. Vogel, eds., *De Nieuwe Wereld en de lage landen: onbekende aspecten van vijfhonderd jaar ontmoetingen tussen Latijns-Amerika en Nederland* (Amsterdam: Meulenhoff, 1992), pp. 97-114.

2465. Oostindie, Gert, and Alex van Stipriaan. "Slavery and Slave Cultures in a Hydraulic Society," in Palmié, ed., *Slave Cultures and the Cultures of Slavery*, pp. 78-99.

2466. Oostindie, Gert, ed. *Fifty Years Later: Antislavery, Capitalism and Modernity in the Dutch Orbit*. Leiden: KITLV Press, 1995.

For contents see Drescher (2), Emmer, Engerman, Horlings, Knaap, Kuitenbrouwer, Oostindie (2), Oostindie and van Stipriaan, Ross, Sens, and van Stipriaan.

2467. Palm, Layo de (Layo). *E lantamentu di 1795: datos oral: 200 ana lantamentu di katibu*. Curacao: n.p., 1995.

2468. Paula, A. F. "Van slaaf tot quasi-slaaf: een sociaal-historische studie over de dubbelzinnige slavenemancipatie op Nederlands Sint-Maarten, 1816-1863" (Dissertation, Utrecht, 1992).

2469. Paula, A. F. *"Vrije" slaven: een sociaal-historische studie over de dualistische slavenemancipatie op Nederlands Sint Maarten, 1816-1863*. Curaçao: Centraal Historisch Archief, Universiteit van de Nederlandse Antillen; Zutphen, Neth.: Walburg Pers, 1993.

2470. Postma, Johannes. "The Fruits of Slave Labor: Tropical Commodities from Surinam to Holland, 1683-1794" (Unpublished paper, Eleventh International Economic History Congress, Milan, 11-16 September 1994).

2471. Price, Richard, and Sally Price, eds. *Stedman's Surinam: Life in an Eighteenth-Century Slave Society: an Abridged, Modernized Edition of "Narrative of a Five Years Expedition Against the Revolted Negroes of Surinam" by John Gabriel Stedman.* Baltimore: The Johns Hopkins University Press, 1992.

2472. Römer-Kenepa, Nolda C. "Curaçaose vrouwen in de slavenmaatschappij (eind 18de eeuw en eerste helft 19de eeuw)," in Richenel Ansano *et al.*, eds., *Mundu yama sinta mira: Womanhood in Curaçao* (Curaçao: Fundashon Publikashon, 1992), pp. 21-41.

2473. Roos, Doeke. *Zeeuwen en de Westindische Compagnie (1621-1674).* Hulst, Neth.: Van Geyt, 1992.

2474. Schalkwijk, [J.] Marten [W.] "Colonial State-Formation in Caribbean Plantation Societies: Structural Analysis and Changing Elite Networks in Suriname, 1650-1920" (PhD diss., Cornell University, 1994).

2475. Schalkwijk, Marten. "De situatie van de plantages in 1830," *SWI Forum voor kunst, cultuur en wetenschap*, 8, 2 (1991), pp. 5-18.

2476. Scholtens, Ben. *Bosnegers en overheid in Suriname: de ontwikkeling van de politieke verhouding 1651-1992.* Paramaribo: Afdeling Cultuurstudies/Minov, 1994.

2477. Sens, Angelie. "Dutch Antislavery Attitudes in a Decline-Ridden Society, 1750-1815," in Oostindie, ed., *Fifty Years Later*, pp. 89-104.

2478. Stedman, John Gabriel. "Tagesablauf eines Plantagenbesitzers in Surinam (Kapitel 18, S. 251-254)," in Corinna Raddatz, ed., *Afrika in Amerika* (Hamburg: Hamburgisches Museum für Völkerkunde, 1992), pp. 142-47.

Translated from *Narrative of a Five-Years' Expedition Against the Revolted Negroes of Surinam ....*

2479. Stipriaan, Alex van. "Een culturele Januskop," *Oso (Tijdschrift voor Surinaamse Taalkunde, Letterkunde, Cultuur en geschiedenis)*, 13, 2 (1994), pp. 184-95.

2480. Stipriaan, Alex van. "Het dilemma van plantageslaven: weglopen of blijven," *Oso (Tijdschrift voor Surinaamse Taalkunde, Letterkunde, Cultuur en Geschiedenis)*, 11, 2 (1992), pp. 122-40.

2481. Stipriaan, Alex van. "'Nog nooit zoo een brutalen magt meiden gezien': weglopen als sociaal strijdmiddel op de negentiende-eeuwse plantages," *Mokro*, 15 (no. 86) (1993), pp. 8-9.

2482. Stipriaan, Alex van. "Stemmen van protest," in Brommer, ed., *Ik ben eigendom van ...*, pp. 117-31.

2483. Stipriaan, Alex van. *Surinaams contrast: roofbouw en overleven in een Caraïbische plantagekolonie 1750-1863.* Leiden: KITLV Uitgeverij, 1993.

2484. Stipriaan, Alex van. "Suriname and the Abolition of Slavery," in Oostindie, ed., *Fifty Years Later*, pp. 117-42.

2485. Stipriaan, Alex van. "Tussen slaaf en peasant: de rot van de kleine landbouw in het Surinaamse emancipatie proces," in Gobardhan-Rambocus, Hassankhan, and Egger Egger, eds., *De erfenis van de slavernij*, pp. 29-55.

2486. Stipriaan, Alex van. "'Een verre verwijderd trommelen': ontwikeeling van Afro-Surinaamse muziek en dans in de slavernij," in Ton Bevers, Antoon van den Braembussche, and Berend Jan Langenberg, eds., *De kunstwereld: produktie, distributie en receptie in de wereld van kunst en cultuur* (Hilversum: Verloren, 1993), pp. 143-73.

2487. Stipriaan, Alex van. "Water en de strijd om het bestaan in Suriname: een ecologische paradox in de slaventijd," *Tijdschrift voor Geschiedenis*, 107, 3 (1994), pp. 348-70.

2488. Thoden van Velzen, Bonno. "Into the Labyrinth: the Study of Collective Fantasies," *Focaal*, 24 (1994), pp. 9-26.

2489. Thoden van Velzen, H. U. E. "Dangerous Ancestors: Ambivalent Visions of Eighteenth and Nineteenth-Century of the Eastern Maroons of Suriname," in Palmié, ed., *Slave Cultures and the Cultures of Slavery*, pp. 112-44.

2490. Thoden van Velzen, H. U. E. "Remnants that Cannot Be Shaken: Collective Fantasies in a Maroon Society," *American Anthropologist*, 97, 4 (1995), pp. 723-32.

2491. Thompson, Alvin O. "Amerindian-European Relations in Dutch Guyana."

Reprinted in Beckles and Shepherd, eds., *Caribbean Slave Society and Economy*, pp. 13-27.

2492. *Thompson, A. "The Demerara Slave Revolt of 1795," *Emancipation*, 3 (1995), pp. (??).

2493. Toes, Jaap. *Wanklanken rond een wingewest: in de nadagen van de Surinaamse slavernij*. Hoorn: Drukkerij Noordholand, 1992. (Academisch proefschrift, Vrije Universiteit Amsterdam)

2494. *Varma, F. H. R. Oedayrajsingh. *De slavernij van Hindustanen in Suriname: een kultureel-antropologische en sociaal-geografische benadering van onze verzwegen historie*. Paramaribo: published by the author, 1993.

2495. Voort, Jan P. van de. "Negotie en negotiaties voor Suriname 1750-1780," in Brommer, ed., *Ik ben eigendom van ...* , pp. 81-91.

2496. Wetering, Ineke van. "The Transformation of Slave Experience: Self and Danger in the Rituals of Creole Migrant Women in the Netherlands," in Palmié, ed., *Slave Cultures and the Cultures of Slavery*, pp. 210-38.

2497. Wildeman, M. "Slaven, broeders en emancipatie, de slavenzending van de Moravische broeders in Suriname, 1830-1863" (Doctoraalscriptie, Rijksuniversiteit Leiden, 1993).

2498. Zamuel, Hesdie Stuart. *Johannes King: profeet en apostel van het Surinaamse bosland/Johannes King: Prophet and Apostle of the Surinamese Hinterland*. Zoetermeer: Boekencentrum, 1994.

6. Other

2499. Caron, Aimery P., and Arnold R. Highfield. *The French Intervention in the St. John Slave Revolt of 1733-34*. St. Croix: Department of Conservation and Cultural Affairs, Bureau of Libraries, Museums and Archaeological Services, 1981. (Occasional paper no. 7)

2500. Greene, Sandra E. "From Whence They Came: A Note on the Influence of West African Ethnic and Gender Relations on the Organizational Character of the 1733 St. John Slave Rebellion," in Tyson and Highfield, eds., *Danish West Indian Slave Trade*, pp. 47-68.

2501. Hall, N. A. T. "Maritime Maroons: *Grand Marronage* from the Danish West Indies."

Reprinted in Beckles and Shepherd, eds., *Caribbean Slave Society and Economy*, pp. 387-400.

2502. Hall, N. A. T. *Slave Society in the Danish West Indies: St. Thomas, St. John, and St. Croix*. Ed. B. W. Higman. Baltimore: Johns Hopkins University Press, 1992.

2503. Hall, N. A. T. "Slaves' Use of their 'Free' Time in the Danish Virgin Islands in the Later Eighteenth and Early Nineteenth Century."

Reprinted in Beckles and Shepherd, eds., *Caribbean Slave Society and Economy*, pp. 335-44.

2504. Hall, N. A. T. "The Victor Vanquished: Emancipation in St. Croix; Its Antecedents and Immediate Aftermath."

Reprinted in Beckles and Shepherd, eds., *Caribbean Slave Society and Economy*, pp. 419-34.

2505. Highfield, Arnold R. "Patterns of Accommodation and Resistance: The Moravian Witness to Slavery in the Danish West Indies," *Journal of Caribbean History*, 28, 2 (1994), pp. 138-64.

2506. Highfield, Arnold R. *Slavery in the Danish West Indies: A Bibliography*. St. Croix: The Virgin Islands Humanities Council, 1994.

2507. Highfield, Arnold R., ed. *Observations upon the state of Negro slavery in the island of Santa Cruz, the principal of the Danish West India colonies: with miscellaneous remarks upon subjects relating to the West India question, and a notice of Santa Cruz*. Christiansted USVI: Antilles Press, 1996.

Written by a Lieutenant Brady of the British Royal Navy. "Published under the same title in London in 1829 by Simpkin and Marshall and Longman, Reid and Company, Paternoster-Row".

2508. *Higman, Barry W. "Danish West Indian Slavery in Comparative Perspective: An Appreciation of Neville Hall's Contribution to the Historiography," in George Tyson, ed., *Slavery and Freedom in the Virgin Islands* (forthcoming).

2509. Holsoe, Svend. "Archival Research on Estate Whim and St. Croix: Slave Lifeways and the 1840s Slave Rebellion" (Unpublished paper, Annual Meeting of the Society for Historical Archaeology, Kingston, Jamaica, January 1992).

2510. Meier, Gudrun. "Preliminary Remarks on the Oldendorp Manuscripts and Their History," in Palmié, ed., *Slave Cultures and the Cultures of Slavery*, pp. 67-77.

2511. Missio, Nicole. "The Material Culture of Estate Whim at St. Croix" (Unpublished paper, Annual Meeting of the Society for Historical Archaeology, Kingston, Jamaica, January 1992).

2512. Olwig, Karen Fog. "African Cultural Principles in Caribbean Slave Societies: A View From the Danish West Indies," in Palmié, ed., *Slave Cultures and the Cultures of Slavery*, pp. 23-39.

2513. Olwig, Karen Fog. "African Culture in the Danish West Indies: The Slave Trade and its Aftermath," in Tyson and Highfield, eds., *Danish West Indian Slave Trade*, pp. 69-87.

2514. Olwig, Karen Fog. "West Indian Research in Denmark," *Plantation Society in the Americas*, 3, 2 (1993), pp. 51-62.

2515. Pope, Polly. "A Maroon Settlement on St. Croix," *Negro History Bulletin*, 35, 7 (1972), pp. 153-54.

2516. Rupp-Eisenreich, Britta. "L'ethnicité, critère descriptif au XVIIIe siècle: le cas de la traite danoise," in Jean-Pierre Chrétien and Gérard Prunier, eds., *Les ethnies ont une histoire* (Paris: Karthala, 1989), pp. 49-60.

2517. Rupp-Eisenreich, Britta. "Les Frères moraves, ethnologues de la condition esclave? (Isles Vierges, Petites Antilles, 1731-1768)," in Claude Blanckaert, ed., *Naissance de l'Ethnologie? Anthropologie et missions en Amérique XVIe-XVIIIe siècle* (Paris: Éditions du Cerf, 1985), pp. 125-73.

2518. Rupp-Eisenreich, Britta. "Les 'informateurs' africains des missionaries pietistes et moraves," in Daniel Droixhe and Klaus H. Kiefer, eds., *Images de l'Africain de l'antiquité au XXe siècle* (Frankfurt: Peter Lang Verlag, 1987), pp. 45-61.

2519. Steege, Thomas. "Alltäglicher Widerstand von Sklaven in der Karibik am Beispiel von St. Croix 1770-1807," in Raddatz, ed., *Afrika in Amerika*, pp. 148-55.

2520. Stein, Peter. "Die Anfänge der Verschriftung einer Kreolsprache: das Negerhollands im 18. Jahrhundert," in P. Sture Ureland, ed., *Entstehung von Sprachen und Völkern* (Tübingen: Niemeyer, 1985), pp. 437-57.

2521. Stein, Peter. "Bemerkungen zur Edition der 'Sklavenbriefe' aus St. Thomas, 1737-1768 (Kurzfassung)," in Norbert Boretzky, Werner Enninger, and Thomas Stolz, eds., *Akten des 1. Essener Kolloquiums über 'Kreolsprachen und Sprachkontakte' vom 26.1.1985 an der Universität Essen* (Bochum: Brockmeyer, 1985), pp. 135-42.

2522. Stein, Peter. "When Creole Speakers Write the Standard Language: An Analysis of Some of the Earliest Slave Letters from St. Thomas," in Martin Pütz and René Dirven, eds., *Wheels within Wheels: Papers of the Duisburg Symposium on Pidgin and Creole Languages* (Frankfurt: Peter Lang, 1989), pp. 153-78.

2523. Tyson, George F. [Jr.] "On the Periphery of the Peripheries: The Cotton Plantations of St. Croix, Danish West Indies, 1735-1815," *Journal of Caribbean History*, 26, 1 (1992), pp. 1-36.

2524. Tyson, George F., ed. *The Kamina Folk: Slavery and Slave Life in the Danish West Indies*. [St. Thomas], U.S. Virgin Islands: Virgin Islands Humanities Council, 1994.

VI. AFRICA

1. General (Non-Muslim)[6]

2525. Abwa, Daniel. "The Banen and Slavery," *Paideuma* (special issue), 41 (1995), pp. 107-25.

2526. Afolayan, Funso. "Slavery, Warfare and Society in the Nineteenth Century: The Witness of Samuel Johnson," in Toyin Falola, ed., *The Pioneer, Patriot and Patriarch: Samuel Johnson and Yoruba*

[6] Including coastal European enclaves in Africa (French Senegal and Gorée, British and Danes on the Gold Coast), but not the Portuguese colonies or the Dutch and English Cape Colony.

History (Madison: University of Wisconsin Press, 1993), pp. 183-96.

2527. Alagoa, Ebiegberi J., and Atei M. Okorobia. "Pawnship in Nembe, Niger Delta," in Falola and Lovejoy, eds., *Pawnship in Africa*, pp. 71-81.

2528. Allen, Richard B. (Review essay: Manning, *Slavery and African Life*, Morton, *Children of Ham*, and Watson, *Slave Question*), *African Studies Review*, 35, 2 (1992), pp. 114-19.

2529. Austen, Ralph A. "Slavery and the Slave Trade on the Atlantic Coast: The Duala of the Littoral," *Paideuma* (special issue), 41 (1995), pp. 127-52.

2530. Austin, Gareth. "Human Pawning in Asante, 1800-1950: Markets and Coercion, Gender and Cocoa," in Falola and Lovejoy, eds., *Pawnship in Africa*, pp. 119-59.

2531. Ayom, Awak'. "L'esclavage des Noirs africains dans les colonies françaises et la Révolution française de 1789," *Zaire-Afrique*, 32 (no. 265) (1992), pp. 287-310.

2532. Bazémo, Maurice. "La captivité en société Lobi et le patriarcat" (Presentation at Colloquium on "Les dépendances serviles", Paris 1996).

2533. Bazémo, M[aurice]. "Captivité et pouvoirs dans l'ancien royaume Mossi de Ouagadougou (XVIe-XIXe s.)" (Unpublished paper, Colloque International de Recherches sur l'Esclavage Antique [GIREA]. Colloque [19ème] sur "Captifs et prisonniers de guerre dans leurs rapports avec l'esclavage", 2 - 5 October, 1991, Palma, Mallorca).

2534. Bazémo, Maurice. "Captivité et pouvoirs dans l'ancien royaume de Ouagadougou à la fin du XIXe siècle," *Dialogues d'histoire ancienne*, 19, 1 (1993), pp. 191-204.

2535. Bley, Helmut, Clemens Dillmann, Gesine Krüger, and Hans-Hermann Pogarell, eds. *Sklaverei in Afrika: Afrikanische Gesellschaftsformen im Zusammenhang von europäischer und interner Sklaverei und Sklavenhandel*. Pfaffenweiler: Centaurus-Verlagsgesellschaft, 1991.

For contents see Bley and Lehmann-Grube, Füsser, Graebert and Pogarell, Hebenbrock, Kaese (2), Krüger and Hintze, and Sievers.

2536. Bredwa-Mensah, Yaw. "Slavery and Plantation Life at the Danish Plantation Site of Bibease, Gold Coast (Ghana)," *Ethografisch-Archäologische Zeitschrift*, 38 (1996), pp. 445-58.

2537. Brown, Carolyn A. "Testing the Boundaries of Marginality: Twentieth-Century Slavery and Emancipation Struggles in Nkanu, Northern Igboland, 1920-29," *Journal of African History*, 37, 1 (1996), pp. 51-80.

2538. Burnham, Philip. "Raiders and Traders in Adamawa: Slavery as a Regional System," *Paideuma* (special issue), 41 (1995), pp. 153-76.

2539. el-Cheikh, Abdurrahman Abdellah. "[Some New Notes about Slavery in Africa until the End of the 19th Century] (English summary of 'Sab' Mulahazat Jadida 'an al-Riqq fi Ifriqya hatta Nihayat al-Qarn al-Tasi' 'Ashar ... '," *Revue d'histoire maghrébine*, 14 (nos. 45-46) (1987), pp. 49-61.

2540. Chem-Langhëë, Bongfen. "Introduction (to 'Slavery and Slave-Dealing in Cameroon in the Nineteenth and Early Twentieth Centuries')," *Paideuma* (special issue), 41 (1995), pp. 95-106.

2541. Chem-Langhëë, Bongfen. "Slavery and Slave Marketing in Nso' in the Nineteenth Century," *Paideuma* (special issue), 41 (1995), pp. 177-90.

2542. Chem-Langhëë, Bongfen, and E. S. D. Fomin. "Slavery and Slave Trade among the Banyang in the Nineteenth and Early Twentieth Centuries," *Paideuma* (special issue), 41 (1995), pp. 191-206.

2543. Chem-Langhëë, Bongfen, ed. "Slavery and Slave-Dealing in Cameroon in the Nineteenth and Early Twentieth Centuries," *Paideuma* (special issue), 41 (1995).

For contents see Abwa, Austen, Burnham, Chem-Langhëë (2), Chem-Langhëë and Fomin, Geschiere, Njoya, Nkwi, and Warnier.

2544. Ekechi, Felix K. "Pawnship in Igbo Society," in Falola and Lovejoy, eds., *Pawnship in Africa*, pp. 83-104.

2545. "The End of the Atlantic Slave Trade: Its Impact on Africa" (Centre of Commonwealth Studies, University of Stirling, 17-18 April 1993).

See papers listed under XI.13 (Slave Trade: Effects on Africa).

2546. Fall, Babacar. *Le travail forcé en Africa Occidentale Française, 1900-1946.* Paris: Karthala, 1993.

2547. Falola, Toyin. "Slavery and Pawnship in the Yoruba Economy of the Nineteenth Century," in Lovejoy and Rogers, eds., *Unfree Labour in the Development of the Atlantic World*, pp. 221-45.

2548. Falola, Toyin, and Paul E. Lovejoy. "Pawnship in Historical Perspective," in Falola and Lovejoy, eds., *Pawnship in Africa*, pp. 1-26.

2549. Falola, Toyin, and Paul E. Lovejoy, eds. *Pawnship in Africa: Perspectives on Debt Bondage.* Boulder: Westview Press, 1993.

For contents see Alagoa and Okorobia, Austin, Ekechi, Falola, Falola and Lovejoy, Giblin, Howard, Law, Morton, O'Hear, and Usuanlele.

2550. Fioupou, Christiane. "La route: stabilité, transition et exil dans la vision du monde Yoruba: un exemple d'interprétation littéraire" (Unpublished paper, UNESCO conference on "La route de l'esclave", Ouidah, Bénin, 1-5 Sept. 1994).

2551. Forbes, Ella. "African Resistance to Enslavement: The Nature and the Evidentiary Record," *Journal of Black Studies*, 23, 1 (1992), pp. 39-59.

2552. Füsser, Willi. "Vorkoloniale Gesellschaftsstrukturen und Sklaverei: das Beispiel Buganda," in Bley, Dillman, Krüger, and Pogarell, eds., *Sklaverei in Afrika*, pp. 119-36.

2553. Geschiere, Peter. "Slavery and Kinship in the Old Political Economy of the Maka (Cameroon, Eastern Province)," *Paideuma* (special issue), 41 (1995), pp. 207-25.

2554. Gewald, Jan-Bart. "The Issue of Forced Labour in the *Onjembo*: German South West Africa 1904-1908," *Itinerario*, 19, 1 (1995), pp. 97-104.

2555. Giblin, James L. "Pawning, Politics, and Matriliny in Northeastern Tanzania," in Falola and Lovejoy, eds., *Pawnship in Africa*, pp. 43-54.

2556. Glassman, Jonathon. "No Words of Their Own (review essay: Meillassoux, *Anthropology of Slavery*)," *Slavery and Abolition*, 16, 1 (1995), pp. 131-45.

2557. Gondorf, Bernhard. *Das deutsche Antisklaverei-Kommittee in Koblenz: Eine Episode in der deutschen Kolonialgeschichte.* Koblenz: Landesmuseum Koblenz, 1991.

2558. Goodridge, Richard A. "The Issue of Slavery in the Establishment of British Rule in Northern Cameroun to 1927," *African Economic History*, 22 (1994), pp. 19-36.

2559. Graebert, Jochen, and Hans-Hermann Pogarell. "Sklaverei und Sklavenhandel in staatenlosen Gesellschaften: der Fall Südostnigeria," in Bley, Dillman, Krüger, and Pogarell, eds., *Sklaverei in Afrika*, pp. 21-42.

2560. Hansen, Holger Bernt. "Forced Labour in a Missionary Context: A Study of *Kasanvu* in Early Twentieth-Century Uganda," in Twaddle, ed., *The Wages of Slavery*, pp. 186-206.

2561. Hebenbrock, Klaus. "Sklaven aus dem 'Bauch des Dan': Sklaverei und Sklavenhandel in Dahomey," in Bley, Dillman, Krüger, and Pogarell, eds., *Sklaverei in Afrika*, pp. 43-61.

2562. Howard, Allen M. "Pawning in Coastal Northwest Sierra Leone," in Falola and Lovejoy, eds., *Pawnship in Africa*, pp. 267-83.

2563. Hoyt, Edwin P. *African Slavery.* New York: Abelard-Schuman, 1973.

2564. *Ibrahim, 'Abdallah 'Abd al-Raziq Ibrahim. "al-Juhud al-Dawliyya il-Ilgha al-Riqq fi Ifriqya [The International Efforts towards the Abolition of Slavery in Africa]," *Al-Majalla al-Tarikhiyya al-Misriyya*, 32 (1985), pp. 181-219.

2565. Inikori, Joseph E. "Slavery and Capitalism in Africa," in Pas, coord., *Anais do Seminário internacional da escravidão*, pp. 7-24.

Also translated as "Escravidão e capitalismo na África," in Pas, coord., *Anais do Seminário internacional da escravidão*, pp. 25-41.

2566. Jones, Adam. "Female Slave-Owners on the Gold Coast: Just a Matter of Money," in Palmié, ed., *Slave Cultures and the Cultures of Slavery*, pp. 100-11.

2567. Kaese, Wolfgang. "Sklaverei in Afrika: Annäherung an eine Definition," in Bley, Dillman,

Krüger, and Pogarell, eds., *Sklaverei in Afrika*, pp. 1-20.

2568. Kaese, Wolfgang. "Sklaverei und Staat in Afrika: das Beispiel Asante," in Bley, Dillman, Krüger, and Pogarell, eds., *Sklaverei in Afrika*, pp. 62-80.

2569. Kea, Ray A. "Plantations and Labor in the South-East Gold Coast from the Late Eighteenth to the Mid-Nineteenth Century," in Law, ed., *From Slave Trade to "Legitimate" Commerce*, pp. 119-43.

2570. Klein, A. Norman. "Slavery and Akan Origins? (review essay: Wilks, *Forests of Gold: Essays on the Akan and the Kingdom of Asante* [Cambridge: Cambridge University Press, 1994])" *Ethnohistory*, 41, 4 (1994), pp. 627-56.

With commentary by Ivor Wilks, "Slavery and Akan Origins?", pp. 657-65, and reply by Klein, pp. 666-67.

2571. Klein, Martin A. "The Export Slave Trade and the Use of Slaves in West Africa" (Presentation at Colloquium on "Les dépendances serviles", Paris 1996).

2572. Klein, Martin A. "From Kopytoff to Meillassoux: Colonialism and the Analysis of African Slavery" (Unpublished paper, Annual Meeting of the African Studies Association, Seattle, 20-23 November 1992).

2573. Klein, Martin A. "Slavery and Emancipation in French West Africa," in idem, ed., *Breaking the Chains*, pp. 171-96.

2574. Kosack, Godula. "Aus der Zeit der Sklaverei (Nord-Kamerun): alte Mafa erzählen," *Paideuma*, 38 (1992), pp. 177-94.

2575. Krüger, Gesine, and Andrea Hintze. "Sklaverei in Ostafrika: von der Schuldknechtschaft zur Zwangsarbeit," in Bley, Dillman, Krüger, and Pogarell, eds., *Sklaverei in Afrika*, pp. 103-18.

2576. Lange, Dierk. "Ein vernachlässigtes Forschungsgebiet: die Geschichte des westafrikanischen Mittelalters," *Saeculum: Jahrbuch für Universalgeschichte*, 43, 4 (1992), pp. 291-306.

2577. Law, Robin [C. C.] "On Pawning and Enslavement for Debt in the Pre-Colonial Slave Coast," in Falola and Lovejoy, eds., *Pawnship in Africa*, pp. 55-69.

2578. Lovejoy, Paul E., and Alexander Sydney Kanya-Forstner, eds. *Slavery and its Abolition in French West Africa: The Official Reports of G. Poulet, E. Roume, and G. Deherme.* Madison WI: African Studies Program, University of Wisconsin-Madison, 1994.

Includes Georges Poulet, *Enquête sur la captivité en A.O.F.*, Ernest Roume, *Rapport au Ministre des Colonies*, and Georges Deherme, *L'esclavage en Afrique Occidentale Française.*

2579. Martin, Susan. "Slaves, Igbo Women and Palm Oil in the Nineteenth Century," in Law, ed., *From Slave Trade to "Legitimate" Commerce*, pp. 172-94.

2580. Mbodj, Mohamed. "The Abolition of Slavery in Senegal, 1820-1890: Crisis or the Rise of a New Entrepreneurial Class," in Klein, ed., *Breaking the Chains*, pp. 1-36.

2581. Memel-Fotê, Harris. "La fête de l'homme riche dans le Golfe de Guinée au temps de l'esclavage, XVIIe-XIXe siècles," *Cahiers d'études africaines*, 33, 3 (no. 131) (1993), pp. 363-79.

2582. Moitt, Bernard. "Slavery, Flight and Redemption in Senegal, 1819-1905," *Slavery and Abolition*, 14, 2 (1993), pp. 70-86.

2583. Morton, Fred. "Pawning and Slavery on the Kenya Coast: The Miji Kenda Case," in Falola and Lovejoy, eds., *Pawnship in Africa*, pp. 27-42.

2584. Morton-Williams, Peter. "A Yoruba Woman Remembers Servitude in a Palace of Dahomey in the Reigns of Kings Glele and Behanzin," *Africa*, 63, 1 (1993), pp. 102-17.

2585. *Al-Munazzama al-'Arabiyya li-l-Tarbiyya wa-l-Thaqafa wa-l-'Ulum, ed. *Mas'alat al-Riqq fi Ifriqya*. (Arab Organization for Education, Culture, and Sciences seminar, Tunis 27-29 June 1985) (Tunis, 1989).

For contents (English, French, and Arabic) see ... Sengo.

2586. Njoya, Aboubakar Njiasse. "Slavery in the Bamum Kingdom in the 19th and 20th Centuries," *Paideuma* (special issue), 41 (1995), pp. 227-37.

2587. Nkwi, Paul Nchoji. "Slavery and Slave Trade in the Kom Kingdom of the 19th Century," *Paideuma* (special issue), 41 (1995), pp. 239-49.

2588. Ofusu-Appiah, L. H. *People in Bondage: African Slavery in the Modern Era*. Minneapolis: Lerner, 1971.

2589. Perbi, Akosua. "The Abolition of Domestic Slavery by Britain: Asante's Dilemma," *Legon Journal of the Humanities* (Ghana), 6 (1992), pp. 1-23.

2590. Piot, Charles. "Of Slaves and the Gift: Kabre Sale of Kin during the Era of the Slave Trade," *Journal of African History*, 37, 1 (1996), pp. 31-49.

2591. Searing, James. "The Master's Household and the Slave Family: Runaway Slaves in Senegal, 1870-1905" (Unpublished paper, Annual Meeting of the Canadian Association of African Studies/Association Canadienne des Études Africaines, Montréal, May 1992).

2592. *Senghor, Daniel-Sédar. "Commentaire d'acte notarié d'affranchissement d'esclave dressé en île de Gorée (Sénégal) le 2 avril 1817 par maitre Victor-Gervais-Protais Mangeard, greffier notaire," *Gnomon*, n° 93 (1994), pp. 4-10.

2593. *Sengo, T. Shaaban Y. "[title??]," in Al-Munazzama, ed., *Mas'alat al-Riqq fi Ifriqya*, pp. [??].

2594. Shields, Francine. "The History of Women in 19th-Century Yorubaland: Untapped Sources" (Unpublished paper presented at conference on "Source Material for Studying the Slave Trade and the African Diaspora", Stirling, Scotland, 13-14 April 1996).

2595. Sievers, Barbara. "Königsmacht und Sklaven der Krone: Sklavenhandel und Staatenbildung in Kayor," in Bley, Dillman, Krüger, and Pogarell, eds., *Sklaverei in Afrika*, pp. 81-102.

2596. *Slattery, Dennis J. "The Transition from Slavery to a Free Labour Movement in Nigeria, 1850-1948" (MA thesis, Catholic University, 1949).

2597. Sundiata, I. K. *From Slaving to Neoslavery: The Bight of Biafra and Fernando Po in the Era of Abolition, 1827-1930*. Madison: University of Wisconsin Press, 1995.

2598. Sunseri, Thaddeus. "Slave Ransoming in German East Africa, 1885-1922," *International Journal of African Historical Studies*, 26, 3 (1993), pp. 481-511.

2599. "Symposium: The End of the Atlantic Slave Trade: Its Impact on Africa" (Centre of Commonwealth Studies, 17-18 April 1993, University of Stirling).

See papers listed under XI.13 (Slave Trade: Effects on Africa).

2600. Thésée, Françoise. "Documents autour de la Société des Amis des Noirs: au Sénégal en 1789: La Société Africaine dans les royaumes de Sallum, de Sin et de Cayor: une enquête ethnographique avant la lettre," in Toumson (with Porset), eds., *La période révolutionnaire aux Antilles*, pp. 573-91.

2601. Usuanlele, Uyilawa. "Pawnship in Edo Society: From Benin Kingdom to Benin Province Under Colonial Rule," in Falola and Lovejoy, eds., *Pawnship in Africa*, pp. 107-17.

2602. Vignonde, Jean-Norbert. "Esclaves & esclavage dans la parémiologie fon du Bénin" (Unpublished paper, UNESCO conference on "La route de l'esclave", Ouidah, Bénin, 1-5 Sept. 1994).

2603. Warnier, Nea-Pierre. "Slave-Trading without Slave-Raiding in Cameroon," *Paideuma* (special issue), 41 (1995), pp. 251-72.

2604. Wright, Marcia. *Strategies of Slaves and Women: Life-Stories from East/Central Africa*. New York: Lilian Barber Press, 1993.

2. Cape of Good Hope[7]

2605. Adhikari, Mohamed. "The Sons of Ham: Slavery and the Making of Coloured Identity," *South African Historical Journal/Suid-Afrikaanse Historiese Joernaal*, 27 (1992), pp. 95-112.

2606. Armstrong, James C., and Nigel Worden. "The Slaves".

Translated as "Die slawe, 1652-1834," in H. Giliomee and R. Elphick, eds., *'n Samelewing in wording: Suid-Afrika 1652-1840* (2nd rev. ed.) (Cape Town: Maskew Miller Longman, 1990), pp. 110-66.

[7] Including trade supplying the slaves and extensions of Dutch slavery and slave-trading into the interior portions of southern Africa.

2607. Bank, Andrew. *The Decline of Urban Slavery at the Cape, 1806 to 1843*. Cape Town: University of Cape Town, 1991. (Centre for African Studies Communication, No. 22)

2608. Bank, Andrew. "The Erosion of Urban Slavery at the Cape," in Worden and Crais, eds., *Breaking the Chains*, pp. 79-88.

2609. Bank, Andrew. "Slavery Without Slaves: Robert Shell's Social History of Cape Slave Society (review essay: *Children of Bondage*)," *South African Historical Journal*, 33 (1995), pp. 182-93.

2610. Bley, Helmut, and Uta Lehmann-Grube. "Sklaverei in Südafrika," in Bley, Dillman, Krüger, and Pogarell, eds., *Sklaverei in Afrika*, pp. 137-52.

2611. Boeyens, Jan. "'Zwart Ivor': Inboekelinge in Zoutpansberg, 1848-1869".

Republished as "'Black Ivory': The Indenture System and Slavery in Zoutpansberg, 1848-1869," in Eldredge and Morton, eds., *Slavery in South Africa*, pp. 187-214.

2612. Crais, Clifton [C.]. "Slavery and Emancipation in the Eastern Cape," in Worden and Crais, eds., *Breaking the Chains*, pp. 271-87.

2613. Crais, Clifton C. "Slavery and Freedom in South Africa (review essay: Elphick and Giliomee, eds., *Shaping of South African Society*, and Watson, *Slave Question*)," *Slavery and Abolition*, 13, 3 (1992), pp. 201-06.

2614. Cuthbertson, Greg. "Cape Slave Historiography and the Question of Intellectual Dependence," *South African Historical Journal/Suid-Afrikaanse Historiese Joernaal*, 27 (1992), pp. 3-25.

2615. Davids, A. "Words the Cape Slaves Made: A Socio-Historical-Linguistic Study," *South African Journal of Linguistics*, 8, 1 (1990), pp. 1-24.

2616. Dooling, Wayne. "'The Good Opinion of Others': Slavery and Community in the Cape Colony, c. 1760-1830," in Worden and Crais, eds., *Breaking the Chains*, pp. 1-23.

2617. Dooling, Wayne. "Law and Community in a Slave Society: Stellenbosch District, c1760-1820" (MA thesis, University of Cape Town, 1991).

Published in University of Cape Town, Center for African Studies, *Communications*, no. 23 (1992).

2618. Dooling, Wayne. "Slavery and Amelioration in the Graaff-Reinet District, 1823-1830," *South African Historical Journal/Suid-Afrikaanse Historiese Joernaal*, 27 (1992), pp. 75-94.

2619. Elbourne, Elizabeth. "The Meaning of Freedom: Britain and the Cape Colony, 1799 to 1842" (Unpublished paper, conference on "Unfree Labor in the Development of the Atlantic World", 13-14 April 1993, York University, Ontario).

2620. Eldredge, Elizabeth A. "Delagoa Bay and the Hinterland in the Early Nineteenth Century: Politics, Trade, Slaves, and Slave Raiding," in Eldredge and Morton, eds., *Slavery in South Africa*, pp. 127-65.

2621. Eldredge, Elizabeth A. "Slave Raiding across the Cape Frontier," in Eldredge and Morton, eds., *Slavery in South Africa*, pp. 93-126.

2622. Eldredge, Elizabeth A., and Fred Morton, eds. *Slavery in South Africa: Captive Labor on the Dutch Frontier*. Boulder, San Francisco and Oxford: Westview Press, 1994.

For contents see Boeyens, Eldredge (2), Mason, B. Morton, F. Morton (3), Penn, and Shell.

2623. Elphick, Richard, and Robert C.-H. Shell. "Intergroup Relations".

Translated as "Onderlinge gropverhoudinge: Khoikhoi, Koloniste, Slawe, en Vryswartes, 1652-1795," in Richard Elphick and Hermann Giliomee, eds., *'n Samelewing in Wording* (Cape Town: Maskew Miller Longman, 1982), pp. 188-247.

2624. Elphick, Richard, and Robert C.-H. Shell. "A Response to Hans Heese," *Kronos*, 18 (1991), pp. 67-70. With response by Heese, pp. 70-71.

2625. Hattingh, J. L. "Slawerny in die VOC-gebied," *Kronos*, 17 (1990), pp. 3-18.

2626. Heese, Hans. "South African Sources on the Slave Trade with Madagascar and Madagascan Slaves at the Cape of Good Hope," in *Fanandevozana ou esclavage*, pp. 105-16.

2627. Hoetink, Hermannus, and Gert Oostindie. "A Note on the Dutch Historiography of Slavery: Robert Shell's 'Rangton van Bali'," *Kronos*, 20 (1993), pp. 107-09.

2628. Kellenbenz, Hermann. "Südamerikafahrer am Kap der Guten Hoffnung," in Zoller, ed., *Amerikaner wider Willen*, pp. 43-124.

2629. Ludlow, E. "Missions and Emancipation in the South Western Cape: A Case Study of Groenekloof (Mamre) 1838-1852" (MA thesis, University of Cape Town, 1992).

2630. Markell, Ann B. "The Archaeology of Slavery in South Africa" (Unpublished paper, Annual Meeting of the Society for Historical Archaeology, Kingston, Jamaica, January 1992).

2631. Mason, John Edwin. "'Fit for Freedom': The Slaves, Slavery, and Emancipation in the Cape Colony, South Africa, 1805 to 1842" (PhD diss., Yale University, 1992).

2632. Mason, John Edwin. "Fortunate Slaves and Artful Masters: Labor Relations in the Rural Cape Colony during the Era of Emancipation, ca. 1825 to 1838," in Eldredge and Morton, eds., *Slavery in South Africa*, pp. 67-91.

2633. Mason, John [Edwin]. "Paternalism Under Siege: Slavery in Theory and Practice During the Era of Reform, *c.* 1825 Through Emancipation," in Worden and Crais, eds., *Breaking the Chains*, pp. 25-43.

2634. Meltzer, Lalou. "Emancipation, Commerce and the Role of John Fairbairn's *Advertiser*," in Worden and Crais, eds., *Breaking the Chains*, pp. 169-99.

2635. Morgan, Annelize. *Slavin van La Liberté*. Kaapstad: Human & Rousseau, 1984.

2636. Morton, Barry. "Servitude, Slave Trading, and Slavery in the Kalahari," in Eldredge and Morton, eds., *Slavery in South Africa*, pp. 215-50.

2637. Morton, Fred. "Captive Labor in the Western Transvaal after the Sand River Convention," in Eldredge and Morton, eds., *Slavery in South Africa*, pp. 159-77.

2638. Morton, Fred. "Slave-Raiding and Slavery in the Western Transvaal after the Sand River Convention," *African Economic History*, 20 (1992), pp. 99-118.

Republished as "Captive Labor in the Western Transvaal after the Sand River Convention," in Eldredge and Morton, eds., *Slavery in South Africa*, pp. 167-85.

2639. Morton, Fred. "Slavery and South African Historiography," in Eldredge and Morton, eds., *Slavery in South Africa*, pp. 1-9.

2640. Morton, Fred. "Slavery in South Africa," in Eldredge and Morton, eds., *Slavery in South Africa*, pp. 251-69.

2641. Newton-King, Susan. "The Enemy Within," in Worden and Crais, eds., *Breaking the Chains*, pp. 225-70.

2642. Penn, Nigel. "Droster Gangs of the Bokkeveld and the Roggeveld, 1770-1800".

Republished as "*Drosters* of the Bokkeveld and the Roggeveld, 1770-1800," in Eldredge and Morton, eds., *Slavery in South Africa*, pp. 41-65.

2643. Ross, Robert. "Abolitionism, the Batavian Republic, the British, and the Cape Colony," in Oostindie, ed., *Fifty Years Later*, pp. 179-92.

2644. Ross, Robert. "Emancipations and the Economy of the Cape Colony," in Twaddle, ed., *The Wages of Slavery*, pp. 131-48.

2645. Ross, Robert. "Paternalism, Patriarchy and Afrikaans," *South African Historical Journal*, 32 (1995), pp. 34-47.

2646. Ross, Robert. "'Rather Mental than Physical': Emancipations and the Cape Economy," in Worden and Crais, eds., *Breaking the Chains*, pp. 145-67.

2647. Saunders, Christopher. "'Free, Yet Slaves': Prize Negroes at the Cape Revisited," in Worden and Crais, eds., *Breaking the Chains*, pp. 99-115.

2648. Schoeman, Karel. "'Maart van Mosambiek': Andreas Verhoogd, a Slave in the Service of the London Missionary Society," *Quarterly Bulletin of the South African Library*, 49, 3 (1995), pp. 140-49.

2649. Schutte, Gerrit J. "Nogmaals Rangton van Bali," *Kronos*, 19 (1992), pp. 161-66.

2650. Scully, Pamela [Frederika]. "Liberating the Family? Gender, Labor and Sexuality in the Rural

Western Cape, South Africa 1823-1853" (2 vols.) (PhD diss., University of Michigan, 1993).

2651. Scully, Pamela. "Narratives of Infanticide in the Aftermath of Slave Emancipation in the Nineteenth-Century Cape Colony, South Africa," *Canadian Journal of African Studies/Revue Canadienne des Études Africaines*, 30, 1 (1996), pp. 88-105.

2652. Scully, Pamela. "Private and Public Worlds of Emancipation in the Rural Western Cape, *c.* 1830-42," in Worden and Crais, eds., *Breaking the Chains*, pp. 201-23.

2653. Shell, Robert C.-H. *Children of Bondage: A Social History of the Slave Society at the Cape of Good Hope, 1652-1838*. Hanover NH: University Press of New England, 1994.

2654. Shell, Robert C.-H. "A Family Matter: The Sale and Transfer of Human Beings at the Cape, 1658 to 1830," *International Journal of African Historical Studies*, 25, 2 (1992), pp. 285-336.

2655. Shell, Robert C.-H. "Hudson's Cape Town," *Quarterly Bulletin of the South African Library*, 47, 4 (1993), pp. 133-49.

2656. Shell, Robert C.-H. "Land, Labor, and Cape Families: The Introduction of Slavery and Serfdom" (Unpublished paper, American Historical Association, Washington DC, 27-30 Dec. 1992).

2657. Shell, Robert C.-H. "(A Note on Indigenous Slavery)," *Quarterly Bulletin of the South African Library*, 43, 2 (1988), pp. 91-92.

Response from Alan G. Morris, "Dental Mutilation in Historic and Prehistoric South Africa," *Quarterly Bulletin of the South African Library*, 43, 3 (1989), pp. 132-34.

2658. Shell, Robert C.-H. "Rangton van Bali (1673-1720): Roots and Resurrection," *Kronos*, 19 (1992), pp. 167-99.

2659. Shell, Robert C.-H. "Religion, Civic Status and Slavery from Dordt to the Trek," *Kronos*, 19 (1992), pp. 28-63.

2660. Shell, Robert C.-H. "The Short Life and Personal Belongings of one Slave: Rangton of Bali, 1673-1720," *Kronos*, 18 (1991), pp. 1-6.

2661. Shell, Robert C.-H. "Tender Ties: Women and the Slave Household, 1652-1834," in *The Societies of Southern Africa in the 19th and 20th Centuries* (London: University of London, Institute of Commonwealth Studies, 1992), vol. 17, pp. 1-33.

2662. Shell, Robert C.-H. "The Tower of Babel: The Slave Trade and Creolization at the Cape, 1652-1834," in Eldredge and Morton, eds., *Slavery in South Africa*, pp. 11-39.

2663. Southey, N. "From Periphery to Core: The Treatment of Cape Slavery in South African Historiography," *Historia*, 37, 2 (1992), pp. 13-25.

2664. *Van der Spuy, Patricia. "A Collection of Discrete Essays with the Common Theme of Gender and Slavery" (MA thesis, University of Cape Town, 1993).

2665. Van der Spuy, Patricia. "Slave Women and the Family in Nineteenth-Century Cape Town," *South African Historical Journal/Suid-Afrikaanse Historiese Joernaal*, 27 (1992), pp. 50-74.

2666. Visser, D. "The Role of Roman Law in the Punishment of Slaves of the Cape of Good Hope under Dutch Rule," in J. A. Ankum, C. A. Cannata, R. Feenstra, Y. Le Roy, J. E. Spruit, and P. Weimar, eds., *Mélanges Félix Wubbe (offerts par ses amis à l'occasion de son soixante-dixième anniversaire* (Fribourg: Editions Universitaires Fribourg Suisse, 1993), pp. 541-49.

2667. Worden, Nigel. "Between Slavery and Freedom: The Apprenticeship Period, 1834-8," in Worden and Crais, eds., *Breaking the Chains*, pp. 117-44.

2668. Worden, Nigel. *The Chains that Bind Us*. Cape Town: Juta, 1996.

2669. Worden, Nigel. "Coercion and Freedom in the Cape Colony, c. 1700-1856" (Unpublished paper, "Ball and Chain" conference, University of New South Wales and British Australian Studies Association, 4-6 December 1996).

2670. Worden, Nigel. "'A Necessary Evil'? Slavery and Emancipation in the Nineteenth Century Cape," *Cabo*, 6, 1 (1994), pp. 3-11.

2671. Worden, Nigel. "Slavery and Amnesia: Towards a Recovery of Malagasy Heritage

Representations of Cape Slavery," in *Fanandevozana ou esclavage*, pp. 93-104.

2672. Worden, Nigel, and Clifton Crais, eds. *Breaking the Chains: Slavery and Its Legacy in the Nineteenth-Century Cape Colony*. Johannesburg: Witwatersrand University Press, 1994.

For contents see Bank, Crais, Dooling, Mason, Meltzer, Newton-King, Ross, Saunders, Scully, and Worden.

3. Portuguese Colonies

2673. Caley, Cornélio. "Angola nos séculos XV-XVIII: populações, espaços, políticos e relações de complementaridade," in Medina and Castro Henriques, eds., *A rota dos escravos*, pp. 207-20.

2674. Capela, José. *O escravismo colonial em Moçambique*. Porto: Afrontamento, 1993.

2675. Clarence-Smith, W. Gervase. "Cocoa Plantations and Coerced Labor in the Gulf of Guinea, 1870-1914," in Klein, ed., *Breaking the Chains*, pp. 150-70.

2676. Clarence-Smith, W. Gervase. "Labour Conditions in the Plantations of São Tomé and Príncipe," in Twaddle, ed., *The Wages of Slavery*, pp. 149-67.

2677. *Escravatura, trabalho, trabalho indígena, trabalho forçado: fontes primárias e secundárias*. Luanda: Central Nacional de Documentação e Investigação Histórica (Angola)/Lito-Tipo, 1988.

2678. Heintze, Beatrix. "Gefährdetes Asyl: Chancen und Konsequenzen der Flucht angolanischer Sklaven im 17. Jahrhundert," *Paideuma*, 39 (1993), pp. 321-41.

Translated as *Asilo ameaçado: oportunidades e consequências da fuga de escravos em Angola no século XVII*. Luanda: Ministério da Cultura, 1995. (Cadernos do Museu da Escravatura, no. 2)

Reprinted in Heintze, *Studien zur Geschichte Angolas im 16. und 17. Jahrhundert: ein Lesebuch* (Köln: Rüdiger Köppe Verlag, 1996), pp. 232-49.

2679. Mastrobuono, Luisa. "Ovimbundu Women and Coercive Labour Systems, 1850-1940: From Still Life to Moving Picture" (MA thesis, University of Toronto [Canada], 1992).

2680. Medina, João. "África cativa," in Medina and Castro Henriques, eds., *A rota dos escravos*, pp. 17-79.

4. Madagascar

2681. Andrianasolo Benoît. "Aux origines de l'esclavage à Madagascar," in *Fanandevozana ou esclavage*, pp. 249-64.

2682. Beaujard, Philippe, and Tsaboto Jean. "Les parias Antemoro: les Antevolo," in *Fanandevozana ou esclavage*, pp. 533-47.

2683. Benoît, Norbert. "Les séquelles de l'esclavage: le malaise créole," in *Fanandevozana ou esclavage*, pp. 572-92.

2684. Campbell, Gwyn. "The Origins and Demography of Slaves in Nineteenth Century Madagascar: A Chapter in the History of the African Ancestry of the Malagasy," in *Fanandevozana ou esclavage*, pp. 5-38.

2685. Dina, Jeanne. "Les Makoa au XIXe siècle (sud-ouest de Madagascar)" (Unpublished paper, "Fanandevozana ou esclavage" [Colloque international, 1996]).

2686. Domenichini, Jean-Pierre, and Bakoly D. Ramiaramanana. "1877: la première abolition de l'esclavage?" in *Fanandevozana ou esclavage*, pp. 367-77.

2687. Evers, Sandra. "Solidarity and Antagonism in Migrant Societies on the Southern Highlands," in *Fanandevozana ou esclavage*, pp. 565-71.

2688. *Fanandevozana ou esclavage* (Proceedings of Colloque international sur l'esclavage à Madagascar, 24-28 sept. 1996). Antananarivo: Musée d'Art et d'Archéologie de l'Université d'Antananarivo). Coord. Rajaoson François.

For contents see Andrianasolo, Beaujard and Tsaboto, Benoît, Camara, Campbell, Domenichini and Ramiaramanana, Evers, Hebert, Heese, Ho, Jacob, Larson, Lupo, Rabearimanana, Rabemananjara, Raison-Jourde, Rajaoson, Rakoto, Rakotondrabe, Rakotosamimanana, Ramahatra, Ramanantsoa Ramarcel, Ramarcel, Ramiandrasoa, Ramilisonina, Randriamarolaza, Rantoandro, Rasolomanana, Ratsimandrava, Ratsivalaka, Razafiarivony, Razafintsalama, Rouad, Spindler, and Worden.

For additional presentations listed on the program but not included in the advance proceedings, see Chan Low, Dina, Gerbeau, Morabito, Mosca, Raharijaona, Rakotoarisoa, Randriamampionona, Randriamaro, Reverzy, Sala Molins, Wanquet.

2689. Jacob, Guy. "L'abolition de l'esclavage à Madagascar: les perspectives françaises," in *Fanandevozana ou esclavage*, pp. 400-12.

2690. Jacquier-Dubourdieu, Lucile. " Représentation de l'esclavage et conversion: un aspect du mouvement du réveil à Madagascar," *Cahiers des sciences humaines*, 32, 3 (1996), pp. 597-610.

2691. Lupo, Pietro. "Perception de l'esclavage dans quelques documents catholiques à Madagascar," in *Fanandevozana ou esclavage*, pp. 378-85.

2692. Morabito, Vittorio. "L'esclavage à travers des images inédites" (Unpublished paper, "Fanandevozana ou esclavage" [Colloque international, 1996]).

2693. Mosca, Liliana. *L'esclavage et son abolition à Madagascar d'après des documents peu connus ou inédits*. N.p., 1996.

Also as "L'abolition de l'esclavage à Madagascar d'après des documents inédits ou peu connus" (Unpublished paper, "Fanandevozana ou esclavage" [Colloque international, 1996]).

2694. Rabearimanana, Lucile. "Les descendants d'Andevo dans la vie économique et sociale au XXe siècle: le cas de la plaine d'Ambohibary Sambaina," in *Fanandevozana ou esclavage*, pp. 519-32.

2695. Rabemananjara, R. W. "Analyse et commentaire de l'arrêté résidential du 26 Septembre 1896, proclamant l'abolition de l'esclavage à Madagascar," in *Fanandevozana ou esclavage*, pp. 413-28.

2696. Raharijaona, Henri. "Le contexte social et juridique lors de la mise en oeuvre de l'arrêté du 27 Septembre 1896 proclamant l'abolition de l'esclavage à Madagascar" (Unpublished paper, "Fanandevozana ou esclavage" [Colloque international, 1996]).

2697. Raison-Jourde, Françoise. "Familiarisation de l'esclavage, asservissement des libres: le paradoxe merina d'une mutuelle privation du désir de liberté (Madagascar, XIXe siècle)," in *Fanandevozana ou esclavage*, pp. 187-99.

2698. Rajaoson François. "Séquelles et résurgences de l'esclavage en Imerina," in *Fanandevozana ou esclavage*, pp. 489-97.

2699. Rakoto Ignace. "Être ou ne pas être: sur les traces de l'esclave malgache andevo, un non-sujet de droit," in *Fanandevozana ou esclavage*, pp. 119-42.

2700. Rakotoarisoa, J. A. "Les esclaves, une race de seigneurs" (Unpublished paper, "Fanandevozana ou esclavage" [Colloque international, 1996]).

2701. Rakotosamimanana, Berthe. "Distances biologiques entre isolats castiques des Hautes Terres de l'Imerina: interprétations et conséquences," in *Fanandevozana ou esclavage*, pp. 474-88.

2702. Ramahatra, Olivier. "L'esclavage intérieur en Imerina au XIXe siècle," in *Fanandevozana ou esclavage*, pp. 272-98.

2703. Ramanantsoa Ramarcel Benjamina. "*Mainty = andevo*: un amalgame statutaire de l'Imerina," in *Fanandevozana ou esclavage*, pp. 200-13.

2704. Ramiandrasoa Fred. "Un aperçu sur la vie quotidienne des esclaves en Imerina au XIXe siècle," in *Fanandevozana ou esclavage*, pp. 143-51.

2705. Ramilisonina. "*Nahoana no lasa andevo?*" in *Fanandevozana ou esclavage*, pp. 265-71.

2706. Randriamampionona Lalao. "Le rôle des esclaves dans le développement de l'art et de la culture à Madagascar" (Unpublished paper, "Fanandevozana ou esclavage" [Colloque international, 1996]).

2707. Randriamaro Jean Roland. "L'émergence politique des Mainty et Andevo au XXe siècle" (Unpublished paper, "Fanandevozana ou esclavage" [Colloque international, 1996]).

2708. Randriamarolaza, Louis Paul. "Proximité physique, distance psychologique et exclusion sociale à Madagascar, ou de l'esclavage doux à l'esclavage dur," in *Fanandevozana ou esclavage*, pp. 299-308.

2709. Rantoandro, G. A. "Après l'abolition de l'esclavage à Madagascar, le devinir immédiat des affranchis," in *Fanandevozana ou esclavage*, pp. 458-72.

2710. Rasolomanana, Dénis. "Approche de l'intégration sociale du phénomène d'esclavage à travers les proverbes des Hautes Terres de Madagascar," in *Fanandevozana ou esclavage*, pp. 498-518.

2711. Ratsimandrava Juliette. "Maralahy, 'De ma vie et de certaines de mes activités,' Introduction," in *Fanandevozana ou esclavage*, pp. 143-51.

2712. Razafiarivony, Michel. "Les Zazamanaga d'Antanetibe Ambato: de la servitude à la lutte continue pour la reconnaissance réelle," in *Fanandevozana ou esclavage*, pp. 548-64.

2713. Razafintsalama, Claudia Tovonirina. "Le prix de la liberté: l'affranchissement individuel pendant la 2e moitié du XIXe siècle (Antananarivo, Fianarantsoa, Toamasina)," in *Fanandevozana ou esclavage*, pp. 323-44.

2714. Reverzy, Dr. "Méditations sur l'esclavage" (Unpublished paper, "Fanandevozana ou esclavage" [Colloque international, 1996]).

2715. Spindler, Marc. "La position des missions protestantes au XIXe siècle sur l'esclavage," in *Fanandevozana ou esclavage*, pp. 386-99.

2716. Wanquet, Claude. "Les conséquences indirectes à Madagascar de la première abolition de l'esclavage par la France" (Unpublished paper, "Fanandevozana ou esclavage" [Colloque international, 1996]).

5. Ethiopia

2717. Gemeda, Guluma. "Subsistence, Slavery and Violence in Lower Omo Valley, ca. 1898-1940s," *Northeast African Studies*, 12, 1 (1990), pp. 5-19.

2718. Rouad, Alain. "Les édits anti-esclavagistes du Ras Täfäri (1923, 1924, 1931)," in *Fanandevozana ou esclavage*, pp. 445-57.

2719. Salamon, Hagar. "Slavery among the 'Beta-Israel' in Ethiopia: Religious Dimensions of Inter-Group Perceptions," *Slavery and Abolition*, 15, 1 (1994), pp. 72-88.

VII. MUSLIM

1. General and Comparative

2720. Akgunduz, Ahmet. *Islam hukukunda kolelik: cariyelik muessesesi ve Osmanli'da harem.* Istanbul: Osmanli Arastirmalari Vakfi, 1995. (Series Osmanli Arastirmalari Vakfi yayinlari; no. 8)

2721. Ayalon, David. *Islam and the Abode of War: Military Slaves and Islamic Adversaries.* Aldershot: Variorum, 1994. (Variorum Collected Studies Series, CS456)

See studies listed separately, individually paginated, in sequence by Roman numerals.

2722. Ayalon, David. "Mamluk Military Aristocracy: A Non-Hereditary Nobility," *Jerusalem Studies in Arabic and Islam*, 10 (1987), pp. 205-10.

Republished in idem, *Islam and the Abode of War*, pp. VI:205-10.

2723. Ayalon, David. "Preliminary Remarks on the Mamluk Military Institution in Islam," in V. J. Parry and M. E. Yapp, eds., *War, Technology and Society in the Middle East* (London: School of Oriental and African Studies, 1975), pp. 44-58.

2724. Comhaire, J. "Some Notes on Africans in Muslim History," *Muslim World*, 46 (1956), pp. 336-44.

2725. Crone, Patricia. "'Even an Ethiopian Slave': The Transformation of a Sunni Tradition," *Bulletin of the School of Oriental and African Studies*, 57, 1 (1994), pp. 59-67.

2726. Daura, Maiwa'azi Dan. *Islam: the Seed of Slavery?* Tulsa OK: Vincom Publishing Co., 1996.

2727. Donner, Fred M. [Review of Crone, *Slaves on Horses*], *Journal of the American Oriental Society*, 102 (1982), pp. 367-71.

2728. Garcin, Jean-Claude. "The Mamluk Military System and the Blocking of Medieval Moslem Society," in Jean Beachler *et al.*, *Europe and the Rise of Capitalism* (Oxford: Basil Blackwell, 1988), pp. 113-30.

2729. Gost, Roswitha. *Der Harem.* Köln: Dumont, 1993.

2730. Hunwick, John O. *West Africa and the Arab World: Historical and Contemporary Perspectives.* Accra: Ghana Academy of Arts & Sciences, 1991.

2731. Lewis, Bernard. *Race and Slavery in Islam.*

Translated as *Race et esclavage au Proche-Orient* (Paris: Gallimard, 1993).

2732. Marmon, Shaun [E.] *Eunuchs and Sacred Boundaries in Islamic Society.* New York: Oxford University Press, 1995.

2733. Marmon, Shaun E. "Slavery, Islamic World," in Joseph R. Strayer, ed., *Dictionary of the Middle Ages* (New York: Charles Scribner's Sons, 1988), vol. 11, pp. 330-33.

2734. Philips, John Edward. "Some Recent Thinking on Slavery in Islamic Africa and the Middle East," *Middle East Studies Bulletin*, 27, 2 (1993), pp. 157-62.

2735. Philips, John Edward. "World Conference on Slavery and Society in History [Ahmadu Bello University, Nigeria, 1990]," *Annals of the Japan Association of Middle East Studies*, 6 (1991), pp. 271-87.

2736. Reynolds, Jonathon T. "Pilgrims, Slaves and Emigres: Colonial Sources on Nigerian Communities in Sudan and the Middle East in the Early 20th Century" (Unpublished paper, "The African Diaspora and the Nigerian Hinterland").

2737. Ze'ev, Dror. "Slavery," in John L. Esposito, ed., *Oxford Encyclopedia of the Modern Islamic World* (New York: Oxford University Press, 1995), vol. 4, p. 1995.

2738. Zoghby, Samir M. "Blacks and Arabs: Past and Present," *Current Bibliography on African Affairs*, 3, 5 (1970), pp. 5-22.

2. Caliphate and Arabia

2739. Ayalon, David. "On the Term *khadim* in the Sense of 'Eunuch' in the Early Muslim Sources," *Arabica*, 32, 3 (1985), pp. 289-308.

Republished in idem, *Islam and the Abode of War*, pp. XI:289-308.

2740. Cheikh-Moussa, Abdallah. "Figures de l'esclave à l'époque 'abbaside," in Bresc, ed., *Figures de l'esclave*, pp. 31-76.

2741. *Haykal, 'Abd al-'Alim 'Ali 'Abd al-Wahhab Abu. "Al-Raqiq al-Afriqi bi-l-Hijaz khilal al-Nisf al-Awwal min al-Qarn al-'Ishrin," *Al-Majalla al-Tarikhiyya al-Misriyya*, 36 (1989), pp. 317-51.

2742. Patton, Douglas. "Badr al-Din Lu'lu' and the Establishment of a Mamluk Government in Mosul," *Studia Islamica*, 74 (1991), pp. 79-103.

2743. Ragib, Yusuf. "Les esclaves publics aux premiers siècles de l'Islam," in Bresc, ed., *Figures de l'esclave*, pp. 7-30.

2744. Trabelsi, Salah. "Domesticité urbaine et esclavage dominial en Terre d'Islam" (Presentation at Colloquium on "Les dépendances serviles", Paris 1996).

2745. Yahya Oyewole Imam. "Emancipation of Slaves in the First Century of Islam," *Islamic Quarterly*, 40, 2 (1996), pp. 118-26.

3. Ottoman Empire - Muslim Turkey[8]

2746. Alexandrescu-Dersca Bulgaru, Marie-Mathilde. "Coutumes appliquées aux esclaves dans l'Empire ottoman," in *La coutume/Custom* (Transactions of the Jean Bodin Society for Comparative Institutional History) (Brussels: De Boeck Université, 1992), part 3, pp. 299-310.

2747. Ayalon, David. "The End of the Mamluk Sultanate: Why Did the Ottomans Spare the Mamluks of Egypt and Wipe Out the Mamluks of Syria," *Studia Islamica*, 65 (1987), pp. 125-48.

Republished in idem, *Islam and the Abode of War*, pp. IX:125-48.

2748. Ayalon, David. "Mamluk: Military Slavery in Egypt and Syria," in idem, *Islam and the Abode of War*, pp. II:1-21.

---

[8] Studies focusing on particular areas within the Ottoman empire (outside of Turkey) have been distributed to the appropriate regional sections, especially Egypt.

Full version of abridged essay, "Mamluk," in *Encyclopedia of Islam* (2nd ed.) (Leiden: E. J. Brill, 1987), vol. 6, fasc. 103-04, pp. 314-21.

2749. Ayalon, David. "The Mamluks of the Seljuks: Islam's Military Might at the Crossroads," *Journal of the Royal Asiatic Society*, ser. 3, 6, 3 (1996), pp. 305-33.

2750. Erdem, Hakan. *Slavery in the Ottoman Empire and its Demise, 1800-1909*. New York: St. Martin's Press, 1996.

2751. Fendoglu, H. Tahsin. *Islam ve Osmanli hukukunda kolelik ve cariyelik: kamu hukuku acisindan mukayeseli bir inceleme*. Istanbul: Beyan, 1996.

2752. Jennings, Ronald C. "Black Slaves and Free Blacks in Ottoman Cyprus, 1590-1640".

Reprinted in Manning, ed., *Slave Trades, 1500-1800*, pp. 166-82.

2753. Parlatir, Ismail. *Tanzimat edebiyatinda kölelik*. Ankara: Turk Tarih Kurumu Basimevi, 1992.

2754. Peirce, Leslie P. *The Imperial Harem: Women and Sovereignty in the Ottoman Empire*. New York: Oxford University Press, 1993.

2755. Regnault, Hikmet and Félix. "Les eunuques de Constantinople," *Bulletins et Mémoires de la Société d'Anthropologie de Paris* (série V), 2 (1901), pp. 234-40.

2756. *Sagaster, Börte. "Ottoman Attitudes to Slavery in Literary Sources as a Reflection of Ottoman Society at the Turn of the Twentieth Century" (diss. in preparation, 1994).

2757. Seng, Yvonne J. "Fugitives and Factotums: Slaves in Early Sixteenth-Century Istanbul," *Journal of the Economic and Social History of the Orient*, 39, 2 (1996), pp. 136-69.

2758. *Toledano, Ehud R. "Agricultural and Harem Slavery among Ottoman Circassians," in idem, *Slavery & Abolition*, forthcoming.

Revised from "Circassian Slavery and Slave Trade – An Ottoman Solution," in idem, *Ottoman Slave Trade*, ch. 4.

2759. Toledano, Ehud R. "The Imperial Eunuchs of Istanbul".

*Revised as "The Eunuchs of the Imperial Household at the Beginning of the Twentieth Century," in idem, *Slavery & Abolition*, forthcoming.

2760. Toledano, Ehud R. "Ottoman Concepts of Slavery in the Period of Reform, 1830s-1880s," in Klein, ed., *Breaking the Chains*, pp. 37-63.

Reprinted as "Late Ottoman Concepts of Slavery (1830s-1880s)," in Israel Gershoni and Ehud R. Toledano, eds., "Cultural Processes in Muslim and Arab Societies", special issue of *Poetics Today*, 14, 3 (1993), pp. 477-506.

*Revised as "Slavery and Abolition as Viewed by the Ottoman Elite (1830s-1880s)," in idem, *Ottoman Slave Trade*, ch. 5.

2761. *Toledano, Ehud R. "Ottoman Slavery and the Slave Trade," in idem, *Slavery & Abolition*, forthcoming.

2762. Toledano, Ehud R. "Slave Dealers, Women, Pregnancy, and Abortion".

*Revised as part of "Semsigül: A Circassian Female Slave in Mid-Nineteenth-Century Cairo," in idem, *Slavery & Abolition*, forthcoming.

2763. *Toledano, Ehud R. *Slavery & Abolition: Studies in Ottoman Social History*. Forthcoming.

Contents also listed separately.

4. Muslim Egypt

2764. Amitai, Reuven. "The Remaking of the Military Elite of Mamluk Egypt, by Al-Nasir Muhammad B. Qalawan," *Studia Islamica*, 72 (1990), pp. 145-63.

2765. Ayalon, David. "The Auxiliary Forces of the Mamluk Sultanate," *Der Islam: Zeitschrift für Geschichte und Kultur des islamischen Orients*, 65 (1988), pp. 13-37.

Republished in idem, *Islam and the Abode of War*, pp. VII:13-37.

2766. Ayalon, David. "Bahri Mamluks, Burji Mamluks: Inadequate Names for the Two Reigns of the Mamluk Sultanate," *Tarih (Taarainh:A Volume of Occasional Papers in Near Eastern Studies)* (Philadelphia: Annenberg Institute, 1990), vol. 1, pp. 3-53.

Republished in idem, *Islam and the Abode of War*, pp. IV:3-53.

2767. Ayalon, David. "From Ayyubids to Mamluks," *Revue des études islamiques*, 49 (1981), pp. 43-57.

Republished in idem, *Islam and the Abode of War*, pp. III:43-57.

2768. Ayalon, David. "Mamluk Military Aristocracy During the First Years of the Ottoman Occupation of Egypt," in C. E. Bosworth, C. Issawi, R. Savory, and A. L. Udovitch, eds., *Islamic World, from Classical to Modern Times: Essays in Honor of Bernard Lewis* (Princeton: Darwin Press, 1989), pp. 413-31.

Republished in idem, *Islam and the Abode of War*, pp. X:413-41.

2769. Ayalon, David. "The Mamluk Novice (On His Youthfulness and on his Original Religion)," *Revue des études islamiques*, 54 (1986), pp. 1-8.

Republished in idem, *Islam and the Abode of War*, pp. V:1-8.

2770. Ayalon, David. "Some Remarks on the Economic Decline of the Mamluk Sultanate," *Jerusalem Studies in Arabic and Islam*, 16 (1993), pp. 108-24.

Republished in idem, *Islam and the Abode of War*, pp. VIII:108-24.

2771. Clot, André. *L'Égypte des mamelouks: l'empire des esclaves, 1250-1517*. Paris: Perrin, 1996.

2772. *Lamba, H. "L'esclavage en Egypte," *Revue de l'Islam*, 6 (1901), pp. 69-75.

2773. Levanoni, Amalia. "The Mamluks' Ascent to Power in Egypt," *Studia Islamica*, 72 (1990), pp. 121-44.

2774. Meinardus, Otto. "The Upper Egyptian Practice of the Making of Eunuchs in the XVIIIth and XIXth Century," *Zeitschrift für Ethnologie*, 94, 1 (1969), pp. 47-58.

2775. Petry, Carl F. "From Slaves to Benefactors: The Habashis of Mamluk Cairo," *Sudanic Africa*, 5 (1994), pp. 57-66.

2776. *Tamam, Tamam Humam. "Al-Raqiq wa-l-Jundiyya fi Nazar Muhammad 'Ali [Slaves and the Army in Muhammad Ali's View]," *Al-Majalla al-Tarikhiyya al-Misriyya*, 27 (1981), pp. 120-57.

2777. Toledano, Ehud R. "Shemsigul: A Circassian Slave in Mid-Nineteenth-Century Cairo," in Edmund Burke, III, ed., *Struggle and Survival in the Modern Middle East* (Berkeley: University of California Press, 1993), pp. 59-74.

*Revised as part of "Semsigül: A Circassian Female Slave in Mid-Nineteenth-Century Cairo," in idem, *Slavery & Abolition*, forthcoming.

5. North Africa and the Sahara[9]

2778. *Abd, El-Keihil Ould Mohamed el. "Colonisation française et mutations sociales en Mauritanie: cas de l'esclavage en milieu maure 1900-1960" (Unpublished mémoire de maîtrise, Université de Nouackchott, 1986-87).

2779. Aouad-Badoual, Ghita. "L'esclavage tardif au Maroc sous le protectorat," *Revue Maroc-Europe*, 1 (1991), pp. 135-44.

2780. Baepler, Paul Michel. "White Slavery in Africa: The Barbary Captivity Narrative in American Literature" (PhD diss., University of Minnesota, 1996).

2781. Bakker, J. C. de. "Slaves, Arms and Holy War: Moroccan Policy vis-a-vis the Dutch Republic During the Establishment of the 'Alawī Dynasty (1600-1727)" (MA thesis, Universiteit van Amsterdam).

2782. Blanc, François-Paul. "L'esclavage au Maroc au temps du protectorat (analyse juridique)," in Michel Vovelle, Jean Imbert, and Gérard Chianéa, eds., *Les droits de l'Homme et la conquête des libertés* (Actes du Colloque de Grenoble-Vizille 1986) (Grenoble: Presses Universitaires de Grenoble, 1988), pp. 282-93.

2783. Blili, L. "Captives européennes dans la Régence de Tunis aux XVIe et XVIIe siècles" (Unpublished paper, Colloque International de Recherches sur l'Esclavage Antique [GIREA]. Colloque [19ème] sur "Captifs et prisonniers de guerre dans leurs rapports avec l'esclavage", 2-5 October, 1991, Palma, Mallorca).

2784. *Dermenghem, E. "Les confréries noires du Mzab," *Bulletin de Liaison Saharienne*, 15 (1953), pp. 18-20.

---

[9] Includes the "Barbary captivity" of Mediterranean Christians as well as military slavery and enslavement of Africans.

2785. Ennaji, Mohammed. *Soldats, domestiques et concubines: l'esclavage au Maroc au XIXe siècle.* Tunis: Cérès Editions, 1994.

2786. Ennaji, Mohammed. "La transition de l'esclavage au métayage dans le Sud marocain" (Presentation at Colloquium on "Les dépendances serviles", Paris 1996).

2787. Galland, Antoine. *Histoire de l'esclavage d'un marchand de la ville de Cassis, à Tunis.* Paris: Editions La Bibliotheque, 1992. (Author lived 1646-1715)

2788. *Gaston, Joseph. *L'esclavage en Tunisie.* Tunis: [pub??], 1980.

2789. Jamoussi, Habib. "Mariano Stinca: image d'un esclave au pouvoir sous le regne de Hammouda-Pacha Bey," *Revue d'histoire maghrébine,* 23, 1 (1996), pp. 431-64.

2790. *Komorowski, Zygmunt. "Les descendants des Soudanais en Algérie et leurs traditions," *Africana Bulletin* (Warsaw), 15 (1971), pp. 43-53.

2791. Kossentini, K. "Les esclaves espagnols à Tunis au XVIIe siècle" (Unpublished paper, Colloque International de Recherches sur l'Esclavage Antique [GIREA]. Colloque [19ème] sur "Captifs et prisonniers de guerre dans leurs rapports avec l'esclavage", 2-5 October, 1991, Palma, Mallorca).

2792. Largueche [LaGueche], Abdelhamid. "L'abolition de l'esclavage en Tunisie (1841-1846)," in Dorigny, ed. *Les abolitions de l'esclavage,* pp. 371-81.

2793. LaGueche [Largueche], Abdelhamid. "La minorité noire de Tunis au XIXe siècle," in Fanny Colonna (with Zakya Daoud), ed., *Être marginal au Maghreb* (extrait de l'*Annuaire de l'Afrique du Nord,* 1991) (Paris: CNRS Editions, 1993), pp. 135-54.

2794. Makris, G. P. "Slavery, Possession and History: The Construction of the Self among Slave Descendants in the Sudan," *Africa,* 66, 2 (1996), pp. 158-82.

2795. McDougall, E. Ann. "In Search of a Desert-Edge Perspective: The Sahara-Sahel and the Atlantic Trade, 1815-1900," in Law, ed., *From Slave Trade to "Legitimate" Commerce,* pp. 215-39.

2796. *al-Naji, Mahuammad. "Hawla al-Raqiq fi al-Maghrib ma qabla al-Isti'mar [Concerning the Slaves in the Maghrib before Imperialism]," *Abhath* (Rabat), 1 (1983), pp. [??]-57.

2797. *Naji, Mohamed. "Slavery and Social Relations in 19th Century Morocco" (French title not available) (PhD diss., Mohammed V University, Rabat, 1987).

2798. *al-Razuq, Muhammad. "Qadiyyat al-Riqq fi Tarikh al-Maghrib [The Problem of Slavery in the History of the Maghrib," *Majallat al-Buhuth al-Tarikhiyya,* 8, 2 (1986), pp. 269-89.

2799. *Sauvaget, Jean. "L'appel au secours des esclaves des états barbaresques par le seigneur de Fayolle et de Comporté," *Amis pays civraisien,* n.s. 88 (1992), pp. 11-12.

2800. *Senillou, Pierre. "Au secours des esclaves chrétiens au XVIIIe siècle," *Revue de la Société d'Études Folkloriques Centre-Ouests,* 25, 3 (1993), pp. 230-32.

2801. Tauzin, Aline. "Le gigot et l'encrier: maîtres et esclaves en Mauritanie à travers la littérature orale," *Revue du monde musulman et de la Méditerranée,* 51 (1989), pp. 74-90.

2802. Temimi, A[bdeljelil]('Abd al-Jalil al-Tamimi). "Itq al-'Abid wa-'Adaduhum fi Muntasaf al-Qarn al-Tasi' 'Ashar bi-Iyalat Tunis [L'affranchissement des esclaves et leurs recensements au milieu du XIXe siècle dans la Régence de Tunis]," *Revue d'histoire maghrébine,* 12 (nos. 39-40) (1985), pp. 213-18.

2803. Temimi, Abdeljelil. "Pour une histoire social de la 'minorité africaine noire' en Tunisie au 19ème siècle," *Revue d'histoire maghrébine,* 14 (nos. 45-46) (1987), pp. 101-09.

2804. Teyssier, Paul. *Esclave à Alger: récit de captivité de João Mascaranhas (1621-1626).* Paris: Editions Changeigne, 1993.

2805. Vissière, Jean-Louis. "Les Pères Trinitaires et la rédemption des captifs: cartes postales d'Afrique du Nord," in *La Méditerranée au XVIIIe siècle* (Actes du Colloque International tenu à Aix-en-Provence les 4, 5, 6 septembre 1985) (Aix-en-Provence: Université de Provence, 1987), pp. 209-16.

2806. *Webb, Allison Jones. "Nineteenth-Century Slavery in the Mauritanian Sahara" (MA thesis, Johns Hopkins University, 1984).

6. Nilotic Sudan and the Horn

2807. Besteman, C. "Invention of Gosha: Slavery, Colonialism and Stigma in Somali History" (Unpublished paper, Annual Meeting of the African Studies Association, Boston, 4-7 December 1993).

2808. Kapteijns, Lidwien, and Jay Spaulding. "From Slaves to Coolies: Two Documents from the Nineteenth-Century Somali Coast," *Sudanic Africa*, 3 (1992), pp. 1-8.

2809. Sikainga, Ahmad Alawad. *Slaves into Workers: Emancipation and Labor in Colonial Sudan*. Austin: University of Texas Press, 1996.

7. Muslim West Africa

2810. Camara, Ousmane. "Les politiques d'abolition de l'esclavage au Sénégal et en Mauritanie, XIXe-XXe siècles," in *Fanandevozana ou esclavage*, pp. 429-44.

2811. Clark, Andrew F. "Freedom Villages in the Upper Senegal Valley, 1887-1910: A Reassessment," *Slavery and Abolition*, 16, 2 (1995), pp. 311-30.

2812. Clark, Andrew F. "Slavery and Its Demise in the Upper Senegal Valley, West Africa, 1890-1920," *Slavery and Abolition*, 15, 1 (1994), pp. 51-71.

2813. *Cleaveland, Tim. "Slavery and Service in Kaarta and the Hodh in the Nineteenth Century" (Unpublished paper, Annual Meeting of the Canadian Association of African Studies/Association Canadienne des Études Africaines, Montréal, May 1992).

2814. Frank, Barbara E. "Reconstructing the History of an African Ceramic Tradition: Technology, Slavery and Agency in the Region of Kadiolo (Mali)," *Cahiers d'études africaines*, 33, 3 (no. 131) (1993), pp. 381-401.

2815. Jumare, Ibrahim M. "The Ideology of Slavery in the Context of Islam and the Sokoto Jihad," *Islamic Quarterly*, 40, 1 (1996), pp. 31-38.

2816. Klein, Martin A., and E. Ann McDougall. "Desert-Edge Communities in Transition: Slavery and Social Change, 1830-1900" (Unpublished paper, Annual Meeting of the Canadian Association of African Studies/Association Canadienne des Études Africaines, Montréal, May 1992).

2817. Kodjo, Georges Niamkey. "Les esclaves de la couronne dans l'Empire Songaï au XVIe siècle," in Gerbeau and Saugera, eds., *La dernière traite*, pp. 45-58.

2818. Lovejoy, Paul E. "*Murgu*: The Wages of Slavery in the Sokoto Caliphate," in Twaddle, ed., *The Wages of Slavery*, pp. 168-85.

2819. Lovejoy, Paul E. "Slave Labour in the Agricultural Economy of the Sokoto Caliphate: Land Tenure in Kano Emirate" (Unpublished paper, conference on "Unfree Labor in the Development of the Atlantic World", 13-14 April 1993, York University, Ontario).

2820. Lovejoy, Paul E., and Jan S. Hogendorn. *Slow Death for Slavery: The Course of Abolition in Northern Nigeria, 1897-1936*. New York: Cambridge University Press, 1993.

2821. Nast, Heidi J. "Islam, Gender, and Slavery in West Africa circa 1500: A Spatial Archaeology of the Kano Palace, Northern Nigeria," *Annals of the Association of American Geographers*, 86, 1 (1996), pp. 44-77.

2822. O'Hear, Ann. "British Intervention and the Slaves and Peasant Farmers of Ilorin, c. 1890 - c. 1906," *Paideuma*, 40 (1994), pp. 129-48. (Special number, A. S. Kanya-Forstner and Paul E. Lovejoy, eds., "The Sokoto Caliphate and the European Powers 1890-1907".)

2823. O'Hear, Ann. "Pawning in the Emirate of Ilorin," in Falola and Lovejoy, eds., *Pawnship in Africa*, pp. 217-44.

2824. Philips, John Edward. "Military and Administrative Slavery in the Sokoto Caliphate 1804-1903" (Unpublished paper, "The African Diaspora and the Nigerian Hinterland").

2825. Stillwell, Sean. "Oral Data and the Reconstruction of the History of Royal Slavery in the Sokoto Caliphate" (Unpublished paper presented at conference on "Source Material for Studying the

Slave Trade and the African Diaspora", Stirling, Scotland, 13-14 April 1996).

2826. Ubah, C. N. "The Colonial Administration in Northern Nigeria and the Problem of Freed Slave Children," *Slavery and Abolition*, 14, 3 (1993), pp. 208-33.

8. Muslim East Africa

2827. Trevis, Giacomo. "Considerazioni sulla schiavitù," in Giuseppina Finazzo, *L'Italia nel Benadir: l'azione di Vincenzo Filonardi 1884-1896* (Rome: Ateneo, 1966), pp. 467-72.

9. Muslim Asia[10]

2828. Babyan, Kathryn. "The Waning of the Qizilbash: The Spiritual and the Temporal in Seventeenth-Century Iran" (PhD diss., Princeton University, 1993).

2829. *Beckwith, Christopher. "Aspects of the Early History of the Central Asian Guard Corps in Islam," *Archivum Eurasiae Medii Aevi*, 4 (1984), pp. 29-43.

2830. Basu, Helene. *Habshi-Sklaven, Sidi-Fakire, muslimische Heiligenverehrung im westlichen Indien.* Berlin: Das Arabische Buch, 1995.

2831. Findly, Ellison Banks. *Nur Jahan: Empress of Mughal India.* New York: Oxford University Press, 1993.

2832. *Kumar, Sunil. "When Slaves were Nobles: The Shamsi *Bandagan* in the Early Delhi Sultanate," *Studies in History*, 10, 1 (1994), pp. 23-52.

2833. Lal, K. S. *The Mughal Harem.* New Delhi: Aditya Prakashan, 1988.

2834. Lal, K. S. *Muslim Slave System in Medieval India.* New Delhi: Aditya Prakashan, 1994.

2835. Paul, Jürgen. *The State and the Military: The Samanid Case.* Bloomington IN: Indiana University Research Institute for Inner Asian Studies, 1994. (Papers on Inner Asia: Central Asia, no. 26)

[10] See Section X.2-4 for non-Muslim slavery in east, southeast, and south Asia.

10. Other

VIII. Ancient

1. General and Comparative

2836. Annequin, Jacques. "L'esclavage antique," *Dialogues d'histoire ancienne*, 16, 2 (1990), pp. 323-40.

2837. Annequin, Jacques. "Esclavage et dépendances dans l'Antiquité: remarques sur et pour un débat" (Presentation at Colloquium on "Les dépendances serviles", Paris 1996).

2838. Annequin, Jacques. "Histoire et anthropologie de l'esclavage," *Dialogues d'histoire ancienne*, 17, 2 (1991), pp. 185-214. (Annales littéraires de l'Université de Besançon, 458; Centre de recherches d'histoire ancienne, vol. 112)

See also Garrido-Hory.

2839. Annequin, Jacques. "Recherches sur l'esclavage et la dépendance: chronique 1992," *Dialogues d'histoire ancienne*, 18, 2 (1992), pp. 271-300.

2840. Annequin, Jacques. "Recherches sur l'esclavage et la dépendance: chronique 1994," *Dialogues d'histoire ancienne*, 20, 2 (1994), pp. 331-53.

2841. Annequin, Jacques, and Marguerite Garrido-Hory, eds. *Religion et anthropologie de l'esclavage et des formes de dépendance* (Groupe International de Recherches sur l'Esclavage Antique [GIREA], Colloque, 4-6 novembre 1994, Besançon). Paris: Belles Lettres, 1994. (Centre de Recherches d'Histoire Ancienne, vol. 133). (Annales Littéraires de l'Université de Besançon, no. 534).

For contents see Alvar Ezquerra, Capogrossi Colognesi, Cels-Saint Hilaire, Citti, Debord, Ducat, Gonzales, Jourdain-Annequin, Kolendo, Kuzicin, Lomas, Mactoux, Mele, Mossé, Nouailhat, Plácido, and Taceva. Also "Discussions" and "Conclusions".

2842. Biezunska-Malowist, Iza. "La captivité comme source de l'esclavage dans l'Antiquité" (Unpublished paper, Groupe International de Recherches sur l'Esclavage Antique [GIREA]. Colloque [19ème] sur "Captifs et prisonniers de guerre dans leurs rapports avec l'esclavage", 2-5 October, 1991, Palma, Mallorca).

2843. Biezunska-Malowist, Iza. *Schiavitù nel mondo antico*. Napoli: Edizioni Scientifiche Italiane, 1991.

2844. Calabria, Antonio. *Per la critica dell'ideologia proprietaria*. Vol I/1: *La filosofia schiavistica: filosofia della polis*. Siena: Lalli, 1990.

2845. *Esclavos y semilibres en la antigüedad clasica*. Madrid: Editorial de la Universidad Complutense, 1989.

For contents see Annequin, Garrido-Hory, López Barja de Quiroga, Mangas, Plácido, Prieto Arciniega, Rodríguez Cerezo, and Santero Saturnino.

2846. *"Femme-esclave: modèles d'interprétation anthropologique, économique et juridique" (Groupe International de Recherches sur l'Esclavage Antique [GIREA], Colloque, 1994, Naples).

2847. Finley, Moses I., ed. *Classical Slavery*.

Translated as *La schiavitù nel mondo antico* (Roma-Bari: Laterza, 1990); with introduction by A. Momigliano.

2848. Fontela, Carlos Alonso. *La esclavitud a travès de la biblia*. Madrid: Consejo Superior de Investigaciones Científicas, 1986.

2849. Gabba, Emilio. "Il nuovo libro di M. Finley sulla schiavitù antica (*Ancient Slavery and Modern Ideology*)," *Athenaeum*, 60, 1-2 (1982), pp. 276-81.

2850. Garnsey, Peter. *Ideas of Slavery from Aristotle to Augustine*. Cambridge: Cambridge University Press, 1996.

2851. Garnsey, Peter. "Philo Judaeus and Slave Theory," *Scripta Classica Israelica*, 13 (1994), pp. 30-45.

2852. Garrido-Hory, Margarite. "Les captifs et prisonniers de guerre dans les dix-huit premiers colloques du GIREA" (Unpublished paper, Groupe International de Recherches sur l'Esclavage Antique [GIREA]. Colloque [19ème] sur "Captifs et prisonniers de guerre dans leurs rapports avec l'esclavage", 2-5 October, 1991, Palma, Mallorca).

2853. Garrido-Hory, Margarite. "Le Centre de recherches d'histoire ancienne et l'esclavage: Colloques. Publications d'index thématiques. Banques de donées," *Dialogues d'histoire ancienne*, 17, 2 (1991), pp. 185-214. (Annales littéraires de l'Université de Besançon, 458; Centre de recherches d'histoire ancienne, vol. 112)

See also Annequin.

2854. Garrido-Hory, Marguerite [Margarite]. "Réflexions autour de l'index thematique," in *Esclavos y semilibres*, pp. 9-35.

2855. Groupe International de Recherches sur l'Esclavage Antique (GIREA). "Captifs et prisonniers de guerre dans leurs rapports avec l'esclavage" (Colloque [19ème]: 2-5 October 1991, Palma, Mallorca).

For proceedings (unpublished) see Annequin, Bazémo (2), Biezunska-Malowist, Blili, Bosch, Garrido-Hory, Giuffrè, Kolendo, Kossentini, Kuziscin, Lobo Cabrera, Lopez-Nadal, Martín-Corrales, Montaner Alonso, Nicosia, Pena, Placido, Prieto, Sanchez-León, and Taceva.

2856. Groupe International de Recherches sur l'Esclavage Antique (GIREA). "Religion et anthropologie de l'esclavage et des formes de dépendance" (Colloque, 4-6 November 1993, Besançon).

For contents see Annequin and Garrido-Hory, eds., *Religion et anthropologie de l'esclavage*.

2857. *Groupe International de Recherches sur l'Esclavage Antique (GIREA). "Femme-esclave: modèles d'interprétation anthropologique, économique et juridique" (Colloque, 1994, Naples).

2858. *Groupe International de Recherches sur l'Esclavage Antique (GIREA). "Schiavi e dipendenti nell'ambito dell' 'oikos' e della 'familia'" (Colloque, 19-20 November 1995, Siena).

For contents see Bellocci, Bertinelli, Bresson, Buti, Cataldi, Citti, Garrido-Hory, Gonzales, Hodkinson, Lombardo, Mangas, Marino, Martini, Mele, Menacacci, Paradiso, Plácido, Prieto, Ragone, Scardigli, Schiavone, and Smadja.

2859. Groupe International de Recherches sur l'Esclavage Antique (GIREA). "Dépendants et esclaves dans l'Afrique Mineure et l'Egypte de l'Antiquité" (Colloque [22ème]: 12-15 December 1996, L'Africa Romana: XII Convegno Internazionale di Studi, Olbia, Sardinia).

For proceedings (unpublished) see Alvar and Plácido, Blázquez Martinez, Carlsen, Chausa, Garrido-Hory,

Gómez Pallarés, Gonzales, Khanoussi, Lengrand, and Smadja.

2860. Guizzi, Jr., Francesco. "Schiavi e dipendenti: 'oikos' e 'familia' (summary of GIREA colloque, 19-20 November 1995, Siena)," *Labeo: rassegna di diritto romano*, 42, 1 (1996), pp. 133-37.

Primary reference: Groupe International de Recherches sur l'Esclavage Antique (GIREA). "Schiavi e dipendenti nell'ambito dell' 'oikos" e della 'familia'" (Colloque, 1995, Siena), in the bibliographical supplement for 1995.

2861. Hunt, Peter Alan. "Slaves and Soldiers in Classical Ideologies" (PhD diss., Stanford University, 1994).

2862. Kudlien, Fridolf. *Sklaven-Mentalität im Spiegel antiker Wahrsagerei*. Stuttgart: Franz Steiner Verlag, 1991. (Forschungen zur antiken Sklaverei, no. 23)

2863. Kyrtatas, Dimitris J. "Slavery as Progress: Pagan and Christian Views of Slavery as Moral Training," *International Sociology*, 10, 2 (1995), pp. 219-34.

2864. Lens, Jesús. "Sepúlveda y la historiografía clásica I: Aristóteles y Posidonio sobre el Esclavo por naturaleza en el *Democrates Alter*," in *Actas del Congreso Internacional "V Centenario del nacimiento del Dr. Juan Ginés de Sepúlveda"* (Celebrado en Pozoblanco, del 13 al 16 de febrero de 1991) (Córdoba: Excmo. Ayuntamiento de Pozoblanco; Excma. Diputación Provincial de Córdoba, 1993), pp. 71-81.

2865. Ludwig, Jörg Peter. "Historische Metamorphosen der Wertform: zur Genese der Geldform in der antiken Sklaverei," in *Historisch-archäologische Quellen und Geschichte bis zur Herausbildung des Feudalismus* (Berlin: Zentralinstitut für alte Geschichte und Archäologie der Akademie der Wissenschaften der DDR, 1983), pp. 9-11.

2866. Marinovitch, Ljudmila P. "Problèmes de l'esclavage antique dans l'historiographie soviétique," *Index: Quaderni camerti di studi romanistici*, 21 (1993), pp. 325-30.

2867. Mele, Alfonso. "Rites d'initiation des jeunes," in Annequin and Garrido-Hory, eds., *Religion et anthropologie de l'esclavage*, pp. 37-58.

2868. Metzler, D. "Die Freiheitsmütze und ihre antike Vorgeschichte," in *Geschichte und Geschichtsbewußtsein: Festschrift für K. E. Jeismann zum 65. Geburtstag* (Münster, 1990), pp. 706-25.

2869. Ota, Hidemichi. "Les différents aspects de l'esclave et de l'esclavage," in Toru Yuge, ed., *Le monde méditerranéen et l'esclavage: recherches japonaises* (Paris: Belles Lettres, 1991), pp. 97-112. (Annales littéraires de l'Université de Besançon, 426)

2870. Ota, Hidemichi. "Esclavage et société esclavagiste," in Toru Yuge, ed., *Le monde méditerranéen et l'esclavage: recherches japonaises* (Paris: Belles Lettres, 1991), pp. 79-95. (Annales littéraires de l'Université de Besançon, 426)

2871. Ota, Hidemichi. "Réexamen du concept d'esclave," in Toru Yuge, ed., *Le monde méditerranéen et l'esclavage: recherches japonaises* (Paris: Belles Lettres, 1991), pp. 55-77. (Annales littéraires de l'Université de Besançon, 426)

2872. Pereira-Menaut, Gerardo. "From Slavery-Research to Political Economy," in Marie-Madeleine Mactoux and Evelyne Geny, eds., *Mélanges Pierre Lévêque: 5, Anthropologie et société* (Paris: Belles Lettres, 1990), pp. 307-14. (Annales littéraires de l'Université de Besançon, 429; Centre de recherches d'histoire ancienne, vol. 101)

2873. Pérez, Christine. "Recherches sur l'esclavage et la dépendance: chronique 1993," *Dialogues d'histoire ancienne*, 19, 2 (1993), pp. 301-32.

2874. Prieto [Arciniega], A. "Index tematico de las formas de dependencia antiguas según las fuentes epigraficas" (Unpublished paper, Groupe International de Recherches sur l'Esclavage Antique [GIREA]. Colloque [19ème] sur "Captifs et prisonniers de guerre dans leurs rapports avec l'esclavage", 2-5 October, 1991, Palma, Mallorca).

2875. *Reduzzi Merola, F. *"Servo parere": Studi sulla condizione giuridica degli schiavi vicari e dei sottoposti a schiavi nelle esperienze greca e romana*. Naples, 1990.

2876. *Religion et anthropologie de l'esclavage et des formes de dépendance*. Groupe International de Recherches sur l'Esclavage Antique (GIREA) (Colloque, 4-6 novembre 1994, Besançon).

For contents see Annequin and Garrido-Hory, eds., *Religion et anthropologie de l'esclavage.*

2877. Rogers, Guy Maclean. "Freedom in the Making of Western Culture," *Arethusa*, 28, 1 (1995), pp. 87-97.

Forum on Patterson, *Freedom in the Making of Western Culture*; see also Lefkowitz and Millar.

2878. Rubinsohn, Wolfgang Zeev. *Die grossen Sklavenaufstande der Antike: 500 Jahre Forschung.* Darmstadt: Wissenschaftliche Buchgesellschaft, 1993.

2879. Rubinsohn, Zeev W. "Post World-War II Japanese Historiography on Slavery and Slave Revolts in Antiquity," *Scripta Classica Israelica*, 13 (1994), pp. 187-93.

2880. Scheidel, Walter. "Die Frau als Ware: Sklavinnen in der Wirtschaft der griechisch-römischen Welt," in Edith Specht, ed., *Frauenreichtum: Die Frau als Wirtschaftsfaktor im Altertum* (Vienna: Wiener Frauenverlag, 1994), pp. 143-80.

2881. Scheidel, Walter. "Sexualität, Ehe und Sklaverei: zu einem zentralen Aspekt persönlicher Unfreiheit" (Tagung der Arbeitsgruppe "Antike Sklaverei", Mainz, Germany, 9 October 1996).

2882. Scheidel, Walter. "Slavery and the Shackled Mind: On Fortune-telling and Slave Mentality in the Graeco-Roman World (review essay: Kudlien, *Sklaven-Mentalität*)," *Ancient History Bulletin*, 7, 3 (1993), pp. 107-14.

2883. "Schiavi e dipendenti nell'ambito dell' 'oikos' e della 'familia'" (*Groupe International de Recherches sur l'Esclavage Antique [GIREA], Colloque, 1995, Siena).

For contents see *Groupe International de Recherches sur l'Esclavage Antique (GIREA), "Schiavi e dipendenti nell'ambito dell' 'oikos' e della 'familia'".

2884. *Schiavone, A. "La schiavitú-merce fra paradigma naturalistico e convenzione sociale: da Aristotele alla giurisprudenza romana" (Unpublished paper, Colloque International de Recherches sur l'Esclavage Antique [GIREA], "Schiavi e dipendenti nell'ambito dell' 'oikos' e della 'familia'", 19-21 November 1995, Siena).

2885. Schulz-Falkenthal, Heinz. "Die antike Sklaverei als Gegenstand der Forschung vom Ausgang des 15. Jahrhunderts bis zur Mitte des 19. Jahrhunderts: historiographische Bemerkungen und sachliche Erläuterungen zu einer Spezialbibliographie," *Wissenschaftliche Zeitschrift der Martin-Luther-Universität Halle-Wittenberg*, 35, 4 (1986), pp. 64-77.

2886. Thompson, Hugh. "Iron Age and Roman Slave-Shackles," *Archaeological Journal*, 150 (1993), pp. 57-168.

2887. Wiedemann, Thomas E. J. *Slavery*. Oxford and New York: Oxford University Press, for the Classical Association, 1992. (1987 original, with addenda)

2888. Yuge, Toru, ed. *Le monde méditerranéen et l'esclavage: recherches japonaises*. Paris: Belles Lettres, 1991. (Annales littéraires de l'Université de Besançon 426). (Centre de Recherches d'Histoire Ancienne, vol. 99)

2. Ancient Near East[11]

2889. Brown, Truesdell S. "A Miniscule History of the Slaves of Tyre: Justin 18.3.6-19," Ancient History Bulletin, 5, 3 (1991), pp. 59-65.

2890. Chirichigno, Gregory. *Debt Slavery in Israel and the Ancient Near East*. Sheffield: Sheffield Academic Press, 1993.

2891. Cobin, David M. "A Brief Look at the Jewish Law of Manumission," *Chicago-Kent Law Review*, 70, 3 (1995), pp. 1339-48. (Symposium on the Law of Freedom, Part 2)

2892. Dandamaev, Muhammad A., and Vladimir G. Lukonin. *The Culture and Social Institutions of Ancient Iran*. Trans. Philip L. Johl, with the assistance of D. J. Dadson. Cambridge: Cambridge University Press, 1989.

2893. Farber, W. "Hanum kauft Gadagada: eine altassyrische selbstverkaufts-Urkunde," *Aula orientalis: revista de estudios del Próximo Oriente antiguo*, 8, 2 (1990), pp. 197-205.

---

[11] See VIII.3 (Greece and Dependencies) for works on this area from Hellenistic perspectives and VIII.4 (Rome and Provinces) for works in terms of Roman and Christian (New Testament) law, philosophy, and theology.

2894. Grosz, Katarzyna. "On Some Aspects of the Adoption of Women at Nuzi," in D. I. Owen and M. A. Morrison, eds., *Studies on the Civilization and Culture of Nuzi and the Hurrians* (Winona Lake IN: Eisenbrauns, 1987), pp. 131-52.

2895. Hallo, William W. "Slave Release in the Biblical World in Light of a New Text," in Ziony Zevit, Seymour Gitin, and Michael Sokoloff, eds., *Solving Riddles and Untying Knots: Biblical, Epigraphic, and Semitic Studies in Honor of Jonas C. Greenfield* (Winona Lake IN: Eisenbrauns, 1995), pp. 79-93.

2896. Hurowitz, V. A. "Joseph's Enslavement of the Egyptians (Genesis 47.13-26) in Light of Famine Texts from Mesopotamia," *Revue biblique*, 101, 3 (1994), pp. 355-62.

2897. *Jursa, M. "Zu Edubba 1, 10," *Nouvelles assyriologiques brèves et utilitaires*, (1994-95), pp. (??).

2898. Kippenberg, H. G. "Die Entlassung aus Schuldknechtschaft im antiken Judäa: eine Legitimitätsvorstellung von Verwandtschaftsgruppen," in Gunter Kehrer, ed., *"Vor Gott sind alle gleich": Soziale Gleichheit, soziale Ungleichheit und die Religionen* (Düsseldorf: Patmos, 1983), pp. 74-104.

2899. Levi, Mario Attilio. "Templi e schiavi sacri in Asia Minore," in Marta Sordi, ed., *Santuarie politica nel mondo antico* (Milan: Università Cattolica Milano, 1983), pp. 51-56. (Contributi dell'Istituto di Storia Antica dell'Università del Sacro Cuore, 9)

2900. Lindenberger, James M. "How Much for a Hebrew Slave? The Meaning of Misneh in Deut 15:18," *SBL: Journal of Biblical Literature*, 110, 3 (1993), pp. 479-82.

2901. MacGinnis, John. "The Manumission of a Royal Slave," *Acta Sumerologica* (Hiroshima, Japan), 15 (1993), pp. 99-106.

2902. Maidman, M. P. "JEN VII 812: an Unusual Personnel Text from Nuzi," in D. I. Owen and M. A. Morrison, eds., *Studies on the Civilization and Culture of Nuzi and the Hurrians* (Winona Lake IN: Eisenbrauns, 1987), pp. 157-66.

2903. Marello, P. "Esclaves et reines," in Dominique Charpin and Jean-Marie Durand, eds., *Florilegium marianum II: Recueil d'études à la mémoire de Maurice Birot* (Paris, 1994), pp. 115-29. (Mémoires de NABU, 3)

2904. Matthews, Victor H. "The Anthropology of Slavery in the Covenant Code," in Bernard M. Levinson, ed., *Theory and Method in Biblical and Cuneiform Law: Revision, Interpolation and Development* (Sheffield, Eng.: Sheffield Academic Press, 1994), pp. 119-35. (Journal for the Study of the Old Testament, Supplement series, 181)

2905. Oelsner, J. "Recht im hellenistischen Babylonien: Tempel - Sklaven - Schuldrecht - allgemeine Charakterisierung," in Markham J. Geller and Herwig Maehler, eds., *Legal Documents of the Hellenistic World* (London: The Warburg Institute, 1995), pp. 106-48.

2906. Osiek, Carolyn. "Slavery in the Second Temple World," *Biblical Theology Bulletin*, 22, 4 (1992), pp. 174-79.

2907. Roth, Martha T. "The Material Composition of the Neo-Babylonian Dowry," *Archiv für Orientforschung*, 36-37 (1989-90), pp. 1-55.

2908. Schneider, Thomas. "Die semitischen und ägyptischen Namen der syrischen Sklaven des Papyrus Brooklyn 35.1446 verso," in Kurt Bergerhof, Manfried Dietrich, and Oswald Loretz, eds., *Ugarit-Forschungen* (Internationales Jahrbuch für die Altertumskunde Syrien-Palästinas) (Neukirchen-Vluyn: Verlag Butzon & Bercker Kevelaer, 1989), vol. 19, pp. 255-82.

2909. Shapira, Hayim Tsevi. *Sefer Maarkhot Hayim: al Masekhet Gitin: al perek rishon, sheni u-revii; Uve-sofo Kuntres Be-inyene avadim*. Bene-Berak: H. Ts. Shapira, 1994.

2910. Swartley, Willard M. "Slavery, Sabbath, War and Women: Case Issues in Biblical Interpretation" (Scottdale PA and Kitchener, Ont.: Herald Press, 1983). (Conrad Grebel Lectures, 1982)

2911. Tsevat, Matitiahu. "The Hebrew Slave According to Deuteronomy 15:12-18: His Lot and the Value of His Work, with Special Attention to the Meaning of *Misneh*," *SBL: Journal of Biblical Literature*, 113, 4 (1994), pp. 587-95.

2912. Tumbarello, Giacomo. "La schiavitù nella Bibbia," *Bibbia e Oriente*, 35, 2 (1993), pp. 65-74.

2913. Vajman, A. A. "Die Bezeichnung von Sklaven und Sklavinnen in der protosumerischen Schrift," *Baghdader Mitteilungen*, 20 (1989), pp. 121-33.

2914. Vajman, A. A. "Die Deutung einiger Zeichen in proto-sumerischen Sklaven und Sklavinnen," *Baghdader Mitteilungen*, 21 (1990), pp. 116-23.

2915. Westbrook, Raymond. "Slave and Master in Ancient Near Eastern Law," *Chicago-Kent Law Review*, 70, 4 (1995), pp. 1631-76. (Symposium on Ancient Law, Economics and Society, part 1)

2916. Westbrook, Raymond. "Slavery in Early Law" (Unpublished paper, Société Internationale "Fernand de Visscher" pour l'Histoire des Droits de l'Antiquité, New Orleans/Baton Rouge, 18-21 September 1995).

2917. Ziegler, N. "Deux esclaves en fuite à Mari," in Dominique Charpin and Jean-Marie Durand, eds., *Florilegium marianum II: Recueil d'études à la mémoire de Maurice Birot* (Paris, 1994), pp. 11-21. (Mémoires de NABU, 3)

3. Greece and Dependencies[12]

2918. Ambler, Wayne. "Aristotle on Nature and Politics: The Case of Slavery," Political Theory, 15, 3 (1987), pp. 390-410.

2919. Barja de Quiroga, Pedro López. "El beneficium manumissionis, la obligación de manumitir y la virtud estoica," *Dialogues d'histoire ancienne*, 19, 2 (1993), pp. 47-64.

2920. Beringer, Walter. "Freedom, Family and Citizenship in Early Greece," in John W. Eadie and Josiah Ober, eds., *The Craft of the Ancient Historian: Essays in Honor of Chester G. Starr* (Lanham, New York, London: University Press of America, 1985), pp. 41-56.

2921. Beyer, Jeorjios Martin. "Aesop: eine Sklavenbiographie," *Antike Welt*, 25, 2 (1994), pp. 290-91.

[12] With the exception of Hellenistic Egypt (see Section VIII.5) and Hellenistic aspects of Christian theology of slavery (see Rome and Provinces, Section VIII.4).

2922. *Bresson, A. "Noms d'esclaves dans le monde rhodien" (Unpublished paper, Colloque International de Recherches sur l'Esclavage Antique [GIREA], "Schiavi e dipendenti nell'ambito dell' 'oikos' e della 'familia'", 19-21 November 1995, Siena).

2923. Bruneau, Philippe. "L'esclavage à Délos," in Marie-Madeleine Mactoux and Evelyne Geny, eds., *Mélanges Pierre Lévêque: 3, Anthropologie et société* (Paris: Belles Lettres, 1990), pp. 41-52. (Annales littéraires de l'Université de Besançon, 404; Centre de recherches d'histoire ancienne, vol. 99)

2924. Brunt, Peter A. "Aristotle and Slavery," in idem, *Studies in Greek History and Thought* (Oxford: Clarendon Press, 1993), pp. 343-88.

2925. Cartledge, Paul. "Like a Worm i' the Bud? A Heterology of Classical Greek Slavery," *Greece & Rome*, 40, 2 (1993), pp. 163-80.

2926. Cartledge, Paul. "Richard Talbert's Revision of the Spartan-Helot Struggle: A Reply," *Historia: Zeitschrift für Altegeschichte*, 40, 3 (1991), pp. 379-81.

2927. *Cataldi, S. "I '*PLOUSIOI DOULOI*' nella '*ATHENAION POLITEIA*' dello Pseudo-Senofonte" (Unpublished paper, Colloque International de Recherches sur l'Esclavage Antique [GIREA], "Schiavi e dipendenti nell'ambito dell' 'oikos' e della 'familia'", 19-21 November 1995, Siena).

2928. Citti, V. "Esclavage et sacré dans le langage tragique," in Annequin and Garrido-Hory, eds., *Religion et anthropologie de l'esclavage*, pp. 91-99.

2929. *Citti, V. "'*PORNE KAI DOULE*': una coppia nominale in Lisia" (Unpublished paper, Colloque International de Recherches sur l'Esclavage Antique [GIREA], "Schiavi e dipendenti nell'ambito dell' 'oikos' e della 'familia'", 19-21 November 1995, Siena).

2930. Cohen, Edward E. "Banking as a 'Family Business': Legal Adaptations Affecting Wives and Slaves," in *Symposion 1990: Vorträge zur griechischen und hellenistischen Rechtsgeschichte* (Pacific Grove, California, 24 - 26 September 1990) (Weimar/Vienna: Böhlau, 1991), pp. 239-63.

With response by Josiah Ober, pp. 265-71.

2931. Crowther, N. B. "Slaves and Greek Athletes," *Quaderni Urbinati di Cultura Classica*, n.s. 40 (1992), pp. 35-42.

2932. Debord, P. "Religion et mentalité des esclaves," in Annequin and Garrido-Hory, eds., *Religion et anthropologie de l'esclavage*, pp. 147-59.

2933. Ducat, J. "Les conduites et les idéologies intégratrices concernant les esclaves de type hilotique," in Annequin and Garrido-Hory, eds., *Religion et anthropologie de l'esclavage*, pp. 17-28.

2934. Ducat, J. *Les hilotes*. Paris: de Boccard, 1990. (Also *Bulletin de correspondance hellénique*, supp. 212)

2935. Ducat, Jean. *Les Pénestes de Thessalie*. Paris: Belles Lettres, 1994.

2936. Fisher, Nick. "Hybris, Status and Slavery," in Anton Powell, ed., *The Greek World* (London and New York: Routledge, 1995), pp. 44-84.

2937. Fisher, N. R. E. (Nicolas Ralph Edmund) *Slavery in Classical Greece*. Bristol: Bristol Classical Press, 1993.

Reprint, with corrections: London: Bristol Classical Press, 1995.

2938. Gagarin, Michael. "The Torture of Slaves in Athenian Law," *Classical Philology*, 91, 1 (1996), pp. 1-18.

2939. Garlan, Yvon. "À propos des esclaves dans l'*Économique* de Xénophon," in Marie-Madeleine Mactoux and Evelyne Geny, eds., *Mélanges Pierre Lévêque: 2, Anthropologie et société* (Paris: Belles Lettres, 1989), pp. 237-43. (Annales littéraires de l'Université de Besançon, 377; Centre de recherches d'histoire ancienne, vol. 82)

2940. Garlan, Yvon. "L'anti-esclavagisme a-t-il existé en Grèce antique?" (Presentation at Colloquium on "Les dépendances serviles", Paris 1996).

2941. Garlan, Yvon. *Les esclaves en Grèce ancienne*.

Translated (by. S. Demichele) as *Gli schiavi nella Grecia antica dal mondo miceneo all'ellenismo* (Milan: Mondadori, 1984).

2942. Gschnitzer, Fritz. "Sklaverei im Recht von Gortyn" (Tagung der Arbeitsgruppe "Antike Sklaverei", Mainz, Germany, 9 October 1996).

2943. Hanson, Victor Davis. "Thucydides and the Desertion of Attic Slaves during the Decelean War," *Classical Antiquity*, 11, 2 (1992), pp. 210-28.

2944. *Hodkinson, S. "Servile and Free Dependents in the Classical Spartan 'oikos'" (Unpublished paper, Colloque International de Recherches sur l'Esclavage Antique [GIREA], "Schiavi e dipendenti nell'ambito dell' 'oikos' e della 'familia'", 19-21 November 1995, Siena).

2945. Iordanov, Stéphan. "*DOULOPOLIS*: sur l'origine d'une image mythologique," *Diologues d'histoire ancienne*, 19, 1 (1993), pp. 173-90.

2946. Johne, Renate. "Griechische und barbarische Frauengestalten bei Heliodor," *Das Altertum*, 38, 3 (1993), pp. 177-85.

2947. Jourdain-Annequin, C. "Servitude et liberté d'un héros," in Annequin and Garrido-Hory, eds., *Religion et anthropologie de l'esclavage*, pp. 61-90.

2948. Klees, Hans. "Zur Beurteilung der Helotie im historischen und politischen Denken der Griechen im 5. und 4. Jh. v. Chr.," *Laverna*, 2 (1991), pp. 27-52.

2949. Klees, Hans. "Zur Beurteilung der Helotie im historischen und politischen Denken der Griechen im 5. und 4. Jh. v. Chr., II," *Laverna*, 3 (1992), pp. 1-31.

2950. Kotula, Tadeusz. "Les grands domaines et l'esclavage face à la 'crise du IIIe siècle," *Eos*, 79 (1991), pp. 71-83.

2951. Kyrtatas, Dimitris [J]. "The Athenian Democracy and Its Slaves," *History Today*, 44, 2 (1994), pp. 43-48.

2952. Lévy, Edmond. "Le théorie aristotélicienne de l'esclavage et ses contradictions," in Marie-Madeleine Mactoux and Evelyne Geny, eds., *Mélanges Pierre Lévêque: 3, Anthropologie et société* (Paris: Belles Lettres, 1990), pp. 197-213. (Annales littéraires de l'Université de Besançon, 404; Centre de recherches d'histoire ancienne, vol. 99)

2953. *Lombardo, M. "Schiavitú e 'oikos' nelle società magno-greche" (Unpublished paper, Colloque International de Recherches sur l'Esclavage Antique

[GIREA], "Schiavi e dipendenti nell'ambito dell' 'oikos' e della 'familia'", 19-21 November 1995, Siena).

2954. Mactoux, Marie-Madeleine. "Esclaves et rites de passage," in *Mélanges de l'École française de Rome: Antiquité*, 102, 1 (1990), pp. 53-81.

2955. Mactoux, Marie-Madeleine. "Logique rituelle et *polis* esclavagiste," in Annequin and Garrido-Hory, eds., *Religion et anthropologie de l'esclavage*, pp. 101-25.

2956. Martin-Beyer, Jeorjios. "Aesop - eine Sklavenbiographie," *Antike Welt*, 25, 3 (1994), pp. 290-91.

2957. *Martini, R. "Osservazioni sugli '*APELEUTHEROI*' nella Grecia classica" (Unpublished paper, Colloque International de Recherches sur l'Esclavage Antique [GIREA], "Schiavi e dipendenti nell'ambito dell' 'oikos' e della 'familia'", 19-21 November 1995, Siena).

2958. McKeown, Niall. "The Slave Mode of Production in Classical Athens: A Very Peculiar Institution" (PhD diss., Cambridge University, 1991).

2959. *Mele, Alfonso. "La lana e la lavorazione domestica della lana a Taranto" (Unpublished paper, Colloque International de Recherches sur l'Esclavage Antique [GIREA], "Schiavi e dipendenti nell'ambito dell' 'oikos' e della 'familia'", 19-21 November 1995, Siena).

2960. Mossé, Claude. "Les esclaves banquiers à Athènes au IVe siècle a.c.: une forme originale d'ascension sociale" (Presentation at Colloquium on "Les dépendances serviles", Paris 1996).

2961. Mossé, Claude. "Peut-on parler de patronage dans l'Athènes archaique et classique?" in Annequin and Garrido-Hory, eds., *Religion et anthropologie de l'esclavage*, pp. 29-36.

2962. Mulliez, Dominique. "Les actes d'affranchissement delphiques," *Cahiers du Centre G. Glotz*, 3 (1992), pp. 31-44.

2963. Oelsner, J. "Recht im hellenistischen Babylonien: Tempel - Sklaven - Schuldrecht - allgemeine Charakterisierung," in Markham J. Geller and Herwig Maehler (in collaboration with A. D. E. Lewis), eds., *Legal Documents of the Hellenistic World* (London: The Warburg Institute, 1995), pp. 106-48. (Papers from a seminar arranged by the Institute of Classical Studies, Institute of Jewish Studies, and the Warburg Institute, University of London, February - May 1986)

2964. Osborne, Robin. "The Economics and Politics of Slavery at Athens," in Anton Powell, ed., *The Greek World* (London and New York: Routledge, 1995), pp. 27-43.

2965. Papazoglou, Fanoula. "La *patrios politeia* et l'abolition de l'hilotie," *Ancient Society*, 24 (1993), pp. 5-25.

2966. Papazoglou, Fanoula. "Sur la condition des hilotes affranchis," *Historia: Zeitschrift für Altegeschichte*, 44, 3 (1995), pp. 370-75.

2967. Paradiso, Annalisa. *Forme di dipendenza nel mondo greco: ricerche sul VI libro di Ateneo*. Bari: Edipuglia, 1991. (Dipartimento di scienze dell'antichità dell'Università di Bari, Sezione storica: Documenti e studi, 10).

2968. *Paradiso, A[nnalisa]. "Gli iloti e l''okos'" (Unpublished paper, Colloque International de Recherches sur l'Esclavage Antique [GIREA], "Schiavi e dipendenti nell'ambito dell' 'oikos' e della 'familia'", 19-21 November 1995, Siena).

2969. Paradiso, Annalisa. "Schiavi e miniere: le condizioni di lavoro degli schiavi minatori e la valutazione dell'estrazione mineraria presso gli Stoici," *Atti della Accademia delle Scienze di Torino: Classe di Scienze morali, storiche e filologiche*, 124 (1990), pp. 23-40.

2970. Paradiso, Annalisa. "Schiavi e miniere: le condizioni di lavoro degli schiavi minatori e la valutazione dell'estrazione mineraria presso gli Stoici," *Atti della Accademia delle Scienze di Torino: Classe di Scienze morali, storiche e filologiche*, 124 (1990), pp. 23-40.

2971. Plácido, Domingo. "La esclavización de griegos cautivos durante el periodo de la crisis de la ciudad-estado" (Unpublished paper, Groupe International de Recherches sur l'Esclavage Antique [GIREA]. Colloque [19ème] sur "Captifs et prisonniers de guerre dans leurs rapports avec l'esclavage", 2-5 October, 1991, Palma, Mallorca).

2972. Plácido, Domingo. "Los lugares sagrados de los hilotas," in Annequin and Garrido-Hory, eds., *Religion et anthropologie de l'esclavage*, pp. 127-35.

2973. Plácido, Domingo. "'Nombres de libres que son esclavos ...' (Pólux, III, 82)," in *Esclavos y semilibres*, pp. 55-79.

2974. *Plácido, Domingo. "Los '*OIKÉTAI*' entre la dependencia personal y la produción para el mercado" (Unpublished paper, Colloque International de Recherches sur l'Esclavage Antique [GIREA], "Schiavi e dipendenti nell'ambito dell' 'oikos' e della 'familia'", 19-21 November 1995, Siena).

2975. Plácido, Domingo. *Tucidides: index thématique des références à l'esclavage et à la dépendance.* Paris: Belles Lettres, 1992. (Annales littéraires de l'Université de Besançon, Centre de Recherches d'histoire ancienne, vol. 452)

2976. Pomeroy, Sarah B. "Slavery in the Greek Domestic Economy in the Light of Xenophon's 'OEconomicus'," *Index: Quaderni camerti di studi romanistici*, 17 (1989), pp. 11-18.

2977. *Preito, A. "El 'oikos' en el cine: la 'Odisea'" (Unpublished paper, Colloque International de Recherches sur l'Esclavage Antique [GIREA], "Schiavi e dipendenti nell'ambito dell' 'oikos' e della 'familia'", 19-21 November 1995, Siena).

2978. *Ragone, G. "La schiavitú di Esopo: storie e romanzo" (Unpublished paper, Colloque International de Recherches sur l'Esclavage Antique [GIREA], "Schiavi e dipendenti nell'ambito dell' 'oikos' e della 'familia'", 19-21 November 1995, Siena).

2979. Rihll, T[racey] E. "EKTHMOPOI: Partners in Crime?" *Journal of Hellenic Studies*, 111 (1991), pp. 101-27.

2980. Rihll, Tracey. "The Origin and Establishment of Ancient Greek Slavery," in Bush, ed., *Serfdom and Slavery*, pp. 89-111.

2981. Rihll, Tracey [E.]. "War, Slavery, and Settlement in Early Greece," in John Rich and Graham Shipley, eds., *War and Society in the Greek World* (London and New York: Routledge, 1993), pp. 77-107.

2982. Rosivach, Vincent J. "Agricultural Slavery in the Northern Colonies and in Classical Athens: Some Comparisons," *Comparative Studies in Society and History*, 35, 3 (1993), pp. 551-67.

2983. Sanchez-León, M.-L. "'*APOROI*' y '*DOULOI*' en Pergamo" (Unpublished paper, Groupe International de Recherches sur l'Esclavage Antique [GIREA]. Colloque [19ème] sur "Captifs et prisonniers de guerre dans leurs rapports avec l'esclavage", 2-5 October, 1991, Palma, Mallorca).

2984. Schofield, M. "Ideology and Philosophy in Aristotle's Theory of Slavery," in G. Patzig, ed., *Aristoteles' "Politik": Akten des XI. Symposium Aristotelicum* (Friedrichshafen am Bodensee, 25 Aug. - 3 Sept. 1987) (Göttingen: Vandenhoeck & Ruprecht, 1990), pp. 1-27.

With comments by Charles H. Kahn, pp. 28-31.

2985. Schoufour, Christiaan Jacobus Wilhelm. "A Slave by Nature: Aristotle's Apologia in the 'Politics'" (MA thesis, Dalhousie University [Canada], 1994).

2986. Smith, N. D. "Aristotle's Theory of Natural Slavery," in D. Keyt and F. D. Miller, eds., *A Companion to Aristotle's Politics* (Oxford: Oxford University Press, 1991), pp. 145-55.

2987. Taceva, M. "Entre la liberté et l'esclavage en Thrace ancienne" (Unpublished paper, Groupe International de Recherches sur l'Esclavage Antique [GIREA]. Colloque [19ème] sur "Captifs et prisonniers de guerre dans leurs rapports avec l'esclavage", 2-5 October, 1991, Palma, Mallorca).

2988. Tsets'hladze, Revazovic Goca. "On Colchian Slaves in the Ancient World," *Acta antiqua Academiae Scientiarum Hungaricae*, 33 (1990-92), pp. 255-60.

2989. Velkov, Velizar. "Zur Frage der Sklaverei in den westpontischen griechischen Kolonien (4.-3. Jahrhundert)," *Acta Antiqua Academiae Scientiarum Hungaricae*, 32 (1989), pp. 51-53.

2990. Yamakawa, Hiroshi. "'Slaves of the Deity' in the Linear B Land Tenure Tablets," *Kodai*, 5 (1994), pp. 1-15.

4. Rome and Provinces[13]

2991. Abramenko, Andrik. "Liberti als Dekurionen: einige Überlegungen zur lex Malacitana," Laverna, 3 (1992), pp. 94-103.

2992. Albasi, Tiziana, and Claudia Marchioni. "Schiavi, liberti e donne in Orazio," in Tiziana Albasi, Elda Biggi, Giuseppe Consiglio, Nicola Criniti, Laura Magnani, Claudia Marchioni, and Laura Montanini, *Gli affanni del vivere e del morire: schiavi, soldati, donne, bambini nelle Roma imperiale* (Rome: Grafo, 1991), pp. 17-71.

2993. *Alvar, Jaime, and Domingo Plácido. "Transformaciones desde la explotación colonial a la esclavista" (Unpublished paper, Colloque International de Recherches sur l'Esclavage Antique [GIREA]. Colloque [22ème] sur "Dépendants et esclaves dans l'Afrique Mineure et l'Egypte de l'Antiquité", 12-15 December 1996, L'Africa Romana: XII Convegno Internazionale di Studi, Olbia [Sardinia]).

2994. Alvar Ezquerra, J. "Integración social de esclavos y dependientes en la Península Ibérica a través de los cultos mistéricos," in Annequin and Garrido-Hory, eds., *Religion et anthropologie de l'esclavage*, pp. 275-93.

2995. *Amaya Calero, Manuel. "La responsibilidad en la compraventa de esclavos y animales" (Unpublished paper at conference of the Société Internationale Fernand de Visscher pour l'Histoire des Droits de l'Antiquité, Miskok, 16-20 Sept. 1991).

2996. Andreau, Jean. "The Freedman," in Andrea Giardina, ed., *The Romans* (translated by Lydia G. Cochrane) (Chicago and London: University of Chicago Press, 1993), pp. 175-98.

2997. Annequin, Jacques. "L'esclavage et la crise des institutions à Rome: La *Conjuration de Catilina* de Mérimée," *Dialogues d'histoire ancienne*, 18, 1 (1992), pp. 37-58.

2998. Annequin, Jacques. "Les esclaves rêvent aussi ... remarques sur 'La clé des songes' d'Artemidore," *Dialogues d'histoire ancienne*, 13, (1987), pp. 71-113. (Annales littéraires de l'Université de Besançon, 366; Centre de recherches d'histoire ancienne, vol. 78)

2999. Annequin, Jacques. "Fugitiva (?), fugitivi, litterati: quelques réflexions sur trois passages des 'Métamorphoses' d'Apulée: VI, I sq.; VII, XV sq.; IX, XI, sq.," in *Esclavos y semilibres*, pp. 91-115.

3000. Baba, Noriaki. "Slave-owning Slaves and the Structure of Slavery in the Early Roman Empire," *Kodai*, 1 (1990), pp. 24-35.

3001. *Bellocci, N. "Il tentato suicidio del servo: aspetti socio-familiari nei giuristi dell'ultima epoca dei Severi" (Unpublished paper, Colloque International de Recherches sur l'Esclavage Antique [GIREA], "Schiavi e dipendenti nell'ambito dell' 'oikos' e della 'familia'", 19-21 November 1995, Siena).

3002. *Bergada, M. M. "La condamnation de l'esclavage dans l'Homélie IV," in S. G. Hall, ed., *Gregory of Nyssa, Homilies on Ecclesiastes: An English Version with Supporting Studies* (Proceedings of the Seventh International Colloquium on Gregory of Nyssa, St. Andrews, 5-10 September 1990) (Berlin and New York: de Gruyter, 1993), pp. [??].

3003. *Bertinelli, M. G. Angeli. "Lo schiavo nelle relazioni familiari (a margine delle epigrafi lunensi)" (Unpublished paper, Colloque International de Recherches sur l'Esclavage Antique [GIREA], "Schiavi e dipendenti nell'ambito dell' 'oikos' e della 'familia'", 19-21 November 1995, Siena).

3004. Betzig, Laura. "Roman Polygyny," *Ethology and Sociobiology*, 13 (1992), pp. 309-49.

3005. Blänsdorf, Jürgen. "Sklaverei in Ciceros Briefen" (Tagung der Arbeitsgruppe "Antike Sklaverei", Mainz, Germany, 9 October 1996).

3006. *Blázquez Martinez, José Maria. "Representaciones de esclavos en los mosaicos africanos" (Unpublished paper, Colloque International de Recherches sur l'Esclavage Antique [GIREA]. Colloque [22ème] sur "Dépendants et esclaves dans l'Afrique Mineure et l'Egypte de l'Antiquité", 12-15 December 1996, L'Africa Romana: XII Convegno Internazionale di Studi, Olbia [Sardinia]).

---

[13] Includes literature on Christianity and slavery (including Hellenistic regions), in addition to issues arising from Roman law; excludes Roman Egypt (see Section VIII.5) and Byzantium (Section IX.2).

3007. Bodel, John Putnam. "Freedmen in the Satyricon of Petronius" (PhD diss., University of Michigan, 1984).

3008. Bonelli, Guido. "Plinio il Giovane e la schiavitù: considerazioni e precisazioni," *Quaderni Urbinati di Cultura Classica*, 77 (1994), pp. 141-48.

3009. Bonfils, Giovanni de. "L'obbligo di vendere lo schiavo cristiano alla chiesa e la clausola del *competens pretium*," *Atti dell'Accademia Romanistica Costantiniana* (X Congresso Internazionale, 1991), 10 (1995), pp. 503-28.

3010. Bonfils, Giovanni de. *Gli schiavi degli Ebrei nella legislazione del IV secolo: storia di un divieto.* Bari: Cacucci, 1993.

3011. Boston, Linda. "A Womanist Reflection on I Corinthians 7:21-24 and I Corinthians 14:33-35," *Journal of Women and Religion*, 9-10 (1990-92), pp. 81-89.

3012. Bradley, Keith R. *Slavery and Society at Rome.* New York: Cambridge University Press, 1994.

3013. Bradley, Keith R. "The *vicesima libertatis*: Its History and Significance," *Klio*, 66, 1 (1984), pp. 175-82.

3014. Brown, Truesdell S. "A Miniscule History of the Slaves of Tyre: Justin 18.3.6-19," *Ancient History Bulletin*, 5, 3 (1991), pp. 59-65.

3015. Brunt, P. A. "Evidence Given under Torture in the Principate," *Zeitschrift der Savigny-Stiftung für Rechtsgeschichte (Romanistische Abteilung)*, 97 (1980), pp. 256-65.

3016. Buckland, W. W. *The Roman Law of Slavery: The Condition of the Slave in Private Law from Augustus to Justinian.*

Reprinted: Homes Beach FL: William W. Gaunt & Sons, 1994.

3017. Bürge, Alfons. "Cum in familia nubas: Zur wirtschaftlichen und sozialen Bedeutung der familia libertorum," *Zeitschrift der Savigny-Stiftung für Rechtsgeschichte (Romanistische Abteilung)*, 105 (1988), pp. 312-33.

3018. Bürge, Alfons. "Der mercennarius und die Lohnarbeit," *Zeitschrift der Savigny-Stiftung für Rechtsgeschichte (Romanistische Abteilung)*, 107 (1990), pp. 80-136.

3019. *Buti, I. "Si serva servo quasi dotem dederit" (Unpublished paper, Colloque International de Recherches sur l'Esclavage Antique [GIREA], "Schiavi e dipendenti nell'ambito dell' 'oikos' e della 'familia'", 19-21 November 1995, Siena).

3020. Callahan, Allen Dwight. "Paul's Epistle to Philemon: Toward an Alternative *Argumentum*," *Harvard Theological Review*, 86, 4 (1993), pp. 357-76.

3021. Capogrossi Colognesi, Luigi. "La '*summa divisio de iure personarum*': quelques considérations à propos des formes de dépendance dans la réalité romaine," in Annequin and Garrido-Hory, eds., *Religion et anthropologie de l'esclavage*, pp. 163-77.

3022. Carcaterra, Antonio. "La schiavitù nel secolo IV: 'spinte' e 'stimoli' cristiani nelle leggi a favore degli schiavi," *Atti dell'Accademia romanistica costantiniana: VIII Convegno internazionale* (Napoli: Edizioni Scientifiche Italiane, 1990), pp. 147-79. (Università degli Studi di Perugia, Facoltà di Giurisprudenza)

3023. *Carlsen, Jesper. "Considerazioni su schiavi privati e schiavi imperiali nelle province del Nord Africa" (Unpublished paper, Colloque International de Recherches sur l'Esclavage Antique [GIREA]. Colloque [22ème] sur "Dépendants et esclaves dans l'Afrique Mineure et l'Egypte de l'Antiquité", 12-15 December 1996, L'Africa Romana: XII Convegno Internazionale di Studi, Olbia [Sardinia]).

3024. Carlsen, Jesper. "Dispensatores in Roman North Africa," in Attilio Mastino, ed., *L'Africa romana: Atti del IX convegno di studio, Nuoro, 13-15 dicembre 1991* (Sassari: Edizioni Gallizzi, 1992), pp. 97-104.

3025. Carlsen, Jesper. "The *f* and Roman Estate Management," in Heleen Sancisi-Weerdenburg *et al.*, eds., *De Agricultura: In memoriam Pieter Willem de Neeve (1945-1990)* (Amsterdam: J. C. Gieben, 1993), pp. 197-205.

3026. Carlsen, Jesper. "*Magister pecoris*: The Nomenclature and Qualifications of the Chief Herdsman in Roman Pasturage," *Analecta romana Instituti Danici*, 20 (1991), pp. 59-65.

3027. Carlsen, Jesper. *Vilici and Roman Estate Managers until AD 284*. Rome: "L'Erma" di Bretschneider, 1995. (Analecta Romana Instituti Danici, Supplementum 24)

3028. Cavallini, Eleonora. "Legge di natura e condizione dello schiavo," *Labeo: rassegna di diritto romano*, 40, 1 (1994), pp. 72-86.

3029. Cels-Saint Hilaire, J. "*Histoire d'un 'Saturnalicius princeps'*: dieux et dépendants dans l'*Apocolyncotose* du divin Claude," in Annequin and Garrido-Hory, eds., *Religion et anthropologie de l'esclavage*, pp. 179-208.

3030. Ceska, Josef. "Die Politik der Söhne Konstantins d. Gr. mit Rücksicht auf den Übergang der Sklavenhalterordnung zum Feudalismus," *Sborník prací Brno*, 10 (1963), pp. 17-24.

3031. *Chausa, Antonio. "Esclavos y libertos de veteranos en el Africa romana" (Unpublished paper, Colloque International de Recherches sur l'Esclavage Antique [GIREA]. Colloque [22ème] sur "Dépendants et esclaves dans l'Afrique Mineure et l'Egypte de l'Antiquité", 12-15 December 1996, L'Africa Romana: XII Convegno Internazionale di Studi, Olbia [Sardinia]).

3032. Christol, Michel. "Les ambitions d'un affranchi à Nimes sous le Haut-Empire: l'argent et la famille," *Cahiers du Centre G. Glotz*, 3 (1992), pp. 241-58.

3033. Coarelli, Filippo. "Magistri Capitolini e mercanti di schiavi nella Roma repubblicana," *Index: Quaderni camerti di studi romanistici*, 15 (1987), pp. 175-90.

3034. Collins, Matthew Scott. "Rhetoric, Household and Cosmos: A Rhetorical and Sociological Analysis of the Letter to the Colossians with Particular Focus on Colossians 3:18-4:1" (PhD diss., Vanderbilt University, 1995).

3035. *Combes, I. "Doulos Theou: The Metaphor of Slavery in the Writings of the Early Church, from the New Testament to the Beginning of the Fifth Century" (PhD diss., Cambridge University, 1991).

3036. Corcoran, Gervase. *Saint Augustine on Slavery*. Rome: Institutum Patristicum "Augustinianum", 1985.

3037. Crespo Ortiz de Zárate, J. "Doble cognomen en -anus/-ianus como forma de filiación en el régimen esclavista," in Pedro Sáez and Salvador Ordónez, eds., *Homenáje al Profesor Presedo* (Sevilla and Jerez: Caja San Fernando, 1994), pp. 365-74.

3038. Crespo Ortiz de Zárate, Santos. "La subdependencia personal en Hispania romana: *servus vicarius* y las relaciones de dependencia entre siervos y libertos," *Hispania antiqua: revista de historia antigua*, 15 (1991), pp. 239-61.

3039. D'Arms, John H. "Slaves at Roman *Convivia*," in William J. Slater, ed., *Dining in a Classical Context* (Ann Arbor: University of Michigan Press, 1991), pp. 171-83.

3040. Daube, David. "*Mancipatio* of *res nec mancipi* in Cicero".

Reprinted in David Cohen and Dieter Simon, eds., *Collected Studies in Roman Law* (Frankfurt: Vittorio Klostermann, 1991), pp. 1315-20.

3041. Daube, David. "Slave-Catching".

Reprinted in David Cohen and Dieter Simon, eds., *Collected Studies in Roman Law* (Frankfurt: Vittorio Klostermann, 1991), pp. 501-13.

3042. Daube, David. "Two Early Patterns of Manumission".

Reprinted in David Cohen and Dieter Simon, eds., *Collected Studies in Roman Law* (Frankfurt: Vittorio Klostermann, 1991), pp. 165-91.

3043. Daube, David. "What Price Equality? Some Historical Reflections," *Rechtshistorisches Journal*, 5 (1986), pp. 185-208.

3044. Dennis, T. J. "The Relationship between Gregory of Nyssa's Attack on Slavery in his Fourth Homily on Ecclesiastes and his Treatise 'De Hominis Opificio'," *Studia Patristica*, 17 (1982), pp. 1065-72.

3045. *Doi, Masaoki. "Dating the Outbreak of the Spartacus War," *Senshu Jinbun Ronshu*, 50 (1992), pp. 1-33 (in Japanese).

3046. Doi, Masaoki. "Female Slaves in the Spartacus Army," in Marie-Madeleine Mactoux and Evelyne Geny, eds., *Mélanges Pierre Lévêque: 2, Anthropologie et société* (Paris: Belles Lettres, 1989), pp. 161-72. (Annales littéraires de l'Université de Besançon, 377; Centre de recherches d'histoire ancienne, vol. 82)

3047. Doi, Masaoki. "Luttes de classes à la fin de la république romaine: caractère de la revolte de Spartacus," in Toru Yuge, ed., *Le monde méditerranéen et l'esclavage: recherches japonaises* (Paris: Belles Lettres, 1991), pp. 147-68. (Annales littéraires de l'Université de Besançon, 426)

3048. Doi, Masaoki. "The Origin of Spartacus and the Anti-Roman Struggle in Thracia," *Index: Quaderni camerti di studi romanistici*, 20 (1992), pp. 31-40.

3049. *Doi, Masaoki. "The Present State of Studies on Spartacus' Uprising and Its Problems," *Studies in Humanities*, 35 (1985), pp. 17-45.

3050. *Doi, Masaoki. "The Problems of the Retreat Southwards of Spartacus' Army," *Senshu Shigaku*, 24 (1992), pp. 1-32 (in Japanese).

3051. Doi, Masaoki. "Révoltes serviles et problèmes agraires: l'exemple sicilien," in Toru Yuge, ed., *Le monde méditerranéen et l'esclavage: recherches japonaises* (Paris: Belles Lettres, 1991), pp. 113-45. (Annales littéraires de l'Université de Besançon, 426)

3052. Donderer, Michael, and Ioanna Spiliopoulou-Donderer. "Spätrepublikanische und kaiserzeitliche Grabmonumente von Sklavenhändlern," *Gymnasium*, 100 (1993), pp. 254-66.

3053. Downing, F. Gerald. "A Cynic Preparation for Paul's Gospel for Jew and Greek, Slave and Free, Male and Female," *New Testament Studies*, 42, 3 (1996), pp. 454-62.

3054. Eck, Werner. "Grabinschrift einer Sklavin des Egrilius Plarianus," *Zeitschrift für Papyrologie und Epigraphik*, 86 (1991), pp. 115-16.

3055. Eck, Werner. "*Superiumentari et muliones* im privaten Personal eines römischen Statthalters," *Zeitschrift für Papyrologie und Epigraphik*, 90 (1992), pp. 207-10.

3056. Eck, Werner, and Johannes Heinrichs. *Sklaven und Freigelassene in der Gesellschaft der römischen Kaiserzeit: Textauswahl und Übersetzung*. Darmstadt: Wissenschaftliche Buchgesellschaft, 1993. (Texte zur Forschung, Band 61)

3057. *Elayi, J. "La révolte des esclaves de Tyr relatée par Justin," *Mitteilungen des Deutschen Archäologischen Instituts (Abteilung Berlin)*, 12 (1981), pp. 139-50.

3058. Evans-Grubbs, Judith. "'Marriage More Shameful than Adultery': Slave-Mistress Relationships, 'Mixed Marriages', and Late Roman Law," *Phoenix*, 47, 2 (1993), pp. 125-54.

3059. Fabre, Georges. "Les affranchis et serviteurs impériaux sous Domitien," *Pallas*, 40 (1994), pp. 337-55.

3060. Faro, Silvano. *La libertas ex divi Claudii edicto: schiavitù e valori morali nei I secolo d.C.* Catania: Edizioni de Prisma, 1996.

3061. Fear, A. T. "*Cives latini, servi publici* and the *Lex Irnitana*," *Revue internationale des droits de l'antiquité*, sér. 3, 37 (1990), pp. 149-66.

3062. Fear, A. T. "The Dancing Girls of Cadiz," *Greece and Rome*, 38 (1991), pp. 75-79.

3063. Ferenczy, Endre. "Die Freigelassenen und ihre Nachkommen im öffentlichen Leben des republikanischen Rom," *Klio*, 70, 2 (1988), pp. 468-76.

3064. Fernández Ulbina, J. "Marx, MacMullen, Ste Croix: esclavos y campesinos del Bajo Imperio," in Pedro Sáez and Salvador Ordónez, eds., *Homenáje al Profesor Presedo* (Sevilla and Jerez: Caja San Fernando, 1994), pp. 403-22.

3065. Firpo, G. "Il problema servile tra Costantino e Giustiniano: pensiero cristiano e legislazione imperiale," in Marta Sordi, ed., *L'impero romano-cristiano: problemi politici, religiosi, culturali* (Roma: Coletti, 1991), pp. 95-119.

3066. Fitzgerald, William. "Labor and Laborer in Latin Poetry: The Case of the *Moretum*," *Arethusa*, 29 (1996), pp. 389-418.

3067. Ford, John D. "Stair's Title 'Of Liberty and Servitude'," in Andrew D. E. Lewis and D. J. Ibbetson, eds., *The Roman Law Tradition* (Cambridge: Cambridge University Press, 1994), pp. 135-58.

3068. Frend, W. "Fathers and Slaves: St. Augustine and Some Eastern Contemporaries," *Antiquitas*, 18 (1993), pp. 59-68.

3069. Gaide, Françoise. "Primogenius et les oiseaux (Pétrone, Sat. 46)," *Latomus*, 52 (1993), pp. 386-88.

3070. Garland, Andrew. "Cicero's *familia urbana*," *Greece & Rome*, 39, 2 (1992), pp. 163-72.

3071. *Garrido-Hory, M[argarite]. "Les esclaves africains dans l'oeuvre de Martial" (Unpublished paper, Colloque International de Recherches sur l'Esclavage Antique [GIREA]. Colloque [22ème] sur "Dépendants et esclaves dans l'Afrique Mineure et l'Egypte de l'Antiquité", 12-15 December 1996, L'Africa Romana: XII Convegno Internazionale di Studi, Olbia [Sardinia]).

3072. *Garrido-Hory, Marguerite [Margarite]. "'*Puer*' et '*minister*' dans Martial et Juvénal" (Unpublished paper, Colloque International de Recherches sur l'Esclavage Antique [GIREA], "Schiavi e dipendenti nell'ambito dell' 'oikos' e della 'familia'", 19-21 November 1995, Siena).

3073. *Gebbia, Clara. "Il SC. Claudianum e l'emancipazione femminile dal I al IV secolo," *Seia*, 3 (1986 [1990]), pp. 25-37.

3074. *Gianotti, Gian Franco. "Asini e schiavi nelle Metamorfosi di Apuleio," in Mariagrazia Vacchina, ed., *Attualità dell'antico* (Aosta: Associazione italiana di cultura classica, 1988), pp. 83-105.

3075. Giménez-Candela, Teresa. "Manumisión en provincias," in Carmén Castillo, ed. (with collaboration of Jesús María Bañales, Ramón Martinez, and Ramón Serrano), *Novedades de epigrafía jurídica romana en el ultimo decenio* (Pamplona: Servicio de Publicaciones de la Universidad de Navarra, 1989), pp. 217-25.

3076. Giuffré, Vincenzo. "Schiavi soldati, soldati schiavi" (Unpublished paper, Groupe International de Recherches sur l'Esclavage Antique [GIREA]. Colloque [19ème] sur "Captifs et prisonniers de guerre dans leurs rapports avec l'esclavage", 2-5 October, 1991, Palma, Mallorca).

3077. Golubcova, E. D., I. S. Sifman, and A. I. Pavlovskaja. *Die Sklaverei in den östlichen Provinzen des römischen Reiches im 1. - 3. Jahrhundert*. Translated by Jaroslav Kriz, with Günter Prinzing and Elisabeth Herrmann-Otto. Stuttgart: Steiner, 1992. (Übersetzungen ausländischer Arbeiten zur antiken Sklaverei, 5)

3078. *Gómez Pallarés, Joan, and Joaquin Gómez Pantoja. "Hierros pastoriles en Africa y en el Occidente romano" (Unpublished paper, Colloque International de Recherches sur l'Esclavage Antique [GIREA]. Colloque [22ème] sur "Dépendants et esclaves dans l'Afrique Mineure et l'Egypte de l'Antiquité", 12-15 December 1996, L'Africa Romana: XII Convegno Internazionale di Studi, Olbia [Sardinia]).

3079. *Gonzales, A[ntonio]. "L'esclave, la famille et la '*familia*' dans la correspondance de Pline le Jeune" (Unpublished paper, Colloque International de Recherches sur l'Esclavage Antique [GIREA], "Schiavi e dipendenti nell'ambito dell' 'oikos' e della 'familia'", 19-21 November 1995, Siena).

3080. *Gonzales, Antonio. "Historiographie et esclavage: le cas de l'Afrique" (Unpublished paper, Colloque International de Recherches sur l'Esclavage Antique [GIREA]. Colloque [22ème] sur "Dépendants et esclaves dans l'Afrique Mineure et l'Egypte de l'Antiquité", 12-15 December 1996, L'Africa Romana: XII Convegno Internazionale di Studi, Olbia [Sardinia]).

3081. Gonzales, A[ntonio]. "Le révélation chrétienne chez l'esclave du péplum," in Annequin and Garrido-Hory, eds., *Religion et anthropologie de l'esclavage*, pp. 303-16.

3082. Grieser, Heike. "Sklavenfreilassungen in den christlichen Quellen des merovingischen Galliens: Formen, Motive und Status der liberti" (Tagung der Arbeitsgruppe "Antike Sklaverei", Mainz, Germany, 9 October 1996).

3083. Guarino, Antonio. "Ineptiae Iuris Romani: IX. 1. Lo stato giuridico di Titirio," *Labeo: rassegna di diritto romano*, 35 (1989), pp. 336-39.

3084. Guarino, Antonio. "Le murene di Pollione," in *Iusculum Iuris* (Napoli: Jovene, 1985), pp. 247-50.

3085. Günther, Rigobert. "Probleme der Sklaverei in der Spätantike," in Helena Kurzová, Stepánka Brozová, and Zuzana Vanecková, eds., *Speculum antiquitatis graeco-romanae: Studia Ioanni Burian sexagenario oblata* (Prague: Kabinet pro studia recká, rimská a latinská CSAV, 1990), pp. 78-85.

3086. *Günther, Rosmarie. *Frauenarbeit - Frauenbindung: Untersuchungen zu unfreien und freigelassenen Frauen in den stadtrömischern Inschriften*. Munich, 1987.

3087. Günther, Rosmarie. "Die Grösse des Grabplatzes von servae und libertae als Ausweis ihrer wirtschaftlichen Lage und sozialen Reputation," *Laverna*, 1 (1990), pp. 101-24.

3088. Harrill, J. Albert. "Ignatius *ad Polycarp. 4.3* and the Corporate Manumission of Christian Slaves," *Journal of Early Christian Studies*, 1, 2 (1993), pp. 107-42.

3089. Harrill, J. Albert. *The Manumission of Slaves in Early Christianity*. Tübingen: J. C. B. Mohr, 1995.

3090. Harrill, J. Albert. "Paul and Slavery: The Problem of 1 Cor. 7:21," *Biblical Research*, 39 (1994), pp. 5-28.

3091. Havas, L. "Les révoltes des esclaves: la critique des textes," *Acta antiqua Academiae Scientiarum Hungaricae*, 33 (1990-92), pp. 287-93.

3092. Herrmann[-Otto], Elisabeth. *Ex ancilla natus: Untersuchungen zu den "hausgeborenen" Sklaven und Sklavinnen im Westen des Romischen Kaiserreiches*. Stuttgart: F. Steiner, 1994. (Forschungen zur antiken Sklaverei, Bd. 24)

3093. Herschbell, J. P. "Epictetus: A Freedman on Slavery," *Ancient Society*, 26 (1996), pp. 185-204.

3094. Highet, Gilbert. "*Libertino Patre Natus*," *American Journal of Philology*, 94, 3 (1973), pp. 268-81.

3095. Hopkins, Keith. "Novel Evidence for Roman Slavery," *Past and Present*, no. 138 (1993), pp. 3-27.

3096. Huchthausen, Liselot. "Sklavenkrankheiten in Rom," *Antiquitas*, 15 (1992), pp. 81-86.

3097. Huwiler, B. "*Homo et res*: Skizzen zur hellenistischen Theorie der Sklaverei und deren Einfluss auf das römische Recht," in J. A. Ankum, C. A. Cannata, R. Feenstra, Y. Le Roy, J. E. Spruit, and P. Weimar, eds., *Mélanges Félix Wubbe (offerts par ses amis à l'occasion de son soixante-dixième anniversaire* (Fribourg: Editions Universitaires Fribourg Suisse, 1993), pp. 273-94.

3098. *Imfeld, M. M. "Ein Sklave als Prätor: der Fall Barbarius Philippus (D. 1,14,3)" (Unpublished paper, 47th meeting of the Société Internationale "Fernand de Visscher" pour l'Histoire des Droits de l'Antiquité, Oxford, September 1993).

3099. Ivanov, Veselin. "Proucvanija varkhy istorijata na Sparakovoto vastanie, Cast I (Studies in the History of Spartacus' Revolt, Part 1)," *Izvestija na narodnija Muzej - Varna*, 26 (no. 41) (1990), pp. 21-32. (In Bulgarian, with Italian summary.)

3100. *Jakob, Eva. "Sklavenkäufe mit Gewährleistung in der Kaiserzeit" (Unpublished paper, Société Internationale "Fernand de Visscher" pour l'Histoire des Droits de l'Antiquité, Amsterdam and Utrecht, 21-26 September 1992).

3101. Jones, Michael Ridgway, Jr. "Voluptatis Artifices: The Social Position of Roman Theatrical Performers During the Republic and the Principate of Augustus" (PhD diss., Yale University, 1995).

3102. Jorquera Nieto, José Miguel. "*Servus*: Rome et l'esclavage sous la République (review essay: Dumont, *Servus: Rome et l'esclavage sous la République*)," *Dialogues d'histoire ancienne*, 19, 2 (1993), pp. 65-116 (in Spanish).

3103. Joshel, Sandra. "The Question of Women in Classical Rome: Femininity, Slavery, and Imperial Discourse" (Unpublished paper, American Historical Association, Chicago, 5-8 Jan. 1995).

3104. Kamienik, Roman. "La dernière bataille de Spartacus," *Antiquitas*, 16 (1992), pp. 29-43. (In Polish, with French summary)

3105. Kamienik, R[oman]. "Spartacus und das Meer," *Antiquitas*, 18 (1993), pp. 89-96.

3106. Karabélias, Evanghelos. "La pratique du concubinat avec une femme libre, affranchie ou esclave dans le droit postclassique," in *Atti dell'Accademia romanistica costantiniana: VII Convegno internazionale* (Perugia: Università degli studi di Perugia, Facoltà di giurisprudenza) (Naples: Edizioni Scientifiche Italiane, 1988), pp. 183-201.

3107. Khanoussi, Mustapha. "Disp(ensator) m(armorum) n(umidicorum)," *Africa*, 10 (1988), pp. 208-11.

3108. *Khanoussi, Mustapha. "Les *officiales marmorum Numidicorum*" (Unpublished paper, Colloque International de Recherches sur l'Esclavage Antique [GIREA]. Colloque [22ème] sur "Dépendants et esclaves dans l'Afrique Mineure et l'Egypte de l'Antiquité", 12-15 December 1996, L'Africa Romana: XII Convegno Internazionale di Studi, Olbia [Sardinia]).

3109. Klees, Hans. "Griechisches und Römisches in den Traumdeutung Artemidors für Herren und Sklaven," in Christoph Börker and Michael Donderer, eds., *Das antike Rom und der Osten: Festschrift für K. Parlasca zum 65. Geburtstag* (Erlangen: Universitätsbund Erlangen-Nürnberg, 1990), pp. 53-76.

3110. Klein, Richard. "Die Bestellung von Sklaven zu Priestern: ein rechtliches und soziales Problem in Spätantike und Frühmittelalter," *Klio*, 73, 2 (1991), pp. 601-05.

Reprinted in Karlheinz Dietz, Dieter Hennig, and Hans Kaletsch, eds., *Klassisches Altertum, Spätantike und frühes Christentum: Adolf Lippold zum 65. Geburtstag gewidmet* (Würzburg: Selbstverlag des Seminars für Alte Geschichte der Universität Würzburg, 1993), pp. 473-93.

3111. Kolendo, Jerzy. "La religion des esclaves dans le *De agricultura* de Caton," in Annequin and Garrido-Hory, eds., *Religion et anthropologie de l'esclavage*, pp. 267-74.

3112. Kolendo, Jerzy. "Les romains prisonniers de guerre des Barbares au temps des guerres marcomanniques et la 'redemptio ab hostibus'" (Unpublished paper, Groupe International de Recherches sur l'Esclavage Antique [GIREA]. Colloque [19ème] sur "Captifs et prisonniers de guerre dans leurs rapports avec l'esclavage", 2-5 October, 1991, Palma, Mallorca).

3113. Kontoulis, Georg. *Zum Problem der Sklaverei (DOULEIA) bei den kappadokischen Kirchenvätern und Johannes Chrysostomus*. Bonn: Habelt, 1993.

3114. Koptev, A. V. "'Svoboda' i 'rabstvo' kolonov v pozdnej rimskoj Imperii," *Vestnik Drevnej Istorii*, 13 (1990), pp. 24-40. (In Russian, with English summary)

3115. Kotula, Tadeusz. "Les grands domaines et l'esclavage face à la 'crise du IIIe siècle'," *Eos*, 79 (1991), pp. 71-83.

3116. Kousishchin [Kuziscin], Vasilij I. "Efficacité du travail servile à Rome: ses avantages et défauts," *Graecolatina Pragensia. Acta Universitatis Carolinae: Philologica*, 13 (1991), pp. 53-63.

3117. Kuziscin, V[asilij] I. "Slaves captivi and non-captivi in Ancient Rome" (Unpublished paper, Groupe International de Recherches sur l'Esclavage Antique [GIREA]. Colloque [19ème] sur "Captifs et prisonniers de guerre dans leurs rapports avec l'esclavage", 2-5 October, 1991, Palma, Mallorca).

3118. Kuzsicin, V. "Transformation from *servus* through *libertinus* to *civis romanus*: The Social and Religious Adaptation," in Annequin and Garrido-Hory, eds., *Religion et anthropologie de l'esclavage*, pp. 229-40.

3119. Labruna, L. "Minima de servis, II: I misteri del servus recepticius," *Index: Quaderni camerti di studi romanistici*, 17 (1989), pp. 167-84.

3120. Lazzaro, Luciano. *Esclaves et affranchis en Belgique et Germanies romaines d'après les sources épigraphiques*. Paris: Belles Lettres, 1993. (Annales littéraires de l'Université de Besançon, 430). (Centre de Recherches d'Histoire Ancienne, vol. 102)

3121. Lazzaro, Luciano. "Schiavi e liberti nelle iscrizioni di Padova romana," in Marie-Madeleine Mactoux and Evelyne Geny, eds., *Mélanges Pierre Lévêque: 3, Anthropologie et société* (Paris: Belles Lettres, 1990), pp. 181-95. (Annales littéraires de l'Université de Besançon, 404; Centre de recherches d'histoire ancienne, vol. 99)

3122. *Lebedeva, G. E. "The Evolution of the Slave Laws in Proto-Byzantine Legislation," *Vizantijskij Vremennik*, 55 (1994), pp. 85-90. (in Russian)

3123. Lefkowitz, Mary R. "Women and Freedom," *Arethusa*, 28, 1 (1995), pp. 107-11.

3124. *Lengrand, D. "Dédicaces religieuses, affranchis, esclaves en Afrique romaine" (Unpublished paper, Colloque International de Recherches sur l'Esclavage Antique [GIREA]. Colloque [22ème] sur "Dépendants et esclaves dans l'Afrique Mineure et l'Egypte de l'Antiquité", 12-15 December 1996, L'Africa Romana: XII Convegno Internazionale di Studi, Olbia [Sardinia]).

3125. Leuregans, Pierre. " ... achat sous la couronne d'esclaves ...," *Index*, 15 (1987), pp. 191-206.

3126. Levi, Mario Attilio. "Deux recueils sur l'esclavage dans l'Empire," *Dialogues d'histoire ancienne*, 19, 2 (1993), pp. 400-04.

3127. Linderski, Jerzy. "'Partus ancillae': A 'vetus quaestio' in the Light of a New Inscription," *Labeo: rassegna di diretto romano*, 33 (1987), pp. 192-98.

3128. Llewelyn, S. R. "'He Gives Authority to his Slaves, to Each his Work ... ' Mark.13.34," in Llewelyn (*et al.*), *New Documents Illustrating Early Christianity*, pp. 60-63.

3129. Llewelyn, S. R. "'If You Can Gain Your Freedom': Manumission and 1 Cor.7.21," in Llewelyn (*et al.*), *New Documents Illustrating Early Christianity*, pp. 63-70.

3130. Llewelyn, S. R. "Manumission in Thessaly and at Delphi," in Llewelyn (*et al.*), *New Documents Illustrating Early Christianity*, pp. 76-81.

3131. Llewelyn, S. R. "A Petition Concerning a Runaway: Paul's Letter to Philemon," in Llewelyn (*et al.*), *New Documents Illustrating Early Christianity*, pp. 55-60.

3132. Llewelyn, S. R. "The Sale of a Slave-Girl: The New Testament's Attitude to Slavery," in Llewelyn (*et al.*), *New Documents Illustrating Early Christianity*, pp. 48-55.

3133. Llewelyn, S. R. "The Slave of God (Rom.6.22) and Sacral Manumission," in Llewelyn (*et al.*), *New Documents Illustrating Early Christianity*, pp. 70-76.

3134. Llewelyn, S. R. (with the collaboration of R. A. Kearsley). *New Documents Illustrating Early Christianity: A Review of the Greek Inscriptions and Papyri Published in 1980-81*. Ancient History Documentary Research Centre, Macquarie University, 1992.

Contents listed under Llewelyn (5).

3135. Lomas, F. "Dépendance et autorité dans les églises hispaniques au VIe siècle," in Annequin and Garrido-Hory, eds., *Religion et anthropologie de l'esclavage*, pp. 209-27.

3136. López Barja de Quiroga, Pedro. "La dependencia económica de los libertos en el Alto Imperio Romano," *Gerión*, 9 (1991), pp. 163-74.

3137. López Barja de Quiroga, Pedro. "Freedmen Social Mobility in Roman Italy," *Historia: Zeitschrift für Altegeschichte*, 44, 3 (1995), pp. 326-48.

3138. López Barja de Quiroga, Pedro. "Latinus Iunianus: 'status' jurídico y realidad historica," in *Esclavos y semilibres*, pp. 85-89.

3139. Los, Andrzej. *Les affranchis à Pompéi: étude socio-économique*. Wroclaw: Wydawnictwo Uniwersytetu Wroclawskiego, 1991. (In Polish with French summary)

3140. Los, Andrzej. "Les affranchis dans la vie politique à Pompéi," in *Mélanges de l'École française de Rome: Antiquité*, 99, 2 (1987), pp. 847-73.

3141. Los, Andrzej. "Les affranchis impériaux à Pompéi," *Antiquitas*, 18 (1993), pp. 149-56.

3142. Los, Andrezej. "La condition sociale des affranchis privés au 1er siècle après J.-C.," *Annales: économies, sociétés, civilisations*, 50, 5 (1995), pp. 1011-43.

3143. Los, Andrzej. "Les intérets des affranchis dans l'agriculture italienne," *Mélanges d'archéologie et d'histoire de l'École Française de Rome*, 104, 2 (1992), pp. 709-53.

3144. Los, Andrzej. "La vie privée des affranchis à Pompéi," *Antiquitas*, 16 (1992), pp. 77-94 (in Polish with French summary).

3145. Lowe, J. C. B. "Cooks in Plautus," *Classical Antiquity*, 4, 1 (1985), pp. 72-102.

3146. Lucrezi, F. "Pictores servi," *Opus: International Journal for Social and Economic History of Antiquity*, 3 (1984), pp. 85-92.

3147. MacMullen, Ramsay. "Late Roman Slavery".

Republished in MacMullen, *Changes in the Roman Empire: Essays in the Ordinary* (Princeton: Princeton University Press, 1990), pp. 236-49.

3148. Mactoux, Marie-Madeleine. "Esclaves et rites de passage," *Mélanges de l'Ecole française de Rome (Antiquité)*, 102, 1 (1990), pp. 53-81.

3149. Major, A. "Claudius' Edict on Sick Slaves," *Scholia*, 3 (1994), pp. 84-90.

3150. Manfredini, Arrigo Diego. "'Ad ecclesiam confugere', 'ad statuas confugere', 'nell'età di Teodosio I," in *Atti dell'Accademia romanistica costantiniana: VI Convegno internazionale* (Perugia: Università degli studi di Perugia, Facoltà di giurisprudenza) (Naples: Edizioni Scientifiche Italiane, 1986), pp. 39-58.

3151. Manfredini, A[rrigo]. D[iego]. "Sugli schiavi ordinati 'invito domino'," in *Atti dell'Accademia Romanistica Costantiniana* (X Congresso Internazionale, 1991), 10 (1995), pp. 529-40.

3152. Mangas, Julio. "Esclavos y libertos en Asturia Augusta," in *Esclavos y semilibres*, pp. 207-19.

3153. *Mangas, Julio. "Niños esclavos en el ambito de la 'familia'" (Unpublished paper, Colloque International de Recherches sur l'Esclavage Antique [GIREA], "Schiavi e dipendenti nell'ambito dell' 'oikos' e della 'familia'", 19-21 November 1995, Siena).

3154. *Marino, A. Storchi. "Schiavitú e forme di dipendenza in Roma arcaica: alcune riflessioni" (Unpublished paper, Colloque International de Recherches sur l'Esclavage Antique [GIREA], "Schiavi e dipendenti nell'ambito dell' 'oikos' e della 'familia'", 19-21 November 1995, Siena).

3155. Martin, Dale B. *Slavery as Salvation: The Metaphor of Slavery in Pauline Christianity*. New Haven: Yale University Press, 1990.

3156. Martino, Francesco de. "Schiavi e coloni tra antichità e medioevo," in *Hestiasis: Studi di tarda antichità offerti a Salvatore Calderone* (Sicania, 1986), vol. 2, pp. 7-44. (Università degli Studi di Messia, Facoiltà di Lettere e Filosofia, Centro di Studi Umanistici: Studi tardoantichi, II, 1986)

3157. Martorana, Giuseppe. "Il riso di Demetria in Sicilia," *Kokalos*, 28-29 (1982-83), pp. 105-12.

3158. Mastino, Attilio, and Paola Ruggeri. "*Claudia Augusta liberta Acte*, la liberta amata da Nerone ad Olbia," *Latomus*, 54 (1995), pp. 513-44.

3159. McCarthy, Kathleen. "Masterful Inventions: The Art of Authority in Plautine Comedy" (PhD diss., Princeton University, 1994).

3160. *Menacacci, F. "Relazioni di parentela nella comunità servile: gli schiavi gemelli" (Unpublished paper, Colloque International de Recherches sur l'Esclavage Antique [GIREA], "Schiavi e dipendenti nell'ambito dell' 'oikos' e della 'familia'", 19-21 November 1995, Siena).

3161. Millar, Fergus. "The Roman *Libertus* and Civic Freedom," *Arethusa*, 28, 1 (1995), pp. 99-105.

3162. Morabito, Marcel. "Les esclaves privilégiés à travers le Digeste: témoins et acteurs d'une société en crise," *Index*, 13 (1985), pp. 477-90.

3163. Morabito, Marcel. "Études de stratégies serviles," in Jean Andreau and Hinnerk Bruhns, eds., *Parenté et stratégies familiales dans l'antiquité romaine (Actes de la table ronde des 2-4 octobre 1986)* (Rome: École française de Rome, 1990), pp. 439-46.

3164. *Mrozek, Stanislaw. "Le role économique et sociale des affranchis à la fin de la République et au début de l'Empire," *Roczniki Dziejów Spoleczno-Gospodarczych*, 37 (1976), pp. 33-45. (in Polish)

3165. Munzi, Massimiliano. "Un grammatico greco a *Grumentum*: società e cultura in un centro della Lucania," *Archeologia Classica*, 45, 1 (1993), pp. 375-87.

3166. Nicosia, G. "Prigionia di guerra e perdita della libertà nell'esperienza giuridica romana" (Unpublished paper, Groupe International de Recherches sur l'Esclavage Antique [GIREA]. Colloque [19ème] sur "Captifs et prisonniers de guerre dans leurs rapports avec l'esclavage", 2-5 October, 1991, Palma, Mallorca).

3167. Nielsen, Hanne Sigismund. "Delicia in Roman Literature and in the Urban Inscriptions," *Analecta Romana Instituti Danici*, 19 (1990), pp. 79-88.

3168. Nielsen, Hanne Sigismund. "Ditis examen domus? On the Use of the Term '*verna*' in the Roman Epigraphical and Literary Sources," *Classica et Mediaevalia*, 42 (1991), pp. 221-40.

3169. Nikiprowetzky, Valentin. "Quelques observations sur la répudiation de l'esclavage par les Thérapeutes et les Esséniens d'après les notices de Philon et de Flave Joséphus," in *Mélanges à la mémoire de Marcel-Henri Prévost* (Paris, 1982), pp. 229-71.

3170. Nouailhat, R. "Esclave, serviteur, moine: structure de dépendance à Lérins au début du ve siècle," in Annequin and Garrido-Hory, eds., *Religion et anthropologie de l'esclavage*, pp. 241-66.

3171. Osiek, Carolyn. "Captivity and Slavery: Early Christian Experience," *The Bible Today*, 31, 6 (1993), pp. 348-52.

3172. Osiek, Carolyn. "Slavery in the New Testament World," *The Bible Today*, 22 (1984), pp. 151-55.

3173. Pawlak, Malgorzata. "The Pagan Cults of Slaves and Freedmen in Roman Africa," *Antiquitas*, 18 (1993), pp. 175-81.

3174. Pawlak, Malgorzata. "*Vernae* en Afrique romaine," *Antiquitas*, 16 (1992), pp. 107-21. (In Polish with French summary)

3175. Pena, M. J. "Reflexiones sobre la condición juridica y social de la población rural de Mallorca en época romana" (Unpublished paper, Groupe International de Recherches sur l'Esclavage Antique [GIREA]. Colloque [19ème] sur "Captifs et prisonniers de guerre dans leurs rapports avec l'esclavage", 2-5 October, 1991, Palma, Mallorca).

3176. Plácido, Domingo. "La cuestión del esclavismo antiguo: el caso de las sociedades hispanas," *Historia social* (Instituto de Historia Social U.N.E.D. Valencia), no. 20 (1994), pp. 5-22.

3177. Pomeroy, Arthur J. "Trimalchio as *deliciae*," *Phoenix*, 46, 1 (1992), pp. 45-53.

3178. Prieto Arciniega, A. "Aproximación a las formas de dependencia en los territorios de Baetula e Iluro," in *Esclavos y semilibres*, pp. 179-85.

3179. Puglisi, Gaetano. "Il microcosmo di C. Pompeius Trimalchio Maecenatianus: schiavi e liberti nella casa di un mercante romano (Petr. 27-28)," *Index: Quaderni camerti di studi romanistici*, 15 (1987), pp. 207-26.

3180. Querzoli, Serena. "La prostituzione della schiava nel diritto fra Augusto e gli Antonini," *Ostraka: Rivista di antichità*, 2, 2 (1993), pp. 399-404.

3181. *Reekmans, Tony. "Slaven en hun meesters in het prozaische oeuvre van Seneca de Wijsgeer," *Medelingen van de koninklijke Academie voor Wetenschappen, Letteren & Schone Kunsten van Belgie, Kl. der Letteren*, 43, 1 (1981), pp. 179-96.

3182. Ricl, Marijana. "Consécrations d'esclaves en Macédonie sous l'Empire," *Ziva Antika*, 43, 1-2 (1993), pp. 129-44. (in Croatian, with French summary on pp. 143ff.)

3183. Rink, Bernhard. "Sklavenfreilassungen in der späten römischen Republik als Beispiel für soziale Mobilität," *Laverna*, 4 (1994), pp. 45-54.

3184. Rix, Helmut. *Die Termini der Unfreiheit in den Sprachen Alt-Italiens*. Stuttgart: Franz Steiner Verlag, 1994.

3185. Rodger, Alan. "Labeo and the Fraudulent Slave," in A. D. E. Lewis and David J. Ibbetson, eds., *The Roman Law Tradition* (Cambridge: Cambridge University Press, 1994), pp. 15-31.

Also as the Rt. Hon. Lord Rodger of Earlsferry, Q.C., F.B.A, (Unpublished paper, 47th meeting of the Société Internationale "Fernand de Visscher" pour l'Histoire des Droits de l'Antiquité, Oxford, September 1993).

3186. Rodríguez Cerezo, T. M. "Historia antigua de Roma (libros I-VI), de Dionisio de Halicarnaso. un nuevo índice temático," in *Esclavos y semilibres*, pp. 81-84.

3187. Rubinsohn, Wolfgang Zeev. *Spartacus' Uprising and Soviet Historical Writing*. Trans. John G. Griffith. Oxford: Oxbow Books, 1987.

3188. Saller, Richard. "The Hierarchical Household in Roman Society: A Study of Domestic Slavery," in Bush, ed., *Serfdom and Slavery*, pp. 112-29.

3189. Salles, Catherine. *Spartacus et la révolte des gladiateurs*. Bruxelles: Complexe, 1990. (La mémoires des siècles, vol. 217)

3190. Sanchez León, Juan Carlos. *Les sources de l'histoire de Bagaudes: traduction et commentaire*. Paris: Belles Lettres, 1996. (Annales littéraires de l'Université de Besançon, 603; Centre de recherches d'histoire ancienne, vol. 153)

3191. Santero Saturnino, José M.[a] "Esclavos y libertos de colegios," in *Esclavos y semilibres*, pp. 139-56.

3192. *Scacchetti, M. G. *Manumissione testamentaria e doloso de pauperamento dell'eredità giacente: lettura esegetica del Titolo 47, 4 del Digesto*. Milan: Giuffrè, 1993.

3193. *Scardigli, B. Forster. "Serve private di vestali?" (Unpublished paper, Colloque International de Recherches sur l'Esclavage Antique [GIREA], "Schiavi e dipendenti nell'ambito dell' 'oikos' e della 'familia'", 19-21 November 1995, Siena).

3194. Schäfer, Christoph. "Zur [SPHRAGIS] von Sklaven in der lex portorii provinciae Asiae," *Zeitschrift für Papyrologie und Epigraphik*, 86 (1991), pp. 193-98.

3195. Scheidel, Walter. "*Agricola, colonus, cultor, rusticus*: Beobachtungen zum rechtlichen und sozialen Status der 'Landwirte' in Columellas Schrift *de re rustica*," *Maia: Revista di letterature classiche*, 42, n.s. 3 (1990), pp. 257-65.

3196. Scheidel, Walter. "Columellas privates *ius liberorum*: Literatur, Recht, Demographie: einige Probleme," *Latomus*, 53, 3 (1994), pp. 513-27.

3197. Scheidel, Walter. "The Demography of Slavery and Manumission in the Roman Empire" (Unpublished paper, Premier Colloque International de Démographie Historique Antique, Arras, France, 22 November 1996).

3198. Scheidel, Walter. *Grundpacht und Lohnarbeit in der Landwirtschaft des römischen Italien*. Frankfurt am Main: Peter Lang, 1994.

3199. Scheidel, Walter. "Instrumentum vocale: Bauern und Sklaven in der römischen Landwirtschaft," *Historicum*, 47 (1996), pp. 11-16.

3200. Scheidel, Walter. "Quasikolonen bei Vergil?" *Klio*, 72, 1 (1990), pp. 166-72.

3201. Scheidel, Walter. "*Servi alieni* als Erben: zum gesellschaftlichen Hintergrund," *Zeitschrift der Savigny-Stiftung für Rechtsgeschichte (Romanistische Abteilung)*, 110 (1993), pp. 648-51.

3202. Scheidel, Walter. "Sklaven und Freigelassene als Pächter und ihre ökonomische Funktion in der römischen Landwirtschaft," in Heleen Sancisi-Weerdenburg *et al.*, eds., *De Agricultura: In memoriam Pieter Willem de Neeve (1945-1990)* (Amsterdam: J. C. Gieben, 1993), pp. 182-96.

3203. Schlinkert, Dirk. "Der Hofeunuch in der Spätantike: ein gefährlicher Aussenseiter?" *Hermes: Zeitschrift für Klassische Philologie*, 122, 3 (1994), pp. 342-59.

3204. Scholten, Helga. *Der Eunuch in Kaisernahe: zur politischen und sozialen Bedeutung des "praepositus sacri cubiculi" im 4. und 5. Jahrhundert n.Chr.* Frankfurt am Main: Lang, 1995.

3205. Schulze-Oben, Heidrun. *Freigelassene in den Städten des römischen Hispanien: Juristische, wirtschaftliche und soziale Stellung nach dem Zeugnis der Inschriften*. Bonn: Habelt, 1989.

3206. Sebai, Leila Ladjimi. "A propos du collier d'esclave trouvé à Bulla Regia: 'Nunc mors perpetua(m) libertatem dedit' (Epitaphe d'esclave, Carthage, CIL, VIII, 25006)," *Africa*, 10 (1988), pp. 212-19.

3207. Segenni, Simonetta. *I liberti ad Amiternum: ricerche di onomastica*. Pisa: Giardini Editori Stempatori, 1990.

3208. Serrano Delgado, José Miguel. *Status y promoción social de los libertos en Hispania Romana*. Sevilla: Servicio de Publicaciones de la Universidad de Sevilla, 1988.

3209. *Shima, Sohei. "The Relationship between Master and Slave in the Household Codes of the Ancient Mediterranean Society: Examination of the First Letter of Peter," *Seiyoshi Kenkyu*, 22 (1993), pp. 111-23. (in Japanese)

3210. Shima, Sohei. "Roman Slavery and Christianity: The Historical Background of the Letter to Colossans 3:22-4:1," *Kodai: Journal of Ancient History*, 4 (1993), pp. 67-73.

3211. Sicari, Amalia. *Prostitutzione e tutela giuridica della schiava: un problema di politica legislativa nell'impero romano*. Bari: Cacucci, 1991. (Pubblicazioni della Facoltà Giuridica dell'Università di Bari, 99)

3212. Sirks, A. J. Boudewijn. "Ad senatus consultum Claudianum," *Zeitschrift der Savigny-Stiftung für Rechtsgeschichte, Romanistische Abteilung*, 111 (1994), pp. 436-37.

3213. *Smadja, Elisabeth. "Esclavage et systèmes de production en Afrique romaine" (Unpublished paper, Colloque International de Recherches sur l'Esclavage Antique [GIREA]. Colloque [22ème] sur "Dépendants et esclaves dans l'Afrique Mineure et l'Egypte de l'Antiquité", 12-15 December 1996, L'Africa Romana: XII Convegno Internazionale di Studi, Olbia [Sardinia]).

3214. *Smadja, E[lisabeth]. "Les esclaves et l'argent dans le théâtre romain" (Unpublished paper, Colloque International de Recherches sur l'Esclavage Antique [GIREA], "Schiavi e dipendenti nell'ambito dell' 'oikos' e della 'familia'", 19-21 November 1995, Siena).

3215. Solin, Heikki. *Die stadtrömischen Sklavennamen: Ein Namenbuch. Vol. 1: Lateinische Namen. Vol. 2: Griechische Namen. Vol. 3: Barbarische Namen. Indices*. Stuttgart: Franz Steiner Verlag, 1996.

3216. Soraci, Rosario. "La legislazione di Costantino sulla schiavitù: Ettore Ciccotti e il dibattito storiografico moderno," *Quaderni catanesi di studi classici e medievali*, 5 (1983), pp. 57-77.

3217. Sordi, Marta. *Paolo a Filemone: o della schiavitù*. Milan: Jaca Book, 1987.

3218. Speidel, Michael P. "The Soldiers' Servants," *Ancient Society*, 20 (1989), pp. 239-48.

3219. Stains, David R. "Gregory of Nyssa's Ethic of Slavery and Emancipation" (PhD diss., University of Pittsburgh, 1994).

3220. Susini, Giancarlo. "L'*actor* di Rofello, sul dorso dell'Appennino," *Caesarodunum*, 29 (1995), pp. 181-88.

3221. Szulczyk, Jerzy. "Investigations on the History of Spartacus' Insurrection," *Antiquitas*, 16 (1992), pp. 155-63. (In Polish with English summary)

3222. Szulczyk, Jerzy. "Problèmes de l'approvisionnement en nourriture des esclaves dans la révolte de Spartacus et difficultés de recrutement à l'armée romaine," *Antiquitas*, 15 (1992), 197-205. (In Polish with French summary)

3223. Taceva, M. "Religion et anthropologie de l'esclavage en Mésie et en Thrace (Ier-IIIe s. ap. J.-C.)," in Annequin and Garrido-Hory, eds., *Religion et anthropologie de l'esclavage*, pp. 295-302.

3224. Thébert, Yvon. "The Slave," in Andrea Giardina, ed., *The Romans* (translated by Lydia G. Cochrane) (Chicago and London: University of Chicago Press, 1993), pp. 138-74.

3225. Thompson, Lloyd A. *Romans and Blacks*. Norman: Oklahoma University Press, 1989.

3226. Thurmond, David L. "Some Roman Slave Collars in *CIL*," *Athenaeum*, 82, 2 (1994), pp. 459-93.

3227. Van Houte, Samuel. "The Freedmen at Pompeii" (PhD diss., University of Maryland - College Park, 1971).

3228. Volkmann, Hans. *Die Massenversklavungen der Einwohner erorberter Städte in der helenistisch-römischen Zeit*. Zweite durchgesehene und erweiterte Auflage von Gerhard Horsmann. Stuttgart: Steiner, 1990. (Forschungen zur Antiken Sklaverei, 22)

New ed., with revisions and expansion by Gerhard Horsmann (Stuttgart: Franz Steiner Verlag, 1990).

3229. Wallinga, H. T. "*Bellum spartacium*: Florus' Text and Spartacus' Objective," *Athenaeum*, 80, 1 (1992), pp. 25-43.

3230. Watson, Alan. "Seventeenth-Century Jurists, Roman Law, and the Law of Slavery," *Chicago-Kent Law Review*, 68, 3 (Symposium on the Law of Slavery) (1993), pp. 1343-54.

3231. Watson, Alan. "A Slave's Marriage: Dowry or Deposit," *Journal of Legal History*, 12, 2 (1991), pp. 132-39.

3232. Watson, Alan. "Thinking Property at Rome," *Chicago-Kent Law Review*, 68, 3 (Symposium on the Law of Slavery) (1993), pp. 1355-71.

3233. Weaver, P. R. C. "Where have All the Junian Latins Gone? Nomenclature and Status in the Early Empire," *Chiron*, 20 (1990), pp. 275-305.

3234. Weaver, P. R. C., and P. I. Wilkins. "A Lost Alumna," *Zeitschrift für Papyrologie und Epigraphik*, 99 (1993), pp. 241-44.

3235. Welwei, Karl-Wilhelm. *Unfreie im antiken Kriegsdienst. Dritter Teil: Rom.* Stuttgart: Franz Steiner Verlag, 1988.

3236. Zecchini, Giuseppe. "Salustio, Lucullo e I tre schiavi di C. Giulio Cesare (due nuovi frammenti delle *Historiae*)," *Latomus*, 54, 3 (1995), pp. 592-607.

3237. Zoz de Biasio, Maria Gabriella. "Nota minima sulla tutela dei nuclei familiari servili," in *Studi in onore di Arnaldo Biscardi* (Milan: Istituto Editoriale Cisalpino - La Goliardica, 1983), vol. 4, pp. 537-44.

5. Egypt

3238. Arzt, Peter. "Brauchbare Sklaven: Ausgewählte Papyrustexte zum Philemonbrief," *Protokolle zur Bibel*, 1, 1 (1992), pp. 44-58.

3239. Bagnall, Roger S. "Freedmen and Freedwomen with Fathers?" *Journal of Juristic Papyrology*, 21 (1991), pp. 7-8.

3240. Bagnall, Roger S. "Slavery and Society in Late Roman Egypt," in Baruch Halpern and Deborah W. Hobson, eds., *Law, Politics and Society in the Ancient Mediterranean World* (Sheffield: Academic Press, 1993), pp. 220-40.

3241. Borkowski, Zbigniew, and Jean A. Straus. "P. Colon. inv. 4781 verso: vente d'une esclave," *Zeitschrift für Papyrologie und Epigraphik*, 98 (1993), pp. 249-52.

3242. Clarysse, W. "Slaven en papyri," *Kleio N.R.*, 19, 1 (1989), pp. 1-22.

3243. Gundlach, Rolf. *Die Zwangsumsiedlung auswärtiger Bevölkerung als middle Ägyptischer Politik bis zum Ende des mittleren Reiches.* Stuttgart: Franz Steiner Verlag, 1994.

3244. Helck, Wolfgang. "Kriegsgefangene," in Wolfgang Helck and Wolfhard Westendorf, eds., *Lexikon der Ägyptologie* (Wiesbaden: Otto Harrassowitz, 1979), Bd. 3, Lieferung 5, cols. 786-88.

3245. Helck, Wolfgang. "Sklaven," in Wolfgang Helck and Wolfhard Westendorf, eds., *Lexikon der Ägyptologie* (Wiesbaden: Otto Harrassowitz, 1984), Bd. 5, cols. 982-87.

3246. Holton Pierce, Richard. "A Sale of an Alodian Slave Girl: A Reexamination of Papyrus Strassburg Inv. 1404," *Symbolae Osloenses*, 70 (1995), pp. 148-66.

3247. Keenan, James G. "The Will of Gaius Longinus Castor," *Bulletin of the American Society of Papyrologists*, 31, 3-4 (1994), pp. 101-07.

3248. Loprieno, Antonio. "Lo schiavo," in Sergio Donadoni, ed., *L'uomo egiziano* (Rome: Laterza, 1990), pp. 197-233.

3249. *Samuel, A. A. "The Role of Paramone Clauses in Ancient Documents," *Journal of Juristic Papyrology*, 12 (1965), pp. 221-311.

3250. Scholl, Reinhold. "Zum ptolemäischen Sklavenrecht," in Markham J. Geller and Herwig Maehler, eds., *Legal Documents of the Hellenistic World* (London: The Warburg Institute, 1995), pp. 149-72.

3251. Scholl, Reinhold. "Zur Höhe der Salzsteuer für Sklaven," *Zeitschrift für Papyrologie und Epigraphik*, 76 (1989), pp. 95-97.

3252. Scholl, Reinhold. "Zur Sklaverei am Hof der Ptolemäer," in Lucia Criscuolo and Giovanni Geraci, eds., *Egitto e storia antica dall'ellenismo all'età araba: Bilancio di un confronto* (Atti del Colloquio Internazionale Bologna, 31 agosto - 2 settembre 1987) (Bologna: Cooperativa Libraria Universitaria Editrice Bologna, 1989), pp. 671-81.

3253. Smither, P. "The Report Concerning the Slave Girl Senbet," *Journal of Egyptian Archaeology*, 34 (1948), pp. 31-34.

3254. Straus, Jean A. "Remarques sur quelques contrats de vente d'esclaves conservés sur papyrus," *Zeitschrift für Papyrologie und Epigraphik*, 104 (1994), pp. 227-29.

6. Other

IX. Medieval and Early Modern Europe

1. General and Comparative

3255. Davies, Wendy. "On Servile Status in the Early Middle Ages" (Unpublished paper, Conference on "Serfdom and Slavery", University of Manchester, 5-7 Sept. 1994).

3256. Fontenay, Michel. "L'esclave galérien dans la Méditerranée des temps modernes," in Bresc, ed., *Figures de l'esclave*, pp. 115-43.

3257. Heers, Jacques. *Esclaves et domestiques au Moyen Âge dans le monde mediterranéen*. Paris: Hachette/Pluriel, 1996.

3258. Hunwick, John O. "African Slaves in the Mediterranean World: A Neglected Aspect of the African Diaspora".

Republished in Harris, ed., *Global Dimensions of the African Diaspora* (2nd ed.), pp. 289-323.

3259. Hunwick, John O. "A Working Bibliography on Africans in Slavery in the Mediterranean World," *Saharan Studies Newsletter*, 3, 2 (1995), pp. 5-14.

3260. Koningsveld, P. S. van. "Muslim Slaves and Captives in Western Europe during the Late Middle Ages," *Islam and Christian-Muslim Relations*, 6, 1 (1995), pp. 5-23.

3261. Morabito, Marcel. "Signes médiévaux de survie de l'esclavage antique: le témoinage des pénitentiels (VIe-XIe s.)," in Marie-Madeleine Mactoux and Evelyne Geny, eds., *Mélanges Pierre Lévêque: 5, Anthropologie et société* (Paris: Belles Lettres, 1990), pp. 259-85. (Annales littéraires de l'Université de Besançon, 429; Centre de recherches d'histoire ancienne, vol. 101)

3262. Stella, Alessandro. "Les galères dans la Méditerranée (XVIe-XVIIIe siècles): miroir des formes de la mise en servitude" (Presentation at Colloquium on "Les dépendances serviles", Paris 1996).

3263. Stuard, Susan Mosher. "Ancillary Evidence for the Decline of Medieval Slavery," *Past and Present*, no. 149 (1995), pp. 3-28.

3264. Vauchez, André. "Note sur l'esclavage et le changement de religion en Terre Sainte au XIIIe siècle," in Bresc, ed., *Figures de l'esclave*, pp. 791-96.

3265. Verlinden, Charles. "Slavery, Slave Trade," in Joseph R. Strayer, ed., *Dictionary of the Middle Ages* (New York: Charles Scribner's Sons, 1988), vol. 11, pp. 334-40.

2. Byzantine

3266. Bartusis, Mark C. "Douloparoikos," in Alexander P. Kazhdan, ed., *Oxford Dictionary of Byzantium* (New York: Oxford University Press, 1991), vol. 1, pp. 658-59.

3267. Cappell, Andrew J. "Slavery," in Alexander P. Kazhdan, ed., *Oxford Dictionary of Byzantium* (New York: Oxford University Press, 1991), vol. 3, pp. 1915-16.

3268. *Caserta, Also. "Tratta dei negri e Regno di Napoli," *Campania sacra*, n[os] 12-13 (1982-83), pp. 186-237.

3269. Kazhdan, Alexander P. "Doulos," in Alexander P. Kazhdan, ed., *Oxford Dictionary of Byzantium* (New York: Oxford University Press, 1991), vol. 1, p. 659.

3270. Letsios, Dimitrios. "Die Kriegsgefangenschaft nach Auffassung der Byzantiner," *Byzantinoslavica (Revue internationale des études byzantines)*, 53, 2 (1992), pp. 213-27.

3271. MacCoull, Leslie S. B. "A Cinderella Story from Byzantine Egypt: P. Cair. Masp. I 67089 and III 67294," *Byzantion: Revue internationale des études byzantines*, 57 (1992), pp. 380-88.

3272. Morris, Rosemary. "Emancipation in Byzantium: Roman Law in a Medieval Society," in Bush, ed., *Serfdom and Slavery*, pp. 130-43.

3. Italy and Colonies

3273. Balard, Michel. "Esclavage en Crimée et sources fiscales génoises au XVe siècle," in Bresc, ed., *Figures de l'esclave*, pp. 77-87.

3274. Bono, Salvatore. "Esclaves musulmans en Italie".

Also as "Schiavi musulmani in Italia nell'etá moderna," *Erdem*, 3, 9 (1987), pp. 829-38.

3275. Bresc, Henri. "Esclaves auliques et main-d'œuvre servile agricole dans la Sicilie des XIIe et XIIIe siècles," in Bresc, ed., *Figures de l'esclave*, pp. 97-114.

3276. Camerano, Alessandra. "Courtesans and Slaves from Eastern Countries: Vices and Virtues in Sixteenth-Century Rome" (Unpublished paper, Sixteenth-Century Studies Conference, 9-12 December 1993, St. Louis).

3277. Williams, John Ryan. "From the Commercial Revolution to the Slave Revolution: The Development of Slavery in Medieval Genoa" (PhD diss., University of Chicago, 1995).

4. Iberia[14]

3278. *Alvarèz Alonso, Clara. "Libertad y propiedad: el primer liberalismo y la esclavitud," *Anuario de historia del derecho español*, 65 (1995), pp. 585-632.

3279. Bosch, M. del C. "'Servam et captivam meam'" (Unpublished paper, Groupe International de Recherches sur l'Esclavage Antique [GIREA]. Colloque [19ème] sur "Captifs et prisonniers de guerre dans leurs rapports avec l'esclavage", 2-5 October, 1991, Palma, Mallorca).

3280. Bravo Lozano, Jesús. "Mulos y esclavos: Madrid, 1670," *Cuadernos de historia moderna y contemporánea*, 1 (1980), pp. 11-30.

3281. Bunes Ibarra, M. A. de. *La imagen de los musulmanes y del Norte de África en la España de los siglos XVI y XVII: los caracteres de una hostilidad*. Madrid: Consejo Superior de Investigaciones Científicas, 1989.

3282. Cabrera Muños, Emilio. "Cautivos cristianos en el reino de Granada durante la segunda mitad del siglo XV," in Christina Segura Graiño, ed., *Relaciones exteriores del Reino de Granada* (IV Coloquio de historia medieval andaluza) (Almería: Instituto de Estudios Almerienses, 1988), pp. 227-36.

3283. Coca Castañer, J. E. López de. "Institutions on the Castilian-Granadan Frontier, 1369-1482," in R. Bartlett and A. MacKay, eds., *Medieval Frontier Societies* (Oxford: Clarendon Press, 1989), pp. 135-41.

3284. Fernández Martín, Luis. *Comediantes, esclavos y moriscos en Valladolid, siglos XVI y XVII*. Valladolid: Secretariado de Publicaciones de la Universidad de Valladolid, 1988.

3285. Ferrer i Mallol, Maria Teresa. "Els redemptors de captius: mostolafs, eixees o alfaquecs (segles XII-XIII)," *Medievalia*, 9 (1990), pp. 85-106.

3286. Franco Silva, Alfonso. *La esclavitud en Andalucia, 1450-1550*. Granada: Universidad de Granada, 1992.

3287. Franco Silva, Alfonso. "La esclavitud en la peninsula ibérica a fines del medievo: estado de la cuestión - fuentes y problemas relacionados con sus actividades" (Presentation at "Seminário internacional: Escravos com e sem açucar", Madeira, 17-21 June 1996).

3288. Furio, Antoni. "Esclaves et salariés: la fonction économique de l'esclavage en Péninsule Ibérique au Bas Moyen-Age" (Presentation at Colloquium on "Les dépendances serviles", Paris 1996).

3289. Lahon, Didier. "Les Confréries de Noirs et leurs privilèges royaux d'affranchissement: relations avec le pouvoir au XVIIIe siècle" (Presentation at Colloquium on "Les dépendances serviles", Paris 1996).

3290. Larquié, Claude. "L'esclavage dans une capitale: Madrid au XVIIe siècle," in Bresc, ed., *Figures de l'esclave*, pp. 177-200.

3291. Lobo Cabrera, Manuel. "Canárias: escravos e açucar" (Presentation at "Seminário internacional: Escravos com e sem açucar", Madeira, 17-21 June 1996).

3292. Lobo Cabrera, Manuel. "La esclavitud en España en la edad moderna: su investigación en los últimos cincuenta años," *Hispania: Revista española de historia*, 50, 4 (no. 176) (1990), pp. 1091-1104.

3293. Lobo Cabrera, Manuel. "El trabajo esclavo en las islas atlanticas" (Unpublished paper, Colloque

[14] Includes the Balearic Islands, the Canaries, and Madeira and the Azores; see Brazil (Section IV), Caribbean (Section V.3) and Africa - Portuguese (Section VI.3) for Iberian colonization in the Atlantic beyond Madeira.

International de Recherches sur l'Esclavage Antique [GIREA]. Colloque [19ème] sur "Captifs et prisonniers de guerre dans leurs rapports avec l'esclavage", 2-5 October, 1991, Palma, Mallorca).

3294. López Molina, Manuel. "Cartas de horro y libertad de esclavos en Martos: 1610-1630," in *Comunicaciones Presentadas al XI Congreso de Profesores-Investigadores* (Palos de la Frontera, 21-24 September 1992) (Granada: Asociación de Profesores de Geografia e Historia de Bachillerato de Andalucia "Hespérides", 1994), pp. 145-55.

3295. *López Molina, Manuel. "La esclavitud en Martos en la segunda mitad del siglo XVI," *Comunicaciones presentadas al IX Congreso de Profesores Investigadores*, pp. 191-201.

3296. López-Nadal, G. "Corsarismo y esclavitud en el Mediterraneo occidental (ss. XVI-XVII)" (Unpublished paper, Groupe International de Recherches sur l'Esclavage Antique [GIREA]. Colloque [19ème] sur "Captifs et prisonniers de guerre dans leurs rapports avec l'esclavage", 2-5 October, 1991, Palma, Mallorca).

3297. Marcos Martin, Alberto. *De esclavos a señores: estudios de historia moderna*. Valladolid: Universidad de Valladolid, Secretariato de Publicaciones, 1992.

3298. *Marcos Martín, Alberto. "La esclavitud en la ciudad de La Laguna durante la segunda mitad del siglo XVI a travès de los registros parroquiales," *Investigaciones históricas*, 2 (1980), pp. 7-35.

3299. Martín Corrales, E. "La esclavitud en la Cataluña del siglo XVIII" (Unpublished paper, Colloque International de Recherches sur l'Esclavage Antique [GIREA]. Colloque [19ème] sur "Captifs et prisonniers de guerre dans leurs rapports avec l'esclavage", 2-5 October, 1991, Palma, Mallorca).

3300. Meyerson, Mark D. "Slavery and the Social Order: Mudejars and Christians in the Kingdom of Valencia," *Medieval Encounters: Jewish, Christian and Muslim Culture in Confluence and Dialogue*, 1, 1 (1995), pp. 144-73.

3301. Meyerson, Mark D. "Slavery and Solidarity: Mudejars and Foreign Muslim Captives in the Kingdom of Valencia," *Medieval Encounters: Jewish, Christian and Muslim Culture in Confluence and Dialogue*, 2, 3 (1995), pp. 286-343.

3302. Montaner Alonso, Pre de. "Amos y esclavos en la Mallorca moderna" (Unpublished paper, Colloque International de Recherches sur l'Esclavage Antique [GIREA]. Colloque [19ème] sur "Captifs et prisonniers de guerre dans leurs rapports avec l'esclavage", 2-5 October, 1991, Palma, Mallorca).

3303. Penafiel Ramón, Antonio. *Amos y esclavos en la Murcia del setecientos*. Murcia: Real Academia Alfonso X el Sabio, 1992.

3304. Pimental, Maria do Rosário. *Viagem ao fundo das consciências: a escravatura na época moderna*. Lisbon: Ediçoes Colibri, 1995.

3305. Sanchez de Madariaga, Elena. "From Brother to Slave: Religious 'Esclavitudes' in Seventeenth-Century Madrid" (Unpublished paper, Sixteenth-Century Studies Conference, 9-12 December 1993, St. Louis).

3306. Saunders, Alastair de C. M. "The Legacy of Black Slavery in Renaissance Portugal," *Camões Center Quarterly*, 4, 1-2 (1992), pp. 14-19.

3307. Stella, Alessandro. "L'esclavage en Andalousie à l'époque moderne," *Annales: Économies, Sociétés, Civilisations*, 47, 1 (1992), pp. 35-63.

3308. Stella, Alessandro. "'Herrado en el rostro con una S y un clavo': l'homme-animal dans l'Espagne des XVe-XVIIIe siècles," in Bresc, ed., *Figures de l'esclave*, pp. 147-63.

3309. Stevens-Arroyo, Anthony M. "The Inter-Atlantic Paradigm: The Failure of Spanish Medieval Colonization of the Canary and Caribbean Islands," *Comparative Studies in Society and History*, 35, 3 (1993), pp. 515-43.

3310. Vieira, Alberto. "Canaviais e escravos na Madeira" (Presentation at "Seminário internacional: Escravos com e sem açucar", Madeira, 17-21 June 1996).

3311. Vila Vilar, Enriqueta. "Los estudios sobra la esclavitud africana en España en el último medio siglo: su significación en las revistas: 'Hispania' y 'Revista de Índias'," *Revista de Índias*, 49 (n° 187) (1989), pp. 657-81. Special issue: "Cincuenta años de historiografia americanista en España".

3312. Vincent, Bernard. "L'esclavage en milieu rural espagnol au XVIIe siècle: l'example de la région d'Alméria," in Bresc, ed., *Figures de l'esclave*, pp. 165-76.

3313. Vincke, Johannes. "Königtum und Sklaverei im aragonischen Staatenbund während des 14. Jahrhunderts," *Gesammelte Aufsätze zur Kulturgeschichte Spaniens*, 25 (1970), pp. 19-112.

5. France

3314. Bart, Jean. "Esclavage et servage tardif," in Dorigny, ed., *Les abolitions de l'esclavage*, pp. 27-29.

3315. Bathélemy, Dominique. "Qu'est-ce que le servage, en France, au XIe siècle," *Revue historique*, 582 (1992), pp. 233-84.

3316. *Kincl, Jaromír. *Studie o otrouch, kolonech a propustenuch ve vizigotskem state 5.-8. stoleh*. Praha: Universita Karlova, 1968. (Summary in French) (Acta Universitatis Carolinae, série Juridica, Monographia 8)

3317. Koufinkana, Marcel. "Esclaves et esclavage dans la France d'Ancien Régime (1600-1794): nombre, provenance, conditions et statuts. représentation dans la société, vie quotidienne" (Thèse de doctorat en histoire, Toulouse II, 1989).

3318. *Koufinkana, Marcel. "Les esclaves noirs en France et la Révolution (1700-1794)," *Les idéaux de la Révolution française chez les Maghrébins: Horizons maghrébins* (Toulouse), 18-19 (1992), pp. 144-61.

3319. Le Bail, Louis. "L'Amérique et la Basse-Loire au XVIIIe siècle," *Généalogie et histoire de la Caraïbe*, 76 (1995), p. 1467.

3320. Peabody, Sue. "'There are No Slaves in France': Law, Culture, and Society in Early Modern France, 1685-1789" (PhD diss., University of Iowa, 1993).

3321. Peabody, Sue. "Race, Slavery, and French Law: The Legal Context of the 'Police des Noirs'" (Unpublished paper, American Historical Association, Washington DC, 27-30 Dec. 1992).

3322. Peabody, Sue. *There Are No Slaves in France: The Political Culture of Race and Slavery in Eighteenth-Century France*. New York: Oxford University Press, 1996.

3323. Samson, Ross. "Slavery: The Roman Legacy," in John Drinkwater and Hugh Elton, eds., *Fifth-century Gaul: A Crisis of Identity?* (Cambridge: Cambridge University Press, 1992), pp. 218-27.

3324. *Tanneau, J. "Révolution féodale et réorganisation sociale: Le Nivernais de l'esclavage au servage Xe-XIIIe siècles," (??), pp. 109-343.

3325. *Villard, Madeleine. "Esclavage et bagne," *Bulletin de l'Académie du Var* (Toulon), 160 (1992), pp. 67-79.

3326. Weinberger, St. "The Reordering of Society in Medieval Provence," *Revue belge de philologie et d'histoire*, 70, 4 (1992), pp. 907-20.

6. England[15]

3327. Brady, Niall. "Labor and Agriculture in Early Medieval Ireland: Evidence from the Sources," in Frantzen and Moffat, eds., The Work of Work, pp. 125-45.

3328. Cotter, William R. "The Somerset Case and the Abolition of Slavery in England," *History*, 79 (n° 255) (1994), pp. 31-56.

3329. Frantzen, Allen J. "The Work of Work: Servitude, Slavery, and Labor in Medieval England," in Frantzen and Moffat, eds., *The Work of Work*, pp. 1-15.

3330. Frantzen, Allen J., and Douglas Moffat, eds. *The Work of Work: Servitude, Slavery, and Labor in Medieval England*. Glasgow: Cruithne Press, 1994.

For contents see Brady, Frantzen, Girsch, Karras, Moffat, and Samson.

3331. *Fusujima, Masayoshi. "A Reexamination of Slavery in Anglo-Saxon Society," *Josai Journal of Economics*, 25, 2 (1993), pp. 1-137, and 25, 3 (1993), pp. 1-105.

---

[15] Including Anglo-Saxon, Norman, eighteenth/nineteenth-century England, and Ireland.

3332. Girsch, Elizabeth Stevens. "Metaphorical Usage, Sexual Exploitation, and Divergence in the Old English Terminology for Male and Female Slaves," in Frantzen and Moffat, eds., *The Work of Work*, pp. 30-54.

3333. Karras, Ruth Mazo. "Desire, Descendants, and Dominance: Slavery, the Exchange of Women, and Masculine Power," in Frantzen and Moffat, eds., *The Work of Work*, pp. 16-29.

3334. Moffat, Douglas. "Sin, Conquest, Servitude: English Self-Image in the Chronicles of the Early Fourteenth Century," in Frantzen and Moffat, eds., *The Work of Work*, pp. 146-68.

3335. Morris, Thomas D. "'Villeinage ... as it Existed in England Reflects but Little Light on our Subject'".

Reprinted in Finkelman, ed., *Race, Law and American History*, vol. 2 (*Race and Law Before Emancipation*), pp. 331-73.

3336. Myers, Norma. *Reconstructing the Black past: Blacks in Britain, c. 1780-1830*. Portland OR: F. Cass, 1996. (Studies in Slave and Post-Slave Societies and Culture)

3337. Myers, Norma. "Servant, Sailor, Soldier, Tailor, Beggarman: Black Survival in White Society 1780-1830," *Immigrants & Minorities*, 12, 1 (1993), pp. 47-74.

3338. Pelteret, David Anthony Edgell. *Slavery in Early Mediaeval England: From the Reign of Alfred until the Twelfth Century*. Woodbridge, Suffolk, and Rochester NY: Boydell Press, 1995. (Studies in Anglo-Saxon History, 8)

3339. Samson, Ross. "The End of Early Medieval Slavery," in Frantzen and Moffat, eds., *The Work of Work*, pp. 95-124.

3340. Scammell, Jean. "The Formation of the English Social Structure: Freedom, Knights, and Gentry, 1066-1300," *Speculum*, 68, 3 (1993), pp. 591-618.

3341. Shyllon, Folarin. "Blacks in Britain: A Historical and Analytical Overview," in Harris, ed., *Global Dimensions of the African Diaspora* (2nd ed.), pp. 223-48.

3342. Strickland, Matthew. "Slaughter, Slavery or Ransom: The Impact of the Conquest on Conduct in Warfare," in Carola Hicks, ed., *England in the Eleventh Century* (Proceedings of the 1990 Harlaxton Symposium) (Stamford: Paul Watkins, 1992), pp. 41-59. (Harlaxton Medieval Studies, II)

3343. Walvin, James. "Black People in Britain," in Tibbles, ed., *Transatlantic Slavery*, pp. 82-86.

3344. Walvin, James. "Freedom and Slavery in the Shaping of Victorian Britain" (Unpublished paper, conference on "Unfree Labor in the Development of the Atlantic World", 13-14 April 1993, York University, Ontario).

3345. Walvin, James. "In Black and White: Recent Publications on British Black Writings (review essay: Edwards and Dabydeen, eds., *Black Writers in Britain*; Fyfe, ed., *Our Children Free and Happy*; and McCalman, *Horrors of Slavery*)," *Slavery and Abolition*, 16, 2 (1995), pp. 376-82.

7. Eastern Europe and Russia

3346. Hammer, Carl I. "The Handmaid's Tale: Morganatic Relationships in Early-Medieval Bavaria," *Continuity and Change*, 10, 3 (1995), pp. 345-68.

3347. Hammer, Carl I. "Servile Names and Seigneurial Organization in Early-Medieval Bavaria," *Studi Medievali*, 3rd serie, 36, 2 (1995), pp. 917-28.

3348. Hammer, Carl T. "A Slave Marriage Ceremony from Early Medieval Germany: A Note and a Document in Translation," *Slavery and Abolition*, 16, 2 (1995), pp. 243-49.

8. Scandinavia

3349. Iversen, Tore. "Trelldommen: Norwegian Slavery in the Middle Ages" (Unpublished summary of paper, Conference on "Serfdom and Slavery", University of Manchester, 5-7 Sept. 1994).

9. Other

X. OTHER

1. Asia - General and Comparative

3350. Harris, Joseph E. "Africans in Asian History," in Harris, ed., *Global Dimensions of the African Diaspora* (2nd ed.), pp. 325-36.

2. East Asia

3351. Ikemoto, Kozo. *Kindai sekai ni okeru rodo to iju: riron to rekishi no taiwa*. Kyoto-shi: Aunsha, 1992.

3352. Palais, James B. "Slavery: The Slow Path to Abolition," in idem, *Confucian Statecraft and Korean Institutions* (Seattle: University of Washington Press, 1996), pp. 208-70.

3353. Sinn, Elizabeth. "Chinese Patriarchy and the Protection of Women in 19th-Century Hong Kong," in Jaschok and Miers, eds., *Women and Chinese Patriarchy*, pp. 141-70.

3354. *Tong, Enzheng. "The Ancient Slave Societies in Southeast China," *Tianfu Xinlun*, 5 (??), pp. 1-3.

3. Southeast Asia

3355. Bowie, Katherine A. "Slavery in Nineteenth-Century Northern Thailand: Archival Anecdotes and Village Voices," in E. Paul Durrenberger, ed., *State Power and Culture in Thailand* (New Haven: Yale University Southeast Asia Studies, 1996), pp. 100-38.

3356. Feeny, David. "The Demise of Corvée and Slavery in Thailand, 1782-1913," in Klein, ed., *Breaking the Chains*, pp. 83-111.

3357. Knaap, Gerrit. "Slavery and the Dutch in Southeast Asia," in Oostindie, ed., *Fifty Years Later*, pp. 193-206.

3358. Reid, Anthony. "The Decline of Slavery in Nineteenth-Century Indonesia," in Klein, ed., *Breaking the Chains*, pp. 64-82.

3359. Thomaz, Luís Filipe F. R. "A escravatura em Malaca no século XVI," *Studia*, no. 53 (1994), pp. 253-316.

4. Non-Muslim India[16]

3360. Chatterjee, Indrani. "Slavery in the Nizamut of Murshidabad, 1800-1890" (Unpublished paper, n.d. [1995]).

3361. Chauhan, R. R. S. *Africans in India: From Slavery to Royalty*. New Delhi: Asian Publication Services, 1995.

3362. Ghosh, Amitav. "The Slave of ms. H.6," in Partha Chatterjee and Gyanendra Pandey, eds., *Subaltern Studies VII: Writings on South Asian History and Society* (New York: Oxford University Press, 1993), pp. 159-220.

3363. Joshi, Varsha. *Polygamy and Purdah: Women and Society among Rajputs*. Jaipur: Rawat Publications, 1995.

3364. Kumar, Dharma. "Colonialism, Bondage, and Caste in British India," in Klein, ed., *Breaking the Chains*, pp. 112-30.

3365. Negi, Jaideep. *The Begar & Beth System in Himachal Pradesh: A Study of Erstwhile Shimla Hill States*. New Delhi: Reliance Pub. House, 1995.

3366. *Parpola, A. "The Coming of the Aryans to Iran and India and the Cultural and Ethnic Identity of the Dasas," *Studia Orientalia*, 64 (1988), pp. 195-302.

3367. Pescatello, Ann M. "The African Presence in Portuguese India".

Reprinted in Manning, ed., *Slave Trades, 1500-1800*, pp. 143-65.

3368. Pinto, Jeanette. *Slavery in Portuguese India, 1510-1842*. Bombay: Himalaya Publishing House, 1992.

3369. Pouchepadass, Jacques. "La main d'œuvre rurale non-libre dans l'Inde orientale après l'abolition de l'esclavage" (Presentation at Colloquium on "Les dépendances serviles", Paris 1996).

---

[16] Includes Portuguese India (Goa) but excludes Muslim slavery in India except when approached regionally, rather than in terms of Islamic institutions; see Section VII.9 "Muslim Asia".

3370. Prakash, Gyan. *Bonded Histories: Genealogies of Labor Servitude in Colonial India*. Cambridge: Cambridge University Press, 1989.

3371. Prakash, Gyan. "Terms of Servitude: The Colonial Discourse on Slavery and Bondage in India," in Klein, ed., *Breaking the Chains*, pp. 131-49.

3372. Silk, Jonathan A. "A Bibliography on Ancient Indian Slavery," *Studien zur Indologie und Iranistik*, 16-17 (1992), pp. 277-85.

3373. Vijaya, T. P. "Aspects of Slavery in Coorg in the Nineteenth Century," *Indica*, 29, 2 (no. 55) (1992), pp. 107-22.

5. Oceania

3374. Duffield, Ian. "'Set My People Free?': The Relocation to NEW of VDL Convicts from Britain's Slave Colonies" (Unpublished paper, "Ball and Chain" conference, University of New South Wales and British Australian Studies Association, 4-6 December 1996).

3375. Finn, Jeremy. "Offering to Sell Person as a Slave - Definition of Slave - Expert Evidence - Admissibility of Expert Opinion Evidence as to Defendant's Competence in English (New Zealand)," *Criminal Law Journal*, 17, 2 (1993), pp. 117-20.

3376. Munro, Doug. "Degrees of Unfreedom: The Indenture Experience in the Pacific Islands" (Unpublished paper, "Ball and Chain" conference, University of New South Wales and British Australian Studies Association, 4-6 December 1996).

3377. Salman, Michael. "The United States and the End of Slavery in the Philippines, 1898-1914: A Study of Imperialism, Ideology and Nationalism" (2 vols.) (PhD diss., Stanford University, 1993).

3378. Schwalbenberg, Henry M. "The Economics of Pre-Hispanic Visayan Slave Raiding," *Philippine Studies*, 42, 3 (1994), pp. 376-84.

3379. Scott, William Henry. *Slavery in the Spanish Philippines*. Manila, Philippines: De la Salle University Press, 1991.

6. Amerindian[17]

3380. Abel, Annie Heloise. *Slaveholding Indians*. 3 vols. Cleveland: Arthur H. Clark. 1915-25.

Reprinted New York: Scholarly Press, 1972; including Vol. 1: "The American Indian as Slaveholder and Secessionist".

Vols. 1-2 reprinted Lincoln: University of Nebraska Press, 1992.

3381. Baker, Julie Philips. "Black Slavery Among the American Indians," *AB Bookman's Weekly*, 89, 7 (1992), pp. 613-14, 616-18.

3382. Bartl, Renate. "Die Beziehungen zwischen Schwarzen und Indianern in Nordamerika" (MA thesis, Department of American Cultural History, Universität zu Munich, 1986).

3383. Bartl, Renate. "Native American Tribes and Their African Slaves," in Palmié, ed., *Slave Cultures and the Cultures of Slavery*, pp. 162-75.

3384. Dobyns, Henry F., Paul H. Ezell, Alden W. Jones, and Greta S. Ezell. "What were Nixoras?" *Southwestern Journal of Anthropology*, 16, 2 (1960), pp. 230-58.

3385. *Griffin, Larry D. "Black Slaves in the Cherokee Nation" (Unpublished manuscript, Cherokee Nation Collection, John Vaughan Library, Northeastern State College, Tahlequah, OK).

3386. Martin, Joel W. "Southeastern Indians and the English Trade in Skins and Slaves," in Charles Hudson and Carmen Chaves Tesser, eds., *The Forgotten Centuries: Indians and Europeans in the American South, 1521-1704* (Athens GA: University of Georgia Press, 1994), pp. 304-24.

3387. McLoughlin, William G. "Red Indians, Black Slavery and White Racism: America's Slaveholding Indians," *American Quarterly*, 26, 4 (1974), pp. 367-85.

3388. *Montané, Julio. "De nijoras y 'españoles a medias'," *Memoria del XV Simposio de Historia y Antropología de Sonora* (Hermosillo, 1991) (Place: Pub, date?),. vol. 1, pp. 105-24.

---

[17] Pre-contact forms of slavery and "Indian captivities" of Europeans, as well as relations with enslaved Africans, throughout the Americas.

3389. Neilson, John C. "Indian Masters, Black Slaves: An Oral History of the Civil War in Indian Territory," *Panhandle-Plains Historical Review*, 65 (1992), pp. 42-54.

3390. Porter, Kenneth Wiggins. "Florida Slaves and Free Negroes in the Seminole War, 1835-1842," *Journal of Negro History*, 28, 4 (1943), pp. 390-421.

3391. Porter, Kenneth Wiggins. "Negroes and Indians on the Texas Frontier," *Journal of Negro History*, 41, 3 (1956), pp. 185-214; 41, 3 (1956), pp. 285-310.

3392. Porter, Kenneth Wiggins. "Negroes and the Seminole War, 1817-1818," *Journal of Negro History*, 36, 3 (1951), pp. 249-80.

3393. Porter, Kenneth Wiggins. "Negroes and the Seminole War, 1824-1842," *Journal of Southern History*, 30, 4 (1964), pp. 427-50.

3394. Porter, Kenneth Wiggins. "Negroes on the Southern Frontier, 1670-1763," *Journal of Negro History*, 33, 1 (1946), pp. 53-78.

3395. Porter, Kenneth Wiggins. "Notes Supplementary to Relations Between Negroes and Indians within the Present Limits of the United States," *Journal of Negro History*, 18, 3 (1933), pp. 282-321.

3396. Porter, Kenneth Wiggins. "Three Fighters for Freedom," *Journal of Negro History*, 28, 1 (1943), pp. 51-72.

3397. Ruby, Robert H., and John A. Brown. *Indian Slavery in the Pacific Northwest*. Spokane: A. H. Clark, 1993.

3398. Sekora, John. "Red, White, and Black: Indian Captivities, Colonial Printers, and the Early African-American Narrative," in Frank Shuffelton, ed., *A Mixed Race: Ethnicity in Early America* (New York: Oxford University Press, 1993), pp. 92-104.

3399. Shadow, Robert D., and Maria Rodríguez-Shadow. "Aztec Slavery: A Historical Panorama of Anthropological Perspectives," in Zoller, ed., *Amerikaner wider Willen*, pp. 321-48.

3400. "Slavery," in Frederick Webb Hodge, *Handbook of American Indians North of Mexico* (Washington DC: U.S. Government Printing Office, 1907-10), vol. 2, pp. 597-600. Reprinted 1975.

3401. Socolow, Susan Migden. "Spanish Captives in Indian Societies: Cultural Contact Along the Argentine Frontier, 1600-1835," *Hispanic American Historical Review*, 72, 1 (1992), pp. 73-99.

3402. Sweet, David. *A Rich Realm of Nature Made Poor: The Peoples of the Amazon Heartland and Transfrontier Colonialism, 1540-1755*. Forthcoming.

3403. Tallant, Harold D. "Slavery," in *American Indians* (consulting ed. Harvey Markowitz) (Pasadena: Salem Press, 1995), vol. 3, pp. 727-29.

3404. Thomson, Norman. *El libro rojo del Putumayo: precedido de una introducción sobre el verdadero escandalo de las atrocidades del Putumayo*. Santa Fe de Bogotá: Planeta, 1995. Prologo de Roberto Pineda Camacho. (1a ed. de Planeta Colombiana; Series "Lista negra") Original English ed. published by and attributed to Norman Thomson.

3405. Usner, Daniel H. "Indian-Black Relations in Colonial and Antebellum Louisiana," in Palmié, ed., *Slave Cultures and the Cultures of Slavery*, pp. 145-61.

7. Indian Ocean (Mascarene Islands, etc.)

3406. Barker, Anthony J. "Distorting the Record of Slavery and Abolition: The British Anti-Slavery Movement and Mauritius, 1826-37," *Slavery and Abolition*, 14, 3 (1993), pp. 185-207.

3407. Barker, Anthony J. *Slavery and Anti-Slavery in Mauritius, 1810-33: The Conflict between Economic Expansion and Humanitarian Reform under British Rule*. New York: St. Martin's Press, 1996.

3408. *Brouwer, C. G. "Die Madagaskar 'Connection': holländische Beiträge zur Erforschung der jeminitischen Sklavengeschichte," *Orientations*, 1 (1993), pp. 54-86.

3409. Carter, Marina. "The Transition from Slave to Indentured Labour in Mauritius," in Twaddle, ed., *The Wages of Slavery*, pp. 114-30.

3410. Fuma, Sudel. *L'esclavagisme à la Réunion, 1794-1848*. Paris and St. Dénis, Réunion: l'Harmattan, 1992.

3411. Gerbeau, Hubert. "L'esclavage des 'races intelligentes' aux Mascareignes" (Presentation at Colloquium on "Les dépendances serviles", Paris 1996).

3412. Gerbeau, Hubert. "Histoire oubliée, histoire occultée: la diaspora malgache à la Réunion: entre esclavage et liberté" (Unpublished paper, "Fanandevozana ou esclavage" [Colloque international, 1996]).

3413. Ho Hai Quang. "L'esclavage à l'Île Bourbon de 1664 à 1714," in *Fanandevozana ou esclavage*, pp. 39-65.

3414. Ly-Tio-Fane Pineo, Huguette. "Les esclaves 'de plantation' de l'Île Maurice à la veille de l'abolition, d'après le recensement de 1823," in Colette Dubois, Hubert Gerbeau, Yvan G. Paillard, and Pierre Soumille, eds., *Histoires d'outre-mer: mélanges en l'honneur de Jean-Louis Miège* (Aix-en-Provence: Université de Provence, 1992), vol. 2, pp. 635-55. (Offerts par l'Institute d'Histoire des Pays d'Outre-Mer)

3415. Nagapen, Amédée. "Le Catholicisme des esclaves à l'Île Maurice".

Also published as "*Le Catholicisme des esclaves à l'Île Maurice*". Port-Louis: Diocèse de Port-Louis, 1989.

3416. Noël, Karl. *L'esclavage à l'Île de France: Île Maurice de 1715 à 1810*. Paris: Editions Two Cities, 1991.

3417. Payet, J. V. *Histoire de l'esclavage à l'Île Bourbon*. Paris: Harmattan, 1990.

3418. *al-Tamimi, 'Abd al-Malik Khalaf. "Baritanya wa-Tajarat al-Raqiq fi Mintaqat al-Khalij al-'Arabi, 1820-1898 [??]," *Al-Majalla al-Tarikhiyya al-'Arabiyya li-l-Dirasat al-'Uthmaniyya* (Arab Historical Review for Ottoman Studies), 1-2 (1990), pp. 73-91.

3419. Teelock, Vijaya. *A Select Guide to Sources on Slavery in Mauritius* and *Slaves Speak Out: The Testimony of Slaves in the Era of Sugar*. Bell Village, Mauritius: African Cultural Centre, 1995.

3420. Wanquet, Claude. "Le tentative de Baco et Burnel d'application de l'abolition aux Mascareignes en 1796: analyse d'un échec et de ses conséquences," in Dorigny, ed., *Les abolitions de l'esclavage*, pp. 231-40.

8. Modern

3421. Ali, Miriam. *Without Mercy: A Woman's Struggle Against Modern Slavery*. London: Little, Brown, 1995.

3422. Anderson, Bridget. *Britain's Secret Slaves: An Investigation into the Plight of Overseas Domestic Workers*. London: Anti-Slavery International, 1993. With contributions from Anti-Slavery International and Kalayan and the Migrant Domestic Workers, no. 5 Human Rights Series.

3423. Asia Watch Committee. *A Modern Form of Slavery: Trafficking of Burmese Women and Girls into Brothels in Thailand*. New York: Human Rights Watch, 1993.

3424. Australian Council for Overseas Aid. Burma Human Rights Project. *Slave Labor in Burma: An Examination of the SLORC's Forced Labour Policies*. Australian Council for Overseas Aid, 1996.

3425. "Ball and Chain" (Conference, University of New South Wales and British Australian Studies Association, 4-6 December 1996).

3426. Booth, David. "Comfort Women" (Unpublished paper, University of Hawaii, 1995).

3427. [Calica, Dan, and Sancho Nelia, eds.] *War Crimes on Asian Women: Military Sexual Slavery by Japan During World War II: The Case of the Filipino Comfort Women*. Manila: Task Force on Filipina Victims of Military Slavery by Japan, Asian Women Human Rights Council, 1993.

3428. Clarkson, Wensley. *Slave Girls*. New York: St. Martin's Paperbacks, 1996.

3429. Fierce, Milfred C. *Slavery Revisited: Blacks and the Southern Convict Lease System, 1865-1933*. Brooklyn: Africana Studies Research Center, Brooklyn College, 1994.

3430. Gregory, Joseph R. "African Slavery 1996," *First Things: A Monthly Journal of Religion and Public Life*, no. 63 (May 1996), pp. 37-39.

3431. Harding, Christopher. "Under Western Eyes: Contemporary Problems in the Removal of Conditions of Slavery and Servitude," *Cambrian Law Review*, 14 (1983), pp. 48-62.

3432. Heagney, Brenda. *The Long Days of Slavery: Fellows and Members of the RACP Who Were Prisoners-of-War in South East Asia: An Exhibition*. Sydney: Royal Australasian College of Physicians, 1996.

3433. Hicks, George L. *The Comfort Women: Sex Slaves of the Japanese Imperial Forces*. London: Souvenir Press, 1995.

American edition: *The Comfort Women: Japan's Brutal Regime of Enforced Prostitution in the Second World War*. New York: Norton, 1995

3434. Holland, Alison. "Feminism, Colonialism and Aboriginal Workers: An Anti-Slavery Crusade," *Labour History* (Sydney: Australian Society for the Study of Labour History), 69 (1995), pp. 52-64.

3435. Howard, Keith. *True Stories of the Korean Comfort Women: Testimonies Compiled by the Korean Council for Women Drafted for Military Sexual Slavery by Japan and the Research Association on the Women Drafted for Military Sexual Slavery by Japan*. London: Cassell, 1995.

3436. Iokoi, Zilda Márcia Gricoli. "Trabalho escravo no Brasil atual," *Revista de história* (São Paulo), no. 120 (1989), pp. 109-20.

3437. Jaschok, Maria. "Chinese 'Slave' Girls in Yunnan-Fu: Saving (Chinese) Womanhood and (Western) Souls, 1930-1991," in Jaschok and Miers, eds., *Women and Chinese Patriarchy*, pp. 171-97.

3438. Jaschok, Maria, and Suzanne Miers, eds. *Women and Chinese Patriarchy: Submission, Servitude, and Escape*. Hong Kong: Hong Kong University Press, 1994.

For contents see Jaschok, Miers, and Sinn.

3439. Karay, Felicja. *Ha-Mavet be-Tsahov: Mahaneh ha-Avodah Skarz'isko Kamyenah*. Yerushalayim and Tel Aviv: Yad va-shem; Universitat Tel Aviv, 1994. (Pirsume ha-Makhon le-Heker ha-Tefutsot; sefer 95).

Title on added title page: *Death Comes in Yellow, Skarzysko-Kamienna Slave Labor Camp*.

3440. Karim, Farhad. *Contemporary Forms of Slavery in Pakistan*. New York: Human Rights Watch, 1995.

3441. Katyal, Neal Kumar. "Men Who Own Women: A Thirteenth Amendment Critique of Forced Prostitution," *Yale Law Journal*, 103, 3 (1993), pp. 791-826.

3442. Kazuko, Watanabe. "Militarism, Colonialism, and the Trafficking of Women: 'Comfort Women' Forced into Sexual Labor for Japanese Soldiers," *Bulletin of Concerned Asian Scholars*, 26, 4 (1994), pp. 3-17.

3443. Lichtenstein, Alex. "Good Roads and Chain Gangs in the Progressive South: 'The Negro Convict is a Slave'," *Journal of Southern History*, 59, 1 (1993), pp. 31-62.

3444. Martin, Aurelia, and Bernard Vincent. "Esclavage et domesticité dans l'Espagne moderne" (Presentation at Colloquium on "Les dépendances serviles", Paris 1996).

3445. Matzner, David, and David Margolis. *The Muselmann: The Diary of a Jewish Slave Laborer*. Hoboken NJ: Ktav, 1994.

3446. McDermott, M. Joan, and Sarah J. Blackstone. "White Slavery Plays of the 1910s: Fear of Victimization and the Social Control of Sexuality," *Theatre History Studies*, 16 (1996), pp. 141-56.

3447. McGrath, Ann. "'Modern Stone Age Slavery': Images of Aboriginal Labour and Sexuality," *Labour History* (Sydney: Australian Society for the Study of Labour History), 69 (1995), pp. 30-51.

3448. McGrath, Ann, and Kay Saunders, with Jackie Huggins, eds. "Aboriginal Workers," *Labour History* (Sydney: Australian Society for the Study of Labour History), 69 (1995), special issue.

For contents see Holland and McGrath.

3449. Miers, Suzanne. "Contemporary Forms of Slavery (review essay: [Anti-Slavery International], Sutton, *Slavery in Brazil*; Anderson, *Britain's Secret*

Slaves; Sattaur, *Child Labour in Nepal*; Smith, *Ethnic Groups in Burma*)," *Slavery and Abolition*, 17, 3 (1996), pp. 238-46.

3450. Miers, Suzanne. "Mui Tsai Through the Eyes of the Victim: Janet Lim's Story of Bondage and Escape," in Jaschok and Miers, eds., *Women and Chinese Patriarchy*, pp. 108-21.

3451. *Muwakkil, Salim. "Slavery in the Sudan," *In These Times*, 20, 11 (1996), pp. 22-[?].

3452. Perbi, Akosua. "The Legacy of Indigenous Slavery in Contemporary Ghana," *FASS Bulletin* (Faculty of Social Studies, University of Ghana - Legon), 1, 1 (1996), pp. 83-92.

3453. Posel, Sherab. "Kamaiya: Bonded Labor in Western Nepal," *Columbia Human Rights Law Review*, 27, 1 (1995), pp. 123-75.

3454. [Rone, Jemera.] *Children in Sudan: Slaves, Street Children and Child Soldiers*. London: Human Rights Watch/Africa and Human Rights Watch Children's Rights Project, 1995.

3455. Rose, R. S. "Slavery in Brazil: Does it Still Exist?" *Review of Latin American Studies*, 4, 1 (1991), pp. 96-113.

3456. Sattaur, Omar. *Child Labour in Nepal*. London: Anti-Slavery International, 1993. (A report by Anti-Slavery International and Child Workers in Nepal Concerned Centre, no. 5, Child Labour Series).

3457. Shelley, Lore, ed. *The Union Kommando in Auschwitz: The Auschwitz Munition Factory Through the Eyes of its Former Slave Laborers*. Lanham MD: University Press of America, 1996. (Studies in the Shoah, v. 13)

3458. *"Slave Nation [Burma]," *New Internationalist*, no. 280 (June 1996), pp. 12-[?].

3459. Smith, Martin. *Ethnic Groups in Burma: Development, Democracy and Human Rights*. London: Anti-Slavery International, 1994. (A report by Anti-Slavery International, no. 8 Human Rights Series.)

3460. Spiegel, Marjorie. *The Dreaded Comparison: Human and Animal Slavery*. (Rev. and expanded ed.) New York: Mirror Books, 1996.

3461. Sutton, Alison. *Slavery in Brazil: A Link in the Chain of Modernization: The Case of Amazonia*. London: Anti-Slavery International, 1994. (A report by Anti-Slavery International, no. 7, Human Rights Series.)

3462. Tessier, Kevin. "The New Slave Trade: The International Crisis of Immigrant Smuggling," *Indiana Journal of Global Legal Studies*, 3, 1 (1995), pp. 261-65. (Indiana Journal of Global Legal Studies Immigration Project, Kevin Tessier)

3463. "'That was Slavery Days': Aboriginal Domestic Servants in the Twentieth Century," *Labour History* (Sydney: Australian Society for the Study of Labour History), 69 (1995), pp. 196-209.

3464. Thomas, Laurence Mordekhai. *Vessels of Evil: American Slavery and the Holocaust*. (Philadelphia: Temple University Press, 1993).

Also as 6 sound cassettes (New York: Jewish Braille Institute of America, 1995).

3465. Torres, Dominique. *Esclaves: 200 millions d'esclaves aujourd'hui*. Paris: Phébus, 1996.

3466. United States. Congress. House. Committee on International Relations. Subcommittee on International Operations and Human Rights. "Slavery in Mauritania and Sudan: Joint Hearing before the Subcommittees on International Operations and Human Rights and Africa of the Committee on International Relations, House of Representatives, One Hundred Fourth Congress, second session, March 13, 1996" (Washington: U.S. G.P.O., 1996).

3467. Washington Coalition for Comfort Women Issues. *Comfort Women's Testimony of Military Sexual Slavery by Japan*. Washington DC: The Coalition, 1995.

3468. Waterford, Van. *Prisoners of the Japanese in World War II: Statistical History, Personal Narratives, and Memorials Concerning POWs in Camps and on Hellships, Civilian Internees, Asian Slave Laborers, and Others Captured in the Pacific Theater*. Jefferson, N.C.: McFarland, 1994.

3469. Weiss, Theodore. *"Personal Memoirs of the Holocaust": From Slavery to Freedom*. [S.l.]: TEDO, 1994. (Written in 1945 in Hungarian, translated to English in 1993)

3470. Williams, Rhonda. "The Contemporary International Slave Traffic in Women and Children: A Comparison of Institutional Responses with Feminist Responses" (MA thesis, Carleton University, 1991).

3471. Yoon, Youngik. "International Sexual Slavery," *Touro International Law Review*, 6 (1995), pp. 417-36.

9. Other

3472. Murray, Stephen O. "Czaplicka's Interpretation of Kamchadal Slavery and of Siberian Transformed Shamans as a Third Gender," in idem, ed., *Oceanic Homosexualities* (New York: Garland, 1992), pp. 329-40.

XI. SLAVE TRADE

1. Atlantic - General

3473. *Adeqoye, Omoniyi. "The United States Naval Squadrons and the Suppression of Slave Trade in West Africa, 1820-1862" (MA thesis, Columbia University, 1966).

3474. "African Slave Migration," in Simon Collier, Harold Blakemore, and Thomas E. Skidmore, eds., *Cambridge Encyclopedia of Latin America and the Caribbean* (Cambridge: Cambridge University Press, 1991), pp. 138-42.

3475. "The Atlantic Slave Trade: A Demographic Simulation". ("Migration in World History", Northeastern University, Annenberg/CPB Project; dir. Patrick Manning).

http://www.afr.neu.edu/simulation/afrintro.html

3476. Benot, Yves. "De la traite négrière au sous-développement" (Unpublished paper, UNESCO conference on "La route de l'esclave", Ouidah, Bénin, 1-5 Sept. 1994).

3477. Binder, Wolfgang. "Uses of Memory: The Middle Passage in African American Literature," in Binder, ed., *Slavery in the Americas*, pp. 539-64.

3478. Bradley, Michael. *Chosen People from the Caucasus: Jewish Origins, Delusions, Deceptions and Historical Role in the Slave Trade, Genocide & Cultural Colonization*. Foreword by John H. Clarke. New York: Third World Press, 1993.

3479. Bruner, Edward M. "Tourism in Ghana: the Representation of Slavery and the Return of the Black Diaspora," *American Anthropologist*, 98, 2 (1996), pp. 290-304.

3480. Burton, Ann M. "British Evangelicals, Economic Warfare and the Abolition of the Atlantic Slave Trade, 1795-1810," *Anglican and Episcopal History*, 65, 2 (1996), pp. 197-225.

3481. Clarence-Smith, W[illiam] Gervase. "The Dynamics of the African Slave Trade (review essay: Miller, *Way of Death*; Law, *Slave Coast of West Africa*; Thornton, *Africa and Africans in the Making of the Atlantic World*; Savage, ed., *Human Commodity*; Solow, ed., *Slavery and the Rise of the Atlantic System*; Inikori and Engerman, eds., *Atlantic Slave Trade*; Manning, *Slavery and African Life*; Wright, *Strategies of Slaves and Women*; and Meillassoux, *Anthropology of Slavery*)," *Africa*, 64, 2 (1994), pp. 275-86.

3482. Cowley, Malcolm, and Daniel P. Mannix. "The Middle Passage".

Reprinted (from *The Middle Passage*) in Northrup, ed., *The Atlantic Slave Trade*, pp. 99-112.

3483. Cummins, Light Townsend. "Keeping Score: Winners and Losers in the Transatlantic Slave Trade (review essay: Inikori and Engerman, eds. *Atlantic Slave Trade*)," *Reviews in American History*, 21, 3 (1993), pp. 379-84.

3484. Curtin, Philip D. "From Guesses to Calculations".

Reprinted (from *The Atlantic Slave Trade*) in Northrup, ed., *The Atlantic Slave Trade*, pp. 39-50.

3485. Curtin, Philip D. "The Slavery Hypothesis for Hypertension among African-Americans: The Historical Evidence," *American Journal of Public Health*, 82 (1992), pp. 1681-86.

3486. Curtin, Philip D. "The Tropical Atlantic in the Age of the Slave Trade," in Michael Adas, ed., *Islamic and European Expansion: The Forging of a Global Order* (Philadelphia: Temple University Press, 1993), pp. 165-98.

3487. D'Anjou, Leo. *Social Movements and Cultural Change: The First Abolition Campaign Revisited.* New York: Aldine de Gruyter, 1996.

3488. Daget, Serge. "Les croisières françaises de répression de la traite des Noirs sur les côtes occidentales de l'Afrique (1817-1850)," *Enquêtes et documents* (Nantes: Centre de Recherches sur l'Histoire du Monde Atlantique), vol. 14 (1988), pp. 23-35.

3489. Daget, Serge. "Droit de visite, Droits de l'Homme et traite des Noirs," in Coquery-Vidrovitch, ed., *Esclavage, colonisation, libérations nationales de 1789 à nos jours*, pp. 195-202.

3490. Daget, Serge. "Le prix de la traite des Noirs: des siècles de trafic, des millions de morts et d'esclaves: des épreuves et des gains difficiles à mesurer," *Les anneaux de la mémoire* (Exhibition catalogue, Nantes, 1992), pp. 151-53.

3491. Davis, David Brion. "The Slave Trade and the Jews," *New York Review of Books*, 41, 21 (22 Dec. 1994), pp. 14-16.

3492. Deveau, Jean-Michel. *Pour une pédagogie de l'histoire de la traite négrière.* La Rochelle: Centre Départemental de Documentation Pédagogique de la Charante-Maritime, 1994.

3493. Deveau, Jean-Michel. "Towards the Pedagogy of the History of the Slave-Trade" (Unpublished paper, UNESCO conference on "La route de l'esclave", Ouidah, Bénin, 1-5 Sept. 1994).

3494. Drescher, Seymour. "The Atlantic Slave Trade and the Holocaust: A Comparative Analysis," in Alan S. Rosenbaum, ed., *Is the Holocaust Unique?* (Boulder: Westview Press, 1996), pp. 65-85.

3495. Drescher, Seymour. "The Role of Jews in the Trans-atlantic Slave Trade," *Immigrants & Minorities*, 12, 2 (1993), pp. 113-25.

3496. Eltis, David. "Cuba, Brazil and the Atlantic Slave System," in Richard J. Salvucci, ed., *Latin America and the World Economy: Dependency and Beyond* (Lexington MA: D.C. Heath, 1996), pp. 52-59.

3497. Eltis, David, and Stanley L. Engerman. "Fluctuations in Sex and Age Ratios in the Transatlantic Slave Trade, 1664-1864," *Journal of Economic History*, 46, 2 (1993), pp. 308-23.

3498. Eltis, David, and Stanley L. Engerman. "Was the Slave Trade Dominated by Men?" *Journal of Interdisciplinary History*, 23, 2 (1992), pp. 237-57.

3499. *Eltis, David, and David Richardson. "The Structure of the Transatlantic Slave Trade, 1595-1867" (Unpublished paper, Social Science History Association, Chicago 1995).

3500. Eltis, David, David Richardson, and Stephen Behrendt. "The Structure of the Transatlantic Slave Trade: Some Preliminary Indications of African Origins of Slaves Arriving in the Americas" (Unpublished paper, Colloquium for African-American Research, Feb. 1995, Tenerife, Canary Islands).

3501. Eltis, David, Stephen D. Behrendt, Herbert S. Klein, David Richardson, and Barbara Solow. "The Transatlantic Slave Trade: A Database" (in preparation, W. E. B. Dubois Institute for Afro-American Research, Harvard University, 1993-).

3502. Emmer, Pieter C. "Afrikanischer Sklavenhandel und Sklaverei im Atlantischen Gebiet, 1500-1900," in Corinna Raddatz, ed., *Afrika in Amerika* (Hamburg: Hamburgisches Museum für Völkerkunde, 1992), pp. 63-79.

3503. Feelings, Tom. *The Middle Passage.* New York: Dial Press, 1995.

3504. *Fenoaltea, Stefano. *The Atlantic Slave Trade: An Economic Analysis.* Princeton: Princeton University Press, forthcoming.

3505. Füllberg-Stolberg, Claus. "Der transatlantische Sklavenhandel: Zahlen und Kakten der Herkunft der farbigen Unterschichten Amerikas," *Journal für Geschichte*, 1, 3 (1979), pp. 21-25.

3506. Geggus, David P. "Sex Ratio, Age and Ethnicity in the Atlantic Slave Trade: Data from French Shipping and Plantation Records".

Reprinted in Manning, ed., *Slave Trades, 1500-1800*, pp. 257-78.

3507. Glausser, Wayne. "Three Approaches to Locke and the Slave Trade," *Journal of the History of Ideas*, 51, 2 (1990), pp. 199-216.

3508. Goldfarb, Stephen J. "An Inquiry into the Politics of the Prohibition of the International Slave Trade," in Whitten, ed., "Eli Whitney's Cotton Gin," pp. 20-34.

3509. Guéront. "Submarine Archaeology and the History of the Slave Trade" (Unpublished paper, UNESCO conference on "La route de l'esclave", Ouidah, Bénin, 1-5 Sept. 1994).

3510. Gwyn, Julian. "The Economics of the Transatlantic Slave Trade: A Review (of Eltis, *Economic Growth and the Ending of the Transatlantic Slave Trade*)," *Histoire sociale/Social History*, 25, 1 (no. 49) (1992), pp. 151-62.

3511. Henige, David P. "A Skeptical View of How Much Can Be Known".

Reprinted (from "Measuring the Immeasurable") in Northrup, ed., *The Atlantic Slave Trade*, pp. 60-64.

3512. Hertzog, Keith P. "Naval Operations in West Africa and the Disruption of the Slave Trade during the American Revolution," *American Neptune*, 55, 1 (1995), pp. 42-48.

3513. Heywood, Linda. "The African Diaspora," in *A Slave Ship Speaks*, pp. 24-39.

3514. Hopkins, A. G. "The 'New International Economic Order' in the Nineteenth Century: Britain's First Development Plan for Africa," in Law, ed., *From Slave Trade to "Legitimate" Commerce*, pp. 240-64.

3515. Inikori, Joseph E. "Africa in World History: The Export Slave Trade from Africa and the Emergence of the Atlantic Economic Order," in B. A. Ogot, ed., *General History of Africa, Vol. 5: Africa from the Sixteenth to the Eighteenth Century* (Berkeley/Paris/London: University of California Press/UNESCO/Heinemann, 1992), pp. 74-112.

3516. Inikori, Joseph E. "Export versus Domestic Demand: The Determinants of Sex Ratios in the Transatlantic Slave Trade," *Research in Economic History*, 14 (1992), pp. 117-66.

3517. Inikori, Joseph E. "The Unmeasured Hazards of the Atlantic Slave Trade: Sources, Causes, and Historiographical Implications" (Unpublished paper, UNESCO conference on "La route de l'esclave", Ouidah, Bénin, 1-5 Sept. 1994).

3518. Inikori, Joseph E., and Stanley L. Engerman. "A Skeptical View of Curtin's and Lovejoy's Calculations".

Reprinted (from *The Atlantic Slave Trade*) in Northrup, ed., *The Atlantic Slave Trade*, pp. 65-66.

3519. Kaké, Ibrahima Baba. "Popularization of the History of the Slave-Trade" (Unpublished paper, original in French, UNESCO conference on "La route de l'esclave", Ouidah, Bénin, 1-5 Sept. 1994).

3520. Klein, Herbert S. "Profits and the Causes of Mortality".

Reprinted (from "Economic Aspects of the Eighteenth-Century Atlantic Slave Trade") in Northrup, ed., *The Atlantic Slave Trade*, pp. 112-20.

3521. Klein, Herbert S. "Recent Trends in the Study of the Atlantic Slave Trade."

Translated as "Novas interpretações do tráfico de escravos do Atlântico," *Revista de história* (São Paulo), no. 120 (1989), pp. 3-26.

3522. Klein, Martin A. "Simulating the African Slave Trade," *Canadian Journal of African Studies/Revue canadienne des études africaines*, 28, 2 (1994), pp. 296-99.

3523. Kordes, Hagen. "De la traite négrière au triage des immigrants" (Unpublished paper, UNESCO conference on "La route de l'esclave", Ouidah, Bénin, 1-5 Sept. 1994).

3524. Law, Robin C. C. "A Lagoonside Port on the Eighteenth-Century Slave Coast: The Early History of Badagri," *Canadian Journal of African Studies/Revue canadienne des études africaines*, 28, 1 (1994), pp. 32-59.

3525. Law, Robin [C. C.] "The Slave Trade in Seventeenth-Century Allada: A Revision," *African Economic History*, 22 (1994), pp. 59-92.

3526. Law, Robin [C. C.] "The Transition from the Slave Trade to 'Legitimate Commerce'" (Unpublished paper, UNESCO conference on "La route de l'esclave", Ouidah, Bénin, 1-5 Sept. 1994).

3527. Littlefield, Daniel C., Greg Robinson, and Petra E. Lewis. "Slave Trade," in Jack Salzman, David Lionel Smith, and Cornel West, eds., *Encyclopedia of African-American Culture and History* (New York: Macmillan Library Reference, 1996), vol. 5, pp. 2471-86.

3528. Lokossou, Clément. "Les monuments de la traite: traite négrière et tourisme culturel" (Unpublished paper, UNESCO conference on "La route de l'esclave", Ouidah, Bénin, 1-5 Sept. 1994).

3529. Loth, Heinrich. "The Slave Trade Between Dahomey and the 'Congo Free State' in the Period of the Expansion and Stabilization of Colonial Rule as Reported in German Sources," in Thea Büttner, ed., *African Studies/Afrika-Studien* (Dedicated to the IVth International Congress of Africanists in Kinshasa) (Berlin: Akademie-Verlag, 1978), pp. 221-34.

3530. Lovejoy, Paul E. "Curtin's Calculations Refined but Not Refuted".

Reprinted (from "The Volume of the Atlantic Slave Trade") in Northrup, ed., *The Atlantic Slave Trade*, pp. 50-59.

3531. Lovejoy, Paul E. "The Volume of the Atlantic Slave Trade: A Synthesis".

Reprinted in Manning, ed., *Slave Trades, 1500-1800*, pp. 37-64.

3532. Manning, Patrick. "Introduction," in Manning, ed. *Slave Trades, 1500-1800*, pp. xv-xxiv.

3533. Manning, Patrick, ed. *Slave Trades, 1500-1800: Globalization of Forced Labor*. Brookfield VT: Variorum, 1996.

For contents see Alencastro, Austen, Bush, Deyle, Drescher, Filliot, Geggus, Jennings, Lovejoy, Manning (2), Miller, Monteiro, Pescatello, Rathbone, Richardson, Ricks, and Thornton.

3534. Miller, Joseph C. "Deaths Before the Middle Passage".

Reprinted (from *Way of Death*) in Northrup, ed., *The Atlantic Slave Trade*, pp. 120-32.

3535. Miller, Joseph C. "The Slave Trade," in *Encyclopedia of Latin American History* (Barbara Tenenbaum, ed.) (5 vols.) (New York: Charles Scribner's Sons, 1995), vol. 4, pp. 122-27.

3536. Morgan, Philip D. "African Migration," in *Encyclopedia of American Social History*, vol. 2, pp. 795-809.

3537. Northrup, David, ed. *The Atlantic Slave Trade*. Lexington MA: D. C. Heath, 1994. (Problems in World History series)

For contents see Cowley and Mannix, Craton, Curtin, Davis, Eltis, Henige, Inikori and Engerman, Jordan, Klein, Lovejoy, Manning, Miller, Rodney, Temperley, and Williams (2).

3538. Nwachuku, Levi A. "The European Slave Trade: An Overview," in Sudarkasa, Nwachuku, Millette, and Thomas, eds., *The African-American Experience*, pp. 25-42.

3539. Nwauwa, Apollos O. "The British Abolition of the Slave Trade: A Reappraisal of the Humanitarian and Economic Controversy," *Africa Quarterly* (New Delhi), 31 (3-4) (1991-92), pp. 45-59.

3540. Palmer, Colin. "African Slave Trade: The Cruelest Commerce," *National Geographic*, 182, 3 (1992), pp. 62-91.

3541. Palmer, Colin. "The Atlantic Slave Trade and Its Abolition in Hemispheric Perspective," in Tyson and Highfield, eds., *Danish West Indian Slave Trade*, pp. 1-10.

3542. Pardue, Jeffrey David. "The Imperialism of Suppressing the Slave Trade: Captain Owen and the British in Fernando Po" (MA thesis, University of Waterloo [Canada], 1993).

3543. Pedersen, Carl. "Middle Passages: Representations of the Slave Trade in Caribbean and African-American Literature," *Massachusetts Review*, 34, 2 (1993), pp. 225-38.

3544. Price, Jacob M. "Transaction Costs: A Note on Merchant Credit and the Organization of Private Trade," in James D. Tracy, ed., *The Political Economy of Merchant Empires* (New York: Cambridge University Press, 1991), pp. 276-79.

3545. Quénum, Alphonse. "L'église catholique et la traite négrière atlantique au XIXe siècle," in Gerbeau and Saugera, eds., *La dernière traite*, pp. 191-211.

3546. Quénum, Alphonse. *Les églises chrétiennes et la traite atlantique du XVe au XIXe siècle*. Paris: Karthala, 1993.

3547. Quénum, Alphonse. "Les églises chrétiennes et la traite négrière atlantique du XVème au XIXème siècle" (Unpublished paper, UNESCO conference on "La route de l'esclave", Ouidah, Bénin, 1-5 Sept. 1994).

3548. Reikat, Andrea. "Textile Imports into West Africa in the Slave Trade" (Unpublished paper presented at conference on "Source Material for Studying the Slave Trade and the African Diaspora", Stirling, Scotland, 13-14 April 1996).

3549. Reynolds, Edward. "Human Cargoes: Enslavement and the Middle Passage," in Tibbles, ed., *Transatlantic Slavery*, pp. 29-34.

3550. Richardson, David. "The Rise of Atlantic Empires," in Tibbles, ed., *Transatlantic Slavery*, pp. 13-14.

3551. Richardson, David. "The Transatlantic Slave Trade 1595-1867: Evidence from the Harvard Database" (Unpublished paper presented at conference on "Source Material for Studying the Slave Trade and the African Diaspora", Stirling, Scotland, 13-14 April 1996).

3552. Richardson, David, and David Eltis. "Productivity in the Transatlantic Slave Trade," *Explorations in Economic History*, 32, 4 (1995), pp. 465-84.

3553. *Richardson, David, David Eltis, and Stephen Behrendt. "The Structure of the Transatlantic Slave Trade 1595-1867," in H. L. Gates, Jr., C. Pedersen, and M. Diedrich, eds., *Transatlantic Passages* (forthcoming).

3554. *Richardson, David, and Paul E. Lovejoy. "The Yoruba Factor in the Export Slave Trade from the Bight of Benin, 1750-1870" (forthcoming).

3555. Scott, Julius. "Slavery and Freedom at Work: British Sailors and Opposition to the Slave Trade in the 1780s and 1790s" (Presentation at Colloquium on "Les dépendances serviles", Paris 1996).

3556. Sen, Indrani. "Eighteenth-Century Prices of Slaves on the Gold Coast" (Unpublished paper presented at conference on "Source Material for Studying the Slave Trade and the African Diaspora", Stirling, Scotland, 13-14 April 1996).

3557. Sorrenson-Gilmore, Caroline. "European Written Sources During the Abolitionist Era in Coastal West Africa: The Case of Badagry" (Unpublished paper presented at conference on "Source Material for Studying the Slave Trade and the African Diaspora", Stirling, Scotland, 13-14 April 1996).

3558. Soumonni, Elisée. "The Compatibility of the Slave and Palm Oil Trades in Dahomey, 1818-1858," in Law, ed., *From Slave Trade to "Legitimate" Commerce*, pp. 78-92.

3559. Soumonni, Elisée. "The Neglected Local Sources for Studying the Slave Trade in Dahomey" (Unpublished paper presented at conference on "Source Material for Studying the Slave Trade and the African Diaspora", Stirling, Scotland, 13-14 April 1996).

3560. *The Slave Trade, 1858-92*. (British Foreign Office: File 541, Confidential Print Series) (microfilm, 10 rolls) Wilmington DE: Scholarly Resources, n.d.

3561. Thornton, John K. "The African Background to American Colonization," in Stanley L. Engerman and Robert E. Gallman, eds., *Cambridge Economic History of the United States* (New York: Cambridge University Press, 1996), vol. 1, pp. 53-94.

3562. Uya, Okon Edet. "The Middle Passage and Personality Change Among Diaspora Africans," in Harris, ed., Global Dimensions of the African Diaspora (2nd ed.), pp. 83-97.

3563. Yarak, Larry. "Dutch Military Recruitment in Asante and the Gold Coast, 1831-72" (Unpublished paper presented at conference on "Source Material for Studying the Slave Trade and the African Diaspora", Stirling, Scotland, 13-14 April 1996).

2. Atlantic - Individual Voyages and Captains

3564. Alsop, J. D. "The Career of William Towerson, Guinea Trader," *International Journal of Maritime History*, 4, 2 (!992), pp. 45-82.

3565. *The Amistad Incident: Four Perspectives*. Middletown CT: Published under a grant to Middlesex Community College by the Connecticut Humanities Council, 1992.

3566. Appleby, John C. "'A Business of Much Difficulty': A London Slaving Venture 1651-1654," *Mariner's Mirror*, 81, 1 (1995), pp. 3-14.

3567. Appleby, John C. "A Guinea Venture, *c*. 1657: A Note on the Early English Slave Trade," *Mariner's Mirror*, 79, 1 (1993), pp. 84-87.

3568. Behrendt, Stephen D. "The Journal of an African Slaver, 1789-1792, and the Gold Coast Slave Trade of William Collow," *History in Africa*, 22 (1995), pp. 61-71.

3569. Benoît, Norbert. "La dernière traite de Jean Vincent Morice" (Unpublished paper, UNESCO conference on "La route de l'esclave", Ouidah, Bénin, 1-5 Sept. 1994).

3570. Delcourt, André. "Le voyage négrier de la *Favorite* (10 mai 1743 - 2 juin 1744)," *Enquêtes et documents* (Nantes: Centre de recherche sur l'histoire du monde atlantique), 17 (1990), pp. 5-19.

3571. Jennings, Judith. "Joseph Woods, 'Merchant and Philosopher': The Making of the British Anti-Slave Trade Ethic," *Slavery and Abolition*, 14, 3 (1993), pp. 162-84.

3572. Meyer, Jean. "Un portrait d'armateur: Guillaume Grou," *Les anneaux de la mémoire* (Exhibition catalogue, Nantes, 1992), p. 54.

3573. Mosneron, Joseph. *Moi, Joseph Mosneron: armateur négrier nantais (1748-1833): portrait culturel d'une bourgeoisie négociante au siècle des Lumières*. (Ed. Olivier Petre-Grenouilleau,) Rennes: Editions Apogée, 1995. (Collection Moi.)

3574. Passot, Eric. "Le capitaine Landolphe: de la traite à la course," *Revue historique des Armées*, n° 4 (1994), pp. 98-104.

3575. Saugera, Éric. "De Sidoine à Sophie Raphel, ou les lettres d'un capitaine négrier à sa femme pendant la traite illégale, 1824-1831," in Gerbeau and Saugera, eds., *La dernière traite*, pp. 119-50.

3576. Saugera, Éric. "Une expédition négrière nantaise sous la Restauration: les comptes du *Cultivateur*, 1814-1818," *Enquêtes et documents* (Nantes: Centre de recherche sur l'histoire du monde atlantique), 16 (1989), pp. 5-55.

3577. Saugera, Éric. "Un exemple de traite à la Côte d'Afrique," *Les anneaux de la mémoire* (Exhibition catalogue, Nantes, 1992), pp. 28-29.

3578. Saugera, Éric. "Le 'portefeuille' du Capitaine Jalaber," *Les anneaux de la mémoire* (Exhibition catalogue, Nantes, 1992), p. 24.

3579. Saugera, Éric. "Le prise d'un négrier anglais par la *Belle Poule*," *Les anneaux de la mémoire* (Exhibition catalogue, Nantes, 1992), p. 25.

3580. Schwarz, Suzanne. *Slave Captain: the Career of James Irving in the Liverpool Slave Trade*. Wrexham: Bridge Books, 1995.

3581. Svaleson, Leif. "The Slave Ship *Fredensborg*: History, Shipwreck, and Find," *History in Africa*, 22 (1995), pp. 455-58.

3582. Thornton, John K. "African Background of the Slave Cargo of the Henrietta Maria" (Unpublished, 1993).

3583. Watt, Sir James. "James Ramsay, 1733-1789: Naval Surgeon, Naval Chaplain and Morning Star of the Anti-Slavery Movement," *Mariner's Mirror*, 81, 2 (1995), pp. 156-70.

3584. Wisnes, Selena Axelrod, ed. *Letters on West Africa and the Slave Trade: Paul Erdmann Isert's Journey to Guinea and the Caribbean Islands in Columbia (1788)*. Oxford: Oxford University Press, 1991. (Fontes Historiae Africanae, Series Varia VII)

3585. Zahedieh, Nuala. "The Capture of the Blue Dove, 1664: Policy, Profits and Protection in Early English Jamaica," in McDonald, ed., *West Indies Accounts*, pp. 29-47.

3. Atlantic - Portuguese and Brazilian

3586. Aparício, Alexandra, and Rosa Cruz e Silva. "O fundo documental sobre o tráfico de escravos e escravatura no Arquivo Histórico Nacional," *Fontes e estudos (Revista do Arquivo Histórico Nacional)* (Luanda, Angola), 3 (1996), pp. 141-46.

3587. Böttcher, Nikolaus. *Aufstieg und Fall eines atlantischen Handelsimperiums: portugiesische Kaufleute und Sklavenhändler in Cartagena de Indias von 1580 bis zur Mitte des 17. Jahrhunderts*. Frankfurt: Vervürt Verlag, 1995.

3588. Caldeira, José de Ribamar C. (Review essay: Conrad, *Tumbeiros*), *Revista de história* (São Paulo), no. 119 (1985-88), pp. 239-42.

3589. *Carvalho, Platão Eugênio de. "Na origem do tráfico de escravos para o Brasil: a captura em

Angola, 1482-1589" (Dissertação - Mestrado, Universidade de São Paulo, 1989).

3590. Castro Henriques, Isabel. "A rota dos escravos: Angola e a rede do comércio negreiro," in Medina and Castro Henriques, eds., *A rota dos escravos*, pp. 81-203.

3591. Conrad, Robert C. "Slave Trade: Abolition of, Brazil," in *Encyclopedia of Latin American History* (Barbara Tenenbaum, ed.) (New York: Charles Scribner's Sons, 1995), pp. 127-28.

3592. Cruz e Silva, Rosa da. "Rotas do tráfico: do corredor do Kwanza ao sertão de Benguela," in Medina and Castro Henriques, eds., *A rota dos escravos*, pp. 221-28.

3593. Curto, José C. "Alcohol and Slaves: The Luso-Brazilian Alcohol Commerce at Mpinda, Luanda, and Benguela during the Atlantic Slave Trade, c. 1480-1830 and Its Impact on the Societies of West Central Africa" (PhD diss., University of California - Los Angeles, 1996).

3594. Curto, José C. "The Legal Portuguese Slave Trade from Benguela, Angola, 1730-1828: A Quantitative Reappraisal," *África* (São Paulo), 16-17, 1 (1993-94), pp. 101-16.

3595. Curto, José C. "A Quantitative Reassessment of the Legal Portuguese Slave Trade from Luanda, Angola, 1710-1830," *African Economic History*, 20 (1992), pp. 1-25.

3596. *Curto, José C., and Raymond Gervaise. "The Population of Luanda under the Weight of the Trans-Atlantic Slave Trade, 1781-1845" (1994, forthcoming)

3597. Elbl, Ivana. "Sex and Age in the Early Portuguese Slave Trade in West Africa, 1450-1521" (Unpublished paper, Annual Meeting of the Canadian Association of African Studies/Association Canadienne des Études Africaines, Toronto, May 1991).

3598. Ferreira, Roquinaldo Amaral. "Dos sertões ao Atlântico: tráfico ilegal de escravos e comércio lícito em Angola, 1830-1860" (Dissertação de Mestrado, Universidade Federal do Rio de Janeiro - Instituto de Filosofia e Ciências Sociais, Programa de Pós-Graduação em História Social, n.d. [1996]).

3599. Ferreira, Roquinaldo A[maral]. "Padrões de investimentos durante o tráfico ilegal de escravos em Angola (1830-1860)," *Fontes e estudos (Revista do Arquivo Histórico Nacional)* (Luanda, Angola), 3 (1996), pp. 189-227.

3600. Ferreira, Roquinaldo Amaral, ed. "Documento: o relatório Alcoforado," *Estudos afro-asiáticos*, 28 (1995), pp. 219-29.

3601. Florentino, Manolo Garcia. *Em costas negras: uma história do tráfico Atlântico de escravos entre a África e o Rio de Janeiro (séculos XVIII e XIX)*. Rio de Janeiro: Arquivo Nacional, 1995.

3602. *Fontes e estudos (Revista do Arquivo Histórico Nacional)* (Luanda, Angola), 3 (1996).

Special issue on the slave trade in Angola: includes documents from Benguela, 1796-99, and the Luso-Britannic Mixed Commission, 1844-45; for contents also see Aparício and Silva, Ferreira, and Miller.

3603. Fragoso, João Luís Ribeiro. *Homens de grossa aventura: acumulação e hierarquia na praça mercantil do Rio de Janeiro (1790-1830)*. Rio de Janeiro: Arquivo Nacional, 1992.

3604. Graden, Dale T. "An Act 'Even of Public Security': Slave Resistance, Social Tensions and the End of the International Slave Trade to Brazil, 1835-1856," *Hispanic American Historical Review*, 76, 2 (1996), pp. 249-82.

Translated as "'Uma lei ... até de segurança pública': resistência escrava, tensões sociais e o fim do tráfico internacional de escravos para o Brasil (1835-1856)," *Estudos afro-asiáticos*, 30 (1996), pp. 113-49.

3605. Gutiérrez, Horácio. "O tráfico de crianças escravas para o Brasil durante o século XVIII," *Revista de história* (São Paulo), no. 120 (1989), pp. 59-73.

3606. Hall, Trevor Paul. "The Role of Cape Verde Islanders in Organizing and Operating Maritime Trade Between West Africa and Iberian Territories, 1441-1616" (PhD diss., Johns Hopkins University, 1993).

3607. Heintze, Beatrix. "'Stücke' Handel in Angola: zur Sklaverei in den ersten hundert Jahren portugiesischer Okkupation".

Reprinted in Heintze, *Studien zur Geschichte Angolas im 16. und 17. Jahrhundert: ein Lesebuch* (Köln: Rüdiger Köppe Verlag, 1996), pp. 212-31.

3608. Klein, Herbert S. "Angola Slave Trade in the Eighteenth Century, 1723-1771" (Data-set, Data and Program Library Service, University of Wisconsin - Madison).

3609. Klein, Herbert S. "Slave Trade to Rio de Janeiro, 1795-1811" (Data-set, Data and Program Library Service, University of Wisconsin - Madison).

3610. Klein, Herbert S. "Slave Trade to Rio de Janeiro, 1825-1830" (Data-set, Data and Program Library Service, University of Wisconsin - Madison).

3611. Klein, Herbert S. "Tráfico de escravos," in *Estatísticas históricas do Brasil* (Rio de Janeiro: IBGE, 1987), vol. 3 (Estatísticas retrospectivas), pp. 51-59.

3612. Marques, João Pedro. "A abolição do tráfico de escravos na imprensa portuguesa (1810-1840)," *Revista internacional de estudos africanos*, 16-17 (1992-94), pp. 7-30.

3613. Medina, João, and Isabel Castro Henriques, eds. *A rota dos escravos: Angola e a rede do comércio negreiro*. Lisbon: Cegia, 1996.

For contents see Arruda, Caley, Castro Henriques, Cruz e Silva, and Medina.

3614. Miller, Joseph C. "A Marginal Institution on the Margin of the Atlantic System".

Reprinted in Manning, ed., *Slave Trades, 1500-1800*, pp. 214-44.

Translated as "O tráfico português de escravos no Atlântico sul no século dezoito: uma instituição marginal nas margens do sistema atlântico," in *Fontes e estudos (Revista do Arquivo Histórico Nacional)* (Luanda, Angola), 3 (1996), pp. 147-88.

3615. Rocha, Aurélio. "Contribuição para o estudo das relações entre Moçambique e o Brasil no século XIX (Tráfico de escravos e relações políticas e culturais)," *Estudos afro-asiáticos*, 21 (1991), pp. 199-233.

Also in *Studia* (Lisbon), 51 (1992), pp. 61-118.

3616. *Rodrigues, Jaime. "O infame comércio: propostas e experiências no final do tráfico de Africanos para o Brasil (1800-1850)" (Dissertação de Mestrado, UNICAMP, 1994).

3617. Rodrigues, Jaime. "Os traficantes de africanos e seu 'infame comércio' (1827-1860)," *Revista Brasileira de História*, 15 (no. 29) (1995), pp. 139-55.

3618. Santos, Corcino Medeiros dos. *O Rio de Janeiro e a conjuntura atlântica*. Rio de Janeiro: Expressão e Cultura, 1993.

3619. Santos, Maria Emília Madeira. "Abolição do tráfico de escravos e reconversão da economia de Angola: um confronto participado por 'brasileiros'," *Studia*, no. 52 (1994), pp. 221-44.

3620. Tavares, Luís Henrique Dias. *Comércio proibido de escravos*. São Paulo: Editora Ática, 1988.

4. Atlantic - Spanish

3621. Anglarill, Nilda Beatriz. "La route de l'esclave vers le Rio de la Plata: de la traite au dialogue culturel contemporain" (Unpublished paper, UNESCO conference on "La route de l'esclave", Ouidah, Bénin, 1-5 Sept. 1994).

3622. Eltis, David. "Slave Trade, Abolition of: Spanish America," in *Encyclopedia of Latin American History* (Barbara Tenenbaum, ed.) (New York: Charles Scribner's Sons, 1995), pp. 128-29.

3623. Fuente García, Alejandro de la. "El mercado esclavista habanero, 1580-1699: las armazones de esclavos," *Revista de Índias*, 50 (no. 189) (1990), pp. 371-95.

3624. García Fuentes, Lutgardo. "La introducción de esclavos en Indias desde Sevilla en el siglo XVI," in *Andalucía y América en el siglo XVI* (Actas de las II Jornadas de Andalucía y América - Universidad de Santa María de la Rábida, March 1982) (Seville: Escuela de Estudios Hispano-Americanos de Sevilla, 1993), vol. 1, pp. 249-74. (Publicaciones, no. 292)

3625. Klein, Herbert S. "Slave Trade to Havana, Cuba, 1790-1820" (Data-set, Data and Program Library Service, University of Wisconsin - Madison).

3626. López y Sebastián, Lorenzo E., and Justo L. del Río Moreno. "Comercio y transporte en la economia del azucar antillano durante el siglo XVI," *Anuario de estudios americanos*, 49 (1992), pp. 55-87.

3627. Mazzeo de Novó, Cristina Ana. "Esclavitud y acumulación mercantil: el tráfico negrero en el contexto de las reformas borbónicas," *Historica* (Lima), 17 (1993), pp. 149-78.

3628. Mira Caballos, Esteban. "Las licencias de esclavos negros a Hispanoamérica (1544-1550)," *Revista de Indias*, nº 201 (1994), pp. 273-99.

3629. Pérez Vega, Ivette. "Las grandes introducciones y ventas de esclavos en Ponce 1816-1830," in *[Primer] Congreso internacional de historia economica y social de la cuenca del Caribe 1763-1898* (Centro de Estudios Avanzados de Puerto Rico y el Caribe, San Juan de Puerto Rico, 1992), pp. 61-76.

3630. Torres Ramírez, Bibiano. "La trata negrera en Hispanoamérica durante los años de la Independencia norteamericana," in *Hispanoamérica hacia 1776* (Actas de la "Mesa Redonda sobre la América Hispana en 1776") (Madrid: Instituto "Gonzalo Fernández de Oviedo", Instituto de Cooperación Iberoamericana, 1980), pp. 25-30.

3631. Vila Vilar, Enriqueta. "Aspectos marítimos del comercio de esclavos con Hispanoamérica en el siglo XVIII," *Revista de historia naval*, 5, 19 (1987), pp. 113-31.

3632. Vila Vilar, Enriqueta. "La trata libre de esclavos en el Caribe: reconducción de un compilado comercio," in *[Primer] Congreso internacional de historia economica y social de la cuenca del Caribe 1763-1898* (Centro de Estudios Avanzados de Puerto Rico y el Caribe, San Juan de Puerto Rico, 1992), pp. 1-26.

5. Atlantic - British

3633. Behrendt, Stephen D. "British Merchants and the Marketing of Slaves in the Americas" (Unpublished paper, 1996).

3634. Behrendt, Stephen D. "The British Slave Trade, 1785-1807: Volume, Profitability, and Mortality" (PhD diss., University of Wisconsin - Madison, 1993).

3635. Burhard, Trevor. "Who Bought Slaves in Early America? Purchasers of Slaves from the Royal African Company in Jamaica, 1674-1704," *Slavery and Abolition*, 17, 2 (1996), pp. 68-92.

3636. Carlos, Ann M., and Jamie Brown Kruse. "The Decline of the Royal African Company: Fringe Firms and the Role of the Charter," *Economic History Review*, 49, 2 (1996), pp. 291-313.

3637. Carrington, Selwyn H. H. "The United States and the British West Indian Trade 1783-1807," in McDonald, ed., *West Indies Accounts*, pp. 149-68.

3638. Curtin, Philip D., and Herbert S. Klein. "Slave Ship Records of Nineteenth-Century England" (Data-set, Data and Program Library Service, University of Wisconsin - Madison; also Economic and Social Research Council Data Archive, University of Essex).

3639. Doom, Peter K., J. Thomas Lindblad, and L. Jeroen Touwen. "The Marion Johnson Data on African Trade," in Johnson, *Anglo-African Trade*, pp. 13-35.

3640. Drescher, Seymour. "Whose Abolition? Popular Pressure and the Ending of the British Slave Trade," *Past and Present*, no. 143 (1994), pp. 136-66.

3641. Drescher, Seymour. "The Slaving Capital of the World: Liverpool and National Opinion in the Age of Abolition".

Reprinted in Manning, ed., *Slave Trades, 1500-1800*, pp. 334-50.

3642. Elder, Melinda. *The Slave Trade and the Economic Development of Eighteenth-Century Lancaster*. Keele: Ryburn, 1992.

3643. Eltis, David. "British Slave Voyages from the 1640s through the 1730s" (Data-set, unpublished).

3644. Eltis, David. "The British Transatlantic Slave Trade before 1714: Annual Estimates of Volume and Direction," in Engerman and Paquette, eds., *The Lesser Antilles in the Age of European Expansion*, pp. 182-205.

3645. Farias, Paulo de Moraes, and Margaret Peil. "Marion Johnson: An Historian Turns to Computers," in Johnson, *Anglo-African Trade*, pp. 1-3.

3646. Fogel, Robert W. "The Relationship of the Abolition of the Slave Trade to Parliamentary Reform and the Repeal of Religious Restriction," in Fogel, Galantine, and Manning, eds., *Evidence and Methods (Without Consent or Contract)*, pp. 401-02.

3647. Gragg, Larry. "'To Procure Negroes': The English Slave Trade to Barbados, 1627-60," *Slavery and Abolition*, 16, 1 (1995), pp. 65-84.

3648. Hogendorn, Jan S., and Henry A. Gemery. "'Anglo-African Trade in the Eighteenth Century': The Significance of the Marion Johnson Data Set," in Johnson, *Anglo-African Trade*, pp. 37-51.

3649. Inikori, Joseph E. "Measuring the Unmeasured Hazards of the Atlantic Slave Trade: Documents Relating to the British Trade," *Revue française d'histoire d'outre-mer*, 83, 1 (no. 312) (1996), pp. 53-92.

3650. Inikori, Joseph E. "The Volume of the British Slave Trade, 1655-1807," *Cahiers d'études africaines*, 32, 4 (no. 128) (1992), pp. 643-88.

3651. Johnson, Marion. *Anglo-African Trade in the Eighteenth Century*. (Eds. J. Thomas Lindblad and Robert Ross) Leiden: Centre for the History of European Expansion, 1990. (Intercontinenta No. 15)

For contents see Doorn, Lindblad and Touwen, Farias and Peil, Hogendorn and Gemery, Johnson, and Touwen and Doorn.

3652. Johnson, Marion. "Commodities, Customs, and the Computer," in idem, *Anglo-African Trade*, pp. 5-11.

3653. Klein, Herbert S. "English Slave Trade, 1791-1799 (House of Lords Survey)" (Data-set, Data and Program Library Service, University of Wisconsin - Madison; also Economic and Social Research Council Data Archive, University of Essex).

3654. Klein, Herbert S., and Stanley L. Engerman. "Slave Trade to Jamaica, 1782-1788, 1805-1808" (Data-set, Data and Program Library Service, University of Wisconsin - Madison).

3655. *Law, Robin [C. C]. *The English in West Africa, 1681-99: The Local West African Correspondence of the Royal African Company of England*. 3 vols. Forthcoming. (Fontes Historiae Africanae)

3656. Law, Robin [C. C.]. "The Royal African Company of England in West Africa, 1681-99" (Unpublished paper presented at conference on "Source Material for Studying the Slave Trade and the African Diaspora", Stirling, Scotland, 13-14 April 1996).

3657. Law, Robin C. C. "The Royal African Company of England's West African Correspondence, 1681-1699," *History in Africa*, 20 (1993), pp. 173-84.

3658. Lynn, Martin. "Trade and Politics in 19th-Century Liverpool: The Tobin and Horsfall Families and Liverpool's African Trade," *Transactions of the Historic Society of Lancashire and Cheshire*, 142 (1992), pp. 99-120.

3659. Manning, Richard L. "The Cost of British Slave Trade Suppression," in Fogel, Galantine, and Manning, eds., *Evidence and Methods (Without Consent or Contract)*, pp. 398-401.

3660. Midgley, Clare. *Women against Slavery: The British Campaigns, 1780-1870*. London: Routledge, 1992.

3661. Minchinton, Walter E. "The Seaborne Slave Trade of North Carolina," *North Carolina Historical Review*, 71, 1 (1994), pp. 1-61.

3662. Morgan, Kenneth. "Bristol and the Atlantic Trade in the Eighteenth Century," *English Historical Review*, 107, 4 (1992), pp. 626-50.

3663. Morgan, Kenneth. *Bristol and the Atlantic Trade in the Eighteenth Century*. New York: Cambridge University Press, 1993.

3664. Mouser, Bruce J. "Iles de Los as Bulking Center in the Slave Trade, 1750-1800," *Revue française d'histoire d'outre-mer*, 83, 1 (no. 312) (1996), pp. 77-90.

3665. Oldfield, John R. *Popular Politics and British Anti-Slavery: The Mobilisation of Public Opinion Against the Slave Trade, 1787-1807*. Manchester: Manchester University Press; St. Martin's Press, 1995.

3666. Palmer, Colin. "The Middle Passage," in *A Slave Ship Speaks*, pp. 10-23.

3667. Rawley, James A. "London's Defense of the Slave Trade," *Slavery and Abolition*, 14, 2 (1993), pp. 48-69.

3668. *Richardson, David. "The British Empire and the Atlantic Slave Trade, 1660-1807," in P. J. Marshall, ed., *Oxford History of the British Empire:*

The Eighteenth Century (5 vols.) (Oxford: Oxford University Press, forthcoming 1997-98), vol. 5.

3669. Richardson, David. "Cape Verde, Madeira and Britain's Trade to Africa, 1698-1740," *Journal of Imperial and Commonwealth History*, 22, 1 (1994), pp. 1-15.

3670. Richardson, David. "Liverpool and the English Slave Trade," in Tibbles, ed., *Transatlantic Slavery*, pp. 70-76.

3671. *Richardson, David, ed. *Bristol, Africa and the Slave Trade to America*. Vol. 4: "The Final Years, 1770-1807". Glouchester: Bristol Record Society, forthcoming. (Bristol Record Society Publications, vol. 47)

3672. Richardson, David, K. Beedham, and Maurice M. Schofield, eds. *Liverpool Shipping and Trade 1744-1786: A Computerised Edition of the Liverpool Plantation Registers* (Economic and Social Research Council Data Archive, University of Essex, 1992).

3673. Richardson, David, and Steven Behrendt. "Inikori's Odyssey: Measuring the British Slave Trade, 1655-1807," *Cahiers d'études africaines*, 35, 2-3 (nos. 138-39) (1995), pp. 599-615.

3674. Richardson, David, and E. W. Evans. "Empire and Accumulation in Eighteenth-Century Britain," in Terry Brotherstone and Geoff Pilling, eds., *History, Economic History and the Future of Marxism: Essays in Memory of Tom Kemp (1921-1993)* (London: Porcupine Press, 1996), pp. 79-102.

3675. Richardson, David, and M[aurice] M. Schofield. "Whitehaven and the Eighteenth-Century British Slave Trade," *Transactions of the Cumberland and Westmorland Antiquarian and Archaeological Society*, 92 (November 1992), pp. 183-204.

3676. Shaughnessy, Carol. "The Archaeology of the *Henrietta Marie*: A Conversation with David Moore," in *A Slave Ship Speaks*, pp. 40-52.

3677. *A Slave Ship Speaks: The Wreck of the Henrietta Marie*. Key West FL: Mel Fisher Maritime Heritage Society, 1995.

For contents see Heywood, Palmer, Shaughnessy, and Sykes.

3678. Small, Stephen, and James Walvin. "African Resistance to Enslavement," in Tibbles, ed., *Transatlantic Slavery*, pp. 42-49.

3679. Stammers, M. K. "'Guineamen': Some Technical Aspects of Slave Ships," in Tibbles, ed., *Transatlantic Slavery*, pp. 35-42.

3680. Sykes, Oswald. "Up Close and Personal with the Henrietta Marie," in *A Slave Ship Speaks*, pp. 8-9.

3681. Tibbles, Anthony. "Introduction," to Tibbles, ed., *Transatlantic Slavery*, pp. 13-14.

3682. Tibbles, Anthony. "Oil not Slaves: Liverpool and West Africa after 1807," in Tibbles, ed., *Transatlantic Slavery*, pp. 77-81.

3683. Tibbles, Anthony, ed. *Transatlantic Slavery: Against Human Dignity*. London: HMSO, 1994. (National Museums & Galleries on Merseyside)

For contents see Cummins, King, Kolawole, Manning, Morgan, Reynolds, Richardson (2), Small (2), Small and Walvin, Stammers, Tibbles (2), and Walvin (2).

3684. Touwen, L. Jeroen, and Peter K. Doom, comps. "Statistics on Anglo-African Trade 1699-1808," in Johnson, *Anglo-African Trade*, pp. 53-96.

3685. Walvin, James. "British Abolitionism, 1787-1838," in Tibbles, ed., *Transatlantic Slavery*, pp. 87-95.

3686. Watt, Sir James. "Sea Surgeons and Slave Ships: A Nineteenth Century Exercise in Life-Saving," *Transactions of the Medical Society of London*, 104 (1987-88), pp. 130-48.

3687. Zahedieh, Nuala. "Trade, Plunder, and Economic Development in Early English Jamaica, 1655-89," *Economic History Review*, 39, 2 (1986), pp. 205-22.

6. Atlantic - Dutch

3688. Eijgenraam, M. J. "'Menschlievenheid en eigen belang'; de behandeling van de slaven aan boord van de schepen van de Middelburgsche Commercie Compagnie," in *Archief: vroegere en latere mededelingen voornamelijk in betrekking tot Zeeland* (Middelburg: Zeeuwsch Genootschap der Wetenschappen, 1990), pp. 77-103.

3689. Flinkenflögel, Willem. *Nederlandse slavenhandel (1621-1803).* Utrecht: Kosmos, (1994).

3690. Parmentier, J. "De rederij Radermacher & Steenhart (1730-1741): zeeuwse Guinea-vaart en slavenhandel met Zuidnederlandse participatie," *Tijdschrift voor zeegeschiedenis*, 11, 2 (1993), pp. 137-51.

3691. Schmidt, Benjamin. "'O Fortunate Land!': Karel van Mander, A West Indies Landscape, and the Dutch Discovery of America," *New West Indian Guide - Nieuwe West-Indische Gids*, 69, 1-2 (1994), pp. 5-44.

7. Atlantic - French

3692. "Les Anneaux de la Mémoire": Nantes, Europe, Afrique, Amériques (Exposition: Nantes, Château des Ducs de Bretagne, 5 déc. 1992 - 4 févr. 1994). Rochefort: Centre International de la Mer-Corderie Royale, 1992.

For contents see Benoist, Bienvenu and Lelièvre, Bodinier (3), Bodinier and Saugera, Boudriot, Breteau, Cauna (3), Daget, Debrunfaut, Deveau, Ducoin and Guéront, Ekanza, Fallope, Gonçalves, Hesse, Kodjo, Leray (2), Mabeux, Marchand, Martin, Meyer (2), Quénum, Saugera (4), Souza-Ayari, and Weber.

3693. Benoist, Joseph-Roger de. "Gorée, l'île mémoire," *Les anneaux de la mémoire* (Exhibition catalogue, Nantes, 1992), p. 67.

3694. Bienvenue, Gilles, and Françoise Lelièvre. "L'Hôtel Grou: 2 place de la Petite-Hollande - 32 rue de Kervégan," *Les anneaux de la mémoire* (Exhibition catalogue, Nantes, 1992), p. 55.

3695. Bodinier, Jean-Louis. "Les indiennes," *Les anneaux de la mémoire* (Exhibition catalogue, Nantes, 1992), pp. 56-57.

3696. Bodinier, Jean-Louis. "Nantes: mémoire ou amnésie autour de la traite?" *Les anneaux de la mémoire* (Exhibition catalogue, Nantes, 1992), pp. 134-36.

3697. Bodinier, Jean-Louis. "Pacotille: du sens d'un mot," *Les anneaux de la mémoire* (Exhibition catalogue, Nantes, 1992), p. 68.

3698. Bodinier, Jean-Louis, and Éric Saugera, "Le campagne négrière," *Les anneaux de la mémoire* (Exhibition catalogue, Nantes, 1992), pp. 16-18.

3699. Boudriot, Jean. "Le navire négrier à la fin de l'Ancien Régime," *Les anneaux de la mémoire* (Exhibition catalogue, Nantes, 1992), pp. 19-20.

3700. Curtin, Philip D., and Herbert S. Klein. "Slave Ship Records of Eighteenth-Century France" (Data-set, Data and Program Library Service, University of Wisconsin - Madison).

3701. Daget, Serge. "Dans l'illegalité: la traite négrière française vers Cuba et Porto-Rico, 1817-1831," in Butel, ed., *Commerce et plantation dans la Caraïbe*, pp. 81-98.

3702. Daget, Serge. "A Model of the French Abolitionist Movement and its Variations," in Christine Bolt and Seymour Drescher, eds., *Essays in Memory of Roger T. Anstey* (Folkestone: W. Dawson, 1980), pp. 64-69.

3703. Daget, Serge. "La traite," in *Voyage aux îles d'Amérique* (Exhibition catalogue, Archives Nationales, Paris, 1992), pp. 77-81.

3704. Daget, Serge. *La traite des noirs: bastilles négrières et velléités abolitionnistes.* [Paris]: Ouest-France Université, 1990.

3705. Danet, Jean. *Bleus, blancs, nègres: Nantes 1793, quel génocide?* Préface de Henri Leclerc. Nantes: Le Passeur-CECOFOP, 1991.

3706. Deveau, Jean-Michel. *La France au temps des négriers.* Paris: France-Empire, 1994.

3707. Deveau, Jean-Michel. "Les illusions de la traite négrière rochelaise," *Les anneaux de la mémoire* (Exhibition catalogue, Nantes, 1992), p. 53.

3708. Dubrunfaut, Paul. "*Boucaniers, Long-Dean* et autres *Mousquets*: essai d'une définition du fusil de traite," *Les anneaux de la mémoire* (Exhibition catalogue, Nantes, 1992), p. 26.

3709. *Ducoin, Jacques. "La traite des Noirs et les assurances maritimes," *Neptunia*, n° 195 (1994), pp. 11-18.

3710. Ducoin, Jacques, and Max Guéront. "Les risques maritimes de la traite," *Les anneaux de la mémoire* (Exhibition catalogue, Nantes, 1992), p. 146.

3711. Eltis, David. "Mettas-Daget Catalogue of French Slaving Voyages" (Data-set, unpublished).

3712. Emmer, Pieter C. "Capitalism after Slavery? The French Slave Trade and Slavery in the Atlantic, 1500-1900 (review essay: Daget, *Traite des noirs*, and Fallope, *Esclaves et citoyens*)," *Slavery and Abolition*, 14, 3 (1993), pp. 234-47.

Also in *Itinerario*, 17, 1 (1993), pp. 103-16.

3713. Etienne, Raymonde. "La Révolution, la traite des Noirs et La Rochelle," in Coquery-Vidrovitch, ed., *Esclavage, colonisation, libérations nationales de 1789 à nos jours*, pp. 27-30.

3714. Everaert, John G. "Off the Beaten Track: The Dunkirk Slave Trade 1763-1778," in Binder, ed., *Slavery in the Americas*, pp. 131-40.

3715. Fallope, Josette. "Les racines africaines aux Antilles," *Les anneaux de la mémoire* (Exhibition catalogue, Nantes, 1992), pp. 137-39.

3716. Follez, Christophe. "L'échec de l'expédition du navire *Les Dames Elisabeth et Victoire*: tentative d'explication," in Gerbeau and Saugera, eds., *La dernière traite*, pp. 115-18.

3717. Foté, Harris Memel. "La résistance à la traite dans les comptoirs d'Afrique," in Dorigny, ed. *Les abolitions de l'esclavage*, pp. 73-76.

3718. Gerbeau, Hubert. "De l'esclavage à la liberté: l'énigme de la diffusion des *Trois Jours*," in Gerbeau and Saugera, eds., *La dernière traite*, pp. 163-90.

3719. Gonçalvès, Aimé P. "Les forts européens à Ouidah et les comptoirs de Savi (Bénin)," *Les anneaux de la mémoire* (Exhibition catalogue, Nantes, 1992), pp. 21-23.

3720. Grenier, Paulette. *La Rochelle et la traite des Noirs*. La Rochelle: Centre Departemental de Documentation Pédagogique, 1978.

3721. *L'indienne de traite à Nantes, d'après un livre d'empreintes du* XVIII*e siècle de la manufacture Favre-Petit Pierre et Cie, conservée au Musée du Château de Nantes*. Nantes: Ed. Memo, 1993.

3722. Iroko, A. Félix. "Les hommes d'affaires français et le commerce des cauris du XVIIe au XIXe siècle," *Revue française d'histoire d'outre-mer*, 78, 2 (no. 292), pp. 359-74.

3723. Klein, Herbert S. "Nantes Slave Trade in the Eighteenth Century, 1711-1791" (Data-set, Data and Program Library Service, University of Wisconsin - Madison).

3724. Klein, Herbert S. "Virginia Slave Trade in the Eighteenth Century, 1727-1769" (Data-set, Data and Program Library Service, University of Wisconsin - Madison).

3725. Klein, Herbert S., and Stanley L. Engerman. "Facteurs de mortalité dans le trafic français d'esclaves au XVIIIe siècle".

Translated and revised as "Factors in Mortality in the French Slave Trade in the Eighteenth Century" in Fogel and Engerman, eds., *Conditions of Life and the Transition to Freedom: Technical Papers*, vol. 2 (*Without Consent or Contract*), pp. 473-84.

3726. Lemarchand, Yannick. "Copropriété des navires négriers et comptes d'armement," *Les anneaux de la mémoire* (Exhibition catalogue, Nantes, 1992), p. 27.

3727. Lesage, Isabelle. "Lettre d'un citoyen de La Rochelle à M. le comte de Mirabeau: affiche de La Rochelle datée du 24 novembre 1789," in Coquery-Vidrovitch, ed., *Esclavage, colonisation, libérations nationales de 1789 à nos jours*, pp. 31-34.

3728. Mampuya, Samba. *Survivance et répression de la traite négrière du Gabon au Congo de 1840 à 1880*. Vol. 1. Paris: La Bruyère, 1990.

3729. Maheux, Hubert. "Le mobilier de port nantais," *Les anneaux de la mémoire* (Exhibition catalogue, Nantes, 1992), p. 58.

3730. Picard-Tortorici, Nathalie, and Michel François. *La traite des esclaves au Gabon du* XVIIe *au* XIXe *siècle: essai de quantification pour le* XVIIIe *siècle*. Paris: CEPED [Centre Français sur la Population et le Développement], 1993.

3731. Rupp-Eisenreich, Britta. "Les 'inventaires du genre humain' et la traite des esclaves," in Toumson (with Porset), eds., *La période révolutionnaire aux Antilles*, pp. 539-48.

3732. Samson, Daniel. "Nantes, une histoire entre noir et blanc: l'exposition 'Les anneaux de la mémoire'" (Unpublished paper, UNESCO conference on "La route de l'esclave", Ouidah, Bénin, 1-5 Sept. 1994).

3733. Saugera, Éric. *Bordeaux: port négrier (XVIIe-XIXe siècles)*. Paris: Karthala, 1995.

3734. Saugera, Éric. "Nantes dans la traite négrière française - XVIIIe-XIXe siècles," *Les anneaux de la mémoire* (Exhibition catalogue, Nantes, 1992), pp. 50-52.

3735. Villiers, Patrick. "Commerce colonial, traite des noirs et cabotage dans les ports du Ponant pendant la guerre de Sept-Ans," *Enquêtes et documents*, 17 (1990), pp. 21-45.

3736. Villiers, Patrick. *Marine royale, corsaires et trafic dans l'Atlantique de Louis XIV à Louis XVI*. Lille: Société Dunkerquois d'Histoire et d'Archéologie, 1991.

3737. Villiers, Patrick. "Quelques remarques sur le commerce colonial et le commerce négrier français à la veille de la Révolution," in Gerbeau and Saugera, eds., *La dernière traite*, pp. 87-114.

3738. Villiers, Patrick. "Traite des Noirs, commerce colonial et commerce maritime en 1792," in *Actes des 114e et 115e Congrès nationaux des sociétés savantes, Paris 1989 et Avignon 1990: Section d'histoire des sciences et des techniques* (1991), pp. 27-40.

3739. Weber, Jacques. "Entre traite e *coolie trade*: l'affaire de *L'Auguste* (1854)," in Gerbeau and Saugera, eds., *La dernière traite*, pp. 151-62.

3740. Wismes, Armel de. *Nantes et le temps des négriers*. Paris: Editions France-Empire, 1992.

8. Atlantic - English North American Colonies, United States

3741. Allen, James Cory. "The Inter-Colonial Slave Trade from Charlestown to Georgia and East Florida" (Honors paper, Duke University, 1996).

3742. Coughtry, Jay, ed. *Papers of the American Slave Trade*. Bethesda MD: University Publications of America, 1996. (Microfilm)

Ser. A. Selections from the Rhode Island Historical Society; Pt. 1. Brown Family Collections (23 reels); pt. 2 Selected Collections (30 reels).

3743. Deyle, Steven. "'By Farr the Most Profitable Trade': Slave Trade in Colonial North America".

Reprinted in Manning, ed., *Slave Trades, 1500-1800*, pp. 195-213.

3744. Fogel, Robert W. "Problems in Measuring the Extent of Slave Smuggling," in Fogel, Galantine, and Manning, eds., *Evidence and Methods* (*Without Consent or Contract*), pp. 50-52.

3745. Fogel, Robert W. "Revised Estimates of the U.S. Slave Trade and of the Native-Born Share of the Black Population," in Fogel, Galantine, and Manning, eds., *Evidence and Methods* (*Without Consent or Contract*), pp. 53-58.

3746. Harrison, Maureen, and Steve Gilbert, eds. *Landmark Decisions of the United States Supreme Court*: V. *The Slave Ship Cases: The Antelope (1825) - The Amistad (1840)*. La Jolla CA: Excellent Books, 1995. (Landmark Decision Series)

3747. Marr, Warren, II. "The *Amistad* Incident: A Mutiny Aboard the Slave Schooner *Amistad* Spurs the Legal Struggle for Emancipation," *Sea History*, 71 (1994), pp. 20-21.

3748. McMillan, Richard. "The Coastal Slave Trade in Savannah: A Quantitative Analysis of Ship Manifests, 1840-1850," *Georgia Historical Quarterly*, 78, 2 (1994), pp. 339-59.

3749. Minchinton, Walter. "A Comment on 'The Slave Trade to Colonial South Carolina: A Profile'," *South Carolina Historical Magazine*, 95, 1 (1994), pp. 47-57.

Reply by Daniel Littlefield, p. 57.

3750. Oakley, Christopher Arris. "The Indian Slave Trade in Coastal North Carolina and Virginia" (MA thesis, University of North Carolina at Wilmington, 1996).

3751. Pingeon, Frances D. "An Abominable Business: The New Jersey Slave Trade, 1818," *New Jersey History*, 109, 3-4 (1991), pp. 15-35.

3752. Rawley, James A. "Captain Nathaniel Gordon, the Only American Executed for Violating the Slave Trade Laws," *Civil War History*, 39, 3 (1993), pp. 216-24.

3753. Reilly, Kevin S. "Slavers in Disguise: American Whaling and the African Slave Trade, 1845-1862," *American Neptune*, 53, 3 (1993), pp. 177-89.

3754. Vinson, Robert Trent. "The Law as Lawbreaker: The Promotion and Encouragement of the Atlantic Slave Trade by the New York Judiciary System, 1857-1862," *Afro-Americans in New York Life and History*, 20 (1996), pp. 35-58.

9. Atlantic - Other

3755. Brübach, Nils. "'Seefahrt und Handel sind die fürnembsten Säulen eines Estats': Brandenburg-Preussen und der transatlantische Sklavenhandel," in Zoller, ed., *Amerikaner wider Willen*, pp. 11-42.

3756. *Green-Pedersen, Svend E. "Dansk-vestindisk slavehandel og dens ophaevelse: konklusioner efter uderlandske arkiv- og biblioteksstudier," in *Festschrift til Kristof Glamann* (Odense: Odense Universitetsforlag, 1983), pp. 51-70.

3757. Green-Pedersen, Svend E. "History of the Danish Negro Slave Trade".

Originally in Danish, as "Den danske negerslavehandels historie 1733-1807: en forelobig oversigt med saerligt henblik pa dens omfang og struktur, dens okonomiske betydning samt dans opaevelse," *Fran medeltid till välfardssamhälle* (Nordiska Historiker-mötet i Uppsala, 1974) (Uppsala, 1976), pp. 347-64.

3758. Hernaes, Per O. *Slaves, Danes and the African Coast Society: The Danish Slave Trade from West Africa and Afro-Danish Relations on the Eighteenth-Century Gold Coast.* Trondheim: Department of History - University of Trondheim, 1995.

3759. Highfield, Arnold R. "The Danish Atlantic and West Indian Slave Trade," in Tyson and Highfield, eds., *Danish West Indian Slave Trade*, pp. 11-32.

3760. Holsoe, Svend E. "The Origins, Transport, Introduction and Distribution of Africans on St. Croix: An Overview," in Tyson and Highfield, eds., *Danish West Indian Slave Trade*, pp. 33-46.

3761. Sadji, Uta. "La traite des noirs sur les scènes germanophones du XVIIIe siècle".

Translated as "Der Negersklavenhandel auf der deutschen Bühne des 18. Jahrhunderts," in Daniel Droixhe and Klaus H. Kiefer, eds., *Images de l'africain de l'antiquité au XXe siècle* (Frankfurt: Verlag Peter Lang, 1987), pp. 95-101.

3762. Steege, Thomas. "Vor den Toren Hamburgs: der Holsteinisch-Dänische Guts- und Industriekomplex der Schimmelmanns und der Atlantische Dreieckshandel in der 2. Hälfte des 18. Jh.," in Raddatz, ed., *Afrika in Amerika*, pp. 81-89.

3763. Tyson, George F., and Arnold R. Highfield, eds. *The Danish West Indian Slave Trade: Virgin Islands Perspectives.* St. Croix VI: Virgin Islands Humanities Council, 1994.

For contents see Greene, Highfield, Holsoe, Olwig, and Palmer.

10. American Internal (United States, Brazil, Caribbean, etc.)

3764. Bancroft, Frederic. *Slave Trading in the Old South.*

Republished, with new introduction by Michael Tadman (Columbia: University of South Carolina Press, 1996).

3765. Deyle, Steven H. "The Domestic Slave Trade in America" (PhD diss., Columbia University, 1995).

3766. Deyle, Steven. "The Irony of Liberty: Origins of the Domestic Slave Trade," *Journal of the Early Republic*, 12, 1 (1992), pp. 37-62.

3767. Deyle, Steven. "'The Nastiness of Life': African American Resistance to the Domestic Slave Trade" (Unpublished paper, American Historical Association, Chicago, 5-8 Jan. 1995).

3768. Emmer, P[ieter] C. "'Jesus Christ was Good, but Trade Was Better': An Overview of the Transit Trade of the Dutch Antilles, 1634-1795," in Engerman and Paquette, eds., *The Lesser Antilles in the Age of European Expansion*, pp. 206-22.

3769. Friedman, Gerald, and Ralph A. Galantine. "Regional Markets for Slaves and the Interregional Slave Trade," in Fogel, Galantine, and Manning, eds., *Evidence and Methods (Without Consent or Contract)*, pp. 195-99.

3770. Johnson, Walter Livezey. "Masters and Slaves in the Market of Slavery and the New Orleans Trade, 1804-1864" (PhD diss., Princeton University, 1995).

3771. Klein, Herbert S. "Internal Slave Trade to Rio de Janeiro, 1852" (Data-set, Data and Program Library Service, University of Wisconsin - Madison).

3772. Kotlikoff, Laurence J., and Sebastian E. Pinera. "The Old South's Stake in the Interregional Movement of Slaves".

Reprinted in Fogel and Engerman, eds., *Markets and Production: Technical Papers*, vol. 1 (*Without Consent or Contract*), pp. 80-94.

3773. Marr, Don H. "Slave Trading and Slave Traders in North Carolina" (MA thesis, Eastern Carolina University, 1995).

3774. Medairy, Bernard John. "The Notorious Patty Cannon and her Gang of Kidnappers on the Eastern Shore" (Towson MD: B. Medairy, 1995).

3775. Perdue, Theda. "Slavery," in Frederick E. Hoxie, ed., *Encyclopedia of North American Indians* (Boston: Houghton Mifflin, 1996), pp. 596-98.

3776. Pritchett, Jonathan B., and Richard M. Chamberlain. "Selection in the Market for Slaves: New Orleans, 1830-1860," *Quarterly Journal of Economics*, 108, 2 (1993), pp. 461-74.

3777. Pritchett, Jonathan B., and Herman Freudenberger. "A Peculiar Sample: The Selection of Slaves for the New Orleans Market," *Journal of Economic History*, 52, 1 (1992), pp. 109-27.

3778. Soares, Luiz Carlos. "O roubo de escravos no Rio de Janeiro e o tráfico interno paralelo: 1808-1850," *Revista de história* (São Paulo), no. 120 (1989), pp. 121-34.

3779. Tadman, Michael. "The Hidden History of Slave Trading in Antebellum South Carolina: John Springs III and Other 'Gentlemen Dealing in Slaves'," *South Carolina Historical Magazine*, 97, 1 (1996), pp. 6-29.

3780. Tadman, Michael. *Speculators and Slaves*.

Paperback ed., with new introduction (Madison: University of Wisconsin Press, 1996).

3781. Wiegers, Robert P. "A Proposal for Indian Slave Trading in the Mississippi Valley and Its Impact on the Osage," *Plains Anthropologist*, 33, 2 (1988), pp. 187-202.

11. Indian Ocean

3782. Arasaratnam, S. "Slave Trade in the Indian Ocean in the Seventeenth Century," in K. S. Mathew, ed., *Mariners, Merchants and Oceans: Studies in Maritime History* (New Delhi: Manohar, 1995), pp. 195-208.

3783. Bhacker, M. Reda. "Roots of Domination and Dependency: British Reaction Towards the Development of Omani Commerce at Muscat and Zanzibar in the Nineteenth Century" (PhD diss., University of Oxford, 1988).

3784. Chan Low, Jocelyn. "La colonisation Néerlandaise de l'Île Maurice et la traite des esclaves de Madagascar" (Unpublished paper, "Fanandevozana ou esclavage" [Colloque international, 1996]).

3785. Eldredge, Elizabeth. "The Delagoa Bay Slave Trade, 1720-1830" (Unpublished paper, Annual Meeting of the Canadian Association of African Studies/Association Canadienne des Études Africaines, Toronto, May 1991).

3786. Filliot, Jean-Michel. "La traite vers l'Île de France: Colonial Trade and Neutrality".

Reprinted in Manning, ed., *Slave Trades, 1500-1800*, pp. 245-56.

3787. Gutiérrez, Horácio. (Review essay: Capela and Medeiros, *O tráfico de escravos de Moçambique para as ilhas do Índico*)," *Revista de história* (São Paulo), no. 120 (1989), pp. 163-82.

3788. Hebert, J. C. "Le 'Journal du traitant inconnu' en Imerina, en 1808," in *Fanandevozana ou esclavage*, pp. 214-49.

3789. Larson, Pier M. "A Census of Slaves Exported from Central Madagascar to the Mascarenes Between 1775 and 1820," in *Fanandevozana ou esclavage*, pp. 175-86.

3790. *Larson, Pier M. "The Slave Trade from Central Madagascar to the Mascareines: Origins, Numbers, Organization, 1770-1820" (forthcoming).

3791. Pierson, Gerald J. "U.S. Consuls in Zanzibar and the Slave Trade, 1870-1890," *The Historian*, 55, 1 (1992), pp. 53-68.

3792. Prasad, U. V. Sambhu. "Plantation Slaves of India: A Study of the Seventeenth and Eighteenth Century Slaves of East India Company" (Unpublished paper, 1993).

3793. Prasad, U. V. Sambhu. "Slavc Tradc and Migration in Late Medieval Indian Littoral" (PhD diss., Pondicherry University, 1992).

3794. Prasad, U. V. Sambhu. "Slavery and Famine: A Study of Slave Trade Under British East India Company in Coromandel Coast" (Unpublished paper, 1993).

3795. Rakotondrabe, Daniela Tovonirina. "L'oligarchie merina, les Anglais et la traite des esclaves: contraintes et enjeux de l'affranchissement des Mozambiques à Madagascar (1865-1878)," in *Fanandevozana ou esclavage*, pp. 345-66.

3796. Ratsivalaka, R. G. "La traite des esclaves dans les îles du Sud-Ouest de l'océan Indien à la veille du traité malgacho-britannique du 23 octobre 1817," in *Fanandevozana ou esclavage*, pp. 65-82.

3797. Ricks, Thomas M. "Slaves and Slave Traders in the Persian Gulf: 18th and 19th Centuries: An Assessment".

> Reprinted in Manning, ed., *Slave Trades, 1500-1800*, pp. 279-90.

3798. Souza, Teotonio R. de. "French Slave-Trading in Portuguese Goa (1773-1791)," in idem, ed., *Essays in Goan History* (New Delhi: Concept Publishing Company, 1989), pp. 119-31.

12. Trans-Saharan and Red Sea

3799. Austen, Ralph A. "The Mediterranean and Islamic Slave Trade Out of Africa: A Tentative Census".

> Reprinted in Manning, ed., *Slave Trades, 1500-1800*, pp. 1-36.

3800. *Bramley, W. E. Jennings. "Tales of the Wadai Slave Trade in the Nineties," *Sudan Notes and Records*, 21 (1940), pp. 169-84.

3801. Cordell, Dennis D. "The Trans-Saharan Slave Trade and the Reproduction of Saharan Oases: Some Hypotheses and Preliminary Research" (Unpublished paper, Annual Meeting of the African Studies Association, Boston, 4-7 December 1993).

3802. Goldsmith, Sandra. "Abdul Momen's Mission: One Man's Crusade to End the Slave Trade in Asia and the Middle East," *Student Lawyer*, 22, 8 (1994), pp. 30-33.

3803. Lavers, John E. "Trans-Saharan Trade Before 1800: Towards Quantification," *Paideuma*, 40 (1994), pp. 243-78. (Special number, A. S. Kanya-Forstner and Paul E. Lovejoy, eds., "The Sokoto Caliphate and the European Powers 1890-1907".)

3804. *Le Gall, Michel. "The End of the Trans-Saharan Slave Trade to Tripoli: A Reassessment," *Princeton Papers in Near Eastern Studies*, 2 (1993), pp. [??].

3805. Lovejoy, Paul E. "The Transsaharan and Trans-Atlantic Slave Trades from the Sokoto Caliphate" (Unpublished paper, Annual Meeting of the African Studies Association, Boston, 4-7 December 1993).

3806. Mohammadou, Eldredge. "Adamawa and the Transsaharan Slave Trade in the Nineteenth Century" (Unpublished paper, Annual Meeting of the African Studies Association, Boston, 4-7 December 1993).

3807. Naqd, Muhammad Ibrahim. *Alaqat al-riqq fi al-mujtama al-Sudani: tawthiq wa-taliq*. al-Qahirah: Dar al-Thaqafah al-Jadidah, 1995.

3808. Renault, François. "Essai de synthèse sur la traite transsaharienne et orientale des esclaves en Afrique," in Gerbeau and Saugera, eds., *La dernière traite*, pp. 23-44.

3809. Renault, François. "La traite transsaharienne des esclaves (review essay: Savage, ed., *Human Commodity*)," *Revue française d'histoire d'outre-mer*, 80, 3 (no. 300) (1993), pp. 467-77.

3810. *Starratt, P. E. "A Historical Study of Tuareg Slave Trade in the Nineteenth Century" (MA thesis, University of Birmingham, 1971).

3811. Toledano, Ehud R. *The Ottoman Slave Trade and Its Suppression*.

> *Translated as *Osmanli köle ticareti, 1840-1890*. Istanbul: [pub??], 1994. (Tarih Vakji Yurt Yayinlari)

3812. Wright, John. "The Mediterranean Middle Passage: The Nineteenth Century Slave Trade between Tripoli and the Levant," *Journal of North African Studies*, 1, 1 (1996), pp. 42-58.

13. Effects on Africa

3813. Aînamon, Augustin. "Aperçu historique sur Savalou," in *Le Bénin et la route de l'esclave*, pp. 109-12.

3814. Alpern, Stanley B. "What Africans Got for their Slaves: A Master List of European Trade Goods," *History in Africa*, 22 (1995), pp. 5-43.

3815. Anignikin, Sylvain C. "Abomey cité des rois," in *Le Bénin et la route de l'esclave*, pp. 118-20.

3816. Anignikin, Sylvain C. "Dassa-Zoumé," in *Le Bénin et la route de l'esclave*, pp. 101-03.

3817. Austin, Gareth. "Between Abolition and *Jihad*: The Asante Response to the Ending of the Atlantic Slave Trade, 1807-1896," in Law, ed., *From Slave Trade to "Legitimate" Commerce*, pp. 93-118.

3818. Bancole, Alexis. "Agoué et la traite négrière," in *Le Bénin et la route de l'esclave*, pp. 85-88.

3819. Bancole, Alexis, and Gilles Raoul Soglo. "Porto-Novo et la traite négrière," in *Le Bénin et la route de l'esclave*, pp. 76-78.

3820. Beyan, Amos J. "Transatlantic Trade and the Coastal Area of Pre-Liberia," *The Historian*, 57, 4 (1995), pp. 757-68.

3821. Botte, Roger. "Les rapports Nord-Sud, la traite négrière et le Fuuta Jaloo à la fin du XVIIIe siècle," *Annales: Économies, Sociétés, Civilisations*, 46, 6 (1991), pp. 1411-35.

3822. Cobbing, Julian. "Grasping the Nettle: The Slave Trade and the Early Zulu," in R. Edgecombe, J. P. C. Laband, and P. S. Thompson, eds., *The Debate on Zulu Origins* (Pietermaritzburg: University of Natal, 1992), n.p.

3823. Codo, Bellarmin C. "Les Afro-Brésiliens de retour" (Unpublished paper, UNESCO conference on "La route de l'esclave", Ouidah, Bénin, 1-5 Sept. 1994).

3824. Codo, Bellarmin C. "Quelques aspects du Bénin sur la route de l'esclave," in *Le Bénin et la route de l'esclave*, pp. 63-65.

3825. Comité National pour le Bénin du Projet "La Route de l'Esclave". "Le conférence de lancement du project 'La Route de l'Esclave," in *Le Bénin et la route de l'esclave*, pp. 43-60.

3826. Comité National pour le Bénin du Projet "La Route de l'Esclave". "Note de présentation," in *Le Bénin et la route de l'esclave*, pp. 39-42.

3827. Comité National pour le Bénin du Projet "La Route de l'Esclave" (Eds. Elisée Soumonni, Bellarmin C. Codo, and Joseph Adande). *Le Bénin et la route de l'esclave*. Cotonou: ONEPI, 1994.

For contents see Aînamon, Anignikin (2), Bancole, Bancole and Soglo, Codo, Comité Nationale, Degbelo, Gonçalves, Ichola, Iroko (4), Lokossou, Nouhouayi, Sacramento, Soglo, Vodoume, and Zinsou.

3828. "The 'Crisis of Adaptation': A Bibliography," in Law, ed., *From Slave Trade to "Legitimate" Commerce*, pp. 265-71.

3829. Curto, José C. "Demografia histórica e os efeitos do tráfico de escravos em África: uma análise dos principais estudos quantitativos," *Revista internacionial de estudos africanos*, 14-15 (1991), pp. 243-77.

Also as "Historical Demography and the Effects of the Slave Trade in Africa: An Analysis of the Major Quantative Studies" (CDAS Discussion Paper no. 77) (Centre for Developing-Area Studies, McGill University, Québec, 1992).

3830. Degbelo, Amélie. "La route de l'esclave et les amazones du Danxomé," in *Le Bénin et la route de l'esclave*, pp. 130-34.

3831. Ekanza, Simon-Pierre [M'Bra]. "Les populations africaines face à la traite," *Les anneaux de la mémoire* (Exhibition catalogue, Nantes, 1992), pp. 62-64.

3832. Ekanza, Simon-Pierre. "Zone côtière et échanges commerciaux dans la Côte d'Ivoire précoloniale, XVIe-XIXe siècle," in Gerbeau and Saugera, eds., *La dernière traite*, pp. 23-44.

3833. Eltis, David. "The Economics of African Participation in the Slave Trade".

Reprinted (from "Precolonial Western Africa and the Atlantic Economy") in Northrup, ed., *The Atlantic Slave Trade*, pp. 161-73.

3834. Fakambi, Justin. *Routes des esclaves au Bénin (ex-Dahomey) dans une approche régionale.* Cotonou: Graphic Express (privately published), n.d. [1990, 1993].

3835. Gonçalves, Aimé. "L'architecture 'afro-brésilienne'," in *Le Bénin et la route de l'esclave*, pp. 121-23.

3836. Hopkins, Anthony. "From Abolition to Partition: A Continental Study" (Unpublished paper, Symposium: The End of the Atlantic Slave Trade: Its Impact on Africa, 17-18 April 1993, Centre of Commonwealth Studies, University of Stirling).

3837. Ichola, Nourou Dine. "Note explicative du logo," in *Le Bénin et la route de l'esclave*, pp. 135-38.

3838. Inikori, Joseph E. "Ideology Versus the Tyranny of Paradigm: Historians and the Impact of the Atlantic Slave Trade on African Societies," *African Economic History*, 22 (1994), pp. 59-92.

3839. Inikori, Joseph E. "Slavery in Africa and the Transatlantic Slave Trade," in Jalloh and Maizlish, eds., *African Diaspora*, pp. 39-72.

3840. Inikori, Joseph E. "The Sources of Supply for the Atlantic Slave Trade from the Bight of Benin and the Bight of Bonny (Biafra)".

Also in *Odu (A Journal of West African Studies)*, no. 31 (1987), pp. 104-23.

3841. Iroko, A. Félix. "Condemnations penales et ravitaillement en esclaves de la traite négrière," in *Le Bénin et la route de l'esclave*, pp. 93-95.

3842. Iroko, A. Félix. "Ketu dans la traite négrière aux XVIIIè-XIXè siècles," in *Le Bénin et la route de l'esclave*, pp. 104-08.

3843. Iroko, A. Félix. "La monnaie de la traite négrière à la Côte des Esclaves," in *Le Bénin et la route de l'esclave*, pp. 70-72.

3844. Iroko, A. Félix. "Traite négrière et corruption des moeurs à la Côte des Esclaves," in *Le Bénin et la route de l'esclave*, pp. 82-84.

3845. Kea, Ray. "Plantations and Labour in the Accra Urban Hinterland from the Late Eighteenth to the Mid-Nineteenth Century" (Unpublished paper, Symposium: The End of the Atlantic Slave Trade: Its Impact on Africa, 17-18 April 1993, Centre of Commonwealth Studies, University of Stirling).

3846. Kodjo, Georges-Niamkey. "Les esclaves à Kong (Côte-d'Ivoire)," *Les anneaux de la mémoire* (Exhibition catalogue, Nantes, 1992), pp. 65-66.

3847. *Larson, Pier M. "Social Transformation in an International Economy: Rural Communities and the Slave Trade from Highland Madagascar, 1770-1800" (forthcoming).

3848. Law, Robin [C. C.] "An African Response to Abolition: Anglo-Dahomian Negotiations on Ending the Slave Trade, 1838-77," *Slavery and Abolition*, 16, 2 (1995), pp. 281-310.

3849. Law, Robin [C. C.]. "Introduction," in Law, ed., *From Slave Trade to "Legitimate" Commerce*, pp. 1-31.

3850. Law, Robin [C. C.]. "'Legitimate' Trade and Gender Relations in Yorubaland and Dahomey," in Law, ed., *From Slave Trade to "Legitimate" Commerce*, pp. 195-214.

3851. Law, Robin C. C. "'Here is no Resisting the Country': The Realities of Power in Afro-European Relations on the West African 'Slave Coast'," *Itinerario*, 18, 2 (1994), pp. 50-64.

3852. Law, Robin [C. C.] "The Transition from the Slave Trade to 'Legitimate' Commerce," *Studies in the World History of Slavery Abolition, and Emancipation* (Aug. 1996).

http://h-net.msu.edu/~slavery

3853. Law, Robin [C. C.], ed. *From Slave Trade to "Legitimate" Commerce: The Commercial Transition in Nineteenth-Century West Africa*. New York: Cambridge University Press, 1995.

For contents see Austin, Hopkins, Kea, Law, Lovejoy and Richardson, Lynn, McDougall, Martin, and Soumonni.

3854. Lindsay, Lisa A. "'To Return to the Bosom of their Fatherland': Brazilian Immigrants in Nineteenth-Century Lagos," *Slavery and Abolition*, 15, 1 (1994), pp. 22-50.

3855. Lovejoy, Paul E., and David Richardson. "British Abolition and Its Impact on Slave Prices Along the Atlantic Coast of Africa, 1783-1850," *Journal of Economic History*, 55, 1 (1995), pp. 98-119.

3856. Lovejoy, Paul E., and David Richardson. "The Initial 'Crisis of Adaptation': The Impact of British Abolition on the Atlantic Slave Trade in West Africa, 1808-1820," in Law, ed., *From Slave Trade to "Legitimate" Commerce*, pp. 32-56.

3857. Lynn, Martin. "The West African Palm Oil Trade in the Nineteenth Century and the 'Crisis of Adaptation'," in Law, ed., *From Slave Trade to "Legitimate" Commerce*, pp. 57-77.

3858. Mahoney, Florence. "The Liberated Slaves and the Question of the Return to Africa" (Unpublished paper, UNESCO conference on "La route de l'esclave", Ouidah, Bénin, 1-5 Sept. 1994).

3859. Mann, Kristin. "Owners, Slaves and the Struggle for Labour in the Commercial Transition in Lagos," in Law, ed., *From Slave Trade to "Legitimate" Commerce*, pp. 144-71.

3860. Manning, Patrick. "The Advantages and Limitations of Simulation in Analysing the Slave Trade" (Unpublished paper presented at conference on "Source Material for Studying the Slave Trade and the African Diaspora", Stirling, Scotland, 13-14 April 1996).

3861. Manning, Patrick. "The Impact of the slave Trade on the Societies of West and Central Africa," in Tibbles, ed., *Transatlantic Slavery*, pp. 96-103.

3862. Manning, Patrick. "The Slave Trade and the Demographic Evolution of Africa" (Unpublished paper, UNESCO conference on "La route de l'esclave", Ouidah, Bénin, 1-5 Sept. 1994).

3863. Manning, Patrick. "Social and Demographic Transformations".

Reprinted (from "Contours of Slavery and Social Change in Africa") in Northrup, ed., *The Atlantic Slave Trade*, pp. 148-60.

3864. Martin, Susan. "Slaves, Igbo Women and Palm Oil in the Nineteenth Century" (Unpublished paper, Symposium: The End of the Atlantic Slave Trade: Its Impact on Africa, 17-18 April 1993, Centre of Commonwealth Studies, University of Stirling).

3865. Notables de Savi. "Contribution à l'histoire de Sahe (Savi)," in *Le Bénin et la route de l'esclave*, pp. 73-75.

3866. Nouhouayi, Albert. "Zagnanado (Agoonlin) et la route de l'esclave," in *Le Bénin et la route de l'esclave*, pp. 113-17.

3867. Pavanello, Mariano. "Il cano e il fuoco: storia e mito nel commercio di schiavi e armi tra gli Nzema del Ghana," *Africana (Rivista di studi extraeuropei)* (1996), pp. 141-53.

3868. Rathbone, Richard. "Resistance to Enslavement in West Africa".

Reprinted in Manning, ed., *Slave Trades, 1500-1800*, pp. 183-94.

3869. Rodney, Walter. "The Unequal Partnership Between Africans and Europeans".

Reprinted (from *How Europe Underdeveloped Africa*) in Northrup, ed., *The Atlantic Slave Trade*, pp. 135-47.

3870. *La route de l'esclave* - Colloque International. "De la traite négrière au defi du développement: réflexion sur les conditions de la paix mondiale" (Ouidah, Bénin - 1-5 September 1994).

For papers presented see Adande, Adoukonou, Almeida, Anglarill, Assonga, Bebel-Gisler, Behanzin, Benoît (2), Benot, Codo, Dabla, Deveau, Diagne, Dorigny, Dovonon, Fiopou, Garcia, Gbnamankou, Guéront, Inikori, Irele, Kabengele, Kazadi wa Mukuna, Kaké, Ki-zerbo, Kordes, Law, Liborel, Lirius-Galap, Lokossou, López Segrera, Lovejoy, Mahoney, Manning, Miller, Montilius, Peyrière, Quénum, Restrepo, Roumeguère, Sala-Molins, Samson, Somé, Ravares, Vignonde, Villaverde, Walker, and Yai.

3871. Sacramento, Léon. "Cotonou: de la traite esclavagiste aux relations économiques internationales," in *Le Bénin et la route de l'esclave*, pp. 89-92.

3872. Searing, James F. *West African Slavery and Atlantic Commerce: The Senegal River Valley, 1700-1860*. New York: Cambridge University Press, 1993.

3873. Soglo, Gilles. "Notes sur la traite des esclaves à Glexwe (Ouidah)," in *Le Bénin et la route de l'esclave*, pp. 66-69

3874. Soumonni, Elisée. "The Compatibility of the Slave and Palm Oil Trades in Dahomey, 1818-1858" (Unpublished paper, Symposium: The End of the Atlantic Slave Trade: Its Impact on Africa, 17-18

April 1993, Centre of Commonwealth Studies, University of Stirling).

3875. Thornton, John K. "Sexual Demography: The Impact of the Slave Trade on Family Structure".

Reprinted in Manning, ed., *Slave Trades, 1500-1800*, pp. 133-43.

3876. Voduume, Clément Cakpo. "Place d'Abomey dans la traite négrière," in *Le Bénin et la route de l'esclave*, pp. 96-100.

3877. Yarak, Larry. "Dutch Military Recruitment in Kumase, 1837-52" (Unpublished paper, Symposium: The End of the Atlantic Slave Trade: Its Impact on Africa, 17-18 April 1993, Centre of Commonwealth Studies, University of Stirling).

3878. Young, Reginald. *The Transatlantic Slave Trade and the Development of Tropical Africa: A Brief Scan*. London: R. Young, 1995.

3879. Zinsou, Edgar Okiki. "Ganvié: un exemple de cité-refuge," in *Le Bénin et la route de l'esclave*, pp. 79-81.

14. Trade within Africa

3880. Hogendorn, Jan S. "Economic Modelling of Price Differences in the Slave Trade between the Central Sudan and the Coast," *Slavery and Abolition*, 17, 3 (1996), pp. 209-22.

3881. Law, Robin [C. C.]. "Reconstructing the Social History of Slave-Trading: The Port of Whydah" (Unpublished paper, "The African Diaspora and the Nigerian Hinterland").

3882. Lovejoy, Paul E. "The Central Sudan and the Atlantic Slave Trade," in Robert W. Harms, Joseph C. Miller, David S. Newbury, and Michele D. Wagner, eds., *Paths toward the African Past: Essays in Honor of Jan Vansina* (Atlanta: ASA Press, 1994), pp. 345-70.

3883. Lovejoy, Paul E., and David Richardson. "Competing Markets for Male and Female Slaves: Prices in the Interior of West Africa, 1780-1850," *International Journal of African Historical Studies*, 28, 2 (1995), pp. 261-93.

3884. Moffa, Claudio. "Il Katanga 'terra di nessuno' fra tratta schiavista e nuovo ordine coloniale: la construzione dello Stato coloniale nei Rapporti del Sostituto," *Africana (Rivista di study extraeuropei)* (1996), pp. 109-21.

3885. Richardson, David, and E. W. Evans. "Hunting for Rents: The Economics of Slaving in Pre-Colonial Africa," *Economic History Review*, 48, 4 (1995), pp. 665-86.

15. Medieval and Early Modern Mediterranean

3886. Arbel, Benjamin. "Slave Trade and Slave Labor in Frankish Cyprus (1191-1571)," in J. A. S. Evans and R. W. Unger, eds., *Studies in Medieval and Renaissance History* (New York: AMS Press, 1993), vol. 14 (old series vol. 24) (1993), pp. 149-90.

3887. Balard, Michel. "Esclavage en Crimée et sources fiscales génoises au XVe siècle," *Byzantinische Forschungen*, 22 (1996), pp. 9-17.

3888. Buccianti, Cinzia. "Il commercio degli schiavi negri a Tripoli nel XVIII secolo: brevi note su alcuni documenti dell'archivio di Stato di Venezia," *Africana (Rivista di studi extraeuropei)* (1996), pp. 61-67.

3889. Constable, Olivia Remie. "Muslim Spain and Mediterranean Slavery: The Medieval Slave Trade as an Aspect of Muslim-Christian Relations," in Scott L. Waugh and Peter D. Diehl, eds., *Christendom and its Discontents: Exclusion, Persecution, and Rebellion, 1000-1500* (New York: Cambridge University Press, 1996), pp. 264-84.

3890. *Corrado, Marciani. "Il commercio degli schiavi alle fiere di Lanciano nel sec. XVI," *Archivio storico per le provincie Napoletane*, 41 (1961), pp. 269-82.

3891. Kolendo, Jerzy. "Les barbares et le monde méditerranéen: l'afflux des esclaves" (Presentation at Colloquium on "Les dépendances serviles", Paris 1996).

3892. *Larquié, Claude. "La Méditerranée, l'Espagne et le Maghreb au XVIIe siècle: le rachat des chrétiens et le commerce des hommes," *Actes du Ve Congrès d'Histoire et de Civilisation du Maghreb*, vol. 2, pp. 75-90.

3893. *Poujol, Sylvain. "Marins et esclaves," *Provence généalogie*, 89 (1993), pp. 32-37.

16. Other

3894. Alam, Muzaffar. "Trade, State Policy and Regional Change: Aspects of Mughal-Uzbek Commercial Relations, c. 1550-1750," *Journal of the Economic and Social History of the Orient*, 37, 3 (1994), pp. 202-27.

3895. Gbnamankou, Dieudonné. "La traite des noirs en direction de la Russie" (Unpublished paper, UNESCO conference on "La route de l'esclave", Ouidah, Bénin, 1-5 Sept. 1994).

3896. Luengo, Jose Maria Salutan. *A History of the Manila-Acapulco Slave Trade, 1565-1815*. Tubigon, Bohol (Philippines): Mater Dei Publications, 1996.

3897. Munro, Doug. "The Pacific Islands Labour Trade: Approaches, Methodologies, Debates," *Slavery and Abolition*, 14, 2 (1993), pp. 87-108.

AUTHOR INDEX

THIS INDEX refers users to all authors and editors in the bibliography by the numbers of the entries for their works listed. Numbers without parentheses indicate a primary author, or editor, as alphabetized within the bibliography's regional sections. Numbers in parentheses refer to secondary authorship or editorship. The entry-numbers of works edited are preceded by "ed.", and "(ed.)" indicates a secondary editorship. Series of entries by the same scholar are inclusive (e.g. 9359-62 = 9359, 9360, 9361, 9362).

The names of authors whose works have appeared under variant forms are here consolidated under the most common form, with the elements of the variations enclosed in square brackets: e.g. Robert W[illiam] Fogel, P. Dieudonné [de Thulin] Rinchon, Mirtha Teresa González [Moreno]. Listings in the bibliography have been standardized to the most common form, with variant elements of the names enclosed in square brackets.

A slash (/) indicates duplicated entries and unintegrated translations that turned up on final editing, in spite of efforts to eliminate the inevitable repetition that built up during the years over which the bibliography was compiled.

A

B

D

E

F

H

I

J

K

L

M

N

Q

R

S

W

Y

Z

Subject/Keyword Index

Note for Users: This index refers readers to terms and concepts sufficiently central to the arguments made in materials listed in the bibliography to merit reference in their titles, by entry numbers. It is thus a composite of subject terms and key-words - places, concepts, persons - but is not remotely exhaustive in terms of the detailed contents of the materials cited.

The entries do not repeat the geographical organization of the bibliography itself, although they do include references to prominent secondary regional emphases in materials listed under other, primary, headings. Examples would be a comparative study of slavery in Russia and the United States placed in the "General and Comparative" section (I) and indexed under "Russia" and "United States", or an article on slavery and the slave trade in Cuba placed in the "Caribbean - Spanish" section of the bibliography and indexed under "Cuba" and "Trade: Cuba".

In general, only aspects of the contents of the bibliography germane to the subject of slavery (or the slave trade) are indexed.

In general, geographical index entries are found for the specific focus of the work. More inclusive index categories refer users to these detailed levels of analysis wherever they exist. The literature for the Americas, for example, tends to fall in categories running from individual plantations, then counties or parishes, and finally states or colonies, all within the broader regional categories of the bibliography itself. Thus, a work on Montepellier plantation will be listed as the property studied, and not under St. James Parish or Jamaica, all within the "Caribbean - British" section of the bibliography. But users will find a notation under the Jamaica entry reminding them to consult the names of individual plantations located on that island. Similarly, studies on the Boni War are indexed as such, although they are also relevant to the categories of "Maroons" and "Suriname", where the "*see also*" sections of both entries cite "Boni".

The subtleties of distinguishing between slavery in a given location and the slave trade to or from it have resulted in placing a number of entries in the regional and "Slave Trade" sections on a relatively arbitrary basis. The index provides a limited guide through this maze by including entries under "Trade" for the regions where it is mentioned and second entries under countries, colonies, and regions for the slave trade there.

Some other logical distinctions rendered in related, and otherwise potentially overlapping, terms employed in the index include:

Abolition: political movements opposing slavery or the slave trade (under the authority of another state, and including U.S.); *Anti-slavery*: ideology (cf. *Pro-slavery*); *Emancipation*: political freeings of enslaved groups (within a state's own jurisdiction, including colonies in Africa and elsewhere), and the process of the freed people's construction of new lives, identities, and communities; *Suppression*: naval and other pressures applied to slaving ships; *Free blacks/coloureds*: communities of freedpersons; *Freedmen*: status or activities of the individuals freed; *Freedom*: ideology and/or status; *Manumission*: individual acts of freeing individuals

Trade: generally within Section XI (Slave Trade), but see index under "Trade:" for additional materials listed within the other, geographical, sections of the bibliography (e.g. Trade: Rio de Janeiro). Works in Section XI emphasizing specific regional flows are indexed under the relevant geographical designation (e.g. Italy: trade).

Cross-references are provided for synonyms and alternate phrasings common in the literature.

Technical legal distinctions have not generally been indexed (except for manumission) but will be found within the listings for "Law(s) of slavery" (modern) and "Roman Law".

Listings for broad conceptual areas (e.g. Law, Economics) include further references to specific cases, economic concepts, and so on. Headings for "Ships" and "Plantations" list all specific such entities mentioned.

Reviews of works are listed, under authors' names.

A slash (/) indicates duplicated listings (e.g. 2921/2956) that survived proof-reading to emerge after the entries in the bibliography had been numbered and could thus no longer be eliminated without interrupting the numerical sequence established.

A

C

D

E

F

I

J

K

L

Q

R

S

T

U